Lectures in applied mathematics and informatics

edited by

Luigi M. Ricciardi

Manchester University Press

Manchester and New York

Distributed exclusively in the USA and Canada by St. Martin's Press

Published by Manchester University Press
Oxford Road, Manchester M13 9PL, UK
and Room 400, 175 Fifth Avenue,
New York, NY 10010, USA

Distributed exclusively in the USA and Canada
by St. Martin's Press, Inc.,
175 Fifth Avenue, New York, NY 10010, USA

British Library cataloguing in publication data

Lectures in applied mathematics and informatics.
  1. Applied mathematics
  I. Ricciardi, Luigi, *1942–*
  510

Library of Congress cataloging in publication data

Lectures in applied mathematics and informatics/edited by Luigi M. Ricciardi.
    p.   cm.
  ISBN 0–7190–2671–7
  1. Mathematics. 2. Information theory. I. Ricciardi, Luigi M., 1942– .
  QA7.L43 1989
  510—dc20   89–12620

  ISBN 0 7190 2671 7 *hardback*

Typeset by Graphicraft Typesetters Ltd., Hong Kong
Printed in Great Britain
by Biddles Ltd, Guildford and King's Lynn

Lectures in applied mathematics and informatics

Contents

Preface   ix

Chapter 1 Analysis of algorithms *Paul Cull*   1
    1 Introduction   1
    2 Towers of Hanoi–analysis of a problem   6
    3 Divide-and-conquer   19
    4 Average case   31
    5 Lower bounds   35
    6 Exhaustive search   41
    7 Hard problems   48
    References   61

Chapter 2 Rational and recognizable languages *Jean Enric Pin*   62
    1 Rational and recognizable subsets   63
    2 Languages and automata   75
    3 The minimal automaton, the syntactic monoid   82
       and varieties
    4 Rational operations and rational languages   90
    References   104

Chapter 3 On generalized entropies with applications   107
    Inder Jeet Taneja
    1 Introduction   107
    2 Characterizations of generalized entropies   109
    3 Properties of generalized entropies   124
    4 Applications to statistical pattern recognition   133
    5 Applications to fuzzy sets   155
    References   165

Chapter 4   On the spatial distributions of dispersing animals   170
             Nanako Shigesada
             1   Introduction   170
             2   Density-dependent dispersal: theory of
                 environmental density   171
             3   Behavioural version of Morisita's equation   173
             4   Dispersal in a continuously varying environment   175
             5   Further applications of the model: dispersal in
                 homogeneous environments   177
             6   Effect of interspecific population pressure on the
                 spatial structure of a competitive community   182
             7   Spatial distribution of rapidly dispersing animals
                 in heterogeneous environments: multiple-scale
                 method   190
             8   Population with general logistic growth   193
             9   Multi-species systems   196
            10   Summary   200
             Appendix: proof of theorem   200
             References   203

Chapter 5   Diffusion processes and first-passage-time problems   206
             Luigi M. Ricciardi and Shunsuke Sato
             1   Introduction   206
             2   Preliminaries   207
             3   Kinetic equations   208
             4   Diffusion equations   212
             5   Wiener and Ornstein–Uhlenbeck processes   218
             6   Stochastic differential equations   222
             7   The first-passage-time problem   239
             8   The Laplace transform approach   244
             9   The moments of the first-passage-time   256
            10   Algorithms for evaluation of first-passage-time   264
                 p.d.f.'s
            11   Asymptotic results   276
             References   283

Chapter 6   Functionals of Brownian motion   *Takeyuki Hida*   286
             1   Introduction   286
             2   White noise and Brownian functionals   288
             3   Applications of the integral representation   295
             4   Infinite-dimensional rotation group $O(E)$ 302
             5   Generalized Brownian functionals   312
             6   Causal calculus   315
             7   Multi-dimensional parameter case   323

8   Concluding remarks   325
References   328

Chapter 7   Random semicontinuous functions   330
Gabriella Salinetti and Roger J.-B. Wetts
1   Stochastic processes: the classical view   330
2   Some questions, some examples   332
3   Some topological considerations   334
4   Separability, measurability and stochastic   337
equivalence
5   The epigraphical approach   338
6   The epigraphical random set   340
7   Distributions and distribution functions   343
8   . . . and finite-dimensional distributions!   344
9   Weak convergence and convergence in   346
distribution
10   Convergence in distribution and convergence of   347
the finite-dimensional distributions
11   Bounded random l.sc. functions   349
12   An application to goodness-of-fit statistics   350
References   353

Name index   354
Subject index   358

Preface

Since the establishment in 1983 of a new doctoral programme in applied mathematics and informatics at the University of Naples, we have enjoyed the presence of well known mathematicians and applied scientists from different countries who have gladly accepted our invitation to offer special topics courses for our students, often in collaboration with Italian colleagues. Because of the heterogeneity of the audience's background, these courses have been designed to be as self-contained as possible.

The positive response of our graduate students induced me to ask some of our former guests to write down a text of their lectures with the aim of making this material available to a wider audience. The immediate cooperative response by the contributors to the present volume, as well as an encouraging conversation with the Editor of the Manchester University Press series *Nonlinear Science: Theory and Applications*, Dr Arun V. Holden, has finally led to the birth of this book.

The first three chapters are devoted to basic topics of informatics, namely analysis of algorithms, algebraic fundamentals of rational and recognizable languages and measures of information. Chapter 1 starts with the very basic and often misunderstood notion of *algorithm*. It continues with an analysis of fundamental questions such as correctness and comparison of algorithms with specific reference to concrete examples. NP-problems and approximation algorithms are also throughly discussed.

Chapter 2 starts with the algebraic characterization of rational and recognizable subsets. The connection between the recognizable subsets of a finitely generated free monoid and finite automata follows. It is then shown how one can associate and algorithmically compute a monoid (the *syntactic monoid*) to each recognizable language in such a way that the properties of recognizable languages can be studied through properties of their syntactic monoid. An outline of Hashiguchi's theory and a discussion of star and concatenation operations conclude this chapter.

The notion of *generalized entropy* was introduced in information theory literature by A. Rényi in 1961. The motivation was that for certain purposes, other than Shannon's communication theory, measures of information different from Shannon's entropy may serve just as well or even better. This is the leitmotif of Chapter 3 in which a thorough discussion of measures of information in terms of generalized entropies is provided. Specific applications to statistical pattern recognition and to fuzzy sets are included.

Chapter 4 is, I believe, a paradigm of the modern approach to the construction of mathematical models in ecology and population dynamics, a real challenging task for the applied mathematician. It focuses on the analysis of the spatial distribution of dispersing animals via mathematical models of density-dependent dispersal in heterogeneous environments both for single and for multiple-species systems.

The last three chapters deal with topics and problems within the area of stochastic processes. For instance, Chapter 5 contains an introduction to the essential elements of one-dimensional diffusion processes with emphasis on the available theoretical and computational methods to evaluate first-passage-time probability density functions and moments through generally time dependent boundaries.

As is well known, Brownian motion plays a fundamental role not only in pure mathematics but also in a wide variety of significant applications in various fields of science such as quantum dynamics, biology, engineering, and psychology. This is why Chapter 6 starts with a brief introduction in which Brownian motion and its probability measure (the Wiener measure) are rigorously defined. There follows a self-contained synthesis of the author's numerous and fundamental contributions to the analysis of generalized Brownian functionals. Here an important role is played by the integral representation and by the infinite dimension rotation group. Interesting examples and an outline of stimulating applications are included.

Chapter 7, which concludes the volume, discusses a novel approach to the description and the analysis of random phenomena. After a brief review of the classical theory of stochastic processes, the authors indicate the usefulness of the epigraphical approach that relies on modeling the paths of random phenomena by semicontinuous functions. A comparison of the two theories and an application to the convergence of stochastic processes are finally provided.

I trust that the compact and self-contained style of each chapter, the basic and up-to-date nature of the subjects discussed and the abundance of references will make this volume of interest not only to undergraduate and graduate students of mathematics and information sciences, but also to any one who is interested in applied or interdisciplinary mathematical research.

Naples
March 1990 L. M. R.

1

Analysis of algorithms

Paul Cull   *Department of Computer Science, Oregon State University, Corvallis, Oreg. 97331, USA*

1   Introduction

1.1   What is an algorithm?

An algorithm is a procedure which solves a problem and is suitable for implementation as a program for a digital computer. This informal definition makes two important points. First, an algorithm solves a problem. A computer program may not solve a problem. For example, there are computer programs which never terminate. It would be very difficult to say that such a program does anything, let alone solve a problem. Second, each step of the algorithm should be well-defined and be representable, at least in principle, by a program. For example, $s := P/q$ would not be well-defined if q could be 0; 'find the smallest x such that $P(x)$ is true' would not be well-defined if no such x existed, or if x were allowed to range over the positive and negative integers and $P(x)$ were true for all negative x. 'Add a dash of salt' would not be an acceptable instruction in a computer program unless one had created a model world and a mapping which would translate the instruction into the modification of some location in a computer's memory.

For our purposes, and for many purposes, the above informal definition of algorithm is sufficient, but we should point out that a formal definition of algorithm can be created. This has been done by Turing, Markoff, and others (Rogers, 1967). The satisfying thing about all these formal definitions is that they define the same class of algorithms. If we have an algorithm in one of these senses, then there is an equivalent algorithm in any one of the other senses. Further, the existence of a formal definition means that if we run into difficulties with the informal definition, we could use the formal definition to unravel the difficulty.

1.2 What is analysis of algorithms?

The task of analysis of algorithms is threefold:

(a) to produce provably correct algorithms, that is, algorithms which not only solve the problem they are designed to solve, but which also can be demonstrated to solve the problem;
(b) to compare algorithms for a problem with respect to various measures of resources (e.g. time and space), so that one can say when one algorithm is better than another;
(c) to find, if possible, the best algorithm for a problem with respect to a particular measure of resource usage.

Each of these tasks will be examined in more detail later, but first I want to say a few words about where analysis of algorithms fits in the worlds of mathematics and computer science. Mathematics has two great branches, pure mathematics and applied mathematics. Mathematics also has two major techniques, proof and computation. It would be tempting to suggest that pure mathematics uses proof and applied mathematics uses computation, but both pure and applied mathematics use both proof and computation. The difference between the two branches is the world they work in. Pure mathematics works in an abstract world. It needs no reference to a real world. Applied mathematics, on the other hand, assumes there is a real world and then constructs an abstract world. The mapping or correspondence between entities of the real and abstract worlds form an essential part of applied mathematics.

Where does computer science fit in? Computer science is the science which deals with computation and computing devices. In its theoretical branches, computer science uses the mathematical techniques of proof and computation, while in its more practical branches, computer science uses engineering techniques and experimental techniques.

Analysis of algorithms, like applied mathematics, assumes a real world. This real world contains actual computers and actual computer programs. From this real world, an abstract world of abstract computers and abstract programs is constructed. This construction is usually informal and exact definitions of abstract entities are often not stated, but a number of real-world limitations disappear in the abstract world. For example, real computers have a fixed finite memory size and they have an upper bound on the size of numbers which can be represented. In the abstract world, these limitations do not exist. Finite but unbounded memories are assumed to exist. No bound on the size of numbers exists.

Again, like applied mathematics, analysis of algorithms uses the techniques of proof and computation to deal with the entities in its abstract world, and like applied mathematics, one must be cautious in applying results from the abstract world to the real world. There are examples of algorithms which would work very quickly if arbitrarily large numbers could be used, but implementing these algorithms on real computers results in algorithms which are much slower. As another example, there are algorithms which can be shown to be quicker than other algorithms, but only if the input is astronomically large. These examples make perfect sense in the abstract world, but have little or no relevance for the real world.

Analysis of algorithms is the applied mathematics of computer science. Whether it should be called mathematics or computer science usually depends on who is doing it. If a mathematician does analysis of algorithms, it may be called mathematics, but if a computer scientist does analysis of algorithms, it is usually called computer science.

1.2.1 *Proofs of correctness*

The first of the three tasks of analysis of algorithms is to produce provably correct algorithms. This task suggests that we need a methodology to both produce algorithms and to produce proofs of the correctness of these algorithms. Later we will consider two design strategies: (a) to solve a problem, break it into smaller problems of the same kind; (b) to solve a problem, search an answer space until you find the answer to the problem you have.

Proving correctness of algorithms based on a search strategy is usually relatively easy: show that the answer to your problem is in the space; show that your algorithm searches the whole space, or that if your algorithm decides not to search a portion of the space, then your algorithm has established that your answer cannot lie in the portion not to be searched.

Proving correctness of algorithms based on breaking a problem into smaller problems can most readily be done by using mathematical induction. You establish that your algorithm correctly solves all small enough cases of the problem. Your algorithm will usually have a section which deals with these small cases, but particularly when the small cases may be of size 0 and no action by the algorithm is required, the section for small cases may not exist. The other section of your algorithm will deal with larger cases by breaking them into smaller cases and combining the solutions to the smaller cases to give the solution to the larger problem. You then have to show that if the smaller problems are solved correctly, then your algorithm combines these solutions correctly to yield the solution to the larger problem.

The proof procedure just outlined assumes that your algorithm is recursive, that is, to solve large problems the algorithm calls itself to solve smaller problems, but proofs by mathematical induction are not limited to recursive algorithms. Inductive proofs are also natural when dealing with interative algorithms which are based on loops, for example, white loops,

for loops, **do** loops, or **repeat** ... **until** loops. Inductive proofs of correctness of loop programs involve the creation of a 'loop invariant', a truth-valued function, which is true on each iteration of the loop and which states that the loop has completed the desired computation when the loop is exited. Such a proof also requires one to show that the loop does in fact terminate. When there are several loops, the correctness of each loop must be established, and then it must be shown that the correctness of each loop implies the correctness of the whole algorithm. The most difficult part of such proofs is usually the identification of the loop invariants. Without a knowledge of how and why the algorithm was designed, such proofs are nearly impossible. Some programming languages, like EUCLID, now allow the specification of the loop invariants and other propositions so that at least in principle it would be possible to mechanically establish the correctness of a fully annotated program.

While it is often easier to establish the correctness of a recursive algorithm, the overwhelming majority of programs are iterative rather than recursive. Why is this true? One reason is that a number of common programming languages like FORTRAN, BASIC, and COBOL do not permit recursion. Another reason is that many programmers believe that recursive programs are always slower than iterative programs. While this may have been true in languages like ALGOL and PL/1, and when recursive programs in ALGOL were compared to iterative programs in FORTRAN, the speed advantage of iterative over recursive programs has disappeared in languages like PASCAL and C.

1.2.2 *Comparing algorithms*

For any (solvable) problem there will be an infinity of algorithms which solve the problem. How do we decide which is the 'best' algorithm? There are a number of possible ways to compare algorithms. We will concentrate on two measures: time and space. We would like to say that one algorithm is faster, uses less time, than another algorithm if when we run the two algorithms on a computer the faster one will finish first. Unfortunately, to make this a fair test we would have to keep a number of conditions constant. For example, we would have to code the two algorithms in the same programming language, compile the two programs using the same compiler, and run the two programs under the same operating system on the same computer, and have no interference with either program while it is running. Even if we could practically satisfy all these conditions, we might be chagrined to find that algorithm A is faster under conditions C, but that algorithm B is faster under conditions D.

To avoid this unhappy situation we will only calculate time to order. We let n be some measure of the size of the problem, and give the running time as a function of n. For example: we could use the number of digits as the measure of problem size if the problem is the addition or multiplication of two integers; we could use the number of elements if the problem is to sort several elements; we could use the number of edges or the number of vertices if the problem is to determine if a graph has a certain property. We do not distinguish running times of the same order. For our purposes two functions of n, $f(n)$ and $g(n)$, have the same order if for some N there are two positive constants C_1 and C_2 so that $C_1|g(n)| \leqslant |f(n)| \leqslant C_2|g(n)|$ for all $n \geqslant N$. We symbolize this relation by $f(n) = \theta(g(n))$, read '$f(n)$ is order $g(n)$'. Thus we will consider two algorithms to take the same time if their running times have the same order. In particular, we do not distinguish between algorithms whose running times are constant multiples of one another.

If we find that algorithm A has a time order which is strictly less than algorithm B, then we can be confident that for any large enough problem algorithm A will run faster than algorithm B, regardless of the actual conditions. On the other hand, if algorithms A and B have the same time order, then we will not predict which one will be faster under a given set of actual conditions.

The space used by an algorithm is the number of bits the algorithm uses to store and manipulate data. We expect the space to be an increasing function of n, the size of the problem. This space measurement ignores the number of bits used to specify the algorithm, which has a fixed constant size independent of the size of the problem. Since we have chosen bits as our unit, we can be more exact about space than we can be about time. We can distinguish an algorithm which uses $3n$ bits from an algorithm which uses $2n$ bits. But we will not distinguish an algorithm which uses $3n + 7$ bits from an algorithm which uses $3n + 1$ bits, because we can hide a constant number of bits within the algorithm itself.

1.2.3 *Best algorithms*
The third task of analysis of algorithms is to find the best algorithm with respect to a particular measure of resource usage. This involves proving 'lower bounds', that is, showing that every algorithm which solves the problem must use at least so much of the particular resource. To establish a best algorithm, one must have both a proof of a lower bound and an algorithm which uses no more than this lower bound. Here a distinction should be made between bounds for an algorithm and bounds for a problem. If one establishes an upper bound on a particular resource used by an algorithm for a problem, then one has an upper bound both for the algorithm and for the problem. If one establishes a lower bound for a problem, then one has a lower bound for all algorithms which solve the problem. But demonstrating a lower bound for one algorithm for a problem does not establish a lower bound for the problem.

2   Towers of Hanoi: an analysis of a problem

2.1   The Towers of Hanoi problem

In this section, we will demonstrate the threefold task of analysis of
algorithms using the Towers of Hanoi problem. We have chosen the
Towers of Hanoi problem because each of the tasks can be demonstrated
rather easily, and a best algorithm can be discovered. Material in this
section is based on Cull and Ecklund (1985).

In the Towers of Hanoi problem, one is given three towers, usually
called A, B, and C, and n disks of different sizes. Initially the disks are
stacked on tower A in order of size with disk n, the largest, on the
bottom, and disk 1, the smallest, on the top. The problem is to move the
stack of disks to tower C, moving the disks one at a time in such a way
that a disk is never stacked on top of a smaller disk. An extra constraint is
that the sequence of moves should be as short as possible. An algorithm
solves the Towers of Hanoi problem if, when the algorithm is given as
input n, the number of disks, and the names of the towers, then the
algorithm produces the shortest sequence of moves which conforms to the
above rules.

2.2   A recursive algorithm

The road to a best algorithm starts with some algorithm which one then
attempts to improve. One often uses some sort of strategy to create an
algorithm. A very useful strategy is to look at the problem and see if the
solution can be expressed in terms of the solutions of several problems of
the same kind, but of smaller size. This strategy is usually called divide-
and-conquer. If the problem yields to the divide-and-conquer approach,
one can construct a recursive algorithm which solves the problem. This
construction also gives almost immediately an inductive proof that the
algorithm is correct. Time and space analyses of a divide-and-conquer
algorithm are often straightforward, since the algorithm directly gives
difference equations for time and space usage.

While these divide-and-conquer algorithms have many nice properties,
they may not use minimal time and space. They may, however, serve as a
starting-point for constructing more efficient algorithms.

Consideration of the Towers of Hanoi problem leads to the key
observation that moving the largest disk requires that all of the other
disks are out of the way. Hence the $n - 1$ smaller disks should be moved
to tower B, but this is just another Towers of Hanoi problem with fewer
disks. After the largest disk has been moved, the $n - 1$ smaller disks can
be moved from B to C; again this is a smaller Towers of Hanoi problem.
These observations lead to the following recursive algorithm:

procedure HANOI (A,B,C,n)
  if n = 1 **then** move the top disk from tower A to tower C
       else HANOI (A,C,B,n−1)
           move the top disk from tower A to tower C
           HANOI (B,A,C,n−1).

Is this the best algorithm for the problem? We will show that this algorithm has minimum time complexity, but does not have minimum space complexity. First, though, we prove that the algorithm correctly solves the problem, the first task of analysis of algorithms as outlined in the Introduction.

Proposition 1 The recursive algorithm HANOI correctly solves the Towers of Hanoi problem.

Proof Clearly the algorithm gives the correct minimal sequence of moves for 1 disk. If there is more than 1 disk the algorithm moves $n - 1$ disks to tower B, then moves the largest disk to tower C, and then moves and $n - 1$ disks from tower B to tower C. This is precisely what is required in a minimum move algorithm because, according to the rules, the largest disk can only be moved when all the other $n - 1$ disks are on a single tower. So the $n - 1$ disks must be moved from tower A to some other tower. Clearly at least one move is required to move the largest disk from tower A to tower C. When the largest disk is moved to tower C, the other $n - 1$ disks are on a single tower and still have to be moved to tower C. By inductively assuming $n - 1$ disks are moved in the minimum number of moves, we see that the algorithm for n disks makes no more than the minimal number of moves and finishes with all the n disks moved from tower A to tower C. $\square$

Here we should remark that we have not only produced a provably correct algorithm for the problem; we have also shown that the minimal sequence of moves is unique. This uniqueness makes the proof of correctness easy. The proof would be more complicated if more than one minimum sequence were possible.

We would like to calculate the running time of HANOI, but we don't know how long various operations will take. How long will it take to move a disk? How long will it take to subtract 1 from n? How long will it take to test if $n = 1$? How long will it take to issue a procedure call? Because we only wish to calculate time to order we don't have to answer these questions exactly, but we do have to make a distinction between operations which take a constant amount of time, independent of n, and operations whose running time depends on n.

One possibility is to assume that each operation takes constant time independent of n. AHU (Aho, Hopcroft, and Ullman, 1974) calls this assumption the uniform cost criterion. With this uniform cost assumption and letting $T(n)$ be the running time for n disks, we have the difference equation

$$T(n) = 2T(n - 1) + c,$$

because there are 2 calls to the same procedure with $n - 1$ disks and c is the sum of the constant running times for the various operations. Letting $T(1)$ be the running time of the algorithm for 1 disk, we find

$$T(n) = (T(1) + c)2^{n-1} - c,$$

which can be verified by direct substitution. This gives

$$T(n) = \theta(2^n),$$

since

$$\frac{T(1)}{2} 2^n \leq T(n) < \left(\frac{T(1) + c}{2}\right)2^n.$$

Another possibility is to assume that some of the operations have running times which are a function of n. But which function of n should we use? Each of the numbers in the algorithm is between 1 and n, and the disks can also be represented by numbers between 1 and n. Since such numbers can be represented using about log n bits, it seems reasonable to assume that each operation which manipulates numbers or disks has running time which is a constant times log n. AHU calls this the logarithmic cost criterion and suggests using it when the numbers used by an algorithm do not have fixed bounds. Using the logarithmic cost criterion we have the difference equation

$$T(n) = 2T(n - 1) + c \log n$$

for the running time of the algorithm. This difference equation has the solution

$$T(n) = 2^n \left[\frac{T(1)}{2} + c \sum_{i=1}^{n} \frac{\log i}{2^i}\right]$$

which can be verified by substitution. Since the summation in this solution converges, as one can demonstrate by the ratio test, and assuming that the constants are positive, we have

$$T(n) = \theta(2^n).$$

Since both cost criteria give the same running time, we conclude:

Proposition 2   The algorithm HANOI has running time $\theta(2^n)$.

Although we have established the running time for a particular algorithm which solves the Towers of Hanoi problem, we have have not yet established the time complexity of the problem. We need to establish a lower bound so that every algorithm which solves the problem must have running time greater than or equal to the lower bound. We establish $\theta(2^n)$ as the lower bound in the proof of the following proposition.

Proposition 3 The Towers of Hanoi problem has time complexity $\theta(2^n)$.

Proof Following the proof of Proposition 1, a straightforward induction shows that the minimal number of moves needed to solve the Towers of Hanoi problem is $2^n - 1$. Since each move requires at least constant time we have established the lower bound on time complexity.

An upper bound for the time complexity of the problem comes from Proposition 2. Since the upper bound and lower bound are equal to order, we have established the $\theta(2^n)$ time complexity of the problem. $\square$

Now that we know HANOI's time complexity we would like to consider its space complexity. First we will establish a lower bound on space which follows from the lower bound on time.

Proposition 4 Any algorithm which solves the Towers of Hanoi problem must use at least $n +$ constant bits of storage.

Proof Since the algorithm must produce $2^n - 1$ moves to solve the problem, the algorithm must be able to distinguish 2^n different situations. If the algorithm did not distinguish this many situations, then the algorithm would halt in the same number of moves after each of the two non-distinguished situations, which would result in an error in at least one of the cases.

The number of situations distinguished by an algorithm is equal to the number of storage situations times the number of internal situations within the algorithm. Since the algorithm has a fixed finite size, it can have only a constant number of different internal situations. The number of storage situations (states) is 2 to the number of storage bits. Thus $C \cdot 2^{BITS} \geq 2^n$, and so $BITS \geq n - \log C = n +$ constant. $\square$

In order to discuss the space complexity of the recursive algorithm, let us now consider the data structure used. Two possible data structures are the array and the stack. An array is a set of locations indexed by a set of consecutive integers so that the information stored at a location in the array can be referenced by indicating the integer which indexes the location. For example, the information at location I in the array ARRAY would be referenced by ARRAY[I]. A stack is a linearly ordered set of locations in which information can be inserted or deleted only at the beginning of the stack.

The towers could each be represented by an array with n locations, and each location would need at most log n bits. So an array data structure with $\theta(n \log n)$ bits would suffice. Alternatively, each tower could be represented by a stack. Each stack location would need log n bits, so again this is an $\theta(n \log n)$ bit structure. Actually savings would be made. Since only n disks have to be represented, the stack structure needs only n locations versus the $3n$ locations used by the array structure. Another possible structure is an array in which the ith element holds the name of the tower on which the ith disk is located. This structure uses only $\theta(n)$ bits. Yet another possibility is to not represent the towers, but to output the moves in the form FROM ___ TO ___. Thus we could use no storage for the towers.

The recursive algorithm still requires space for its recursive stack. When a recursive algorithm calls itself, the parameters for this new call will take the places of the previous parameters, so these previous parameters are placed on a stack from which they can be recalled when the new call is completed. Also placed on the stack is the return address, the position in the algorithm at which execution of the old call should be resumed. All of this information, the parameters and the return address, for a single call are referred to as a stack frame. At most n stack frames will be active at any time and each frame will use a constant number of bits for the names of the towers and log n bits for the number of disks. So the recursive algorithm will use $\theta(n \log n)$ bits whether or not the towers are actually represented. We summarize these considerations by the following proposition.

Proposition 5 The recursive algorithm HANOI correctly solves the Towers of Hanoi problem and uses $\theta(2^n)$ time and $\theta(n \log n)$ space.

The recursive algorithm uses more than minimal space. We are faced with several possibilities:

(a) minimal space is only a lower bound and is not attainable by any algorithm;
(b) minimal space can only be achieved by an algorithm which uses more than minimal time;
(c) some other algorithm attains both minimal time and minimal space.

By developing a series of iterative algorithms, we will arrive at an algorithm which uses both minimal time and minimal space.

2.3 Improved algorithms

As a first step in obtaining a better algorithm, we will consider an iterative algorithm which simulates the recursive algorithm for $n \geqslant 2$. In this algorithm, RECURSIVE SIM, we have chosen to explicitly keep track of the stack counter because this will aid us in finding an algorithm using even less space.

```
procedure RECURSIVE SIM (A,B,C,n)
  I:= 1
  L1[1]:= A; L2[1]:= C; L3[1]:= B
  NUM[1]:= n − 1; PAR[1]:= 1; PAR[0]:= 1
  while I ⩾ 1 do
    if NUM[I] > 1
      then L1[I + 1]:= L1[I]
           L2[I + 1]:= L3[I]
           L3[I + 1]:= L2[I]
           NUM[I + 1]:= NUM[I] −1
           PAR[I + 1]:= 1
           I:=I + 1
      else  MOVE FROM L1[I] TO L3[I]
            while PAR[I] = 2 do
                  I:= I − 1
            if I ⩾ 1 then MOVE FROM L1[I] TO L2[I]
                          PAR[I]:= 2
                          TEMP:= L1[I]
                          L1[I]:= L3[I]
                          L3[I]:= L2[I]
                          L2[I]:= TEMP
```

The names of the towers are stored in the three arrays L1, L2, L3; the number of disks in a recursive call is stored in NUM; and the value of PAR indicates whether a call is the first or second of a pair of recursive calls.

RECURSIVE SIM sets up the parameters for the call HANOI (A,C, B,$n-1$). When the last move for this call is made, the arrays will contain the parameters for calls with 1 through $n - 2$ disks, where each of these calls will have PAR = 2. The arrays will still contain the parameters for the (A,C,B,$n-1$) call with PAR = 1. The inner **while** loop will pop each of the calls with PAR = 2, leaving the array counter pointing at the (A,C,B,$n-1$) call. Since I will be 1 at this point, the **if** condition is satisfied and the MOVE FROM L1[I] TO L2[I] accomplishes the MOVE FROM A TO C of the recursive algorithm HANOI. The following assignment statements set up the call (B,A,C,$n-1$) with PAR = 2. So when the moves for this call are completed, all of the calls in the array will have PAR = 2, and the inner **while** loop will pop all of these calls setting I to 0. Then the **if** condition will be false, so no operations are carried out, and the outer **while** condition will be false, so the algorithm will terminate.

Proposition 6 The RECURSIVE SIM algorithm correctly solves the Towers of Hanoi problem, and uses $\theta(2^n)$ time and $\theta(n \log n)$ space.

Proof Correctness follows since this algorithm simulates the recursive algorithm which we have proved correct. The major space usage is in the arrays. Since each time I is incremented the corresponding NUM[I] is decremented and since NUM[I] never falls below 1, there are at most $n - 1$ locations ever used in an array. The four arrays L1, L2, L3, and PAR use only a constant amount of space for each element, but NUM must store a number as large as $n - 1$ so it uses $\theta(\log n)$ bits for an element. Thus the arrays use $\theta(n \log n)$ bits.

Now we have to argue about time usage. Most of the operations deal with constant-sized operands so these operations will take constant time. The exceptional operations are incrementing, decrementing, assigning, and comparing numbers which may have $\theta(\log n)$ bits. A difference equation for the time is

$$T(n) = 2T(n - 1) + C \log n,$$

where $T(n)$ is the time to solve a problem with n disks, and $C \log n$ is the time for manipulating the numbers with $\theta(\log n)$ bits. As in the proof of Proposition 1, we have $T(n) = \theta(2^n)$. $\square$

Notice that this algorithm does not improve on the recursive algorithm, but study of this form can lead to a saving of space. Storing the array NUM causes the use of $\theta(n \log n)$ space. If we did not have to store NUM, the algorithm would use only $\theta(n)$ space. Do we need to save NUM? NUM is used as a control variable so it seems necessary. But if we look at NUM[1] + 1 we get n. When NUM[I + 1] is set, it is set equal to NUM[I] $- 1$, but then

NUM[I + 1] + I + 1 = NUM [I] $- 1 + $ I $+ 1$
                                    = NUM[I] + I = n.

Thus the information we need about NUM is stored in I and n. So if we replace the test on NUM[I] $= 1$ with a test on I $= n - 1$, we can dispense with storing NUM and improve the space complexity from $\theta(n \log n)$ to $\theta(n)$. This replacement does not increase the time complexity of any step in the algorithm, so the time complexity remains $\theta(2^n)$.

Our new procedure is

procedure NEW SIM (A,B,C,n)
    I:= 1
    L1[1]:= A; L2[1]:= C; L3[1]:= B
    PAR[1]:= 1; PAR[0]:= 1
    while I ⩾ 1 **do**
      if I ≠ n − 1
        then L1[I + 1]:= L1[I]
               L2[I + 1]:= L3[I]
               L3[I + 1]:= L2[I]

```
        PAR[I + 1]:= 1
        I:= I + 1
else  MOVE FROM L1[I] TO L3[I]
      while PAR[I] = 2 do
          I:= I - 1
      if I ≥ 1 then MOVE FROM L1[I] TO L2[I]
                    PAR[I]:= 2
                    TEMP:= L1[I]
                    L1[I]:= L3[I]
                    L3[I]:= L2[I]
                    L2[I]:= TEMP
```

From the above observation we have:

Proposition 7 NEW SIM correctly solves the Towers of Hanoi problem and uses $\theta(2^n)$ time and $\theta(n)$ space.

Although we have reached $\theta(n)$ space we would like to decrease the space even further, hopefully to $n +$ constant bits. If we look at the array PAR, we find that the algorithm scans PAR to find the first element not equal to 2, replaces that element by 2, and then replaces all the previous 2s by 1s. This is analogous to the familiar operation of adding 1 to a binary number, in which we find the first 0, replace it by a 1, and replace all the previous 1s by 0s. So it seems that we can replace the array PAR by a simple counter. The number of bits in the counter will, of course, depend on n.

So far this has not resulted in any saving of space. Will there be enough information in the counter to determine from which tower we should move a disk? The affirmative answer will enable us to achieve a minimal space algorithm. To motivate the design of our minimal space algorithm, we will examine the sequence of 31 moves needed to solve the problem with 5 disks. This sequence is shown in Table 1.

Every other move in the solution involves moving disk 1. So if we know which tower contains disk 1 we would know from which tower to move, in alternate moves, but we might not know which tower to move to. When we consider the three towers to be arranged in a circle, we see from Table 1 that disk 1 always moves in a counter-clockwise direction when we have an odd number of disks. Similarly disk 1 always moves in a clockwise direction when we have an even number of disks. Thus by keeping track of the tower which contains disk 1 and whether n is odd or even, we would know how to make every other move.

For the moves which do not involve disk 1, we know that the move involves the two towers which do not contain disk 1. Looking again at Table 1, we see that the odd-numbered disks always move in the same direction as disk 1 and that the even-numbered disks always move in the

Table 1.   Towers of Hanoi solution for 5 disks

Tower 0	Tower 1	Tower 2	Decimal Count	Count	Disk	From	To
12345	–	–	0	00000	1	0	2
2345	–	1	1	00001	2	0	1
345	2	1	2	00010	1	2	1
345	12	–	3	00011	3	0	2
45	12	3	4	00100	1	1	0
145	2	3	5	00101	2	1	2
145	–	23	6	00110	1	0	2
45	–	123	7	00111	4	0	1
5	4	123	8	01000	1	2	1
5	14	23	9	01001	2	2	0
25	14	3	10	01010	1	1	0
125	4	3	11	01011	3	2	1
125	34	–	12	01100	1	0	2
25	34	1	13	01101	2	0	1
5	234	1	14	01110	1	2	1
5	1234	–	15	01111	5	0	2
–	1234	5	16	10000	1	1	0
1	234	5	17	10001	2	1	2
1	34	25	18	10010	1	0	2
–	34	125	19	10011	3	1	0
3	4	125	20	10100	1	2	1
3	14	25	21	10101	2	2	0
23	14	5	22	10110	1	1	0
123	4	5	23	10111	4	1	2
123	–	45	24	11000	1	0	2
23	–	145	25	11001	2	0	1
3	2	145	26	11010	1	2	1
3	12	45	27	11011	3	0	2
–	12	345	28	11100	1	1	0
1	2	345	29	11101	2	1	2
1	–	2345	30	11110	1	0	2
–	–	12345	31	11111			

opposite direction. So knowing the towers involved and whether the disk to be moved is odd or even would allow us to decide which way to move.

Can we determine from a counter whether the disk being moved is odd or even? If we look at the *Count* column of Table 1 we see that the position of the rightmost 0 tells us the number of the disk to be moved. Thus a single counter with n bits is sufficient to solve the Towers of Hanoi problem.

We use these facts to construct the algorithm which follows.

procedure TOWERS (n)
  T:= 0 (*TOWER NUMBER COMPUTED MODULO 3*)
  COUNT:= 0 (*COUNT HAS n BITS*)
  $P:= \begin{cases} 1 \text{ if } n \text{ is even} \\ -1 \text{ if } n \text{ is odd} \end{cases}$
  while TRUE **do**
    MOVE DISK 1 FROM T TO T + P
    T:= T + P
    COUNT:= COUNT + 1
    if COUNT = ALL 1s **then** RETURN
    if RIGHTMOST 0 IN COUNT IS IN EVEN POSITION
      then MOVE DISK FROM T − P TO T + P
      else MOVE DISK FROM T + P TO T − P
    COUNT:= COUNT + 1
  endwhile

	n	... 2 1
COUNT	0	... 0 0

A picture of the storage used for COUNT.

Notice that it has n bits, and that we have called the rightmost bit position 1. The positions from right to left are then odd, even, odd, even....

Remarks We can still improve this algorithm by removing the first COUNT:= COUNT + 1 statement and deleting the rightmost bit of COUNT. This would also require changing the numbering of the bits in COUNT so that the rightmost bit is bit 0. An algorithm similar to our TOWERS has recently been published by Walsh (1982).

We have to show that TOWERS correctly solves the Towers of Hanoi problem. We do this by proving that a certain sequence of moves has been accomplished when COUNT contains a number of the form $2^k - 1$, so that when $k = n$, the sequence of moves for HANOI (A,B,C,n) has been completed and the procedure will terminate since COUNT contains all 1's.

Proposition 8   When COUNT $= 2^k - 1$, that is, COUNT $= \boxed{00\ldots01\ldots1}$

with k 1s, then:

> if $k \not\equiv n(\bmod 2)$ the correct moves for HANOI (A,C,B,k) have been
> completed and T contains 1 (which represents B);
> if $k \equiv n(\bmod 2)$ the correct moves for HANOI (A,B,C,k) have been
> completed and T contains 2 (which represents C).

Proof   If $k = 1$ the single move T to T + P has been completed, which is A to C if n is odd, and is A to B if n is even, and T contains T + P which is 2 if n is odd and is 1 if n is even. This agrees with our claim.

Notice that COUNT can only take on the value $2^k - 1$ immediately before the **if** ... RETURN statement. Assume that the moves for either HANOI (A,B,C,k) or HANOI (A,C,B,k) have been completed. If $k \not\equiv n(\bmod 2)$, the next move will be A to C since by assumption T now contains 1; if k is odd, the move is T − P to T + P which is 1 − (1) to 1 + 1 which represents A to C, and if k is even, the move is T + P to T − P which is 1 + (−1) to 1 − (−1) which represents A to C. If $k \equiv n(\bmod 2)$, the next move will be A to B since by assumption T now contains 2; if k is odd, the move is T − P to T + P which is 2 − (−1) to 2 + (−1) which represents A to B, and if k is even, the move is T + P to T − P which is 2 + 1 to 2 − 1 which represents A to B.

Next, COUNT will be incremented to $\boxed{0\ldots010\ldots0}$, i.e. k trailing 0s. When COUNT $= 2^{k+1} - 1$, the algorithm will have repeated the same sequence of moves as before since it only 'sees' the rightmost information in COUNT, with the difference that T will have started with a different value. The different starting value of T will result in a cyclic permutation of the labels. If $k \not\equiv n(\bmod 2)$, then the completed moves will be

> HANOI (A,C,B,k)
>   A to C
> HANOI (B,A,C,k),

giving HANOI (A,B,C,$k+1$) with $k + 1 \equiv n(\bmod 2)$, and T will contain 2 (i.e. 1 + 1). If $k \equiv n(\bmod 2)$, then the completed moves will be

> HANOI (A,B,C,k)
>   A to B
> HANOI (C,A,B,k),

giving HANOI (A,C,B,$k+1$) with $k + 1 \neq n(\mathrm{mod}\ 2)$, and T will contain 1 (i.e. $2 + 2$). $\Box$

Proposition 9 The algorithm TOWERS uses $\theta(2^n)$ time and n + constant bits of space.

Proof For space usage, there are n bits in COUNT, and a constant number of bits are used for T and P.

For time, the initialization takes $\theta(n)$ and the **while** loop is iterated $2^n - 1$ times. If each iteration took a constant amount of time we would have $\theta(2^n)$, but the test and increment instruction on COUNT could take time $\theta(n)$ giving $\theta(n2^n)$. So we have to show that only $\theta(2^n)$ time is used.

If the value in COUNT is even then incrementing and testing will only require looking at one bit. If the value in COUNT is odd and $(\mathrm{COUNT} - 1)/2$ is even, then the algorithm only looks at 2 bits. In fact, the algorithm will look at k bits in COUNT in 2^{n-k} cases. Thus the time

used will be $\theta\left(\sum_{k=1}^{n} k \cdot 2^{n-k}\right) = \theta(2^n)$ since $\sum_{k=1}^{\infty} k \cdot 2^{-k}$ converges. $\Box$

We summarize these results in the following theorem.

Theorem Any algorithm which solves the Towers of Hanoi problem for n disks must use at least $\theta(2^n)$ time and n + constant bits of storage. The algorithm TOWERS solves the problem and simultaneously uses minimum time and minimum space.

2.4 Exercises

For the following two algorithms for the Towers of Hanoi problem, prove that the algorithms are correct and compute the time and space they use.

(a) **procedure** HANOI ITERATIVE (A,B,C,n)
        if n mod $2 = 0$ **then** MOVE[1]:= A TO B
                          else MOVE[1]:= A TO C
        K:= 1
        while $n > 1$ **do**
          $n := n - 1$; K:= 2*K
          if n mod $2 = 0$ **then** MOVE[K]:= A TO B
                                    L1:= C; L2:= A; L3:= B
                    else MOVE[K]:= A TO C
                                  L1:=B; L2:= C; L3:=A
        for I:= 1 **to** K $- 1$ **do**

case MOVE[I] **of**
    A TO B: MOVE[K + I]:= L1 TO L2
    A TO C: MOVE[K + I]:= L1 TO L3
    B TO A: MOVE[K + I]:= L2 TO L1
    B TO C: MOVE[K + I]:= L2 TO L3
    C TO A: MOVE[K + I]:= L3 TO L1
    C TO B: MOVE[K + I]:= L3 TO L2

Hints: For correctness you may want to introduce a new variable and prove a statement which says that on each iteration of the **while** loop the new variable increases (or if you want decreases), and that at the end of each iteration a Hanoi problem whose size depends on the new variable has been solved. You will need to give the tower names for the problem which has been solved. You will also need to specify the value of the new variable.

For space, you should know that the algorithm is storing each move in the array MOVE.

For time, you may want to consider both the uniform and the logarithmic cost measures.

(b)   (Buneman and Levy, 1980)

MOVE SMALLEST DISK ONE TOWER CLOCKWISE
while A DISK (OTHER THAN THE SMALLEST) CAN BE MOVED **do**
    MOVE THAT DISK
    MOVE THE SMALLEST DISK ONE TOWER CLOCKWISE
endwhile

Hints: For correctness, you should be careful since this algorithm only solves the original Towers of Hanoi problem when the number of disks is even. You will probably want to introduce a new variable and prove a statement about the configuration of the disks when the number of moves completed is a specific function of your new variable.

For time and space, the above algorithm is incomplete since it does not specify the data structure used to determine if a disk can be moved. You might consider representing each tower by a stack of integers with the integers representing the disks on the tower. Alternately you might consider representing the information by an array DISK, so that DISK[I] contains the name of the tower which contains the Ith largest disk. You may also find it useful to show that the ith disk is moved 2^{n-i} times.

3 Divide-and-conquer

3.1 What is divide-and-conquer?

The algorithm design strategy which breaks a given problem into several smaller problems of the same type is usually called the divide-and-conquer strategy. In the previous section, the recursive algorithm for the Towers of Hanoi problem is an example of a divide-and-conquer algorithm. Given a problem with n disks, this algorithm converts it into two problems with $n - 1$ disks. Each of the subproblems is successively broken into subproblems until problems which can be solved immediately are reached. The Towers of Hanoi algorithm continues forming problems with fewer disks until it reaches problems with 1 disk which can be solved immediately. After the subproblems are solved the divide-and-conquer algorithm then combines the solutions of the subproblems to give a solution to the original problem. In the Towers of Hanoi example, there is no explicit combining, because the necessary combination is simply to solve one subproblem after the other subproblem has been solved. This combination is handled by the ordering of the statements in the algorithm.

The recursive structure of a divide-and-conquer algorithm leads directly to an inductive proof of correctness, and also gives directly a difference equation for the running time of the algorithm.

Consider designing by divide-and-conquer an algorithm to sort the elements of an n element array. One way to do this is to find the largest element in the array, interchange it with the last element of the array, and then sort the remaining $n - 1$ element array. This algorithm could be written as

procedure SORT (n)
  if $n > 1$ **then** LARGEST (n)
                SORT $(n - 1)$,

where LARGEST is an algorithm which handles the largest element. If LARGEST works correctly then it is easy to prove that SORT works correctly. Similarly if we know how many comparisons LARGEST used, then we could compute the number of comparisons used by SORT from the formula

$$S(n) = S(n - 1) + L(n),$$

where $S(n)$ is the number of comparisons used by SORT (n), $S(n - 1)$ is the number of comparisons used by SORT $(n - 1)$, and $L(n)$ is the number of comparisons used by LARGEST (n). It is easy to design

LARGEST (n) so that it uses exactly $n - 1$ comparisons. This gives the difference equation

$$S(n) = S(n - 1) + n - 1.$$

When there is only 1 element in the array SORT does nothing. This gives the initial condition $S(1) = 0$. It is easy to check that $S(n) = n(n - 1)/2$ satisfies both the difference equation and the initial condition.

This recursive sorting algorithm can be easily converted to an iterative algorithm because the recursive algorithm is tail-recursive, that is, the only time the algorithm calls itself is at the end of the algorithm. The corresponding iterative algorithm is

> **for** I:= n **downto** 2 **do**
>   LARGEST (I).

It is still easy to write an inductive proof of the correctness of this algorithm. The number of comparisons used by this iterative algorithm can be computed by

$$\sum_{I=n}^{2} L(I) = \sum_{I=n}^{2} (I - 1) = n(n - 1)/2.$$

Both the recursive and iterative sorting algorithms use the same number of comparisons. They also both use space to store the original array. The recursive algorithm has the disadvantage that it uses a stack to keep track of the recursion. This stack requires some space. Further, the recursive algorithm spends some time in manipulating this stack. So in this case, the iterative algorithm would be preferred to the recursive algorithm.

In the above example, we have broken a problem of size n into a single problem of size $n - 1$. Instead we could try to break the problem of size n into two problems of size $n/2$. If we could solve the two problems of size $n/2$, then we would be left with the problem of combining two sorted sequences of size $n/2$ to form a single sorted sequence of size n. Let us assume that the algorithm MERGE takes as input two sorted sequences and outputs a single sorted array which contains all the elements of the input. From the MERGE algorithm we can construct a divide-and-conquer algorithm MERGESORT:

> **procedure** MERGESORT (A,n)
>   **if** $n > 1$ **then** BREAK A into two arrays A_1 & A_2
>   EACH OF SIZE $n/2$
>   MERGESORT $(A_1,n/2)$
>   MERGESORT $(A_2,n/2)$
>   MERGE (A_1,A_2).

As usual it is easy to construct an inductive proof of correctness of this algorithm.

To calculate the number of comparisons used by this sort, we need to know the number of comparisons used by MERGE. Although this number will depend on which elements are actually in the two subarrays A_1 and A_2, it is clear that at most $n - 1$ comparisons are used because each comparison results in an element being merged into its proper place in the output array. So in the worst case the number of comparisons used by MERGESORT is given by the difference equation

$$C(n) = 2C(n/2) + n - 1$$

because the algorithm with input of size n calls itself twice with input of size $n/2$ and MERGE uses at most $n - 1$ comparisons. For an initial condition we have $C(1) = 0$ since the algorithm does nothing when $n = 1$. The solution to this equation is

$$C(n) = n \log n - n + 1$$

where log means logarithm to the base 2. The solution can be easily verified using induction. This solution can also be written as $C(n) = \theta(n \log n)$.

If the number of comparisons is the measure of resource usage, then MERGESORT is preferred to the previous sorting algorithms because MERGESORT is $\theta(n \log n)$ while the other sorting algorithms are $\theta(n^2)$.

3.2 Divide-and-conquer difference equations

Consider a divide-and-conquer algorithm which breaks a problem of size n into subproblems each of size n/c. Assume that there are a such subproblems and that the algorithm takes bn^m time to split the original problem into subproblems and to combine the solutions of the subproblems to give the solution to the original problem. A difference equation for the time used by the algorithm is

$$T(n) = aT(n/c) + bn^m.$$

The solution for the time used by the algorithm is

$$T(n) = \begin{cases} \theta(n^m) & \text{if } a < c^m, \\ \theta(n^m \log n) & \text{if } a = c^m, \\ \theta(n^{\log_c a}) & \text{if } a > c^m. \end{cases}$$

The derivation of the solution is not too complicated but it involves a number of details, so we will not give it in full. To derive the solution, you can first convert the divide-and-conquer equation to a standard linear constant coefficient difference equation by the substitution $n = c^r$ and $T(n) = t_r$. Use standard techniques to solve this difference equation. Determine which term in the solution will be largest, and from the assumptions that a, b, and c are positive and the initial condition is non-negative, show that the coefficient of this largest term is positive.

The above solution for the time used by the algorithm also holds for the divide-and-conquer equation

$$T(n) = aT(n/c) + P(n),$$

where $P(n)$ is a polynomial of degree m. This holds because the equation is linear, so the solutions due to the various terms in the polynomial can be linearly combined, and therefore the solution due to the highest-power term in the polynomial will dominate.

Time here should be taken in a broad sense. It could mean actual time as measured by a clock, but it could also mean the number of times a particular operation is used. For example, when we considered sorting, 'time' was the number of comparisons used. In many numerical algorithms, time is the number of multiplications and divisions used.

3.3 Some divide-and-conquer examples

For the running time of MERGESORT we have the equation: $T(n) = 2T(n/2) + bn$. This equation holds for either the number of comparisons or for the total running time. Since $a = 2$, $c = 2$, $m = 1$, we have $a = c^m$ and the solution is $T(n) = \theta(n \log n)$.

A fairly common numeric problem is calculating the product of two polynomials. The input is the coefficients of the two polynomials, and the desired output is the coefficients of the product polynomial. The usual algorithm for this problem proceeds iteratively by multiplying each coefficient of the first polynomial by the first coefficient of the second polynomial, then multiplying each coefficient of the first polynomial by the second coefficient of the second polynomial, and adding these products to the appropriate partial coefficient of the product polynomial; this process is continued until all of the coefficients of the second polynomial have been used. If each of the polynomials has n coefficients then this algorithm will use $\theta(n^2)$ multiplications and $\theta(n^2)$ total operations.

The polynomial multiplication problem can also be solved by a divide-and-conquer algorithm which breaks each polynomial in half, multiplies four half-size polynomials, and then adds the half-size products in the appropriate way to give the product polynomial. More explicitly, let $P(X)$ and $Q(X)$ be two polynomials with n coefficients each. Write

$$P(X) = P_0(X) + P_1(X) X^{n/2},$$
$$Q(X) = Q_0(X) + Q_1(X) X^{n/2}.$$

Then $P(X) Q(X) = P_0(X) Q_0(X) + [P_0(X) Q_1(X) + P_1(X) Q_0(X)] X^{n/2} + P_1(X) Q_1(X) X^n$.

For the number of multiplications $M(n)$, we have

$$M(n) = 4 M(n/2),$$

and since $a = 4$, $c = 2$, $m = 0$, we have $a > c^m$ and the solution is $M(n) = \theta(n^{\log_2 4}) = \theta(n^2)$. For the total number of operations $T(n)$, we have

$$T(n) = 4T(n/2) + bn$$

because all of the polynomial additions can be carried out with a multiple of n coefficient additions, and the multiplications by powers of X simply shift a sequence of coefficients. Since $a = 4$, $c = 2$, $m = 1$, we have $a > c^m$ and $T(n) = \theta(n^2)$.

There seems little point to this divide-and-conquer approach since it gives us the same running time as the usual algorithm, but it suggests that all four of the half-size multiplications might not be necessary because we only need the sum $(P_0 Q_1 + P_1 Q_0)$ rather than both these products. This sum can be computed using only one multiplication if we have $P_0 Q_0$ and $P_1 Q_1$ because $(P_0 Q_1 + P_1 Q_0) = (P_0 + P_1)(Q_0 + Q_1) - P_0 Q_0 - P_1 Q_1$.

Our new divide-and-conquer algorithm is $P(X) Q(X) = P_0(X) Q_0(X) + \{[P_0(X) + P_1(X)][Q_0(X) + Q_1(X)] - P_0(X) Q_0(X) - P_1(X) Q_1(X)\} X^{n/2} + P_1(X) Q_1(X) X^n$. This algorithm uses only three half-size multiplications, so

$$M(n) = 3 M(n/2)$$

and

$$T(n) = 3 T(n/2) + bn$$

because the number of additions and subtractions is still proportional to n. For $M(n)$ we have $a = 3$, $c = 2$, $m = 0$, so $a > c^m$ and $M(n) = \theta(n^{\log_2 3})$. For $T(n)$ we have $a = 3$, $c = 2$, $m = 1$, so $a > c^m$ and $T(n) = \theta(n^{\log_2 3})$. This divide-and-conquer algorithm will be faster than the usual $\theta(n^2)$ algorithm because $\log_2 3 < 2$.

Another problem in which divide-and-conquer leads to a faster algorithm is matrix multiplication. If $n \times n$ matrices are broken into four $n/2 \times n/2$ matrices then the problem is to compute the matrix C, where

$$\begin{bmatrix} C_{11} & C_{12} \\ C_{21} & C_{22} \end{bmatrix} = \begin{bmatrix} A_{11} & A_{12} \\ A_{21} & A_{22} \end{bmatrix} \begin{bmatrix} B_{11} & B_{12} \\ B_{21} & B_{22} \end{bmatrix}.$$

The straightforward algorithm is

$$C_{11} = A_{11} B_{11} + A_{12} B_{21},$$
$$C_{12} = A_{11} B_{12} + A_{12} B_{22},$$
$$C_{21} = A_{21} B_{11} + A_{22} B_{21},$$
$$C_{22} = A_{21} B_{12} + A_{22} B_{22}.$$

The equation for the running time of this algorithm is

$$T(n) = 8\ T(n/2) + bn^2,$$

because there are eight half-size multiplications and the additions can be done in time proportional to n^2. This equation has $a = 8$, $c = 2$, $m = 2$, so $a > c^m$ and $T(n) = \theta(n^{\log_2 8}) = \theta(n^3)$.

A faster divide-and-conquer algorithm was designed by Strassen (1969). This faster algorithm uses only seven half-size multiplications. Strassen's algorithm is

$$
\begin{aligned}
M_1 &= (A_{12} - A_{22})\ (B_{21} + B_{22}),\\
M_2 &= (A_{11} + A_{22})\ (B_{11} + B_{22}),\\
M_3 &= (A_{11} - A_{21})\ (B_{11} + B_{12}),\\
M_4 &= (A_{11} + A_{12})\ B_{22},\\
M_5 &= A_{11}(B_{12} - B_{22}),\\
M_6 &= A_{22}(B_{21} - B_{11}),\\
M_7 &= (A_{21} + A_{22})\ B_{11},\\
C_{11} &= M_1 + M_2 - M_4 + M_6,\\
C_{12} &= M_4 + M_5,\\
C_{21} &= M_6 + M_7,\\
C_{22} &= M_2 - M_3 + M_5 - M_7.
\end{aligned}
$$

It is a simple exercise in algebra to prove this algorithm correct. The very real difficulty was discovering the algorithm in the first place. The running time of Strassen's algorithm obeys the equation

$$T(n) = 7\ T(n/2) + bn^2$$

because there are seven half-size multiplications and the additions and subtractions of matrices can be carried out in time proportional to n^2. Thus Strassen's algorithm has $\theta(n^{\log_2 7})$ running time.

As the final example of this section, consider solving for X, the system of linear equations $AX = B$. A divide-and-conquer approach to this problem would attempt to break it into several subproblems of the same kind. By adding multiples of some $n/2$ of the rows of A to the other $n/2$ rows of A, we can reduce A to the form $\begin{bmatrix} A_1 & A_2 \\ 0 & A_3 \end{bmatrix}$ and by using the same transformation the vector B will be transformed to $\begin{pmatrix} B_1 \\ B_2 \end{pmatrix}$. If we also split X into $\begin{pmatrix} X_1 \\ X_2 \end{pmatrix}$ the solution to the original problem can be given as the solutions to

$$
\begin{aligned}
A_3 X_2 &= B_2,\\
A_1 X_1 &= B_1 - A_2 X_2.
\end{aligned}
$$

The equation for the running time of this algorithm is

$$T(n) = 2\ T(n/2) + bn^3$$

because we have two half-size subproblems and it takes time proportional to n^3 to reduce A to the required special form. Since $a = 2$, $c = 2$, $m = 3$, we have $a < c^m$ and $T(n) = \theta(n^m) = \theta(n^3)$.

There is nothing that particularly recommends this algorithm – it has the same running time as the standard Gaussian elimination algorithm – but it is an example of a divide-and-conquer algorithm with $a < c^m$. An example of a divide-and-conquer algorithm with $a = c^m$ is MERGE-SORT. Examples of divide-and-conquer algorithms with $a > c^m$ are the polynomial multiplication and matrix multiplication algorithms.

3.4 Polynomial multiplication and fast Fourier transform

In practice the polynomial multiplication algorithms of the last section are not used because there is a much faster algorithm. The faster algorithm is based on the idea that there are two ways to represent a polynomial. A polynomial with n coefficients may be represented by its coefficients or it may be represented by the values of the polynomial at n distinct points. Either representation can be calculated from the other representation. This can be represented schematically by:

$$\text{coefficients} \ \underset{\text{interpolation}}{\overset{\text{evaluation}}{\rightleftarrows}} \ \text{values}.$$

If we have the coefficients of two polynomials each with $n/2$ coefficients and we want the $n - 1$ coefficients of the product polynomial, we could evaluate each of the input polynomials at the same $n - 1$ points and multiply the corresponding values to obtain the values of the product polynomial at these $n - 1$ points. To obtain the desired coefficients we could interpolate a polynomial with $n - 1$ coefficients through these points.

The difficulty with this approach is that the standard methods for evaluation and interpolation are both $\theta(n^2)$, so using them would result in an $\theta(n^2)$ method for multiplying polynomials. On the other hand, there is nothing in the above discussion which forces us to use any particular set of points as evaluation and interpolation points. It is easy to evalate a polynomial at certain points. For example, the value of a polynomial at 0 is simply one coefficient of the polynomial, and the value of a polynomial at 1 is simply the sum of the coefficients.

It is difficult to see how to generalize the idea of evaluation at 0, but the idea of evaluation at 1 can be generalized if we are willing to allow complex numbers. A complex number w is an nth root of unity if $w^n = 1$. We know by the fundamental theorem of algebra that there are n complex numbers which are n^{th} roots of unity. A primitive n^{th} root of unity is a complex number w such that $w^n = 1$ and $w^j \neq 1$ for $1 \leq j \leq n - 1$. A primitive root is useful because its powers $w^0, w^1, w^2, \ldots, w^{n-1}$ give us the n numbers which are n^{th} roots of unity. We can use as our primitive roots the complex numbers $e^{2\pi i/n}$ which can be calculated by $\cos(2\pi/n) + i \sin(2\pi/n)$. These numbers only need to be calculated once and stored in a table. This table will also be useful because a primitive $n/2$ root of unity is w^2 which will already be in your table.

To evaluate a polynomial $a_0 + a_1 X + \ldots + a_{n-1} X^{n-1}$ at the n roots of unity we should compute

$$\begin{bmatrix} w^0 & w^0 & \ldots & w^0 \\ w^0 & w^1 & \ldots & w^{n-1} \\ w^0 & w^{1\cdot 2} & \ldots & w^{(n-1)\cdot 2} \\ & \cdot & & \\ & \cdot & & \\ & \cdot & & \\ w^0 & w^{1\cdot(n-1)} & \ldots & w^{(n-1)\cdot(n-1)} \end{bmatrix} \begin{pmatrix} a_0 \\ a_1 \\ \cdot \\ \cdot \\ \cdot \\ \cdot \\ a_{n-1} \end{pmatrix}.$$

Unfortunately if we do this by the obvious algorithm it will take time $\theta(n^2)$ even if we have already calculated the entries in the matrix. However, the matrix has a very special structure and if we can make use of this structure we may be able to construct a faster algorithm.

To display the structure of the matrix we will permute some of the columns. Since we are planning to break things in half we will assume that n is a power of 2. Also we will number the rows and columns from 0 to $n - 1$, so the indices can be represented by using $\log n$ bits. Our permutation will interchange column j with column $\text{Rev}(j)$, where $\text{Rev}(j)$ is a number formed by reading the bits of j in reverse order. In our permuted matrix location i, j will contain $w^{i\text{Rev}(j)}$.

In the lower-left quadrant the matrix will have $i \geq n/2$, $j < n/2$, and $\text{Rev}(j)$ will be even. So

$$w^{i\text{Rev}(j)} = w^{(n/2 + i - n/2)\text{Rev}(j)} = [w^{n/2}]^{\text{Rev}(j)} w^{(i-n/2)\text{Rev}(j)}$$
$$= (-1)^{\text{Rev}(j)} w^{(i-n/2)\text{Rev}(j)} = w^{(i-n/2)\text{Rev}(j)},$$

and the lower-left quadrant will be identical to the upper-left quadrant.

The lower-right quadrant has $i \geq n/2$, $j \geq n/2$, and $\text{Rev}(j)$ is odd. So

$$w^{i\text{Rev}(j)} = -w^{(i-n/2)\text{Rev}(j)},$$

and the lower-right quadrant is the negative of the upper-right quadrant.

The upper-right quadrant has $i < n/2$, $j \geq n/2$ and $\text{Rev}(j) - 1 = \text{Rev}(j - n/2)$. So

$$w^{i\text{Rev}(j)} = w^i \, w^{i(\text{Rev}(j)-1)} = w^i \, w^{i\text{Rev}(j-n/2)},$$

and the upper-right quadrant is identical to the upper-left quadrant multiplied by the diagonal matrix whose i^{th} diagonal entry is w^i.

The upper-left quadrant has $i < n/2$, $j < n/2$, and $\text{Rev}(j)$ is even. So

$$w^{i\text{Rev}(j)} = [w^2]^{i\text{Rev}(j)/2}.$$

The half-size permuted matrix will contain w^2 raised to the $i\text{Rev}(j)$ power because w^2 is a principal $(n/2)^{\text{nd}}$ root of unity. Of course, in the half-size matrix $\text{Rev}(j)$ will have $(\log n) - 1$ bits. In the larger matrix $\text{Rev}(j)/2$ simply removes the low-order bit, which is 0. Thus the upper-left quadrant will be idential to the half-size permuted matrix.

From these considerations we have

$$F_{2n} = \begin{bmatrix} F_n & DF_n \\ F_n & -DF_n \end{bmatrix},$$

where D is a diagonal matrix whose k^{th} entry is w^k where w is a principal $(2n)^{\text{th}}$ root of unity. As we have seen, the matrix can be used to evaluate a polynomial at all the $2n$ roots of unity, and since it turns out that this evaluation gives the coefficients of the discrete Fourier expansion of the polynomial, the matrix is called the (permuted) Fourier matrix.

The form of the above matrix suggests a divide-and-conquer algorithm to compute the discrete Fourier tranform of a vector. Since the algorithm will be faster than a method based directly on the definition of Fourier transform, the algorithm is usually called the fast Fourier transform (FFT). Assume X is a vector with 2n components. Let X_1 be the first n components of X, and let X_2 be the last n components of X. Then

$$F_{2n} X = \begin{pmatrix} F_n X_1 + DF_n X_2 \\ F_n X_1 - DF_n X_2 \end{pmatrix}.$$

Notice that $F_n X_1$ and $F_n X_2$ need only be computed once each. Their values can then be combined to give $F_{2n} X$. To obtain the nice form the columns of the original matrix had to be permuted, so to obtain the effect of the original matrix on a vector the vector must be permuted before the permuted matrix is applied. The whole algorithm to compute the discrete Fourier tranform of $\overline{X}$ is:

$$\overline{X} \xrightarrow{\text{permute}} X = \begin{pmatrix} X_1 \\ X_2 \end{pmatrix} \xrightarrow{\text{half-size } F} \begin{pmatrix} F_n X_1 \\ F_n X_2 \end{pmatrix} \xrightarrow{\text{combine}} \begin{pmatrix} F_n X_1 + DF_n X_2 \\ F_n X_1 - DF_n X_2 \end{pmatrix}.$$

In this process the matrix F never really needs to exist. The F's in the above scheme are simply recursive calls to the procedure F. The non-zero elements of D are powers of w. So the powers of w can be computed once, stored in an array, and used from the array when necessary.

The running time for this algorithm can be considered in two parts: the time to permute, and the time for the recursive procedure F. The permutation uses the bit reversals of the numbers 0 through $2n - 1$. Since these numbers can be represented using $\log n + 1$ bits, the permutation can be computed in $\theta(n \log n)$. The permutation can be done in $\theta(n)$ if the bit reversals are pre-computed. The running time for the procedure for F obeys the difference equation:

$$T(2n) = 2 \, T(n) + bn$$

because there are two half-size recursive calls, and the multiplication by D and the additions and subtractions can be carried out in time proportional to n. Thus

$$T(2n) = \theta(n \log n).$$

To use this fast algorithm for polynomial multiplication, we need a fast way to interpolate, or what is the same, a fast way to multiply a vector by the inverse of the F matrix. For the inverse procedure we need the idea of conjugate. The conjugate of a complex number $a + bi$ is $a - bi$. We represent the conjugate of the complex number Z by Z^*. The product $ZZ^* = a^2 + b^2$, which is the square of the length of the vector which represents Z. For a root of unity w, the product $ww^* = 1$ because the length of w is 1. The conjugate of a complex matrix is the transpose of the matrix with each element replaced by its conjugate. The inverse of matrix F is its conjugate divided by the dimension because

$$F_{2n} \cdot F_{2n}^* = \begin{bmatrix} F & DF \\ F & -DF \end{bmatrix} \begin{bmatrix} F^* & F^* \\ F^*D^* & -F^*D^* \end{bmatrix}$$

$$= \begin{bmatrix} FF^* + DFF^*D^* & FF^* - DFF^*D^* \\ FF^* - DFF^*D^* & FF^* + DFF^*D^* \end{bmatrix} = \begin{bmatrix} 2nI & 0 \\ 0 & 2nI \end{bmatrix}.$$

So F^*X can be computed quickly because

$$F^*X = F^*X^{**} = (F^\mathrm{T}X^*)^* = P(FPX^*)^*,$$

where F^T is the transpose of F, and P is the bit-reversal permutation matrix. The last equality follows because $F^\mathrm{T} = PFP$.

Finally the whole algorithm to compute the coefficients of the product polynomial is:

(1) Place the n coefficients of the first polynomial in the first n components of the vector X of dimension $2n$. The other n components of X will contain 0.
(2) Similarly place the n coefficients of the second polynomial in the vector Y.

(3) Permute both X and Y.

(4) Use the recursive algorithm to compute both FX and FY.

(5) Componentwise multiply FX and FY to obtain a vector Z.

(6) Permute and conjugate Z.

(7) Use the recursive algorithm to compute FZ.

(8) Conjugate and divide each component of FZ by $2n$.

The resulting vector will contain the $2n - 1$ coefficients of the product polynomial as its first $2n - 1$ components. The last component should contain 0. Since this algorithm will most likely be carried out using floating point arithmetic, the last component will likely not be exactly 0, but the value in this component will give us an estimate of how exact the other components are.

3.5 How practical are divide-and-conquer algorithms?

After creating algorithms in the abstract world of analysis of algorithms, we should now look back to the real world of programs and ask if the divide-and-conquer algorithms, which are theoretically faster, will be practically faster, and whether they will be practical at all. There are several reasons to be sceptical about the practicality of these algorithms. In our abstract world recursion was available at no cost. In the real world recursion may be unavailable or it may have a high cost. In the abstract world we computed time only to order, not distinguishing $10^{23}n^2$ from $2n^2$, but in the real world these functions are very different.

Let us address recursion first. The tempting thing for a theoretician is to say that all 'modern' programming languages have recursion so there is no problem. Unfortunately large amounts of programming are done in older languages which do not support recursion. So there is still some reason for considering converting recursive algorithms to iterative algorithms. Even when recursion is available it may not be a good idea to use it. Theoretically we often assume that passing data to procedures is free. In the analysis in this section we have ignored space usage, and we have particularly ignored extra space used to maintain stacks for the recursive procedures. In the real world neither of these should be ignored. Sometimes by doing a space analysis we find that the recursive stack does not get very big, so we are justified in ignoring it. In other cases, we find that the recursive stack gets very large because we are putting copy after copy of the same data on the stack. This problem can often be overcome by having only a single global copy of the data and, instead of passing the data to the recursive procedure, passing only a pointer to the particular part of the global copy that is needed. In some cases, we find that data passed to the recursive routine may be replaced by a much simpler global structure. In the Towers of Hanoi example, the number of disks was

repeatedly passed to the recursive procedure, but the equivalent information could be maintained in a global counter. There are a number of
methods which will suffice to convert a recursive routine to an iterative
routine, but if they are general enough to work for all recursive routines,
they are too general to result in any saving in time or space. Special
features of a particular recursive routine can often be exploited in produc-
ing a more efficient iterative routine. We have seen how special features
can be exploited in the Towers of Hanoi example. As another example,
the MERGESORT algorithm works from the top down, splitting a big
array and passing each half to the recursive routine. This routine can be
made iterative by working bottom-up. Consider each element as a sorted
array of size 1 and merge these in pairs until you have sorted arrays of
size 2. Again merge these in pairs until you have sorted arrays of size 4.
Continue merging until the entire array is sorted. This can be accomplished without passing any arrays to procedures by keeping track of the
size and the beginning and ending indices of the subaarrays you are
merging.

In summary, it is often worthwhile to convert recursive algorithms to
iterative algorithms, but you should exploit the special features of the
problem to create an efficient iterative algorithm.

Are faster algorithms always faster? Probably not. In our analysis we
have concentrated on asymptotic time order. We expect our faster algorithms to be faster than slower algorithms for big enough inputs, but the
slower algorithms may well be faster for small inputs. For example, in
sorting there are $\theta(n^2)$ algorithms which are faster than an $\theta(n \log n)$
algorithm for $n < 20$, but for $n > 20$ the $\theta(n \log n)$ algorithm is faster.
In this case, unless we are dealing with very small data sets, the faster
algorithm really is faster. On the other hand, there are $\theta(n^{2.5})$ algorithms
for matrix multiplication. These algorithms don't become faster than the
standard $\theta(n^3)$ algorithm until one is dealing with $50\,000 \times 50\,000$ matrices. Since no one is presently trying to multiply matrices this large, the
$\theta(n^{2.5})$ algorithm is only theoretically interesting.

The algorithms we have designed may fail to be practical in other ways.
The algorithms are not foolproof, that is, the algorithms assume that they
will receive the type of data they are expecting, and their behaviour on
unexpected data may well be rather strange. Practical programs should
check the input data to make sure it is of the expected kind and issue a
warning if the data is not of the expected kind. The algorithm may also
not be practical if it solves the wrong problem. For example, the FFT-
based polynomial multiplication algorithm is designed for dense polynomials, that is, polynomials in which all or almost all the coefficients are
non-zero, but many large-scale polynomial multiplication problems arise
in which the polynomials are sparse, that is, have almost all the coefficients equal to zero. For such sparse problems there are algorithms

which will easily outperform the FFT-based algorithm. Similarly there are special algorithms for sorting which will be slow in general but will be very fast when the input data is almost sorted.

In summary, there are practical issues which should be considered before a theoretically good algorithm is used as a practical program.

3.6 Exercises

(a) You have a large number of coins and a pan balance. You may put any number of coins in each pan of the balance. The balance will tell you if the set of coins in one pan weighs the same as the set of coins in the other pan, or it will tell you which set is heavier. Somewhere among your coins is one coin which has a different weight from the other coins. All the coins except this odd coin have exactly the same weight. The problem is to find the odd coin.

Design a divide-and-conquer algorithm to solve this problem. You may assume that the number of coins is a power of 3. Prove that your algorithm is correct. Give and solve a difference equation for the number of times your algorithm uses the balance.

(b) Design a divide-and-conquer algorithm to find the two largest elements in an array. Prove that your algorithm is correct. Calculate the number of comparisons it uses. Show by example that your algorithm uses more comparisons than necessary.

(c) Two string C_1 and C_2 commute (that is, $C_1C_2 = C_2C_1$) iff there is a string w such that $C_1 = w^{k_1}$ and $C_2 = w^{k_2}$. Start from an inductive proof that w exists and construct an algorithm to find w.

4 Average case

4.1 What is average case?

Up till now we have considered the running time of an algorithm to be a function of the size of the input, but what happens when there are several different inputs of the same size? An algorithm may treat all inputs of the same size in the same way, or it may handle some inputs more quickly and some inputs more slowly. The maximum of the running time over all inputs of the same size is called the worst-case running time. The minimum running time over all inputs of the same size is called the best-case running time. The running times averaged over all inputs of the same size is called the average-case running time. The average-case running time is not the same as the average of the worst case and the best case. It is often difficult to calculate the average-case time because the probability associated with each of the various inputs of a particular size is unknown. For definiteness and simplicity, it is often assumed that each input with the same size is equally likely to occur. With this assumption average case can be calculated.

4.2 Some examples of average case behaviour

As an example of average case behaviour, consider the following algorithm:

```
procedure LARGETWO
   FIRST:= B[1]
   SEC:= B[2]
   for I:= 2 to n do
     if B[I] > FIRST
       then SEC:= FIRST; FIRST:= B[I]
       else if B[I] > SEC
             then SEC:= B[I].
```

This algorithm should find the two largest elements in an array. We will consider the number of comparisons of array elements it uses to accomplish this task. In the **for** loop, for each I the algorithm makes either 1 or 2 comparisons. In best case the algorithm makes 1 comparison for each I giving a total of $n - 1$ comparisons. In worst case the algorithm makes 2 comparisons for each I giving a total of $2(n - 1)$ comparisons.

Let $A(n)$ be the number of comparisons used on average by this algorithm. Since the algorithm proceeds in one direction across the array, we may reasonably assume that for the first $n - 1$ elements the algorithm will on average use $A(n - 1)$ comparisons, that is, the same number it would use if the last element did not exist. For the last element it will use at least one comparison. It will use a second comparison exactly when $B[n] \leq$ FIRST, but since FIRST will be the largest of the first $n - 1$ elements, the algorithm will use a second comparison as long as $B[n]$ is not the largest element in the array. The probability that $B[n]$ is not the largest element is $(n - 1)/n$, if we assume that each element is equally likely to be the largest element. From these considerations we have:

$$A(n) = A(n - 1) + 1 + \frac{n - 1}{n} = A(n - 1) + 2 - 1/n.$$

For an initial condition we have $A(2) = 3/2$, since for two elements the algorithm is equally likely to use one or two comparisons. The solution to this difference equation is

$$A(n) = 2(n - 1) - \sum_{j=1}^{n} 1/j$$

and for large n

$A(n) \to 2(n - 1) - \ln n + \text{constant}.$

So we have that the average case of this algorithm is very close to the algorithm's worst case. Notice that if we took (worst + best)/2 we would get $3/2(n - 1)$, which will be a severe underestimate of the average case. (As an aside, we should mention that this is a poorly set up algorithm since it assumes that the array has at least two locations. If this algorithm were used with an array containing a single element, the results would be unpredictable.)

The QUICKSORT algorithm has a more complicated average case analysis. The algorithm is:

procedure QUICKSORT(A)
    PICK AN ELEMENT α OF A AT RANDOM
    DIVIDE A INTO A_1 (THE ELEMENTS OF A WHICH ARE
                LESS THAN α.)
              A_2 (THE ELEMENTS OF A WHICH EQUAL
                  α. WE WILL ASSUME THERE IS ONLY
                  ONE SUCH ELEMENT.)
              A_3 (THE ELEMENTS OF A WHICH ARE
                  GREATER THAN α.)
    RETURN (QUICKSORT$(A_1) \cdot A_2 \cdot$ QUICKSORT(A_3)).

The worst case for QUICKSORT occurs when A_1 or A_3 contains $n - 1$ elements. If we let $W(n)$ stand for the worst-case running time of QUICKSORT, we have

$W(n) = W(n - 1) + bn$

because the separation into A_1, A_2, A_3 takes time proportional to n. From this we have $W(n) = \theta(n^2)$. The best case for QUICKSORT occurs when A_1 and A_3 are each approximately $n/2$. If we let $B(n)$ be the best-case running time, we have approximately

$B(n) = 2B(n/2) + bn$

and $B(n) = \theta(n \log n)$. For the worst case to occur each recursive splitting must have one of the sets A_1 or A_3 empty. For the best case to occur each recursive splitting must have A_1 and A_3 of approximately equal size.

Will the average case be like the worst case or like the best case? We might expect nearly equal splits to occur more frequently than one-sided splits, so we could guess that average case is probably closer to best case than to worst case. If we let $A(n)$ be the average case running time and assume that every split is equally likely, we have

$$A(n) = \frac{1}{n} \sum_{k=1}^{n} [A(k-1) + A(n-k) + b(n+1)],$$

where $b(n+1)$ is the time to split and combine. Then

$$nA(n) - (n-1) A(n-1)$$
$$= \sum_{k=1}^{n} A(k-1) - \sum_{k=1}^{n-1} A(k-1) + \sum_{k=1}^{n} A(n-k)$$
$$- \sum_{k=1}^{n-1} A(n-1-k) + bn(n+1) - bn(n-1)$$
$$= 2A(n-1) + 2bn$$

and $nA(n) = (n+1) A(n-1) + 2bn$ and $\dfrac{A(n)}{n+1} = \dfrac{A(n-1)}{n} + \dfrac{2b}{n+1}$.

Letting $Z(n) = A(n)/(n+1)$, we have $Z(n) = Z(n-1) + \dfrac{2b}{n+1}$, which

has the solution $Z(n) = C_1 + 2b \sum_{j=1}^{n} \dfrac{1}{(j+1)}$. But $Z(n) \to C_2 + C_3 \log n$,

so $A(n) \to C_2(n+1) + C_3(n+1) \log n$, giving $A(n) = \theta(n \log n)$.

In summary, the average case behaviour of an algorithm is somewhere between the worst case and the best cast behaviour, but it may be very close to the best case behaviour or very close to the worst case behaviour.

4.3   Exercises

(a) A number of useful tricks were used in deriving the average case behaviour of QUICKSORT. For the procedure LARGETWO set up a difference equation with a summation by assuming that each element is equally likely to be the largest element. Then employ the techniques used on QUICKSORT to obtain the simple difference equation we used for LARGETWO.

(b) For the following procedure do an average case analysis. Is the average case nearer to worst case or to best case?

```
procedure BIGTWO
    FIRST:= B[1]
    SEC:= B[2]
    for I:= 2 to n do
        if B[I] ⩾ SEC
            then if B[I] > FIRST
                then SEC:= FIRST; FIRST:= B[I]
                else SEC:= B[I].
```

5 Lower bounds

5.1 Trivial lower bounds

A lower bound is a statement that every algorithm which solves a particular problem must use at least so much of a particular resource. We have already met some lower bounds in the Towers of Hanoi example. There we argued that every algorithm for the problem must take at least $\theta(2^n)$ time because the output must contain $2^n - 1$ moves. Such a lower bound is called a trivial lower bound because it is obvious that an algorithm must take at least as much time as it takes to print its output. Although such a bound is called trivial it may not be trivial to compute the length of the output. For example, it was not immediately obvious that the output for the Towers of Hanoi must have length $2^n - 1$.

Trivial lower bounds can also depend on the input. If we can show that to compute the correct answer an algorithm must read all of its input, then the algorithm must use time which is at least as great as the length of the input. For example, if an algorithm is supposed to multiply an $n \times n$ matrix by an n-component vector, we have the trivial lower bound of $\theta(n^2)$ because if the algorithm does not read some of the input, then there are vectors and matrices for which the algorithm gives the wrong answer. As another example, consider an algorithm which is supposed to find the largest element in an n-element array. This algorithm must take time at least $\theta(n)$, since if it does not look at all the elements in the array there are arrays for which the algorithm will give an incorrect answer. There are problems in which an algorithm does not have to look at the whole input. For example, to determine if a list is empty an algorithm only has to look at the first element of the list; it does not need to look at all elements of the list.

Input and output lower bounds can vary widely. Sometimes the output bound will be larger than the input bound. Sometimes the input bound will be larger than the output bound. In the Towers of Hanoi problem the output bound is $\theta(2^n)$, but the input bound is only $\theta(\log n)$ because n and the names of the towers can be specified in $\theta(\log n)$ bits. In the variant of the Towers of Hanoi in which one is asked if a given configuration is used in moving the disks from tower A to tower C, the output bound is $\theta(1)$ since the yes or no answer can be specified with a single bit, while the input bound is $\theta(n)$ because $\theta(n)$ bits are needed to specify which tower contains which disk.

So far our lower bounds have been best case bounds, that is, even in the best case every algorithm must use at least the time specified by the lower bound. Consider the problem of determining if a list contains a particular element. The desired element could be the first element in the list, so the best case lower bound is $\theta(1)$. On the other hand, to be sure that the desired element is not in the list an algorithm must look at every element, so the worst case lower bound is $\theta(n)$.

5.2   Lower bounds on specific operations

The trivial lower bounds merely state that an algorithm must do the required input and output; they say nothing about any computation the algorithm must perform. To obtain lower bounds involving specific operations, the operations which the algorithm is allowed to use must be specified. In this section we will consider algorithms in which the only allowed operations on input elements are comparisons. This will suffice for the problems considered. For other problems, the operations of addition, subtraction and multiplication might be allowed. We refer the interested reader to Winograd (1980).

Let us consider deriving a lower bound on the number of comparisons needed to find the largest element in an array. We use an input bound argument. If some element is not compared to any other element then either the algorithm says that the uncompared element is the largest element, which will be false in some cases, or the algorithm says that some other element is largest, which will be false when the uncompared element is largest. Since elements can be compared two at a time, we have that any algorithm which correctly finds the largest using only comparisons must use at least $n/2$ comparisons.

We know that $n/2$ comparisons are needed, but we expect that $n - 1$ comparisons are needed because our methods for finding the largest use $n - 1$ comparisons. We can consider an algorithm as forming a directed graph. Each time a comparison is made, a directed edge from the larger to the smaller element is put into the graph. When the largest element has been found, then for every other element there will be a directed path in the graph from the largest to the other element. If not, we could replace the element without a path by an element larger than the element that the algorithm reports to be largest. Since the algorithm is assumed to use only comparisons, the algorithm cannot detect this replacement. So if not all these paths exist, then the algorithm will give incorrect answers. If all these paths exist, then the graph formed from the directed graph by replacing the directed edges with undirected edges will be connected. Since a connected graph has at least $n - 1$ edges and since each edge corresponds to a comparison, $n - 1$ comparisons are needed.

A different way to obtain this lower bound is to think of finding the largest as a dynamic system. As an algorithm proceeds it classifies each element as belonging to one of three sets: the set U which contains elements which have been compared to no other element; the set S of elements which have been compared to some other element and have been found to be smaller; and the set L of elements which have been compared to some other element and have been found to be larger than any element they have been compared to. The states of the dynamic system will be vectors with three integer components giving the sizes of the sets U, S and L. When the algorithm starts the dynamic system will be in state $(n,0,0)$, and when the algorithm correctly terminates the dynamic system will be in state $(0,n-1,1)$. In each comparison of the algorithm, the state changes in one of the following six ways, where the sets from which the elements to be compared are indicated by the names of the sets above the arrows:

$$(U,S,L) \xrightarrow{U:U} (U-2,S+1,L+1)$$

$$(U,S,L) \xrightarrow{S:S} (U,S,L)$$

$$(U,S,L) \xrightarrow{L:L} (U,S+1,L-1)$$

$$(U,S,L) \xrightarrow{U:S} (U-1,S+1,L) \text{ or } (U-1,S,L+1)$$

$$(U,S,L) \xrightarrow{U:L} (U-1,S+1,L)$$

$$(U,S,L) \xrightarrow{S:L} (U,S+1,L-1) \text{ or } (U,S,L)$$

Since we have a model of the action of any algorithm which finds the largest element using only comparisons, we can establish a lower bound for the algorithm by establishing a lower bound on the number of transitions in the dynamic system required to go from state $(n,0,0)$ to state $(0,n-1,1)$. Consider the middle component. It must increase from 0 to $n - 1$, but this component can increase by at most 1 in any of the tansitions. Hence at least $n - 1$ transitions in the dynamic system and $n - 1$ comparisons in the algorithm are required.

It is important to notice that this result really does depend on the type of algorithm being considered. By allowing different operations the largest element can be located using only $\log n$ comparisons. Consider the following algorithm:

```
for I:= 1 to n do
    NUM[I]:= n**a₁
function BIG (i,j)
    if j = i + 1
        then if aᵢ ≥ aⱼ
                then BIG:= i
                else BIG:= j
```

$$\textbf{else if } \sum_{k=i}^{(i+j)/2} \text{NUM}[k] \geq \sum_{k=\frac{i+j}{2}+1}^{j} \text{NUM}[k]$$

$$\textbf{then } \text{BIG}:= \text{BIG } (i,(i+j)/2)$$
$$\textbf{else } \text{BIG}:= \text{BIG}((i+j)/2+1,j)$$

end function
$\text{LARGEST}:= a_{\text{BIG}(1,n)}.$

In this algorithm we are assuming that the elements are distinct positive integers. The ** indicates exponentiation. Let $C(n)$ be the number of comparisons used by the algorithm with n elements; then $C(n) = C(n/2) + 1$ and $C(2) = 1$. Thus $C(n) = \log n$. (If you also want to count the comparison between i and $j + 1$, there are 2 log n comparisons.) The trick here is to make sure that the largest element is in the half-size subset with the largest sum. Consider the case in which LARGEST is in the first half. Then

$$\sum_{k=\frac{n}{2}+1}^{n} \text{NUM}[k] \leq \frac{n}{2} n^{\text{LARGEST}-1}$$
$$= \frac{n}{2}^{\text{LARGEST}} < n^{\text{LARGEST}} + \frac{n}{2} - 1 \leq \sum_{k=1}^{n/2} \text{NUM}[k],$$

so this algorithm will work correctly. The use of exponentiation allows us to make the largest element so large that we can do a binary search through the subsets and locate the largest element quickly.

This example should indicate that lower-bound proofs are sensitive to operations allowed in the algorithm. It is thus important in lower-bound arguments to indicate the class of algorithms being considered.

5.3 Lower bounds on sorting

A very traditional and ubiquitous problem is sorting. Given n elements from a totally ordered set, put them in order from the smallest to the largest. We have already encountered several algorithms for this problem. Some had $\theta(n^2)$ worst case running time. Some had $\theta(n \log n)$ worst case running time. Some has $\theta(n \log n)$ average case running time. Some had $\theta(n \log n)$ best case running time. From these examples, one might conjecture that an $\theta(n \log n)$ lower bound could be established for best case and hence for average and worst cases, at least for algorithms which sort by using only comparisons. Unfortunately this conjecture is false. If the elements are already sorted, an algorithm could check in only $n - 1$ comparisons that the elements were in order. It is not essential that

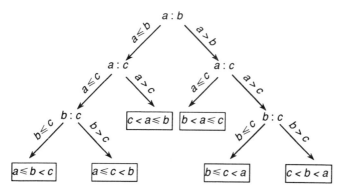

Fig. 1.1 Comparison tree for sorting algorithm

the elements actually be in order; for any particular arrangement of the elements, an algorithm can be created which tests for this arrangement using $n - 1$ comparisons, and if the elements are in this particular arrangement the algorithm will sort them with no additional comparisons. So any best case lower bound for sorting must be less than or equal to $n - 1$ comparisons. But no smaller lower bound is possible because if an array is sorted then the largest element can be found using no comparisons, since the largest element is the last element in the array. Since we have already demonstrated a best case lower bound of $n - 1$ comparisons to find the largest element, $n - 1$ comparisons is also the best case lower bound for sorting.

It still is reasonable to believe that a lower bound of $\theta(n \log n)$ may be possible for worst case and average case. To obtain these bounds we introduce a model of computation called the comparison tree. Each internal node of a comparison tree contains an expression like $a:b$ which means compare a to b. From a comparison node there are two arrows to other nodes. One arrow is labelled $a \leq b$ and the other arrow is labelled $a > b$. There are also external nodes or leaves which indicate the termination of the tree. The comparison tree should capture the idea of an algorithm which uses only comparisons. The algorithm starts at the root of the tree, does the comparison there, and then follows the appropriate arrow. This process continues until a leaf is reached. Figure 1 shows a comparison tree for an algorithm which sorts 3 elements. In this example there are 6 leaves because there are 3! possible orderings of 3 elements. A comparison tree for sorting n elements will have $n!$ leaves. In this example there are sets which will be sorted using only 2 comparisons, but there are also sets for which this algorithm uses 3 comparisons.

Let us define the depth of the root of a tree as depth 0, and the depth of a node in the tree as 1 + depth of its parent node. Then the maximum number of comparisons to sort any set using a particular comparison tree algorithm is the maximum depth of a node in the tree. In the example, there is a node (a leaf) of depth 3 and there is a set on which this algorithm uses 3 comparisons.

To obtain a worst case lower bound, we will consider the depth of comparison trees for sorting. Since there are only two arrows from each node, the number of nodes can only double when the depth is increased by 1. So there are at most 2^D nodes at depth D, and summing the nodes at every depth there are at most 2^{D+1} nodes in a tree with maximum depth D. Since there are $n!$ possible orderings of n things, a comparison tree for sorting must have at least $n!$ leaves. From these two facts we have $2^{D+1} \geq n!$. Taking logs and using Stirling's approximation that $n! \sim n^n e^{-n} \sqrt{2\pi n}$, we have

$$D \geq \theta(n \log n),$$

and hence $\theta(n \log n)$ is a worst case lower bound for the number of comparisons used by an algorithm which sorts using only comparisons.

The comparison tree model can also be used to produce an average-case lower bound. The average number of comparisons will be the average depth of a leaf of the comparison tree. By average here we mean that we assume that each ordering of the n elements is equally likely and hence each ordering has probability $1/n!$ Now the average depth of a leaf will be at least as great as the average depth of a node. To minimize the average depth of a node, we will consider the full tree with total depth L where $\log n! - 1 < L \leq \log n!$. By a full tree we mean a tree which has exactly 2^i nodes at depth i. This full tree will give us a lower bound because any comparison tree for sorting has at least $\log n!$ nodes and we are making their depths as small as possible. The average depth of a node in our full tree is at least

$$\frac{1}{n!} \sum_{i=0}^{L} i 2^i = \frac{2}{n!} \{(L-1) 2^L + 1\} \geq \frac{2}{n!} \{(\log n! - 2) \frac{n!}{2} + 1\}.$$

Again using Stirling's approximation this is asymptotic to $\theta(n \log n)$, and $\theta(n \log n)$ is an average case lower bound for sorting. We summarize these results in the following proposition.

Proposition 10 Any algorithm which sorts using only comparisons must use at least

(a) $\theta(n)$ comparisons in best case,
(b) $\theta(n \log n)$ comparisons in average case,
(c) $\theta(n \log n)$ comparisons in worst case.

We close this section with two reminders. First, average case here assumes that all $n!$ orderings are equally likely. If there are significantly fewer orderings which are very likely to occur, then the above average case bound does not hold. For example, if the inputs are almost-sorted then there are $\theta(n)$ average case algorithms. Secondly, the bounds in the proposition apply for algorithms which sort using only comparisons. If different types of operations are allowed, then these bounds may not hold.

5.4 Exercises

(a) Prove a worst case lower bound of $\frac{3n}{2} - 2$ comparisons for any algorithm which finds the largest and smallest elements in an array by using only comparisons. Devise a divide-and-conquer algorithm for this problem. Show that your algorithm uses $\frac{3n}{2} - 2$ comparisons.

(b) Create an algorithm which finds the largest and second largest elements in an array and uses only $n + (\log n) - 2$ comparisons. (Hint: Keep track of the elements which are potentially the largest, and for each such element keep track of those elements which have 'lost' only to this element.)

6 Exhaustive search

6.1 Straightforward exhaustive search

The algorithms which we have considered so far have been based on the divide-and-conquer strategy, that is, try to break the problem into several smaller problems of the same kind. An exhaustive search is a different strategy for designing algorithms. This strategy is based on the idea of trying all possible answers. Either the solution is located or no solution exists.

A simple problem for which this strategy is reasonable is: given a list, and a value, is there an element of the list which contains the given value? An exhaustive search algorithm would look at each element in turn until either one with the given value is found or until all of the elements have been viewed. If there are n elements in the list, then this algorithm will take $\theta(1)$ in best case and $\theta(n)$ in worst case, and these are the best possible running times for any algorithm for this problem.

There are also problems for which straightforward exhaustive search gives very poor algorithms. Consider sorting. A straightforward exhaustive search would try each possible ordering until the sorted ordering is found. Unfortunately, there are $n!$ possible orderings so in worst case (when the last ordering is the correct one) this algorithm will take at least

$\theta(n!)$, which is much, much greater than the $\theta(n \log n)$ taken by algorithms we have already found.

Satisfiability is another problem to which exhaustive search can be applied. The satisfiability problem is: given a Boolean expression, is there an assignment of true and false to the variables which makes the expression true? If there are n variables, there are 2^n possible true/false assignments for the variables, and since a Boolean expression of length L can evaluated in $\theta(L)$ time, the exhaustive search algorithm will take $\theta(L \, 2^n)$ time in worst case. Unlike sorting, it is not clear that there are faster algorithms for this problem. Also unlike the find value problem, it is not clear that this is the best running time possible for this problem.

6.2 Backtracking

While straightforward exhaustive search may be useful in some problems, there is usually additional information available which will allow an algorithm to eliminate some of the possibilities. One way to make use of this additional information is called backtracking. In a backtrack algorithm the search is broken into stages, and at each stage only the possibilities which can still lead to a solution are considered. The name 'backtracking' comes from a method for finding a way through a maze. At a choice-point in the maze, pick an arbitrary path which has not yet been used. Continue making such choices until you reach a dead-end or a choice-point at which all paths have already been used. Then go back on the path you have come down to the previous choice-point and continue the method. This last step, going back on a path, is called backtracking, and this name is also given to the general method. So in the general backtracking method the search is broken into stages; at each stage a choice is made; when the algorithm determines that none of the choices at a stage can lead to a solution, then the algorithm backtracks by returning to the previous stage and taking one of the unused choices.

A problem to which backtracking can be directly applied is the Hamiltonian path: given a graph, find a sequence of vertices which contains each vertex exactly once and such that adjacent vertices in the sequence are connected by an edge in the graph. At each stage in the backtrack algorithm an unused vertex sharing an edge with the current vertex is chosen. If it is impossible to choose such a vertex, the algorithm backtracks to the previous vertex and tries to choose a vertex other than the one that led to the dead-end. If the graph contains a Hamiltonian path, this algorithm will eventually find it, because the algorithm generates all sequences of vertices with adjacent vertices connected by an edge and no repeated vertices. A straightforward exhaustive search for this problem would generate a permutation of the vertices and then test to see if the vertices

Table 2

X_1	X_2	X_3	Expression
F	F	F	F
F	F	T	F
F	T	F	F
F	T	T	F
T	F	F	F
T	F	T	F
T	T	F	T
T	T	T	T

adjacent in the permutation were also adjacent in the graph. In worst case all permutations would be generated and the exhaustive search algorithm would take at least $n!$ time. The backtrack algorithm in worst case would generate at most $\prod_{i=1}^{n} d_i$ paths, where d_i is the degree of vertex i. So in worst case we expect the backtrack algorithm to be faster than the exhaustive search algorithm. The backtrack algorithm also has the advantage that it uses information about the graph in generating a path. If the backtrack algorithm uses more information about the graph in picking the next vertex, we can reasonably expect the backtrack algorithm to work much more quickly in average case.

We will next consider backtracking and exhaustive search for the satisfiability problem. Consider the Boolean expression: $X_1 \cdot (X_1 \vee \bar{X}_2 \vee \bar{X}_3)$ $\cdot (\bar{X}_1 \vee X_2)$. Since this expression has 3 variables, there are 8 possible truth assignments, which we show in Table 2. An exhaustive search algorithm would generate 7 out of 8 of these assignments before it found that the expression was satisfiable. A backtrack algorithm could proceed according to the tree shown in Figure 2. It picks the first variable X_1 and assigns it F, then $X_1 = F$ is substituted in the expression yielding the expression F. Since F is not satisfiable, the algorithm backtracks and tries the assignment $X_1 = T$. When this is substituted into the expression, it yields the expression X_2. A reasonably clever algorithm would notice that this expression can be satisfied by the assignment $X_2 = T$, and hence that the whole expression is satisfiable. A less clever algorithm might try $X_2 = F$, and have to backtrack once more before finding a satisfying assignment. In either case, it seems that the backtrack algorithm will be better than the exhaustive search algorithm.

The backtrack algorithm should simplify the expression at each stage. While this might seem complicated in general, it is very easy when the expression is in clause form. In clause form a Boolean expression is a set of clauses ANDed together, and within each clause are a set of literals

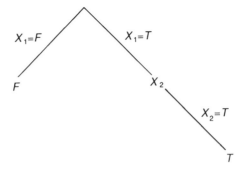

Fig. 1.2   Backtrack algorithm

(that is, complemented and uncomplemented variables) ORed together. When a variable X is assigned the value T, all the clauses containing the literal X become true and can be removed from the expression, while all the clauses containing $\bar{X}$ are simplified by the removal of $\bar{X}$. Similarly, if X is assigned the value F, then each clause containing $\bar{X}$ can be removed from the expression and each clause containing X can be simplified by the removal of X. One special case should be noted: if a clause containing a single variable has that variable removed, then the whole expression becomes false.

   How should the backtrack algorithm choose which variable to assign at each stage? An algorithm could try assigning X_1, then X_2, and so forth, but this method does not take advantage of the structure of the expression. If an expression contains a clause with a single literal, then that literal must be set to true for the entire expression to be true. If an expression contains a variable X which only appears in the form X and never in the form $\bar{X}$, then X can be assigned true and all the clauses containing X can be removed without affecting the satisfiability of the expression. These two rules can be used to simplify the expression. There is one complication: if the expression contains a clause with the single literal X and another clause with a single literal $\bar{X}$, then the expression is not satisfiable.

   After the expression has been simplified as much as possible by the above rules, a method for choosing which assignment to make next is still needed. A method which seems reasonable is to pick the literal which appears in the most clauses and to make this literal true. This method is not guaranteed to find a satisfying assignment, but it will simplify the expression. Such a method which is reasonable but not guaranteed to lead to a solution is called a *heuristic*. A backtrack algorithm will still have to backtrack when the heuristic does not lead to a solution, but a well-chosen heuristic can greatly reduce the number of times the algorithm has to backtrack.

6.3 Knight's tour

We have already mentioned the Hamiltonian path problem. A specialization of this problem is the knight's tour problem. In the knight's tour problem, the vertices of the graph are the squares of an $n \times m$ chessboard. Two squares are connected by an edge if and only if a knight can legally move from one square to the other. The knight can move two squares in one direction and one square in an orthogonal direction. The knight's tour problem is to find a Hamiltonian path in this graph, or equivalently move the knight legally around the chessboard so that it visits each square exactly once.

If nm is odd then from some starting squares there is no knight's tour. The traditional chessboard has squares of two colours, so that orthogonally adjacent squares are of different colours. If nm is odd, then there are more squares of one colour. Since the knight always moves from one colour to the other, a tour starting from a square of the less numerous colour is impossible.

To find a knight's tour one could use the backtrack algorithm for a Hamiltonian path, but as the last section suggests, some sort of heuristic should be used to choose the next square. One plausible idea is based on the degree of a square. The degree of a square is the number of unused squares the knight could go to if it were on this square. If the square has large degree then there are many ways into and out of the square, and it is not too important to deal with this square immediately. If a square has degree 2, then there is one way in and one way out of the square, and this square should probably be used as soon as possible. So the heuristic is: next visit a possible square of lowest degree.

Even without this heuristic a backtrack algorithm will find a knight's tour if one exists. With this heuristic, the backtrack algorithm may work faster. As well as picking the next square the degree can also be used in deciding when to backtrack. Clearly a backtrack is called for when the tour reaches a dead-end, a square from which no unused square can be reached in one step. Just before the move into this dead-end, the dead-end square had degree 1. A square of degree 1 should be entered only if it is the last square on the board. So if the lowest degree among possible next squares is 1 and there is more than one unused square, then the algorithm should backtrack. Further, if there are ever two unused squares of degree 1, then the algorithm should backtrack since both of these squares cannot be the last square.

Initially squares near the centre of the board will have degree 8, squares nearer an edge will have degree less than 8, and the corner squares will have degree 2. As a partial tour is constructed the degrees of the squares will decrease.

How well will this heuristic work? Is backtracking ever needed? We will answer these questions in a moment, but first we want to consider a

1	14	9	20	3
24	19	2	15	10
13	8	25	4	21
18	23	6	11	16
7	12	17	22	5

Fig. 1.3 Knight's tour on a 5 × 5 board

special case. In the special case $n = m = 4k + 1$, for k a positive integer, and the tour starts in one of the corner squares. For this special case a knight's tour can be found using a simple rule with no backtracking. The simple rule is: choose as the next square the possible square nearest the edge of the board. Figure 3 shows a 5 × 5 board with each square containing a number indicating the order in which the knight visits the squares. Notice that the knight starts in a corner and finishes the tour at the centre of the board. It is clear that the simple rule needs some amplification. How did the knight at the square numbered 2 decide to go to the square numbered 3 rather than the square numbered 21 or the square numbered 13, and how did the knight at square 8 decide to go to square 9 rather than square 17? The extra tie-breaking rules are: choose the square with lowest initial degree, and choose the first square in clockwise order. With these rules one can prove inductively that a knight's tour will be found in the special case. The induction considers a $[4(k + 1) + 1] \times [4(k + 1) + 1]$ board as a $(4k + 1) \times (4k + 1)$ board surrounded by a two-square border.

From the special case, we can see that in the general case we will also need tie-breaking rules to determine which square should be picked when two possible next squares have the same degree. From the special case, we could try the rule which says: choose the first such square in clockwise order. Unfortunately, it can be shown that for some starting squares this tie-breaking rule does not give a knight's tour. Another possible tie-breaking rule is to 'look-ahead': choose the next possible square of lowest degree which has the lowest degree following square. But again this tie-breaking rule may fail. Further look-ahead would be possible but it would take considerably more computation.

In spite of the fact that the heuristic, even with tie-breaking rules, does not work in all cases, it still works in a large majority of cases. Some empirical studies show that a backtracking algorithm using the heuristic uses no backtracks in most cases, one backtrack in a few cases, and two backtracks in rare cases, and never uses more than two backtracks. A proof of any of these empirical results would be interesting, but it is probably very difficult.

When heuristics work so well on a problem one should consider whether there is a reasonable non-exhaustive algorithm for the problem. Cull and DeCurtins (1978) proved that if $\min(n,m) \geq 5$, then there is a knight's tour from at least one starting square on an $n \times m$ board, and if nm is even there is a knight's tour starting from any square on the board. Their proof technique is constructive and takes $\theta(nm)$ time to construct the knight's tour. Their paper does not contain a proof that if nm is odd then there is a knight's tour starting from every square of the more numerous colour.

6.4 The *n*-queens problem

Backtracking is an effective method for the *n*-queens problem. Can *n* queens be placed on an $n \times n$ board so that no queen can take another queen: that is, can *n* objects be placed on an $n \times n$ board so that no two objects are in the same row, the same column, or the same diagonal? The answer to this question is 'no' when $n = 2$ or 3, and 'yes' otherwise. The problem becomes more difficult when one is asked for all the different ways to place *n* non-taking queens on an $n \times n$ board. Two ways are different if one cannot be obtained from the other by rotating and/or reflecting the board.

Since one queen will be placed in each row, we will take placing a queen in a row as a stage in a backtracking algorithm. The algorithm starts by placing a queen in column 1 of row 1, then it successively places queens in the lowest-numbered allowed column of each successive row, until either every row has a queen or there is no allowed place for a queen in the present row. If there is no allowed place to put a queen in the present row, then the algorithm backtracks and tries to place a queen in the next allowed place in the previous row. If a queen has been placed in each row then this solution is output and the algorithm backtracks. The algorithm terminates when it has backtracked to row 1 and the queen in row 1 is in column *n*. This algorithm can be written as either a recursive or an iterative program. Since the algorithm is tail-recursive, we suggest writing it as an iterative algorithm. We leave the actual program as an exercise and refer the reader to Wirth (1976).

The algorithm we have outlined will produce all allowed placements, not all different allowed placements. We still need a method which determines if two placements are different. Two placements are the same if one is the rotation-reflection of the other. The rotation by 45° and the reflection generate the 8-element group of the symmetries of a square. By applying each element of this group to a placement, one will obtain the 8 placements which are equivalent. If one had a table of the different placements found so far, then one could look in the table and see if any of these 8 equivalent placements had already been found. But there is an easier way. Since a placement will consist of n numbers indicating the columns in which each of the n queens are placed, and each column number will be between 1 and n, a solution can be viewed as a single number in base n. The algorithm is set up so that it generates the placements in numerical order. Thus to see if a placement is different, apply to it each of the 7 non-identity elements of the group and determine if any of these equivalent placements gives a lower number. If one of these equivalent placements gives a lower number, then this placement is equivalent to an already generated placement. If each of the 7 equivalent placements gives a number greater than or equal to the present placement, then the present placement is different from all previous placements.

How fast is this backtrack algorithm for n queens? A straightforward exhaustive search would generate all permutations of n things and hence take about $n!$ time. Empirical studies suggest that the backtrack algorithm runs in time proportional to $(n/2)^{n/2}$. This is much, much smaller than $n!$. A proof that this algorithm runs in the time suggested by the empirical studies would be very interesting.

6.5 Exercises

(a) Use the heuristics of Section 6.3 to construct a knight's tour of a 6 × 6 board.
(b) Pick starting squares and show that the heuristics of Section 6.3 do not find a knight's tour of a 5 × 5 board even when such a tour is possible.
(c) Determine all the different placements of 8 non-taking queens on an 8 × 8 board.

7 Hard problems

7.1 Classification of algorithms and problems

We have encountered various algorithms, particularly of the divide-and-conquer type, which have running times like $\theta(n)$, $\theta(n \log n)$, and $\theta(n^3)$, where n is some measure of the size of the input. We have also encountered algorithms, particularly of the exhaustive search type, which have running times like $\theta(2^n)$ and $\theta(n!)$. For algorithms of the first type, doubling the size of the input increases the running time by a constant factor, while for algorithms of the second type, doubling n increases the running time by a factor proportional to the running time. If we double the speed of the computer we are using, then the largest input size which our computer can solve in a given time will increase by a constant factor if we have an algorithm of the first type; for an algorithm of the second type, the input size our computer can solve will only increase by an additive constant, at best. These considerations led Edmonds (pers. comm.) to propose that algorithms of the first type are computationally reasonable, while algorithms of the second type are computationally unreasonable. More specifically, he suggested the definitions:

Reasonable algorithm: an algorithm whose running time is bounded by a polynomial in the size of the input.

Unreasonable algorithm: an algorithm whose running time cannot be bounded by any polynomial in the size of the input.

This suggests that we should try to replace unreasonable algorithms by reasonable algorithms. Unfortunately, this goal is not always attainable. For the Towers of Hanoi problem, any algorithm must have running time at least $\theta(2^n)$. Since some problems do not have reasonable algorithms, we should classify problems as well as algorithms. Corresponding to the Edmonds definition for algorithms, Cook (1971) and Karp (1972) suggested the following definitions for problems:

Easy problem: a problem which has a polynomial time bounded algorithm.

Hard problem: a problem for which there is no polynomial time bounded algorithm.

As easy problem may have unreasonable algorithms. For example, we have seen an $\theta(n!)$ exhaustive search algorithm for sorting, but sorting is an easy problem because we also have an $\theta(n \log n)$ sorting algorithm. A hard problem, on the other hand, can never have a reasonable algorithm.

Some problems like the Towers of Hanoi are hard for the trivial reason that their output is too large. To avoid such output-bound problems, Cook (1971) suggested considering only yes/no problems; that is, problems whose output is limited to be either yes or no. One such yes/no problem is the variant of the Towers of Hanoi problem in which the input is a configuration and the question is: is this configuration used in moving the disks from tower A to tower C? Furthermore, this variant is an easy problem. Usual easy problems can be transformed into easy yes/no problems by giving as the instance of the yes/no problem both the input and the output of the usual problem and asking if the output is correct. For example, sorting can be converted into a yes/no problem when we give both the input and the output and ask if the output is the input in sorted order. As another example, matrix multiplication can be converted into a yes/no problem in which we give three matrices A, B, and C and ask if $C = AB$. There are also other ways to transform usual problems into yes/no problems. Examples are the above variant of the Towers of Hanoi, and the variant of sorting in which we ask if the input is in sorted order.

To avoid problems which are hard only because of the length of their output, Cook defined:

P = the class of yes/no problems which have polynomial time algorithms. (Some authors call this class PTIME.)

For many problems, it is easy to show that they are in P. One gives an algorithm for the problem and demonstrates a polynomial upper bound on its running time. It may be quite difficult to show that a problem is not in P, but it is clear that there are problems which are not in P. For example, the halting problem, which asks if an algorithm ever terminates when given a particular input, is not in P because the halting problem has no algorithm.

Classification of problems would not be very useful if we only could say that some problems have polynomial time algorithms and some problems have no algorithms. We would like a finer classification, particularly one that helps classify problems which arise in practice. In the next section we introduce some machinery which is needed for a finer classification.

7.2 Non-deterministic algorithms

Up to this point we have discussed only deterministic algorithms. In a deterministic algorithm there are no choices; the result of an instruction determines which instruction will be executed next. In a non-deterministic algorithm choices are allowed; any one of a set of instructions may be executed next. Non-deterministic algorithms can be viewed as 'magic': if there is a correct choice, the magic forces the non-deterministic algorithm to make this correct choice. A less magic view is that if there are several possibilities the non-deterministic algorithm does all of them in parallel. Since the number of possibilities multiply at each choice-point, there may be arbitrarily many possibilities being executed at once. Therefore, a non-deterministic algorithm gives us unbounded parallelism.

This view of non-determinism as unbounded parallelism makes clear that non-determinism does not take us out of the realm of things which can be computed deterministically, because we could build a deterministic algorithm which simulates the non-deterministic algorithm by keeping track of all the possibilities. However, a non-deterministic algorithm may be faster than any deterministic algorithm for the same problem. We define the time taken by a non-deterministic algorithm as the fewest instructions the non-deterministic algorithm needs to execute to reach an answer. (This definition is not precise since what an instruction means is undefined. This could be made precise by choosing a model of computation like the Turing machine in which an instruction has a well-defined meaning, but this imprecise definition should suffice for our purposes.) With this definition of time, a non-deterministic algorithm could sort in $\theta(n)$ time because it always makes the right choice, whereas a deterministic algorithm would take at least $\theta(n \log n)$ time in some cases. In some sense we are comparing the best case of the non-deterministic algorithm with the worst case of the deterministic algorithm, so it is not surprising that the non-deterministic algorithm is faster.

For yes/no problems we give non-deterministic algorithms even more of an edge. We divide the inputs into yes-instances and no-instances. The yes-instances eventually lead to yes answers. The no-instances always lead to no answers. We assume that our non-deterministic algorithms cannot lead to yes as a result of some choices, and to a no as a result of some other choices. For a yes-instance, the running time of a non-deterministic algorithm is the fewest instructions the algorithm needs to execute to reach a yes answer. The running time of the non-deterministic algorithm is the maximum over all yes-instances of the running time of the algorithm for the yes-instances. We ignore what the non-deterministic algorithm does in no-instances.

As an example of non-deterministic time, consider the yes/no problem: given a set of n numbers each containing $\log n$ bits, are there two identical numbers in the set? In a yes-instance, a non-deterministic algorithm could guess which two numbers were identical and then check the bits of the two numbers, so the running time for this non-deterministic algorithm is $\theta(\log n)$. On the other hand, even in a yes-instance, a deterministic algorithm would have to look at almost all the bits in worst case, so the running time for any deterministic algorithm is at least $\theta(n \log n)$.

The definition of non-deterministic time may seem strange, but it does measure an interesting quantity. If we consider a yes/no problem, the yes-instances are all those objects which have a particular property. The non-deterministic time is the length of a proof that an object has a certain property. We ignore no-instances because we are not interested in the lengths of proofs that an object does not have the property.

7.3 NP and reducibility

Now that we have a definition of the time used by a non-deterministic algorithm, we can, in analogy with the class P, define

NP = the class of yes/no problems which have polynomial time non-deterministic algorithms.

It is immediate from this definition that $P \leqslant NP$, because every problem in P has a deterministic polynomial time algorithm and we can consider a deterministic algorithm as a non-deterministic algorithm which has exactly one choice at each step. It is not clear, however, whether P is properly contained in NP or whether P is equal to NP.

Are there problems in NP which may not be in P? Consider the yes/no version of satisfiability: given a Boolean expression, is there an assignment of true and false to the variables which makes the expression true? This problem is in NP because if there is a satisfying assignment we could guess the assignment, and in time proportional to the length of the expression we could evaluate the expression and show that the expression is true. We discussed exhaustive algorithms for satisfiability because these seem to be the fastest deterministic algorithms for satisfiability. No polynomial time deterministic algorithm for satisfiability is known. Similarly, the problem: given a graph does it contain a Hamiltonian path?, seems to be in NP but not in P. Hamiltonian path is in NP because we can guess the Hamiltonian path and quickly (i.e. in polynomial time) check to see if the guessed path really is a Hamiltonian path. Hamiltonian path does not seem to be in P, because exhaustive search algorithms seem to be the fastest deterministic algorithms for this problem and these search algorithms have worst case running times which are at least $\theta(2^n)$, and hence their running times cannot be bounded by any polynomial.

Another problem which is in NP but may not be in P is composite number: given a positive integer n, is n the product of two positive integers which are both greater than 1? Clearly this is in NP because we could guess the two factors, multiply them, and show that their product is n. Why isn't this problem clearly in P? Everyone knows the algorithm which has running time at most $\theta(n^2)$ and either finds the factors or reports that there are no factors. This well-known algorithm simply tries to divide n by 2 and by each odd number from 3 to $n - 1$. While this algorithm is correct, its running time is not bounded by a polynomial in the size of the input. Since n can be represented in binary, or in some other base, the size of the input is only log n bits, and n cannot be bounded by any polynomial in log n. This example points out that we have been too loose about the meaning of size of input. The official definition says that the size of the input is the number of bits used to represent the input. According to the official definition, the size of the input for this problem is log n if n is represented in binary. But if n were represented in unary then the size of the input would be n. So the representation of the input can affect the classification of the problem.

There is a great variety of problems known to be in NP, but not known to be in P. Some of these problems may not seem to be in NP because they are optimization problems rather than yes/no problems. An example of this kind of optimization problem is the travelling salesman problem: given a set of cities and distances between them, what is the length of the shortest circuit which visits each city exactly once and returns to the starting city? This optimization problem can be changed into a yes/no problem by giving an integer B as part of the input. The yes/no question becomes: is there a circuit which visits each city exactly once and returns to the starting city and has length at most B? At first glance the optimization problem seems harder than the yes/no problem, because we can solve the yes/no problem by solving the optimization problem, and solving the yes/no problem does not give a solution to the optimization problem. But we can use the yes/no problem to solve the optimization problem. Set B to n times the largest distance; then the answer to the yes/no problem is yes. Set $STEP$ to $B/2$. Now set B to $B - STEP$, and $STEP$ to $STEP/2$. Now do the yes/no problem with this new B and this new $STEP$. If the answer is yes, set B to $B - STEP$ and $STEP$ to $STEP/2$. If the answer is no, set B to $B + STEP$ and $STEP$ to $STEP/2$. Continue this process until $STEP = 0$. The last value of B will be the solution to the optimization problem. How long will this take? Since $STEP$ is halved at each call to the yes/no procedure, the number of calls will be the log of the initial value of $STEP$. But $STEP$ is initially n times the largest distance, so the number of calls is log n + log (largest distance) which is less than the size of the input. Thus the optimization problem can be solved by solving the yes/no problem a number of times which is less than the length of the input.

This example suggests the idea that two problems are equally hard if both of them can be solved in polynomial time if either one of them can be solved in polynomial time. This equivalence relation on problems also suggests a partial ordering of problems. A problem A is no harder than problem B if a polynomial time deterministic algorithm for B can be used to construct a polynomial time deterministic algorithm for A. We symbolize this relation by A $\leq$ B. If A is the yes/no travelling salesman problem, and B is the travelling salesman optimization problem, then we have both A $\leq$ B and B $\leq$ A. If A and B are any two problems in P then we have both A $\leq$ B and B $\leq$ A, because we could take the polynomial time deterministic algorithm for one problem and make it a subroutine of the polynomial deterministic algorithm for the other problem and never call the subroutine. While in these examples the relation $\leq$ works both ways, there are cases in which $\leq$ only works one way. For example, let A be any problem in P, and let HALT be the halting problem; then A $\leq$ HALT, but HALT $\nleq$ A, because we don't need an algorithm for HALT to construct a polynomial time algorithm for A, and the polynomial time algorithm for A cannot help in constructing any algorithm for HALT, let alone a polynomial time algorithm for HALT.

This relation A $\leq$ B which we are calling 'A is no harder than B', is usually called polynomial time reducibility, and is read 'A is polynomial time reducible to B'. There are many other definitions of reducibility in the literature. We refer the interested reader to Rogers (1967) and Garey and Johnson (1979).

The notion of a partial ordering on problems should aid us in our task of classifying problems. In particular, it may aid us in saying that two problems in NP are equally hard. Further, it suggests the question: is there a hardest problem in NP? We consider this question in the next section.

7.4 NP-complete problems

In this section, we will consider the relation $\leq$ defined in the last section, and answer the question: is there a hardest problem in NP? Since we have a partial order $\leq$, we might think of two very standard instances of partial orders: the partial (and total) ordering of the integers, which has no maximal element; and the partial ordering of sets, which has a maximal element. From these examples, we see that our question cannot be answered on the basis that we have a partial order. If we consider $\leq$ applied to problems, is there a hardest problem? The answer is no, because the Cantor diagonal proof always allows us to create harder problems. On the other hand, one may recall that the halting problem is the hardest recursively enumerable (RE) problem. So on the analogy with RE, there may be a hardest problem in NP. Cook (1971) proved that there is a hardest problem in NP. A problem which is the hardest problem in NP is called an NP-complete problem. Cook proved the more specific result:

Cook's Theorem: Satisfiability is NP-complete.

The proof of this theorem requires an exact definition of non-deterministic algorithm; since we have avoided exact definitions, we will only be able to give a sketch of the proof. We refer the interested reader to Garey and Johnson (1979) for the details. The basic idea of the proof is to take any instance of a problem in NP which consists of a non-deterministic algorithm, a polynomial that gives the bound on the non-deterministic running time, and an input for the algorithm, and to show how to construct a Boolean expression which is satisfiable iff the non-determinist algorithm reaches a yes answer within the number of steps specified by the polynomial applied to the size of the input. The construction proceeds by creating clauses which can be interpreted to mean that at step 0 the algorithm is in its proper initial state. Then for each step, a set of clauses is constructed which can be interpreted to mean that the state of the algorithm and the contents of the memory are well-defined at this step. Further, for each step a set of clauses is constructed which can be interpreted to mean that the state of the algorithm and the contents of memory at this step follow from the state and contents at the previous step by an allowed instruction of the algorithm. Finally, some clauses are constructed which can be interpreted to mean that the algorithm has reached a yes answer. The polynomial time bound is used to show that the length of this Boolean expression is bounded by a polynomial in the length of the input.

An interesting consequence of the proof is that satisfiability of Boolean expressions in clause form is NP-complete. This result can be refined to show that satisfiability in clause form with exactly 3 literals in each clause is also NP-complete.

After Cook's result, Karp (1972) quickly showed that a few dozen other standard problems are NP-complete. Garey and Johnson's book (1979) contains several hundred NP-complete problems. Johnson also writes a column for the *Journal of Algorithms* which contains even more information on NP-complete problems.

Why is this business of NP-complete problems so interesting? The NP-complete problems are the hardest problems in NP in the sense that for any problem A in NP, A $\leq$ NP-complete. So if there were a polynomial time deterministic algorithm for any NP-complete problem, there would be a polynomial time deterministic algorithm for any problem in NP; that is, P and NP would be the same class. Conversely, if P $\neq$ NP, then there is no point to looking for a polynomial time deterministic algorithm for an NP-complete problem. Simply knowing that a problem is in NP without knowing that it is NP-complete leaves open the question of whether or not the problem has a polynomial time bounded algorithm even on the supposition that P $\neq$ NP. The fact that a number of NP-complete problems have been well-known problems for several hundred years and no one has managed to find a reasonable algorithm for any one of them suggests to most people that P $\neq$ NP and that the NP-complete problems really are hard.

One of the virtues of Cook's theorem is that to show that an NP problem A is NP-complete you only have to show that satisfiability $\leq$ A. As a catalogue of NP-complete problems is built, the task of showing that an NP problem A is NP-complete gets easier because you only have to pick some NP-complete problem B and show that B $\leq$ A.

We have already mentioned the travelling salesman problem (TSP). This problem is NP-complete. Let us show that if the Hamiltonian circuit is NP-complete then TSP is NP-complete. The Hamiltonian circuit problem (HC) is: given a graph, is there a circuit which contains each vertex exactly once and uses only edges in the graph? Given an instance of HC, we create an instance of TSP by letting each vertex from HC become a city for TSP, and defining the distance between cities by $d(i,j) = 1$ if there is an edge in HC between vertices i and j, and $d(i,j) = 2$ if there is no such edge. Now if there were n vertices in HC, we use $B = n$ as our bound for TSP. If the answer to TSP is yes, then there is a circuit of length n, but this means that the circuit can only contain edges of distance 1 and hence this circuit is also a Hamiltonian circuit of the original graph. Conversely, if there is a Hamiltonian circuit, then there is a TSP circuit of length n. To complete our proof, we must make sure that this transformation from HC to TSP can be accomplished in polynomial time in the size of the instance of HC. Since HC has n vertices and TSP can be specified by giving the $n(n-1)/2$ distances between the n cities, we only have to check for each of the $n(n-1)/2$ distances whether or not it corresponds to an edge in the original graph. Even with a very simple algorithm this can be done in at worst $\theta(n^4)$, which is bounded by a polynomial in the size of the HC instance.

This is a very simple example of proving that one problem in NP is NP-complete by reducing a known NP-complete problem to the problem. We refer the reader to Garey and Johnson (1979) for more complicated examples.

7.5 Dealing with hard problems

In the theoretical world there are hard problems. Some of these hard problems are NP-complete problems and there are other problems which are harder than NP-complete problems. How can these hard problems be handled in the real world?

The simplest way to handle hard problems is to ignore them. Many practical programmers do not know what hard problems are. Their programming involves tasks like billing and payroll which are theoretically trivial, but practically quite important. Ignoring hard problems may be a reasonable strategy for these programmers.

Another way to handle hard problems is to avoid them. To avoid hard problems, you have to know what they are. One of the major virtues of lists of NP-complete problems is that they help the programmer to identify hard problems and to point out that no reasonable algorithms for these problems are known. It is often unfortunately the case that a programmer is approached with a request for a program and the person making the request has tried to remove all the specific information about the problem and generalize the problem as much as possible. Over-generalization can make a problem very hard. If the programmer can get the specific information, he may be able to design a reasonable algorithm for the real problem and avoid the hard generalization.

Sometimes real problems are really hard but not too big. For example, many real scheduling problems turn out to be travelling salesman problems with 30 to 50 cities. For these situations an exhaustive algorithm may still solve the problem in reasonable time. The programmer should still try to tune the algorithm to take advantage of any special structure in the problem, and to take advantage of the instructions of the actual computer which will be used. Exhaustive search is a way to handle some NP-complete problems when the size of the input is not too large.

Heuristics are another way to deal with hard problems. We have already mentioned heuristics in discussing backtrack algorithms. A heuristic is a method to solve a problem which doesn't always work. To be useful a heuristic should work quickly when it does work. The use of heuristics is based on the not unreasonable belief that the real world is usually not as complicated as the worst case in the theoretical world. This belief is supported by the observation that creatures which seem to have less computing power than computers can make a reasonable living in the real world. Artificial intelligence has been using heuristics for years to solve problems like satisfiability. These heuristics seem to be very effective on the instances of satisfiability which arise in artificial intelligence contexts. Heuristics are also widely used in the design of operating systems. Occasional failures in these heuristics lead to software crashes. Since we usually see only a couple of such crashes per year these heuristics seem to be very effective.

Sometimes the behaviour of heuristics can be quantified so that we can talk about the probability of the heuristic being correct. For example, a heuristic to find the largest element in an n-element array is to find the largest element among the first $n - 1$ elements. If the elements of the array are in random order, then this heuristic fails with probability $1/n$, and as $n \to \infty$ the probability that this heuristic gives the correct answer goes to 1. Such probabilistic algorithms are now being used for a wide variety of hard problems. For example, large primes are needed for cryptographic purposes. While it seems to be hard to discover large primes, there are tests which are used so that if a number passes all the tests then the number is probably a prime.

Many hard problems can be stated as optimization problems: find the smallest or largest something which has a particular property. While actually finding the optimum may be difficult, it may be much easier to find something which is close to optimum. For example, in designing a computer circuit one would like the circuit with the fewest gates which carries out a particular computation. This optimization problem is hard. But from a practical point of view, no great disaster would occur if you designed a circuit with 10% more gates than the optimum circuit. For various hard problems, approximation algorithms have been produced which give answers close to the optimum answer. We will consider an example of approximation in the next section.

7.6 Approximation algorithms

Let us consider the travelling salesman optimization problem: given a set of cities and distances between them, find the shortest circuit which contains each city exactly once. This problem arises in many real scheduling situations. We will try to approximate the shortest circuit.

To make an approximation possible, we will assume that the distances behave like real distances, that is, the distances obey the triangle inequality $d(i,j) \leq d(i,k) + d(k,j)$, so that the distance from city i to city j is no longer than the distance from city i to city k plus the distance from city k to city j.

A simpler task than finding the minimum circuit is finding the minimum spanning tree. The minimum spanning tree is a set of links which connects all the cities and has smallest sum of distances. In the minimum spanning tree, the cities are not all directly connected; several links may have to be traversed to get from city i to city j. There is a reasonable algorithm for the minimum spanning tree because the shortest link is in this tree. So one can proceed to find this tree by putting in the shortest link and continuing to add the shortest link which does not complete a cycle.

A circuit can be constructed from the minimum spanning tree by starting at some city and traversing the links of the tree to visit every other city and return to the starting city. This circuit is twice as long as the sum of the distances of the links in the minimum spanning tree. But this circuit may visit some cities more than once. To 'clean up' this circuit, we use this circuit while no city is repeated and, if city j is the first repeated city and if city i is the city before city j and if city k is the next city after city j which has not yet been visited, we connect city i to city k. We continue to use this procedure to produce a circuit in which each city is visited exactly once. From the triangle inequality we have that the length of this new circuit is at most as long as the circuit with cities repeated, and hence that this new circuit is no longer than twice the length of the minimum spanning tree.

The optimum circuit must be at least as long as the minimum spanning tree because the optimum circuit connects every city. Thus we have

$$OPT \leq ALG \leq 2\,OPT$$

where OPT is the length of the optimum circuit and ALG is the length of the circuit produced by the approximation algorithm.

It would be pleasant if all hard optimization problems had approximation algorithms. Unfortunately this is not the case. We really needed the triangle inequality to produce an approximation for the travelling salesman problem. Consider an instance of Hamiltonian circuit with n vertices. We can convert this to an instance of travelling salesman without triangle inequality by assigning distance 1 to all the edges which are in the original graph, and assigning distance $n + 2$ to all the edges which were not in the original graph. Now if there were a Hamiltonian circuit in the original graph, then there would be a travelling salesman circuit of length n. If we could approximate this travelling salesman problem within a factor of 2, the travelling salesman circuit would have length at most $2n$ exactly when the original graph had a Hamiltonian circuit, because if the travelling salesman circuit used even one of the edges not in the original graph, it would have length at least $2n + 1$. So approximating the travelling salesman problem without triangle inequality is as hard as Hamiltonian circuit.

This example can be generalized to show that no approximation within a factor of $f(n)$ is possible by assigning each edge not in the graph a distance greater than $nf(n)$. To make sure the transformation can be carried out in polynomial time in the size of the instance of Hamiltonian circuit, $f(n)$ must be bounded by $2^{P(n)}$ where $P(n)$ is a polynomial. Thus no reasonable approximation to the travelling salesman problem is possible unless the Hamiltonian circuit problem can be solved quickly; that is, unless $P = NP$.

7.7 The world of NP

The fact that various NP-complete problems have resisted attempts to find reasonable algorithms for them suggests to many people that $P \neq NP$. Even if we accept this belief, there are still other open questions about classes of problems associated with NP. The class NP is defined in terms of the yes-instances of its problems. A class could also be defined in terms of no-instances. In correspondence with NP, we define the class co-NP as problems whose complements are in NP; that is, for each problem in co-NP there is a non-deterministic algorithm which has polynomial bounded running time for the no-instances of the problem. This definition suggests the questions:

Does NP = co-NP?
Does   P = NP ∩ co-NP?

Unfortunately, these questions are unsolved.

While the above questions are unsolved, many people believe that the answer to each of these questions is no. The basis for this belief is the analogy between NP and RE. For RE, Figure 4a can be shown to be valid. If the analogy between NP and RE is valid, the world of NP should look like Figure 4b. A minor difference in the two diagrams is that RE ∩ co-RE has the name RECURSIVE, but NP ∩ co-NP has not been assigned a name. If this diagram is correct then there are several types of hard problems which are not NP-complete. In particular, there may be problems which are in NP ∩ co-NP but are not in P. Composite number is a candidate problem for this status. We know that composite is in NP. The complement of composite number is prime number. While it is not immediately obvious, for every prime number there is a proof that the number is prime and the length of the proof is bounded by a polynomial in the log of the number. So the complement of composite is also in NP, and composite is in NP ∩ co-NP. But everyone (including the National

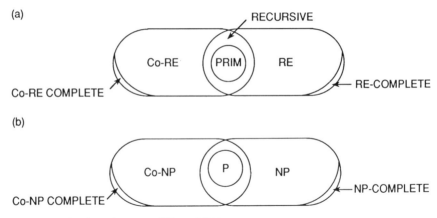

Fig. 1.4   Analogy between NP and RE

Security Agency) assumes that composite and prime do not have reasonable algorithms. Unfortunately, proving that composite/prime is not in P
is probably very difficult since this would imply P ≠ NP.

We conclude by mentioning that our diagram of the world of NP may
be incorrect, but there is some reasonable circumstantial evidence to
support it.

7.8   Exercises

(a) Show that if Hamiltonian circuit is NP-complete then Hamiltonian
    path is NP-complete.
(b) Show that if Hamiltonian path is NP-complete then Hamiltonian
    circuit is NP-complete.

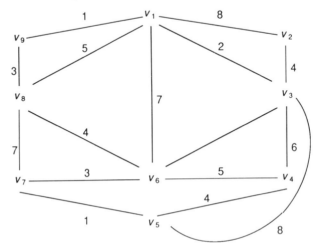

Fig. 1.5

(c) For figure 5 use the minimum spanning tree method to construct a short travelling salesman circuit. Assume that any missing edges have the shortest distance consistent with the triangle inequality. How close to the minimum circuit is your constructed circuit?

References

Aho, A. V., Hopcroft, J. E. and Ullman, J. D. (1974) *The Design and Analysis of Computer Algorithms*, Addison-Wesley, Reading, Mass.

Buneman, P. and Levy, L. (1980) The Towers of Hanoi problem, *Information Processing Letters*, **10**, 243–4.

Cook, S. A. (1971) The complexity of theorem-proving procedures, in *Proceedings of the 3rd ACM Symposium on Theory of Computing*, pp. 151–8.

Cull, P. and DeCurtins, J. (1978) Knight's Tour revisited, *Fibonacci Quarterly*, **16**, 276–85.

Cull, P. and Ecklund, E. F. Jr (1985) Towers of Hanoi and analysis of algorithms, *American Mathematical Monthly*, **92**, 407–20.

Garey, M. R. and Johnson, D. S. (1979) *Computers and Intractability: a Guide to the Theory of NP-Completeness*, W. H. Freeman, San Francisco.

Greene, D. H. and Knuth, D. E. (1981) *Mathematics for the Analysis of Algorithms*, Birkhäuser, Boston.

Horowitz, E. and Sahni, S. (1978) *Fundamentals of Computer Algorithms*, Computer Science Press, Potomac, Md.

Karp, R. M. (1972) Reducibility among combinatorial problems, in *Complexity of Computer Computations*, R. E. Miller and J. W. Thatcher (eds), Plenum, New York, pp. 85–104.

Knuth, D. E. (1968) *The Art of Computer Programming. Vol. 1 Fundamental Algorithms*, 2nd edn 1973, Addison-Wesley, Reading, Mass.

Knuth, D. E. (1969) *The Art of Computer Programming. Vol. 2 Seminumerical Algorithms*, 2nd edn 1981, Addison-Wesley, Reading, Mass.

Knuth, D. E. (1973) *The Art of Computer Programming. Vol. 3 Sorting and Searching*, Addison-Wesley, Reading, Mass.

Pan, V. (1984) *How to Multiply Matrices Faster*, Lecture Notes in Computer Science 179, Springer, Berlin.

Rogers, H. (1967) *Theory of Recursive Functions and Effective Computability*, McGraw-Hill, New York.

Sedgewick, R. (1983) *Algorithms*, Addison-Wesley, Reading, Mass.

Strassen, V. (1969) Gaussian elimination is not optimal, *Numerische Mathematik*, **13**, 354–6.

Traub, J. F. and Woźniakowski, H. (1980) *A General Theory of Optimal Algorithms*, Academic Press, New York.

Walsh, T. R. (1982) The Towers of Hanoi revisited: moving the rings by counting the moves, *Information Processing Letters*, **15**, 64–7.

Winograd, S. (1980) *Arithmetic Complexity of Computations*, SIAM, Philadelphia, Pa.

Wirth, N. (1976) *Algorithms + Data Structures = Programs*, Prentice-Hall, Englewood Cliffs, NJ.

2

Rational and recognizable languages

Jean Enric Pin   *Université Paris VI and CNRS, LITP, Tour 55–65, 4 place Jussieu, 75252 Paris Cedex 05, France*

This chapter contains an account of a course of lectures given at the University of Naples in 1984, supplemented by some recent research on rational languages. The lectures were given for mathematicians wanting an introduction to this branch of theoretical computer science. It deals with concepts that mathematicians do not normally use: we speak of semigroups rather than groups, semirings rather than rings, automata, and so on. It is none the less a mathematical theory, and one that is both rich and elegant, although the present chapter can unfortunately only sketch a very brief outline.

The range of subjects dealt with is one of various possible alternatives. The first section presents basic general research findings on recognizable and rational subsets of a monoid, and on rational transductions. I have followed Berstel's account (1979) closely – sometimes even very closely! – it remains the best reference work on the subject. Section 2 contains a demonstration of Kleene's (1956) theorem. Section 3 gives a basic outline of Eilenberg's (1974, 1976) theory of varieties which forms the basis for the classification of languages. For further details the reader should refer to works by Eilenberg (1978), Lallement (1979), or the present author (Pin, 1984). Section 4 contains the main research findings on the three rational operations: union, product and star. Hashiguchi's findings are presented in algebraic form, which avoids having to use automata. Sections 4.2 and 4.3 begin to locate some ways of approaching the problems of hierarchies (star height and concatenation). I also present there very briefly the links with formal logic.

1   Rational and recognizable subsets

Carrying on the comparison with classical mathematics touched on in the introduction, one could say that this section is somewhat analogous to a chapter on topology in a book of analysis. The reader will see that the abstract definition of rational and recognizable sets makes it difficult to imagine further developments. As with topology, the definition only takes its full form when seen alongside the examples contained in this section and following sections.

1.1   A little algebra

In this subsection we introduce the three algebraic structures we shall be using later on: semigroups, monoids and semirings.

A *semigroup* is a set with an internal associative law of composition which is usually written in a multiplicative form. If this operation is commutative, the semigroup is called *commutative*. Given two semigroups, S and T, *a morphism of semigroups* $\varphi: S \to T$ is an application of S in T such that for all $x, y \in S$, $(xy)\varphi = (x\varphi)(y\varphi)$.

A *monoid M* is a semigroup containing an identity, 1, that is to say, an element such that for all $x \in M$, $1x = x1 = x$. Given two monoids, M and N, *a morphism of monoids* is a morphism of semigroups such that $1\varphi = 1$.

Let S be a semigroup. A *subsemigroup T* of S is a subset of S such that if $t, t' \in S$ then $tt' \in S$. If S is a monoid, a subsemigroup T of S is a submonoid if $1 \in T$. A semigroup T is (a *quotient semigroup* of S if there is a surjective morphism $\varphi: S \to T$. A quotient monoid is defined in similar fashion.

Given a family $(S_i)_{i \in I}$ of semigroups (respectively monoids), the product $\prod_{i \in I} S_i$ is the semigroup (monoid) defined on the set $\prod_{i \in I} S_i$ by the multiplication

$$(s_i)_{i \in I} (s_i')_{i \in I} = (s_i s_i')_{i \in I}.$$

As the semigroup 1 formed from a single element is an identity for the operation produced, let us set, as is customary, $\prod_{i \in \varnothing} S_i = 1$.

Let A be a set, called an *alphabet*, whose elements are called *letters*. We will denote by A^+ (respectively A^*) the *free semigroup (monoid)* with base A. In practical terms, A^+ is constructed in the following fashion: the elements of A^+ are the finite non-empty sequences of letters called *words*. For the sake of simplicity, they are shown by simple juxtaposition:

$a_1 \ldots a_n$, and the product of the words $a_1 \ldots a_p$ and $b_1 \ldots b_q$ is the word $a_1 \ldots a_p b_1 \ldots b_q$. In the case of the free monoid, we must add the empty word, denoted by 1, which corresponds to the empty sequence.

The universal property of the free semigroup (monoid) on A can be expressed as follows: if S is a semigroup and if $\varphi: A \to S$ is an application of A in S, there is a unique morphism of semigroups (monoids) $\bar{\varphi}: A^+ \to S(A^* \to S)$ such that $a\varphi = a\bar{\varphi}$ for all $a \in A$. Moreover, $\bar{\varphi}$ is surjective if and only if the set A generates the semigroup (monoid) S. One particular result is that any semigroup (monoid) is a quotient of a free semigroup (monoid).

We denote by $|u|$ the *length* of a word $u \in A^*$. Formally, the application $u \to |u|$ is the morphism of monoids of A^* in $(\mathbb{N},+)$ defined by $|a| = 1$ for all $a \in A$. In particular, $|1| = 0$.

A word u is a *left factor* (or *prefix*) of a word w if there is a word v such that $uv = w$. If $v \neq 1$, we say that u is a proper left factor of w. The notion of *right factor* (or *suffix*) is defined in a dual fashion. A word u is a factor of a word v if there are words x and y such that $v = xuy$. We say u is a *proper factor* if $xy \neq 1$. A word $u = a_1 \ldots a_n$ (where $a_1, \ldots, a_n$ are letters) is a *subword* of v if there are words $v_0, \ldots, v_n \in A^*$ such that $v = v_0 a_1 v_1 a_2 \ldots a_n v_n$. For example, if $u = abacbacb$, aba is a left factor of u, acb is a right factor, $bacb$ is a factor and $bcbb$ is a subword of u.

A *semiring* K is a set equipped with two binary operations $+$ and $\cdot$ obeying the following conditions:

  (i) $(K,+)$ is a commutative monoid with identity 0,
  (ii) $(K,.)$ is a semigroup,
(iii) multiplication is distributive with respect to addition,
(iv) for all $x \in K$, $0 \cdot x = 0 = x \cdot 0$.

If, moreover, $(K,.)$ is a monoid, we call K a unitary semiring.

The properties of subsemiring and of semiring morphisms conform to what one would expect.

Let S be a semigroup. The power set $\mathcal{P}(S)$ of the subsets of S is given its natural semiring structure by taking the union as addition (and the empty set as 0) and the following multiplication:

$$XY = \{xy \mid x \in X \text{ and } y \in Y\} \text{ for all } X, Y \in \mathcal{P}(S).$$

If $\varphi: S \to T$ is a function, we define a function $\bar{\varphi}$ of $\mathcal{P}(S)$ in $\mathcal{P}(T)$ by putting $X\bar{\varphi} = \{x\varphi \mid x \in X\}$.

Proposition 1.1.1 If $\varphi: S \to T$ is a morphism of semigroups, $\bar{\varphi}: \mathcal{P}(S) \to \mathcal{P}(T)$ is a semiring morphism. If, moreover, φ is injective (surjective), then $\bar{\varphi}$ is injective (surjective).

Demonstration of this is obvious and left to the reader.

1.2 Recognizable subsets

Definition 1.2.1 Let M be a monoid. A subset P of M is called recognizable if there is a finite monoid N, a morphism (of monoids) $\alpha\colon M \to N$ and a subset Q of N such that $P = Q\alpha^{-1}$.

In this case, M is also a finite monoid and $P\alpha = Q \cap M\alpha$, hence $P = P\alpha\alpha^{-1}$. As a result, we have the following equivalent definition.

Definition 1.2.1′ A subset P of M is recognizable if there is a finite monoid N and a surjective morphism $\alpha\colon M \to N$ such that $P = P\alpha\alpha^{-1}$. The set of recognizable subsets of M is denoted by $\mathrm{Rec}(M)$.

Examples

(1) If M is finite, $\mathrm{Rec}(M) = \mathscr{P}(M)$ since if we denote by ι the identity map on M, we have $P = P\iota^{-1}$ for any subset P of M.

(2) Let $M = \mathbb{Z}$ and let $\alpha\colon \mathbb{Z} \to N$ be a surjective morphism onto a finite monoid. N is necessarily a quotient group of $\mathbb{Z}$, therefore of the form $\mathbb{Z}/n\mathbb{Z}$. It follows that if $Q \subset \mathbb{Z}/n\mathbb{Z}$, $Q\alpha^{-1} = \bigcup_{\dot{q}\in Q} q + n\mathbb{Z}$ (where q is any element of the class $\dot{q}$). Therefore a recognizable subset of $\mathbb{Z}$ is a finite union of arithmetical progressions. (The converse is also true.)

The following sums up the principal properties of $\mathrm{Rec}(M)$.

Theorem 1.2.1 Let M be a monoid

(i) $\mathrm{Rec}(M)$ is a Boolean algebra (for union, intersection and complementation).

(ii) Let $\varphi\colon M \to N$ be a morphism of monoids. If $Q \in \mathrm{Rec}(N)$ then

$$Q\varphi^{-1} \in \mathrm{Rec}(M).$$

(iii) Let $P \in \mathrm{Rec}(M)$ and let K be a subset of M. Then we have

$$KP^{-1}, PK^{-1} \in \mathrm{Rec}(M) \text{ where}$$
$$K^{-1}P = \{m \in M \mid \exists k \in K \; km \in P\} \text{ and}$$
$$PK^{-1} = \{m \in M \mid \exists k \in K \; mk \in P\}$$

Proof (i) Let $P, Q \in \mathrm{Rec}(M)$. Then there exist finite monoids N, R and morphisms $\alpha\colon M \to N$ and $\beta\colon M \to R$ such that $P = P\alpha\alpha^{-1}$ and $Q = Q\beta\beta^{-1}$. This produces $(M\backslash P) = (M\backslash P)\alpha\alpha^{-1}$ which shows that $\mathrm{Rec}(M)$ is closed by complementation. Similarly, let $\alpha \times \beta\colon M \to N \times R$ be the morphism defined by $m(\alpha \times \beta) = (m\alpha, m\beta)$. It follows that $(P\alpha \times Q\beta)$ $(\alpha \times \beta)^{-1} = P \cap Q$ and thus $\mathrm{Rec}(M)$ is closed under intersection. Finally, let 1 be the trivial monoid with one element. There is a unique morphism $\gamma\colon M \to 1$, for which $\varnothing\gamma^{-1} = \varnothing$. Therefore $\varnothing \in \mathrm{Rec}(M)$ and $\mathrm{Rec}(M)$ is a Boolean algebra.

(ii) Let $Q \in \mathrm{Rec}(N)$. We then have a morphism $\alpha: N \to F$ with finite F such that $Q\alpha\alpha^{-1} = Q$.

We then have $(Q\varphi^{-1})(\varphi\alpha)(\varphi\alpha)^{-1} = Q\varphi^{-1}\varphi\alpha\alpha^{-1}\varphi^{-1} = Q\alpha\alpha^{-1}\varphi^{-1} = Q\varphi^{-1}$. Therefore $Q\varphi^{-1}$ is recognizable since $\varphi\alpha: M \to F$ is a morphism.

(iii) Let $P \in \mathrm{Rec}(M)$. We then have a finite monoid N and a surjective monoid $\alpha: M \to N$ such that $P = P\alpha\alpha^{-1}$. There follows

$$
\begin{aligned}
(K^{-1}P)\alpha\alpha^{-1} &= \{u \in M \mid \exists m \in K^{-1}P \; u\alpha = m\alpha\} \\
&= \{u \in M \mid \exists m \in M \; \exists k \in K \; km \in P \text{ and } u\alpha = m\alpha\} \\
&\subset \{u \in M \mid \exists m \in M \; \exists k \in K \; (ku)\alpha = (km)\alpha \text{ and } \\
&\quad km \in P\} \\
&\subset \{u \in M \mid \exists k \in K \; (ku)\alpha \in P\alpha\} \\
&\subset \{u \in M \mid \exists k \in K \; ku \in P\} \text{ (since } P\alpha\alpha^{-1} = P) \\
&= K^{-1}P
\end{aligned}
$$

The opposite inclusion being obvious, we have $K^{-1}P = (K^{-1}P)\alpha\alpha^{-1}$ and therefore $K^{-1}P \in \mathrm{Rec}(M)$. The demonstration for PK^{-1} is analogous.

1.3   Rational subsets

Let S be a semigroup and X a subset of S. we put $X^1 = X$, and by induction, $X^{n+1} = X^n X$ for all $n > 0$. Finally we put

$$X^+ = \bigcup_{n>0} X^n.$$

One can see that X^+ is the subsemigroup of S generated by X. If S is a monoid with identity 1, we also put

$$X^0 = \{1\} \quad \text{and} \quad X^* = \bigcup_{n>0} X^n.$$

X^* is therefore the submonoid of S generated by X.

Definition 1.3.1   Let M be a monoid. The set $\mathrm{Rat}(M)$ of rational subsets of M is the smallest set $\mathscr{R}$ of $\mathscr{P}(M)$ satisfying the following conditions:

(i) For every $m \in M$, $\{m\} \in \mathscr{R}$ and $\varnothing \in \mathscr{R}$.
(ii) If $X, Y \in \mathscr{R}$ then $X \cup Y \in \mathscr{R}$.
(iii) If $X, Y \in \mathscr{R}$ then $XY \in \mathscr{R}$.
(iv) If $X \in \mathscr{R}$, $X^* \in \mathscr{R}$.

We can see that a subset of M is rational if and only if it is obtained from the finite subsets of M by a finite number of unions, products, or star operations.

The rational subsets are closed under morphisms. More precisely we have the following.

Proposition 1.3.1 Let $\varphi: M \to N$ be a morphism of monoids. Then φ induces a morphism of the semiring $\bar{\varphi}: \text{Rat}(M) \to \text{Rat}(N)$. Moreover, if φ is injective (surjective), $\bar{\varphi}$ is injective (surjective).

Proof The main difficulty is to show that if $X \in \text{Rat}(M)$, then $X\bar{\varphi} \in \text{Rat}(N)$. Let us denote by $\mathcal{R}$ the set of the subsets X of M such that $X\bar{\varphi} \in \text{Rat}(N)$. We have $\varnothing \in \mathcal{R}$ and $\{m\} \in \mathcal{R}$ for any $m \in M$. Moreover, if $X, Y \in \mathcal{R}$, then $(XY)\bar{\varphi} = (X\bar{\varphi})(Y\bar{\varphi})$, $(X \cup Y)\bar{\varphi} = X\bar{\varphi} \cup Y\bar{\varphi}$ and $X^*\bar{\varphi} = (X\bar{\varphi})^*$. Therefore $X \cup Y \in \mathcal{R}$, $XY \in \mathcal{R}$ and $X^* \in \mathcal{R}$, and consequently $\mathcal{R}$ contains $\text{Rat}(M)$.

Let us suppose that φ is injective and $X\bar{\varphi} = Y\bar{\varphi}$. For every $x \in X$ there exists $y \in Y$ such that $x\varphi = y\varphi$, whence $x = y$. Consequently, $X \subset Y$ and, by a symetrical argument, $Y \subset X$. Therefore $\bar{\varphi}$ is injective.

Suppose that φ is surjective and let $\mathcal{S}$ be the set of the subsets Y of N such that $X\bar{\varphi} = Y$ for some $X \in \text{Rat}(M)$. Since φ is surjective, $\mathcal{S}$ contains the singletons and the empty set. Moreover, $\mathcal{S}$ is closed under union, product and star. Therefore $\mathcal{S}$ contains $\text{Rat}(M)$, which concludes the demonstration.

The rational subsets of a monoid are clearly closed under the operations of union, product and star. On the other hand, they are not generally closed under complementation and intersection (cf. Berstel, 1979, p. 58). None the less we have:

Proposition 1.3.2 Let M be a monoid. If $X \in \text{Rat}(M)$ and $Y \in \text{Rec}(M)$, then $X \cap Y \in \text{Rat}(M)$.

The following statements allow us to compare the sets $\text{Rec}(M)$ and $\text{Rat}(M)$.

Theorem 1.3.3 (Kleene, 1956). Let M be a finitely generated free monoid. Then $\text{Rec}(M) = \text{Rat}(M)$.

Kleene's theorem will be proved in the next section.

Theorem 1.3.4 (McKnight, 1964). Let M be a monoid. Then $\text{Rec}(M)$ is contained in $\text{Rat}(M)$ if and only if M is finitely generated.

Proof If M is finitely generated, there is a finite alphabet A and a surjective morphism $\alpha: A^* \to M$. Now if $X \in \text{Rec}(M)$, $X\alpha^{-1} \in \text{Rec}(A^*)$ by Theorem 1.2.1, and $X\alpha^{-1} \in \text{Rat}(A^*)$ by Kleene's theorem. Finally, $X = X\alpha^{-1}\alpha$ and therefore $X \in \text{Rat}(M)$ by Proposition 1.3.1. Therefore $\text{Rec}(M) \subset \text{Rat}(M)$.

The converse is based on another interesting result:

Proposition 1.3.5   If X is a rational subset of a monoid M, X is contained in a finitely generated submonoid N of M and $X \in \text{Rat}(N)$.

Proof   Let us denote by $\mathscr{R}$ the set of all subsets of M contained in a finitely generated submonoid by M. Of course, $\mathscr{R}$ contains the singletons and the empty set. Let $X, Y \in \mathscr{R}$. We then have two finite subsets of M, A and B, such that $X \subset A^*$ and $Y \subset B^*$. In this case, $X \cup Y$ and XY are contained in $(A \cup B)^*$ and X^* is contained in A^*. Therefore $X \cup Y$, XY and X^* are in $\mathscr{R}$ and $\mathscr{R}$ contains $\text{Rat}(M)$.

In particular, if $\text{Rec}(M) \subset \text{Rat}(M)$, M is a recognizable and therefore rational subset, of M. As a result, M is finitely generated, which concludes Theorem 1.3.4.

1.4   Particular monoids

We have seen that if M is a free monoid with a finite base, $\text{Rec}(M) = \text{Rat}(M)$. One can thus, in certain particular cases, demonstrate some additional properties of rational and recognizable subsets. This section contains the most striking of these particular cases.

1.4.1   *Groups*

The case of the subgroups of a group is a good illustration of the difference between rational and recognizable subsets.

Theorem 1.4.1   Let G be a group and H be a subgroup of G. Then

 (i) $H \in \text{Rec}(G)$ if and only if H has finite index.
(ii) $H \in \text{Rat}(G)$ if and only if H is finitely generated.

1.4.2   *Finitely generated free groups*

In the case of finitely generated free groups, one can be more precise. Let A be a finite alphabet. $\bar{A}$ a disjoint copy of A and let $B = A \cup \bar{A}$. We know that the free group with base A, $F(A)$, is the quotient of B^* by the congruence produced by the relations $a\bar{a} = 1 = \bar{a}a$ for all $a \in A$. Let us denote by $\pi: B^* \to F(A)$ the morphism defined by this congruence. A word of B^* is called reduced if it contains no factor of the form $a\bar{a}$ or $\bar{a}a$ with $a \in A$. We can demonstrate that any element of B^* is congruent to a unique reduced word $u\delta$. This defines an application $\delta: B^* \to B^*$ called Dyck's reduction. Since, moreover, $u\delta = v\delta$ implies $u\pi = v\pi$, there is a (unique) injective function ι such that $\pi\iota = \delta$.

We then have:

Theorem 1.4.2 (Benois, 1969)

(i) If $X \in \text{Rat}(B^*)$, then $X\delta \in \text{Rat}(B^*)$,
(ii) $X \in \text{Rat}(F(A))$ if and only if $X\iota \in \text{Rat}(B^*)$.

Theorem 1.4.3 (Fliess, 1971). $\text{Rat}(F(A))$ is closed under Boolean operations (union, intersection, complementation).

1.4.3 *Monoids* $\mathbb{N}^k$

The case of finitely generated commutative free monoids (therefore isomorphic to $\mathbb{N}^k$ for a certain positive integer k) provides another interesting example. Let us denote $\mathbb{N}^k$ additively and let us say that a subset of $\mathbb{N}^k$ is semilinear if it is a finite union of subsets of the form

$$L(x; x_1,\ldots,x_r) = \{x + n_1 x_1 + \ldots + n_r x_r \mid n_1, \ldots, n_r \in \mathbb{N}\}$$

Proposition 1.4.4 A set of $\mathbb{N}^k$ is rational if and only it is semilinear.

Proof Any semilinear set is rational by construction. Conversely, the empty set and all the singletons are semilinear. Moreover, the union and the product (here the sum!) of two semilinear subsets is again semilinear. Lastly, the submonoid generated by $L(x; x_1, \ldots, x_r)$ is the semilinear set $L(0; x, \ldots, x_r)$. Consequently, all rational sets are semilinear.

We will state the following result, which is much more difficult.

Proposition 1.4.5 (Eilenberg and Schützenberger, 1969). For any $k > 0$, $\text{Rat}(\mathbb{N}^k)$ is a Boolean algebra (for union, intersection and complementation).

1.4.4 *Product of monoids*

The following theorem allows us to describe the recognizable subsets of a product of monoids.

Theorem 1.4.6 (Mezei, unpublished). Let M_1 and M_2 be two monoids and $M = M_1 \times M_2$. Then $X \in \text{Rec}(M)$ if and only if X is a finite union of subsets of the form $X_1 \times X_2$ with $X_1 \in \text{Rec}(M_1)$ and $X_2 \in \text{Rec}(M_2)$.

Proof Let $\pi_i: M \to M_i$ ($i = 1, 2$) be the natural projections. We then have for all subsets X_1 of M_1 and X_2 of M_2,

$$X_1\pi_1^{-1} \times X_2\pi_2^{-1} = (X_1 \times M_2) \cap (M_1 \times X_2) = X_1 \times X_2.$$

Consequently, according to Theorem 1.2.1, if $X_1 \in \text{Rec}(M_1)$ and $X_2 \in \text{Rec}(M_2)$, then $X_1 \times X_2 \in \text{Rec}(M)$. The condition of the statement is thus sufficient since a finite union of recognizable subsets is recognizable.

Conversely, let X be a recognizable subset of M. Then there exist a finite monoid N, a subset P of N and a morphism $\alpha: M \to N$ such that $X = P\alpha^{-1}$. Let $\gamma: M \to N \times N$ be the morphism defined by

$$(m_1, m_2)\gamma = ((m_1, 1)\alpha, (1, m_2)\alpha)$$

Let us set

$$Q = \{(n_1, n_2) \in N \times N \mid n_1 n_2 \in P\}.$$

We then have

$$\begin{aligned} Q\gamma^{-1} &= \{(m_1, m_2) \in M \mid (m_1, 1)\alpha(1, m_2)\alpha \in P\} \\ &= \{(m_1, m_2) \in M \mid (m_1, m_2)\alpha \in P\} = X. \end{aligned}$$

Let $\alpha_1: M_1 \to N$ and $\alpha_2: M_2 \to N$ be the morphisms defined respectively by $m_1\alpha_1 = (m_1, 1)\alpha$ and $m_2\alpha_2 = (1, m_2)\alpha$. There follows for all $(n_1, n_2) \in N \times N$, $(n_1, n_2)\gamma^{-1} = n_1\alpha_1^{-1} \times n_2\alpha_2^{-1}$ and therefore $X = Q\gamma^{-1} = \bigcup_{(n1, n_2) \in Q} n_1\alpha_1^{-1} \times n_1\alpha_2^{-1}$. Since the sets $n_i\alpha_i^{-1}$ $(i = 1, 2)$ are recognizable in M_i, X certainly has the desired form.

Corollary 1.4.7 Let A^* and B^* be two finitely generated free monoids. Then $\text{Rec}(A^* \times B^*)$ is *closed under concatenatim product*. On the other hand, if A and B are non-empty, $\text{Rec}(A^* \times B^*)$ is not closed *under star*.

Proof Let $X, X' \in \text{Rec}(A^* \times B^*)$. According to Mezei's Theorem 1.4.6, X and X' can be written in the form $X = \bigcup_{1 \le i \le n} X_i \times Y_i$ and $X' = \bigcup_{1 \le i \le n'} X_i' \times Y_i'$ with $X_i, X_i' \in \text{Rec}(A^*)$ and $Y_i, Y_i' \in \text{Rec}(B^*)$. It follows that XX' is a finite union of subsets of the form $(X_i \times Y_i)(X_j' \times Y_j') = (X_iX_j') \times (Y_iY_j')$. Now according to Kleene's theorem, $\text{Rec}(A^*) = \text{Rat}(A^*)$, and therefore $X_iX_j' \in \text{Rec}(A^*)$. Similarly, $Y_iY_j' \in \text{Rec}(B^*)$. Consequently, $XX' \in \text{Rec}(A^* \times B^*)$ according to Mezei's theorem.

Let us suppose henceforth that A and B are non-empty and let $a \in A$ and $b \in B$. Then $\{a\}$ is a rational (and hence recognizable) subset of A^*. Similarly $\{b\} \in \text{Rec}(B^*)$. Consequently, $X = \{a\} \times \{b\} \in \text{Rec}(A^* \times B^*)$, according to Mezei's theorem.

Let us suppose that $X^* = \{(a^n, b^n) \mid n \ge 0\}$ be recognizable. We then have a finite monoid N and a morphism $\alpha: A^* \times B^* \to N$ such that $X^*\alpha\alpha^{-1} = X^*$. Since N is finite, there are integers $i < j$ such that $(a, 1)^i\alpha = (a, 1)^j\alpha$. Therefore

$$(a^i, b^i)\alpha = (a, b)^i\alpha = (a, 1)^i\alpha(1, b)^i\alpha = (a, 1)^j\alpha\,(1, b)^i\alpha = (a^j, b^i)\alpha,$$

which contradicts the equality $X^* = X^*\alpha\alpha^{-1}$. Therefore $\text{Rec}(A^* \times B^*)$ is not closed under star.

We can thus characterize the rational subsets of $M_1 \times M_2$.

Theorem 1.4.8 Let M_1 and M_2 be two monoids and $M = M_1 \times M_2$. Then $X \in \text{Rat}(M)$ if and only if there is a finite alphabet A, two monoid morphisms $\alpha_1\colon A^* \to M_1$ and $\alpha_2\colon A^* \to M_2$ and a rational subset R of A^* such that $X = \{(u\alpha_1, u\alpha_2) \mid u \in R\}$.

Proof First of all, if X is of the form indicated, we have $X = R\alpha$ where $\alpha\colon A^* \to M_1 \times M_2$ is the morphism defined by $u\alpha = (u\alpha_1, u\alpha_2)$. Now since $R \in \text{Rat}(A^*)$, we have $X \in \text{Rat}(M)$ according to Proposition 1.3.1.

Let us suppose conversely that $X \in \text{Rat}(M)$. According to Proposition 1.3.5, there exists a finitely generated submonoid N of M such that $X \in \text{Rat}(N)$. There therefore exists a finite alphabet A and a surjective morphism $\beta\colon A^* \to N$. Since $X \in \text{Rat}(N)$, there exists according to Proposition 1.3.1 a language $R \in \text{Rat}(A^*)$ such that $R\beta = X$. Let $\pi_1\colon M \to M_1$ and $\pi_2\colon M \to M_2$ be the natural projections and let us put $\alpha_1 = \beta\pi_1$ and $\alpha_2 = \beta\pi_2$. It follows that $X = R\beta = \{(u\alpha_1, u\alpha_2) \mid u \in R\}$.

We will return to the study of the rational subsets of $M_1 \times M_2$ in Section 1.5.

1.4.5 *Other monoids*
The results we have just looked at have been generalized in various forms. Sakarovitch (1981) has studied the generalizations of the free groups constituted by the monoids presented on the alphabet $A \cup \bar{A}$ by relations of the type

$$\{a\bar{a} = 1 \mid a \in I\} \cup \{\bar{a}a = 1 \mid a \in J\}$$

where I and J are subsets of A.

The partially commutative free monoids, monoids presented on the alphabet A by a certain number of relations of commutation (of the type $ab = ba$ with $a, b \in A$), have been the subject of much research in connection with the problems of synchronization in automata theory.

Another body of work concerns monoids verifying the condition $\text{Rec}(M) = \text{Rat}(M)$. It has been shown that there are monoids that satisfy this condition and which are neither free nor finite.

1.5 **Relations and transductions**

1.5.1 *Rational transductions*
Let M and N be two monoids. A relation on M and N is a subset R of $M \times N$. If $R \in \text{Rat}(M \times N)$, the relation is called rational. Relations can also be viewed in a more lateral way. In fact, with each relation R on M and N there is associated an application $\tau_R\colon M \to \mathcal{P}(M)$ defined by

$m\tau_R = \{n \in N \mid (m,n) \in R\}.$

Any application of M in $\mathscr{P}(N)$ is called a *transduction* of M in N, and τ_R is said to be the transduction defined by the relation R. We will note, conversely, that with any transduction τ of M in N there is associated a relation R, called the *graph* of τ, defined by

$R = \{(m,n) \mid n \in m\tau\}.$

We will say that a transduction is *rational* if its graph is a rational relation.

If τ is a transduction of M in N, we denote by τ^{-1} the transduction of N in M the graph of which is the inverse of the graph of τ

$R_{\tau^{-1}} = \{(n,m) \mid n \in m\tau\}.$

Consequently, τ^{-1} is defined by $n\tau^{-1} = \{m \in M \mid n \in m\tau\}.$

Any transduction τ of M in N induces an application of $\mathscr{P}(M)$ in $\mathscr{P}(N)$, for all $X \in \mathscr{P}(M)$, by

$$X\tau = \bigcup_{x \in X} x\tau.$$

In particular, τ^{-1} induces an application of $\mathscr{P}(N)$ in $\mathscr{P}(M)$, for $Y \in \mathscr{P}(N)$, by

$Y\tau^{-1} = \{m \in M \mid m\tau \cap Y \neq \varnothing\}.$

The following statements are a summary of several important properties of rational transductions. Let us start with a new formulation of Theorem 1.4.8.

Proposition 1.5.1   A transduction τ of M in N is rational if and only if there is a finite alphabet A, morphisms of monoids $\alpha: A^* \to M$, $\beta: A^* \to N$ and a rational language R of A^* such that, for every $m \in M$, $m\tau = (m\alpha^{-1} \cap R)\beta.$

The following statement is a direct result of the definition.

Proposition 1.5.2   If τ is a rational transduction of M in N, τ^{-1} is a rational transduction of N in M.

Here is yet another important result.

Proposition 1.5.3   Let τ be a rational transduction of M in N. If $X \in \mathrm{Rec}(M)$, then $X\tau \in \mathrm{Rat}(N)$.

Proof   Let us use the result and the notations of Proposition 1.1.1. We have $X\tau = (X\alpha^{-1} \cap R)\beta$. Now, according to the results of Section 1, $X \in$

Rec(M) implies $X\alpha^{-1} \in$ Rec(A^*). Since Rat(A^*) = Rec(A^*), we also have $(X\alpha^{-1} \cap R) \in$ Rat(A^*) hence $(X\alpha^{-1} \cap R)\beta \in$ Rat(N).

Let us note that if $X \in$ Rat(M), $X\tau$ is not necessarily rational. Let us finally cite the theorem of Elgot dand Mezei (1965).

Proposition 1.5.4 Let A be a finite alphabet. If τ_1 is a rational transduction of M_1 in A^* and if τ_2 is a rational transduction of A^* in M_2, then $\tau_1\tau_2$ is a rational transduction of M_1 in M_2.

1.5.2 *Examples*
Let A be a finite alphabet and let M be a monoid. According to Theorem 1.4.8, the morphisms of monoids of A^* in M (and their inverses) are rational transductions.

A *substitution* $\sigma: A^* \to M$ is a transduction which satisfies the following conditions:

$$1\sigma = \{1\} \quad \text{and} \quad (uv)\sigma = (u\sigma)(v\sigma) \quad \text{for any } u, v \in A^*.$$

In other words, σ induces a morphism from A^* in $\mathscr{P}(M)$. If this transduction is rational, we say that the substitution is rational. It is easy to see that a substitution is rational if and only if, for every $a \in A$, $a\sigma \in$ Rat(M).

If M is a finitely generated monoid, the identity on M is a rational transduction since if E if is a finite set of generators of M, the graph of the identity is the set

$$D = \{(m,m) \in E \times E\}^*.$$

Moreover, if $X \in$ Rat(M), the transductions

$$m \to Xm \quad \text{and} \quad m \to mX$$

are rational. In fact, their graphs are respectively

$$(X \times \{1\})D \quad \text{and} \quad D(\{1\} \times X).$$

Similarly the transductions

$$m \to X^{-1}m = \{n \in M \; \exists x \in X \; xm = n\} \quad \text{and}$$
$$m \to mX^{-1} = \{n \in M \; \exists x \in X \; mx = n\},$$

the inverses of the preceding transductions, are rational.

Finally, the transduction $\tau: M \times M \to M$ defined by $(m,n)\tau = mn$ is rational since its graph is $\{(x,1,x) \mid x \in E\}^* \{(1,x,x) \mid x \in E\}^*$.

Let A be a finite alphabet. The transduction of A^* in $A^* \times A^*$ defined by $u\tau = (u,u)$ is rational. Observe that if L_1 and L_2 are languages of A^*, $(L_1 \times L_2)\tau^{-1} = L_1 \cap L_2$.

Similarly, it can be shown (exercise!) that the application which associates with a word of A^* the set of its factors (respectively left factors, right factors, subwords, factors of fixed length k, etc.) is a rational transduction.

On the other hand, if $\text{Card}(A) \geq 2$, the application which associates with a word $u = a_1 \ldots a_n$ its 'mirror image' $a_n \ldots a_1$ is *not* a rational transduction.

The reader will find further examples in Berstel (1979, Chapters 3 and 4) and in Pin and Sakarovitch (1983, 1985).

1.5.3 *Matrix representations*

Let M be a monoid and K a semiring. For any integer $n > 0$, we denote by $K^{n \times n}$ the multiplicative monoid of square matrices of dimension n with coefficients in K. (The product of two matrices m and n is defined in the usual way by the formula $(mn)_{ij} = \sum_{1 \leq k \leq n} m_{ik} n_{kj}$ for $1 \leq i, j \leq n$.)

Let τ be an application of M in K.

Definition 1.5.1   We say that τ has a *linear representation* of dimension n with coefficients in K if there is an integer $n > 0$, a monoid morphism μ: $M \to K^{n \times n}$ and vectors $\lambda \in K^{1 \times n}$ and $v \in K^{n \times 1}$ such that for any $m \in M$, $m\tau = \lambda(m\mu)v$.

We then have the following theorem which we will state without proof.

Theorem 1.5.5   Let A be a finite alphabet. A transduction τ of A^* in M is rational if and only if it has a linear representation with coefficients in $\text{Rat}(M)$.

Note that there is an algorithm to calculate a linear representation of a given rational transduction. The following result is much more elementary, but is none the less useful.

Theorem 1.5.6   Let A be a finite alphabet and let τ be a transduction of A^* in M having a linear representation with coefficients in $\mathscr{P}(M)$. If $X \in \text{Rec}(M)$, the $X\tau^{-1} \in \text{Rec}(A^*)$.

Proof   Let (λ,μ,v) be a linear representation of dimension n of τ. Since X is recognizable, there is a finite monoid N, and a morphism α: $M \to N$ such that $X = X\alpha\alpha^{-1}$. We will again denote by α the semiring morphism $\mathscr{P}(M) \to \mathscr{P}(N)$ induced by α. This morphism extends again into a morphism of $\mathcal{P}(M)^{n \times n}$ in $\mathcal{P}(N)^{n \times n}$ (respectively, of $\mathcal{P}(M)^{1 \times n}$ in $\mathcal{P}(N)^{1 \times n}$, of $\mathcal{P}(M)^{n \times 1}$ in $\mathcal{P}(N)^{n \times 1}$). Let us put

$$P = \{n \in M \mid (\lambda \alpha) n (\nu \alpha) \cap X \neq \emptyset\}.$$

First we have

$$\begin{aligned}
P\alpha^{-1} &= \{m \in M \mid (\lambda \alpha)(m\alpha)(\nu\alpha) \cap X \neq \emptyset\} \\
&= \{m \in M \mid \lambda m \nu \cap X \neq \emptyset\}
\end{aligned}$$

since $X\alpha\alpha^{-1} = X$ and α is a morphism. From this we deduce

$$\begin{aligned}
P\alpha^{-1}\mu^{-1} &= \{u \in A^* \mid \lambda(u\mu)\nu \cap X \neq \emptyset\} \\
&= \{u \in A^* \mid u\tau \cap X \neq \emptyset\} = X\tau^{-1}.
\end{aligned}$$

Therefore $X\tau^{-1}$ is recognized by the morphism

$$\mu\alpha: A^* \to \mathcal{P}(N)^{n \times n}.$$

In fact, the above demonstration allows us to show that $X\tau^{-1}$ is recognized by the monoid of matrices $A^*\mu\alpha$ (contained in $\mathcal{P}(N)^{n \times n}$). This supplementary piece of information has many applications (Pin and Saka-vovitch, 1983, 1985). We will content ourselves here with a few examples.

Corollary 1.5.7 If $\sigma: A^* \to M$ is a substitution (rational or not), and if $X \in \text{Rec}(M)$, then $X\sigma^{-1} \in \text{Rec}(A^*)$. Moreover, if X is recognized by the finite monoid N, $X\sigma^{-1}$ is recognized by $\mathcal{P}(N)$.

Proof Indeed, $(1,\sigma,1)$ is a linear representation of dimension 1 for σ.

Let X be any subset of A^*. Then the transduction $\tau: A^* \to A^*$ defined by $u\tau = Xu$ has the linear representation of dimension 1 $(X,\iota,1)$ where ι is the identity of A^*. As $u\tau^{-1} = X^{-1}u$, we obtain a new proof of Theorem 1.2.1 (iii) in the case of A^*.

Let $\tau: A^* \to A^* \times A^*$ be the rational transduction defined by

$$u\tau = \{(u_1, u_2) \mid u_1 u_2 = u\}.$$

τ allows the linear representation of dimension 2 (λ, μ, ν) with $\lambda = (\{(1,1)\}, \emptyset)$, $\nu = \begin{pmatrix} \emptyset \\ \{(1,1)\} \end{pmatrix}$ and $\mu: A^* \to \text{Rat}(A^*)^{2 \times 2}$ defined by $a\mu = \begin{pmatrix} \{(a,1)\} & \{(a,1), (1,a)\} \\ \emptyset & \{(1,a)\} \end{pmatrix}$ for any $a \in A$.

2 Languages and automata

The aim of this section is to establish the connection linking the recognizable subsets of a finitely generated free monoid with finite automata.

In the course of this, we shall demonstrate Kleene's theorem which was stated in Section 1.

2.1 Automata

A finite automaton is a triplet (Q,A,δ) where Q is a finite set called a set of states, A is a finite set called an alphabet and δ is an application of $Q \times A$ in the set of the subsets of Q.

Example Let $\mathcal{A} = (Q,A,\delta)$ with $Q = \{1,2,3,\}$, $A = \{a,b\}$ and

$$\delta(1,a) = \{1,2\} \qquad \delta(1,b) = \{2,3\}$$
$$\delta(2,a) = \varnothing \qquad \delta(2,b) = \{2\}$$
$$\delta(3,a) = \{3\} \qquad \delta(3,b) = \{1,2\}$$

The automaton is said to be *deterministic* if for any $q \in Q$ and for any $a \in A$, $\mathrm{Card}(\delta(q,a)) \leq 1$. In this case δ can be considered as a partial function of $Q \times A$ in Q. The automaton is called *complete* if for any $q \in Q$ and for any $a \in A$, $\mathrm{Card}(\delta(q,a)) \geq 1$. Consequently, in a complete deterministic.automaton, δ is a function of $Q \times A$ in Q.

It is convenient to represent an automaton by a directed graph in which the vertices are the states of the automaton and the edges are the triplets (i,a,j) such that $j \in \delta(i,a)$.

Example (continued) The automaton $\mathcal{A}$ described below can be represented as follows:

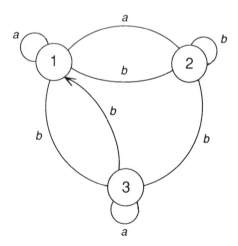

The application δ extends to an application of $Q \times A^*$ in $\mathcal{P}(Q)$ according to the following rules. For any $q \in Q$, $\delta(q,1) = \{q\}$. For any $u \in A^*$ and $n \in A$, $\delta(q,ua) = \bigcup_{q' \in \delta(q,u)} \delta(q',a)$.

Example (continued) Thus we have $\delta(1,ab) = \delta(1,b) \cup \delta(2,b) = \{2,3\}$.

2.2 Automata and recognizable languages

Let A be a finite alphabet and let A^* be the free monoid with base A. We call any subset of A^* a *language*. A language L is recognized by a finite automaton $\mathcal{A} = (Q,A,\delta)$ if there are two subsets I (set of initial states) and F (set of final states) of Q such that

$L = \{u \in A^* \mid$ there is $i \in I$ and $j \in F$ such that $j \in \delta(i,u)\}$.

In graph terminology, L is the set of labels of paths from any initial state to any final state. We usually show initial (or final) states by means of an arrow entering (or leaving).

Example The automaton

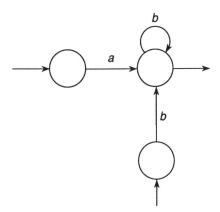

recognizes the language $ab^* \cup bb^*$.

The connection between automata and recognizable subsets is made clear by the following statement.

Theorem 2.2.1 Let L be a language of A^*. The following conditions are equivalent

(i) L is recognizable.
(ii) L is recognized by a deterministic complete finite automaton with a single initial state.

(iii) L is recognized by a finite automaton.

Proof (i) implies (ii). Since L is recognizable, there is a finite monoid M, a subset P of M and a morphism $\alpha: A^* \to M$ such that $L = P\alpha^{-1}$. Let $\mathscr{A} = (M,A,\delta)$ be the automaton defined by $\delta(m,a) = m(a\alpha)$ for any $m \in M$ and for any $a \in A$. Let 1 be the unique initial state and let P be the set of final states. The language recognized by $\mathscr{A}$ is then

$$\{u \in A^* \mid \delta(1,u) \in P\} = \{u \in A^* \mid 1(u\alpha) \in P\} = P\alpha^{-1} = L,$$

which proves (ii).

(ii) obviously implies (iii).

(iii) implies (i). Let $\mathscr{A} = (A,Q,\delta)$ be a finite automaton recognizing L. Let us denote by M the monoid of relations on Q equipped with the composition of relations as multiplication. Since Q is finite, M is a finite monoid. Let $\alpha: A^* \to M$ be the application defined by

$$(i,j) \in u\alpha \text{ if and only if } j \in \delta(i,u).$$

α is a morphism. In fact, 1α is the identity, and if $u \in A^*$ and $a \in A$, we have successively: .

$$(i,j) \in (ua)\alpha \Leftrightarrow j \in \delta(i,ua) \Leftrightarrow \exists k \in \delta(i,u) \text{ such that } j \in \delta(k,a) \Leftrightarrow$$
$$\exists k \in Q \text{ such that } (i,k) \in u\alpha \text{ and } (k,j) \in a\alpha \Leftrightarrow (i,j) \in (u\alpha)(a\alpha).$$

Now let I be the set of initial states and F the set of final states. Put

$$P = \{m \in M \mid m \cap I \times J \neq \varnothing\}.$$

There follows

$$\begin{aligned}
P\alpha^{-1} &= \{u \in A^* \mid \exists (i,j) \in I \times J \ (i,j) \in u\alpha\} \\
&= \{u \in A^* \mid \exists (i,j) \in I \times J \ j \in \delta(i,u)\} = L.
\end{aligned}$$

Therefore L is recognized by M.

2.3 Automata and rational languages

We will first establish the following result, the first step of Kleene's theorem.

Proposition 2.3.1 If $L \in \mathrm{Rat}(A^*)$, then L is recognized by a finite automaton.

Proof First of all, the empty language is recognized by any finite automaton whose set of final states is empty. Language $\{1\}$ is recognized by the automaton $\to\bigcirc\to$ and, if a is a letter, the language $\{a\}$ is recognized by the automaton $\to\bigcirc\overset{a}{\to}\bigcirc\to$. Now, for $i = 1, 2$, let there be automata $\mathscr{A}_i = (Q_i,A,\delta_i)$ recognizing languages L_i, containing the set of initial (and final) states I_i (and F_i). We can always suppose that $Q_1 \cap Q_2 = \emptyset$. We will construct an automaton recognizing $L_1 \cup L_2$ and $L_1 L_2$.

Let us first consider the automaton $\mathscr{A} = (Q, A, \delta)$ defined by $Q = Q_1 \cup Q_2$ and

$$\delta(q, a) = \begin{cases} \delta_1(q, a) & \text{if } q \in Q_1, \\ \delta_2(q, a) & \text{if } q \in Q_2. \end{cases}$$

We take $I = I_1 \cup I_2$ as the set of initial states and $F = F_1 \cup F_2$ as the set of final states. The language recognized by $\mathscr{A}$ is therefore

$$L = \{u \in A^* \mid \exists i \in I_1 \cup I_2, \ \exists j \in F_1 \cup F_2 \ j \in \delta(i, u)\}.$$

Now for any $u \in A^*$, $\delta(q, u) \subset Q_i$ if $q \in Q_i$ $(i = 1, 2)$. Consequently,

$$\begin{aligned} L &= \{u \in A^* \mid \exists i \in I_1 \ \exists j \in F_1 \ j \in \delta(i, u)\} \\ &\quad \cup \{u \in A^* \mid \exists i \in I_2 \ \exists j \in F_2 \ j \in \delta(i, u)\} \\ &= L_1 \cup L_2. \end{aligned}$$

For $L_1 L_2$, let us consider the automaton $\mathscr{A} = (Q, A, \delta)$ defined by $Q = Q_1 \cup Q_2$ and

$$\delta(q, a) = \begin{cases} \delta_2(q, a) & \text{if } q \in Q_2 \\ \delta_1(q, a) \cup \displaystyle\bigcup_{i \in I_2} \delta_2(i, a) & \text{if } q \in F_1 \\ \delta_1(q, a) & \text{if } q \in Q_1 \backslash F_1 \end{cases}$$

Finally, we put $I = I_1$ and

$$F = \begin{cases} F_2 & \text{if } 1 \notin L_2 \\ F_1 \cup F_2 & \text{if } 1 \in L_2 \end{cases}$$

Let $u \in L_1 L_2$. Then u can be factored as $u = u_1 u_2$ with $u_1 \in L_1$ and $u_2 \in L_2$. If $u_2 = 1$, $1 \in L_2$ and $u = u_1$ is recognized by $\mathscr{A}$ since $F = F_1 \cup F_2$ in this case. Otherwise, we write $u_2 = av$ with $a \in A$. Now there exist $i_1 \in I_1$, $j_1 \in F_1$ such that $j_1 \in \delta_1(i_1, u_1)$, $i_2 \in I_2$, $q \in Q_2$ and $j_2 \in F_2$ such that $q \in \delta_2(i_2, a)$ and $j_2 \in \delta_2(q, v)$. From this we deduce $j_1 \in \delta_1(i_1, u_1)$, $q \in \delta(j_1, a)$ and $j_2 \in \delta(q, v)$ hence $j_2 \in \delta(i_1, u)$. Therefore u is recognized by $\mathscr{A}$.

Conversely, let u be a word recognized by $\mathscr{A}$. Let us suppose that $1 \notin L_2$ (the case of $1 \in L_2$ is treated in a similar manner). Since there is no transition from a state of Q_2 to a state of Q_1, any word recognized by $\mathscr{A}$ is factored into $u_1 av$ so that there exist states $i_1 \in I_1$, $j_1 \in Q_1$, $q \in Q_2$ and $j_2 \in F_2$ such that $j_1 \in \delta(i_1, u_1)$, $q \in \delta(j_1, a)$ and $j_2 \in \delta(i_2, v)$. From this we deduce on the one hand that $j_1 \in \delta_1(i_1, u_1)$ and $j_1 \in F_1$, hence $u_1 \in L_1$, and on the other that there exists $i_2 \in I_2$ such that $q \in \delta(i_2, a)$, hence $av \in L_2$. Consequently $u \in L_1 L_2$.

Finally, if $\mathscr{A} = (Q, A, \delta)$ recognizes a language L, with the set of initial (and final) states I (and F), we can construct an automaton $\mathcal{A}'$ which recognizes L^* in the following manner:

$\mathcal{A}' = (Q',A,\delta')$ with $Q' = Q \cup \{q_0\}$ (q_0 being a new state) and, if $q \in Q$,

$$\delta'(q,a) = \begin{cases} \delta(q,a) & \text{if } \delta(q,a) \cap F = \varnothing \\ \delta(q,a) \cup \{q_0\} & \text{if } \delta(q,a) \cap F \neq \varnothing \end{cases}$$

and, by putting $\delta(I,a) = \bigcup_{q \in I} \delta(q,a)$,

$$\delta'(q_0,a) = \begin{cases} \delta(I,a) & \text{if } \delta(I,a) \cap F = \varnothing, \\ \delta(I,a) \cup \{q_0\} & \text{if } \delta(I,a) \cap F \neq \varnothing. \end{cases}$$

We take q_0 as the only initial and final state.

Example   If $\mathcal{A}$ is the automaton

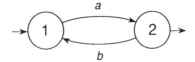

$\mathcal{A}'$ will be represented like this

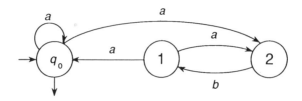

If $u \in L$, u is recognized by $\mathcal{A}'$. This is obvious if u is of length $\leqslant 1$. If not, u is written as avb with $v \in A^*$ and $a, b \in A$ and there exist states p, $q \in Q$ and $j \in F$ such that $p \in \delta(i,a)$, $q \in \delta'(p,v)$ and $j \in \delta(q,b)$. From this follows $p \in \delta'(i,a)$, $q \in \delta'(p,v)$ and $q_0 \in \delta'(q,b)$, hence $q_0 \in \delta(i,avb)$. Therefore u is recognized by $\mathcal{A}'$. Thus any word of L^* is recognized by $\mathcal{A}'$.

Conversely, we can show by induction on the length of u that if u is recognized by $\mathcal{A}'$, then $u \in L^*$. This is clear if u is the empty word. If not, let us put $u = a_1 \ldots a_n$ with $n > 0$. There exist then a sequence of states $q_1, \ldots, q_{n-1}$ such that

$q_1 \in \delta(q_0, a_1)$, $q_{i+1} \in \delta(q_i, a_{i+1})$ $(1 \leqslant i \leqslant n - 2)$ $q_0 \in \delta(q_{n-1}, a_n)$

Let k be the highest index such that $q_k \neq q_0$. Since $q_0 \in \delta'(q_k, q_{k+1})$, we necessarily have $\delta(q_k, a_{k+1}) \cap F \neq \emptyset$. If $k = 0$, we have $q_0 \in \delta'(q_0, a_1)$, whence $\delta(I, a_1) \cap F \neq \emptyset$ and $a_1 \in L$. If not, we have $\delta'(q_0, a_1) = \delta(I, a_1)$ and there exists $i \in I$ such that $q_1 \in \delta(i, a_1)$. It follows that $\delta(i, a_1 \ldots a_{k+1})$ $\cap F \neq \emptyset$ and consequently $a_1 \ldots a_{k+1} \in L$. Now we have $q_0 \in \delta'(q_0, a_{k+2} \ldots a_n)$ and therefore $a_{k+2} \ldots a_n$ is recognized by $\mathscr{A}'$. By induction, $a_{k+2} \ldots a_n \in L^*$ and consequently $u \in L^*$. Therefore $\mathscr{A}'$ recognizes L^*.

Now we will establish the converse of Proposition 2.3.1.

Proposition 2.3.2 If L is recognized by a finite automaton, $L \in \mathrm{Rat}(A^*)$.

Proof According to Theorem 2.2.1, we can assume that L is recognized by a complete deterministic finite automaton $\mathscr{A} = (Q, A, \delta)$. Let us put $Q = \{1, \ldots, n\}$ and, for simplicity, $q \cdot u = \delta(q, u)$ for $q \in Q$ and $u \in A^*$. Finally, let us consider the sets $R_{ij}^k = \{u \in A^* \mid i \cdot u = j$ and, for any prefix v of u different from 1 and from u, $i \cdot v \leqslant k\}$. It is easily seen that these sets are defined recursively by the formulae

$$R_{ij}^0 = \begin{cases} \{a \in A \mid i \cdot a = j\} & \text{if } i \neq j, \\ \{a \in A \mid i \cdot a = j\} \cup \{1\} & \text{if } i = j, \end{cases}$$

$$R_{ij}^k = R_{ik}^{k-1} (R_{kk}^{k-1})^* R_{kj}^{k-1} \cup R_{ij}^{k-1}.$$

Moreover, the language L recognized by $\mathscr{A}$ is

$$L = \bigcup_{i \in I, j \in J} R_{ij}^n.$$

As $R_{ij}^0 \in \mathrm{Rat}(A^*)$ by construction, it follows by induction on k that $R_{ij}^k \in \mathrm{Rat}(A^*)$ for any i, j, $k \in Q$. Hence, finally, $L \in \mathrm{Rat}(A^*)$.

2.4 Conclusion

Summing up the results of Section 2, we arrive at the following statement.

Theorem 2.4.1 (Kleene, 1956). Let L be a language of A^*. The following conditions are equivalent:

(i) $L \in \mathrm{Rec}(A^*)$,
(ii) $L \in \mathrm{Rat}(A^*)$,
(iii) L is recognized by a finite automaton,
(iv) L is recognized by a complete deterministic finite automaton possessing a unique initial state.

3 The minimal automaton, the syntactic monoid and varieties

The aim of this section is to show that we can associate with each recognizable language L a finite monoid, called the syntactic monoid of the language. Sections 3.3 and 3.4 give an algorithm to compute this monoid. We can then study the properties of recognizable languages through properties of their syntactic monoid. This is the purpose of Eilenberg's theory of varieties, the basic terms of which are presented in Section 3.6.

3.1 The syntactic monoid

In this section we propose to show that if P is a recognizable subset of a monoid M, there is a 'minimal' finite monoid which recognizes P. The term 'minimal' is used here in the sense of division, defined as follows.

Definition 3.1.1 We say that a monoid M *divides* a monoid N (denoted by $M \prec N$), if M is the quotient of a submonoid of N.

It is not difficult to prove the following result.

Proposition 3.1.1 The relation $\prec$ is a partial order on finite monoids. Moreover, if M divides N, $\mathrm{Card}(M) \leqslant \mathrm{Card}(N)$.

To prove this result, we will first describe the syntactic monoid of P, and then verify whether this monoid possesses the property of minimality that we are looking for.

Definition 3.1.2 Let P be a subset of M. The syntactic congruence is the congruence $\sim_P$ defined on M by $u \sim_P v$ if and only if for any $x, y \in M$, $xuy \in P \Leftrightarrow xvy \in P$. The quotient monoid $M/\sim_P = M(P)$ is the syntactic monoid of P.

This definition applies to all subsets P *of* M, recognizable or not. Similarly, we will say that a monoid N (finite or not) recognizes P if there is a morphism $\alpha\colon M \to N$ such that $P = P\alpha\alpha^{-1}$. We then have the following properties.

Proposition 3.1.2 Let P be a subset of M and let N be a monoid. Then

(i) $M(P)$ recognizes P.
(ii) If N recognizes P, them $M(P)$ divides N.

Proof (i) Let $\alpha\colon M \to M/\sim_P$ be the natural morphism. We will show that $P = P\alpha\alpha^{-1}$. Inclusion from left to right is clear. Conversely, let $u \in$

$P\alpha\alpha^{-1}$. Then $u\alpha = v\alpha$ for some $v \in P$ and therefore $u \sim_P v$. Now, since $1v1 \in P$, there follows $1u1 \in P$, hence $u \in P$. Therefore $P\alpha\alpha^{-1} \subset P$, which concludes the proof of (i).

(ii) Since N recognizes P, there is a morphism $\beta: M \to N$ such that $P\beta\beta^{-1} = P$. Put $R = M\beta$, and then R is a submonoid of N. Moreover, if $u\beta = v\beta$ and $xuy \in P$, we have $(xuy)\beta = (xvy)\beta \in P\beta$, hence $xvy \in P\beta\beta^{-1} = P$. Consequently, $u\beta = v\beta$ implies $u \sim_P v$, hence $u\alpha = v\alpha$. It follows from this that $M(P) = M\alpha$ is a quotient of R.

From this we deduce

Corollary 3.1.3 If P is a recognizable subset of M, the syntactic monoid of P is minimal for the order $\prec$ amongst finite monoids which recognize P.

Corollary 3.1.4 If P is a recognizable subset of M, the syntactic monoid of P is the monoid with smallest cardinal recognizing P.

3.2 The case of languages

If L is a language of A^*, Proposition 3.1.2 can be completed as follows:

Proposition 3.2.1 Let L be a language of A^* and let N be a monoid. Then N recognizes L if and only if $M(L)$ divides N.

Proof According to Proposition 3.1.2, it remains to be proved that if $M(L)$ divides N, then N recognizes L. Since $M(L)$ divides N, there is a submonoid R of N such that $M(L)$ is a quotient of R. We then use a classic property of free monoids

Lemma 3.2.2 Let $\alpha: A^* \to M$ and $\beta: R \to M$ be two monoid morphisms. If β is surjective, there is a morphism $\gamma: A^* \to R$ such that $\alpha = \gamma\beta$.

Proof Let us associate with each letter $a \in A$ any element $a\gamma$ of the set $a\alpha\beta^{-1}$. According to the universal property of free monoids, γ can be extended into a morphism of A^* in R which verifies by construction $\alpha = \gamma\beta$.

Let us apply the lemma with $M = M(L)$. We then have $L\alpha\alpha^{-1} = L(\alpha\beta^{-1})(\beta\alpha^{-1}) = L\alpha\alpha^{-1} = L$ and therefore N recognizes L.

Corollary 3.2.3 If M recognizes L and M divides N, then N recognizes L.

3.3 The minimal automaton

In this section, a finite deterministic automaton equipped with a set of initial states and a set of final states will be called simply an automaton. The transition function will be denoted by a dot.

Let $\mathscr{A} = (Q,A, . ,I,F)$ be an automaton. We say that a state q is *accessible* if there is a word $u \in A^*$ such that $q \in I \cdot u$. The state q is called *coaccessible* if there is a word $v \in A^*$ such that $q \cdot v \in F$. Let us denote by Q' the set of states which are both accessible and coaccessible. The transition function induces a function $*$ of $Q' \times A$ in Q' defined by

$$q * a = \begin{cases} q \cdot a & \text{if } q \cdot a \in Q', \\ \varnothing & \text{if not.} \end{cases}$$

Let us put $I' = I \cap Q'$, $F' = F \cap Q'$ and let us consider the automaton $\mathscr{A}'$ $= (Q',A,*,I',F')$. Let us denote by L and L' the languages recognized by $\mathscr{A}$ and $\mathscr{A}'$ respectively. The inclusion of $L' \subset L$ is obvious. Conversely, if $u \in L$, there exists $i \in I$ such that $i \cdot u \in F$. We therefore have $i \in I'$ and $i \cdot u \in F'$. Moreover, if $u = u_1u_2$, the state $i \cdot u_1$ is both accessible and coaccessible, since $(i \cdot u_1) \cdot u_2 \in F$. We therefore have $i \cdot u = i * u \in F'$, hence $u \in L'$. Consequently, $L = L'$.

We will say that an automaton is *trim* if all its states are both accessible and coaccessible. The preceding argument shows that any recognizable language can be recognized by a trim automaton.

We defined a partial order on automata as follows. Let $\mathscr{A} = (Q,A, . ,I, F,)$ and $\mathscr{A}' = (Q',A, . ,I',F')$ be two automata. Then $\mathscr{A} \leqslant \mathscr{A}'$ if there is a surjective function $\varphi \colon Q' \to Q$ such that $I\varphi = I'$, $F\varphi = F'$, and, for every $U \in A^*$ and every $q \in Q'$, $(q \cdot u)\varphi = (q\varphi) \cdot u$. We then have

Proposition 3.3.1 Let $\mathscr{A}$ and $\mathscr{A}'$ be two trim automata such that $\mathscr{A} \leqslant \mathscr{A}'$. Then $\mathscr{A}$ and $\mathscr{A}'$ recognize the same language.

Proof Let L and L' be the languages recognized by $\mathscr{A}$ and $\mathscr{A}'$ respectively. We have

$$L' = \{u \in A^* \mid I' \cdot u \cap F' \neq \varnothing\} = \{u \in A^* \mid (I\varphi) \cdot u \cap (F\varphi) \neq \varnothing\}$$
$$= \{u \in A^* \mid (I \cdot u)\varphi \cap (F\varphi) \neq \varnothing\} = \{u \in A^* \mid I \cdot u \cap F \neq \varnothing\} = L.$$

Let L be a recognizable language of A^*. We will show that, amongst the automata which recognize L, there is a trim automaton which possesses a single initial state and is minimal for the order $\leqslant$ amongst the automata with these properties.

To establish this result, we first describe a particular automaton called the 'minimal automaton' of L, then we verify that this automaton possesses the required properties.

Since L is recognizable, L is recognized by a morphism $\alpha: A^* \to M$, where M is a finite monoid. We have seen (Theorem 1.2.1 (iii)) that for any $u \in A^*$, $u^{-1}L$ is also recognized by α. Since α only recognizes a finite number of languages, the set $\{u^{-1}L \mid u \in A^*\}$ is finite.

Let us put $\mathscr{A} = (Q, A, \cdot, q_0, F)$ where $Q = \{u^{-1}L \mid u \in A^* \text{ and } u^{-1}L \neq \varnothing\}$, $q_0 = L$, $F = \{u^{-1}L \mid 1 \in u^{-1}L\} = \{u^{-1}L \mid u \in L\}$, and where the function of transition is given by the formulae

$$(u^{-1}L) \cdot v = (uv)^{-1}L = v^{-1}(u^{-1}L).$$

Proposition 3.3.2 $\mathscr{A}$ is a trim automaton with a single initial state, which recognizes L. Moreover, $\mathscr{A}$ is minimal (for the order $\leqslant$) amongst the automata with these properties.

Proof Any state of $\mathscr{A}$ is accessible since by definition $u^{-1}L = q_0 \cdot u$. Moreover, if $u^{-1}L$ is non-empty, there is $v \in A^*$ such that $uv \in L$. We then have $(uv)^{-1}L \neq \varnothing$ and therefore $(uv)^{-1}L = (u^{-1}L) \cdot v \in F$. Therefore all states are coaccessible. The language recognized by $\mathscr{A}$ is the set

$$\{u \in A^* \mid q_0 \cdot u \in F\} = \{u \in A^* \mid u^{-1}L \in F\} = L.$$

Finally, let $\mathscr{A}' = (Q', A, \cdot, i', F')$ be a trim automaton with a single initial state and recognizing L. If u and v are two words of A^* such that $q = i' \cdot u = i' \cdot v$, we have $u^{-1}L = v^{-1}L = \{w \in A^* \mid q \cdot w \in F\}$. Consequently, we can define a function φ of Q' in Q by putting $q\varphi = u^{-1}L$ where u is such that $i' \cdot u = q$. Since $i' \cdot 1 = i'$, we have $i'\varphi = L = q_0$. On the other hand

$$F'\varphi = \{u^{-1}L \mid i' \cdot u \in F'\} = \{u^{-1}L \mid u \in L\} = F.$$

Finally, φ is surjective since $u^{-1}L = (i' \cdot u)\varphi$. Now, let $q \in Q'$ and $u \in A^*$. Let $v \in A^*$ such that $i' \cdot v = q$. There follows $(q\varphi) \cdot u = (v^{-1}L) \cdot u = (vu)^{-1}L = (i' \cdot vu)\varphi = (q \cdot u)\varphi$. Therefore $\mathscr{A} \leqslant \mathscr{A}'$.

3.4 Algorithms

Let L be a rational language given, for example, by a rational expression. Kleene's theorem states that the syntactic monoid of L is finite. We should now give an effective computation of this syntactic monoid.

Let $\mathscr{A} = (Q, A, \cdot)$ be a deterministic automaton. We denote by $F(Q)$ the monoid of all functions from Q to Q under composition of functions. Define a morphism of A^* in $F(Q)$ by associating with every word u of A^* the function $q \to q \cdot u$. The image of A^* by this morphism is the *monoid of transition* of $\mathscr{A}$, denoted as $M(\mathscr{A})$. $M(\mathscr{A})$ is generated by the functions $q \to q \cdot a$ where $a \in A$, and is therefore easily calculated.

Example   Let $\mathcal{A}$ be the automaton represented below:

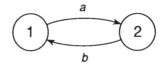

The monoid of transition of $\mathcal{A}$ contains six elements which correspond to the words 1, a, b, ab, ba and aa. If we identify the elements of $M(\mathcal{A})$ with these words, we have the relations $aba = a$, $bab = b$ and $bb = aa$. In addition, aa is a zero of $M(\mathcal{A})$: let us remember that an element 0 of a monoid M is a zero if for every $x \in M$ we have $0x = 0 = x0$. Here is the table of the transitions of $\mathcal{A}$:

	1	2
1	1	2
a	2	–
b	–	1
aa	–	–
ab	1	–
ba	–	2

Further examples of more detailed calculations can be found in Pin (1984, p. 31).

The following proposition allows us to reduce the calculation of the syntactic monoid to the calculation of the minimal automaton.

Proposition 3.4.1   Let L be a recognizable language. The syntactic monoid of L is equal to the monoid of transition of its minimal automaton.

Proof   Let $\mathcal{A}$ be the minimal automaton of L and let α be the morphism of A^* on $M(\mathcal{A})$ as defined above. We have $u\alpha = v\alpha$ if and only if

$$\text{for any state } x^{-1}L \text{ of } \mathcal{A}, \ (x^{-1}L)\cdot u = (x^{-1}L)\cdot v \tag{1}$$

Now, $y \in (x^{-1}L)\cdot u$ if and only if $xuy \in L$. Condition 1 is therefore equivalent to $u \sim_L v$. Consequently, $M(\mathcal{A}) = M(L)$.

There exist (at least) two algorithms to calculate the minimal automaton of a rational language. The first is directly based on the definition of the minimal automaton. We calculate the residuals $u^{-1}L$ from the following formulae, where $a \in A$, $u \in A^*$ and where L, L_1, L_2 are languages:

$$u^{-1}(L_1 \cup L_2) = u^{-1}L_1 \cup u^{-1}L_2, \quad v^{-1}(u^{-1}L) = (uv)^{-1}L$$

$$a^{-1}(L_1 L_2) = \begin{cases} (a^{-1}L_1)L_2 & \text{if } 1 \notin L_1, \\ (a^{-1}L_1)L_2 \cup a^{-1}L_2 & \text{if } 1 \in L_1, \end{cases}$$

$$a^{-1}L^* = (a^{-1}L)L^*.$$

This procedure is very efficient with calculations to be done by hand for small automata since the evaluation of the $u^{-1}L$ is relatively easy with a little practice and the minimal automaton is obtained directly (cf. Pin, 1984, p. 31). The theoretical justification is trickier since we are in reality working on rational expressions and not on languages. It is therefore necessary to test, within the algorithm, whether two rational expressions define the same language.

The second method consists of calculating first a non-deterministic finite automaton $\mathscr{A} = (Q, A, \delta, I, F)$ recognizing L, by using for example the algorithm described in Section 2. We can then determinize this automaton in the following fashion: we put $\mathscr{A}' = (\mathscr{P}(Q), A, \delta', I', F')$ where $I' = \{X \in \mathscr{P}(Q) \mid X \cap I \neq \varnothing\}$, $F' = \{X \in \mathscr{P}(Q) \mid X \cap F \neq \varnothing\}$ and

$$\delta'(X, u) = \bigcup_{x \in X} \delta(x, u) \text{ for } x \in \mathscr{P}(Q) \text{ and } u \in A^*. \text{ We can easily see that}$$

$\mathscr{A}'$ recognizes L. We then construct a trim deterministic automaton with a single initial state. To obtain the minimal automaton it only remains to 'minimize' this automaton.

3.5 The case of free semigroups

All the above can easily be adapted to the case where languages are subsets of the free semigroup A^+. We then define the syntactic congruence of a language L of A^+ in the following fashion:

$u \sim_L v$ if and only if, for any $x, y \in A^*$ $(xuy \in L \Leftrightarrow xvy \in L)$.

The quotient semigroup $A^+/\sim_L$ is the syntactic semigroup of L.

3.6 Varieties

The concept of a syntactic monoid suggests classifying recognizable languages according to the algebraic properties of the monoids which recognize them. This natural idea has been shown to be extremely productive and has been fully developed by Eilenberg (1976). Since most 'good' algebraic properties of a monoid are preserved by taking submonoids, quotient monoids and finite direct products, we are led to introduce the following definition.

Definition 3.6.1 A variety of finite monoids is a class **V** of finite monoids such that

(i) If $M \in \mathbf{V}$ and if N is a submonoid of M, then $N \in \mathbf{V}$.

(ii) If $M \in \mathbf{V}$ and if N is a quotient of M, then $N \in \mathbf{V}$.

(iii) If $(M_i)_{i \in I}$ is a finite family of elements of **V**, then $\prod_{i \in I} M_i \in \mathbf{V}$.

Varieties of finite semigroups are defined in an analogous manner.

Given an alphabet A, we now associate with each variety of monoids **V**, the set $A^*\mathcal{V}$ of the recognizable languages of A^* which are recognized by a monoid of **V**. According to Proposition 3.2.1, a language L is in $A^*\mathcal{V}$ if and only if its syntactic monoid is an element of **V**. We thus obtain a correspondence $\mathbf{V} \to \mathcal{V}$ associating with the variety of finite monoids **V** an object called a '*variety of languages*' for which the precise definition follows.

Definition 3.6.2 A variety of languages $\mathcal{V}$ associates with each alphabet A a set $A^*\mathcal{V}$ of recognizable languages of A^* such that:

(i) For any alphabet A, $A^*\mathcal{V}$ is a Boolean algebra.
(ii) For any alphabet A, if $a \in A$ and $L \in A^*\mathcal{V}$, then $a^{-1}L$ and $La^{-1} \in A^*\mathcal{V}$.
(iii) For any monoid morphism $\varphi: A^* \to B^*$, $L \in B^*\mathcal{V}$ implies $L\varphi^{-1} \in A^*\mathcal{V}$.

The theorem of varieties, due to Eilenberg (1976), is stated as follows.

Theorem 3.6.1 The correspondence $\mathbf{V} \to \mathcal{V}$ induces a bijection between the varieties of finite monoids and the varieties of languages.

There is an analogous theorem for the varieties of finite semigroups if we consider languages as subsets of the free semigroup A^+. In other words, in the definition of a variety of languages, we must replace the word 'monoid' by 'semigroup' and the symbol '*' by the symbol '+'. In this case, we speak of a +-variety of languages.

Here are a few examples of varieties. The first follows directly from Kleene's theorem. Let **M** be the variety of all finite monoids. The corresponding variety of languages is the variety of rational languages.

Let **I** be the trivial variety constituted by the single monoid with an element. For any alphabet A, the variety $\mathcal{V}$ corresponding to **I** is defined by $A^*\mathcal{V} = \{\varnothing, A^*\}$.

Recall that an element e of a semigroup S is idempotent if $ee = e$. A *nilpotent* semigroup is a finite semigroup such that, for any idempotent

$e \in S$ and for any $s \in S$, we have $es = e = se$. A little thought will show that if S is not empty, S contains in fact a zero, which is the only idempotent of S. Moreover, any product of at least Card(S) elements of S is equal to this zero.

One can show that the nilpotent semigroups form a variety of finite semigroups, denoted by **Nil**. The +-variety of corresponding languages, denoted by $\mathscr{Nil}$, is defined by $A^*\mathscr{Nil} = \{$finite or cofinite languages of $A^+\}$. (Recall that a language is cofinite if its complement is finite.)

This example shows the necessity of distinguishing between the varieties and the +-varieties. In fact, the finite-cofinite languages of A^* do not define a variety of languages because they do not verify condition (iii) of Definition 3.6.2. It is sufficient to take $A = B = \{a,b\}$, $a\varphi = a$, $b\varphi = 1$, and $L = \{a\}$ (that is, L is finite but $L\varphi^{-1} = b^*ab^*$ is neither finite, nor cofinite).

The most important variety of languages is certainly the variety of star-free languages. By definition, the set $A^*\mathscr{S}$ of star-free languages of A^* is the smallest set of languages of A^* such that

(i) $\{1\} \in A^*\mathscr{S}$, $\{a\} \in A^*\mathscr{S}$ for any $a \in A$.
(ii) A^* is closed by the finite Boolean operations (including complementation) and concatenation product.

Note that $\varnothing = \bigcup_{i \in \varnothing} L_i$ and A^*, the complement of the empty set, are star-free. Similarly, if $A = \{a,b\}$, $b^* = A^*\backslash A^*aA^*$ is star-free. More complicated, $(ab)^* = A^*\backslash(bA^* \cup A^*a \cup A^*aaA^* \cup A^*bbA^*)$ is a star-free language. On the other hand, $(aa)^*$ and $\{aa,ba\}^*$ are not star-free languages, as we will see.

A finite monoid M is called aperiodic if for any $x \in M$, there is $n > 0$ such that $x^n = x^{n+1}$. This is equivalent to saying that any group which divides M is trivial. In other words, aperiodic monoids are 'the opposite of groups' in semigroup theory. Schützenberger's (1965) theorem is then stated as follows:

Theorem 3.6.2 A recognizable language is star-free if and only if its syntactic monoid is aperiodic.

For example, the syntactic monoid of $(aa)^*$ is the group with two elements. Consequently, $(aa)^*$ is not star-free. In terms of varieties, Schützenberger's theorem is stated as follows:

Theorem 3.6.3 The variety **A** of aperiodic monoids corresponds to the variety of star-free languages.

4 Rational operations and rational languages

In this last section, we will return to the study of the three rational operations: union, product and star.

4.1 Hashiguchi's results

Let us consider the three operators U, P and S which associate with a set $\mathscr{L}$ of languages of A^* the following respective sets

$\mathscr{L}U = \{$finite unions of languages of $\mathscr{L}\}$,
$\mathscr{L}P = \{$finite products of languages of $\mathscr{L}\}$,
$\mathscr{L}S = \mathscr{L} \cup \{L^* \mid L \in \mathscr{L}\}$.

Let ω be a word on the alphabet $\{U,P,S\}$, for example, $\omega = SPUPU$. We can think of ω as an operator obtained by composing in this order the operators S, P, U, P and U. More generally if $\Omega \subset \{U,P,S\}^*$ is a set of words on the alphabet $\{U,P,S\}$ we put

$$\mathscr{L}\Omega = \bigcup_{\omega \in \Omega} \mathscr{L}\omega$$

We can easily see that if Γ is a subset of any kind of $\{U,P,S\}^*$, $\mathscr{L}\Gamma^*$ is the smallest set of languages $\mathscr{L}'$ containing $\mathscr{L}$ and such that for any $\omega \in \Gamma$, $\mathscr{L}'\omega = \mathscr{L}'$. In other words, $\mathscr{L}\Gamma^*$ is the closure of $\mathscr{L}$ by the operators of Γ.

With this formalism Hashiguchi's results can be stated as follows.

Theorem 4.1.1 (Hashiguchi, 1983). Let $\mathscr{L}$ be a finite set of rational languages of A^*. For any subset Γ of $\{U,P,S\}$ there is an algorithm to determine whether a given rational language is an element of $\mathscr{L}\Gamma^*$.

There are eight cases to be considered following the chosen set Γ, and we cannot demonstrate here the eight results *in extenso*. We will in fact show six of the eight cases and deal with the two remaining cases in connection with a problem of semigroup theory which has also been solved by Hashiguchi.

Let us start with a few basic results on operators. If Ω_1 and Ω_2 are two sets of operators, we denote $\Omega_1 \subset \Omega_2$ (respectively $\Omega_1 = \Omega_2$) if for any set $\mathscr{L}$ of languages $\mathscr{L}\Omega_1 \subset \mathscr{L}\Omega_2$ (resp. $\mathscr{L}\Omega_1 = \mathscr{L}\Omega_2$).

Proposition 4.1.2 We have the relations

(i) $UU = U$, $PP = P$ and $SS = S$,
(ii) $UP \subset PU = UPU = PUP$,
(iii) $SUS = US \subset \{U,SPS\}$.

Proof

(i) is obvious.
(ii) follows from the distributivity of the product in relation to the union.
(iii) follows from the formulae

$$(K_1 \cup \ldots \cup K_p \cup L_1^* \cup \ldots \cup L_q^*)^* = (K_1 \cup \ldots \cup K_p \cup L_1$$
$$\cup \ldots \cup L_q)^* \text{ and } (L_1 \cup \ldots \cup L_k)^* = (L_1^* \ldots L_k^*)^*.$$

Corollary 4.1.3 If $\Omega \subset \{U,S\}^*$ and if $\mathscr{L}$ is finite, $\mathscr{L}\Omega$ is a finite set.

Proof Since $SS = S$, $UU = U$ and $SUS = US$, any operator $\omega \in \{U,S\}^*$ is equal to one of the operators 1 (identity), U, S, SU, US, or USU. From this we deduce that in all cases $\mathscr{L}\Omega \subset \mathscr{L}USU$. Now, since $\mathscr{L}$ is finite, $\mathscr{L}U$ finite, therefore $\mathscr{L}US$ is finite, and finally $\mathscr{L}USU$ is finite.

This allows us to state the following result, which in particular demonstrates Theorem 4.1.1 for $\Gamma \subset \{U,S\}$.

Proposition 4.1.4 Let $\mathscr{L}$ be a finite set of rational languages of A^*. For any rational subset Ω of $\{U,S\}^*$ there is an algorithm to decide whether a given rational language L is an element of $\mathscr{L}\Omega$.

Proof According to Corollary 4.1.3, $\mathscr{L}\Omega$ is a finite (and easily calculable) set of rational languages. The problem therefore is to test whether a given rational language L is an element of a given finite list $L_1, \ldots, L_n$ of rational languages. For this, it is sufficient to test separately, for $i = 1, \ldots, n$, whether $L = L_i$, which can be done by checking, for example, that the minimal automata of L and of L_i are isomorphic by an isomorphism which preserves the initial state and the final states.

The last relatively elementary case is that where $\Gamma = \{U,P,S\}$. In this case $\mathscr{L}\Gamma^*$ is called the rational closure of $\mathscr{L}$; this is the smallest set of languages containing $\mathscr{L}$ and closed under union, product and star.

Proposition 4.1.5 Let $\mathscr{L}$ be a finite set of rational languages. There is an algorithm to decide whether a given rational language is in the rational closure of $\mathscr{L}$.

Proof Let $\mathscr{L} = \{L_1, \ldots, L_n\}$, $B = \{1, \ldots, n\}$ and let $\sigma: B^* \to A^*$ be the substitution defined by $i\sigma = L_i$ for $i = 1, \ldots, n$. We denote by L^c the complement of a language L of A^*. Then

Lemma 4.1.6 L is an element of the rational closure of $\mathscr{L}$ if and only if $L = (L^c\sigma^{-1})^c\sigma$.

Proof We have, by definition,

$$L^c \sigma^{-1} = \{i_1 \ldots i_k \in B^* \mid L_{i_1} \ldots L_{i_k} \cap L^c \neq \emptyset\}$$

and consequently,

$$
\begin{aligned}
R = (L^c \sigma^{-1})^c &= \{i_1 \ldots i_k \in B^* \mid L_{i_1} \ldots L_{i_k} \cap L^c = \emptyset\} \\
&= \{i_1 \ldots i_k \in B^* \mid L_{i_1} \ldots L_{i_k} \subset L\} \\
&= \{u \in B^* \mid u\sigma \subset L\}.
\end{aligned}
$$

If L is in the rational closure of $\mathscr{L}$, there exists $K \in \mathrm{Rat}(B^*)$ such that $K\sigma = L$. Consequently, $K \subset R$ and therefore $L = K\sigma \subset R\sigma \subset L$, hence $R\sigma = L$. Conversely, assume that $R\sigma = L$. Since L is recognizable, R is recognizable (see the results of the preceding sections) and therefore rational, and consequently $L = R\sigma$ is in the rational closure of $\mathscr{L}$.

Proposition 4.1.5 can now be easily demonstrated. $(L^c \sigma^{-1})^c \sigma$ is in fact a rational language which we know how to calculate and it only remains to test the equality of two rational languages to decide whether L is in the rational closure of $\mathscr{L}$.

The case $\Gamma = \{P, S\}$ is the last we will demonstrate. Let us start with a formal result on operators.

Proposition 4.1.7

(i) We have $\{U, P, S\}^* = \{P, S\}^* U$.
(ii) If $K \in \mathscr{L}\{U, P, S\}^*$, $K^* \in \mathscr{L}\{P, S\}^*$.

Proof (i) It is sufficient to establish that for any $\omega \in \{U, P, S\}^*$, $\omega \subset \{P, S\}^* U$. We proceed by induction on the length of ω, considered as a word on the alphabet $\{U, P, S\}$. If $\omega = 1$, the result is obvious. Let us suppose the result obtained for ω. We then have

$\omega U \subset \{P, S\}^* UU = \{P, S\}^* U$,
$\omega P \subset \{P, S\}^* UP \subset \{P, S\}^* PU \subset \{P, S\}^* U$ according to Proposition 4.1.2 (ii),
$\omega S \subset \{P, S\}^* US \subset \{P, S\}^* \{U, SPS\}$ according to proposition 4.1.2
(iii) $\subset \{P, S\}^* \cup \{P, S\}^* U \subset \{P, S\}^* U$.

(ii) Let $K \in \mathscr{L}(U, P, S\}^*$. According to (i), we have $K \in \mathscr{L}\{P, S\}^* U$ and therefore K is written $K_1 \cup \ldots \cup K_p$ with $K_1, \ldots, K_p \in \mathscr{L}\{P, S\}^*$. From this we deduce

$$K^* = (K_1 \cup \ldots \cup K_p)^* = (K_1^* \ldots K_p^*)^*$$

hence $K \in \mathscr{L}\{P, S\}^*$.

We can now prove.

Proposition 4.1.8 Let $\Gamma = \{P, S\}$ and let $\mathscr{L}$ be a finite set of rational languages of A^*. There is an algorithm to decide whether a given rational language is in $\mathscr{L}\Gamma^*$.

Proof We will use the same notation as in the proof of Proposition 4.1.5. Let L be a rational language and let M be its syntactic monoid (that we can calculate). We denote by $\eta: A^* \to M$ the syntactic morphism and by $\varphi: B^* \to \mathscr{P}(M)$ the morphism defined by $\varphi = \sigma\eta$. For any $X \in \mathscr{P}(M)$ we put

$$L(X) = \{u \in B^* \mid X(u\varphi) = X\}$$

and we denote by $\mathscr{F}$ the set of languages of B^* of the form $K = L(X_0)i_1L(X_1) \ldots i_pL(X_p)$ with $i_1, \ldots, i_p \in B$, $X_0 = \{1\}$, $X_p \subset L\eta$ and, for $1 \leqslant k \leqslant p$, $X_{k-1}(i_k\varphi) = X_k$ and such that all the X_i are distinct.

Lemma 4.1.9

(i) $\mathscr{F}$ is a finite calculable set of rational languages of B^*.
(ii) For any $K \in \mathscr{F}$, $K\sigma \subset L$.

Proof (i) Since L is rational, M is finite, as is $\mathscr{P}(M)$. Consequently, there exist a finite number of sequences of pairwise distinct elements in $\mathscr{P}(M)$. Since B is also finite, $\mathscr{F}$ is finite. Moreover, for every $X \in \mathscr{P}(M)$, $L(X)$ is recognized by $\mathscr{P}(M)$. This is therefore a recognizable language that can be calculated. Thus each element of $\mathscr{F}$ is a rational set for which one can effectively calculate the minimal automaton.

(ii) Let $K \in \mathscr{F}$. Then $K = L(X_0)i_1L(X_1) \ldots i_pL(X_p)$ with the above conditions and consequently:

$\{1\}L(X_0)\varphi = \{1\}$, $\{1\}i_1 = X_1$, $X_1L(X_1)\varphi = X_1 \ldots X_pL(X_p)\varphi = X_p$, $\{1\}(K\varphi) = X_p \subset L\eta$. It follows that $K\varphi = K\sigma\eta \subset L\eta$, hence $K\sigma \subset K\sigma\eta\eta^{-1} \subset L\eta\eta^{-1} = L$.

Proposition 4.1.8 then follows from the following lemma.

Lemma 4.1.10 We have $L \in \mathscr{L}\{P, S\}^*$ if and only if there exists $K \in \mathscr{F}$ such that $K\sigma = L$.

Proof Let us suppose that there exists $K \in \mathscr{F}$ such that $K\sigma = L$. Using the above notation, we have $L(X) = (L(X))^*$ for any $X \in \mathscr{P}(M)$ and therefore, by Proposition 4.1.7, $L(X)\sigma = (L(X)\sigma)^* \in \mathscr{L}\{P, S\}^*$. Consequently, $K\sigma = (L(X_0)i_1L(X_1) \ldots i_pL(X_p))\sigma = L(X_0)\sigma(i_1\sigma)L(X_1)\sigma \ldots L(X_p)\sigma \in \mathscr{L}\{P, S\}^*$.

Conversely, let us suppose that $L \in \mathscr{L}\{P, S\}^*$. We then have a language R of B^* of the form $u_0R_1^*u_1 \ldots R_p^*u_p$ (with $u_0, \ldots, u_p \in B^*$) such that

$R\sigma = L$. Let us put $u = u_0 \ldots u_p$, and, for $0 \leqslant i \leqslant |u|$, $T_i = (u_0 K_1^* u_1 \ldots u_{r-1} K_r^* x)$ with $|u_0 \ldots u_{r-1} x| = i$. If $T_i = T_j$ with $i < j$ and $T_j = (u_0 K_1^* u_1 \ldots u_{r-1} K_r^* x x' K_{r+1}^* \ldots u_{s-1} K_s^* y)\varphi$ with $xx' = u_r$, we have $T_i(x' K_{r+1}^* \ldots K_s^* y)\varphi = T_j = T_i$ hence $x' K_{r+1}^* \ldots K_s^* y \subset L(T_i)$. It follows from this observation that K is contained in an element F of $\mathcal{F}$. We then have $L = K\sigma \subset F\sigma \subset L$, hence $F\sigma = L$.

The case where $\Gamma = \{U,P\}$ is undoubtedly the most interesting.

Proposition 4.1.11 Let $\Gamma = \{U,P\}$ and let $\mathcal{L}$ be a finite set of rational languages. There is an algorithm to decide whether a given rational language is in $\mathcal{L}\Gamma^*$.

Proof We will use again the notation used in the demonstration for Proposition 4.1.5. In particular we put

$$R = \{u \in B^* \mid u\sigma \subset L\} = (L^c \sigma^{-1})^c \sigma.$$

Let $\tau: A^* \to B^*$ be the transduction defined by

$$v\tau = R \cap v\sigma^{-1}.$$

τ is a rational transduction according to the results of previous sections and therefore has a linear representation (λ, μ, ν), where $\mu: A^* \to \mathcal{P}(B^*)^{n \times n}$ is a monoid morphism. Let K be the semiring $(\mathbb{N} \cup \{\infty\}, \min, +)$. We can easily verify that the function $\varphi: \mathcal{P}(B^*) \to K$ defined by

$$X\varphi = \min \{|x| \mid x \in X\} \quad \text{and} \quad \varnothing\varphi = \infty$$

is a semiring morphism which extends into a monoid morphism

$$\varphi: \mathcal{P}(B^*)^{n \times n} \to K^{n \times n}.$$

Consequently, if we put $\gamma = \tau\varphi$, $\gamma: A^* \to K$ is defined by

$$v\gamma = \min \{|u| \mid u\sigma \subset L \text{ and } v \in u\sigma\}$$

and moreover, for any $v \in A^*$, $v\gamma = (\lambda\varphi) + (v\mu\varphi) + (v\varphi)$. In other words, γ has the linear representation $(\lambda\varphi, \mu\varphi, \nu\varphi)$ with coefficients in K. Let us put $S = A^*\gamma$. We then have

Lemma 4.1.12 We have $L \in \mathcal{L}\{U,P\}^*$ if and only if (a) $L = R\sigma$ and (b) S is finite.

Proof The condition $L = R\sigma$ implies that for any $v \in L$, there exists $u \in F$ such that $v \in u\sigma$. It follows that if $v \in L$, $v\gamma < \infty$. Conversely, if $v\gamma < \infty$, there exists $u \in R$ such that $v \in u\sigma$ and therefore $v \in R\sigma = L$.

If $L \in \mathcal{L}\{U \cdot P\}^*$, there exists a finite set $F \subset B^*$ such that $L = F\sigma$. Let n be the maximal length of the words of F. If $v \in L$, there exists $u \in F$

such that $v \in u\sigma$ and therefore $u\gamma \leq n$. On the other hand, if $v \notin L$, we have seen that $v\gamma = \infty$. Therefore $S = A^*\gamma \subset \{0,1,\ldots,n\} \cup \{\infty\}$.

Conversely, if S is finite, there exists an integer n such that $S \subset \{0,1,\ldots,n\} \cup \{\infty\}$. From this we deduce that $v \in L$ if and only if $v\gamma \leq n$. If we set $F = \{u \in R \mid |u| \leq n\}$, we then have $F\sigma = L$ and therefore $L \in \mathscr{L} \{U,P\}^*$.

The demonstration of Proposition 4.1.11 now rests on the following theorem of Hashiguchi which we will state without proof. Let n be a positive integer and M be a finite set of matrices of $K^{n \times n}$. We denote by $\langle M \rangle$ the multiplicative submonoid of $K^{n \times n}$ generated by M.

Theorem 4.1.13 (Hashiguchi, 1982a). It is decidable whether, given a finite set M of matrices of $K^{n \times n}$ and two integers r, s such that $1 \leq r$, $s \leq n$, the set $\{m_{r,s} \mid m \in \langle M \rangle\}$ is finite or not.

We can now conclude the proof of Proposition 4.1.11. Let us put $\lambda\varphi = (\lambda_1,\ldots,\lambda_n) \in K^{1 \times n}$, $v\varphi = \begin{pmatrix} v_1 \\ \vdots \\ v_n \end{pmatrix} \in K^{n \times 1}$ and $M = \{a\mu\varphi \mid a \in A\}$.

With this notation there follows

$$A^*\gamma = \{ \min_{1 \leq i,j \leq n} (\lambda_i + m_{ij} + v_j) \mid m \in \langle M \rangle\}.$$

Let us put $I = \{i \mid \lambda_i < \infty\}$, $J = \{j \mid v_j < \infty\}$, $\lambda_0 = \max_{i \in I} \lambda_i$ and $v_0 = \max_{j \in J} v_j$. We then have, for any $m \in M$, and with the normal convention $\min \emptyset = \infty$,

$$\min_{1 \leq i,j \leq n} (\lambda_i + m_{ij} + v_j)$$

$$= \min_{i \in I, j \in J} (\lambda_i + m_{ij} + v_j) \leq \lambda_0 + \min_{i \in I, j \in J} (m_{ij}) + v_0.$$

It follows that the set $S = A^*\gamma$ is finite if and only if there exist $i \in I$ and $j \in J$ such that the set $\{m_{ij} \mid m \in \langle M \rangle\}$ is finite. Now this condition is decidable according to Theorem 4.1.13.

The demonstration of the last case uses the arguments of both Propositions 4.1.8 and 4.1.11.

Proposition 4.1.14 Let $\mathscr{L}$ be a finite set of rational languages of A^*. There is an algorithm to decide whether a given rational language is in $\mathscr{L}P^*$.

Proof If L is empty, $L \in \mathscr{L}P^*$ if and only if $\mathscr{L}$ contains an empty language. We will suppose from now on that L is non-empty.

We will again use the notation given in the demonstration for Proposition 4.1.8. Let us put $B_1 = \{i \in B \mid 1 \in i\sigma = L_i\}$. For each subset X of $\mathcal{P}(M)$, we denote by $\mathcal{E}(X)$ the set of the languages of the form $C_0^* i_1 C_1^* i_2 \ldots i_p C_p^*$ with $i_1, \ldots, i_p \in B_1$, $C_0, \ldots, C_p \subset B_1$ and such that if we put $X_0 = X$ and $X_k = X_{k-1}(i_k\varphi)$ for $1 \leq k \leq p$, we have

(a) $X_j(u\varphi) = X_j$ for any $u \in C_j^*$.
(b) The X_j $(0 \leq j \leq p)$ are all distinct.

Let m be the minimal length of the words of L (m is an integer that we can calculate by knowing L). We denote as $\mathcal{F}$ the set of the languages of the form

$$T = u_0 E_1 u_1 E_2 \ldots E_q u_q$$

with

(a) $u_0, \ldots, u_q \in (B \backslash B_1)^*$ and $|u_0 \ldots u_q| \leq m$.
(b) For $1 \leq i \leq q$, $E_i \in \mathcal{E}(Y_i)$ where Y_i is defined by $Y_1 = u_0\varphi$ and $Y_{j+1} = Y_j(E_j u_j)\varphi$ for $1 \leq j \leq p - 1$.
(c) $K\sigma \subset L$ (that is to say, $K\varphi \subset L\eta$).

We then have the following result:

Lemma 4.1.15

(i) $\mathcal{F}$ is a finite calculable set of rational languages of B^*.
(ii) If $L \in \mathcal{L} P^*$, there exist $T \in \mathcal{F}$ and $u \in T$ such that $u\sigma = L$.

Proof (i) We can show that, for any $X \in \mathcal{P}(M)$, $\mathcal{E}(X)$ is finite by imitating the proof of Lemma 4.1.9. The finiteness of $\mathcal{F}$ immediately follows from this.

(ii) If $L \in \mathcal{L}P^*$, there is $u \in B^*$ such that $u\sigma = L$. Since for $i \in B \backslash B_1$, $i\sigma \subset A^+$, the minimal length of the words of $u\sigma$ is greater than or equal to the number of letters of u belonging to $B \backslash B_1$. It follows that u has a factorization of the form $u_0 v_1 u_1 v_2 \ldots v_q u_q$ with $v_1, \ldots, v_q \in B_1^*$, $u_0, \ldots u_q \in (B \backslash B_1)^*$ and $|u_0 \ldots u_q| \leq m$. Let us put $Y_1 = u_0\varphi$ and, for every $1 \leq j \leq p - 1$, $Y_{j+1} = Y_j(v_j u_j)\varphi$. It is sufficient to verify that $v_i \in E$ for some $E \in \mathcal{E}(Y_i)$ such that $Y_i(E\varphi) = Y_i(v_i\varphi)$. To simplify the notation, let us put $v = v_i$ and $Y = Y_i$. Then v has a factorization of the form $v = x_0 i_1 x_1 \ldots i_p x_p$ with $i_1, \ldots, i_p \in B$, $x_0, \ldots, x_p \in B_1^*$ and, if we put $X_0 = Y$ and $X_k = X_{k-1}(i_k\varphi)$ for $1 \leq k \leq P$,

(a) $X_j(x_j\varphi) = X_j$ for $0 \leq j \leq p$,
(b) the X_j are all distinct.

Let us denote by C_j the set of letters of x_j, and let us put

$$E = C_0^* i_1 C_1^* \ldots i_p C_p^*.$$

It is clear that $v \in E$. Moreover, since $x_j \in B_1^*$, we have for any letter i of x_j, $1 \in i\varphi$, hence

$$X_j = X_j \cdot \{1\} \subset X_j(i\varphi).$$

Since $X_j(x_j\varphi) = X_j$, we have necessarily $X_j(i\varphi) = X_j$ for any letter i of x_j and consequently $X_j(u\varphi) = X_j$ for any $u \in C_j^*$. From this follows $E \in \mathscr{E}(Y)$ and $Y(E\varphi) = Y(v\varphi)$ as stated above, which concludes the proof of the lemma.

Let us now proceed with the demonstration of Proposition 4.1.14. For every $T \in \mathscr{F}$, let us denote by $\gamma_T \colon A^* \to K$ the transduction defined by

$$v\gamma_T = \min \{|u| \mid u \in T \text{ and } v \in u\sigma\}.$$

We can demonstrate, as in the demonstration for Proposition 4.1.11, that γ_T has a linear representation $(\lambda_T, \mu_T, \nu_T)$ with coefficients in K. Let us put $S_T = A^*\gamma_T$.

Lemma 4.1.16 $L \in \mathscr{L}P^*$ if and only if there exists $T \in \mathscr{F}$ such that (a) $L = T\sigma$ and (b) S_T is finite.

Proof If $L \in \mathscr{L}P^*$, there exist, according to Lemma 4.1.15, $T \in \mathscr{F}$ and $u \in T$ such that $u\sigma = L$. Since $T \in \mathscr{F}$, we also have $T\sigma \subset L$, hence $L = u\sigma \subset T\sigma \subset L$ and therefore $T\sigma = L$. On the other hand, we have $v\gamma_T \leq |u|$ if $v \in L$ and $v\gamma_T = \infty$ if $v \notin L$ (since $T\sigma = L$). Consequently, S_T is finite.

Conversely, let us suppose that conditions (a) and (b) are satisfied. There is an integer n such that $S_T \subset \{0,1, \ldots,n\} \cup \{\infty\}$. It follows by (a) that $v \in L$ if and only if $v\gamma_T \leq n$. If we put $F = \{u \in T \mid |u| \leq n\}$, we then have $F\sigma = L$ and $F \subset T$. Let us put $F = \{w_1,\ldots,w_r\}$. Since $T \in \mathscr{F}$, T is written in the form $u_0C_1^*u_1 \ldots C_p^*u_p$ with $u_1, \ldots, u_p \in B$ and $C_1, \ldots, C_p \subset B_1$. Therefore, for $1 \leq i \leq r$, $w_i = u_0v_{i,1}u_1v_{i,2} \ldots v_{i,p}u_p$ with $v_{i,j} \in C_j^*$. Let us put, for $1 \leq j \leq p$, $v_j = v_{1,j}v_{2,j} \ldots v_{r,j}$ and $w = u_0v_1u_1 \ldots v_pu_p$. We have $v_j \in C_j^*$ for $1 \leq j \leq p$ and thus $w \in T$. Consequently, $w\sigma \subset L$. On the other hand, since $v_{i,j} \in B_1^*$, we have $1 \in v_{i,j}\sigma$ for any i, j. It follows that $v_{i,j}\sigma = 1 \ldots 1(v_{i,j}\sigma) 1 \ldots 1 \subset (v_{1,j})\sigma \ldots (v_{r,j})\sigma = v_j\sigma$, hence $w_i\sigma \subset w\sigma$ for $1 \leq i \leq r$. Therefore $L = F\sigma = \{w_1,\ldots,w_r\}\sigma \subset w\sigma \in L$, hence $w\sigma = L$. Consequently $L \in \mathscr{L}P^*$.

The end of the demonstration of Proposition 4.1.14 is identical to that of Proposition 4.1.11 and therefore makes use in particular of Theorem 4.1.13.

To conclude Section 4.1 let us note a famous corollary of Proposition 4.1.11. A language L of A^* is called *limited* if there is an integer $k > 0$ such that $L^* = \{1\} \cup L \cup L^2 \cup \ldots \cup L^k$. (Simon, 1978; Hashiguchi, 1979.)

Proposition 4.1.17   It is decidable whether a given rational language is limited or not.

Proof   Let $\mathcal{L} = \{L\}$ Then L is limited if and only if $L^* \in \mathcal{L}\{U,P\}^*$. This property is decidable by Proposition 4.1.11.

4.2   The star operation

This operation remains relatively mysterious despite much research. Problems to do with star height have been particularly difficult, although some progress has recently been made. Let us restate the terms of these problems, which use the notion of rational expression.

Rational expressions on alphabet A are defined recursively by

(a) $\varnothing$, 1 and a (for any $a \in A$) are rational expressions.
(b) If E and F are rational expressions, $(E \cup F)$, (EF) and (E^*) are rational expressions.

Generalized rational expressions on alphabet A are defined recursively by

(a) $\varnothing$, 1 and a (for any $a \in A$) are generalized rational expressions.
(b) If E and F are generalized rational expressions, $(E \cup F)$, $(E \cap F)$, (EF), (E^c) and (E^*) are generalized rational expressions.

The *star height* $h(E)$ of a (generalized) rational expression E is defined recursively by

(a) $h(\varnothing) = 0$, $h(1) = 0$ and, for any $a \in A$, $h(a) = 0$.
(b) If E and F are (generalized) rational expressions, $h(E \cup F) = h(EF)$ $= \max(h(E),h(F))$ and $h(E^*) = h(E) + 1$ (resp. $h(E \cap F) = \max (h(E),h(F))$ and $h(E^c) = h(E)$).

The value $v(E)$ of a rational expression E is the language of A^* represented by E. Formally, v is a function of the set of rational expressions in the set of rational languages of A^* defined by:

(a) $v(\varnothing) = \varnothing$, $v(1) = \{1\}$, $v(a) = \{a\}$ for every $a \in A$.
(b) If E and F are two (generalized) rational expressions, $v(E \cup F) = v(E) \cup v(F)$, $v(EF) = v(E)v(F)$ and $v(E^*) = (v(E))^*$ (resp. $v(E \cap F) = v(E) \cap v(F)$ and $v(E^c) = A^* \backslash v(E)$).

The star height $h(L)$ of a recognizable language L is by definition the minimum of the star heights of the rational expressions which represent it. In other words

$h(L) = \min\{h(E) \mid E$ is a rational expression and $v(E) = L\}$.

The generalized star height $hg(L)$ of a rational language L is similarly defined by:

$hg(L) = \min\{h(E) \mid E$ is a generalized rational expression and $v(E) = L\}$.

The main problem is to find an algorithm to calculate the star height (respectively the generalized star height) of a given rational language. The following are the main results.

Theorem 4.2.1 (Dejean and Schützenberger, 1966). For any positive integer n there is rational language of star height n.

Theorem 4.2.2 (Hashiguchi, 1982b). There is an algorithm to determine whether the star height of a rational language is 1.

Hashiguchi's result is based on a particular case of Proposition 4.1.11, but the complete proof is too lengthy to include here.

Of course, we also know how to determine whether a rational language is of star height 0: it is necessary and sufficient that the language be finite. A complete solution of the star-height problem has been recently announced by Hashiguchi (1988):

Theorem 4.2.3 There is an algorithm to determine the star height of a given rational language.

For generalized star height the known results are more fragmentary. First of all, the languages of generalized star height 0 are precisely the star-free languages which we have already encountered. Schützenberger's Theorem 3.6.2 in particular allows us to state

Theorem 4.2.4 A language is of generalized star height 0 if and only if its syntactic monoid is aperiodic. This property is therefore decidable.

Theorem 4.2.4 suggests that languages of generalized star height bounded by n form a variety of languages, and can therefore be characterized by a property of their syntactic monoid. This hypothesis, which is explicitly mentioned in Henneman's thesis (1971), has never been invalidated but it is non the less unlikely, given the following result.

Theorem 4.2.5 (Pin, 1978). For any finite monoid M there is a finite language F such that M divides the syntactic monoid of F^*.

Corollary 4.2.6 If the languages of generalized star height ≤ 1 form a variety of languages, all rational languages are of generalized star height 0 or 1.

The fact remains that we still have no example of a language with generalized star height >1! To illustrate the difficulty of the problem, here is a famous example which was thought to be of star height 2 until Henneman found an expression of height 1 to represent it:

$$L = (ab^*a \cup b(ab^*a)^*b)^*.$$

The expression found by Henneman is the following:

$(E \cap F) \cup ((b \cup ab^*a)E \cap (a^*ba^*bF))$ where
$E = ((b \cup ab^*a) (b \cup ab^*a))^*$ and $F = (b \cup (b^*ab^*ab^*ab^*a))^*$ and
where $b^* = (A^*aA^*)^c = (\emptyset^c a \emptyset^c)^c$.

Here is another candidate for generalized star height 2, proposed by Thérien (1980):

$$L = (ab^*a \cup ba^*b(ab^*a)^*ba^*b)^*.$$

Positive results are rare. None the less, we should mention the results obtained by Henneman in his thesis.

Theorem 4.2.7 If a language L is recognized by a commutative group, then L is of generalized star height $\leqslant 1$.

Henneman has also obtained upper bounds for the generalized star height of languages recognized by solvable or supersolvable groups and several other more technical partial results. Using a theorem of Straubing's on the varieties of languages closed under concatenation (cf. the following section), we can improve Theorem 4.2.7. We will say that a monoid M is an aperiodic extension of a commutative group if there is a commutative group G and a surjective morphism of monoids $\varphi: M \to G$ such that $1\varphi^{-1}$ is an aperiodic semigroup. We then have

Theorem 4.2.8 If a rational language L is recognized by an aperiodic extension of a commutative group, then L is of generalized star height $\leqslant 1$. Further results can be found in Pin *et al.* (1989).

The star operation has also been studied from the point of view of varieties of languages. A variety of languages $\mathscr{V}$ is closed under star if for every alphabet A, $L \in A^*\mathscr{V}$ implies $L^* \in A^*\mathscr{V}$.

Theorem 4.2.9 The only variety of languages closed under star is that of all rational languages.

Theorem 4.2.9 indicates that the star operation is a very 'powerful' operation. To limit this 'power', one can imagine several restrictions on the star operation. Here is just one example. A language of the form L^* is called 'pure' if for any $n > 0$, $u^n \in L$ implies $u \in L$. We then say that the operation $L \to L^*$ is a pure star.

Theorem 4.2.10 The variety of star-free languages is the smallest variety closed under pure star.

It will be noticed that the concatenation product is not mentioned in this statement, which renders the terminology 'star-free' a little strange. In fact, the product of concatenation is linked to the pure star operation by the following result which derives from Straubing's work (1979, 1981).

Theorem 4.2.11 Any variety of languages closed under concatenation product is closed under pure star.

It is not known whether the converse of this theorem is true or false.

4.3 The concatenation product

This operation is almost as difficult to study as the star when one thinks of the number of problems that still remain unsolved. As with the star, we can define some hierarchies of languages by using the concatenation product. The first hierarchy of this type was introduced by Brzozowski (1980) and has served as a model for hierarchies subsequently proposed. We will present only the simplest of these hierarchies, one which has been proposed by Straubing (1985). Let A be a finite alphabet. Each level of the hierarchy will be constituted by a Boolean algebra formed by recognizable languages. Level 0 is constituted by the trivial Boolean algebra $\{\emptyset, A^*\}$. Level $n + 1$ is the Boolean algebra generated by languages of the form $L_0 a_1 L_1 a_2 \ldots a_k L_k$ where $k \geqslant 0$, $a_1, \ldots, a_k \in A$ and where the languages $L_0, \ldots, L_k$ are languages of level n.

Let us start by looking at level 1. It follows directly from the definition given above that level 1 is the Boolean algebra generated by languages of the form $A^* a_1 A^* a_2 \ldots a_k A^*$ where $k \geqslant 0$ and $a_1, \ldots, a_k \in A$. Simon (1975) has obtained a syntactic characterization of these languages which remains one of the finest results in the theory of varieties. We will say that a finite monoid M is $\mathscr{J}$-trivial if two elements of M which generate the same ideal are equal, i.e. if the condition $MaM = MbM$ implies $a = b$. The $\mathscr{J}$-trivial monoids form a variety of monoids, denoted by $\mathbf{J}$, and (strictly) contained in the variety $\mathbf{A}$ of aperiodic monoids. Simon's theorem is then stated as follows:

Theorem 4.3.1 A recognizable language is of level 1 in Straubing's hierarchy if and only if its syntactic monoid is $\mathscr{J}$-trivial.

This theorem shows that level 1 languages form a variety of languages. In fact, the result is general:

Theorem 4.3.2 For any positive integer n, the languages of level 1 in Straubing's hierarchy form a variety of languages.

Simon's theorem also provides an algorithm to determine whether a language is of level 1 in Straubing's hierarchy. It is not yet known whether such an algorithm exists as from level 2. However, it is known that Straubing's hierarchy is infinite.

Theorem 4.3.3 (Brzozowski and Knast, 1978).   Straubing's hierarchy is strict: for any positive integer n, there are languages of level $n + 1$ which are not of level n. The union of all the levels constitutes the class of star free languages.

A non-trivial description of level 2 of the hierarchy has, however, been obtained by Pin and Straubing (1981). If **V** is a variety of monoids, we denote by **PV** the variety of monoids generated by the monoids of the form $\mathscr{P}(M)$ where M belongs to **V**. We then have

Theorem 4.3.4 Let L be a recognizable languages of A^*. The following conditions are equivalent:

 (i) L is of level 2 in Straubing's hierarchy.
 (ii) L is in the Boolean algebra generated by the languages of form

$A_0^* a_1 A_1^* a_2 \ldots a_k A_k^*$ where $k \geq 0$, $A_i \subset A$ for $0 \leq i \leq k$ and $a \in A$ for $1 \leq i \leq k$.

(iii) The syntactic monoid of L is an element of **PJ**.

Unfortunately, this result provides no algorithm to determine whether a language is of level 2 in Straubing's hierarchy. Such an algorithm has been recently found by Straubing (1986) in the case where the alphabet A contains at most 2 letters. There is also an algebraic description of the hierarchy of varieties of monoids which corresponds to Straubing's hierarchy, but it is too technical to give an account of here.

One of the most remarkable recent results is the link between Straubing's hierarchy and a classic hierarchy of logic. This link has been shown by Thomas (1982) in connection with another hierarchy, but Thomas's result can be adapted without difficulty to Straubing's hierarchy.

Let us consider the language $L = A^* a A^*$ on the alphabet $A = \{a,b\}$. The language L is the set of words of A^* in which a letter is an a. In terms of logic, we will say that L is the set of the words u which satisfy the formula

$\exists x R_a x.$

This formula is intuitively translated by 'there is an occurrence of the word u which is an a'. Similarly, the formula

$$\varphi = \exists x (R_a x \wedge (\forall y (y < x) \rightarrow R_b y))$$

is translated by 'there is an occurrence of the word u which is an a and such that any occurrence which precedes it is a b'. The set of words which satisfy φ is therefore the language $b^* a A^*$.

It remains to formalize the preceding. We will suppose that the base vocabulary of the logic is known. Let A be a finite alphabet. We consider the set of symbols $S = \{<\} \cup \{R_a \mid a \in A\}$. In classical fashion, we construct S-formulae using the symbols of S and logical symbols (equality, logical connectives $\vee$, $\wedge$, $\daleth$, $\rightarrow$, $\leftrightarrow$, variables, quantifiers, and constants 'true' and 'false'). With each word u of A^* we associate an S-structure:

$$M(u) = (M, <, (R_a)_{a \in A})$$

where $M = \{1, \ldots, |u|\}$, $<$ is the usual order on integers, and, for $a \in A$, R_a is the subset of M defined by $R_a x$ if and only if the xth letter of u is an a. We say that a language L of A is defined by a statement φ if L is the set of the words u of A^* such that $M(u)$ is a model for φ. We then have the following results:

Theorem 4.3.5 (Büchi, 1960; Elgot, 1961). A language L of A^* is recognizable if and only if it can be defined by an S-sentence of the second weak monadic order.

Theorem 4.3.6 (McNaughton and Papert, 1971; Ladner, 1977). A language L of A^* is star-free if and only if it can be defined by a first order S-sentence.

We know that any first-order formula is equivalent to a formula in normal prenex form, that is to say, of the form $\varphi = Q(x_1, \ldots, x_k)\psi$ where $Q(x_1, \ldots, x_n)$ is a sequence of quantifiers $\exists x_i$ or $\forall x_i$ and where ψ is a formula without quantifiers. If $Q(x_1, \ldots, x_k)$ is formed of n blocs of quantifiers such that the first bloc contains only existential quantifiers, the second bloc only universal quantifiers, etc., we say that φ is a Σ_n-formula. We denote by Σ_n the set of the Σ_n-formulae and by $B\Sigma_n$ the set of the Boolean combinations of Σ_n-formulae. Thomas's result can then be adapted in the following form:

Theorem 4.3.7 A language of A^* is of level n in Straubing's hierarchy if and only if it can be defined by an S-statement of $B\Sigma_n$.

As with the star operation, we know how to characterize the varieties of closed languages for the concatenation product. We have already defined the aperiodic extensions of a commutative group. It is in fact a particular case of the following definition. A monoid M is an aperiodic extension of a monoid N if there is a surjective morphism $\varphi\colon M \to N$ such that for an idempotent e of N, $e\varphi^{-1}$ is an aperiodic semigroup. If $\mathbf{V}$ is a variety of monoids, we will say that $\mathbf{V}$ is closed by aperiodic extension if a monoid of $\mathbf{V}$ is also in $\mathbf{V}$.

Theorem 4.3.8 (Straubing, 1979). A variety of languages is closed under product if and only if the corresponding variety of monoids is closed by aperiodic extension.

As with the star operation, we can impose various restrictive conditions on the concatenation product (non-ambiguous product, deterministic product and so on) and we have theorems analagous to Theorem 4.3.8 for these restrictions (cf. Pin, 1981).

References

Brzozowski (1980) contains a detailed bibliography on the problems of star height (with the exception of Hashiguchi, 1982b). Similarly, Pin (1984) contains a bibliography on the varieties of languages and semigroups.

Benois, M. (1969) Parties rationnelles du groupe libre, *C.R. Acad. Sci. Paris, Sér. A*, **269**, 1188–90.
Berstel, J. (1979) *Transductions and Context-free Languages*, Teubner, Stuttgart.
Brzozowski, J. A. (1980) Open problems about regular languages. In *Formal Language Theory, Perspectives and Open Problems*, R. V. Book (ed.), Academic Press, New York, pp. 23–47.
Brzozowski, J. A. and Knast, R. (1978) The dot-depth hierarchy of star-free languages is infinite, *J. Comput. Syst. Sci.*, **16**, 37–55.
Büchi, J. R. (1960) Weak second-order arithmetic and finite automata, *Z. Math. Logic Grundlagen Math.*, **6**, 66–92.
Cohen, R. S. and Brzozowski, J. A. (1971) Dot-depth of star-free events, *J. Computer and System Sciences*, **5**, 1–16.
Dejean, F. and Schützenberger, M. P. (1966) On a question of Eggan, *Information and Control*, **9**, 23–5.
Eilenberg, S. (1974, 1976) *Automata, Languages and Machines*, Academic Press, New York, Vol. A, 1974; Vol. B, 1976.
Eilenberg, S. and Schützenberger, M. P. (1969) Rational sets in commutative monoids, *Journal of Algebra*, **13**, 173–91.
Elgot, C. C. (1961) Decision problems of finite automata design and related arithmetics, *Trans. Amer. Math. Soc.*, **98**, 21–52.
Elgot C. C. and Mezei, G. (1965) On relations defined by generalized finite automata. *IBM J. of Res. and Dev.* **9**, 47–65.

Fliess, M. (1971) Deux applications de la représentation matricielle d'une série rationnelle non commutative, *J. of Algebra*, **19**, 344–53.

Hashiguchi, K. (1979) A decision procedure for the order of regular events, *Theoret. Comput. Sci.*, **8**, 69–72.

Hashiguchi, K. (1982a) Limitedness theorem on finite automata with distance functions, *J. of Computer and System Sciences*, **24**, 232–44.

Hashiguchi, K. (1982b) Regular languages of star-height one, *Information and Control*, **53**, 199–210.

Hashiguchi, K. (1983) Representation theorems on regular languages, *J. Comput. System Sci.*, **27**, 101–15.

Hashiguchi, K. (1986) Improved limitedness theorems on finite automata with distance functions, *Rapport LITP 86–72*.

Hashiguchi, K. (1988) Algorithms for determining relative star-height and star-height, *Information and Computation*, **78**, 124–69.

Henneman, W. H. (1971) Algebraic theory of automata, PhD dissertation, MIT.

Kleene, S. C. (1956) Representations of events in nerve nets and finite automata. In *Automata Studies*, C. E. Shannon and J. McCarthy (eds), Princeton, NJ, pp. 3–40.

Ladner, R. (1977) Application of model-theoretic game to discrete linear orders and finite automata, *Information and Control*, **33**, 281–303.

Lallement G. (1979) *Semigroups and Combinatorial Applications*, Wiley, New York.

Lothaire M. (1983) Combinatorics on words, *Encyclopedia of Mathematics 17*, Addison-Wesley, Reading, Mass.

McKnight, J. D. Jr. (1964) Kleene quotient theorems, *Pacific Journal of Math.*, **14**, 1343–52.

McNaughton, R. and Papert, S. (1971) *Counter-free Automata*, MIT Press, Cambridge, Mass.

Mascle, J. P. (1986) Torsion matrix semigroups and recognizable transductions, *13th ICALP, Lecture Notes in Computer Science 226*, Springer, Berlin, pp. 244–53.

Perrot, J. F. (1978) Variétés de langages et opérations, *Theoretical Computer Science*, **7**, 197–210.

Pin, J.-E. (1978) Sur le monoïde de L* lorsque L est un language fini, *Theor. Computer Science*, **7**, 211–15.

Pin, J.-E. (1981) Variétés de langages et variétés de semigroupes. Thesis, Paris.

Pin, J.-E. (1984) *Variétés de languages formels*, Masson, Paris; trans. as *Varieties of Formal Languages*, North Oxford Academic, London and Plenum, New York (1986).

Pin, J.-E. and Sakarovitch, J. (1983) Operations and transductions that preserve rationality, *6ème GI Conference, Lecture Notes in Computer Science 145*, pp. 617–28.

Pin, J.-E. and Sakarovitch, J. (1985) Une application de la représentation matricielle des transductions, *Theoretical Computer Science*, **35**, 271–93.

Pin, J.-E. and Straubing, H. (1981) Monoids of upper triangular matrices, *Colloquia Mathematica Societatis Janos Bolyai, 39, Semigroups, Szeged*, pp. 259–72.

Pin, J.-E., Straubing, H. and Thérien, D. (1989) New results on the generalized star-height problem, *STACS 89, Lecture Notes in Computer Science 349*, pp. 458–67.

Sakarovitch, J. (1981) Description des monoïdes de type fini, *EIK 17*, pp. 417–34.

Schützenberger, M. P. (1965) On finite monoids having only trivial subgroups, *Inform. and Control*, **48**, 190–4.

Simon, I. (1975) Piecewise testable events, *Proc. 2nd GI Conf., Lecture Notes in Computer Science 33*, Springer, Berlin, pp. 214–22.

Simon, I. (1978) Limited subsets of a free monoid, *Proceedings 19th Annual Symposium of Computer Science*, pp. 143–50.

Straubing, H. (1979) Aperiodic homomorphisms and the concatenation product of recognizable sets, *Journal of Pure and Applied Algebra*, **15**, 319–27.

Straubing, H. (1981) Relational morphisms and operations on recognizable sets, *RAIRO Inf. Théor.*, **15**, 149–59.

Straubing, H. (1985) Finite semigroup varieties of the form **V** ∗ **D**, *J. Pure Applied Algebra*, **36**, 53–94.

Straubing, H. (1986) Semigroups and languages of dot-depth two, *Proc. 13th ICALP, Lecture Notes in Computer Science 226*, Springer, Berlin, pp. 416–23.

Thérien, D. (1980) Classification of regular languages by congruences, PhD thesis, Waterloo.

Thomas, W. (1982) Classifying regular events in symbolic logic, *Journal of Computer and System Sciences*, **25**, 360–76.

3

On generalized entropies
with applications

Inder Jeet Taneja   *Departamento de Matemática, Universidade Federal de Santa Catarina, 88.049 Florianópolis, SC, Brazil*

1   Introduction

Information theory is a relatively new branch of mathematics that was made mathematically rigorous only in the 1940s. The term 'information theory' does not possess a unique definition. Broadly speaking, information theory deals with the study of problems concerning any system. This includes information processing, information storage, information retrieval and decision making. In a narrow sense, information theory studies all theoretical problems connected with the transmission of information over communication channels. This includes the study of uncertainty (information) measures and various practical and economical methods of coding information for transmission.

The first studies in this direction were undertaken by Nyquist in 1924 and 1928 and by Hartley in 1928 who recognized the logarithmic nature of the measure of information. In 1948, Shannon published a remarkable paper on the properties of information sources and of the communication channels used to transmit the outputs of these sources. Around the same time, Wiener (1948) also considered the communication situation and came up, independently, with results similar to those of Shannon.

Both Shannon and Wiener considered the communication situation as one in which a signal, chosen from a specified class, is to be transmitted through a channel. The output of the channel is described statistically by giving a probability distribution over the set of all possible outputs for each permissible input. The basic problem of communication is to reconstruct as closely as possible the input signal after observing the received signal at the output.

However, the approach used by Shannon differs from that of Wiener in the nature of the transmitted signal and in the type of decision made at the receiver. In the Shannon model messages are first encoded and then transmitted, whereas in the Wiener model the signal is communicated directly through the channel without being encoded.

In the past forty years the literature on information theory has grown quite voluminous and apart from communication theory it has found deep applications in many social, physical and biological sciences, for example, economics, statistics, accounting, language, psychology, ecology, pattern recognition, computer sciences, fuzzy sets. . . .

A key feature of Shannon information theory is that the term '*information*' can often be given a mathematical meaning as a numerically measurable quantity, on the basis of a probabilistic model, in such a way that the solutions of many important problems of information storage and transmission can be formulated in terms of this measure of the amount of information. This important measure has a very concrete operational interpretation: it roughly equals the minimum number of binary digits needed, on the average, to encode the message in question. The coding theorems of information theory provide such overwhelming evidence for the adequateness of the Shannon information measure that to look for essentially different measures of information might appear to make no sense at all. Moreover, it has been shown by several authors, starting with Shannon (1948), that the measure of the amount of information is uniquely determined by some rather natural postulates. Still, all the evidence that the Shannon information measure is the only possible one, is valid only within the restricted scope of coding problems considered by Shannon. As pointed out by Rényi (1961) in his fundamental paper on generalized information measures, in other sorts of problems other quantities may serve just as well, or even better, as measures of information. This should be supported either by their operational significance or by a set of natural postulates characterizing them, or, preferably, by both. Thus the idea of generalized entropies arises in the literature. It started with Rényi (1961) who characterized a scalar parametric entropy as entropy of order α, which includes Shannon entropy as a limiting case.

In this chapter we shall discuss the existence of various generalized entropies involving one or more scalar parameters. Applications of some of these entropies to statistical pattern recognition and fuzzy set theory will also be discussed. Section 2 deals with the existence and characterizations of various generalized entropies. Section 3 unifies important properties of the main entropies. Both these sections are based on Capocelli and Taneja (1985). Section 4 deals with the applications to statistical pattern recognition. In Section 4.1, bounds on the probability of error are obtained by three different approaches covering most of the entropies. This section unifies some of the author's recent work. Analogues to Fano-type bounds are also given. Section 4.2 deals with the error bounds and distance measures. Two generalized distance measures are considered which cover most of the previously known ones. This is based on Capocelli *et al.* (1985). Section 4.3 deals with the divergence measures arising due to concavity and sum property of the generalized entropies. This is based on Capocelli and Taneja (1984) and Sant'anna and Taneja (1985). Finally, Section 5 deals with the applications of generalized entropies to fuzzy sets. This section reviews most of the previously known work. New information-theoretic examples are added. The idea of dispersion entropy of superposition fuzzy sets is introduced.

2   Characterizations of generalized entropies

Let $\Delta_n = \left\{ P = (p_1,p_2,\ldots,p_n) \colon p_k \geqslant 0,\ \sum_{k=1}^{n} p_k = 1 \right\},\ n = 2,\ 3,\ \ldots$

denote the set of all complete finite (*n*-ary) probability distributions associated with a discrete random variable X having finite number of values.

Throughout this chapter, it is assumed that all the logarithms are with base 2 and that $0 \log 0 = 0$; $0 \sin (\beta \log 0) = 0$ for $\beta \neq 0$; $0^\alpha = 0$ for $\alpha > 0$. Also for the two distributions P and $Q \in \Delta_n$, $p_k = 0$ whenever $q_k = 0$ for each $k = 1, 2, \ldots, n$.

2.1   Shannon entropy

Shannon (1948) for the first time investigated and characterized through certain postulates a measure of information given by

$$\Phi_1 := H(P) = -\sum_{k=1}^{n} p_k \log p_k,$$

for all $P = (p_1,p_2,\ldots,p_n) \in \Delta_n$.

This measure of information known as '*measure of uncertainty*' is now popularly referred to as *Shannon entropy*. $H(p_1,p_2,\ldots,p_n)$ measures the amount of uncertainty before the experiment or the information gained at the end of the experiment. It can also be interpreted (McEliece, 1977) as a measure of the randomness of X. When Shannon proposed and characterized this measure of information he did not explicitly associate the idea of information with an event. He associated entropy with a (complete) probability distribution. However, the idea of information associated with an event is referred to as *self-information*. Entropy can also be interpreted as the average self-information.

In questionnaire theory, $H(p_1,p_2,\ldots,p_n)$ can be interpreted as the minimum number of 'yes or no' questions required to determine the

result of one observation X. This aspect of entropy has been systematically carried to graph theory (Picard, 1980) and to significant developments
in the theory of questionnaires.

The simplest operational justification of the interpretation of Shannon
entropy as a measure of information is contained in the elementary
coding theorems for memoryless sources, one holding for variable-length
codes (requiring exactly decodability) and another holding for fixed-
length codes (requiring decodability with arbitrary small probability of
error). In both cases, entropy is the infimum of the achievable coding
rates (average number of binary codes per messages).

It can be shown that for large n, there are $2^{H(P)}$ typical sequences of
length n, each with a probability $2^{-H(P)}$ approximately. This interpretation of entropy is important since typical sequences are used in one of the
proofs of the fundamental theorem of information theory.

The true significance of Shannon entropy becomes apparent, however,
in the more complex problems of reliable transmission of information
over noisy channels. Here, the mutual information plays the key role.

After Shannon, various authors approached entropy characterizations
by different routes'and mainly adopted two approaches. One is axiomatic; the other is based on functional equations, and goes on by weakening
or changing the regularity conditions. For a brief review we refer to Aczél
and Daróczy (1975), Mathai and Rathie (1975) and Taneja (1979). In
order to characterize this measure of information mainly three properties
have been taken into consideration, either together or individually; they
are popularly referred to as *additivity*, *recursivity* or *branching*, and *the
sum property*.

2.2 Entropy of order α

A systematic attempt to develop a generalization of Shannon entropy was
carried out by Rényi (1961), who characterized an *entropy of order* α as

$$\Phi_2 := H_\alpha(P) = \frac{1}{1-\alpha} \log\left(\sum_{k=1}^{n} p_k^\alpha\right), \quad \alpha \neq 1, \alpha > 0,$$

for all $P = (p_1, p_2, \ldots, p_n) \in \Delta_n$, α being a parameter. This includes
Shannon entropy in a limiting sense, namely $H_\alpha(P) \to H(P)$ as $\alpha \to 1$.

Rényi's (1961) main motivation in considering this generalized information measure appears to be that he wanted to solve some limit theorems.
Later, he demonstrated that entropy of order α naturally occurs in the
solutions of certain search problems. Campbell (1965) has shown that the
variable-length version of the elementary coding theorem carries over
to entropy of order α, if in the definition of average code length one
considers exponential averaging instead of standard arithmetic averaging.

Entropy of order α does have some significance for fixed-length codes too: for optimum binary encoding with rate $R > H(P)$ of messages of length n from a memoryless source with distribution P, Jelinek (1968a) related the error probability $p_n(e)$ in the limiting case with entropy of order α. He also showed (Jelinek, 1968b) that coding with respect to exponentiated average length L' is useful in minimizing the problem of buffer overflow which occurs when the source symbols are being produced at a fixed rate and the codewords must be stored temporarily in a finite buffer. Jelinek and Schneider (1972) proved that the optimum error exponents of variable length to block coding are identical with those of block to variable length coding and are interestingly related with H_α. Kieffer (1979) considered the problem of variable-length noiseless coding of sequence of length n produced by a discrete memoryless source, where the cost of encoding a sequence is assumed to be a function only of the codeword length. A class of decision rules is defined for deciding which of two source symbols can be coded with smaller expected cost as $n \to \infty$. It is shown that for a large family of cost functions there exists a best decision rule that relates to an entropy of order α. Parker (1980) proved that a simple generalization of Huffman algorithm solves the problem of minimizing L' and its increasing functions. Recently, Blumer (1982) considered the problem of minimizing redundancy of order α and obtained bounds sharper than those of Gallager (1978). Recently, Taneja (1984) extended the concept of exponentiated average codeword length to the best one-to-one codes. Arimoto (1975, 1976) related mutual information of order α defined in terms of H_α to the random coding exponent function, $E_0(\alpha,P)$ arising in the simple derivation of a coding theorem proved by Gallager (1965). He also presented an algorithm to compute the capacity of order α. Ben-Bassat and Raviv (1978) showed that H_α, for $\alpha > 1$, provides a better approximation than Shannon entropy in bounding the Bayesian probability of error.

Thus, all the studies above well justify Rényi's (1961) motivation in considering entropy of order α. This appears to serve equally well to, or sometimes better than, Shannon entropy.

Entropy of order α satisfies additivity but lacks recursivity as well as the sum property. Rényi considered an additional axiom generalizing the sum property; this is generally known as quasi-linearity. Based on the same motivation later researchers have generalized it directly or indirectly by changing some of its postulates and came up with the following generalizations.

Aczél and Daróczy (1963)

$$\Phi_3 := H_\alpha^\ell(P) = -\sum_{k=1}^{n} p_k^\alpha \log p_k \Big/ \sum_{k=1}^{n} p_k^\alpha, \quad \alpha > 0;$$

$$\Phi_4 := H_{\alpha,\beta}(P) = \frac{1}{\beta - \alpha} \log \left[\sum_{k=1}^{n} p_k^{\alpha} \bigg/ \sum_{k=1}^{n} p_k^{\beta} \right], \quad \beta \neq \alpha, \ \alpha, \beta > 0;$$

$$\Phi_5 := H_{\alpha,\beta}^{T}(P) = -\frac{1}{\beta} \arctan \left[\sum_{k=1}^{n} p_k^{\alpha} \sin (\beta \log p_k) \bigg/ \right.$$

$$\left. \sum_{k=1}^{n} p_k^{\alpha} \cos (\beta \log p_k) \right], \quad \beta \neq 0, \ \alpha > 0.$$

Varma (1966)

$$\Phi_6 := H_{m,\alpha}^{1}(P) = \frac{1}{m - \alpha} \log \left[\sum_{k=1}^{n} p_k^{\alpha - m + 1} \right], \quad m - 1 < \alpha < m, \ m \geq 1;$$

$$\Phi_7 := H_{m,\alpha}^{2}(P) = \frac{1}{m(m - \alpha)} \log \left[\sum_{k=1}^{n} p_k^{\alpha/m} \right], \quad 0 < \alpha < m, \ m \geq 1.$$

Kapur (1967)

$$\Phi_8 := H_{\delta,\beta}(P) = \frac{1}{1 - \delta} \log \left[\sum_{k=1}^{n} p_k^{\delta + \beta - 1} \bigg/ \sum_{k=1}^{n} p_k^{\beta} \right],$$

$$\delta \neq 1, \ \delta > 0, \ \beta \geq 1.$$

Rathie (1970)

$$\Phi_9 := H_{\delta,\beta_1,\ldots,\beta_n}(P) = \frac{1}{1 - \delta} \log \left[\sum_{k=1}^{n} p_k^{\delta + \beta_k - 1} \bigg/ \sum_{k=1}^{n} p_k^{\beta_k} \right],$$

$$\delta \neq 1, \ \delta > 0, \ \beta_k \geq 1, \ k = 1, 2, \ldots, n$$

for all $P = (p_1, p_2, \ldots, p_n) \in \Delta_n$.

It can be easily seen that Φ_4 and Φ_5 go to Φ_3 when $\beta \to \alpha$ and $\beta \to 0$ respectively. Φ_3 and Φ_4 reduce to Φ_1 and Φ_2 respectively when $\alpha = 1$ and $\beta = 1$. Φ_6 and Φ_7 reduce to Φ_2 when $m = 1$. Φ_9 reduce to Φ_8 when $\beta_k = \beta$ for each $k = 1, 2, \ldots, n$. Finally, Φ_8 is an equivalent version of Φ_4, i.e. it reduces to Φ_4 when $\delta + \beta - 1 = \alpha$. Also, $H_{\alpha,\beta}(P)$ is a linear combination of $H_{\alpha}(P)$, i.e.

$$H_{\alpha,\beta}(P) = \frac{1 - \alpha}{\beta - \alpha} H_{\alpha,1}(P) + \frac{1 - \beta}{\alpha - \beta} H_{1,\beta}(P), \tag{1}$$

where $H_{\alpha,1}(P) = H_{\alpha}(P)$ and $H_{1,\beta}(P) = H_{\beta}(P)$.

2.3   Entropy of degree β

For operational purposes it seems more natural to consider instead of Rényi entropy, the similar expression $\sum_{k=1}^{n} p_k^{\beta}$ as an information measure. So Havrda and Charvát (1967) proposed the following entropy of degree β:

$$\Phi_{10} := H^{\beta}(P) = (2^{1-\beta} - 1)^{-1} \left[\sum_{k=1}^{n} p_k^{\beta} - 1 \right], \quad \beta \neq 1, \beta > 0.$$

This quantity permits simpler axiomatic characterizations too (Havrda and Charvát, 1967). It reduces to Shannon entropy as $\beta \to 1$. It lacks the additivity property but satisfies the sum property and generalized recursive property. In communication problems it is much less used than Rényi's entropy. But as a particular case, when $\beta = 2$ it connects to Bhattacharyya coefficient, information energy, quadratic entropy, Gini's index and Bayesian distance, which are applied to other fields more than to information theory.

2.4 γ-Entropy

Let $f(u)$ be a real-valued continuous function defined and non-negative over $(0,1]$ with a continuous derivative on $(0,1)$ and $f(1) = 0$. Arimoto (1971) defined generalized entropies by

$$H_f(P) = \inf \sum_{k=1}^{n} p_k f(q_k),$$

where the infimum is taken over all probability distributions $Q = (q_1, q_2, \ldots, q_n) \in \Delta_n$ with $q_k > 0$. By defining the generalized entropies such as $H_f(P)$, Arimoto (1971) came up with an example of it consisting of a parametric entropy, referred as γ-entropy. This is given by

$$\Phi_{11} := {}_{\gamma}H(P) = (2^{\gamma-1} - 1)^{-1} \left[\left(\sum_{k=1}^{n} p_k^{\frac{1}{\gamma}} \right)^{\gamma} - 1 \right], \quad \gamma \neq 1, \gamma > 0.$$

In this case also, ${}_{\gamma}H(P) \to H(P)$ as $\gamma \to 1$. Arimoto's main motivation to consider the generalized entropies, $H_f(P)$ was to prove some important results on decision theory connected with Bayesian probability of error and then related it to Bhattacharyya distance, Gallager's random coding exponent function and so on. This entropy is neither additive nor recursive; nor does it satisfy the sum property.

Thus, we see that of the three generalized entropies – entropy of order α, entropy of degree β, and γ-entropy – the first is additive, the second is recursive and satisfies the sum property, and the third does not satisfy any of these properties. However, they all contain the common function $\sum_{k=1}^{n} p_k^{\delta}$, which makes them related as follows:

$$H_{\delta}(P) = \frac{1}{1 - \delta} \log \left[(2^{1-\delta} - 1) H_{\delta}(P) + 1 \right]$$

$$= (2^{\frac{\delta}{\delta-1}} - 1)^{-1} \log [(2^{\frac{\delta}{\delta-1}} - 1) \, {}_\delta H(P) + 1], \quad \delta \neq 1, \delta > 0. \tag{2}$$

2.5   Entropy of order α and degree β

Sharma and Mittal (1975) introduced and characterized the following two entropies called *entropy of order 1 and degree β* and *entropy of order α and degree β* respectively:

$$\Phi_{12} := H_1^\beta(P) = (2^{1-\beta} - 1)^{-1} \left[2^{(\beta-1) \sum\limits_{k=1}^{n} p_k \log p_k} - 1 \right], \quad \beta \neq 1, \beta > 0,$$

and

$$\Phi_{13} := H_\alpha^\beta(P) = (2^{1-\beta} - 1)^{-1} \left[\left(\sum_{k=1}^{n} p_k^\alpha \right)^{\frac{\beta-1}{\alpha-1}} - 1 \right],$$

$$\alpha \neq 1, \beta \neq 1, \alpha, \beta > 0.$$

Sharma and Mittal's main motivation was to unify the three entropies $H_\alpha(P)$, $H^\beta(P)$ and ${}_\gamma H(P)$. And doing so they got $H_\alpha^\beta(P)$ and also $H_1^\beta(P)$. As a particular case, $H_\alpha^\beta(P)$ reduces to $H^\beta(P)$ and ${}_\gamma H(P)$ when $\alpha = \beta$ and $\alpha = 1/\gamma = 1/(2 - \beta)$ respectively. As a limiting case, $H_\alpha^\beta(P)$ reduces to $H_1^\beta(P)$ and $H_\alpha(P)$ when $\alpha \to 1$ and $\beta \to 1$ respectively. Also, $H_1^\beta(P)$ and $H_\alpha^\beta(P)$ reduce to Shannon entropy when $\beta \to 1$ and $\beta = \alpha$ and $\alpha \to 1$ respectively. Furthermore, these two entropies bear a composite relation with Shannon entropy and entropy of order α given by

$$H_1^\beta(P) = g_\beta(H(P)), \tag{3}$$

and

$$H_\alpha^\beta(P) = g_\beta(H_\alpha(P)), \tag{4}$$

where

$$g_\beta(x) = (2^{1-\beta} - 1)^{-1} [2^{(1-\beta)x} - 1], \quad \beta \neq 1, \beta > 0, x \geq 0. \tag{5}$$

Thus, we see that the entropy of order α and degree β contains either as particular or as limiting cases Shannon entropy, entropy of order α, entropy of degree β, γ-entropy, and entropy of order 1 and degree β. In the following theorem, we shall provide a characterization under an axiomatic approach (Sharma and Mittal, 1975; van der Pyl, 1977) that characterizes these entropies one by one.

Theorem 1   Let $H: \Delta_n \to \mathbb{R}$ satisfy the following five axioms:

A1. *Symmetry*: For all $P \in \Delta_n$, $H(P)$ is a symmetric function of its arguments.

A2. *Continuity*: $H(\{p\})$ is a continuous function for all p satisfying $0 < p \leqslant 1$.

A3. *Unity*: $H(\{1/2\}) = 1$.

A4. *Preadditivity*: There exists a family of functions $f_n: \Delta_n \to \mathbb{R}$ such that

$$H(P * Q) = H(P) + f_n(P)H(Q),$$

for all $P \in \Delta_n$, $Q \in \Delta_m$, and $P * Q \in \Delta_{nm}$.

A5. *ψ-average*: There exists a continuous and strictly monotonic function such that for every $P \in \Delta_n$,

$$\psi(H(P)) = \sum_{k=1}^{n} p_k \psi(H(\{p_k\})).$$

Then the only non-trivial continuous solutions of the above system of axioms are given by either $H(P)$, $H_\alpha(P)$, $H_1^\beta(P)$, or $H_\alpha^\beta(P)$. While $H^\beta(P)$ and $_\gamma H(P)$ follows after an immediate substitution of values of α and β in $H_\alpha^\beta(P)$.

Proof By axioms A1 and A4, we have

$$H(\{pq\}) = H(\{p\}) + f_1(\{p\}) H(\{q\})$$
$$= H(\{q\}) + f_1(\{q\}) H(\{p\}). \tag{6}$$

This gives

$$\frac{f_1(\{p\}) - 1}{H(\{p\})} = \frac{f_1(\{q\}) - 1}{H(\{q\})} = c \text{ (say)}, \tag{7}$$

where c is a constant. If $H(\{p\}) = 0$ or $H(\{q\}) = 0$, we put $f_1(\{p\}) = 1$ or $f_1(\{q\}) = 1$. By taking $c = 0$, $f_1(\{p\}) = 1$ for every $p \in (0,1]$ so that

$$H(\{pq\}) = H(\{p\}) + H(\{q\}). \tag{8}$$

The continuous solution of the functional equation (8) (Aczél, 1966) is given by

$$H(\{p\}) = c_1 \log p.$$

From axiom A3, we have

$$H(\{p\}) = -\log p.$$

Let us write

$$P = (p_1, p_2, \ldots, p_n) = p(p_1', p_2', \ldots, p_n'), \text{ where } p_k = pp_k',$$
$$k = 1, 2, \ldots, n.$$

From axiom A4, we have

$$H(pp_1', pp_2', \ldots, pp_n') = H(\{p\}) + f_1(\{p\})H(p_1', p_2', \ldots, p_n'), \tag{9}$$

or, by symmetry,

$$H(pp_1', pp_2', \ldots, pp_n') = H(p_1', p_2', \ldots, p_n') + f_n(p_1', p_2', \ldots, p_n')H(\{p\}).$$
$$(10)$$

Now, (9) and (10) together give

$$H(p_1', p_2', \ldots, p_n')[1 - f_1(\{p\})] = H(\{p\})[1 - f_n(p_1', \ldots, p_n')].$$

Then $f_1(\{p\}) = 1$ implies $f_n(p_1, p_2, \ldots, p_n) = 1$, for every $P \in \Delta_n$. Now, axiom A4 just reduces to additivity. The axiom A5 with the only solutions $\psi(x) = ax + b$ and $\psi(x) = 2^{(1-\alpha)x}$ obtained by Rényi (1961) leads to $H(P)$ and $H_\alpha(P)$. Assuming now $c \neq 0$, from (6) and (7) we get

$$f_1(\{p\}) - 1 = c\, H(\{p\}),$$

and then

$$f_1(\{pq\}) = f_1(\{p\})\, f_1(\{q\}).$$
$$(11)$$

The non-trivial continuous solution of the above functional equation (11) is given by

$$f_1(\{p\}) = p^\alpha, \quad \alpha > 0,$$

i.e. $H(\{p\}) = \dfrac{p^\alpha - 1}{c}.$

By axiom A3, we get $c = 2^{-\alpha} - 1$. Now,

$$H(pq_1, pq_2, \ldots, pq_n) = H(\{p\}) + f_1(\{p\})\, H(q_1, \ldots, q_n)$$
$$= p^\alpha \psi^{-1}\left[\sum_{k=1}^{n} q_k \psi\left(\frac{q_k^\alpha - 1}{c} \right) \right].$$
$$(12)$$

From Hardy *et al.* (1934), the solutions of (12) are given by

$$\psi(x) = \log(cx + 1) \quad \text{and} \quad \psi(x) = (cx + 1)^t.$$

Putting $\alpha = \beta - 1$, i.e. $c = (2^{1-\beta} - 1)^{-1}$ ($\beta \neq 1$), $t = (\alpha - 1)/(\beta - 1)$, $\alpha \neq 1$, $\beta \neq 1$, we finally get $H_1^\beta(P)$ and $H_\alpha^\beta(P)$.

In the following theorem we give a simpler axiomatic approach to characterize the entropy of order α and degree β.

Theorem 2 Let $H: \Delta_n \to \mathbb{R}$ be a function satisfying the following axioms:

B1. $H(P) = \eta\left(\sum_{k=1}^{n} f(p_k) \right)^\delta + \zeta, \quad \eta,\, \delta,\, \zeta \neq 0,$

   where f is a continuous function defined on $[0,1]$;
B2. For $P \in \Delta_n$, $Q \in \Delta_m$, $P * Q \in \Delta_{nm}$,

$$H(P*Q) = H(P) + H(Q) - \frac{1}{\zeta}H(P)\,H(Q);$$

B3. $H(\frac{1}{2},\frac{1}{2}) = 1;$

where η and ζ are arbitrary constants and δ is a parameter. Then

$$H(P) = (2^{(1-\sigma)\delta} - 1)^{-1}\left[\left(\sum_{k=1}^{n} p_k^\sigma\right)^\delta - 1\right], \quad \sigma > 0, \tag{13}$$

which is the same as $H_\alpha^\beta(P)$ for $\sigma = \alpha$ and $\delta = (\beta - 1)/(\alpha - 1)$

Proof From axioms B1 and B2, we have

$$\left[\sum_{k=1}^{n}\sum_{j=1}^{m} f(p_k q_j)\right]^\delta = \left(-\frac{\eta}{\zeta}\right)\left[\sum_{k=1}^{n} f(p_k)\right]^\delta\left[\sum_{j=1}^{m} f(q_j)\right]^\delta,$$

i.e. $$\sum_{k=1}^{n}\sum_{j=1}^{m} f(p_k q_j) = \left(-\frac{\eta}{\zeta}\right)^{\frac{1}{\delta}}\sum_{k=1}^{n}\sum_{j=1}^{m} f(p_i)\,f(q_j). \tag{14}$$

The functional equation (14) is equivalent to (Chaundy and McLeod, 1960)

$$f(pq) = \left(-\frac{\eta}{\zeta}\right)^{\frac{1}{\delta}} f(p)\,f(q), \quad p, q \in [0,1]. \tag{15}$$

Now, substituting in (15),

$$\left(-\frac{\eta}{\zeta}\right)^{\frac{1}{\delta}} f(p) = \phi(p), \tag{16}$$

we get

$$\phi(pq) = \phi(p)\,\phi(q). \tag{17}$$

The most general (non-trivial) continuous solution of the functional equation (17) is given by

$$\phi(p) = p^\sigma, \quad \sigma > 0. \tag{18}$$

Now (16) and (18) together give

$$f(p) = \left(-\frac{\eta}{\zeta}\right)^{\frac{1}{\delta}} p^\sigma, \tag{19}$$

Finally, axioms B1, B3 and (19) together give (13).

The quantity $\left(\sum_{k=1}^{n} p_k^\sigma\right)^\delta$ arising in (13) was called a generalized measure of certainty by van der Lubbe *et al.* (1984). They characterized it by using arguments similar to those of Theorem 1 and studied its properties. They related it to many important functions including generalized entropies.

2.6 Generalized additive entropies

We know that the entropy of degree β is not additive like Shannon entropy and entropy of order α. But it satisfies the following relations:

$$H^\beta(P*Q) \begin{cases} \leqslant H^\beta(P) + H^\beta(Q), & \beta \geqslant 1, \\ \geqslant H^\beta(P) + H^\beta(Q), & \beta \leqslant 1, \end{cases} \tag{20}$$

for all $P \in \Delta_n$, $Q \in \Delta_m$ and $P*Q \in \Delta_{nm}$. That is, either it is sub-additive or super-additive, depending on the values of β. Motivated by this property, Sharma and Taneja (1977) considered the following generalized relation called *generalized additivity*:

$$H(P*Q) = G(P)\,H(Q) + G(Q)\,H(P), \tag{21}$$

where the functions H and G satisfy the well-known sum property, i.e.

$$H(P) = \sum_{k=1}^{n} f(p_k), \tag{22}$$

and

$$G(P) = \sum_{k=1}^{m} g(p_k), \tag{23}$$

where f and g are continuous functions defined over $[0,1]$. Relation (21) together with (22) and (23) then leads to the following functional equation:

$$\sum_{k=1}^{n}\sum_{j=1}^{m} f(p_k q_j) = \sum_{k=1}^{n}\sum_{j=1}^{m} f(p_k)\,g(q_j) + \sum_{k=1}^{n}\sum_{j=1}^{m} f(q_j)\,g(p_k), \tag{24}$$

for all $P = (p_1, p_2, \ldots, p_n) \in \Delta_n$, $Q = (q_1, q_2, \ldots, q_m) \in \Delta_m$ and $P*Q = (p_1 q_1, p_1 q_2, \ldots, p_1 q_m, \ldots, p_n q_1, \ldots, p_n q_m) \in \Delta_{nm}$.

The functional equation (24) generalizes the one considered long ago by Chaundy and McLeod (1961) in order to characterize Shannon entropy. A relation similar to (21) turns out to be an important property of entropy of fuzzy set theory (De Luca and Termini, 1972).

The following theorem gives the continuous solutions of the functional equation (24).

Theorem 3 (Sharma and Taneja, 1977). The most general non-trivial real continuous solutions of the functional equation (24) are given by

$$f(p) = c\,p^\alpha \log p, \quad g(p) = p^\alpha, \tag{25}$$

$$f(p) = \tfrac{1}{2}d(p^\alpha - p^\beta), \quad g(p) = \tfrac{1}{2}(p^\alpha + p^\beta), \tag{26}$$

and

$$f(p) = \frac{1}{r} p^\alpha \sin(\beta \log p), \quad g(p) = p^\alpha \cos(\beta \log p), \tag{27}$$

where c, d, r $(\neq 0)$ are arbitrary real constants and α, β are arbitrary real positive parameters.

Proof Let a, b, a', b' be positive integers such that $1 \leqslant a \leqslant a'$, and $1 \leqslant b' \leqslant b$. Setting $n = a - a' + 1$, $m = b - b' + 1$,

$$p_i = \frac{1}{a} \ (i = 1,2,\ldots,a-a'), \quad p_{a-a'+1} = \frac{a'}{a},$$

$$q_j = \frac{1}{b} \ (j = 1,2,\ldots,b-b'), \quad q_{b-b'+1} = \frac{b'}{b},$$

in (24), we get

$$(a - a')(b - b')f(1/ab) + (b - b')f(a'/ab)$$
$$+ (a - a')f(b'/ab) + f(a'b'/ab)$$

$$= (b - b')g(1/b) + g(b'/b)(a - a')f(1/a) + f(a'/a)$$

$$+ (a - a')g(1/a) + g(a'/a)(b - b')f(1/b) + f(b'/b). \tag{28}$$

Putting $a' = b' = 1$ in (28) we get

$$f(1/ab) = g(1/b)f(1/a) + g(1/a)f(1/b). \tag{29}$$

Taking $a' = 1$ in (28) and using (29), we get

$$f(b'/ab) = g(b'/b)f(1/a) + g(1/a)f(b'/b). \tag{30}$$

Similarly, taking $b' = 1$ in (28) and using (29), we get

$$f(a'/ab) = g(1/b)f(a'/a) + g(a'/a)f(1/b). \tag{31}$$

Now, (28) together with (29), (30) and (31) gives

$$f(a'b'/ab) = g(b'/b)f(a'/a) + g(a'/a)f(b'/b),$$

i.e. $f(pq) = g(q)f(p) + g(p)f(q)$, \hfill (32)

for all rationals p, $q \in [0,1]$.

By the continuity of the functions f and g, (32) is true for all reals p, $q \in [0,1]$.

The most general complex solutions (Aczél, 1966) of (32) are given by

$$f(p) \equiv 0, \quad g(p) \ \text{arbitrary}, \tag{33}$$

$$f(p) = e_0(p)h(p), \quad g(p) = e_0(p), \tag{34}$$

and

$$f(p) = \tfrac{1}{2}d[e_1(p) - e_2(p)], \quad g(p) = \tfrac{1}{2}[e_1(p) + e_2(p)], \tag{35}$$

where $d \neq 0$ is an arbitrary complex constant and $h(p)$, $e_w(p)$, $w = 0, 1, 2$ are arbitrary functions satisfying

$$h(pq) = h(p) + h(q), \tag{36}$$

and

$$e_w(pq) = e_w(p)e_w(q), \quad w = 0, 1, 2, \tag{37}$$

respectively.

The real continuous solutions of (32) would depend on the solutions of (36) and (37).

The most general continuous solution of (36) is given by

$$h(p) = c \log p, \quad p > 0, \tag{38}$$

where c is a real or imaginary constant.

Also, the most general non-trivial continuous solution of (37) is given by

$$e(p) = p^\alpha, \quad \alpha > 0, \tag{39}$$

where α is an arbitrary real or imaginary parameter.

Thus, the solutions given in (34) can be put in the following form:

$$f(p) = c\, p^\alpha \log p, \quad g(p) = p^\alpha, \tag{40}$$

where α and c are real or imaginary constants. Now, $g(p)$ in (40) is real and continuous if and only if α is real and non-negative, so $f(p)$ in (40) is real iff c is real. Thus one set of the real continuous solutions of (32) is given by

$$f(p) = c\, p^\alpha \log p, \quad g(p) = p^\alpha,$$

where α (>0) and c are real constants. Also, by (38) and (39) the set of solutions of (32) given by (30) can be written as

$$f(p) = \tfrac{1}{2}d(p^\alpha - p^\beta) \quad \text{and} \quad g(p) = \tfrac{1}{2}(p^\alpha + p^\beta), \tag{41}$$

where α, β and d are constants, real or imaginary. Now, $g(p)$ in (41) would be real if (i) both α and β are real; or (ii) α and β are complex conjugates. Thus another set of real continuous solutions of (32) obtained from (41) is given by

$$f(p) = \tfrac{1}{2}d(p^\alpha - p^\beta), \quad g(p) = \tfrac{1}{2}(p^\alpha + p^\beta),$$

where $\alpha(>0)$, $\beta(>0)$ and d are real arbitrary constants. Next, let $\alpha = \alpha_1 + i\alpha_2$, then by (ii) $\beta = \alpha_1 - i\alpha_2$. For $f(p)$ to be real we must take $d = ir$ (with r real). Then (41) gives

$$f(p) = \frac{1}{r} p^{\alpha_1} \sin(\alpha_2 \log p), \quad g(p) = p^{\alpha_1} \cos(\alpha_2 \log p).$$

If we write $\alpha = \alpha_1$ and $\beta = \alpha_2$ we have the third set of real continuous solutions of (32) given by (27).

2.6.1 *Characterization of generalized entropies*

The generalized entropies of a probability distribution $P = (p_1, p_2, \ldots, p_n) \in \Delta_n$ corresponding to the real continuous solutions (25), (26) and (27) of the functional equation (24) under the boundary condition $f(\frac{1}{2}) = 1$ and sum property (22) are respectively given by

$$\Phi_{14} := H_\ell^\alpha(P) = -2^{\alpha-1} \sum_{k=1}^{n} p_k^\alpha \log p_k, \quad \alpha > 0,$$

$$\Phi_{15} := H_p^{\alpha,\beta}(P) = (2^{1-\alpha} - 2^{1-\beta})^{-1} \left[\sum_{k=1}^{n} p_k^\alpha - \sum_{k=1}^{n} p_k^\beta \right],$$

$$\alpha \neq \beta, \alpha, \beta > 0.$$

and

$$\Phi_{16} := H_s^{\alpha,\beta}(P) = -\frac{2^{\alpha-1}}{\sin \beta} \sum_{k=1}^{n} p_k^\alpha \sin(\beta \log p_k), \quad \beta \neq s\pi, \alpha > 0,$$

$$s = 0, 1, 2, \ldots$$

respectively. The entropies $H_\ell^\alpha(P)$ and $H_p^{\alpha,\beta}(P)$ reduce to $H(P)$ and $H^\beta(P)$ when $\alpha = 1$ and $\beta = \alpha$ respectively. $H_p^{\alpha,\beta}(P)$ and $H_s^{\alpha,\beta}(P)$ both reduce to $H^\beta(P)$ when $\beta \to \alpha$ and $\beta \to 0$ respectively. Also, the generalized entropy $H_p^{\alpha,\beta}(P)$ bears a linear relation with $H^\beta(P)$ given by

$$H_p^{\alpha,\beta}(P) = \frac{2^{1-\alpha} - 1}{2^{1-\alpha} - 2^{1-\beta}} H_p^{\alpha,1}(P) + \frac{2^{1-\beta} - 1}{2^{1-\beta} - 2^{1-\alpha}} H_p^{1,\beta}(P), \qquad (42)$$

where $H_p^{\alpha,1}(P) = H^\alpha(P)$ and $H_p^{1,\beta}(P) = H^\beta(P)$.

The entropy $H_\ell^\alpha(P)$ is referred as *α-log entropy*, $H_p^{\alpha,\beta}(P)$ as *entropy of degree (α, β)* and $H_s^{\alpha,\beta}(P)$ as *sine-entropy*.

2.7 Weighted entropies or entropies with preferences

The cybernetic analogy between man and machine consists precisely of the fact that both are control systems. This means that information is transmitted and processed in view of a goal with regard to which control signals must be efficient. The whole activity of cybernetic systems (biological and technical) is directed towards the fulfilment of a goal. The system must then possess a qualitative differentiating criterion for the signals to be transmitted. This implies the existence of a logical block able to discriminate the quality of various signals according to a given criterion. The cybernetic criterion for a qualitative differentiation of the signals is represented by the relevance, the significance, or the utility of the information carried with respect to the goal.

The occurrence of an event removes a double uncertainty: a qualitative one related to its probability of occurrence and a quantitative one related to its utility for the fulfilment of the goal. Based on this model, Belis and Guiaşu (1968) introduced and characterized (Guiaşu, 1977) the following *weighted or useful entropy*:

$$\Phi_{17} := H(P; U) = -\sum_{k=1}^{n} p_k u_k \log p_k,$$

where u_k's (≥ 0) are the *weights* or *utilities* associated with each event x_k having probability p_k, $k = 1, 2, \ldots, n$.

The motivation of Belis and Guiaşu (1968) in introducing this weighted entropy was to emphasize the importance of the occurrence of the event along with its probability. On the other hand, the entropy introduced by Shannon (1948) does not take this aspect into consideration. Later, Longo (1976) justified the importance of weights in communication systems and proved some noiseless coding theorems. In the literature this aspect of weights to fuzzy set theory related to image processing has also been considered. Bouchon (1976) took it to questionnaire theory.

Based on the model of Belis and Guiaşu, Picard (1979) gave generalizations of the weighted entropy in the following forms:

$$\Phi_{18} := H(P; V) = -\frac{\sum_{k=1}^{n} v_k \log p_k}{\sum_{k=1}^{n} v_k},$$

$$\Phi_{19} := H_\alpha(P; V) = \frac{1}{1-\alpha} \log \left(\frac{\sum_{k=1}^{n} p_k^{\alpha-1} v_k}{\sum_{k=1}^{n} v_k} \right), \quad \alpha \neq 1, \alpha > 0,$$

$$\Phi_{20} := H_1^\beta(P; V) = (2^{1-\beta} - 1)^{-1} \left\{ 2^{(\beta-1)\sum_{k=1}^{n} v_k \log p_k / \sum_{k=1}^{n} v_k} - 1 \right\},$$
$$\beta \neq 1, \beta > 0,$$

and

$$\Phi_{21} := H_\alpha^\beta(P; V) = (2^{1-\beta} - 1)^{-1} \left\{ \left(\frac{\sum_{k=1}^{n} p_k^{\alpha-1} v_k}{\sum_{k=1}^{n} v_k} \right)^{\frac{\beta-1}{\alpha-1}} - 1 \right\},$$

$$\alpha \neq 1, \beta \neq 1, \alpha, \beta > 0.$$

Picard (1979) called $V = (v_1, v_2, \ldots, v_n)$, $v_k > 0$, $\forall\, k$, a distribution of *preferences* rather than utilities. In particular, when $v_k = p_k u_k$, V reduces to the same model as considered by Belis and Guiaşu (1968). If the distribution $V = (v_1, v_2, \ldots, v_n) \in \Delta_n$, then all the above entropies reduce to a measure of inaccuracy between the two distributions (Kerridge, 1961) and its generalizations.

The characterization of the above entropies given by Picard (1979) goes along the lines of Theorem 2.

2.8 Hypoentropy

Irrespective of its characterization, Ferreri (1980) introduced a generalization of Shannon entropy called *hypoentropy* given by

$$\Phi_{22} := H_\lambda(P) = \left(1 + \frac{1}{\lambda}\right) \log\,(1 + \lambda)$$

$$- \frac{1}{\lambda} \sum_{k=1}^{n} (1 + \lambda p_k) \log\,(1 + \lambda p_k), \quad \lambda > 0.$$

In this case, $H_\lambda(P) \to H(P)$ as $\lambda \to \infty$.

Ferreri (1980) showed that some of its properties are similar to those holding for Shannon entropy and specified some of its applications to statistics. Hypoentropy satisfies recursivity and the sum property but is not additive.

2.9 Trigonometric entropies

We have seen above that there are only two kinds of trigonometric entropies that have been studied so far. One by Aczél and Daróczy (1963) involves three trigonometric functions, sine, cosine and tangent. The second, by Sharma and Taneja (1977), involves only one trigonometric function, the sine function. It has two parameters, α and β. If we put $\alpha = 1$, then

$$\Phi_{23} := S_1^\beta(P) = -\frac{1}{\sin \beta} \sum_{k=1}^{n} p_k \sin\,(\beta \log p_k),$$

$$\beta \neq s\pi, s = 0, 1, 2, \ldots .$$

In this case, $S_1^\beta(P) \to H(P)$ as $\beta \to 0$. In this entropy the $\log(.)$ function is inside the sine function. Still, one can generalize Shannon entropy by trigonometric functions, where sine is inside the $\log(.)$. Motivated by this, recently, Sant'anna and Taneja (1985) introduced and characterized the following *trigonometric entropies*:

$$\Phi_{24} := S_2^\beta(P) = -\sum_{k=1}^{n} p_k \log\left(\frac{\sin \beta p_k}{2 \sin \frac{\beta}{2}}\right), \quad \beta \neq 0,$$

$$\Phi_{25} := S_3^\beta(P) = -\sum_{k=1}^{n} \left(\frac{\sin \beta p_k}{2 \sin \frac{\beta}{2}}\right) \log\left(\frac{\sin \beta p_k}{2 \sin \frac{\beta}{2}}\right), \quad \beta \neq 0,$$

and

$$\Phi_{26} := S_4^\beta(P) = \sum_{k=1}^{n} \left(\frac{\sin \beta p_k}{2 \sin \frac{\beta}{2}}\right), \quad \beta \neq 0,$$

for all $P \in \Delta_n$.

Both $S_2^\beta(P)$ and $S_3^\beta(P)$ reduce to Shannon entropy as $\beta \to 0$, while $S_4^\beta(P)$ goes to 1 as $\beta \to 0$. Thus we end up with an entropy which no longer reduces to Shannon entropy, but from the applications point of view it is as good as Shannon's (Sant'anna and Taneja, 1985).

Figure 1 depicts all the limiting and special cases and shows how all the generalized entropies can be brought to Shannon entropy.

3 Properties of generalized entropies

In this section, we shall study some important properties of the entropies introduced in Section 2. We shall see that some of these properties are frequently applied in the subsequent sections devoted to statistical pattern recognition and fuzzy set theory. In order to study these properties, we have selected eight of them, namely Shannon entropy, and four with one parameter and three with two parameters. For proofs we refer to Aczél and Daróczy (1975), van der Pyl (1977), El-Sayed (1977), Ben-Bassat and Raviv (1978) and Capocelli and Taneja (1985). To simplify the notations, let us rewrite them as follows:

$$E_1(P) = -\sum_{k=1}^{n} p_k \log p_k,$$

$$E_2(P) = \frac{1}{1-\alpha} \log\left(\sum_{k=1}^{n} p_k^\alpha\right), \quad \alpha \neq 1, \alpha > 0,$$

$$E_3(P) = (2^{1-\beta} - 1)^{-1}\left[\sum_{k=1}^{n} p_k^\beta - 1\right], \quad \beta \neq 1, \beta > 0,$$

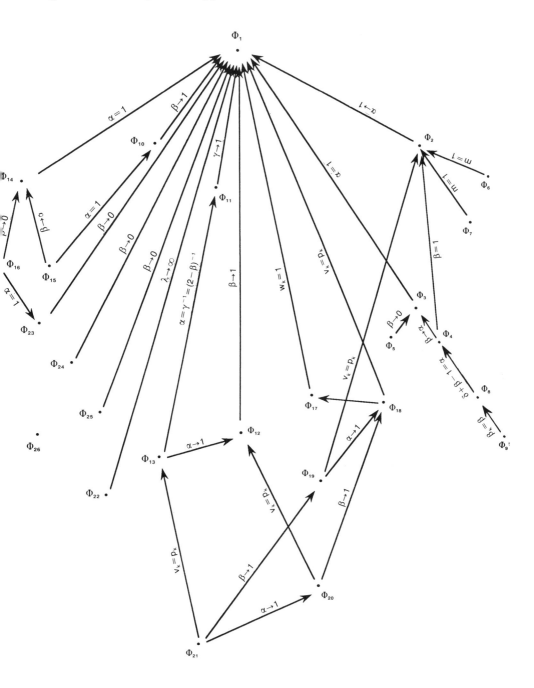

Fig. 3.1 Entropy graph

$$E_4(P) = (2^{\gamma-1} - 1)^{-1}\left[\left(\sum_{k=1}^{n} p_k^{\frac{1}{\gamma}}\right)^{\gamma} - 1\right], \quad \gamma \neq 1, \gamma > 0,$$

$$E_5(P) = (2^{1-\beta} - 1)^{-1}\left[2^{(\beta-1)\sum_{k=1}^{n} p_k \log p_k} - 1\right], \quad \beta \neq 1, \beta > 0,$$

$$E_6(P) = (2^{1-\beta} - 1)^{-1}\left[\left(\sum_{k=1}^{n} p_k^{\alpha}\right)^{\frac{\beta-1}{\alpha-1}} - 1\right], \quad \alpha \neq 1, \beta \neq 1, \alpha, \beta > 0,$$

$$E_7(P) = (\beta - \alpha)^{-1} \log\left[\sum_{k=1}^{n} p_k^{\alpha} \Big/ \sum_{k=1}^{n} p_k^{\beta}\right], \quad \alpha \neq \beta, \alpha, \beta > 0,$$

and

$$E_8(P) = (2^{1-\alpha} - 2^{1-\beta})^{-1}\left[\sum_{k=1}^{n} p_k^{\alpha} - \sum_{k=1}^{n} p_k^{\beta}\right], \quad \alpha \neq \beta, \alpha, \beta > 0,$$

for all $P = (p_1, p_2, \ldots, p_n) \in \Delta_n$. Also let $p_{max} = \max\{p_1, p_2, \ldots, p_n\}$.

(i) *Non-negativity*: For all $P \in \Delta_n$, $E_i(P) \geq 0$, $i = 1, 2, \ldots, 8$ with equality iff there exists a k for which $p_k = 1$, while $p_r \neq 0$ for $r \neq k$.

(ii) *Continuity*: For all $P \in \Delta_n$, $E_i(P)$, $i = 1, 2, \ldots, 8$ are all continuous functions of P.

(iii) *Symmetry*: For all $P \in \Delta_n$, $E_i(P)$, $i = 1, 2, \ldots, 8$ are all symmetric functions of their arguments, i.e.

$$E_i(p_1, p_2, \ldots, p_n) = E_i(p_{\rho(1)}, p_{\rho(2)}, \ldots, p_{\rho(n)}),$$

where ρ is any permutation from 1 to n.

(iv) *Expansibility*: For all $P = (p_1, p_2, \ldots, p_n) \in \Delta_n$,

$$E_i(p_1, p_2, \ldots, p_n, 0) = E_i(p_1, p_2, \ldots, p_n), \quad i = 1, 2, \ldots 8.$$

(v) *Normality*: $E_i(\frac{1}{2}, \frac{1}{2}) = 1$, $i = 1, 2, \ldots, 8$.

(vi) *Decisivity*: $E_i(1, 0) = E_i(0, 1) = 0$, $i = 1, 2, \ldots, 8$.

(vii) For all $P \in \Delta_n$, $Q \in \Delta_m$, $P * Q \in \Delta_{nm}$, we have

(a) *Additivity*: $E_i(P * Q) = E_i(P) + E_i(Q)$, $i = 1, 2,$ and 7.

(b) *Non-additivity* or *Pseudo-additivity*:

$$E_i(P * Q) = E_i(P) + E_i(Q) + C_i E_i(P) E_i(Q),$$
$$i = 3, 4, 5 \text{ and } 6,$$

where $C_3 = C_5 = C_6 = 2^{1-\beta} - 1$ and $C_4 = 2^{\gamma-1} - 1$.

(c) *Generalized additivity*: $E_8(P * Q) = G(P) E_8(Q) + G(Q) E_8(P)$,

where $G(P) = \sum_{k=1}^{n} \dfrac{p_k^{\alpha} + p_k^{\beta}}{2}$ and $G(Q) = \sum_{j=1}^{m} \dfrac{q_j^{\alpha} + q_j^{\beta}}{2}$.

(d) *Sub-additivity*: $E_i(P * Q) \leq E_i(P) + E_i(Q)$, $i = 3, 4, 5, 6$ and 8, for $i = 3, 5,$ and $6, \beta \geq 1$; $i = 4, \gamma \leq 1$ and for $i = 8, \alpha, \beta \geq 1$.

  (e) *Super-additivity*: $E_i(P*Q) \geqslant E_i(P) + E_i(Q)$, $i = 3, 4, 5, 6$ and 8, for $i = 3, 5$ and 6, $\beta \leqslant 1$; $i = 4$, $\gamma \geqslant 1$ and for $i = 8$, α, $\beta \leqslant 1$.

(viii) *Sum property*: For all $P \in \Delta_n$, we have

$$E_i(P) = \sum_{k=1}^{n} f_i(p_k), \quad i = 1, 3 \text{ and } 8,$$

where $f_1(p) = -p \log p$,

$$f_2(p) = (2^{1-\beta} - 1)^{-1}(p^\beta - p), \quad \beta \neq 1, \beta > 0,$$

and $f_8(p) = (2^{1-\alpha} - 2^{1-\beta})^{-1}(p^\alpha - p^\beta)$, $\alpha \neq \beta$, $\alpha, \beta > 0, 0 \leqslant p \leqslant 1$.

(ix) *Generalized recursivity*: For all $P = (p_1, p_2, \ldots, p_n) \in \Delta_n$, we have

$$E_i(p_1, p_2, \ldots, p_n) = E_i(p_1 + p_2, p_3, \ldots, p_n) + T_i(p_1, p_2), i = 1 \text{ and } 3,$$

where $T_1(p_1, p_2) = (p_1 + p_2)E_1\left(\dfrac{p_1}{p_1 + p_2}, \dfrac{p_2}{p_1 + p_2}\right),$

and $T_3(p_1, p_2) = (p_1 + p_2)^\beta E_3\left(\dfrac{p_1}{p_1 + p_2}, \dfrac{p_2}{p_1 + p_2}\right),$

with $p_1 + p_2 > 0$.

 (x) Let $h_i(p) = E_i(p, 1-p)$, $i = 1, 2, \ldots, 8$, $(p, 1-p) \in \Delta_2$, then the following holds:

  (a) $h_i(p) = h_i(1 - p)$, $i = 1, 2, \ldots, 8$.

  (b) $h_i(0) = h_i(1) = 0$, $i = 1, 2, \ldots, 8$.

  (c) $h_i(\tfrac{1}{2}) = 1$, $i = 1, 2, \ldots, 8$.

  (d) $h_i(p) + f_i(1 - p)h_i\left(\dfrac{q}{1 - p}\right) = h_i(q) + f_i(1 - q)h_i\left(\dfrac{p}{1 - q}\right),$

    $i = 1$ and 3, for all $p, q \in [0,1)$ with $p + q \leqslant 1$.

  (e) For all $P \in \Delta_n$,

$$E_i(P) = \sum_{k=2}^{n} f_i(p_k)h_i\left(\dfrac{p_k}{P_k}\right), i = 1 \text{ and } 3,$$

$$P_k = p_1 + p_2 + \ldots + p_k, k = 2, \ldots, n,$$

    where $f_1(p) = p$, $f_3(p) = p^\beta$, $0 \leqslant p \leqslant 1$.

(xi) *Strong-additivity*: For all $P = (p_1, p_2, \ldots, p_n) \in \Delta_n$, $(r_{k1}, r_{k2}, \ldots, r_{km}) \in \Delta_m$, $k = 1, 2, \ldots, n$, we have

  (a) $E_i(p_1 r_{11}, \ldots, p_1 r_{1m}, p_2 r_{21}, \ldots, p_2 r_{2m}, \ldots, p_n r_{n1}, \ldots p_n r_{nm})$

$$= E_i(p_1, p_2, \ldots, p_n) + \sum_{k=1}^{n} f_i(p_k)E_i(r_{k1}, r_{k2}, \ldots, r_{km}), i = 1 \text{ and } 3,$$

    where $f_1(p) = p$ and $f_3(p) = p^\beta$, $0 \leqslant p \leqslant 1$.

(b) Also, the following inequality holds:

$$E_i\left(\sum_{k=1}^{n} p_k r_{k1}, \sum_{k=1}^{n} p_k r_{k2}, \ldots, \sum_{k=1}^{n} p_k r_{km}\right)$$

$$\geqslant \sum_{k=1}^{n} f_i(p_k) E_i(r_{k1}, r_{k2}, \ldots, r_{km}), \; i = 1 \text{ and } 3,$$

where $f_1(p) = p$ and $f_3(p) = p^\beta$, $0 \leqslant p \leqslant 1$, $\beta > 1$.

Remark 1   Properties (ix), (x) and (xi) can also be established for $E_8(P)$, for all $P \in \Delta_n$, by using the linearity relation given in (35).

(xii) For all $P = (p_1, p_2, \ldots, p_n) \in \Delta_n$, $Q = (q_1, q_2, \ldots, q_m) \in \Delta_m$, $R = (r_{11}, r_{12}, \ldots, r_{1m}, r_{21}, \ldots, r_{2m}, \ldots, r_{n1}, \ldots, r_{nm}) \in \Delta_{nm}$, we have

(a) *Independence inequality*:

$$E_i(r_{11}, r_{12}, \ldots, r_{1m}, r_{21}, \ldots, r_{2m}, \ldots, r_{n1}, \ldots, r_{nm})$$
$$\leqslant E_i(p_1 q_1, \ldots, p_1 q_m, p_2 q_1, \ldots, p_2 q_m, \ldots, p_1 q_m, \ldots, p_n q_m),$$
$$i = 1, 2, \ldots, 8,$$

The above inequality is always true for $i = 1$ and 5. For $i = 2$, 3, 4, 6, 7 and 8 (for $i = 7$ and 8 under $0 < \alpha \leqslant 1 < \beta$ or $0 < \beta \leqslant 1 < \alpha$) it is true if any one of the following conditions is satisfied:

(c₁) the probability distribution $P \in \Delta_n$ is uniform (in particular, if $R \in \Delta_{nm}$ is uniform);
(c₂) the probability distribution $Q \in \Delta_m$ is uniform (in particular, if the conditional probability distribution $\{q_{k/j}\}$, $k = 1$, 2, ..., n (where $r_{kj} = p_k q_{k/j}$ is uniform);

or

(c₃) the matrix $\{q_{k/j}\}$ has the row-permutation property, i.e. the rows of the probability matrix $\{q_{k/j}\}$ are permutations of the same set of numbers.

Furthermore, if there exists a constant A such that $\sum_{j=1}^{m} q_{k/j}^\alpha = A$, for all $k = 1, 2, \ldots, n$, $\alpha \neq 1$, $\alpha > 0$, then the entropies $E_2(P)$ and $E_3(P)$ also satisfy the above independence inequality.

(b) *Weak-subadditivity*:

$$E_i(r_{11}, r_{12}, \ldots, r_{1m}, r_{21}, \ldots, r_{2m}, \ldots, r_{n1}, \ldots, r_{nm})$$
$$\leqslant E_i\left(\sum_{j=1}^{m} r_{1j}, \sum_{j=1}^{m} r_{2j}, \ldots, \sum_{j=1}^{m} r_{nj}\right)$$

$$+ E_i\left(\sum_{k=1}^{n} r_{k1}, \sum_{k=1}^{n} r_{k2}, \ldots, \sum_{k=1}^{n} r_{kj}\right), i = 1, 2, 3, \text{ and } 7.$$

For $i = 1$ it is always true; for $i = 3$, it is true for $\beta > 1$; and for $i = 2$ and 7 it is true under the above set of conditions (c_1), (c_2) or (c_3).

(xiii) *Limiting cases*: For all $P \in \Delta_n$, we have:

(a) $\lim\limits_{\alpha \to \infty} E_2(P) = -\log p_{max}$.

(b) $\lim\limits_{\gamma \to 0} E_4(P) = 1 - p_{max}$.

(c) $\lim\limits_{\alpha \to \infty} E_6(P) = \dfrac{(p_{max})^{\beta-1} - 1}{2^{1-\beta} - 1}$, $\beta \neq 1$, $\beta > 0$.

(d) $\lim\limits_{\alpha \to \infty} E_7(P) = \lim\limits_{\beta \to \infty} E_7(P) = -\log p_{max}$.

(xiv) *Monotonicity*: For all $P \in \Delta_n$, we have:

(a) $E_2(P)$ is a decreasing function of α.
(b) $E_6(P)$ is a decreasing function of α (β fixed).
(c) $E_7(P)$ is a decreasing function of α (β fixed) and is a decreasing function of β (α fixed).

(xv) *Inequalities among the entropies:*

(a) $E_6(P) \leq E_5(P)$, $\alpha > 1$, $\beta > 0$;
    $ \geq E_5(P)$, $\alpha < 1$, $\beta > 0$.
(b) $E_5(P) \leq E_1(P)$, $\beta > 1$, $E_1(P) \geq 1$;
    $ \geq E_1(P)$, $\beta < 1$, $E_1(P) \leq 1$.
(c) $E_6(P) \leq E_2(P)$, $\beta > 1$, $\alpha > 0$, $E_2(P) \geq 1$;
    $ \geq E_2(P)$, $\beta < 1$, $\alpha > 0$, $E_2(P) \leq 1$.
(d) $E_2(P) \leq E_1(P)$, $\alpha > 1$;
    $ \geq E_1(P)$, $\alpha < 1$.
(e) $E_6(P) \leq E_3(P)$, $\alpha \geq \beta$;
    $ \geq E_3(P)$, $\alpha \leq \beta$.
(f) $E_6(P) \leq E_4(P)$, $\beta \geq 2 - \frac{1}{\alpha}$;
    $ \geq E_4(P)$, $\beta \leq 2 - \frac{1}{\alpha}$.
(g) $E_2^{\alpha}(P) \leq E_7(P) \leq E_2^{\beta}(P)$, $0 < \beta \leq 1 < \alpha$.
(h) $E_3^{\alpha}(P) \leq E_8(P) \leq E_3^{\beta}(P)$, $0 < \beta \leq 1 < \alpha$.

(xvi) *Concavity*: For all $P \in \Delta_n$, we have

(a) $E_1(P)$ is a concave function of P.
(b) $E_2(P)$ is a concave function of P for $0 < \alpha < 1$.
(c) $E_3(P)$ is a concave function of P for $\beta > 0$.
(d) $E_4(P)$ is a concave function of P for $\gamma > 0$.
(e) $E_5(P)$ is a concave function of P for $\beta > 1$.
(f) $E_6(P)$ is a concave function of P for $\alpha > 0$, $\beta \geqslant 2 - \frac{1}{\alpha}$.
(g) $E_8(P)$ is a concave function of P for $0 < \alpha \leqslant 1 < \beta (0 < \beta \leqslant 1 < \alpha)$.
(h) For all $P = (p, 1 - p) \in \Delta_2$, $E_2(P)$ is a concave function of P for $0 < \alpha \leqslant 2$.
(i) For all $P = (p, 1 - p) \in \Delta_2$, $E_7(P)$ is a concave function of P for $0 < \alpha \leqslant 1 < \beta \leqslant 2$ (or $0 < \beta \leqslant 1 < \alpha \leqslant 2$).

Remark 3   All the results given below are true for $E_7(P)$ and $E_8(P)$, when $0 < \alpha \leqslant 1 < \beta$ (or $0 < \beta \leqslant 1 < \alpha$).

(xvii) *Pseudoconcavity*:

Definition 1   A numerical function θ on a convex set $\Gamma \in \mathbb{R}^n$ is pseudo-concave on Γ if for all $x^1, x^2 \in \Gamma$,

$$\nabla \theta(x^1)(x^2 - x^1) \leqslant 0 \quad \text{implies} \quad \theta(x^2) \leqslant \theta(x^1).$$

For all $P \in \Delta_n$, $E_i(P)$, $i = 1, 2, \ldots, 8$ are pseudoconcave functions of P.

(xviii) *Schur-concavity*:

Definition 2   For all $P, Q \in \Delta_n$, we say that P is majorized by Q, i.e. $P \underset{m}{\prec} Q$ if

(a) $p_1 \geqslant p_2 \geqslant \ldots \geqslant p_n, q_1 \geqslant q_2 \geqslant \ldots \geqslant q_n$, with

$$\sum_{k=1}^{m} p_k \leqslant \sum_{k=1}^{m} q_k, 1 \leqslant m \leqslant n,$$

or

(b) there is a double stochastic matrix $\{a_{kj}\}$, $a_{kj} \geqslant 0$, $k, j = 1, 2, \ldots, n$, with $\sum_{k=1}^{n} a_{kj} = \sum_{j=1}^{n} a_{kj} = 1$ such that $p_k = \sum_{j=1}^{n} a_{kj} q_j$, $k = 1, 2, \ldots, n$.

Definition 3   A function $G: \Delta_n \rightarrow \mathbb{R}$ is Schur-concave on Δ_n if $P \underset{m}{\prec} Q$ on Δ_n implies $G(P) \geqslant G(Q)$.
For all $P \in \Delta_n$, $E_i(P)$, $i = 1, 2, \ldots, 8$ are Schur-concave, i.e. if $P \prec Q$ then $E_i(P) \geqslant E_i(Q)$, $i = 1, 2, \ldots, 8$.

(xix) *Maximality*: $E_i(P)$, $i = 1, 2, \ldots, 8$ attain their maximum when the distribution is uniform, i.e.

$$E_i(P) \leq E_i\left(\frac{1}{n}, \frac{1}{n}, \ldots, \frac{1}{n}\right) = \phi_i(n), \quad i = 1, 2, \ldots, 8.$$

Consequently,

$$\phi_i(P) \leq \phi_i(n + 1), \quad i = 1, 2, \ldots, 8,$$

i.e. $\phi_i(i = 1, 2, \ldots, 8)$ are increasing functions of n.

(xx) *Generalized Shannon inequalities*: For all $P, Q \in \Delta_n$, we have

(a) $E_i(P) \leq E_i(P\|Q)$,
(b) $E_i(P) \leq E_i'(P\|Q)$,

where

$$E_1(P\|Q) = E_1'(P\|Q) = -\sum_{k=1}^{n} p_k \log q_k;$$

$$E_2(P\|Q) = \frac{1}{1 - \alpha} \log \left(\frac{\sum_{k=1}^{n} p_k^\alpha}{\sum_{k=1}^{n} p_k^\alpha q_k^{1-\alpha}} \right),$$

$$E_2'(P\|Q) = \frac{\alpha}{1 - \alpha} \log \left(\sum_{k=1}^{n} p_k \, q_k^{\frac{\alpha-1}{\alpha}} \right), \quad \alpha \neq 1, \alpha > 0;$$

$$E_3(P\|Q) = (2^{1-\beta} - 1)^{-1} \left\{ \frac{\sum_{k=1}^{n} p_k^\beta}{\sum_{k=1}^{n} p_k^\beta q_k^{1-\beta}} - 1 \right\},$$

$$E_3'(P\|Q) = (2^{1-\beta} - 1)^{-1} \left[\sum_{k=1}^{n} p_k q_k^{\frac{\beta-1}{\beta}} - 1 \right], \quad \beta \neq 1, \beta > 0;$$

$$E_4(P\|Q) = (2^{\gamma-1} - 1)^{-1} \left\{ \left(\frac{\sum_{k=1}^{n} p_k^{\frac{1}{\gamma}}}{\sum_{k=1}^{n} p_k^{\frac{1}{\gamma}} q_k^{1-\frac{1}{\gamma}}} \right)^\gamma - 1 \right\},$$

$$E_4'(P\|Q) = (2^{\gamma-1} - 1)^{-1}\left[\sum_{k=1}^{n} p_k q_k^{1-\gamma} - 1\right], \ \gamma \neq 1, \ \gamma > 0;$$

$$E_5(P\|Q) = E_5'(P\|Q) = (2^{1-\beta} - 1)^{-1}\left[2^{(\beta-1)\sum\limits_{k=1}^{n} p_k \log q_k} - 1\right],$$

$$\beta \neq 1, \ \beta > 0;$$

$$E_6(P\|Q) = (2^{1-\beta} - 1)^{-1}\left\{\left(\frac{\sum\limits_{k=1}^{n} p_k^{\alpha}}{\sum\limits_{k=1}^{n} p_k^{\alpha} q_k^{1-\alpha}}\right)^{\frac{\beta-1}{\alpha-1}} - 1\right\},$$

$$E_6'(P\|Q) = (2^{1-\beta} - 1)^{-1}\left\{\left(\sum_{k=1}^{n} p_k q_k^{\frac{\alpha-1}{\alpha}}\right)^{\alpha\frac{\beta-1}{\alpha-1}} - 1\right\},$$

$$\alpha \neq 1, \ \beta \neq 1, \ \alpha, \ \beta > 0;$$

$$E_7(P\|Q) = (\beta - \alpha)^{-1}\log\left\{\frac{\left(\sum\limits_{k=1}^{n} p_k^{\alpha}\right)\left(\sum\limits_{k=1}^{n} p_k^{\beta} q_k^{1-\beta}\right)}{\left(\sum\limits_{k=1}^{n} p_k^{\beta}\right)\left(\sum\limits_{k=1}^{n} p_k^{\alpha} q_k^{1-\alpha}\right)}\right\},$$

$$E_7'(P\|Q) = (\beta - \alpha)^{-1}\log\left\{\left(\sum_{k=1}^{n} p_k q_k^{\frac{\alpha-1}{\alpha}}\right)^{\alpha}\bigg/\left(\sum_{k=1}^{n} p_k q_k^{\frac{\beta-1}{\beta}}\right)^{\beta}\right\},$$

$$\alpha \neq \beta, \ \alpha, \ \beta > 0;$$

$$E_8(P\|Q) = (2^{1-\alpha} - 2^{1-\beta})^{-1}\left\{\frac{\sum\limits_{k=1}^{n} p_k^{\alpha}}{\sum\limits_{k=1}^{n} p_k^{\alpha} q_k^{1-\alpha}} - \frac{\sum\limits_{k=1}^{n} p_k^{\beta}}{\sum\limits_{k=1}^{n} p_k^{\beta} q_k^{1-\beta}}\right\},$$

$$E_8'(P\|Q) = (2^{1-\alpha} - 2^{1-\beta})^{-1}\left\{\left(\sum_{k=1}^{n} p_k q_k^{\frac{\alpha-1}{\alpha}}\right)^{\alpha} - \left(\sum_{k=1}^{n} p_k q_k^{\frac{\beta-1}{\beta}}\right)^{\beta}\right\},$$

$$\alpha \neq \beta, \ \alpha, \ \beta > 0;$$

Equality sign in (a) holds iff $p_k = q_k$, $k = 1, 2, \ldots, n$. Equality sign in (b) holds iff $p_k = q_k$, $k = 1, 2, \ldots, n$ for $i = 1$ and 5; $q_k = p_k^{\alpha}\bigg/\sum\limits_{k=1}^{n} p_k^{\alpha}$ for $i = 2$ and 6; $q_k = p_k^{\alpha}\bigg/\sum\limits_{k=1}^{n} p_k^{\alpha}$ for $i = 3$ and $q_k = p_k^{1/\gamma}\bigg/\sum\limits_{k=1}^{n} p_k^{1/\gamma}$ for $i = 4$.

(xxi) *Generalized Fano-type inequalities*: Let $P \in \Delta_n$ with $q_m = 1 -$

$\sum_{k=1}^{m} p_k$, $1 \leqslant m \leqslant n$. Take

$$Q = \left(p_1, p_2, \ldots, p_m, \frac{q_m}{n-m}, \ldots, \frac{q_m}{n-m}\right) \in \Delta_n, \text{ then}$$

(a) $E_i(P) \leqslant E_i(Q)$,

(b) $E_i(q_m, 1 - q_m) \leqslant E_i(P)$, $i = 1, 2, \ldots, 8$.

In particular the following hold:

(c) $E_i(P) \leqslant E_i\left(\dfrac{1 - p_{max}}{n-1}, \dfrac{1 - p_{max}}{n-1}, \ldots, \dfrac{1 - p_{max}}{n-1}, p_{max}\right)$;

(d) $E_i(1 - p_{max}, p_{max}) \leqslant E_i(P)$, $i = 1, 2, \ldots, 8$.

(xxii) For all $P \in \Delta_n$, we have

$$1 - p_{max} \leqslant \tfrac{1}{2} E_i(P), \quad i = 1, 2, \ldots, 8$$

under the following conditions:

(a) for $i = 1$ it is true when $p_{max} > \tfrac{1}{2}$;

(b) for $i = 2$ it is true either for $\alpha \neq 1$, $\alpha > 0$, $\tfrac{1}{n} p_{max} \leqslant \tfrac{1}{2}$ or for $\alpha \neq 1$, $0 < \alpha \leqslant 2$, $p_{max} > \tfrac{1}{2}$;

(c) for $i = 3$ it is true for $\beta \neq 1$, $\beta > 0$, $p_{max} > \tfrac{1}{2}$;

(d) for $i = 4$ it is true for $\gamma \neq 1$, $\gamma > 0$, $p_{max} > \tfrac{1}{2}$;

(e) for $i = 5$ it is true either for $\beta > 1$, $\tfrac{1}{n} < p_{max} \leqslant \tfrac{1}{2}$ or for $0 < \beta < 1$, $p_{max} > \tfrac{1}{2}$;

(f) for $i = 6$ it is true either for $\alpha \neq 1$, $\alpha > 0$, $\beta \neq 1$, $0 < \beta \leqslant 2$, $p_{max} > \tfrac{1}{2}$ or for any one of the conditions: $\alpha > 0$, $\beta \geqslant 2$; $\alpha > 0$, $\beta \geqslant 2 - \tfrac{1}{\alpha}$; $0 < \alpha \leqslant 2$, $\beta > 1$ with $p_{max} \leqslant \tfrac{1}{2}$, $\alpha \neq 1$, $\beta \neq 1$;

(g) for $i = 7$ it is true either for α, $\beta > 0$, $\tfrac{1}{n} < p_{max} \leqslant \tfrac{1}{2}$ or for $0 < \alpha \leqslant 1 < \beta \leqslant 2$, $p_{max} > \tfrac{1}{2}$ with $\alpha \neq 1$, $\beta \neq 1$;

(h) for $i = 8$ it is true for all α, β satisfying $0 < \alpha \leqslant 1 < \beta$, $p_{max} > \tfrac{1}{2}$.

Remark 3 (i) Properties (xxi) (b) and (d) are not Fano-type inequalities but they are being added together simply to unify the results; (ii) Property (xxii) is discussed in more detail in Section 4.1.

4 Applications to statistical pattern recognition

In statistical pattern recognition the key problem is feature selection. Usually the performance of a recognition system is expressed in terms of the probability of error or misclassification. The aim of feature selection is to reduce the number of features without adversely affecting error performance. The feature selection problem can be viewed as the selection of the set of features which minimizes the probability of error, P_e. The computation of P_e unfortunately is usually very difficult, involving as it does, the determination of the decision regions and integration of the appropriate class-conditional densities over multi-dimensional spaces. We are therefore led to seek an auxiliary criterion for determining the relative importance of the features and use that in the selection process. However, unless we know the connection between the auxiliary criterion and the error probability, the use of a feature set chosen according to this criterion instead of any other, cannot be justified. We are thus led to the choice of an auxiliary criterion which provides a measure of the separability or distance between classes and which has a direct relationship with the probability of error. A variety of such measures have been proposed in the literature, and bounds relating P_e to the various distance and information measures can be found in Kanal (1974) and Chen (1976). The classification problem is stated as follows.

Suppose we have n pattern classes $C = \{C_1, C_2, \ldots, C_n\}$ with 'a priori' probability $p_k = \Pr\{C = C_k\}$, $k = 1, 2, \ldots, n$. Let the feature x on X have a class-conditional probability density function $P(x/C_k)$, $k = 1, 2, \ldots, n$. We assume that p_k and $P(x/C_k)$ are known. Given a feature x on X, we can calculate the conditional (*a posteriori*) probability $P(C_k/x)$ for each k, by the Bayes rule:

$$P(C_k/x) = \Pr\{C = C_k/X = x\} = \frac{p_k\, P(x/C_k)}{\displaystyle\sum_{j=1}^{n} p_j P(x/C_j)}, \quad k = 1, 2, \ldots, n.$$

It is well known that the decision rule which minimizes the probability of error is the Bayes decision rule which chooses the hypotheses (pattern classes) with the largest posterior probability. Using this rule, the partial probability of error for given $X = x$ is expressed by

$$P(e/x) = 1 - \max\{P(C_1/x),\ P(C_2/x),\ \ldots,\ P(C_n/x)\}.$$

Prior to observing X, the probability of error P_e, associated with X is defined as the expected probability of error, i.e.

$$P_e = E_X\{P(e/x)\} = \int_x P(e/x)\, p(x)\, \mathrm{d}x,$$

where $p(x) = \displaystyle\sum_{k=1}^{n} p_k\, P(x/C_k)$ is the unconditional density of X evaluated at x.

In recent years researchers have paid attention to the problem of bounding this probability of error for the multiple class problem taking into consideration such information measures as the Shannon entropy, quadratic entropy, cubic entropy, entropy of order α, entropy of degree β, entropy of order α and degree β. Our aim here is to give briefly the bounds on the probability of error in terms of generalized entropies. Divergence and distance measures arising from these entropies are also considered in obtaining error bounds. Some other bounds based on divergence measures can be found in Kailath (1967), Kanal (1974), Chen (1976) and Boekee and van der Lubbe (1979).

4.1 Generalized entropies and error bounds

This section deals with the bounds on the probability of error in terms of the generalized entropies studied in previous sections. These bounds have been presented in three different approaches. These approaches are mainly for upper bounds on the probability of error. Analogues to the Fano-type bounds are also presented.

4.1.1 *First approach*
Kovalevski (1968) gave a pointwise upper bound for P_e in terms of the parameter t, and a Fano bound taking the Shannon entropy into consideration. Based on Kovalevski's idea, Ben-Bassat (1978) extended his results to the general class of functions satisfying the sum property, defined by

$$T(f) = \left\{ F(P)/F: \Delta_n \to \mathbb{R}, n \geqslant 2, F(P) = \sum_{k=1}^{n} f(p_k), f \text{ is strictly} \right.$$
$$\left. \text{concave}, f'' \text{ exists}, f(0) = \lim_{p \to 0} f(p) = 0 \right\}. \tag{43}$$

The bounds are given by

$$F(P) \geqslant tf\left(\frac{1}{t}\right) + t(t+1)\left[(t+1)f\left(\frac{1}{t+1}\right) - tf\left(\frac{1}{t}\right)\right]\left[P_e - \frac{t-1}{t}\right], \tag{44}$$

and by

$$F(P) \leqslant f(1 - P_e) + (n-1)f\left(\frac{P_e}{n-1}\right), \tag{45}$$

where t is an integer such that

$$\frac{t-1}{t} \leqslant p_e \leqslant \frac{t}{t+1},$$

and

$$P_e = 1 - \max\{p_1, p_2, \ldots, p_n\}.$$

For $t = 1$, $0 < P_e \leqslant \frac{1}{2}$, we have from (44)

$$P_e \leqslant \tfrac{1}{2}F(P). \tag{46}$$

Substituting $P(C/x)$ for P in (45) and (46) and taking expectation on both sides with respect to x, we get

$$F(C/X) \leqslant f(1 - P_e) + (n - 1)f\left(\frac{P_e}{n - 1}\right), \tag{47}$$

and

$$P_e \leqslant \tfrac{1}{2}F(C/X). \tag{48}$$

The particular cases of (47) and (48) considered by Ben-Bassat (1978) are the Shannon entropy, the quadratic entropy, the entropy of degree β. Taneja (1983) extended them to α-log entropy, sine entropy and the entropy of degree (α,β). Recently, Sant'anna and Taneja (1985) extended these for the trigonometric entropies. These bounds are as follows.

Example 1 (*Shannon entropy*).   When $f(p) = -p \log p$, we have

$$H(C/X) \leqslant -P_e \log P_e - (1 - P_e) \log (1 - P_e) + P_e \log (n - 1), \tag{49}$$

and

$$P_e \leqslant \tfrac{1}{2}H(C/X), \quad 0 < P_e \leqslant \tfrac{1}{2}, \tag{50}$$

where

$$H(C/X) = \int_X \left(\sum_{k=1}^{n} P(C_k/x) \log P(C_k/x) \right\} p(x) \, dx.$$

The bound (49) is the well-known Fano bound. The upper bound (50) has been studied by Hellman and Raviv (1970) by using the branching property and by Chu and Chueh (1966) by using the Shannon inequality.

Example 2 (*Quadratic entropy*).   When $f(p) = p(1 - p)$, we have

$$P_e \leqslant \frac{n - 1}{n}\left\{1 - \sqrt{\left[1 - \frac{nh_2(C/X)}{n - 1}\right]}\right\},$$

and

$$P_e \leqslant h_2(C/X),$$

where

$$h_2(C/X) = \int_X \left\{ \sum_{k=1}^{n} P(C_k/x)[1 - P(C_k/x)] \right\} p(x) \, dx.$$

Example 3 (*Cubic entropy*). When $f(p) = p - p^3$, we have

$$h_3(C/X) \leqslant (1 - P_e)^3 + (n - 1) \left(\frac{P_e}{n-1} \right)^3 - 1,$$

and

$$P_e \leqslant \tfrac{1}{2} h_3(C/X), \quad 0 < P_e \leqslant \tfrac{1}{2},$$

where

$$h_3(C/X) = 1 - \int_X \left\{ \sum_{k=1}^{n} P(C_k/x)^3 \right\} p(x) \, \mathrm{d}x.$$

Example 4 (*Entropy of degree* β). When $f(p) = (2^{1-\beta} - 1)^{-1} (p^\beta - p)$, $\beta \neq 1, \beta > 0$, we have

$$H^\beta (C/X) \leqslant (2^{1-\beta} - 1)^{-1} \left\{ (1 - P_e)^\beta + (n - 1) \left(\frac{P_e}{n-1} \right)^\beta - 1 \right\},$$

and

$$P_e \leqslant \tfrac{1}{2} H^\beta(C/X), \quad 0 < P_e \leqslant \tfrac{1}{2},$$

where

$$H^\beta (C/X) = (2^{1-\beta} - 1)^{-1} \int_X \left\{ \sum_{k=1}^{n} P(C_k/x)^\beta - 1 \right\} p(x) \, \mathrm{d}x.$$

Example 5 (*α-log entropy*). When $f(p) = -2^{\alpha-1} p^\alpha \log p, \frac{1}{2} \leqslant \alpha \leqslant 1$, we have

$$H_\ell^\alpha(C/X) \leqslant -2^{\alpha-1} \left\{ (1-P_e)^\alpha \cdot \log (1-P_e) + (n-1)^{1-\alpha} P_e^\alpha \log \left(\frac{P_e}{n-1} \right) \right\},$$

and

$$P_e \leqslant \tfrac{1}{2} H_\ell^\alpha (C/X), \quad 0 < P_e \leqslant \tfrac{1}{2},$$

where

$$H_\ell^\alpha(C/X) = -2^{\alpha-1} \int_X \left\{ \sum_{k=1}^{n} P(C_k/x)^\alpha \log P(C_k/x) \right\} p(x) \, \mathrm{d}x.$$

Example 6 (*Entropy of degree* (α,β)). When $f(p) = (2^{1-\alpha} - 2^{1-\beta})^{-1} (p - p^\beta), 0 < \alpha \leqslant 1 < \beta \ (0 < \beta \leqslant 1 < \alpha)$, we have

$$H^{\alpha,\beta}(C/X) \leqslant (2^{1-\alpha} - 2^{1-\beta})^{-1} \left\{ (1 - P_e)^\alpha - (1 - P_e)^\beta \right.$$

$$+ (n - 1) \left[\left(\frac{P_e}{n - 1} \right)^\alpha - \left(\frac{P_e}{n - 1} \right)^\beta \right] \Big\} ,$$

and

$$P_e \leq \tfrac{1}{2} H^{\alpha, \beta} (C/X), \quad 0 < P_e \leq \tfrac{1}{2},$$

where

$$H^{\alpha, \beta}(C/X) = (2^{1-\alpha} - 2^{1-\beta})^{-1} \int_X \left\{ \sum_{k=1}^n [P(C_k/x)^\alpha \right. $$
$$\left. - P(C_k/x)^\beta] \right\} p(x) \, dx.$$

Example 7 (*Hypoentropy*).   When $f(W) = -W \log \left(\dfrac{(n + \lambda) W^{1 + \frac{n}{\lambda}}}{\left(1 + \frac{1}{\lambda} \right)^{1 + \frac{1}{\lambda}}} \right) ,$

where $W = \dfrac{1 + \lambda p}{n + \lambda}$, $\lambda > 0$, we have

$$H_\lambda(C/X) \leq \left(1 + \frac{1}{\lambda} \right) \log \left(1 + \frac{1}{\lambda} \right)$$
$$- \frac{1}{\lambda} [1 + \lambda(1 - P_e)] \log [1 + \lambda(1 - P_e)]$$
$$- (n - 1) \left[(1 + \lambda \left(\frac{P_e}{n - 1} \right) \right] \log \left[1 + \lambda \left(\frac{P_e}{n - 1} \right) \right] ,$$

and

$$P_e \leq \frac{(n + \lambda) H_\lambda(C/X) - 2}{2},$$

where

$$H_\lambda(C/X) = \left(1 + \frac{1}{\lambda} \right) \log \left(1 + \frac{1}{\lambda} \right)$$
$$- \frac{1}{\lambda} \int_X \left\{ \sum_{k=1}^n [1 + \lambda P(C_k/x)] \log [1 + \lambda P(C_k/x)] \right\} p(x) \, dx.$$

Example 8 (*Weighted entropy*).   When $f(p) = -pu \log p$, we have

$$H(C/X; U) \leq -(1 - P_e) u_{p_{\max}} \cdot \log (1 - P_e)$$
$$- u_{p_{\max}} \cdot P_e \log \left(\frac{P_e}{n - 1} \right) ,$$

and

$$P_e \leq \tfrac{1}{2} H(C/X;\, U), \quad 0 < P_e \leq \tfrac{1}{2},$$

where

$$H(C/X;\, U) = - \int_X \left\{ \sum_{k=1}^{n} P(C_k/x)u_k \, \log \, P(C_k/x) \right\} p(x) \, dx.$$

Example 9 (*Weighted entropy of degree* β). When $f(p) = (2^{1-\beta} - 1)^{-1}$ $(p^\beta - p)u$, $\beta \neq 1$, $\beta > 0$, we have

$$H^\beta(C/X;\, U) \leq (2^{1-\beta} - 1)^{-1} \left\{ (1 - P_e)^\beta \, u_{p_{\max}} \right.$$

$$\left. + (n - 1)\left(\frac{P_e}{n - 1}\right)^\beta u_{p_{\max}} - 1 \right\},$$

and

$$P_e \leq \tfrac{1}{2} H^\beta(C/X;\, U), \quad 0 < P_e \leq \tfrac{1}{2},$$

where

$$H^\beta(C/X;\, U) = (2^{1-\beta} - 1)^{-1} \int_X \left\{ \sum_{k=1}^{n} [P(C_k/x)^\beta \right.$$

$$\left. - P(C_k/x)]u_k \right\} p(x) \, dx.$$

In Examples 8 and 9, $u_{p_{\max}}$ is the weight associated with $p_{\max}$.

Trigonometric entropies

Example 10 When $f(p) = -\dfrac{2^{\alpha-1}}{\sin \beta} p^\alpha \, \sin\,(\beta \, \log \, p)$, $\beta \in (0,\pi)$, $\beta \, \log \, p$ $\in (-\pi, -\pi/2)$, $0 < \alpha \leq \tfrac{1}{2}$ and $\beta \, \log \, p \in (-\pi/2, 0)$, $\alpha > \tfrac{1}{2}$, we have

$$S_1^\beta(C/X) \leq -\frac{2^{\alpha-1}}{\sin \beta} \left\{ (1 - P_e)^\alpha \, \sin \, [\beta \, \log \, (1 - P_e)] \right.$$

$$\left. + (n - 1)^{1-\alpha} P_e^\alpha \, \sin \left[\beta \, \log \left(\frac{P_e}{n - 1} \right) \right] \right\},$$

and

$$P_e \leq \tfrac{1}{2} S_1^\beta(C/X), \quad 0 < P_e \leq \tfrac{1}{2},$$

where

$$S_1^\beta(C/X) = -\frac{2^{\alpha-1}}{\sin \beta} \int_X \left\{ \sum_{k=1}^{n} P(C_k/x)^\alpha \, \sin \, [\beta \, \log \, P(C_k/x)] \right\} p(x) \, dx.$$

Example 11   When $f(p) = -p \log \left(\dfrac{\sin \beta p}{2 \sin \dfrac{\beta}{2}} \right)$, $0 < \beta \leq \dfrac{\pi}{4}$, we have

$$S_2^{\beta}(C/X) \leq -(1 - P_e) \log \left(\frac{\sin \beta(1 - P_e)}{2 \sin \dfrac{\beta}{2}} \right) - P_e \log \left(\frac{\sin \beta \left(\dfrac{P_e}{n - 1} \right)}{2 \sin \dfrac{\beta}{2}} \right),$$

and

$$P_e \leq \tfrac{1}{2} S_2^{\beta}(C/X), \quad 0 < P_e \leq \tfrac{1}{2},$$

where

$$S_2^{\beta}(C/X) = -\int_X \left\{ \sum_{k=1}^{n} P(C_k/x) \log \left(\frac{\sin \beta P(C_k/x)}{2 \sin \dfrac{\beta}{2}} \right) \right\} p(x) \, dx.$$

Example 12   When $f(p) = -\left(\dfrac{\sin \beta p}{2 \sin \dfrac{\beta}{2}} \right) \log \left(\dfrac{\sin \beta p}{2 \sin \dfrac{\beta}{2}} \right)$, $0 < \beta \leq \dfrac{\pi}{4}$,

we have

$$S_3^{\beta}(C/X) \leq -\left(\frac{\sin \beta(1 - P_e)}{2 \sin \dfrac{\beta}{2}} \right) \log \left(\frac{\sin \beta(1 - P_e)}{2 \sin \dfrac{\beta}{2}} \right)$$

$$- (n - 1) \left(\frac{\sin \beta \left(\dfrac{P_e}{n - 1} \right)}{2 \sin \dfrac{\beta}{2}} \right) \log \left(\frac{\sin \beta \left(\dfrac{P_e}{n - 1} \right)}{2 \sin \dfrac{\beta}{2}} \right),$$

and

$$P_e \leq \tfrac{1}{2} S_3^{\beta}(C/X), \quad 0 < P_e \leq \tfrac{1}{2},$$

where

$$S_3^{\beta}(C/X) = -\int_X \left\{ \sum_{k=1}^{n} \left(\frac{\sin \beta P(C_k/x)}{2 \sin \dfrac{\beta}{2}} \right) \log \left(\frac{\sin \beta P(C_k/x)}{2 \sin \dfrac{\beta}{2}} \right) \right\} p(x) \, dx.$$

Example 13   When $f(p) = \dfrac{\sin \beta p}{2 \sin \dfrac{\beta}{2}}$, $0 < \beta \leq \pi$,

we have

$$S_4^\beta(C/X) \leqslant \left(2 \sin \frac{\beta}{2}\right)^{-1} \left\{\sin \beta(1 - P_e) + (n - 1) \sin \beta\left(\frac{P_e}{n - 1}\right)\right\},$$

and

$$P_e \leqslant \tfrac{1}{2} S_4^\beta(C/X), \quad 0 < P_e \leqslant \tfrac{1}{2},$$

where

$$S_4^\beta(C/X) = \left(2 \sin \frac{\beta}{2}\right)^{-1} \int_X \left\{\sum_{k=1}^{n} \sin \beta P(C_k/x)\right\} p(x)\, dx.$$

4.1.2 *Second approach*

In this part we shall provide an alternative approach to get an upper bound on the probability of error. Most of the examples considered in the first approach will also be met here. But this approach extends the results specially for those entropies which do not satisfy the sum property.

Theorem 4 Let $E_n: \Delta_n \to \mathbb{R}$ (reals) be a continuous function satisfying

(i) $E(p, 1-p)$, $0 \leqslant p \leqslant 1$ is a continuous function of p;
(ii) $E(0,1) = E(1,0) = 0$; $E(\tfrac{1}{2}, \tfrac{1}{2}) = 1$;
(iii) $E(1-p_{max}, p_{max}) \leqslant E(P)$.

Then

$$1 - p_{max} \leqslant \tfrac{1}{2} E(P), \quad p_{max} \geqslant \tfrac{1}{2}, \tag{51}$$

for all $P = (p_1, p_2, \ldots, p_n) \in \Delta_n$, where $p_{max} = \max\{p_1, p_2, \ldots, p_n\}$.

Proof Since the graph of $1 - \max\{p, 1-p\}$, $0 \leqslant p \leqslant 1$ contains two straight lines between $(0,0)$ and $(\tfrac{1}{2}, \tfrac{1}{2})$ and between $(\tfrac{1}{2}, \tfrac{1}{2})$ and $(0,0)$, using (i) and (ii) it is easy to conclude that

$$1 - p_{max} \leqslant \tfrac{1}{2} E(1-p_{max}, p_{max}), p_{max} \geqslant \tfrac{1}{2}. \tag{52}$$

Substituting $P(C/x)$ for P in (51) and then taking expectation on both sides with respect to $p(x)$ we get the upper bound

$$P_e \leqslant \tfrac{1}{2} E(C/X) = \tfrac{1}{2} E_X\{E(C/X = x)\}. \tag{53}$$

Examples 1 to 6 work as examples of (53), too. Now we present a few more cases covering more entropies which do not satisfy the sum property.

Example 14 (*Entropy of order α*).   When $E(P) = H_\alpha(P)$, $0 < \alpha \leqslant 2$, $\alpha \neq 1$, we have

$$P_e \leqslant \tfrac{1}{2} H_\alpha(C/X), \quad 0 < P_e \leqslant \tfrac{1}{2},$$

where

$$H_\alpha(C/X) = (\alpha - 1)^{-1} \cdot \int_X \log \left(\sum_{k=1}^{n} p(C_i/x)^\alpha \right) \cdot p(x)\, \mathrm{d}x.$$

Example 15 (*γ-Entropy*).   When $E(P) = {}_\gamma H(P)$, $\gamma \neq 1$, $\gamma > 0$, we have

$$P_e \leqslant \tfrac{1}{2}\, {}_\gamma H(C/X), \quad 0 < P_e \leqslant \tfrac{1}{2},$$

where

$${}_\gamma H(C/X) = (2^{\gamma-1} - 1)^{-1} \int_X \left\{ \left(\sum_{k=1}^{n} P(C_k/x)^{\frac{1}{\gamma}} \right)^\gamma - 1 \right\} p(x)\, \mathrm{d}x.$$

Example 16 (*Entropy of order 1 and degree β*).   When $E(P) = H_1^\beta(P)$, $\beta > 1$, we have

$$P_e \leqslant \tfrac{1}{2} H_1^\beta(C/X), \quad 0 < P_e \leqslant \tfrac{1}{2},$$

where

$$H_1^\beta(C/X) = (2^{1-\beta} - 1)^{-1} \int_X \left\{ 2^{(\beta-1) \sum_{k=1}^{n} P(C_k/x) \log P(C_k/x)} - 1 \right\} p(x)\, \mathrm{d}x.$$

Example 17 (*Entropy of order α and degree β*).   When $E(P) = H_\alpha^\beta(P)$, $\alpha > 0$, $\beta \geqslant 2 - \dfrac{1}{\alpha}$ or $0 < \alpha \leqslant 2$, $\beta > 1$ with $\alpha \neq 1$, we have

$$P_e \leqslant \tfrac{1}{2} H_\alpha^\beta(C/X), \quad 0 < P_e \leqslant \tfrac{1}{2},$$

where

$$H_\alpha^\beta(C/X) = (2^{1-\beta} - 1)^{-1} \int_X \left\{ \left(\sum_{k=1}^{n} P(C_k/x)^\alpha \right)^{\frac{\beta-1}{\alpha-1}} - 1 \right\} p(x)\, \mathrm{d}x.$$

Example 18 (*Entropy of type (α,β)*).   When $E(P) = H_{\alpha,\beta}(P)$, $0 < \alpha \leqslant 1 < \beta \leqslant 2$ (or $0 < \beta \leqslant 1 < \alpha \leqslant 2$) we have

$$P_e \leqslant \tfrac{1}{2} H_{\alpha,\beta}(C/X), \quad 0 < P_e \leqslant \tfrac{1}{2},$$

where

$$H_{\alpha,\beta}(C/X) = (\beta - \alpha)^{-1} \int_X \log \left(\frac{\sum_{k=1}^{n} P(C_k/x)^\alpha}{\sum_{k=1}^{n} P(C_k/x)^\beta} \right) \cdot p(x)\, \mathrm{d}x.$$

4.1.3 *Third approach*

We can observe from Examples 14 and 17 that the bounds are valid only for $0 < \alpha \le 2$ and $\alpha > 0$, $\beta \ge 2 - \frac{1}{\alpha}$ (or $0 < \alpha \le 2$, $\beta > 1$) respectively. Now we extend the validity of these bounds for other values of the parameters. This we have done in two different ways by using the approach of Ben-Bassat and Raviv (1978). This approach is a little isolated and based on the monotonicity of the entropies with respect to the parameters. It is divided into two parts. Part (a) is due to Ben-Bassat and Raviv (1978) and part (b) to Taneja (1985).

(a) Consider the function

$$f(p) = 1 - p + \tfrac{1}{2} \log_2 p \quad 0 < p \le 1.$$

Then

$$f'(p) = -1 + \frac{1}{2 \ln 2} \frac{1}{p},$$

and

$$f''(p) = -\frac{1}{2 \ln 2} \frac{1}{p^2}.$$

Since $f''(p) < 0$ for all p, $f(p)$ is a strictly concave function attaining its single maximum at $p = 1/(2 \ln 2) \cong 0.72$. A direct computation shows that $f(p) = 0$ at $p = \frac{1}{2}$ and $p = 1$. Because of the concavity, these are the only zeros of $f(p)$. As p approaches 0, $f(p)$ approaches $-\infty$. Therefore

$$1 - p \le -\frac{1}{2} \log_2 p \quad \text{for} \quad \frac{1}{n} < p \le \frac{1}{2}. \tag{54}$$

Let us consider the following three examples.

Example 14' (*Entropy of order α*). We know that $\lim\limits_{\alpha \to \infty} H_\alpha(P) = -\log_2 p_{max}$, and that $H_\alpha(P)$ is a decreasing function of α. Hence

$$1 - p_{max} \le \frac{1}{2} H_\alpha(P), \quad \frac{1}{n} < p_{max} \le \frac{1}{2},$$

which lead to the following upper bound:

$$P_e \le \tfrac{1}{2} H_\alpha(C/X), \quad P_e \ge \tfrac{1}{2}, \alpha > 0,$$

where $H_\alpha(C/X)$ is the same as defined in Example 14.

Example 18' (*Entropy of order (α,β)*). We know that $\lim\limits_{\alpha \to \infty} H_{\alpha,\beta}(P) = -\log_2 p_{max}$ (β fixed) and that $H_{\alpha,\beta}(P)$ is a decreasing function of α (β fixed). From (54) we thus get

$$1 - p_{max} \le \frac{1}{2} H_{\alpha,\beta}(P), \quad \frac{1}{n} < p_{max} \le \frac{1}{2},$$

which lead to the following upper bound:

$$P_e \le \frac{1}{2} H_{\alpha,\beta}(C/X), \quad P_e \ge \frac{1}{2}, \ \alpha, \ \beta > 0, \ \alpha \ne \beta,$$

where $H_{\alpha,\beta}(C/X)$ is the same as defined in Example 18.

Example 19 (*Weighted entropy of order* α). We know that $\lim_{\alpha \to \infty} H_\alpha(P; U) = -\log_2 p_{max}$ and that $H_\alpha(P; U)$ is a decreasing function of α. Hence

$$1 - p_{max} \le \frac{1}{2} H_\alpha(P; U), \quad \frac{1}{n} < p_{max} \le \frac{1}{2},$$

which lead to the following upper bound:

$$P_e \le \frac{1}{2} H_\alpha(C/X; U), \quad P_e \ge \frac{1}{2}, \ \alpha \ne 1, \ \alpha > 0.$$

where

$$H_\alpha(C/X; U) = (1 - \alpha)^{-1} \int_X \log \left(\frac{\sum\limits_{k=1}^{n} P(C_k/x)^\alpha u_k}{\sum\limits_{k=1}^{n} P(C_k/x) u_k} \right) \cdot p(x) \, dx.$$

(b) Consider the function

$$f(p) = 1 - p - \tfrac{1}{2}(2^{1-\beta} - 1)^{-1}(p^{\beta-1} - 1), \quad \beta \ne 1, \ \beta > 0, \ 0 < p \le 1.$$

Then

$$f'(p) = -1 - \tfrac{1}{2}(2^{1-\beta} - 1)^{-1}(\beta - 1)p^{\beta-2}$$

and

$$f''(p) = 2^{-1}(2^{1-\beta} - 1)^{-1}(1 - \beta)(\beta - 2)p^{\beta-3}.$$

Furthermore

$$f(\tfrac{1}{2}) = f(1) = 0. \tag{55}$$

If $0 < \beta < 2$, $f''(p) < 0$ for all $p \in (0,1]$. This implies that the function is strictly concave and attains its unique maximum at $f'(p) = 0$, i.e. when

$$p = [2^{-1}(2^{1-\beta} - 1)^{-1}(1 - \beta)]^{\frac{1}{\beta-2}}.$$

Therefore the only zeros of $f(p)$ are those given in (55), i.e. $p = \tfrac{1}{2}$ and $p = 1$. Thus for $0 < \beta < 2$, we have

$f(p) \leq 0$ if $1/n < p \leq \frac{1}{2}$

$f(p) \geq 0$ if $\frac{1}{2} \leq p \leq 1$.

Similarly for $\beta > 2$, we have

$f(p) \geq 0$ if $1/n < p \leq \frac{1}{2}$,

$ \leq 0$ if $\frac{1}{2} \leq p \leq 1$.

For $\beta = 2$, we have

$f(p) = 0, \quad 0 < p \leq 1$.

Finally,

$$f(p) \leq 0, \quad \text{if } 1/n < p \leq \frac{1}{2}, 0 < \beta \leq 2 \text{ or if } p \geq \frac{1}{2}, \beta \geq 2. \tag{56}$$

Example 17′ (*Entropy of order α and degree β*). We know that $\lim\limits_{\alpha \to \infty} H_\alpha^\beta(P) = (2^{1-\beta} - 1)^{-1}(p_{max}^{\beta-1} - 1)$, $\beta \neq 1$, $\beta > 0$ and $H_\alpha^\beta(P)$ is a decreasing function of α (β fixed). Hence from (56) we have

$$1 - p_{max} \leq \frac{1}{2}H_\alpha^\beta(P), \frac{1}{n} < p_{max} \leq \frac{1}{2}, 0 < \beta \leq 2$$

$$\text{or } p_{max} \geq \frac{1}{2}, \beta \geq 2,$$

which lead to the following upper bound:

$$P_e \leq \frac{1}{2}H_\alpha^\beta(C/X), \quad P_e \geq \frac{1}{2}, 0 < \beta \leq 2, \alpha > 0$$

$$\text{or } P_e \leq \frac{1}{2}, \beta \geq 2, \alpha > 0,$$

where $H_\alpha^\beta(C/X)$ is as defined in Example 17.

Example 20 (*Weighted entropy of order α and degree β*). We know that $\lim\limits_{\alpha \to \infty} H_\alpha^\beta(P; U) = (2^{1-\beta} - 1)^{-1} (p_{max}^{\beta-1} - 1)$, $\beta \neq 1$, $\beta > 0$ and $H_\alpha^\beta(P; U)$ is a decreasing function of α (β fixed). Then from (56) we get

$$1 - p_{max} \leq \frac{1}{2}H_\alpha^\beta(P; U), \quad \frac{1}{n} < p_{max} \leq \frac{1}{2},$$

$$0 < \beta \leq 2 \text{ and for } p_{max} \geq \frac{1}{2}, \beta \geq 2,$$

which lead to the following upper bound:

$$P_e \leq \frac{1}{2}H_\alpha^\beta(C/X; U), P_e \geq \frac{1}{2}, \quad 0 < \beta \leq 2, \alpha > 0$$

$$\text{and for } P_e \geq \frac{1}{2}, \beta \geq 2, \alpha > 0,$$

where

$$H_\alpha^\beta(C/X;U) = (2^{1-\beta} - 1)^{-1}, \int_X \left\{ \left(\frac{\sum\limits_{k=1}^{n} P(C_k/x)^\alpha u_k}{\sum\limits_{k=1}^{n} P(C_k/x)u_k} \right)^{\frac{\beta-1}{\alpha-1}} - 1 \right\} p(x)\, dx.$$

From the inequalities among the entropies (Section 3, property (xv)) we can easily see that for certain values of the parameters some upper bounds are better than others.

4.1.4 *Generalized Fano-type bounds*

In property (xxi)(c) substituting $P(C/x)$ for P and taking expectation on both sides with respect to $p(x)$, we then get the following Fano-type bounds:

$$E_i(C/X) \leqslant E_i\left(\frac{P_e}{n-1}, \frac{P_e}{n-1}, \ldots, \frac{P_e}{n-1}, 1 - P_e \right), \quad i = 1, 2, \ldots, 8.$$

For $i = 1, 3$ and 8 these bounds are the same as given in Examples 1, 4 and 6 respectively.

For the generalized weighted entropies, i.e. weighted entropy of order α and weighted entropy of order α and degree β, the Fano-type bounds are given by

$$H_\alpha(C/X; U) \leqslant (1-\alpha)^{-1} \cdot \log \left\{ (n-1)^{1-\alpha} P_e^\alpha \left(\frac{u_{\max}}{u_{\min}} \right) \right.$$
$$\left. + (1 - P_e)^\alpha \left(\frac{u_{p_{\max}}}{u_{\min}} \right) \right\}, \quad 0 < \alpha < 1,$$

and by

$$H_\alpha^\beta(C/X; U) \leqslant (2^{1-\beta} - 1)^{-1} \left\{ \left[(n-1)^{1-\alpha} P_e^\alpha \left(\frac{u_{\max}}{u_{\min}} \right) \right. \right.$$
$$\left. \left. + (1 - P_e)^\alpha \left(\frac{u_{p_{\max}}}{u_{\min}} \right) \right]^{\frac{\beta-1}{\alpha-1}} - 1 \right\}, 0 < \alpha < 1, \beta \neq 1, \beta > 0,$$

respectively, where $u_{\max} = \max\{u_1, u_2, \ldots, u_n\}$, $u_{\min} = \min\{u_1, u_2, \ldots, u_n\}$ and $u_{p_{\max}}$ is the weight associated with $p_{\max}$.

4.2 **Generalized distance measures and error bounds**

This section deals with the bounds on the probability of error in terms of generalized distance measures arising due to entropies E_6 and E_7. The considered generalized distance measures contain the distance measures studied by Toussaint (1972), Devijver (1974) and Trouborst *et al.* (1974) as particular cases.

Toussaint (1972) considered the following distance measure:

$$R_\alpha(P) = \left(\frac{1}{n} \cdot \sum_{k=1}^{n} p_k^\alpha\right)^{\frac{1}{\alpha}}, \quad \alpha > 0. \tag{57}$$

He obtained bounds on the probability of error given by

$$R_\alpha(C/X) \le 1 - P_e \le n^{1/\alpha} R_\alpha(C/X), \quad \alpha > 0, \tag{58}$$

where

$$R_\alpha(C/X) = \int_X \left(\frac{1}{n} \sum_{k=1}^{n} P(C_k/x)^\alpha\right)^{\frac{1}{\alpha}} p(x) \, dx. \tag{59}$$

Later, Trouborst *et al.* (1974) considered the following distance measures:

$$B'_\alpha(P) = \left(\sum_{k=1}^{n} p_k^\alpha\right)^{\frac{1}{\alpha}}, \quad \alpha > 1, \tag{60}$$

and

$$B_\alpha(P) = \left(\frac{\sum_{k=1}^{n} p_k^\alpha}{\sum_{k=1}^{n} p_k^{\alpha-1}}\right), \quad \alpha > 1. \tag{61}$$

They obtained the following bounds:

$$B_\alpha(C/X) \le 1 - P_e \le B'_\alpha(C/X), \quad \alpha > 1, \tag{62}$$

where

$$B'_\alpha(C/X) = \int_X \left(\sum_{k=1}^{n} P(C_k/x)^\alpha\right)^{\frac{1}{\alpha}} \cdot p(x) \, dx,$$

and

$$B_\alpha(C/X) = \int_X \left(\frac{\sum_{k=1}^{n} P(C_k/x)^\alpha}{\sum_{k=1}^{n} P(C_k/x)^{\alpha-1}}\right) \cdot p(x) \, dx.$$

Györfi and Nemetz (1975) obtained interesting inequalities between B_α and B'_α given by

$$B'_\alpha(C/X)^{\frac{\alpha}{\alpha-1}} \le B_\alpha(C/X) \le 1 - P_e \le B'_\alpha(C/X) \le B_\alpha(C/X)^{\frac{\alpha-1}{\alpha}}, \quad \alpha \ge 2.$$

Taneja (1979) obtained an upper bound for P_e in terms of B'_α given by

$$P_e \leqslant (2 - 2^{1/\alpha})^{-1}[1 - B'_\alpha(C/X)], \quad \alpha \neq 1, \alpha > 0, \tag{63}$$

which is the same as that given in Example 14.

Recently, Capocelli *et al.* (1985) considered the following two generalizations of (60) and (61) involving two parameters, given by

$$G_{\alpha,\beta}(P) = \left(\sum_{k=1}^{n} p_k^\alpha \right)^\beta, \quad \alpha > 0, \beta \neq 0, \tag{64}$$

and

$$T_{\alpha,\beta}(P) = \left(\frac{\sum\limits_{k=1}^{n} p_k^\alpha}{\sum\limits_{k=1}^{n} p_k^\beta} \right)^{\frac{1}{\alpha-\beta}}, \quad \alpha \neq \beta, \alpha, \beta \geqslant 0 \tag{65}$$

respectively.

Generalized distance measures (64) and (65) also arise from the entropies E_6 and E_7 respectively. The following particular cases are easily verified:

$$G_{\alpha,1/\alpha}(P) = B'_\alpha(P); \; T_{\alpha,\alpha-1}(P) = B_\alpha(P); \; G_{\alpha,1/(\alpha-1)}(P) = T_{\alpha,1}(P);$$

$$B'_\alpha(P) = n^{-1/\alpha} R_\alpha(P); \; T_{\alpha,0}(P) = R_\alpha(P) \quad \text{and}$$

$$G_{2,1}(P) = T_{2,1}(P) = \sum_{k=1}^{n} p_k^2 = B_2(P) = 1 - h_2(P),$$

where $B_2(P)$ is the Devijver (1974) Bayesian distance and $h_2(P)$ is the Vajda (1968) quadratic entropy. Boekee and van der Lubbe (1979) also considered the distance measure (64).

Properties of $G_{\alpha,\beta}(P)$: For all $P = (p_1, p_2, \ldots, p_n) \in \Delta_n$, we have

(i) $G_{\alpha,\beta}(P)$ is a $\cup$-convex function for $\alpha > 1$, $\alpha\beta \geqslant 1$ (or $0 < \alpha < 1$, $\beta < 0$);

(ii) $G_{\alpha,\beta}(P)$ is a $\cap$-convex function for $0 < \alpha < 1$, $\beta > 0$, $\alpha\beta \leqslant 1$;

(iii) $G_{\alpha,\beta}(P)$ is a decreasing function of α (β fixed and $\beta > 0$);

(iv) $G_{\alpha,\beta}(P)$ is an increasing function of β (α fixed and $\beta < 0$);

(v) $G_{\alpha,\beta}(P)$ is a decreasing function of β (α fixed and $\alpha > 1$);

(vi) $G_{\alpha,\beta}(P)$ is an increasing function of β (α fixed and $0 < \alpha < 1$);

(vii) $G_{\alpha,\beta}(1-p_{\max}, p_{\max}) \leqslant G_{\alpha,\beta}(P) \leqslant G_{\alpha,\beta}\left(\dfrac{1 - p_{\max}}{n - 1}, \dfrac{1 - p_{\max}}{n - 1}, \right.$

$\left. \ldots, \dfrac{1 - p_{\max}}{n - 1}, p_{\max} \right)$ $0 < \alpha < 1$, $\beta > 0$ (or $\alpha > 1$, $\beta < 0$);

(viii) $G_{\alpha,\beta}(1-p_{max},p_{max}) \geqslant G_{\alpha,\beta}(P) \geqslant G_{\alpha,\beta}\left(\dfrac{1-p_{max}}{n-1},\dfrac{1-p_{max}}{n-1},\right.$

$$\ldots,\left.\dfrac{1-p_{max}}{n-1},p_{max}\right) \quad \alpha > 1, \beta > 0 \text{ (or } 0 < \alpha < 1, \beta < 0).$$

Properties of $T_{\alpha,\beta}(P)$: For all $P = (p_1,p_2,\ldots,p_n) \in \Delta_n$, we have

(i) $T_{\alpha,\beta}(P)$ is an increasing function of α (β fixed);

(ii) $T_{\alpha,\beta}(P)$ is an increasing function of β (α fixed);

(iii) $T_{\alpha,\beta}(P) \leqslant p_{max}$;

(iv) $T_{\alpha,\beta}(P) \geqslant \left(p_{max}^{\beta}\bigg/\sum_{k=1}^{n} p_k^{\beta}\right)^{\frac{1}{\alpha-\beta}} \cdot p_{max}, \quad \alpha > \beta$;

(v) $T_{\alpha,\beta}(P) \geqslant \left(p_{max}^{\alpha}\bigg/\sum_{k=1}^{n} p_k^{\alpha}\right)^{\frac{1}{\beta-\alpha}} \cdot p_{max}, \quad \beta > \alpha$.

These properties lead to the following error bounds:

(a) *Bounds on* $G_{\alpha,\beta}$ *in terms of* P_e: We have

$$G_{\alpha,\beta}(C/X) \geqslant [(n-1)^{1-\alpha}P_e^{\alpha} + (1-P_e)^{\alpha}]^{\beta},$$
$$\alpha > 1, \beta > 0, \alpha\beta \geqslant 1$$
$$\text{(or } 0 < \alpha < 1, \beta < 0); \tag{66}$$

and

$$G_{\alpha,\beta}(C/X) \leqslant [(n-1)^{1-\alpha} P_e^{\alpha} + (1-P_e)^{\alpha}]^{\beta},$$
$$0 < \alpha < 1, \beta > 0, \alpha\beta \leqslant 1, \tag{67}$$

where

$$G_{\alpha,\beta}(C/X) = \int_X \left(\sum_{k=1}^{n} P(C_k/x)^{\alpha}\right)^{\beta} p(x) \, dx.$$

(b) *Bounds on* P_e *in terms of* $G_{\alpha,\beta}$: We have

$$P_e \leqslant 1 - [G_{\alpha,\beta}(C/X)]^{\frac{1}{(\alpha-1)\beta}}, \quad \alpha > 0, \alpha \neq 1, \beta \neq 0, \alpha\beta \leqslant \beta + 1; \tag{68}$$

$$P_e \leqslant 1 - G_{\alpha,\beta}(C/X), \quad \alpha > 1, \beta > 0 \text{ (or } 0 < \alpha < 1, \beta < 0),$$
$$\alpha\beta \geqslant \beta + 1; \tag{69}$$

$$P_e \geqslant 1 - [G_{\alpha,\beta}(C/X)]^{1/\alpha\beta}, \quad \alpha > 1, \beta > 0, \alpha\beta \geqslant 1; \tag{70}$$

and

$$P_e \geqslant 1 - G_{\alpha,\beta}(C/X), \quad \alpha > 1, \beta > 0, \alpha\beta \leqslant 1. \tag{71}$$

(c) *Bounds in terms of* $T_{\alpha,\beta}$: The following bounds hold:

$$P_e \leqslant 1 - T_{\alpha,\beta}(C/X), \quad \alpha, \beta \geqslant 0, \alpha \neq \beta; \tag{72}$$

$$P_e \geqslant 1 - n^{1/\alpha} T_{\alpha,\beta}(C/X), \quad \alpha > \beta \geqslant 0; \tag{73}$$

$$P_e \geqslant 1 - n^{1/\beta} T_{\alpha,\beta}(C/X), \quad \beta > \alpha \geqslant 0; \tag{74}$$

$$P_e \geqslant 1 - [T_{\alpha,\beta}(C/X)]^{(\alpha-\beta)/\alpha}, \quad \alpha > \beta \geqslant 1; \tag{75}$$

and

$$P_e \geqslant 1 - [T_{\alpha,\beta}(C/X)]^{(\alpha-\beta)/\beta}, \quad \beta > \alpha \geqslant 1, \tag{76}$$

where

$$T_{\alpha,\beta}(C/X) = \int_X \left(\sum_{k=1}^n P(C_k/x)^\alpha \Big/ \sum_{k=1}^n P(C_k/x)^\beta \right)^{\frac{1}{\alpha-\beta}} p(x)\, dx.$$

Particular cases:

(i) For $\alpha = 2$, $\beta = 1$, the bounds given in (66), (68), (69), (70), (72) and (75) lead to the following well-known inequalities studied by Devijver (1974):

$$1 - V[G_{2,1}(C/X)] \leqslant \frac{n-1}{n}\left\{ 1 - \sqrt{\left[\frac{nG_{2,1}(C/X) - 1}{n-1} \right]} \right\}$$

$$\leqslant P_e \leqslant 1 - G_{2,1}(C/X). \tag{77}$$

(ii) For $\beta = \dfrac{1}{\alpha}$, the bounds given in (66), (67), (68) and (70) give the following bounds:

$$B'_\alpha(C/X) \geqslant [(n-1)^{1-\alpha} P_e^\alpha + (1 - P_e)^\alpha]^{1/\alpha}, \quad \alpha > 1; \tag{78}$$

$$B'_\alpha(C/X) \leqslant [(n-1)^{1-\alpha} P_e^\alpha + (1 - P_e)^\alpha]^{1/\alpha}, \quad 0 < \alpha < 1; \tag{79}$$

$$P_e \leqslant 1 - (B'_\alpha(C/X))^{\alpha/(\alpha-1)}, \quad \alpha > 0; \tag{80}$$

and

$$P_e \geqslant 1 - B'_\alpha(C/X), \quad \alpha > 1, \tag{81}$$

respectively.

(iii) For $\beta = 0$ and $\alpha > 0$ in (72) and (73) we get the same bound given in (58).

(iv) For $\beta = \alpha - 1$, $\alpha \geqslant 1$ in (72) we get the same bound on P_e as given in (62).

The bounds (78) and (79) are new in the literature; (81) is the same as given in (58) or (62).

(d) *Comparison among the bounds*: It is easy to check that under certain conditions on the parameters the following comparison amongst the bounds hold:

(i) The upper bound given in (74) is better than that given in (58), (62) and (77).
(ii) The lower bound on P_e given in (58) is better than that given in (70), (71), (73) and (75).
(iii) The bound (66) is better than (70).
(iv) The entropy-type bounds given in Examples 17 and 17′ are better than (63) and (69).

4.3 Jensen difference divergence measures and error bounds

Burbea and Rao (1982) and Burbea (1983) have considered three different classes of divergence measures and studied their convexity properties. Two of them are direct generalizations of the Jeffreys–Kullback–Leibler *J*-divergence, and the other is based on the Jensen difference. The measure arising due to Jensen difference has a wide range of applications in biological sciences – information radius (Sibson, 1969), information theory (mutual information (Gallager, 1968), statistics (dissimilarity coefficient (Rao, 1982) – and other related areas.

We shall consider divergence measures arising due to Jensen difference and shall present bounds on the probability of error for the two-class problem. The approach adopted is due to Capocelli and Taneja (1984) and Sant'anna and Taneja (1985).

In terms of the prior probabilities for the two-class case, the φ-Jensen difference divergence measure is written as

$$\mathcal{Y}_\phi = \int_X \left\{ \frac{\phi(P(x/C_1)) + \phi(P(x/C_2))}{2} - \phi\left(\frac{P(x/C_1) + P(x/C_2)}{2} \right) \right\} dx,$$

where φ is a convex function defined on [0,1].

Let us consider the more general class of measure:

$$\mathcal{Y}_\phi(p_1,p_2) = \int_X \left\{ \frac{\phi(p_1 P(x/C_1)) + \phi(p_2 P(x/C_2))}{2} \right.$$
$$\left. - \phi\left(\frac{p_1 P(x/C_1) + p_2 P(x/C_2)}{2} \right) \right\} dx.$$

We know that $p_1 P(x/C_1) = p(x)P(C_1/x)$ and $p_2 P(x/C) = p(x)P(C_2/x)$, where $p(x) = p_1 P(x/C_1) + p_2 P(x/C_2)$ is a mixture distribution. Thus

$$\mathcal{Y}_\phi(p_1,p_2) = \int_X \left\{ \frac{\phi(p(x)P(C_1/x)) + \phi(p(x)P(C_2/x))}{2} - \phi\left(\frac{p(x)}{2} \right) \right\} dx.$$

Let us also consider the φ-Jensen difference divergence measure defined in the following way:

$$\underline{\mathscr{Y}}_\phi(p_1,p_2) = \int_X \underline{\mathscr{Y}}_\phi(x)\cdot p(x)\ dx,$$

where

$$\underline{\mathscr{Y}}_\phi(x) = \frac{\phi(P(C_1/x)) + \phi(P(C_2/x))}{2} - \phi(1/2).$$

Let

$$P_e(x) = \min\{P(C_1/x),\ P(C_2/x)\}.$$

Since $\underline{\mathscr{Y}}_\phi(x)$ is symmetric in $P(C_1/x)$ and $P(C_2/x)$, consider $P(C_1/x) = P_e(x)$; then $P(C_2/x) = 1 - p_e(x)$. This gives

$$\underline{\mathscr{Y}}_\phi(x) = \frac{\phi(p_e(x)) + \phi(1 - p_e(x))}{2} - \phi(1/2).$$

(i) *Lower bound on* $\underline{\mathscr{Y}}_\phi(p_1,p_2)$ *in terms of* P_e: Since ϕ is convex, this gives $\underline{\mathscr{Y}}_\phi(x)$ convex. Thus

$$\underline{\mathscr{Y}}_\phi(p_1,p_2) = E_X(\underline{\mathscr{Y}}_\phi(x)) \geqslant \frac{\phi(P_e) + \phi(1 - P_e)}{2} - \phi(1/2). \quad (82)$$

This is a lower bound on $\underline{\mathscr{Y}}_\phi(p_1,p_2)$ in terms of P_e, which in turn gives a bound on P_e in terms of $\underline{\mathscr{Y}}_\phi(p_1,p_2)$, even though in a complicated form.

(ii) *Upper bound on* P_e *in terms of* $\underline{\mathscr{Y}}_\phi(p_1,p_2)$: In order to obtain an upper bound on P_e, let us put the following conditions on the function ϕ:

$$\phi(1) = \phi(0) = 0 \text{ and } \phi(\tfrac{1}{2}) = -\tfrac{1}{2}.$$

Then we have $\underline{\mathscr{Y}}_\phi(0) = \underline{\mathscr{Y}}_\phi(1) = \tfrac{1}{2}$ and $\underline{\mathscr{Y}}_\phi(\tfrac{1}{2}) = 0$. Consider the function

$$f_\phi(x) = 1 - 2\,\underline{\mathscr{Y}}_\phi(x),$$

then $f_\phi(1) = f_\phi(0) = 0$ and $f_\phi(\tfrac{1}{2}) = 1$. Also f_ϕ is concave. Then from Theorem 4, we have

$$p_e(x) \leqslant \tfrac{1}{2}f_\phi(x),$$

i.e. $p_e(x) \leqslant \tfrac{1}{2}[1 - 2\underline{\mathscr{Y}}_\phi(x)]$,
i.e. $P_e \leqslant \tfrac{1}{2}[1 - 2\underline{\mathscr{Y}}_\phi(p_1,p_2)]. \quad (83)$

The following are information-theoretic examples of (82) and (83):

Example 1   For $\phi(p) = p \log p$, we have

$$1 - H(P_e, 1-P_e) \leqslant 2\mathscr{Y}(p_1,p_2) \leqslant 1 - 2P_e,$$

and

$$1 - H(P_e, 1-P_e) \leq \mathscr{Y} \leq 1 - 2P_e,$$

where

$$\mathscr{Y}(p_1, p_2) = \underline{\mathscr{Y}}(p_1, p_2) = \frac{1}{2} \int_X \{P(C_1/x) \log P(C_1/x)$$
$$+ P(C_2/x) \log P(C_2/x) + 1\} p(x) \, dx,$$

$$\underline{\mathscr{Y}} = \int_X \left\{ \frac{P(x/C_1) \log P(x/C_1) + P(x/C_2) \log P(x/C_2)}{2} \right.$$
$$\left. - \left(\frac{P(x/C_1) + P(x/C_2)}{2} \right) \log \left(\frac{P(x/C_1) + P(x/C_2)}{2} \right) \right\} \, dx,$$

and

$$H(P_e, 1-P_e) = -P_e \log P_e - (1-P_e) \log (1-P_e).$$

Example 2 For $\phi(p) = (1 - 2^{1-\beta})^{-1}(p^\beta - p)$, $\beta \neq 1$, $\beta > 0$, we have

$$1 - H^\beta(P_e, 1-P_e) \leq 2\underline{\mathscr{Y}}^\beta(p_1, p_2) \leq 1 - 2P_e,$$

where

$$\underline{\mathscr{Y}}^\beta(p_1, p_2) = (1 - 2^{1-\beta})^{-1} \int_X \left\{ \frac{P(C_1/x)^\beta + P(C_2/x)^\beta}{2} - \left(\frac{1}{2} \right)^\beta \right\} p(x)^\beta \, dx.$$

It is easy to check that

$$\underline{\mathscr{Y}}^\beta(p_1, p_2) \leq \mathscr{Y}^\beta(p_1, p_2), \quad 0 < \beta < 1,$$
$$\geq \mathscr{Y}^\beta(p_1, p_2), \quad \beta > 1.$$

This gives

$$1 - H^\beta(P_e, 1-P_e) \leq 2\mathscr{Y}^\beta(p_1, p_2), \quad 0 < \beta < 1,$$

and

$$1 - 2P_e \geq 2\mathscr{Y}^\beta(p_1, p_2), \quad \beta > 1,$$

where

$$\mathscr{Y}^\beta(p_1, p_2) = (1 - 2^{1-\beta})^{-1} \frac{1}{2} \int_X \{P(C_1/x)^\beta + P(C_2/x)^\beta - 1\} p(x)^\beta \, dx.$$

For $p_1 = p_2 = \frac{1}{2}$, we have

$$1 - H^\beta(P_e, 1-P_e) \leq 2^{1-\beta} \mathscr{Y}^\beta, \quad 0 < \beta < 1,$$

and

$$1 - 2P_e \geq 2^{1-\beta} \mathscr{Y}^\beta, \quad \beta > 1,$$

where

$$\mathscr{Y}^\beta = \int_X \left\{ \frac{P(x/C_1)^\beta + P(x/C_2)^\beta}{2} - \left(\frac{P(x/C_1) + P(x/C_2)}{2} \right)^\beta \right\} dx.$$

Example 3   For $\phi(p) = 2^{\alpha-1} p^\alpha \log p$, $\frac{1}{2} \leqslant \alpha \leqslant 1$, we have

$$1 - H^\beta(P_e, 1-P_e) \leqslant 2\underline{\mathscr{Y}}^\alpha_\ell(p_1, p_2) \leqslant 1 - 2P_e,$$

where

$$\underline{\mathscr{Y}}^\alpha_\ell(p_1, p_2) = 2^\alpha \int_X \{ P(C_1/x)^\alpha \log P(C_1/x)$$
$$+ P(C_2/x)^\alpha \log P(C_2/x) + 1 \} p(x) \, dx.$$

Example 4   For $\phi(p) = (2^{1-\alpha} - 2^{1-\beta})^{-1}(p^\beta - p^\alpha)$, $0 < \alpha \leqslant 1 < \beta$ (or $0 < \beta \leqslant 1 < \alpha$), we have

$$1 - H_p^{\alpha,\beta}(P_e, 1-P_e) \leqslant 2\underline{\mathscr{Y}}_p^{\,\alpha,\beta}(p_1, p_2) \leqslant 1 - 2P_e,$$

where

$$\underline{\mathscr{Y}}_p^{\,\alpha,\beta}(p_1, p_2) = (2^{1-\alpha} - 2^{1-\beta})^{-1} \cdot \frac{1}{2} \cdot \int_X \{ P(C_1/x)^\beta - P(C_2/x)^\alpha$$
$$+ P(C_1/x)^\beta - P(C_2/x)^\alpha + 1 \} p(x) \, dx.$$

Example 5   For $\phi(p) = \dfrac{2^{\alpha-1}}{\sin \beta} p^\alpha \sin (\beta \log p)$, $\beta \in (0, \pi)$, $\beta \log p \in (-\pi, -\pi/2)$, $0 < \alpha \leqslant \frac{1}{2}$ and $\beta \log p \in (-\pi/2, 0)$, $\alpha > \frac{1}{2}$, we have

$$1 - H_s^{\alpha,\beta}(P_e, 1-P_e) \leqslant 2\underline{\mathscr{Y}}_s^{\alpha,\beta}(p_1, p_2) \leqslant 1 - 2P_e,$$

where

$$\underline{\mathscr{Y}}_s^{\alpha,\beta}(p_1, p_2) = \frac{2^{\alpha-1}}{\sin \beta} \int_X \{ P(C_1/x)^\alpha \sin (\beta \log P(C_1/x))$$
$$+ P(C_2/x)^\alpha \sin (\beta \log P(C_2/x)) + 1 \} p(x) \cdot dx.$$

Example 6   For $\phi(p) = \dfrac{\sin \pi p}{2} \log \left(\dfrac{\sin \pi p}{2} \right)$, we have

$$1 - S_3^\pi(P_e, 1-P_e) \leqslant 2\underline{\mathscr{Y}}_3^\pi(p_1, p_2) \leqslant 1 - 2P_e,$$

where

$$\underline{\mathscr{Y}}_3^\pi(p_1, p_2) = \frac{1}{2} \int_X \left\{ \left(\frac{\sin \pi P(C_1/x)}{2} \right) \log \left(\frac{\sin \pi P(C_2/x)}{2} \right) \right.$$
$$\left. + \left(\frac{\sin \pi P(C_2/x)}{2} \right) \log \left(\frac{\sin \pi P(C_2/x)}{2} \right) + 1 \right\} p(x) \, dx.$$

Example 7 For $\phi(p) = -\dfrac{\sin \pi p}{2}$, we have

$$1 - S_4^\pi(P_e,1-P_e) \leq \underline{\mathscr{Y}}_4^\pi(p_1,p_2) \leq 1 - 2P_e,$$

where

$$\underline{\mathscr{Y}}_4^\pi(p_1,p_2) = \frac{1}{2}\int_X \{1 - \tfrac{1}{2}[\sin \pi P(C_1/x) + \sin \pi P(C_2/x)]\}\, p(x)\, dx.$$

5   Applications to fuzzy sets

The theory of fuzzy sets, introduced by Zadeh (1965), is an effective tool for representing and studying the behaviour of systems in which human judgements, perceptions and emotions play an important role. In these systems, the basic concepts are ambiguous and imprecise, i.e. fuzzy. Here a fundamental role is played by an indefiniteness arising from a sort of intrinsic ambiguity rather than from a statistical variability. The significance of the theory is widely recognized in different areas.

De Luca and Termini (1972) worked on the problems of measuring fuzziness and starting from three very general requirements advanced a measure of the fuzziness of a fuzzy set. This measure is not based on probabilities and is therefore conceptually different from the entropy of information theory which also measures uncertainty but in probabilistic situations. The measure of fuzziness is called entropy of fuzzy set. A proposed form of this measure involves Shannon's information function. The quantity interestingly admits of informational interpretations. This study is pursued further in the work of Capocelli and De Luca (1973), and extended in Knopfmacher (1975). Also, Loo (1977) enlarged the class of measures of fuzziness. Emptoz (1981) and Ebanks (1983) starting from these properties emphasized the work of earlier authors and formulated an axiomatic approach.

Apart from entropy measures of fuzzy sets, De Luca and Termini (1983) have considered superposition sets and their entropies. De Luca (1985) has also introduced 'dispersion measures' of fuzzy sets. These recent studies have enlarged the area of active interest in measures of fuzziness. The basic motivation has come from the field of thermodynamics where the diffused state of a gas compares with the fuzzy characters of a set. In this section we discuss mainly two aspects: first the axiomatic study of fuzziness, and second the entropy of superposition sets along with dispersion measures. Dispersion entropy of superposition sets is also introduced by using matrices. Lower and upper bounds on this entropy are given.

5.1 Measures of fuzziness and generalized entropies

Let X be a universe of objects and $\mathscr{L}(X)$ the class of all fuzzy sets f: $X \to [0,1]$ defined in X. In $\mathscr{L}(X)$ two partial ordering relations, viz. $\leq$ (inclusion ordering) and $\leq'$ (sharpening order) may be defined for all f, (inclusion ordering) and $\leq'$ (sharpening order) may be defined for all f, $g \in \mathscr{L}(X)$ as follows:

$f \leq g$ iff $\forall x \in X, f(x) \leq g(x)$;
$f \leq' g$ iff $\forall x \in X, f(x) \leq g(x) \leq \frac{1}{2}$ or $f(x) \geq g(x) \geq \frac{1}{2}$.

Further, as usual for all f, $g \in \mathscr{L}(X)$, two point-by-point operations $\wedge$ and $\vee$ are defined as follows:

$(f \vee g)(x) = \max \{f(x), g(x)\}$;
$(f \wedge g)(x) = \min \{f(x), g(x)\}$.

Also, for any $f \in \mathscr{L}(X)$, the fuzzy complement $\bar{f}$ of f is defined by

$\bar{f}(x) = 1 - f(x), \forall x \in X.$

Next, we recall the definition of direct product of two fuzzy sets which is as follows. If $f \in \mathscr{L}(X)$, $g \in \mathscr{L}(Y)$, then $f \times g \in \mathscr{L}(X \times Y)$ such that

$(f \times g)(x, y) = f(x) \cdot g(y), \quad x \in X, y \in Y.$

Another very usual concept to be employed is that of power of fuzzy set f. The power $P(f)$ of f is defined by

$$P(f) = \sum_{x \in X} f(x), \quad f \in \mathscr{L}(X).$$

Finally, let I_A be the characteristic function of the ordinary subset A of X and let r be a real number such that $0 \leq r \leq 1$. Then $r I_{\{x\}}$ will denote the fuzzy set satisfying

$r I_{\{x\}}(x) = r, \quad r I_{\{x\}}(y) = 0 \quad \text{for } y \neq x.$

We shall use f_r over X, which is defined by

$f_r(x) = r \quad \text{for all } x \in X, 0 \leq r \leq 1.$

In this section the set X will be finite, i.e. Card $(X) < \infty$. In fact we shall take $X = \{x_1, x_2, \ldots, x_N\}$.

5.1.1 *Entropy measures and axioms*
In an effort to define and characterize entropy of fuzzy set, a measure of fuzziness, De Luca and Termini (1972) laid down three intuitively reasonable properties, which have later been extended by Knopfmacher (1975), Loo (1977), Trillas and Rierra (1978) and Ebanks (1983). Emptoz (1981) combined some of these studies.

An entropy measure h in $\mathscr{L}(X)$ is a map:

$h: \mathcal{L}(X) \to \mathbb{R}_+,$

where $\mathbb{R}_+$ denotes the set of non-negative real numbers, satisfying the following axioms or properties.

P_1. *Sharpness:*
   $h(f) = 0$ iff f is a classical characteristic function, i.e. $\forall x \in X$, $f(x) = 0$ or $f(x) = 1$.

P_2. *Maximality:*
   $h(f)$ takes its maximum value iff $f(x) = \frac{1}{2}$ for all $x \in X$.

P_3. *Resolution:*
   If $f \leq' g$, then $h(f) \leq h(g)$, $f, g \in \mathcal{L}(X)$.

P_4. *Valuation:*
   If h is a valuation on the lattice $\mathcal{L}(X)$: $\forall f, g \in \mathcal{L}(X)$, we have $h(f \vee g) + h(g \wedge f) = h(g) + h(f)$.

P_5. *Continuity:*
   h is a continuous function if $\mathcal{L}(X)$ is a metric space.

P_6. *Convexity:*
   h is a strictly $\cap$-convex function of f.

P_7. *Independence:*
   $h(r\, I_{\{x_k\}})$ is independent of x_k for $k = 1, 2, \ldots, N$.

P_8. *Symmetry:*
   $h(\bar{f}) = h(\bar{f}), \forall f \in \mathcal{L}(X)$.

P_9. *Monotonicity:*
   $h(f_r)$ is a strictly increasing function of r on $[0,\frac{1}{2}]$ and strictly decreasing on $[\frac{1}{2},1]$.

P_{10}. *Convexity:*
   $h(f_r)$ is a strictly $\cap$-convex function of r on $[0,1]$.

P_{11}. *Generalized Additivity:*
   There exist mappings $\tau, \sigma : \mathbb{R}_+ \to \mathbb{R}_+$ such that $h(f \times g) = h(f) \cdot \tau(P(g)) + h(g) \cdot \sigma(P(f))$, for all $f \in \mathcal{L}(X)$, $g \in \mathcal{L}(Y)$.

De Luca and Termini (1972) started with axioms P_1, P_2, and P_3. Taking logarithmic entropy as an example, they proved the properties P_4, P_8 and P_{11}. Knopfmacher (1975), Loo (1977), Trillas and Rierra (1978) extended it to other axioms. Emptoz (1981) unified some of these studies. Sharma and Taneja (1977) considered P_{11} for probabilistic entropies. Ebanks (1983) made a limited application of P_{11} to fuzzy set theory.

The following two theorems are combinations of the results of Emptoz (1981) and Ebanks (1983) whose proofs are easy to verify.

Theorem 5. Let $u: [0,1] \to \mathbb{R}_+$ be such that

$u(0) = 0,$

$$u(p) = u(1 - p),$$

where u is a strictly increasing function on $[0,\tfrac{1}{2}]$, then the mapping $h\colon \mathcal{L}(X) \to \mathbb{R}_+$ defined for all $f \in \mathcal{L}(X)$ by

$$h(f) = \frac{1}{N} \sum_{k=1}^{N} u(f(x_k)),$$

satisfies the axioms P_1 to P_{10}.

Theorem 6 Let $\mathscr{C}$ be the class of entropy measures built on $\mathcal{L}(X)$ satisfying P_1, P_2, P_3, P_4, P_7 and P_8. Then for all $h \in \mathscr{E}$ there exists a unique function $u\colon [0,1] \to \mathbb{R}_+$ satisfying

$u(p) = 0$ iff $p = 0$ or $p = 1$;
u is increasing on $[0,\tfrac{1}{2}]$;
$u(p) = u(1 - p),$

and such that

$$h(f) = \frac{1}{N} \sum_{k=1}^{N} u(f(x_k)).$$

Information-theoretic examples We can built such functions from all classical probabilistic binary entropies as examples of the function u given in Theorems 5 and 6. These information-theoretic examples are commonly referred to as generalized information functions or binary entropies, and are as follows:

1. $u(p) = -p \log p - (1 - p) \log (1 - p)$;
2. $u_\alpha(p) = (1 - \alpha)^{-1} \log [p^\alpha + (1 - p)^\alpha]$, $\alpha \neq 1$, $0 < \alpha \leqslant 2$;
3. $u^\beta(p) = (2^{1-\beta} - 1)^{-1} [p^\beta + (1 - p)^\beta - 1]$, $\beta \neq 1$, $\beta > 0$;
4. $_\gamma u(p) = (2^{\gamma-1} - 1)^{-1}\{[p^{1/\gamma} + (1 - p)^{1/\gamma}]^\gamma - 1\}$, $\gamma \neq 1, \gamma > 0$;
5. $u_1^\beta(p) = (2^{1-\beta} - 1)^{-1}\{2^{(\beta-1)[p \log p + (1-p)\log(1-p)]} - 1\}$, $\beta > 1$;
6. $u_\alpha^\beta(p) = (2^{1-\beta} - 1)^{-1}\{[p^\alpha + (1 - p)^\alpha]^{\frac{\beta-1}{\alpha-1}} - 1\}$,
   $\alpha \neq 1$, $\beta \neq 1$, α, $\beta > 0$, $\beta \geqslant 2 - \tfrac{1}{\alpha}$;
7. $u_{\alpha,\beta}(p) = (\beta - \alpha)^1 \log \left(\dfrac{p^\alpha + (1 - p)^\alpha}{p^\beta + (1 - p)^\beta} \right)$.
   $\alpha \neq \beta$, $0 < \alpha \leqslant 1 < \beta \leqslant 2$ (or $0 < \alpha \leqslant 1 < \beta \leqslant 2$);
8. $u^{\alpha,\beta}(p) = (2^{1-\alpha} - 2^{1-\beta})^{-1} [p^\alpha + (1 - p)^\alpha - p^\beta - (1 - p)^\beta]$, $\alpha \neq \beta$,
   $0 < \alpha \leqslant 1 < \beta$ (or $0 < \beta \leqslant 1 < \alpha$);
9. $u_e^\alpha(p) = -2^{\alpha-1}[p^\alpha \log p + (1 - p)^\alpha \log (1 - p)]$, $\tfrac{1}{2} \leqslant \alpha \leqslant 1$;

10. $u_s^1(p) = - p \log \left(\dfrac{\sin \beta p}{2 \sin \dfrac{\beta}{2}} \right) - (1 - p) \log \left(\dfrac{\sin \beta(1 - p)}{2 \sin \dfrac{\beta}{2}} \right),$

$$0 < \beta \leq \frac{\pi}{4};$$

11. $u_s^2(p) = -\left(\dfrac{\sin \beta p}{2 \sin \dfrac{\beta}{2}}\right) \log \left(\dfrac{\sin \beta p}{2 \sin \dfrac{\beta}{2}}\right)$

$\qquad - \left(\dfrac{\sin \beta(1 - p)}{2 \sin \dfrac{\beta}{2}}\right) \log \left(\dfrac{\sin \beta(1 - p)}{2 \sin \dfrac{\beta}{2}}\right), \quad 0 < \beta \leq \dfrac{\pi}{4};$

12. $u_s^3(p) = \dfrac{\sin \beta p}{2 \sin \dfrac{\beta}{2}} + \dfrac{\sin \beta(1 - p)}{2 \sin \dfrac{\beta}{2}}, \quad 0 < \beta \leq \pi;$

13. $u_s^4(p) = -(\sin \beta)^{-1}[p \sin (\beta \log p) + (1 - p) \sin (\beta \log (1 - p))],$
$\quad \beta \in (0, \pi), \; \beta \log p \in (-\frac{\pi}{2}, 0)$ or when $\beta \log_2 e \cdot \tan (\beta \log p) \leq 1.$

Theorem 7 (Ebanks, 1983). The class $\mathscr{C}$ of entropy measures built on $\mathscr{L}(X)$ satisfy P_1, P_2, P_3, P_4 and P_{11} iff $h \in \mathscr{C}$ has the form

$$h(f) = \sum_{k=1}^{N} u(f(x_k)), \quad f \in \mathscr{L}(X),$$

where the mapping $u: [0,1] \to \mathbb{R}_+$ is given either by

$$u(p) = -cp^\gamma \log p, \quad (c > 0, \; \gamma = \log_2 e), \quad 0 < p \leq 1,$$

or by

$$u(p) = c(p^\alpha - p^\beta), \quad (c > 0, \, 0 < \alpha < \beta, \, \alpha 2^{1-\alpha} = \beta 2^{1-\beta}), \quad \alpha \in [0, \gamma].$$

We observe that the α-log entropy and the entropy of degree (α, β) (Sharma and Taneja, 1977) are the respective examples in building the function u in the above theorem.

Theorem 8 (*Ebanks, 1983*). Let $\mathscr{C}$ be the class of entropy measures built on $\mathscr{L}(X)$ satisfying the axioms P_1, P_2, P_3, P_4, P_8 and P_{11} iff $h \in \mathscr{C}$ has the form

$$h(f) = \sum_{k=1}^{N} f(x_k)(1 - f(x_k)), \quad f \in \mathscr{L}(X).$$

The function h greatly resembles the quadratic entropy (Vajda, 1968) in information theory, i.e. when $f(x) = x$ and $\displaystyle\sum_{k=1}^{N} x_k = 1.$

5.2 Entropy of superposition sets and dispersion measures

In this section we shall revise the ideas of superposition sets due to De Luca and Termini (1983) and dispersion measures due to De Luca (1985). Both these ideas have been combined and written in matrix form. Bounds on the dispersion entropy of superposition sets will also be given.

Let X be a universe set of finite cardinality N, and consider M maps F_j, $j \in [M]$ on X, where $[M] = \{1, 2, \ldots, M\}$ such that

$$F_j: X \rightarrow [0,1],$$

and

$$\sum_{j=1}^{M} F_j(x) = 1, \quad x \in X.$$

We can now define a superposition set $F = (F_1, F_2, \ldots, F_M)$ such that $F(x) = (F_1(x), F_2(x), \ldots, F_M(x))$, $x \in X$, where $F: X \rightarrow [0,1]^M$, and $[0,1]^M$ is the set of all M-tuples with elements from $[0,1]$. In general the set of all M-superposition sets may be defined as follows:

$$\mathscr{L}^M(X) = \{F = (F_1, F_2, \ldots, F_M), \ F_j: X \rightarrow [0,1],$$

$$j \in [M], \ \sum_{j=1}^{M} F_j(x) = 1, \forall x \in X\}.$$

For a usual fuzzy set, map f over X, i.e. for $f: X \rightarrow [0,1]$ we may define a 2-superposition set as $F(x) = \{f(x), 1 - f(x)\}$ with $F_1(x) = f(x)$ and $F_2(x) = 1 - f(x)$.

Also it is possible to define a subset of $\mathscr{L}^M(X)$ in which only one component function F_j takes value 1 and the others take value 0. This is called the class of all *crisp* M-superposition sets and is defined as

$$\mathscr{B}^M(X) = \{F \in \mathscr{L}^M(X): \exists j \in [M] \text{ with } F_j(x) = 1, \forall x \in X\}.$$

Now for every $x \in X$, we shall take $F_{\max} = \max\{F_1(x), F_2(x), \ldots, F_M(x)\}$ and $F_{\min} = \min\{F_1(x), F_2(x), \ldots, F_M(x)\}$. Also we shall denote by T_F a function such that $F_{\min} \leqslant T_F \leqslant F_{\max}$. Now we define in $\mathscr{L}^M(X)$ the $\leqslant'$ relation.

If $F, G \in \mathscr{L}^M(X)$, then

$F \underset{T_F}{\leqslant'} G$ for all $j \in [M]$ if either $F_j \geqslant G_j \geqslant T_F$ or $F_j \leqslant G_j \leqslant T_F$;

$F \leqslant' G$ iff there exists a T_F such that $F \underset{T_F}{\leqslant'} G$; or

$F \leqslant' G$ iff $\forall x \in X[F(x) \leqslant' G(x)]$, i.e.
$$\forall x \in X[F_j(x) \leqslant' G_j(x)], \ j \in [M].$$

For each $F \in \mathscr{L}^M(X)$ denote by $\hat{F}$, the rearrangement of the components of F such that $F_j \geqslant F_{j+1}$. Define

$F < G$ iff $\hat{F} \leqslant' \hat{G}$.

Also

$$F \underset{m}{\leqslant} G \quad \text{iff} \quad \sum_{j=1}^{r} \hat{F}_j(x) \geqslant \sum_{j=1}^{r} \hat{G}_j(x), \quad 1 \leqslant r \leqslant M, \forall\, x \in X.$$

The relation $F \underset{m}{\leqslant} G$ is known as 'F majorized by G'. It is easy to prove that (De Luca, 1984),

$F < G$ implies $F \underset{m}{\leqslant} G$.

5.2.1 *Entropy of M-superposition sets*

The entropy H of M-superposition set is a functional

$H: \mathcal{L}^M(X) \rightarrow \mathbb{R}_+,$

which satisfies the following three axioms:

A_1. $H(F) = 0$ iff $F \in \mathcal{B}^M(X)$.

A_2. $H(F)$ reaches its maximum value iff $F = \left(\dfrac{1}{M}, \dfrac{1}{M}, \ldots, \dfrac{1}{M}\right)$.

A_3. If $F \leqslant' G$, then $H(F) \leqslant H(G)$.

Axiom A_3 can be replaced by stronger axioms: either by

A'_3. If $F < G$, then $H(F) \leqslant H(G)$.

Or by

A''_3. If $F \underset{m}{\leqslant} G$, then $H(F) \leqslant H(G)$.

Axiom A''_3 is equivalent to saying that H is a Schur-concave function (Marshall and Olkin, 1979). Thus as a consequence of A''_3, axioms A_1 and A_2 are obviously satisfied, i.e. if H is Schur-concave then

$$H(1,0,0,\ldots,0) \leqslant H(F) \leqslant H\left(\frac{1}{M}, \frac{1}{M}, \ldots, \frac{1}{M}\right).$$

Example.   Consider

$$H(F) = \sum_{j=1}^{M} T(F_j(x)), \forall\, x \in X,$$

where $T: [0,1] \rightarrow \mathbb{R}_+$ is a suitable map such that $T(1) = T(0) = 0$, T is a continuous and strictly concave function.

5.2.2 *Dispersion measures*

The idea of dispersion measures was introduced by De Luca (1985). It is a functional defined on the class of all fuzzy sets having the same power.

Denote by $\mathscr{L}_P(X)$, the class of all fuzzy sets having the same power $P > 0$. Since X is finite, a fuzzy set $f \in \mathscr{L}_P(X)$ can be represented by an N-dimensional vector $f = (f_1, f_2, \ldots, f_N)$, where $N = \text{card } (X)$ and $f_i = f(x_i) \geqslant 0$, $i = 1, 2, \ldots, N$. For any $f \in \mathscr{L}_P(X)$, we denote by $\hat{f}$ the fuzzy set obtained from f by rearranging the values of f in a non-increasing order, i.e. $\hat{f}_i \geqslant \hat{f}_{i+1}$.

Let us consider in $\mathscr{L}_P(X)$, the following well-known relation studied by Schur (1923):

For all $f, g \in \mathscr{L}_P(X)$,

$$f \underset{m}{\leqslant} g \quad \text{iff} \quad \sum_{i=1}^{k} \hat{f}_i \geqslant \sum_{i=1}^{k} \hat{g}_i, \ 1 \leqslant k \leqslant N.$$

This means that f is majorized by g.

Let $f_{\max} = \max \{f_1, f_2, \ldots, f_N\}$ and $f_{\min} = \min \{f_1, f_2, \ldots, f_N\}$. Let θ be such that $f_{\min} \leqslant \theta \leqslant f_{\max}$. For all $f, g \in \mathscr{L}_P(X)$, define the following relations:

$f \underset{\theta}{\leqslant} g$ if for all $i \in [N]$, either $f_i \geqslant g_i \geqslant \theta$ or $f_i \leqslant g_i \leqslant \theta$;
$f \leqslant' g$ iff   there exists a θ such that $f \underset{\theta}{\leqslant}' g$;
$f < g$ iff $\hat{f} \leqslant' \hat{g}$.

As before, the following relation holds:

$f < g$ implies $f \underset{m}{\leqslant} g$.

Definition   A *dispersion measure* in $\mathscr{L}_P(X)$ is any map:

$$D: \mathscr{L}_P(X) \to \mathbb{R}_+,$$

satisfying the following three axioms:

B_1: $D(f)$ is minimum if f is a classical characteristic function. The minimum value of f is proportional by a fixed constant, to the power of P.
B_2: D takes its maximum iff $f = \left(\dfrac{P}{N}, \dfrac{P}{N}, \ldots, \dfrac{P}{N}\right)$, i.e. $f(x) = \dfrac{P}{N}$,
$\quad x \in X$.
B_3: If $f < g$, then $D(f) \leqslant D(g)$ for all $f, g \in \mathscr{L}_P(X)$.

Let us replace B_3 with a stronger axiom:

B_3': If $f \underset{m}{\leqslant} g$, then $D(f) \leqslant D(g)$ for all $f, g \in \mathscr{L}_P(X)$, i.e. D is Schur-concave function. In this case the following holds:

$$D(P, 0, \ldots, 0) \leqslant D(f) \leqslant D\left(\frac{P}{N}, \frac{P}{N}, \ldots, \frac{P}{N}\right).$$

So by considering B_3' instead of B_3, axioms B_1 and B_2 are obviously satisfied. Thus a dispersion measure in $\mathscr{L}_P(X)$ is simply a map $D: \mathscr{L}_P(X) \to \mathbb{R}_+$ which is Schur-concave.

Example 1 $E_i(P)$, $i = 1, 2, \ldots, 8$ are all dispersion measures in fuzzy sets, where the power is one.

Example 2

$$D(f) = \sum_{x \in X} d(f(x)),$$

where $d:[0,1] \to \mathbb{R}_+$, $d(y) = 0$ iff $y \in \{0,1\}$, and d is continuous and strictly concave.

The above two concepts can be combined as follows.

5.2.3 *Dispersion entropy of superposition sets*

Let $\mathscr{L}_P^M(X)$ be the set of all matrices whose rows represent the members of $\mathscr{L}^M(X)$ and columns represent the members of $\mathscr{L}_P(X)$, i.e.

$$\mathscr{L}_P^M(X) = \left\{ \mathscr{M} \colon \mathscr{M} = \{f_{ji}\}, j \in [M], i \in [N], \right.$$

$$\sum_{j=1}^{M} f_{ji}(x) = 1, \forall x \in X, i \in [N],$$

$$\sum_{i=1}^{N} f_{ji}(x) = P, \forall j \in [M], \forall x \in X, f_{ji} \colon X \to [0,1], j \in [M],$$

$$\left. i \text{ fixed and } f_{ji}(x) = f_j(x_i), i \in [N], j \in [M] \text{ is fixed} \right\}.$$

Let $\mathscr{M} \in \mathscr{L}_P^M(X)$, then $\mathscr{M}$ has the following form:

$$\mathscr{M} = \begin{bmatrix} f_1(x_1) & f_2(x_1) & \cdot & \cdot & \cdot & f_M(x_1) \\ f_1(x_2) & f_2(x_2) & \cdot & \cdot & \cdot & f_M(x_2) \\ \cdot & \cdot & \cdot & \cdot & \cdot & \cdot \\ \cdot & \cdot & \cdot & \cdot & \cdot & \cdot \\ \cdot & \cdot & \cdot & \cdot & \cdot & \cdot \\ f_1(x_N) & f_2(x_N) & \cdot & \cdot & \cdot & f_M(x_N) \end{bmatrix}$$

Thus the dispersion entropy of superposition sets is defined as any map

$$D_H : \mathscr{L}_P^M(X) \to \mathbb{R}_+,$$

such that it satisfies simultaneously the axioms A_1, A_2, A_3'' and B_1, B_2, B_3'.

Particular case:

$$D_H(f) = \sum_{x \in X} d(f(x)) = \sum_{x \in X} \sum_{j=1}^{M} T(f_j(x)), \tag{84}$$

with $d(f(x)) = \sum_{j=1}^{M} T(f_j(x))$,

where $T: [0,1] \to \mathbb{R}_+$ is such that $T(0) = T(1) = 0$ and T is continuous and strictly concave function.

Remark 4 Dispersion entropy of superposition sets, D_H, characterizes explicitly the problem of the measure of the uncertainty in decision making in the setting of fuzzy set theory (Capocelli and De Luca, 1973).

Bounds on D_H Using the concavity of the function T and the definition of D_H given in (84) it is easy to obtain (refer to Section 4.1.1) the following upper and lower bounds on D_H:

$$D_H(f) \leqslant T\left(\sum_{x \in X} f_{\max}(x)\right) + (M - 1)\, T\left(\frac{1 - \sum_{x \in X} f_{\max}}{M - 1}\right) \qquad (85)$$

$$\geqslant 2\left(1 - \sum_{x \in X} f_{\max}(x)\right), \quad f_{\max}(x) \geqslant \frac{1}{2}, x \in X, \qquad (86)$$

where $f_{\max}(x) = \max\{f_1(x), f_2(x), \ldots, f_M(x)\}$, $x \in X$.

Remark 5 The particular case of (86) when $M = 2$ has been studied by De Luca and Termini (1979).

The following are the information-theoretic examples of (84), (85) and (86):

1. $T(x) = -x \log_2 x$;
2. $T^\beta(x) = (2^{1-\beta} - 1)^{-1}(x^\beta - x)$, $\beta \neq 1$, $\beta > 0$;
3. $T_\ell^\alpha(x) = -2^{\alpha-1}x^\alpha \log_2 x$, $\frac{1}{2} \leqslant \alpha \leqslant 1$;
4. $T^{\alpha,\beta}(x) = (2^{1-\alpha} - 2^{1-\beta})^{-1}(x^\alpha - x^\beta)$, $0 < \alpha \leqslant 1 < \beta$ (or $0 < \beta \leqslant 1 < \alpha$);
5. $T_s^1(x) = -\left(\dfrac{\sin \pi x}{2}\right) \log_2 \left(\dfrac{\sin \pi x}{2}\right)$;
6. $T_s^2(x) = \dfrac{\sin \pi x}{2}$.

Remark 6 The particular cases considered above involves the sum representation and consequently the given information-theoretic examples are based on it. It is quite possible that there exist other particular cases too, especially involving the mean-value property. This will be discussed elsewhere.

Acknowledgements

This chapter was written during the author's stay with the Dipartimento di Informatica e Applicazioni, Università di Salerno, Salerno, Italy, for which he is thankful to the above mentioned university for providing facilities and financial support. The author also thanks Prof. L. M. Ricciardi, Dipartimento di Matematica e Applicazioni, Università di Napoli, Napoli, Italy, for giving the opportunity to lecture in his department.

References

Aczél, J. (1966) *Lectures on Functional Equations and their Applications*, Academic Press, New York.

Aczél, J. and Daróczy, Z. (1963) Über verallgemeinerte quasilineare Mittelwerte die mit Gewichtsfunktionen gebildet sind, *Publications Mathematicae*, **10**, 171–90.

Aczél, J. and Daróczy, Z. (1975) *On Measures of Information and their Characterizations*, Academic Press, New York.

Arimoto, S. (1971) Information theoretic considerations on estimation problems, *Information and Control*, **19**, 181–94.

Arimoto, S. (1975) Information measures and capacity of order α for discrete memoryless channels, *Colloquium on Information Theory, Kesthely, Hungary*, pp. 41–52.

Arimoto, S. (1976) Computation of random coding exponent functions, *IEEE Transactions on Information Theory*, **IT-20**, 460–73.

Babu, C. C. (1973) On divergence and probability of error in pattern recognition, *Proceedings IEEE*, 789–99.

Belis, M. and Guiaşu, S. (1968) Quantitative–qualitative measure of information in cybernetic systems, *IEEE Transactions on Information Theory*, **IT-14**, 593–4.

Ben-Bassat, M. (1978) *f*-entropies, probability of error, and feature selection, *Information and Control*, **39**, 227–42.

Ben-Bassat, M. and Raviv, J. (1978) Rényi's entropy and the probability of error, *IEEE Transactions on Information Theory*, **IT-24**, 324–31.

Blumer, A. (1982) Bounds on the redundancy of noiseless source coding, *PhD thesis*, University of Illinois at Urbana-Champaign, Department of Mathematics.

Boekee, D. E. and van der Lubbe, J. C. A. (1979) Some aspects of error bounds in feature selection, *Pattern Recognition*, **11**, 353–60.

Bouchon, B. (1976) Useful information and questionnaires, *Information and Control*, **32**, 368–78.

Burbea, J. (1983) *J*-divergence and related concepts, *Encyclopedia of Statistical Sciences*, **4**, 290–6.

Burbea, J. and Rao, C. R. (1982) On the convexity of some divergence measures based on entropy functions, *IEEE Transactions on Information Theory*, **IT-28**, 489–95.

Campbell, L. L. (1965) A coding theorem and Rényi's entropy, *Information and Control*, **23**, 423–9.

Capocelli, R. M. and De Luca, A. (1973) Fuzzy sets and decision theory, *Information and Control*, **23**, 446–73.

Capocelli, R. M. and Taneja, I. J. (1984) Divergence measures and error bounds, *Proceedings of the 1984 IEEE International Conference on Systems, Man and Cybernetics, Oct. 9–12, Halifax, Canada*, pp. 43–7.

Capocelli, R. M. and Taneja, I. J. (1985) On some inequalities and generalized entropies: a unified approach, *Cybernetics and Systems*, **16**, 341–76.

Capocelli, R. M., Gargano, L., Vaccaro, U. and Taneja, I. J. (1985) Generalized distance measures and error bounds, *Proceedings IEEE International Conference on Systems, Man and Cybernetics, Arizona, USA, November 12–15*.

Chaundy, T. W. and McLeod, J. B. (1960) On a functional equation, *Proceedings of the Edinburgh Mathematical Society, Edinburgh Math. Notes*, **43**, 7–8.

Chen, C. H. (1976) On information and distance measures, error bounds, and feature selection, *Information Sciences*, **10**, 159–71.

Chu, J. T. and Chueh, J. E. (1966) Inequalities between information measures and error probability, *Journal of the Franklin Institute*, **282**, 121–5.

De Luca, A. (1984) Entropy and dispersion for a fuzzy set, *Proc. Fall International Seminar on Applied Logic Conf., Palma de Majorca, 24–8 Sept., Spain*.

De Luca, A. (1985) Dispersion measures of fuzzy sets, in *Approximate Reasoning in Expert Systems*, M. M. Gupta, A. Kandel, W. Bandler and J. B. Kiszka (eds), North-Holland, Amsterdam, pp. 199–216.

De Luca, A. and Termini, S. (1972) A definition of nonprobabilistic entropy in the setting of fuzzy sets theory, *Information and Control*, **20**, 301–12.

De Luca, A. and Termini, S. (1979) Entropy and energy measures of a fuzzy set, in *Advances in Fuzzy Set Theory and Applications* M. M. Gupta, R. K. Ragade and R. R. Yagar (eds), North-Holland, Amsterdam.

De Luca, A. and Termini, S. (1983) Superposition sets and their entropies, *Proc. IEEE Int. Conf. on Systems, Man and Cybernetics, Delhi/Bombay, India*, pp. 493–7.

Devijver, P. A. (1974) On a new class of bounds on Bayes risk in multihypothesis pattern recognition, *IEEE Transactions on Computers*, **C-23**, 70–80.

Ebanks, B. R. (1983) On measures of fuzziness and their representations, *Journal of Mathematical Analysis and Applications*, **94**, 24–37.

El-Sayed, A. B. (1977) The independence inequality and its applications to information theory, *Information and Control*, **35**, 229–45.

Emptoz, H. (1981) Nonprobabilistic entropies and indetermination measures in the setting of fuzzy sets the *l*, *Fuzzy Sets and Systems*, **5**, 307–17.

Ferreri, C. (1980) Hypoentropy and related heterogenity divergency and information measures, *Statistica*, **40**, 155–68.

Gallager, R. G. (1965) A simple derivation of the coding theorem and some applications, *IEEE Transactions on Information Theory*, **IT-11**, 3–18.

Gallager, R. G. (1968) *Information Theory and Reliable Communication*, Wiley, New York.

Gallager, R. G. (1978) Variations on a theme by Huffman, *IEEE Transactions on Information Theory*, **IT-29**, 668–74.

Guiaşu, S. (1977) *Information Theory with Applications*, McGraw-Hill, New York.

Györfi, L. and Nemetz, T. (1975) *f*-dissimilarity: A general class of separation measures and several probability measures, *Colloq. on Inform. Theory, Keszthely, Hungary*, pp. 309–31.

Hardy, G. H., Littlewood, J. E. and Polya, G. (1934) *Inequalities*, Cambridge University Press, Cambridge.

Hartley, R. V. L. (1928) Transmission of information, *Bell System Technical Journal*, **7**, 535–63.

Havrda, J. and Charvát, F. (1967) Quantification method of classification processes: concept of structural a-entropy, *Kybernetika*, **3**, 30–35.

Hellman, M. E. and Raviv, J. (1970) Probability of error, equivocation and Chernoff bound, *IEEE Transactions on Information Theory*, **IT-16**, 368–72.

Jelinek, F. (1968a) *Probabilistic Information Theory*, McGraw-Hill, New York.

Jelinek, F. (1968b) Buffer overflow in variable length coding of a fixed rate sources, *IEEE Transactions on Information Theory*, **IT-14**, 490–501.

Jelinek, F. and Schneider, K. (1972) On variable-length-to-block coding, *IEEE Transactions on Information Theory*, **IT-18**, 765–74.

Kailath, T. (1967) The divergence and Bhattacharya distance measures in signal selection, *IEEE Transactions on Communications*, **COM-15**, 52–60.

Kanal, L. N. (1974) Patterns in pattern recognition, *IEEE Transactions on Information Theory*, **IT-20**, 697–722.

Kapur, J. N. (1967) Generalized entropy of order α and type β, *Mathematical Seminar, Delhi*, **4**, 78–94.

Kerridge, D. F. (1961) Inaccuracy and inference, *Journal of the Royal Statistical Society*, Ser. B, **23**, 184–94.

Kieffer, J. C. (1979) Variable-length source coding with a cost depending only on the codeword length, *Information and Control*, **41**, 136–46.

Knopfmacher, J. (1975) Measures of fuzziness, *Journal of Mathematical Analysis and Applications*, **49**, 529–34.

Kovalevski, V. A. (1968) The problem of character recognition from the point of view of mathematical statistics, in *Character Readers and Pattern Recognition*, V. A. Kovalevski (ed.), Spartan Books, New York, N.Y., pp. 3–30.

Longo, G. (1976) A noiseless coding theorem for sources having utilities, *SIAM Journal of Applied Mathematics*, **30**, 739–48.

Loo, S. G. (1977) Measures of Fuzziness, *Cybernetica*, **20**, 201–10.

McEliece, R. J. (1977) *The Theory of Information and Coding – Encyclopedia of Mathematics and its Applications*, Addison-Wesley, Reading, Mass.

Marshall, A. W. and Olkin, I. (1979) *Inequalities: Theory of Majorization and its Applications*, Academic Press, New York.

Mathai, A. M. and Rathie, P. N. (1975) *Basic Concepts in Information Theory and Statistics*, Wiley Eastern, New Delhi.

Nyquist, H. (1924) Certain factors affecting telegraph speed, *Bell System Technical Journal*, **3**, 324.

Nyquist, H. (1928) Certain topics in telegraph transmission theory, *AIEEE Transactions*, **47**, 617.

Parker, D. S. Jr. (1980) Conditions for optimality of the Huffman algorithm, *SIAM Journal of Computing*, **9**, 470–89.

Picard, C. F. (1979) Weighted probabilistic information measures, *Journal of Combinatorics, Information and System Sciences*, **4**, 343–56.

Picard, C. F. (1980) *Graph Theory and Questionnaire*, North-Holland, Amsterdam.

Rao, C. R. (1982) Diversity and dissimilarity coefficients: a unified approach, *Theoretical Population Biology*, **21**, 24–43.

Rathie, P. N. (1970) On a generalized entropy and a coding theorem, *Journal of Applied Probability*, **7**, 124–33.

Rényi, A. (1961) On measures of entropy and information, *Proc. 4th Berkeley Symposium on Mathematical Statistics and Probability*, Univ. of California Press, Berkeley, **1**, pp. 547–61.

Sant'anna, A. P. and Taneja, I. J. (1985) Trigonometric entropies, Jensen difference divergence measures and error bounds, *Information Sciences*, **35**, 145–55.

Schur, I. (1923) Über eine Klasse von Mittelbildungen mit Anwendungen die Determinanten, *Theorie Sitzungsber, Berlin Math. Gesellschaft*, **22**, 9–20.

Shannon, C. E. (1948) A mathematical theory of communication, *Bell System Technical Journal*, **27**, 379–423.

Sharma, B. D. and Mittal, D. P. (1975) New nonadditive measures of entropy for discrete probability distributions, *Journal of Mathematical Sciences, Delhi*, **10**, 28–40.

Sharma, B. D. and Taneja, I. J. (1975) Entropy of type (α,β) and other generalized measures in information theory, *Metrika*, **22**, 205–15.

Sharma, B. D. and Taneja, I. J. (1977) Three generalized additive measures of entropy, *Electron. Informationsverarb. Kybernet*, **13**, 419–33.

Sibson, R. (1969) Information radius, *Zeitschrift Wahrschelnlichkeitstheorie und Verwandte Gebiete*, **14**, 149–60.

Taneja, I. J. (1979) Some contributions to information theory – I (A Survey): On measures of information, *J. Comb. Inform. and Syst. Sci.*, **4**, 253–74.

Taneja, I. J. (1982) Generalized γ–entropy and probability of error, *Proc. IEEE Intern. Conf. on Systems, Man and Cybernetics, Seattle, Washington*, pp. 463–6.

Taneja, I. J. (1983) Error bounds and generalized f-entropies, *Proc. IEEE Intern. Conf. on Systems, Man and Cybernetics, Bombay/Delhi, India*, pp. 652–6.

Taneja, I. J. (1984) A short note on exponentiated mean codeword length for the best 1:1 code, *Matematica Aplicada e Comput.*, **3**, 199–204.

Taneja, I. J. (1985) Generalized error bounds in pattern recognition, *Pattern Recognition Letters*, **3**, 361–8.

Toussaint, G. T. (1972) Feature evaluation criteria and contextual decoding algorithms in statistical pattern recognition, *PhD Thesis*, Dept. of Electrical Engineering, University of British Columbia, Canada.

Trillas, E. and Rierra, T. (1978) Entropies in finite sets, *Information Sciences*, **15**, 159–68.

Trouborst, P. N., Backer, E., Boekee, D. E. and Boxma, Y. (1974) New families of probabilistic distance measures, *Proc. 2nd Intern. Joint Conf. Pattern Recogn., Copenhagen, Denmark*, pp. 3–5.

Vajda, I. (1968) Bounds on the minimal error probability on checking a finite or countable number of hypotheses, *Problems of Information Transmission*, **4**, 9–19.

van der Lubbe, J. C. A., Boxma, Y. and Boekee, D. E. (1984) A generalized class of certainty and information measures, *Information Sciences*, **32**, 187–215.

van Der Pyl, T. (1977) Propriétés de L'Information d'ordre α et de Type β, *Colloq. Intern. du CNRS, N° 276 – Théorie de L'Information, Cachan, France, 4–8 July*, pp. 161–71.

Varma, R. S. (1966) Generalizations of Rényi's entropy of order α, *J. Math. Sci.*, **1**, 34–48.

Wiener, N. (1948, 2nd Ed. 1961) *Cybernetics*, The MIT Press and Wiley, New York.

Zadeh, L. (1965) Fuzzy sets, *Information and Control*, **8**, 338–53.

4

On the spatial distributions of dispersing animals

Nanako Shigesada *Department of Biophysics, Kyoto University, Kyoto, 606, Japan*

1 Introduction

Spatial pattern formations of animal populations are induced by various kinds of biological effects, of which mutual interactions between individual animals and environmental heterogeneity are considered to be the principal causal factors. It has been noted that the dispersal of most insects is greatly influenced by population density, as well as by environmental conditions. Density-dependent dispersal suggests the presence of a population pressure which acts to enhance the dispersal of the population as its density becomes high. From a theoretical viewpoint, it is interesting to see how population pressure can be defined in quantitative terms and exactly how it influences the process of animal dispersal. Furthermore, if the population pressure is working between two different species, how does this interspecific interaction affect the spatial distribution of each population?

Mathematical models describing the dispersing process of living organisms have been presented by many authors, mostly based on an ordinary diffusion equation. The application of a diffusion equation seems valid for a passive dispersion type, such as the dispersal of spores in the air or phytoplankton in sea water. However, for the active dispersive motions of animals, an ordinary diffusion equation is not applicable, even for the apparently simple dispersive motions of small organisms. We have no guiding laws by which the formulation of dispersal can be logically deduced, and we must therefore begin by the analysis of statistical data of experimental observations.

In the present chapter, we will base our analysis on the elegant experiments of Morisita (1952) on the dispersal of the ant-lion, *Glenuroides japonicus*. He performed two well-designed experiments, one of which was concerned with the dispersal of ant-lions in heterogeneous patchy environments, and the other, in homogeneous environments. On the basis of Morisita's experiments, we derive a model describing density-dependent dispersal in a heterogeneous environment. The model will be extended to multiple-species systems, in which interspecific interference acts to enhance dispersal of animals, and we will show that this interspecific population pressure leads to a spatially segregated population distribution, which facilitates the coexistence of species by relaxing competition between species. Finally, in Sections 7–9, a method will be presented to analyse the model for the special case when the dispersal process is sufficiently rapid compared to the growth process.

Although we restrict ourselves to some special dispersing behaviours, actual dispersive motions of animals show a variety of patterns depending upon the behavioural characteristics of species: migration of birds, schooling of fishes, swarming of insects and so on. There are many excellent references dealing with such processes, and we recommend those who are interested in these topics and in general mathematical analyses of nonlinear diffusion models to consult the following books and reviews: Murray (1977), Fife (1979), Okubo (1980, 1986), Levin (1981) and Mimura and Yamaguti (1982).

2   Density-dependent dispersal: theory of environmental density

We begin by introducing Morisita's first experiment (Morisita, 1952, 1971), in which he observed the spatial distribution of the ant-lion, *Glenuroides japonicus*, in a heterogeneous environment composed of two discrete compartments or habitats. The experimental area consists of a box, one half of which was filled with fine sand, and the other half, coarse sand (see Fig. 4.1). Ant-lions were put on the borderline of the two sand types, one-by-one, and the number of individuals which settled in each compartment was counted after they had formed their pits. This experiment revealed that the ant-lions had a strong tendency to prefer fine sand to coarse for pit formation when the population density was low. However, this tendency gradually diminished with increasing density until, finally, almost equal numbers of individuals were found in both sand types. This suggests the presence of repulsive interference between the individuals.

To obtain a more quantitative picture of this experiment, Morisita calculated P_A and P_B, the probabilities of settlement of an individual in area A and area B, when n_A and n_B individuals had already settled in these areas, respectively. He found the probability P_A (P_B) to be pro-

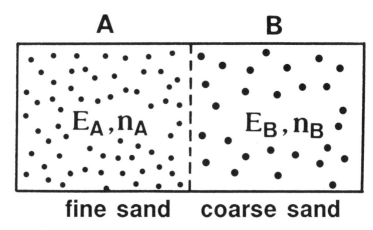

Fig. 4.1 The experimental system to evaluate environmental densities for ant-lion, as devised by Morisita. A box is divided into two compartments. Compartments A and B are filled with fine sand and coarse sand, respectively.

portional to the reciprocal of a quantity, $E_A + n_A (E_B + n_B)$, where E_A (E_B) is a constant parameter. Thus P_A and P_B are given by

$$P_A = (E_B + n_B)/(E_A + E_B + n_A + n_B),$$
$$P_B = (E_A + n_A)/(E_A + E_B + n_A + n_B). \tag{1}$$

Morisita took the value $E_A + n_A (E_B + n_B)$ to represent the degree of unfavourableness of habitat A (B). Thus, unfavourableness increases with population density, and the intrinsic unfavourableness of habitats A and B are characterized by E_A and E_B, respectively. Since E_A (E_B) has the dimension of density, E_A (E_B) is termed the 'environmental density of habitat A (habitat B)'. By using the probabilities (1), Morisita (1971) analysed this Markov process and obtained the average number of individuals found in the fine sand, $\langle n_A \rangle$, after N individuals has been introduced into the box:

$$\frac{\langle n_A \rangle}{N} = \frac{E_B + (N-1)/2}{E_A + E_B + N - 1}. \tag{2}$$

It is clearly evident that the right-hand side of (2) approaches 1/2 as N increases and, as shown in Figure 4.2, equation (2) shows a remarkably close fit with the experimental data.

Morisita also pointed out that his formula is applicable to various other species, including fish and crabs (Kosaka, 1956; Kubo, 1957). How does such a simple relationship derive from seemingly complex behaviours of interacting animals? We proceed to seek the mechanistic basis for Morisita's phenomenological theory in terms of a microscopic dispersal process.

$$\frac{\langle n_A \rangle}{N} \times 100$$

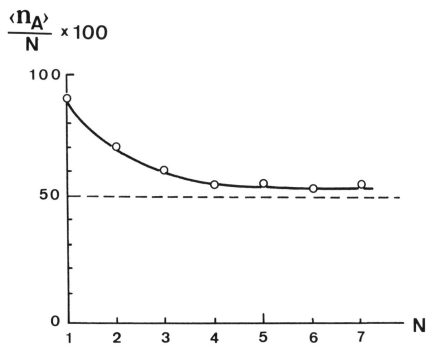

Fig. 4.2 The relation between the percentage of mean number of individuals in fine sand and the total of individuals introduced (from Morisita, 1971).

3 Behavioural version of Morisita's equation

In order to give a mechanistic interpretation to Morisita's phenomenological equation (1), we here assume that movement of an individual animal is influenced by three fundamental forces: (i) a dispersive force associated with random movement of an individual; (ii) population pressure due to mutual interference between individual animals; (iii) an attractive force, which induces directed movement of animals toward favourable environments.

We assume that the first two forces are involved in the dispersion coefficient as follows (Gurney and Nisbet, 1975, 1976):

$$\alpha + \beta n(x) \tag{3}$$

where $n(x)$ is the population density at position x. The quantity α is the intrinsic diffusivity associated with force (i), and βn represents the effect of the population pressure, which is assumed to increase linearly with population density. To measure the attractive force toward favourable regions, we introduce a function called 'environmental potential',

$U(x)$, which indicates the unfavourableness of habitat at position x. We assume that environmental potential induces directed movement of an individual toward favourable regions and its advection velocity is given by $-dU(x)/dx$.

We will now explain the result of the ant-lion experiment in terms of these three forces. When a new ant-lion is put on the sand boundary in the box, it will search for a site to build a pit in the box, in which n_A and n_B individuals have already settled in areas A and B, respectively. If the movement of the ant-lion is induced by the forces mentioned above, and if the elementary transition rate between the two areas due to random dispersion depends only on the condition at the initial point of departure ('repulsive transition', see Okubo, 1980; Teramoto, 1982), the transition probability at which the newly-added ant-lion moves from area B to area A is considered to be given by $\alpha + \beta n_B + \kappa/2$, where κ is proportional to the difference between the two environmental potentials, $U_B - U_A$. In the present case, since the value of the potential in area A with fine sand is lower than that in area B with coarse sand, $U_B - U_A$ is positive. Similarly, the transition rate from A to B is given by $\alpha + \beta n_A - \kappa/2$. Thus, if the probability that the newly-added individual will finally settle in area A (B) is proportional to the transition rate from B (A) to A (B), then we have

$$P_A = (\alpha + \beta n_B + \kappa/2)(2\alpha + \beta n_A + \beta n_B),$$
$$P_B = (\alpha + \beta n_A - \kappa/2)(2\alpha + \beta n_A + \beta n_B). \tag{4}$$

Comparing this expression with (1), we can see that (4) is equivalent to (1) if we set

$$E_A = (\alpha - \kappa/2)/\beta, \quad E_B = (\alpha + \kappa/2)/\beta. \tag{5}$$

Thus (5) can be regarded as a behavioural interpretation of Morisita's environmental density. Substituting (5) into (2), the average number of individuals found in area A is given in terms of new parameters:

$$\frac{\langle n_A \rangle}{N} = \frac{(\alpha + \kappa/2)/\beta + (N - 1)/2}{(2\alpha/\beta) + N - 1}. \tag{6}$$

To evaluate the effect of population pressure under slightly different conditions, let us consider the following experiment, which is modified from the previous one. Instead of introducing individuals one-by-one, if we put all N individuals simultaneously into the box, they move around in the box owing to the heterogeneity of the box and mutual interference of animals. The transition rate from B to A is again given by $\alpha + \beta n_B + \kappa/2$ and, similarly, that from A to B is given by $\alpha + \beta n_A - \kappa/2$, where $n_A + n_B = N$ is kept constant throughout the process. Then the temporal change of the number of individuals in each area is given by the following equations:

$$\frac{d}{dt}n_A = (\alpha + \beta n_B + \kappa/2)n_B - (\alpha + \beta n_A - \kappa/2)n_A,$$

$$\frac{d}{dt}n_B = (\alpha + \beta n_A - \kappa/2)n_A - (\alpha + \beta n_B + \kappa/2)n_B. \tag{7}$$

We can easily obtain the solution of (7), which will approach a stable equilibrium state as follows:

$$\frac{n_A(\infty)}{N} = \frac{(\alpha + \kappa/2)/2\beta + (N - 1)/2}{\alpha/\beta + N - 1}. \tag{8}$$

It can be seen that (6) becomes equivalent to (8), if β in (6) is replaced by 2β. This difference arises from the fact that, in the latter case, each individual is dispersing under the influence of all other individuals during the whole process.

4 Dispersal in a continuously varying environment

In the previous section, we dealt with dispersal between spatially discrete patchy environments. Here we will extend our formulation to a continuously varying environment. To this end, let us consider a linear array of many habitats of different environmental conditions, such as sands of various particle sizes. By a procedure similar to that in (7) for the case of two habitats, we obtain a set of equations, each of which describes the temporal change of the number of individuals, n_i, in the *i*th habitat. If we take the continuous limit of the equations for this discrete-array model, the population flow at position x in a continuously changing environment is obtained as follows (Shigesada *et al.*, 1979):

$$J(t,x) = -\text{grad}_x\{[\alpha + \beta n\,(t,x)]n(t,x)\} - n(t,x)\,\text{grad}_x U(x), \tag{9}$$

where $n(t,x)$ is the population density at position x and time t. The first and second terms of (9) correspond to the flow due to the density-dependent random dispersal and the directed movement induced by the environmental potential, respectively. By using the continuity equation, we have an equation for the temporal change of a density distribution as follows:

$$\frac{\partial}{\partial t}n(t,x) = -\text{div}_x J(t,x). \tag{10}$$

For convenience of analysis, hereafter, we consider the case that animals move in a bounded one-dimensional space, $x \in [0,L] \equiv \sigma$, in which the population is confined. Thus, the model is subject to $J = 0$ at boundaries, $x = 0, L$. The stationary distribution of (10), $n(t=\infty,x) \equiv n^*(x)$, is obtained as a solution of the equation, $J = 0$, i.e.

$$(\alpha + 2\beta n^*)\frac{\mathrm{d}}{\mathrm{d}x}n^* + \frac{\mathrm{d}}{\mathrm{d}x}U \cdot n^* = 0. \tag{11}$$

By integrating (11), we have

$$2\beta\{n^*(x) - n^*(0)\} + \alpha\ln\{n^*(x)/n^*(0)\} = -\{U(x) - U(0)\}, \tag{12}$$

where $n^*(0)$ is uniquely determined from conservation of the total population size, i.e. $\int_0^L n^*(x)\mathrm{d}x = \int_0^L n(0,x)\mathrm{d}x = N$. Furthermore, we can prove that this stationary solution, $n^*(x)$, is globally stable. Let us consider the following function:

$$H = \int_0^L \{\alpha n\ln(n/n^*) - \alpha(n - n^*) + \beta(n - n^*)^2\}\mathrm{d}x \geq 0. \tag{13}$$

The time derivative of the function H is negative definite:

$$\frac{\mathrm{d}H}{\mathrm{d}t} = -\int_0^L (J^2/n)\mathrm{d}x \leq 0. \tag{14}$$

Thus H acts as a Lyapunov function, and hence any solution of (10) starting from an arbitrary non-negative initial distribution, $n(0,x)$, always approaches the equilibrium distribution, $n^*(x)$.

Now we examine characteristic properties of the stationary solution, $n^*(x)$. We may intuitively expect the effect of population pressure to cause the spatial pattern to be flatter, and for this tendency to become stronger as the total number of individuals, N, increases. Figure 4.3 illustrates an example showing such properties. We chose the environmental potential as $U(x) = 1.5(x - 1)^2$ so that it has a minimum at $x = 1$ (Fig. 4.3a). The set of curves in Figure 4.3b represent the stationary distributions, $n^*(x)$, for various values of N and β. Generally speaking, animals gather around the low-potential region. However, we can see that the distribution becomes flatter with the population pressure β, when N remains constant. However, as the total number of animals, N, increases when β remains constant, the animals again tend to gather around the favourable region. Such phenomena were noted in Morisita's experiment (1952) and are also well known in natural systems. For example, a population of aphids on soy bean plants are localized only on new leaves, their most favourable site, when their total population size is small. However, as the population size increases, they expand their habitat to include older leaves, and finally distribute uniformly on all available leaves at a high density (Ito, 1952).

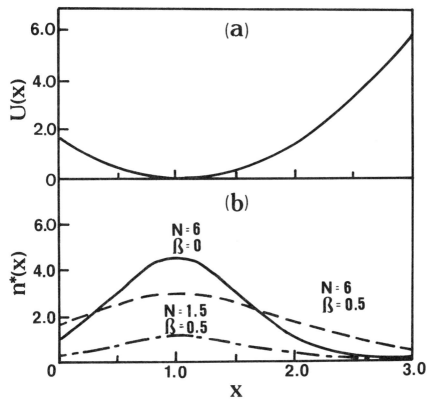

Fig. 4.3   (a) Environmental potential function $U(x) = 1.5 \, (x - 1)^2$. (b) Stationary population densities. N is the total number of individuals. $\alpha = 1$.

5   Further applications of the model: dispersal in homogeneous environments

Here we examine the versatility of the formulation (10) by applying it to another line of Morisita's experiment and also to other experimental data for azuki bean weevils studied by Watanabe *et al.* (1952) and for grasshoppers by Clark (1962).

In order to further evaluate the population pressure, Morisita studied the dispersing process of ant-lions in a uniform experimental field (1954a, b). He placed some ant-lions in the centre of an experimental field which was uniformly covered with soil. The released individuals migrated randomly on the soil until they eventually settled to make pits. He found that the number of individuals, $\tilde{F}(r)$, which settled inside a circle of radius r centred at the releasing point was expressed as

$$\tilde{F}(r) = N\{1 - \exp(-r^2/\sigma_\infty^2)\}, \tag{15}$$

where N is the total number of individuals initially released. Note that this equation coincides with a two-dimensional normal distribution with variance σ_∞^2. He also found that the variance of the distribution σ_∞^2 increased in proportion to the square root of the total number of individuals initially released:

$$\sigma_\infty^2 \propto N^{1/2}. \tag{16}$$

It should be pointed out that if no population pressure acts on individuals, the variance must be independent of N, i.e. $\sigma_\infty^2 \propto N^0$. Conversely, if the population pressure is very high, the individuals may disperse widely enough to maintain a certain minimal distance from one another, and accordingly, variance is expected to be proportional to N, i.e. $\sigma_\infty^2 \propto N^1$. Therefore, since the actual variance found was as given by (16), we may regard the population pressure in the ant-lion population as operating in an intermediate way between these two extreme cases.

Concerning the transient stage of the dispersal, using the data of Watanabe on azuki bean weevils, Morisita (1952) further derived a regression equation for the variance of distribution as a function of time in the following form:

$$\sigma^2(t) = \sigma_\infty^2 \frac{t}{t + T}. \tag{17}$$

Now we will apply the model given (10) to these experimental systems. Consider a two-dimensional uniform space with polar coordinate (r,θ), in which N individuals are released from the origin at time $t = 0$. The individuals are assumed to disperse by random movement and, at the same time, to become sedentary at a constant rate, μ. If we denote the population densities of dispersing and sedentary animals by $n(t,x)$ and $s(t,x)$, respectively, they obey the following equations:

$$\frac{\partial}{\partial t}n(r,t) = \frac{1}{r}\frac{\partial}{\partial r}\left[r\frac{\partial}{\partial r}\{\alpha + \beta n(r,t)\}\,n(r,t)\right] - \mu n(r,t), \tag{18a}$$

$$\frac{\partial}{\partial t}s(r,t) = \mu n(r,t), \tag{18b}$$

subject to the following initial conditions:

$$n(r,0) = \frac{\delta(r)}{2\pi r}N, \quad s(r,0) = 0. \tag{19}$$

For mathematical convenience, we have assumed in the above equations that diffusivity of dispersing animals depends only upon their own density, $n(r,t)$. This assumption may be granted if the migratory animals suffer little interference from the sedentary animals as compared with that from migratory ones. Furthermore, it is known from the experimental data that α is usually relatively small compared with $\beta n(r,t)$, except in peripheral regions. Thus, as a first approximation, we have assumed $\alpha = 0$ in the present analyses. To analyse equation (18), let us introduce the following transformation (Gurtin and MacCamy, 1977; Shigesada, 1980):

$$\tau = \frac{1}{\mu}\{1 - \exp(-\mu t)\}, \quad \xi(r,t) = n(r,t)\exp(\mu t).$$

Then equation (18) can be reduced to

$$\frac{\partial}{\partial \tau}\xi(r,t) = \frac{1}{r}\frac{\partial}{\partial r}\left[r\frac{\partial}{\partial r}\beta n(r,\tau)^2\right], \tag{20}$$

which has already been solved analytically by Pattle (1959) (see also Okubo, 1980). Thus the solutions of (18) subject to initial conditions (19) are given by

$$n(r,t) = \begin{cases} \dfrac{2N\exp(-\mu t)}{\pi R(t)^2}\left[1 - \dfrac{r^2}{R(t)^2}\right] & \text{for } r < R(t), \\ 0 & \text{for } r \geqslant R(t), \end{cases} \tag{21}$$

$$s(r,t) = \begin{cases} \dfrac{\mu R(t)^2}{8\beta}\left[1 - \dfrac{r^2}{R(t)^2} + 2\dfrac{r}{R(t)}\ln\dfrac{r}{R(t)}\right] & \text{for } r < R(t), \\ 0 & \text{for } r \geqslant R(t), \end{cases} \tag{22}$$

where $R(t)$ is the edge of the distribution, which is given by

$$R(t) = \{32\beta N[1 - \exp(-\mu t)]/\pi\mu\}^{1/4}. \tag{23}$$

The characteristic features of these solutions are illustrated in Figure 4.4. The upper curves are the distributions of dispersing animals, and the lower ones are those of sedentary animals. The number of dispersing animals decreases with time, whereas the number of sedentary animals increases with time and finally reaches a stationary distribution. The frontal edge of the distribution given by $R(t)$ increases monotonically with time and tends to an asymptotic value, $R^* = (32\beta N/\pi\mu)^{1/4}$. Thus the population initially placed at the centre never spreads over the entire space.

It may be worthwhile to compare the present results with the case of density-independent dispersal where the diffusion coefficient is constant, i.e. $\beta = 0$. In this case one can obtain

$$n(r,t) = \frac{N}{4\pi\alpha t}\exp(-r^2/4\alpha t - \mu t),$$

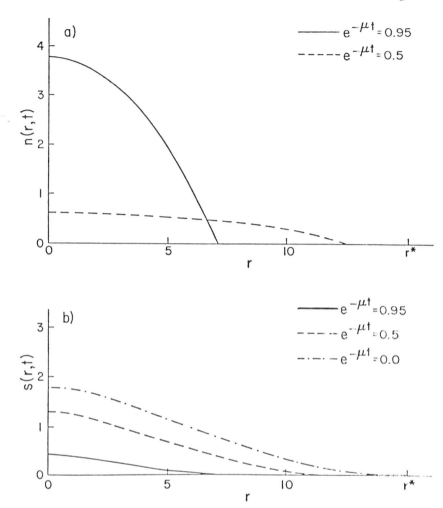

Fig. 4.4 Density distribution of animal population. (a) dispersing animals (eq. (21)). (b) sedentary animals (eq. (22)). Parameters chosen are: $N = 100$; $r_1(t) = 15(1 - \exp(-\mu t))$. Distributions are plotted at different times: ———, $\exp(-\mu t) = 0.95$; — — —, $\exp(-\mu t) = 0.5$; — · —, $\exp(-\mu t) = 0.0$.

$$s(r,t) = \alpha \int_0^t n(r,t')dt', \tag{24}$$
$$\xrightarrow{t \to \infty} \frac{\mu}{2\pi\alpha}K_0[(\mu/\alpha)^{1/2}r].$$

where K_0 and K_1 are the modified Bessel functions of 0th and 1st kinds, respectively. As shown in Figure 5, $s(r,\infty)$ shows a curve convex toward the r-axis, tending to infinity as r approaches zero. Furthermore, the tail

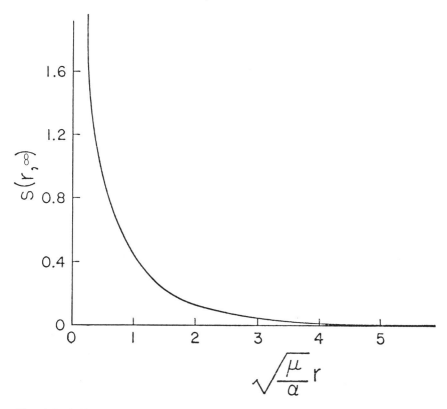

Fig. 4.5 Ultimate density distribution of sedentary animals in the absence of population pressure (eq. (24)). Parameters are chosen as $\mu N/2\pi\alpha = 1$.

of the distribution $s(r,\infty)$ expands to $r = \infty$. This contrasts markedly with the curve obtained in the presence of population pressure shown in Figure 4.4a.

Now, returning to the case of non-zero population pressure, i.e. $\beta \neq 0$, we calculate the total number of animals $F(r,t)$, inside a circle of radius r, and the variance of the distribution $\sigma^2(t)$:

$$F(r,t) = \int_0^r \{n(r,t) + s(r,t)\} \, 2\pi r \, dr$$

$$= \begin{cases} N\left[2\dfrac{r^2}{R(t)^2} - \dfrac{r^4}{R(t)^4} + 2[1 - \exp(-\mu t)] \right. \\ \quad \times \left. \left\{\dfrac{r^2}{R(t)^2} - \dfrac{r^4}{R(t)^4} + 2\,\dfrac{r^4}{R(t)^4}\ln\dfrac{r}{R(t)}\right\}\right] & \text{for } r < R(t), \quad (25) \\ 0 & \text{for } r \geq R(t), \end{cases}$$

$$\sigma^2(t) = \frac{1}{N} \int_0^\infty r^2 \{n(r,t) + s(r,t)\} 2\pi r \, dr$$

$$= \frac{8}{9} \left[\frac{2\beta N}{\pi\mu} \{1 - \exp(-\mu t)\} \right]^{1/2} \left\{ 1 + \frac{1}{2} \exp(-\mu t) \right\}. \tag{26}$$

As $t \to \infty$, they tend to

$$F(r,\infty) = \begin{cases} N\left\{ 4\dfrac{r^2}{R^{*4}} + 3\dfrac{r^4}{R^{*4}} + 4\dfrac{r^4}{R^{*4}} \ln \dfrac{r}{R^*} \right\} & r < R^*, \\ N & r \geqslant R^*, \end{cases} \tag{27}$$

$$\sigma^2(\infty) = \frac{8}{9} \left\{ \frac{2\beta N}{\varepsilon\mu} \right\}^{1/2}. \tag{28}$$

Now, let us compare the variance of the distribution at $t = \infty$ between the theoretical $\sigma^2(\infty)$ given by (28), and the empirical σ^2_∞ given by (16). We can see that they have exactly the same dependency on N, being proportional to the square root of N.

Secondly, let us compare $F(r,\infty)$, given by (27), with Morisita's empirical equation $\tilde{F}(r)$, given by (15). Although the functional form of $F(r,\infty)$ is different from that of (15), we can see that both give very similar curves. In fact, we have only one unknown parameter, R^*, in the function $F(r,\infty)$. If we assign an appropriate value to this single parameter (actually we put $R^* = 21N^{1/4}$), our theoretical curves fit automatically to all the experimental data for varying numbers of N examined by Morisita, as shown in Figure 4.6.

Finally, we examine the time development of the variance given by (26). The characteristic property of this function is similar to Morisita's empirical equation given by (17). We can see in Figure 4.7 that (26) closely fits the original data of Watanabe (1952) with azuki bean weevils, shown by white circles, and also the data of Clark (1962) with grasshoppers, shown by black circles.

6 Effect of interspecific population pressure on the spatial structure of a competitive community

Here we shall consider an ecological community consisting of two competing species. It is generally said that two similar species segregate their habitats or resources in order to minimize interspecific competition, and many supportive experimental data or field observations have been reported. Brian (1956) analysed the segregation process of ants in detail and classified it into two groups: (i) selective segregation – they have already undergone so much selection that they use completely different habitats; (ii) mutual segregation – selection is not so perfect, so that they

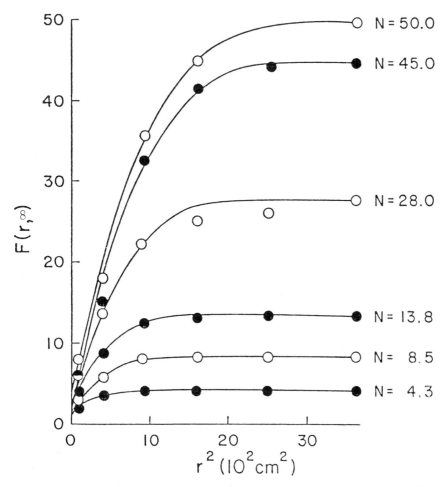

Fig. 4.6 Number of ant-lions settled inside a circle of radius r. Open and solid circles are experimental data for various numbers of ant-lions, $N = 4.3, 8.5, 13.8,$ 28, 45 and 50 (Morisita, 1954b). Solid lines are theoretical curves calculated from eq. (27) under the conditions, $r^* = 21N^{1/4}$.

occupy the same favourable habitats if allowed to live together, but segregate spatially from each other when they do so.

There have been many interesting observations for the latter case. For example, Kawanabe (1959) reported mutual segregation between the anadromous ayu fish and the river-resident pale chub. Both of these similar fish intrinsically favour the central part of a river-rapid. Therefore, when the ayu fish is absent in the river, the pale chub lives in the central part of a river-rapid. However, as the ayu fish ascends the river during the spawning season and settles down in the stream, the pale chub is

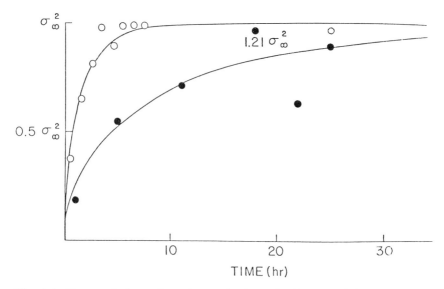

Fig. 4.7 Temporal change in variance of animal distributions. ($\circ$): experimental data of azuki bean weevils obtained by Watanabe *et al.* (1952); the time scale is in hours. ($\bullet$): experimental data for grasshoppers obtained by Clark (1962); the time scale is in days. Solid lines are theoretical curves calculated from eq. (26), in which the parameter μ is chosen as 0.2/hour for the upper curve and 0.03/day for the lower curve.

driven away to less favourable places, such as close to the river bank, so that they finally segregate from each other.

Now we shall look into the behavioural mechanisms for such mutual segregation. Consider two species which favour the same environments. We assume that they migrate in a one-dimensional bounded space under the influence of the population pressure induced by intra-and interspecific interferences. A model describing the dispersal of such species is obtained by extending equation (10) for a single-species population. Thus, the fluxes for species 1 and 2 at position x are given by

$$J_1 = -\frac{\partial}{\partial x}\{(\alpha_1 + \beta_{11}n_1 + \beta_{12}n_2)n_1\} - \frac{dU}{dx}n_1,$$

$$J_2 = -\frac{\partial}{\partial x}\{(\alpha_2 + \beta_{21}n_1 + \beta_{22}n_2)n_1\} - \frac{dU}{dx}n_2. \tag{29}$$

Here term $\beta_{ij}n_j(i \neq j)$ is newly added to (10), and represents the effect of interspecific population pressures on diffusivity. The second term of (29), $U_x n_i$, represents the flux induced by environmental potential. Since the two species are similar to each other, we have assumed that they are exposed to the same environmental potential, $U(x)$. Note that equation (29) is classified as 'repulsive' according to the definition of Okubo (1980). Other types of diffusion, such as Fickian, have been studied by Bertsch *et al.* (1985). The temporal changes in the population densities, n_1 and n_2, are obtained by using the continuity equation as follows:

$$\begin{aligned}
\frac{\partial}{\partial t} n_1 &= -\frac{\partial}{\partial x} J_1, \\
&\qquad\qquad \text{on } x \in [0, L] \equiv \sigma, \\
\frac{\partial}{\partial t} n_2 &= -\frac{\partial}{\partial x} J_2,
\end{aligned} \tag{30}$$

subject to $J_1 = J_2 = 0$ at $x = 0$ and L.

We begin by examining the characteristic properties of the stationary distributions of (30), which are obtained by putting fluxes J_1 and J_2 as zero. Thus we have the following ordinary differential equations:

$$\begin{aligned}
\frac{d}{dx} n_1^* &= -\frac{dU}{dx} n_1^* \{\alpha_2 + \beta_{21} n_1^* + (2\beta_{22} - \beta_{12}) n_2^*\}/A, \\
\frac{d}{dx} n_2^* &= -\frac{dU}{dx} n_2^* \{\alpha_1 + \beta_{12} n_2^* + (2\beta_{11} - \beta_{21}) n_1^*\}/A,
\end{aligned} \tag{31}$$

where

$$\begin{aligned}
A &= (\alpha_1 + 2\beta_{11} n_1^* + \beta_{12} n_2^*)(\alpha_2 + \beta_{21} n_1^* + 2\beta_{22} n_2^*) \\
&\quad - \beta_{12} \beta_{21} n_1^* n_2^* > 0.
\end{aligned} \tag{32}$$

The spatial patterns of $n_1^*(x)$ and $n_2^*(x)$ can be qualitatively studied by applying the isocline method to (31). As shown in Figure 4.8, the phase-plane diagrams of (n_1^*, n_2^*) can be classified into three cases depending on the signs of $D_1 = \beta_{12} - 2\beta_{22}$ and $D_2 = \beta_{21} - 2\beta_{11}$. Corresponding to each case in Figure 4.8, the spatial patterns of population densities are schematically illustrated in Figure 4.9. From this figure, we can see that a spatial segregation may occur if $D_1 D_2 \leq 0$.

As an example showing a segregating pattern, we consider the special case when species 1 is completely dominant over species 2 such that only species 1 exerts population pressure against species 2, but not vice versa (i.e. all β_{ij} except β_{21} are zero). Equation (31) for this case can be analytically solved as follows:

$$\begin{aligned}
n_1^* &= C_1 \exp\{-U(x)/\alpha_1\}, \\
n_2^* &= C_2(\alpha_2 + \beta_{21} n_1^*)^{-1-\alpha_1/\alpha_2} n_1^{*\kappa \alpha_1/\alpha_2}.
\end{aligned} \tag{33}$$

In Figure 10, equation (33) is plotted as a function of x. Figure 4.10a shows the effect of the population pressure of species 1 on species 2, β_{21}. As β_{21} becomes larger, species 2 is forced to escape from species 1 and consequently they segregate sharply. Figure 4.10b shows the effect of the total

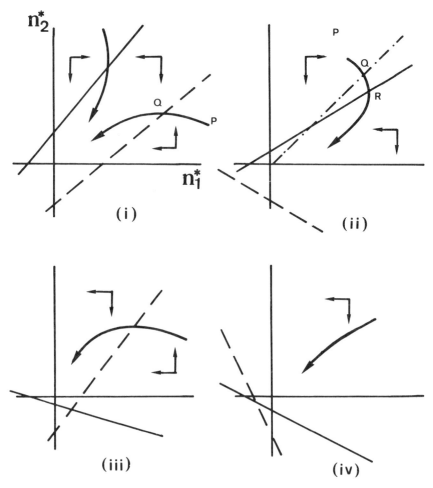

Fig. 4.8   Vector fields in (n_1^*, n_2^*) in the case (i) $(D_1, D_2) = (+, +)$; (ii) $(+, -)$; (iii) $(-, +)$; and (iv) $(-, -)$.

population size of species 1, $N_1 = \int_0^L n_1^*(x)\mathrm{d}x$. When N_1 is small, both species gather around the same favourable region. However, as N_1 increases, species 2 disappears from the favourable region, and consequently the greater part of the favourable region is occupied by species 1. This phenomenon corresponds to the mutual segregation proposed by Brian (1956) and also the segregation observed between ayu fish and pale chub by Kawanabe (1959).

Finally, we shall examine effects of the spatial segregation of habitats on the stability of coexistence of two competing species. Let us first

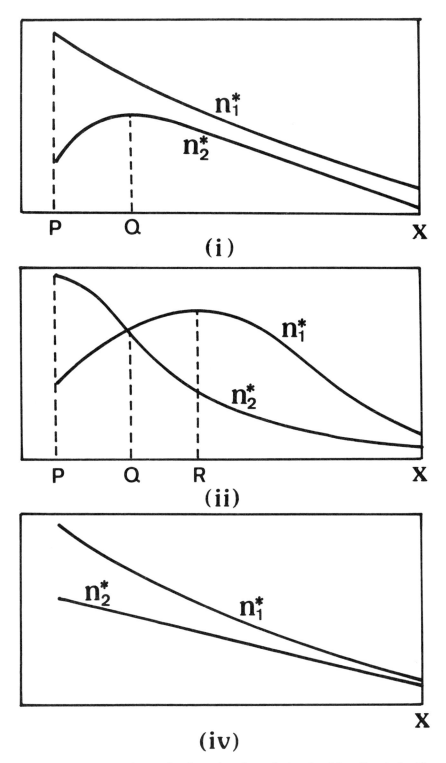

Fig. 4.9   Typical behaviours of trajectories of population densities n_1^* and n_2^* with respect to x corresponding to the cases of (i), (ii) and (iv) of Fig. 4.8. $dU/dx > 0$ is assumed.

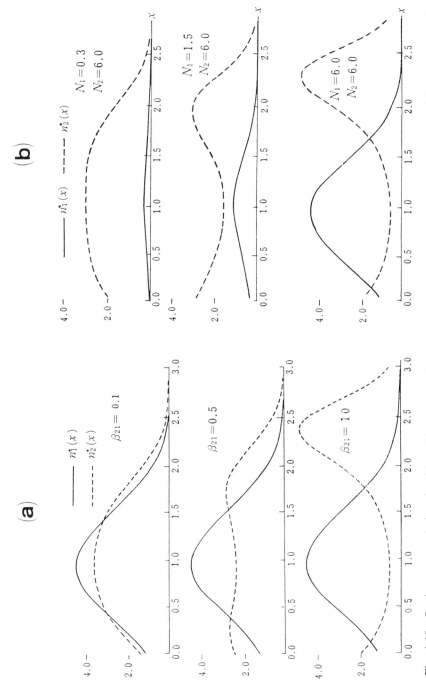

Fig. 4.10   Stationary population densities of two species. Potential function and parameters are $U_1(x) = U_2(x) = 1.5\,(x-1)^2$; (a) $N_1 = N_2 = 6$; $\alpha_1 = \alpha_2 = 1$, $\beta_{11} = \beta_{22} = \beta_{12} = 0$. $\beta_{21} = 0.1$, 0.5 and 10. (b) $\alpha_1 = \alpha_2 = 1$; $\beta_{11} = \beta_{22} = \beta_{12} = 0$, $\beta_{21} = 10$; $N_2 = 6$, $N_1 = 0.3$, 1.5 and 6.0.

consider two competing species which are uniformly distributed in space. If they are not allowed to disperse, the population dynamics for this system are given by the following Lotka–Volterra equations:

$$\frac{d}{dt}n_1 = (\varepsilon_1 - \mu_{11}n_1 - \mu_{12}n_2)n_1,$$

$$\frac{d}{dt}n_2 = (\varepsilon_2 - \mu_{21}n_1 - \mu_{22}n_2)n_2. \tag{34}$$

where ε_1 and ε_2 are intrinsic growth rates of species 1 and 2, μ_{11} and μ_{22} are the coefficients of intraspecific competition and μ_{12} and μ_{21} are those of interspecific competition, respectively. It is well known that the coexistence of two such species becomes possible only when the following conditions are satisfied:

$$\frac{\mu_{11}}{\mu_{21}} > \frac{\varepsilon_1}{\varepsilon_2} > \frac{\mu_{12}}{\mu_{22}}. \tag{35}$$

Otherwise, only one of the species can survive and the other species tends to extinction.

Does the spatial segregation induced by nonlinear dispersal act to relax the interspecific competition and stabilize their coexistence? To examine this problem, we consider an equation which consists of the competition equation (35) combined with a dispersal term given by the right-hand side of (30) as follows:

$$\frac{\partial}{\partial t}n_1 = -\frac{\partial}{\partial x}J_1 + (\varepsilon_1 - \mu_{11}n_1 - \mu_{12}n_2)n_1,$$

$$\frac{\partial}{\partial t}n_2 = -\frac{\partial}{\partial x}J_2 + (\varepsilon_2 - \mu_{21}n_1 - \mu_{22}n_2)n_2. \tag{36}$$

Equation (36) is generally difficult to solve analytically. In the following sections, we present a method to analyse (36) for the special case when the dispersal term is large compared with the growth term. Before doing that, we survey quantitative features of the solutions of (36) by computer simulation.

In Figure 4.11, we chose the competition parameters in such a way that Gause's competitive exclusion principle is satisfied, so that either of two species becomes extinct depending on the initial population sizes of two species ($\varepsilon_1 = \varepsilon_2 = 6$, $\mu_{11} = \mu_{22} = 1.4$, $\mu_{21} = \mu_{22} = 2.8$). As for the flux terms, we used the same parameters as in Figure 4.10, with which the system has shown a typical segregation of habitat. We can see in Figure 4.11 that the initially uniform distributions of the two species will evolve to stationary distributions which show a spatially segregating pattern. Further computer simulations demonstrate that this segregating pattern is locally stable. Thus we can see that two similar and competing species which favour common environments can coexist by segregating their

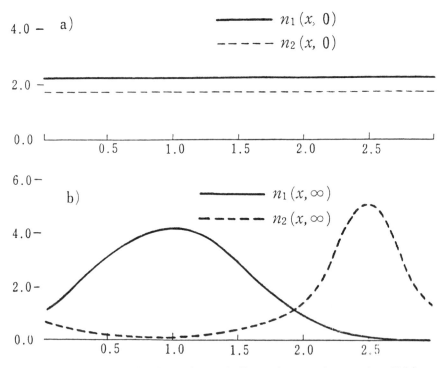

Fig. 4.11 Population densities of two similar and competing species. $U_1(x) =$ $U_2(x) = 1.5(x - 1)^2$; $\alpha_1 = \alpha_2 = 1$; $\beta_{11} = \beta_{22} = \beta_{12} = 0$. $\beta_{21} = 10$; $\varepsilon_1 = \varepsilon_2 = 6$; μ_{11} $= \mu_{22} = 1.4$; $\mu_{21} = \mu_{12} = 2.8$. (a) Initial distributions, $n_1(x,0)$ and $n_2(x,0)$. (b) Stationary distributions finally attained, $n_1(x,\infty)$ and $n_2(x,\infty)$.

habitats, if they are allowed to undergo nonlinear dispersal induced by mutual population pressure.

7 Spatial distribution of rapidly dispersing animals in heterogeneous environments: multiple-scale method

We have dealt with models describing the time development of spatial distributions of populations in a heterogeneous environment for a single-species system in equation (10), and for a two-competing-species system in equation (30). There have been several distinct approaches to the analysis of similar models depending on the system under investigation and the type of method being applied (see reviews by Okubo, 1980, and Levin, 1981). Among them, models for a single species in one-dimensional space have been extensively studied for various types of ecological systems. Okubo (1980) analysed the effects of various kinds of spatially varying dispersal on the spatial structure of populations. Gurney and Nisbet (1975) and Namba (1980) included a spatially varying growth term in their models. In population genetics, Fleming (1975), Nagylaki (1975) and May *et al.* (1975) studied the effect of environmental heterogeneity on the viability of individuals of a single species and presented the condition for the existence of clines in one-dimensional space. As for two-species systems, the effect of dispersal with directed movement was taken into consideration by Comins and Blatt (1974) and Shigesada *et al.* (1979), and the effects of spatially varying growth was considered by Kawasaki and Teramoto (1979) and Pacala and Roughgarden (1982). However, these models incorporated the effect of heterogeneity in either dispersal or growth, but not in both processes.

Here we will extend our models to more general ones which involve effects of environmental heterogeneity in both dispersal and growth processes. Since mathematical analysis of such models is generally a formidable task, we restrict ourselves to the special case when the dispersal process occurs very rapidly compared with the growth process of the species. It is frequently seen in nature that the change in population density as a result of the dispersal process occurs more rapidly than the change due to the growth process. For example, some animals undergo daily migration, seeking resources and settling places, while they reproduce only once or twice a year. In such a case, we can apply a multiple-scale method to our model by means of which the models can be reduced into an ordinary differential equation, thereby simplifying the analysis. We apply this method to a single-species system in Section 8 and to a two-competing-species system in Section 9, and finally compare the results from this method with those from computer calculations.

We start with a model for a single-species population in a bounded heterogeneous habitat as follows:

$$\frac{\partial}{\partial t} n(t,x) = -\frac{\partial}{\partial x} J(x,n) + \varepsilon G(x,n) \quad \text{on } x \in [0,L] \equiv \sigma, \tag{37}$$

where

$$J(x,n) = -\alpha \frac{\partial}{\partial x} n - \frac{d}{dx} U(x) n. \tag{38}$$

The model is subject to the following initial and boundary conditions:

$$n(0,x) = s(x) \geqslant 0 \, (\neq 0),$$
$$J(x,n) = 0 \quad \text{at } x = 0 \text{ and } L, \tag{39}$$

where $n(t,x)$ denotes the popoulation density at time t and position x. The term $J(t,x)$ is the flux of population due to the dispersal process as previously defined in (6). Here we neglect the term due to the population pressure. (The analysis extends without much difficulty to the equation including the population pressure, see Shigesada and Roughgarden, 1982). The second term of (37), $\varepsilon G(x,n)$, represents the net growth rate due to birth and death, which depends both on n and x. For convenience in later discussion, we express the net growth rate by the product of the factor ε and G so that the dispersal term, $-\partial J/\partial x$, and G are of the same order of magnitude. We assume that $G(x,n)$ is a bounded piecewise continuous function of x and has a continuous derivative with respect to n. Further, intraspecific competition is incorporated in the function G such that G becomes negative as n exceeds a certain positive number k.

Since we are interested in the case when the dispersal process occurs very rapidly compared with the growth process, we assume that ε is sufficiently small. For such a case, it is intuitively expected that a rapid change in the spatial distribution of the population due to the dispersal process occurs initially, followed by a slow long-term change in the population size due to the growth process.

To represent this more precisely, let us analyse equation (37) by means of a multiple-scale (two-timing) method (Neyfeh, 1973). For convenience of discussion, we choose the scales of independent variables so as to set the order of magnitude of the dispersal rate to be $O(1)$. Then the multiple-scale method leads to a truncated expansion of the solution as shown in the following theorem (see Appendix for proof: Shigesada, 1984).

Theorem   The solution of (37) with (38) and (39), which is valid for times up to $O(1/\varepsilon)$, is given by

$$n(t,x) = N^0(\varepsilon t)f(t,x) + O(\varepsilon), \tag{40}$$

where $f(t,x)$ and N^0 (εt) are the solutions of the following equations:

$$\frac{\partial}{\partial t}f\,(t,x) = -\frac{\partial}{\partial x}\,J(x,f) \quad \text{on } x \in \sigma,$$

subject to

$$f(0,x) = \frac{s(x)}{\displaystyle\int_\sigma s(x)\mathrm{d}x}\,,$$

$$J(x,f) = 0 \quad \text{at } x = 0 \text{ and } L, \tag{41}$$

$$\frac{\mathrm{d}}{\mathrm{d}t}\,N^0\,(\varepsilon t) = \varepsilon \int_\sigma G(x,N^0(\varepsilon t)\,f^*(x))\mathrm{d}x,$$

subject to $N^0(0) = \displaystyle\int_\sigma s(x)\mathrm{d}x,$ \hfill (42)

where $f^*(x) = \exp\{-U/\alpha\}\Big/\displaystyle\int_\sigma \exp\{-U/\alpha\}\mathrm{d}x.$

It follows from (41) that $f(t,x)$ represents the probability density of the spatial distribution, since $\int_\sigma f(t,x)dx = 1$. Thus $N^0(\varepsilon)$ can be regarded as the total population size in σ. To summarize, when we focus our attention on the behaviour of the rapid dispersal process (in the time range of $O(1)$), the distributional pattern $f(t,x)$ changes so as to satisfy (41), approaching an equilibrium $f(\infty,x) \equiv f^*(x)$ without change in the total population size; conversely, when we turn our attention to the long-term behaviour (in the time range of $O(1/\varepsilon)$), the total population size $N^0(\varepsilon t)$ changes so as to satisfy (42), while the probability density of the spatial distribution always remains in the stationary state, $f^*(x)$. In the following two sections, we will apply the above theorem to typical single- or two-species systems.

8 Population with general logistic growth

Here we will consider the case in which the growth term is of the general logistic type,

$$G(x,n) = \{a(x) - b(x)n\}n, \tag{43}$$

where $a(x)$ and $b(x)$ (>0) are assumed to be piecewise continuous functions of x in σ. The intrinsic growth rate $a(x)$ may have both positive and negative values in the habitat and if regions satisfying $a(x) < 0$ predominate in σ, the population may fail to grow in this habitat as a whole. Thus we are interested in the conditions under which the population can grow in the habitat and how the total population size changes to approach an equilibrium state.

Substituting (43) into (42), we have the equation for the total population size $N^0(\varepsilon t)$;

$$\frac{d}{dt}N^0(\varepsilon t) = \varepsilon(A - BN^0)N^0,$$

$$N^0(0) = \int_\sigma s(x)dx, \tag{44}$$

where

$$A = \int_\sigma a(x)f^*(x)dx, \qquad B = \int_\sigma b(x)f^{*2}(x)dx,$$

$$f^*(x) = \exp\left\{-\frac{U}{\alpha}\right\} \Big/ \int_\sigma \exp\left\{-\frac{U}{\alpha}\right\}dx.$$

The solution of (44) is given by

$$N^0(\varepsilon t) = \frac{AN^0(0)}{BN^0(0) + [A - BN^0(0)] \exp\{-\varepsilon tA\}} \tag{45}$$

which becomes, as $\varepsilon t \to \infty$

$$N^0(\varepsilon t) \to \begin{cases} A/B & \text{when} \quad A \geqslant 0, \\ 0 & \text{when} \quad A < 0. \end{cases} \tag{46}$$

Thus if the average growth rate with respect to $f^*(x)$ is positive, i.e.

$$A = \int_\sigma a(x)f^*(x)dx > 0, \tag{47}$$

then the population can grow in this habitat, and otherwise, the population becomes extinct. In other words, the condition $A > 0$ represents the invasion condition for the population. The value of A depends on the function $U(x)$, and hence even if the average of the intrinsic growth rate $a(x)$ over σ, $\int_\sigma a(x)dx$, is negative, A may be positive when $U(x)$ has such an appropriate form that directed movements are induced toward the region where $a(x)$ is positive.

As we noted previously, the two-timing expansion (40) is applicable as long as we are concerned with the time scale up to $O(1/\varepsilon)$, so that it is not necessarily uniformly valid for all time. However, in the case of the logistic growth of (42), it turns out to be a fairly good approximation even for a longer time range when ε is sufficiently small. Figure 12 shows that the truncated solutions (45) agree well with numerical results derived from (37).

To further examine the validity of our expansion, we will compare the invasion condition (47) with the exact one which is analytically derived from equation (37) combined with (43). When the population is rare throughout the whole habitat, we obtain the invasion condition for the population satisfying equation (37) with (43) by analysing the following linearized equation about the solution $n = 0$:

$$\frac{\partial}{\partial t}n = -\frac{\partial}{\partial x}J(x,n) + \varepsilon a(x)n, \quad x \in \sigma$$

$$J(x,n) = 0 \quad \text{at } x = 0 \text{ and } L. \tag{48}$$

If the equilibrium state $n = 0$ is dynamically unstable, the population can grow in the habitat; that is, the population, even when rare, can invade the habitat. If $n = 0$ is stable, on the other hand, the population finally becomes extinct in the habitat. Fleming (1975) performed a stability

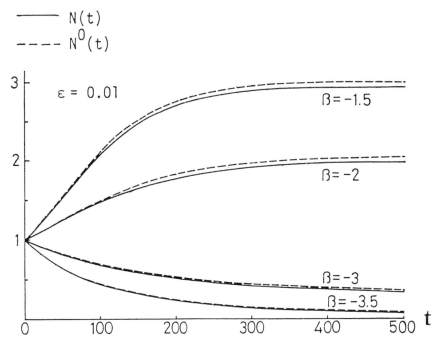

Fig. 4.12 Temporal changes in the total population sizes of single species. The
solid curves are $N(t) = \int_\sigma n(t,x)dx$ derived from (37) by computer calculation.
The broken curves are the truncated solutions of (45), N^0. Parameter values are
$\alpha = 1$, $b(x) = 1$, $\varepsilon = 0.01$, $L = 4$. Advection velocity is given by $-dU/dx = 1$,
so that animals are attracted in the positive direction of the x-axis. The intrinsic
growth rate is $a(x) = \beta + x$. Results for $\beta = -1.5$, -2, -3 and -3.5 are plotted.
The critical value of β for invasion condition in the multiple-scale method is
-3.074 at which $A = 0$.

analysis of (48) for the special case of $U(x) = 0$ and has presented a useful
theorem on the stability condition. By applying his theorem with slight
modifications to our model, we have invasion conditions for our system as
follows:

(i) $A > 0$,

or   (49)

(ii) $A < 0$ and $\varepsilon > \inf \left\{ \dfrac{\displaystyle\int_\sigma n_x^2 \exp\{-U/\alpha\}\,dx}{\displaystyle\int_\sigma a(x)n^2 \exp\{-U/\alpha\}\,dx} \right\} :$

$$\int_\sigma a(x)n^2 \exp\left(-U/\alpha\right) \mathrm{d}x > 0 \Bigg\}.$$

Now if ε tends to zero, the above condition is reduced to $A > 0$, which exactly coincides with our conclusion (47).

9 Multi-species systems

We now extend the previous study to multi-species systems. Consider an M-species system which satisfies the following equation:

$$\frac{\partial}{\partial t}n_i = -\frac{\partial}{\partial x}J_i(x,n_i) + \varepsilon G_i(x,n_1,n_2,\dots,n_M), \quad x \in [0,L] \equiv \sigma$$

for $i = 1, 2, \dots, M$,   (50)

where we put

$$J_i(x,n_i) = -\alpha_i \frac{\partial}{\partial x} n_i - \frac{\mathrm{d}}{\mathrm{d}x} U_i(x) \cdot n_i.$$ (51)

Here $n_i(t,x)$ is the population density of the ith species, and α_i, $U_i(x)$ and εG_i are respectively the diffusion constant, the environmental potential and the growth rate of the ith species. These parameters are defined in the same way as in the single-species system. The model is subject to the following initial and boundary conditions:

$$n_i(0,x) = s_i(x) \geqslant 0 \ (\neq 0),$$

$$J_i(x,n_i) = 0 \quad \text{at } x = 0 \text{ and } L.$$

The multiple-scale method can be applied to the above equation in a similar way as in the case of the single-species system, and the solution, which is valid for all t up to $O(1/\varepsilon)$, is given by

$$n_i(t,x) = N_i^0(\varepsilon t)f_i(t,x) + O(\varepsilon), \quad i = 1, 2, \dots, M,$$ (52)

where $f_i(t,x)$ is the probability density for the spatial distribution of the ith species and satisfies the following equation:

$$\frac{\partial}{\partial t}f_i = -\frac{\partial}{\partial x}J_i(x,f_i), \quad i = 1, 2, \dots, M,$$

$$f_i(0,x) = \frac{s_i(x)}{\displaystyle\int_\sigma s_i(x)\mathrm{d}x},$$ (53)

$$J_i(x,f_i) = 0 \quad \text{at } x = 0 \text{ and } L.$$

Here, $N_i^0(t)$ is the total population size of the ith species in σ and satisfies the dynamical systems,

$$\frac{d}{dt}\, N_i^0 = \varepsilon \int_\sigma G_i(x, N_1^0 f_1^*, N_2^0 f_2^*, \ldots, N_M^0 f_M^*)dx,$$

$$N_i^0(0) = \int_\sigma s_i(x)dx, \quad i = 1, 2, \ldots, M, \tag{54}$$

where

$$f_i^*(x) = \exp\left\{-\frac{U_i}{\alpha_i}\right\} \Big/ \int_\sigma \exp\left\{-\frac{U_i}{\alpha_i}\right\} dx.$$

Now, let us consider a special case of a two-competing-species system, which has the following generalized Lotka–Volterra-type growth functions,

$$G_i(x, n_1, n_2) = \left\{a_i(x) - \sum_j b_{ij}(x)\, n_j\right\} n_i, \quad i = 1, 2, \tag{55}$$

where we assume that $a_i(x)$ and $b_{ij}(x)$ (>0) depend on position x.

As studied in Section 6, if neither of these two species undergoes dispersal (namely when $J_1 = J_2 = 0$), they can coexist at a position x if only if

$$\frac{b_{11}(x)}{b_{21}(x)} > \frac{a_1(x)}{a_2(x)} > \frac{b_{12}(x)}{b_{22}(x)}, \tag{56}$$

and otherwise, one of the species always becomes extinct at x. Since the environment is heterogeneous, (56) may be satisfied at some places in the habitat, but not at other places. In such a case, we are interested in how the total population sizes of the two species in the habitat change with time, if both species undergo dispersal according to equation (51).

The equations for the population sizes in the multiple-scale method are obtained by substituting (55) into (54):

$$\frac{d}{dt}N_i^0 = \varepsilon \left\{A_i - \sum_j B_{ij}N_j^0\right\} N_i^0, \quad i = 1, 2, \tag{57}$$

where

$$A_i = \int_\sigma a_i(x)f_i^*(x)dx,$$

$$B_{ij} = \int_\sigma b_{ij}(x)f_i^*(x)f_j^*(x)dx.$$

Thus if

$$\frac{B_{11}}{B_{21}} > \frac{A_1}{A_2} > \frac{B_{12}}{B_{22}}, \tag{58}$$

the two species can coexist at least for times as large as $O(1/\varepsilon)$, and otherwise, one of the species tends to extinction.

Here it should be noted that equation (57) is analogous to the niche-partitioning theory of MacArthur and Levins (1967), if we take the real habitat space as the niche space. That is, we can see that $f_i^*(x)$ and $a_i(x)$ correspond to their utilization function and resource function. Thus (57) may be interpreted as a behavioural version of the MacArthur–Levins formula for habitat partitioning by competing species.

Now we carry out a numerical calculation of (50) for a two-competing-species system with the following parameters:

$$J_1 = -0.5 \frac{\partial}{\partial x} n_1 - 0.2n_1, \quad J_2 = -0.5 \frac{\partial}{\partial x} n_2 + n_2, \quad L = 2,$$

$$G_1 = (1 - 0.1x - n_1 - n_2)n_1, \quad G_2 = (1 + 0.5x - n_1 - n_2)n_2. \tag{59}$$

We also calculate the total population sizes $N_1(t) = \int_\sigma n_1(t,x)\mathrm{d}x$, $N_2(t)$ $= \int_\sigma n_2(t,x)\mathrm{d}x$, and compare them with the truncated solution by the multiple-scale method given by (57), $N_1^0(t)$ and $N_2^0(t)$. With the parameters chosen in (59), $a_1(x)/a_2(x) < b_{11}/b_{21}$, b_{12}/b_{22} for any $x \in \sigma$, and hence only the second species can survive everywhere in σ in the absence of dispersal. However, if both species undergo dispersal, (57) has a stable positive equilibrium state, because the condition (58) is satisfied ($A_1 = 0.91$, $A_2 = 1.77$, $B_{11} = 0.53$, $B_{12} = B_{21} = 0.40$, $B_{22} = 1.04$), so that both species tend to coexist as a whole in the multiple-scale method. In Figure 13, we show the time developments of the population sizes for three cases, $\varepsilon = 0.01$, 0.1 and 1. The solid and broken lines represent the numerical solutions of $N_1(t)$ and $N_2(t)$ derived from (50) for the case of (59) (hereafter called the exact solution), and the truncated solutions of (57), respectively. From this figure, we can see that for $\varepsilon = 0.01$, the dynamical behaviour of the truncated solution closely coincides with that of the exact solution, and the coincidence persists even for times longer than $O(1/\varepsilon)$. However, as ε increases so that the growth term becomes dominant in equation (50), the truncated solution deviates from the exact one with the lapse of time, and finally the first species becomes extinct in

---

Fig. 4.13 Temporal changes in the total population sizes of the two competing species. The solid curves are $N_1(t) = \int_\sigma n_1(t,x)\mathrm{d}x$ and $N_2(t) = \int_\sigma n_2(t,x)\mathrm{d}x$ derived from eq. (50) for the case of $M = 2$ by computer calculation. The broken curves are the truncated solutions derived from (57), $N_1^0(t)$, $N_2^0(t)$. Parameter values are given by (59). Results for $\varepsilon = 0.01$, 1 and 10 are plotted. The agreement between the two curves becomes better as ε decreases.

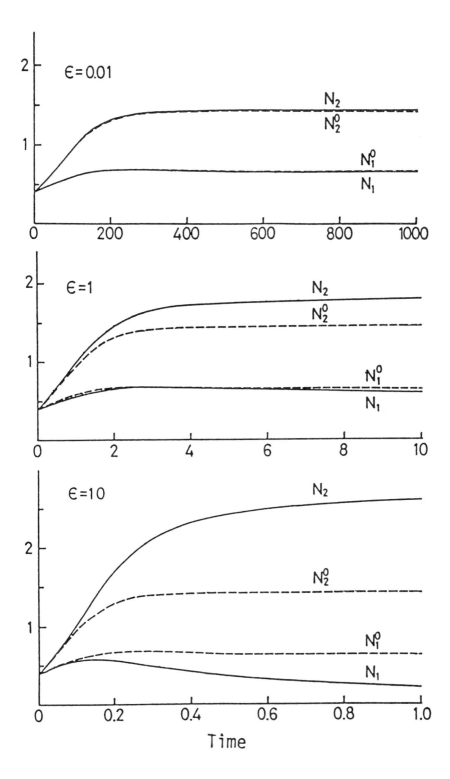

the exact solution, whereas in the truncated solution it remains positive for all time (the case of $\varepsilon = 10$). In the above example, we chose parameters such that the two species undergo dispersal with directed movement toward different favourable places. Thus they segregate their habitats from each other, occupying those places in which they can grow at higher rates. This segregation facilitates the coexistence of species by relaxing the competition between the species.

Further computer calculations with various parameter values have shown that as long as ε is small, the time developments of population sizes according to (57) approximate exact ones fairly well for various kinds of potential functions $U_i(x)$ and growth functions G_i.

10 Summary

Spatial pattern formation of dispersing animals in a heterogeneous environment is a universal biological phenomenon, which involves interactions of animals with the environment as well as among themselves. In this chapter, an attempt has been made to describe the motion of individuals on the basis of microscopic dispersal processes. It is assumed that the movement of an individual animal is influenced by three fundamental forces: (i) a dispersive force associated with random movement of individuals, (ii) population pressure due to mutual interference between individuals, (iii) an attractive force, which induces directed movement of animals toward favourable environments. Thus the dispersal of animals is formulated by a nonlinear diffusion equation combined with a space-dependent growth term. The model is applied to Morisita's experiments on ant-lions and some data on other insects. The model is also extended to a two-competing-species system. It has been demonstrated that the interspecific population pressure leads to spatial segregation of two species, which acts to stabilize their coexistence.

Acknowledgements

The author thanks Drs K. Kawasaki and E. Teramoto for their collaboration and valuable discussion on this work. She is also grateful to Professor L. M. Ricciardi for his continuous encouragement in preparing this chapter.

Appendix: Proof of theorem

Let us introduce the following two different time scales, T_0, T_1 defined as

$$T_0 = t, \quad T_1 = \varepsilon t.$$

We consider the solution of (37) as a function of these two time scales, $n(t,x) = n(T_0, T_1, x; \varepsilon)$ and we attempt to find the solution in the following form, which is valid for times as large as $O(1/\varepsilon)$:

$$n(t,x) = n(T_0, T_1, x; \varepsilon) = n^0(T_0, T_1, x) + \varepsilon n^1(T_0, T_1, x) + \ldots, \quad (A.1)$$

where the remainder is $O(\varepsilon^2)$ and n^1 is bounded for all T_0. We will carry out a perturbation procedure by noting that the time derivative is transformed according to

$$\frac{\partial}{\partial t} = \frac{\partial}{\partial T_0} + \varepsilon \frac{\partial}{\partial T_1}. \quad (A.2)$$

Upon inserting (A.1) and (A.2) into (37) and equating coefficients of like powers of ε, we obtain

$$\frac{\partial}{\partial T_0} n^0 = -\frac{\partial}{\partial x} J(x, n^0),$$

$$n^0(0, 0, x) = s(x), \quad (A.3)$$

$$J(x, n^0) = 0 \quad \text{at } x = 0 \text{ and } L;$$

$$\frac{\partial}{\partial T_0} n^1 + \frac{\partial}{\partial x} J(x, n^1) = -\frac{\partial}{\partial T_1} n^0 + G(x, n^0),$$

$$n^1(0, 0, x) = 0, \quad (A.4)$$

$$J(x, n^1) = 0 \quad \text{at } x = 0 \text{ and } L.$$

The general solution of (A.3) is written in the form

$$n^0(T_0, T_1, x) = N^0(T_1) f(T_0, x), \quad (A.5)$$

where $f(T_0, x)$ is the solution of the following equation:

$$\frac{\partial}{\partial T_0} f = -\frac{\partial}{\partial x} J(x, f),$$

$$f(0, x) = \frac{s(x)}{\displaystyle\int_\sigma s(x) \, dx}, \quad (A.6)$$

$$J(x, f) = 0 \quad \text{at } x = 0 \text{ and } L.$$

By integrating (A.6) over σ, we find $\displaystyle\int_\sigma f(T_0, x) \, dx = 1$. Thus, $f(T_0, x)$ may be regarded as the probability density of the spatial distribution of population in σ, since $f(T_0, x) \geq 0$. Equation (A.6) is a so-called regular Sturm–Liouville problem, and its solution is written as

$$f(T_0, x) = \sum_{i=1}^{\infty} c_i \exp\{-\lambda_i T_0\} \varphi_i(x), \quad (A.7)$$

where φ_i are the eigenfunctions of (A.6) and λ_i are the eigenvalues, which are positive and can be arranged in the following increasing sequence (Berg and McGregor, 1966):

$$0 < \lambda_1 < \lambda_2 < \lambda_3 \ldots$$

Thus $f(T_0,x)$ is bounded for all x and T_0 and asymptotically approaches an equilibrium $f^*(x)$, which is the solution of $J(x,f^*) = 0$:

$$f(T_0,x) \xrightarrow{T_0 \to \infty} f^*(x) = \frac{\exp\{-U(x)/\alpha\}}{\displaystyle\int_\sigma \exp\{-U(x)/\alpha\}\,dx}. \tag{A.8}$$

The function $N^0(T_1)$ remains arbitrary, but we can determine it at the next stage of the perturbation.

To this end, let us integrate (A.4) over σ and put $N^1(T_0,T_1) = \displaystyle\int_\sigma n^1(T_0,T_1,x)\,dx$. We then have

$$\frac{\partial}{\partial T_0} N^1(T_0,T_1) = -\frac{\partial}{\partial T_1} N^0(T_1) + \int_\sigma G\,[x,N^0(T_1)\,f(T_0,x)]\,dx. \tag{A.9}$$

Since $n^1(T_0,T_1,x)$ is required to be bounded for all T_0, $N^1(T_0,T_1)$ should also be bounded for all T_0. However, the solution of (A.9), $N^1(T_0,T_1)$ will become unbounded, because of the occurrence of secular terms, unless we require the right-hand side of (A.9) to tend to zero as $T_0 \to \infty$. So let us try to set the unknown function $N^0(T_1)$ equal to the solution of the following equation,

$$\frac{d}{dT_1} N^0(T_1) = \int_\sigma G[x,N^0(T_1)\,f^*(T_0,x)]\,dx,$$
$$N^0(0) = \int_\sigma s(x)\,dx, \tag{A.10}$$

which is obtained if we substitute $f^*(x)$ into $f(T_0,x)$ in (A.9) and set the right-hand side of (A.9) equal to zero. The solution of (A.10), $N^0(T_1)$, is bounded for all T_1 because we imposed the condition that $G(x,n)$ becomes negative for large n.

Now let us examine whether the solution of (A.9), $N^1(T_0,T_1)$, is actually bounded for all T_0. By substituting (A.10) into (A.9), and integrating over T_0, we obtain the equation,

$$N^1(T_0,T_1) = \int_0^{T_0}\int_\sigma \left\{-G[x,N^0f^*(x)] + G[x,N^0f(T_0',x)]\right\}\,dx\,dT_0'. \tag{A.11}$$

The right-hand side is verified to be bounded for all T_0 if we apply the mean value theorem and take equation (A.7) into consideration. Thus the assumption of N^0 as the solution of (A.10) proves to be appropriate.

To summarize the above analysis, the solution of (37), which is valid for times up to $O(1/\varepsilon)$, is given by

$$n(t,x) = N^0(\varepsilon t)\, f(t,x) + O(\varepsilon), \tag{A.12}$$

where $f(t,x)$ is the probability density of the spatial distribution given by (A.7), and $N^0(\varepsilon t)$ is the solution of the ordinary differential equation (A.10). $\qquad\square$

References

Berg, P. W. and McGregor, J. L. (1966) *Elementary Partial Differential Equations*, Holden-Day, San Francisco.

Bertsch, M. E., Gurtin, D., Hilhorst, D. and Peletier, L. A. (1985) On interacting populations that disperse to avoid crowding: presevation of segregation, *J. Math. Biology*, **23**, 1–13.

Brian, W. J. (1956) Segregation of species of the ant genus *Myrmica*, *J. Anim. Ecol.*, **25**, 319–37.

Clark, D. P. (1962) An analysis of dispersal and movement in *Phaulacridium vittatum* (Sjost) (Acrididae), *Aust. J. Zool.*, **10**, 382–99.

Comins, H. N. and Blatt, D. W. E. (1974) Prey–predator models in spatially heterogeneous environments, *J. Theor. Biol*, **48**, 75–83.

Fife, P. C. (1979) *Mathematical Aspects of Reacting and Diffusing Systems*, Lecture Notes in Biomathematics 28, Springer, Berlin-Heidelberg-New York.

Fleming, W. H. (1975) A selection-migration model in population genetics, *J. Math. Biol.*, **2**, 219–33.

Gurney, W. S. C. and Nisbet, R. M. (1975) The regulation of inhomogeneous populations, *J. Theor. Biol.*, **52**, 441–57.

Gurney, W. S. C. and Nisbet, R. M. (1976) A note on non-linear population transport, *J. Theor. Biol.*, **56**, 249–51.

Gurtin, M. E. and MacCamy, R. C. (1977) On the diffusion of biological populations, *Math. Biosciences*, **33**, 35–49.

Ito, Y. (1952) The growth form of populations in some aphids, with special reference to the relation between population density and movements, *Res. Popul. Ecol.*, **1**, 36–48 (Japanese with English summary).

Kawanabe, H. (1959) Food competition among fishes in some rivers of Kyoto prefecture, Japan, *Memoirs of College of Sci., University of Kyoto, Ser. B*, **26**, (Biology) 253–68.

Kawasaki, K. and Teramoto, E. (1979) Spatial pattern formation of prey-predator populations, *J. Math. Biol.*, **8**, 33–46.

Kosaka, M. (1956) Experimental studies on the habitat preference and evaluation of environment by the flatfishes, *Limanda yokohawae* (Gunthek) and *Kareius bicoloratus* (Basilewsky), *Bull. Jap. Soc. Sci. Fish.*, **22**, 284–92.

Kubo, H. (1957) Experimental studies on the habitat preference of a goby, *Gobius abei Jap. J. Ecol.*, **7**, 80–4, (Japanese with English summary).

Kuno, T. (1952) Time–dispersion curve: experimental studies on the dispersion of insects(2), *Res. Popul. Ecol.*, **1**, 109–18 (Japanese with English summary).

Levin, S. A. (1981) Models in population dispersal. In *Differential Equations and Applications in Ecology, Epidemics, and Population Problems*. S. N. Busenberg, and K. Cooke, (eds), Academic Press, New York.

MacArthur, R. H. and Levins, R. (1967) The limiting similarity, convergence and divergence of coexisting species, *Amer. Natur.*, **101**, 377–85.

May, R. H., Endler, J. A. and McMurtrie, R. E. (1975) Gene frequency clines in the presence of selection opposed by gene flow, *Amer. Natur.*, **109**, 659–676.

Mimura, M. and Yamaguti, M. (1982) Pattern formation in interacting and diffusing systems in population biology. In *Advances in Biophysics* University of Tokyo Press and M. Kotani (ed.), University Park Press, pp. 19–65.

Morisita, M. (1952) Habitat preference and evaluation of environment of an animal: experimental studies on the population density of an ant-lion, *Glenuroides japonicus* M'L. (1), *Physiol. and Ecol.*, **5**, 1–16 (Japanese with English summary).

Morisita, M. (1954a) On the relationship between dispersal of ant-lion and its population density, *Japanese J. Zool.*, **63**, 22–3. (Japanese).

Morisita, M. (1954b) Dispersion and population pressure: experimental studies on the population density of an ant-lion, *Glenuroides japonicus* M'L(2), *Japanese J. Ecol.*, **4**, 71–9 (Japanese with English summary).

Morisita, M. (1971) Measuring of habitat value by the 'environmental density' method. In *Statistical Ecology*, Vol. 1, G. P. Patil, E. C. Pielou and W. E. Waters (eds) Pennsylvania University Press, University Park and London, pp. 379–401.

Murray, J. D. (1977) *Lectures on Nonlinear Differential-Equation Models in Biology*, Clarendon Press, Oxford.

Nagylaki, T. (1975) Conditions for the existence of clines, *Genetics*, **80**, 595–615.

Namba, T. (1980) Density-dependent dispersal and spatial distribution of a population, *J. Theor. Biol.*, **86**, 351–63.

Neyfeh, A. H. (1973) *Perturbation Methods*, Wiley, New York.

Okubo, A. (1980) *Diffusion and Ecological Problems: Mathematical Models*, Springer, Berlin-Heidelberg-New York.

Okubo, A. (1986) Dynamical aspects of animal grouping: swarms, schools, flock, and herds. In *Advances Biophysics 22*, M. Kodani (ed.), University of Tokyo Press and University Park Press, pp. 1–94.

Pacala, S. and Roughgarden, J. (1982) Spatial heterogeneity and interspecific competition, *Theor. Pop. Biol.*, **21**, 92–113.

Pattle, R. E. (1959) Diffusion from an instantaneous point source with a concentration-dependent coefficient. *Quart. J. Mech. Appl. Math.*, **12**, 407–9.

Shigesada, N. (1980) Spatial distribution of dispersing animals, *J. Math. Biol.*, **9**, 85–96.

Shigesada, N. (1984) Spatial distribution of rapidly dispersing animals in heterogeneous environments. In: Lecture Notes in Biomathematics 54: *Mathematical Ecology*, S. A. Levin and T. G. Hallam (eds), Springer 478–91.

Shigesada, N. and Roughgarden, J. (1982) The role of rapid dispersal in the population dynamics of competition. *Theor. Pop. Biol.*, **21**, 353–73.

Shigesada, N., Kawasaki, K. and Teramoto, E. (1979) Spatial segregation of interacting species. *J. Theor. Biol.*, **79**, 83–99.

Shigesada, N., Kawasaki, K. and Teramoto, E. (1986) Traveling periodic waves in heterogeneous environments. *Theor. Popul.* Biol. **30**, 143–60.

Teramoto, E. (1982) A mathematical model of density dependent dispersive motions. In *Biomathematics in 1980*, L. M. Ricciardi and A. C. Scott (eds), North-Holland, Amsterdam, pp. 245–52.

Watanabe, S., Utida, S. and Yosida, T. (1952) Dispersion of insect and change of distribution type in its process: experimental studies on the dispersion of insects (1), *Res. Popul. Ecol.*, **1**, 94–108 (Japanese with English summary).

5

Diffusion processes and first-passage-time problems

Luigi M. Ricciardi   *Dipartimento di Matematica e Applicazioni Università di Napoli, Via Mezzocannone 8, 80134 Napoli, Italy*
and

Shunsuke Sato   *Department of Biophysical Engineering, Faculty of Engineering Science, Osaka University, Toyonaka, Osaka, Japan 560*

1 Introduction

The purpose of these lectures is to bring up, in a somewhat unified way, the essential elements of the theory of one-dimensional diffusion processes with a special emphasis on the available methods to characterize the related first-passage-time distributions. The motivation is twofold: On the one hand, the results thus far worked out on first-passage-time problems appear to be rather fragmentary, so that a unified treatment is desirable *per se*; on the other hand, such problems have been widely recognized to play an important role for applications to fields ranging through biology, physics, engineering and psychology, to name just a few. Hence, the theoretical approaches to the solution of the first-passage-time problems and the associated computational methods will hopefully provide useful tools to a wide category of researchers, irrespective of their specific background and their research field. To this end, the necessary concepts and techniques will be introduced by means of heuristic considerations rather than in an abstract fashion. A special emphasis will thus be given to the pragmatic aspects. As a counterpart to the lack of generality the reader will discover that only the basic notions of probability and differential calculus are essential prerequisites for understanding most of the material discussed in the sequel. The more theoretically inclined applied mathematician will find it useful to use the present notes as an introduction to the subject and refer to one of the excellent treatises on stochastic processes for a more rigorous and complete presentation of the theory of diffusion processes and its related topics. Unfortunately, to our knowledge there is not, as yet, a similarly complete and rigorous treatment in the literature of the first-passage-time problems and of their related computational methods. Several results due to the authors of these notes and to their co-workers will be briefly discussed in the sequel.

2 Preliminaries

Stochastic processes are customarily associated with the outcomes of an (often ideal) experiment whose complexity prevents one from performing deterministic predictions. With reference to one such experiment, let us label by $\omega \in \Omega$ its outcomes and let us assume that certain subsets of Ω (called *events*) and their measures (probabilities of these events) have been specified. Let us now associate with every outcome ω, according to some rule that we do not need to specify here, a real function $X(t,\omega)$, where $t \in T$ will be henceforth identified with the time variable. The family of functions $X(t,\omega)$ is called a *stochastic process* or a *random function*. In the sequel we shall mainly consider stochastic processes for which both T and Ω are continuous sets and we shall identify T with the entire time axis. In summary, the stochastic process $X(t,\omega)$ possesses the following properties: (i) for a specific outcome ω_i, $X(t,\omega_i)$ is a single deterministic function of time; (ii) for a specific time t_j, $X(t_j,\omega)$ is a random variable; and (iii) $X(t_j,\omega_i)$ is a number. In the following, to simplify the notation we shall omit the specification of the random variable and thus denote a stochastic process by $X(t)$. However, the dependence on ω is to be always implicitly assumed.

We shall say that a stochastic process $X(t)$ is known if for any integer n and for any n-tuple of instants $t_1 < t_2 < \ldots < t_n$ the joint n-dimensional probability density function (p.d.f.) $f_n[X(t_1); X(t_2); \ldots; X(t_n)]$ is known. Thus $X(t)$ can be characterized by an infinite sequence of p.d.f.'s of increasing order, namely $f_1[X(t_1)]$, $f_2[X(t_1); X(t_2)]$, $\ldots$, $f_n[X(t_1); X(t_2); \ldots; X(t_n)]$, $\ldots$, related to one another via the so-called compatibility conditions. For instance, a joint p.d.f. of order $(n - 1)$ is obtained by integrating a joint p.d.f. of order n over the domain of one of the random variables:

$$f_{n-1} [X(t_1); X(t_2); \ldots; X(t_j); \ldots; X(t_n)]$$

$$= \int dX(t_j)\, f_n[X(t_1); X(t_2); \ldots; X(t_n)] \quad (1 \leqslant j \leqslant n). \tag{2.1}$$

The knowledge of a stochastic process thus requires the determination of all functions $f_n[X(t_1); X(t_2); \ldots; X(t_n)]$ for all n and $t_1 < t_2 < \ldots < t_n$, which in general is not feasible. Two remarkable exceptions for which such knowledge is attainable are provided by Gaussian and by Markov processes. Hereafter we shall confine our attention to the latter, also known as processes *without after-effect* for a reason that will emerge soon.

We shall say that a process $X(t)$ is Markov if for all integers n and for all n-tuples of instants $t_1 < t_2 < \ldots < t_n$ we have:

$$f_n[X(t_n) \mid X(t_{n-1}); X(t_{n-2}); \ldots; X(t_1)] = f[X(t_n) \mid X(t_{n-1})], \qquad (2.2)$$

where the conditional p.d.f. is defined as:

$$\begin{aligned} &f_n[X(t_n) \mid X(t_{n-1}); X(t_{n-2}); \ldots; X(t_1)] \\ &= \frac{f_n[X(t_1); X(t_2); \ldots; X(t_n)]}{f_{n-1}[X(t_1); X(t_2); \ldots; X(t_{n-1})]}. \end{aligned} \qquad (2.3)$$

The function on the right-hand side of (2.2) is the *transition* p.d.f. of $X(t)$. The Markov property (2.2) can then be stated by saying that given the 'present', $X(t_{n-1})$, the 'future', $X(t_n)$, is independent of the 'past', $X(t_j)$, $(j < n - 1)$. By repeatedly making use of (2.2) and (2.3), one can easily prove that for all integers n and for all n-tuples $t_1 < t_2 < \ldots < t_n$ we have:

$$\begin{aligned} &f_n[X(t_1); X(t_2); \ldots; X(t_n)] \\ &= f_1[X(t_1)]f[X(t_2) \mid X(t_1)]f[X(t_3) \mid X(t_2)] \ldots f[X(t_n) \mid X(t_{n-1})]. \end{aligned}$$

Hence, the description of a Markov process can be obtained solely by the knowledge of the univariate p.d.f. $f_1[X(\tau)]$ and of the transition p.d.f. $f[X(t) \mid X(\tau)]$, for all t and τ. The former is customarily viewed as an 'initial condition', whereas the latter is the actual unknown function when one aims at the specification of the stochastic process. Hence, a problem of primary interest is to formulate some equation involving the transition p.d.f. and then solve it to obtain such function explicitly. Before coming to the formulation of these equations, which will be the object of the next section, it is worth mentioning explicitly that the knowledge of transition and univariate p.d.f.'s only in principle allow us to achieve a complete description of the random function under consideration. Indeed, certain of its features cannot be unveiled unless specific analyses, usually rather cumbersome and often requiring a great deal of numerical computations, are carried out. Arguments in support of this statement will for instance clearly emerge from the discussion of first-passage-time problems.

3   Kinetic equations

The transition p.d.f. is, for any pair of instants $\tau < t$, a function of the variables $y \equiv X(\tau)$ and $x \equiv X(t)$. Such a fourfold dependence on x, t, y and τ is conveniently indicated explicitly by writing $f(x,t \mid y,\tau)$ in place of $f[X(t) \mid X(\tau)]$. By using similar notations, the joint p.d.f. $f_2[X(t); X(t_0)]$ can be expressed in terms of the third-order joint p.d.f. $f_3[X(t); X(\tau); X(t_0)]$ in the following manner:

$$f_2(x,t; x_0,t_0) = \int dy \, f_3(x,t; y,\tau; x_0,t_0) \tag{3.1}$$

for any triple of instants $t_0 < \tau < t$. Hereafter we shall consider t as the present time and t_0 as an arbitrarily preassigned initial time. Making use of (2.3), i.e. under the assumption that $X(t)$ is Markov, from (3.1) we obtain:

$$f(x,t \mid x_0,t_0) \, f_1(x_0,t_0) = \int dy \, f(x,t \mid y,\tau) \, f_2(y,\tau; x_0,t_0)$$

or, making use again of (2.3):

$$f(x,t \mid x_0,t_0) = \int dy \, f(x,t \mid y,\tau) \, f(y,\tau \mid x_0,t_0). \tag{3.2}$$

Equation (3.2) is a compatibility relation that is satisfied by the transition p.d.f. of any Markov process. In the literature it is known as the Chapman–Kolmogorov equation or as the Smolukowski equation. However, it cannot be used directly to determine the transition p.d.f. of the process, unless some further and more stringent assumptions are made on the process itself, as we shall point out soon. To this purpose, it is convenient to rewrite equation (3.2) in a differential form. This can be done by changing in equation (3.2), t into $t + \Delta t$ and τ into t, with $\Delta t > 0$ denoting a small, but finite, increment of the time t. From (3.2) we thus obtain:

$$f(x,t+\Delta t \mid x_0,t_0) - f(x,t \mid x_0,t_0)$$

$$= \int dy \, f(x,t+\Delta t \mid y,t) \, f(y,t \mid x_0,t_0) - f(x,t \mid x_0,t_0). \tag{3.3}$$

Denoting by $R(x)$ any arbitrary function that vanishes sufficiently rapidly at the end-points of the state space together with its derivatives of all orders, from (3.3) we obtain:

$$\int dx \, R(x) \frac{f(x,t+\Delta t \mid x_0,t_0) - f(x,t \mid x_0,t_0)}{\Delta t}$$

$$= \frac{1}{\Delta t} \int dx \, R(x) \int dy \, f(x,t+\Delta t \mid y,t) \, f(y,t \mid x_0,t_0)$$

$$- \frac{1}{\Delta t} \int dx \, R(x) f(x,t \mid x_0,t_0). \tag{3.4}$$

We now expand $R(x)$ as a Taylor series about the point y and substitute such an expansion in the first term on the right-hand side of (3.4). Passing to the limit as $\Delta t \downarrow 0$ we thus obtain:

$$\int dx\, R(x)\, \frac{\partial f}{\partial t} = \lim_{\Delta t \downarrow 0} \frac{1}{\Delta t} \int dy\, R(y) f(y,t \mid x_0,t_0) \int dx\, f(x,t+\Delta t \mid y,t)$$

$$+ \sum_{n=1}^{\infty} \frac{1}{n!} \int dy\, \left\{ \frac{d^n R(y)}{dy^n} f(y,t \mid x_0,t_0) \right.$$

$$\times \lim_{\Delta t \downarrow 0} \frac{1}{\Delta t} \int dx\, (x - y)^n f(x,t+\Delta t \mid y,t) \Big\}$$

$$- \lim_{\Delta t \downarrow 0} \frac{1}{\Delta t} \int dx\, R(x) f(x,t \mid x_0,t_0). \tag{3.5}$$

Let us now remark that

$$\int dx\, f(x,t+\Delta t \mid y,t) = 1, \tag{3.6}$$

since the left-hand side is the probability that the process takes any possible value at time $t + \Delta t$ starting from the value y at time t. Furthermore, let us set

$$A_n(x,t) = \lim_{\Delta t \downarrow 0} \frac{1}{\Delta t} \int dy (y - x)^n f(y,t + \Delta t \mid x,t), \quad (n = 1, 2, \ldots). \tag{3.7}$$

Making use of (3.6) and (3.7), equation (3.5) becomes:

$$\int dx\, R(x)\, \frac{\partial f}{\partial t} = \sum_{n=1}^{\infty} \frac{1}{n!} \int dx\, \frac{d^n R(x)}{dx^n} f(x,t \mid x_0,t_0)\, A_n(x,t). \tag{3.8}$$

The integral on the right-hand side of (3.8) can be calculated by parts. Using the assumed vanishing of $R(x)$ and of its derivatives at the ends of the integration interval, it is easy to prove that

$$\int dx\, \frac{d^n R(x)}{dx^n} f(x,t \mid x_0,t_0)\, A_n(x,t)$$

$$= (-1)^n \int dx\, R(x)\, \frac{\partial^n}{\partial x^n} [A_n(x,t)\, f(x,t \mid x_0,t_0)].$$

Equation (3.8) then yields:

$$\int dx\, R(x) \left\{ \frac{\partial f}{\partial t} - \sum_{n=1}^{\infty} \frac{(-1)^n}{n!} \frac{\partial^n}{\partial x^n} [A_n(x,t)\, f(x,t \mid x_0,t_0)] \right\} = 0. \tag{3.9}$$

Due to the arbitrariness of $R(x)$, we conclude that the following relation holds:

$$\frac{\partial f(x,t \mid x_0,t_0)}{\partial t} = \sum_{n=1}^{\infty} \frac{(-1)^n}{n!} \frac{\partial^n}{\partial x^n} [A_n(x,t)\, f(x,t \mid x_0,t_0)]. \tag{3.10}$$

This is the so-called differential form of the Smolukowski equation, often referred to as the *kinetic equation* of the Markov process $X(t)$. It is an evolution-type equation regulating the time course of the transition p.d.f. The presence of the derivative with respect to time calls for an initial condition. This will henceforth be taken as follows:

$$\lim_{t \downarrow t_0} f(x,t \mid x_0,t_0) = \delta(x - x_0), \tag{3.11}$$

where $\delta(\cdot)$ is the Dirac delta function. The meaning of condition (3.11) is quite obvious: at time t_0 the whole probability mass is located at x_0. As time passes, such a probability mass spreads around so that in general the process $X(t)$ will take values over the entire state space.

In the differential expansion (3.10) the functions $A_n(x,t)$ defined by (3.7) appear. These are the so-called infinitesimal moments of the process $X(t)$. Upon setting

$$\Delta X = X(t + \Delta t) - X(t)$$

we see from (3.7) that for Δt small one has:

$$E\{(\Delta X)^n \mid X(t) = x\} \simeq A_n(x,t)\,\Delta t \quad (n = 1, 2, \ldots) \tag{3.12}$$

showing that for a Markov process the conditional moments of the increment of the process over a small time interval are all proportional to such time interval. Writing (3.12) for $n = 1$ and $n = 2$, the conditional variance $V\{\Delta X \mid X(t) = x\}$ can be calculated. One can then immediately prove that $A_2(x,t)$ can be interpreted as the conditional variance per unit time:

$$A_2(x,t) = \lim_{\Delta t \downarrow 0} \frac{E\{(\Delta X)^2 \mid X(t) = x\}}{\Delta t}. \tag{3.13}$$

Hence, $A_2(x,t)$ is often referred to as to the *infinitesimal variance* of the process. The first-order infinitesimal moment

$$A_1(x,t) = \lim_{\Delta t \downarrow 0} \frac{E\{(\Delta X) \mid X(t) = x\}}{\Delta t} \tag{3.14}$$

is the so-called *drift* of the process.

It should be emphasized that the differential expansion (3.10) of Smolukowski's equation involves the derivatives of the transition p.d.f. with respect to t and x. Hence, t_0 and x_0 are considered as parameters denoting initial time and initial position, respectively, while t and x are viewed as present time and current position variables. However, an alternative differential expansion of Smolukowski's equation can be obtained in which initial time and initial position appear as variables, while present time and current position are taken as parameters. To obtain such an expansion let us perform the substitutions $t_0 \to t_0 - \Delta t$ and $\tau \to t_0$ in (3.2):

$$f(x,t \mid x_0,t_0-\Delta t) = \int dy \, f(y,t_0 \mid X_0,t_0-\Delta t) \, f(x,t \mid y,t_0), \qquad (3.15)$$

where now $x = X(t)$, $x_0 = X(t_0 - \Delta t)$, $y = X(t_0)$ and $\Delta t > 0$ is a small arbitrary increment. Equation (3.15) can be rewritten as:

$$f(x,t \mid x_0,t_0-\Delta t) - f(x,t \mid x_0,t_0)$$

$$= \int dy \, f(y,t_0 \mid x_0,t_0-\Delta t)[f(x,t \mid y,t_0) - f(x,t \mid x_0,t_0)], \qquad (3.16)$$

where use of the identity

$$f(x,t \mid x_0,t_0) = \int dy \, f(x,t \mid x_0,t_0)f(y,t_0 \mid x_0,t_0-\Delta t)$$

has been made. Expanding $f(x,t \mid y,t_0)$ on the right-hand side of (3.16) as a Taylor series about x, dividing both sides by $(-\Delta t)$ and taking the limit as $\Delta t \downarrow 0$, we finally obtain:

$$\frac{\partial f(x,t \mid x_0,t_0)}{\partial t_0} + \sum_{n=1}^{\infty} \frac{A_n(x_0,t_0)}{n!} \frac{\partial^n f(x,t \mid x_0,t_0)}{\partial x_0^n} = 0, \qquad (3.17)$$

where $A_n(x_0,t_0)$ are the infinitesimal moments defined in the foregoing.

We have thus found that the transition p.d.f. of a Markov process evolves according to the *kinetic equations* (3.10) and (3.17), while satisfying the initial condition (3.11). The former is a *forward* equation as the initial variables are fixed, while the latter is a *backward* equation as it describes the unfolding of the process leading to a preassigned state at the present time.

4   Diffusion equations

An important class of Markov processes is characterized by the vanishing of the infinitesimal moments from the third order on. These are the so-called *diffusion processes* for which $A_n(x,t) = 0$ ($n = 3, 4, \ldots$). Hence, in such case the transition p.d.f. satisfies the second-order partial differential *diffusion equations*

$$\frac{\partial f}{\partial t} = -\frac{\partial}{\partial x}[A_1(x,t)f] + \frac{1}{2}\frac{\partial^2}{\partial x^2}[A_2(x,t)f] \qquad (4.1)$$

and

$$\frac{\partial f}{\partial t_0} + A_1(x_0,t_0)\frac{\partial f}{\partial x_0} + \frac{1}{2}A_2(x_0,t_0)\frac{\partial^2 f}{\partial x_0^2} = 0. \qquad (4.2)$$

Hence, the equations describing the evolution of a diffusion process can be written down once the drift and the infinitesimal variance of the process have been determined. Equation (4.1) is known as the *Fokker–Planck* or *forward* equation, whereas (4.2) is the so-called *Kolmogorov* or *backward* equation. In numerous cases either can be used, together with condition (3.11), to determine the transition p.d.f. and thus obtain a description of the considered diffusion process.

Let us now define the *probability current*

$$j(x,t \mid x_0,t_0) = A_1(x,t) f(x,t \mid x_0,t_0) - \frac{1}{2} \frac{\partial}{\partial x} [A_2(x,t) f(x,t \mid x_0,t_0)], \quad (4.3)$$

so that the Fokker–Planck equation (4.1) takes the form:

$$\frac{\partial f}{\partial t} + \frac{\partial j}{\partial x} = 0. \quad (4.4)$$

This can be viewed as the 'conservation equation' for the probability mass of a diffusion process. Indeed, looking at $j(x,t \mid x_0,t_0)$ as the amount of probability crossing the abscissa x in the positive direction per unit time, for any fixed interval (y,z) we have:

$$j(y,t \mid x_0,t_0) \simeq \text{amount of probability } entering \ (y,z) \text{ across } y \text{ in } \Delta t;$$
$$j(z,t \mid x_0,t_0) \simeq \text{amount of probability } leaving \ (y,z) \text{ across } z \text{ in } \Delta t.$$

Hence, the increment of probability in (y,z) between t and $t + \Delta t$ can be roughly expressed as:

$$[j(y,t \mid x_0,t_0) - j(z,t \mid x_0,t_0)]\Delta t$$
$$\simeq \int_y^z dx \ f(x,t+\Delta t \mid x_0,t_0) - \int_y^z dx \ f(x,t \mid x_0,t_0).$$

Therefore,

$$\frac{j(y,t \mid x_0,t_0) - j(z,t \mid x_0,t_0)}{z - y} \simeq \frac{f(v,t+\Delta t \mid x_0,t_0) - f(w,t \mid x_0,t_0)}{\Delta t}, \quad (4.5)$$

with v and w in (y,z). Taking the limit as $z \downarrow y$ and $\Delta t \downarrow 0$ and changing y into x we recover equation (4.4), i.e. we obtain the conservation law mentioned before. This provides a justification of definition (4.3).

Let us now assume that f is non-zero over the 'diffusion interval' (a,b), being zero elsewhere. This implies that at all times the whole probability mass is confined to such an interval. Hence,

$$\int_a^b dx \ f(x,t \mid x_0,t_0) = 1. \quad (4.6)$$

Differentiating (4.6) with respect to t and making use of (4.4) we obtain:

$$\int_a^b dx \ \frac{\partial j(x,t \mid x_0,t_0)}{\partial x} = 0,$$

or:

$$j(a,t \mid x_0,t_0) = j(b,t \mid x_0,t_0). \tag{4.7}$$

However, if no probability mass reaches the end-points of the diffusion interval in finite time, the following stronger condition is expected to hold:

$$j(a,t \mid x_0,t_0) = j(b,t \mid x_0,t_0) = 0. \tag{4.8}$$

Such a situation usually arises when $(a,b) \equiv (-\infty,+\infty)$, in which case one usually expects the vanishing of the transition p.d.f. as $x \to \pm\infty$.

Let us now focus our attention on a diffusion process whose transition p.d.f. does not depend separately on present and initial times but only on their difference:

$$f(x,t \mid x_0,t_0) = f(x,t-t_0 \mid x_0,0) \equiv f(x,t-t_0 \mid x_0). \tag{4.9}$$

We shall say that such a process is temporally homogeneous. A problem of interest is then the investigation of the existence of a *limit* or *steady state* p.d.f. $W(x)$ describing the diffusion process after an infinitely long time interval during which the process progressively 'forgets' its initial state to attain a condition of statistical equilibrium which is independent of both time and initial state. Denoting by $W(x)$ such supposedly existing steady state p.d.f., from equation (4.4) we obtain

$$\frac{\partial W}{\partial x} \equiv 0 = \frac{\partial j_0}{\partial x}, \tag{4.10}$$

implying that the steady state probability current j_0 is a constant. Furthermore, due to assumption (4.9) from (3.7) one sees that drift $A_1(x)$ and infinitesimal variance $A_2(x)$ are now time-independent so that (4.10) reads:

$$\frac{d}{dx}[A_2(x)W(x)] - 2A_1(x)W(x) + 2j_0 = 0. \tag{4.11}$$

The general solution of (4.11) can be written as:

$$W(x) = \frac{c}{A_2(x)} \exp\left[2 \int^x dy\, \frac{A_1(y)}{A_2(y)}\right]$$
$$- \frac{2j_0}{A_2(x)} \int_z^x du\, \exp\left[-2 \int^u dy\, \frac{A_1(y)}{A_2(y)}\right] \exp\left[2 \int_z^x dy\, \frac{A_1(y)}{A_2(y)}\right], \tag{4.12}$$

where c and z are arbitrary constants. However, since changing z is equivalent to changing c, we can look at c and j_0 as the only arbitrary constants. Assuming that no probability mass flows through the end-points of the diffusion interval, we can make use of (4.8) and set $j_0 = 0$ in (4.12). Hence, by making use of the normalization condition

$$\int_a^b dx \ W(x) = 1,$$ (4.13)

we finally obtain:

$$W(x) = \frac{c}{A_2(x)} \exp\left[2 \int_z^x dy \ \frac{A_1(y)}{A_2(y)}\right],$$ (4.14)

with

$$c = \left\{\int_a^b dx \ \frac{1}{A_2(x)} \exp\left[2 \int_z^x dy \ \frac{A_1(y)}{A_2(y)}\right]\right\}^{-1}.$$ (4.15)

Let us now remark that due to (4.9), for a temporally homogeneous diffusion process equations (4.1) and (4.2) can be rewritten as:

$$\frac{\partial f}{\partial t} = \frac{\partial^2}{\partial x^2}[a(x)f] - \frac{\partial}{\partial x}[b(x)f],$$ (4.16a)

$$\frac{\partial f}{\partial t} = a(x_0) \frac{\partial^2 f}{\partial x_0^2} + b(x_0)\frac{\partial f}{\partial x_0},$$ (4.16b)

where we have set

$a(x) = \frac{1}{2} A_2(x),$
$b(x) = A_1(x).$

The theory of integration of the diffusion equations (4.16) is due to Feller. Hereafter we shall limit ourselves to pointing out the main results which are necessary to handle time-homogeneous diffusion equations in many applications. The foundations of Feller theory can be found in Feller (1952 and 1954) and, with several improvements, in Karlin and Taylor (1981).

The integration problem of the above diffusion equations is complicated by the circumstance that $a(x)$ may vanish or $b(x)$ may become singular as x approaches some value x^*, that henceforth will be said to be a singular point. If no such point exists, then equations (4.16) are defined over the entire interval $(-\infty,+\infty)$. The transition p.d.f. can then be determined by solving either equation with the initial condition

$$\lim_{t \downarrow 0} f(x,t \mid x_0) = \delta(x - x_0).$$ (4.17)

This *uniquely* determines the transition p.d.f. However, when the process is singular, condition (4.17) does not suffice and, in fact, one is not even free to choose which of the two diffusion equations to solve in order to find f.

Let us consider an interval $I \equiv (r_1,r_2)$ with $-\infty \leqslant r_1 < r_2 \leqslant +\infty$ and let us assume (which is safe for all cases of practical interest) that the functions $a(x)$, $a'(x)$ and $b(x)$ are continuous for $x \in I$, with the infinite-

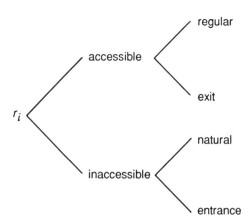

Fig. 5.1   Classification of boundaries

simal variance $a(x) > 0$ inside (r_1,r_2). This means that the only possible singular points are the end-points r_1 and r_2 of I, the 'diffusion interval'. Denoting by r_i the general end-point, it may occur that $X(t)$ never attains, for finite t, the value r_i. In this case r_i is said to be an *inaccessible boundary*. Otherwise, r_i is said to be *accessible*. A finer classification partitions accessible boundaries into *exit* boundaries and *regular* boundaries, whereas inaccessible ones can be either *entrance* boundaries or *natural* boundaries. Also this finer classification reflects specific features of $X(t)$. When r_i is regular, nothing particular happens to $X(t)$ in the neighbourhood of r_i. Thus if we wish to confine the whole probability mass to (r_1,r_2), the initial condition (4.17) must be complemented with boundary conditions, one for each regular boundary. An exit boundary is, instead, one such that a probability flow exists from the inside of the diffusion interval onto the point r_i whereas no probability flow takes place from r_i into the diffusion interval. In other words, r_i acts as an 'absorbing boundary' in the sense that the process sample paths starting at x_0 ($r_1 < x_0 < r_2$) terminate as soon as they attain the value r_i. As for inaccessible boundaries, r_i is entrance if r_i is not attainable from the inside of (r_1,r_2) whereas starting from r_i the process can take values in (r_1,r_2). Finally, natural boundaries are the ones characterized by zero probability flow. Therefore, they are inaccessible from the inside of the diffusion intervals and if some probability mass is initially assigned to them, it stays there forever without being able to spread into the diffusion interval. Figure 1 summarizes the boundary classification.

The interest in this classification rests upon the fact, proved by Feller (1952; 1954), that if one knows the nature of the boundaries of the diffusion interval one can decide what kind of boundary conditions, if any, have to be associated with the diffusion equations in order to determine the transition p.d.f. of the process. Of course, if such a procedure is to be of practical use, one should be able to establish the nature of boundaries without having to know in advance the process transition p.d.f. This is actually the case. Indeed, as proved by Feller, the classification of the boundaries depends solely upon certain integrability properties of the coefficients $a(x)$ and $b(x)$ of the diffusion equations. More specifically, let x' be a point contained inside the diffusion interval $I = (r_1, r_2)$ and let us introduce the following four functions:

$$f(x) = \exp\left[-\int_{x'}^{x} \frac{b(z)}{a(z)}\, dz\right],$$

$$g(x) = [a(x)\, f(x)]^{-1},$$

$$h(x) = f(x) \int_{x'}^{x} g(z)dz, \tag{4.18}$$

$$k(x) = g(x) \int_{x'}^{x} f(z)dz.$$

Let us further denote by $\psi(x) \in L(I_i)$ the (Lebesgue) integrability of a non-negative function $\psi(x)$ in the interval (x', r_i), i.e.

$$\psi(x) \in L(I_i) \leftrightarrow \int_{I_i} dx\psi(x) < \infty \tag{4.19}$$

and by $\psi(x) \notin L(I_i)$ the opposite case, i.e. the case when the integral in (4.19) is divergent. Feller's criterion for the classification of the boundary r_i is then the following:

$$r_i \text{ is } \begin{cases} \text{regular,} & \text{if } f(x) \in L(I_i) \text{ and } g(x) \in L(I_i), \\ \text{exit,} & \text{if } g(x) \notin L(I_i) \text{ and } h(x) \in L(I_i), \\ \text{entrance,} & \text{if } f(x) \notin L(I_i) \text{ and } k(x) \in L(I_i), \\ \text{natural,} & \text{otherwise.} \end{cases}$$

Some interesting and often encountered situations are the following:

(a) *Both boundaries are natural.* Then the initial condition (4.17) alone uniquely determines the transition p.d.f. as a solution of the diffusion equations (4.16). Either equation may thus be used to find f. No boundary conditions, other than $f(r_i, t \mid x_0) = 0$, can be imposed.

(b) *One boundary is natural and the other is exit.* The initial condition (4.17) uniquely specifies the transition p.d.f. as the solution of the Fokker–Planck equation (4.16a). The Kolmogorov equation (4.16b) has, instead, infinitely many solutions all satisfying condition (4.17). In this case use of the Fokker–Planck equation is advisable.

(c) *Both boundaries are exit.* As in (b), again, we can determine $f(x, t \mid x_0)$ as the solution of the Fokker–Planck equation (4.16a) satisfying initial condition (4.17).

(d) *One or both boundaries are regular.* In this case neither of equations (4.16) can be solved with the initial condition (4.17) alone. Boundary conditions also have to be imposed.

Of the various boundary conditions one can associate with the diffusion equations at a regular boundary r_i, the following two are particularly interesting.

(i) *Total reflection at r_i.* By this one means that there is no flow of probability at the boundaries. Therefore the probability density current, j_0 must be zero at the boundary r_i (and, therefore, everywhere due to the assumed stationarity of the p.d.f.). From (4.3), using the stationarity assumption, we thus obtain the following boundary condition for the Fokker–Planck equation:

$$\lim_{x\to r_i}\left\{\frac{\partial}{\partial x}[a(x)f(x,t\mid x_0)] - b(x)f(x,t\mid x_0)\right\} = 0. \tag{4.20}$$

(ii) *Total absorption at r_i.* In this case the boundary condition imposed for the solution of the Fokker–Planck equation is:

$$\lim_{x\to r_i}[a(x)\,f(x)f(x,t\mid x_0)] = 0, \tag{4.21}$$

where $f(x)$ is the function defined in (4.18). In the particular case of non-singular diffusion equations, $a(x)$ and $b(x)$ being bounded and $a(x) > 0$ over the whole interval (r_1,r_2) imply that $f(x)$ is also bounded. Condition (4.21) then becomes

$$\lim_{x\to r_i}f(x,t\mid x_0) = 0. \tag{4.22}$$

Conditions (4.21), and (4.22) for the singular case, ensure that r_i acts as an absorbing boundary in the sense that all sample paths terminate as they reach r_i. Condition (4.20), instead, makes r_i act as reflecting: upon reaching r_i, either sample paths are immediately reflected backward or they stay there for a while but then have to turn back. The boundary plays much the same role as the rigid walls of a container in which the molecules of a gas undergo random motion.

5 Wiener and Ornstein–Uhlenbeck processes

Let us consider the diffusion interval obtained by setting $b(x) = 0$ and $a(x) = \sigma^2/2$ in (4.16), with σ^2 an arbitrary constant. The forward equation (4.16a) then reads

$$\frac{\partial f}{\partial t} = \frac{\sigma^2}{2}\frac{\partial^2 f}{\partial x^2}. \tag{5.1}$$

Since this is non-singular, the diffusion interval is the entire real line with the points at infinity natural boundaries. Hence, to determine the transition p.d.f. we have to look for a solution of (5.1) satisfying the delta condition (4.17). If we assume that the process originates at $x = 0$, this transition p.d.f. is easily recognized to be

$$f(x,t \mid 0) = \frac{1}{\sqrt{(2\pi t)}\sigma} \exp\left(-\frac{x^2}{2\sigma^2 t}\right). \tag{5.2}$$

If instead we solve equation (5.1) under the initial condition (3.11), in place of (5.2) we obtain:

$$f(x,t \mid x_0,t_0) = \frac{1}{\sqrt{[2\pi(t - t_0)]}\sigma} \exp\left[-\frac{(x - x_0)^2}{2\sigma^2 (t - t_0)}\right], \tag{5.3}$$

which is still a normal density. However, now its mean value is x_0 and its variance is $\sigma^2(t - t_0)$.

An important feature of the process $X(t)$ whose transition p.d.f. is given by (5.3) is that, besides being Markov, it has independent increments. Indeed, let $t_0 < t_1 < t_2 < \ldots < t_n$ be arbitrary instants and let $Y_1 = X(t_1) - x_0$, $Y_2 = X(t_2) - X(t_1)$, $\ldots$, $Y_n = X(t_n) - X(t_{n-1})$ be the n random variables representing the increments of the process over the time intervals (t_0,t_1), (t_1,t_2), $\ldots$, (t_{n-1},t_n). Then

$$\begin{aligned}
&\Phi_n(Y_1,Y_2,\ldots,Y_n) \\
&= f(x_0+Y_1,t_1 \mid x_0,t_0) \, f(x_1+Y_2,t_2 \mid x_1,t_1) \ldots f(x_{n-1}+Y_n,t_n \mid x_{n-1},t_{n-1}) \\
&= f(Y_1,t_1-t_0 \mid 0) \, f(Y_2,t_2-t_1 \mid 0) \ldots f(Y_n,t_n-t_{n-1} \mid 0),
\end{aligned} \tag{5.4}$$

where the left-hand side is the joint p.d.f. of the n increments and where for all y and $\tau < t$ the transition p.d.f.

$$\begin{aligned}
f(x,t \mid y,\tau) &= \frac{1}{\sqrt{[2\pi(t - \tau)]}\sigma} \exp\left[-\frac{(x - y)^2}{2\sigma^2(t - \tau)}\right] \\
&\equiv f(x-y,t-\tau \mid 0)
\end{aligned} \tag{5.5}$$

is obtained from (5.3) by identifying x_0 with y and t_0 with τ. Since the right-hand side of (5.4) is the product $\phi_1(Y_1) \, \phi_2(Y_2) \ldots \phi_n(Y_n)$ of the univariate p.d.f.'s of the n considered increments, the independence of these increments follows. Moreover, since the increment $X(t_{k+1}) - X(t_k)$ has the same p.d.f. as $X(t_{k+1} + \alpha) - X(t_k + \alpha)$, whatever $\alpha \in \mathbb{R}$ and t_k, it also follows that these increments are stationary. Note that the stationary-independent-increment property of the process with transition p.d.f. (5.5) is a consequence of the invariance of this function under both space and time shifts.

The diffusion process whose transition p.d.f. is given by (5.3) is said to be a *Wiener process* conditioned upon $X(0) = x_0$ while the process $W(t)$ having transition p.d.f. (5.2) is often referred to as the *standard Wiener process*. This can also be directly defined as the process $W(t)$ such that

(a) $W(0) = 0$.
(b) $W(t)$ has stationary independent increments.
(c) For every $t > 0$, $W(t)$ is normally distributed.
(d) For all $t > 0$, $E[W(t)] = 0$.

It can be seen that these four properties uniquely specify the probability law of $W(t)$ up to the parameter σ^2 appearing in (5.2).

An important feature of the Wiener process $W(t)$ is its being Gaussian. A stochastic process is said to be non-singular *Gaussian* or *normal* if for any finite number of instants $t_1, t_2, \ldots, t_n$ the joint n-dimensional density of the random variables $X(t_1), X(t_2), \ldots, X(t_n)$ is given by

$$f_n(x_1,t_1;x_2,t_2; \ldots; x_n,t_n)$$
$$= (2\pi)^{-n/2} |\Delta|^{-1/2} \exp[-\tfrac{1}{2}(X - m)^T K^{-1}(X - m)], \tag{5.6}$$

where T denotes the transpose of a vector,

$$X^T = [x_1,x_2,\ldots,x_n],$$
$$m^T = [E\{X(t_1)\},E\{X(t_2)\},\ldots,E\{X(t_n)\}]$$
$$K = \|E\{[X(t_i) - E(X(t_i))] [X(t_j) - E(X(t_j))]\}\|,$$

and $\Delta = \det(K) \neq 0$. From (5.6) we see that to specify the probability law of a Gaussian process it is sufficient to know the vector m and the covariance matrix K, which can be calculated if one knows the transition and the univariate p.d.f.'s of the process, or equivalently, the second order joint p.d.f. of the process. Now, for the Wiener process one has:

$$f_2(x_1,t_1; x_2,t_2) = f(x_2,t_2 \mid x_1,t_1) f(x_1,t_1 \mid 0), \tag{5.7}$$

where the functions on the right-hand side are immediately obtained from (5.2) and (5.5). One can then prove that

$$K(t_1,t_2) = \sigma^2 \min (t_1,t_2). \tag{5.8}$$

Since for the Wiener process m is the null vector, from (5.6) and (5.8) the n-dimensional joint p.d.f. can immediately be written down.

Another important diffusion process often met in applications is the *Wiener process with drift*. Its transition p.d.f. is

$$f(x,t \mid x_0,t_0) = \frac{1}{\sqrt{[2\pi(t - t_0)]}\sigma} \exp\left\{-\frac{[x - x_0 - \mu(t - t_0)]^2}{2\sigma^2(t - t_0)}\right\}, \tag{5.9}$$

where the constant μ denotes the drift. The function (5.9) is the solution of the diffusion equation

$$\frac{\partial f}{\partial t} = \frac{\sigma^2}{2} \frac{\partial^2 f}{\partial x^2} - \mu \frac{\partial f}{\partial x} \qquad (5.10)$$

with the initial condition (3.11). The function (5.9) is again a normal density. However, now its mean value $x_0 + \mu(t - t_0)$ linearly shifts in time, the direction being determined by the sign of μ. As one can directly see from (5.9), the Wiener process with drift is also defined over the whole real line, with the points at infinity natural boundaries. However, one can restrict the Wiener process with drift to the interval $(0, +\infty)$ by imposing the reflection condition (4.20) at the zero (regular) boundary, i.e. by requiring that:

$$\left[\frac{\sigma^2}{2} \frac{\partial f(x,t \mid x_0)}{\partial x} - \mu f(x,t \mid x_0) \right]_{x=0} = 0, \qquad (5.11)$$

which expresses the conservation of the probability mass in the interval $(0, +\infty)$. Thus doing, one can prove that the transition p.d.f. $f_r(x,t \mid x_0)$ in the presence of the reflecting boundary is given by:

$$\begin{aligned}
f_r(x,t \mid x_0) = {} & \frac{1}{\sqrt{(2\pi t)}\sigma} \left\{ \exp\left[-\frac{(x - x_0 - \mu t)^2}{2\sigma^2 t} \right] \right. \\
& \left. + \exp\left[-\frac{4\mu x_0 t + (x + x_0 - \mu t)^2}{2\sigma^2 t} \right] \right\} \\
& - \frac{\mu}{\sigma^2} \exp\left[\frac{2\mu x}{\sigma^2} \right] \left[1 - \mathrm{Erf}\left(\frac{x + x_0 + \mu t}{\sqrt{2t}\,\sigma} \right) \right],
\end{aligned} \qquad (5.12)$$

where $\mathrm{Erf}(z)$ is the error function defined as:

$$\mathrm{Erf}(z) = \frac{2}{\sqrt{\pi}} \int_0^z dx\, e^{-x^2}. \qquad (5.13)$$

We now focus our attention on the diffusion equation with constant infinitesimal variance and linear drift with negative slope, say:

$$\frac{\partial f}{\partial t} = \frac{\sigma^2}{2} \frac{\partial^2 f}{\partial x^2} - \frac{\partial}{\partial x} [(\mu - \delta x)f] \qquad (5.14)$$

with $\delta > 0$, μ, and σ^2 arbitrary constants. A straightforward calculation again shows that the points at infinity are natural boundaries so that the transition p.d.f. can be obtained as the solution of (5.14) that satisfies the initial delta condition. The diffusion process whose transition p.d.f. satisfies equation (5.14) is called the *Ornstein–Uhlenbeck* process. Clearly, for $\delta = \mu = 0$ one recovers the Wiener process. Solving equation (5.14) with condition (4.17) one obtains:

$$f(x,t \mid x_0) = \cfrac{1}{\left[\pi \dfrac{\sigma^2}{\delta}(1 - e^{-2\delta t}) \right]^{1/2}}$$

$$\times \exp\left\{ -\cfrac{\left[x - \dfrac{\mu}{\delta} + \left(\dfrac{\mu}{\delta} - x_0 \right)e^{-\delta t} \right]^2}{\dfrac{\sigma^2}{\delta}(1 - e^{-2\delta t})} \right\}. \tag{5.15}$$

Therefore, f is a normal density with conditional mean $E[X(t)]$ and variance $\text{Var}[X(t)]$ given by

$$E[X(t)] = \frac{\mu}{\delta} - \left(\frac{\mu}{\delta} - x_0 \right)e^{-\delta t},$$

$$\text{Var}[X(t)] = \frac{\sigma^2}{2\delta}(1 - e^{-2\delta t}). \tag{5.16}$$

Note that, distinct from the case of the Wiener process, the Ornstein–Uhlenbeck process admits of a steady state distribution. As one can see directly from (5.15), this is a normal density with mean μ/δ and variance $\sigma^2/(2\delta)$. As is well known, the Ornstein–Uhlenbeck process is also Gaussian. The correlation function $R(t,\tau) \equiv E[X(t)X(\tau)]$ can be seen to be given by

$$R(t,\tau) = \frac{\mu^2}{\delta^2} + \frac{\mu}{\delta}\left(x_0 - \frac{\mu}{\delta} \right)(e^{-\delta t} + e^{-\delta\tau})$$

$$+ \left[\left(x_0 - \frac{\mu}{\delta} \right)^2 - \frac{\sigma^2}{2\delta} \right]e^{-\delta(t+\tau)} + \frac{\sigma^2}{2\delta}e^{-\delta|t-\tau|}. \tag{5.17}$$

The expression of the correlation function does not change if we assume that $\delta < 0$. Of course, in this case $X(t)$ is no longer an Ornstein–Uhlenbeck process.

6   Stochastic differential equations

In Section 4 we took into account the diffusion processes and pointed out that the transition p.d.f. of any such process satisfies the diffusion equations (4.1) and (4.2). In order to be able to write down these equations, the drift $A_1(x,t)$ and infinitesimal variance $A_2(x,t)$ must be calculated. Examples of how this task can be accomplished will be provided in the next section. Here we shall sketch heuristically a different procedure to construct diffusion processes that play important roles in many applications. To this end, let us consider the motion of a colloidal particle in a viscous medium and let us focus our attention on the motion of the projection of the particle's position on a fixed coordinate axis. We say that such a projection undergoes a (one-dimensional) Brownian motion. For simplicity, henceforth we shall talk about a particle of mass m moving in one dimension with velocity v. The equation describing such motion is Newton's law:

$$m \frac{dv}{dt} = -\beta v + F(t), \tag{6.1}$$

where the first term on the right-hand side denotes the elastic restoring force due to the friction experienced by the particle, the constant $\beta > 0$ depending on the nature of the medium in which the motion takes place. The second term on the right-hand side, $F(t)$, is the force acting on the particle due to the impacts from the molecules of the medium. In equation (6.1) everything is deterministic and the velocity $v(t)$ is uniquely determined if we know the velocity at some arbitrarily chosen initial time and if we know the force $F(t)$. Alternatively, if we could observe the movement of the particle and measure the velocity $v(t)$ at all times, we could determine the force $F(t)$ acting on the particle:

$$F(t) = m \frac{dv}{dt} + \beta v. \tag{6.2}$$

Similarly, if we could perform the same observation on a (countable) ensemble of colloidal particles, we would determine uniquely an *ensemble* of functions $F_i(t)$:

$$F_i(t) = m \frac{dv_i}{dt} + \beta v_i \quad (i = 1, 2, \ldots), \tag{6.3}$$

where i refers to the ith measurement.

Although in principle possible, such a procedure is not useful. Indeed, what one is interested in is not the precise description of the movement of a single particle but rather some global information of the type: How many particles at a given time have an energy above a preassigned value? How many particles are likely to be found in an assigned region at a given time? And so on. Equivalently formulated, these questions become: What is the probability that at a given time a particle has an energy above a preassigned value? What is the probability that a particle will be found in an assigned region at a given time? And so on. In other words, we are interested in the global properties of an ensemble of macroscopically identical particles. This means that instead of considering the equations:

$$m \frac{dv_i}{dt} + \beta v_i = F_i(t) \quad (i = 1, 2, \ldots), \tag{6.4}$$

where everything is deterministic, we prefer to consider a unique *stochastic equation*:

$$m \frac{\mathrm{d}v}{\mathrm{d}t} + \beta v = F(t) \tag{6.5}$$

with the following interpretation:[1] $F(t)$ is a random function; each and every one of its (continuum of) sample paths, say $F(t,\omega)$, is a deterministic function representing the actual force acting on a particle of the ensemble, thus generating the function $v(t,\omega)$. This, in turn, can be looked upon as the sample path of a stochastic process $v(t)$. Thus (6.5) can be viewed as a transformation mapping a stochastic process $F(t)$ into another stochastic process $v(t)$. The latter is specified if one knows $F(t)$ and $v(0) = v_0$. In general v_0 is not unique but is described by an initial p.d.f. $\psi(v_0)$.

Extending the situation above, we can consider an equation of the type

$$\frac{\mathrm{d}x}{\mathrm{d}t} = G[x,t,\Lambda(t)], \tag{6.6}$$

where $\Lambda(t)$ is a stochastic process and G is an assigned function. Then $x(t)$, the 'solution' of (6.6), is itself a random function. Clearly, its determination cannot be accomplished unless $\Lambda(t)$ is specified.

In the following we shall confine ourselves to considering the more modest, although in practice very interesting, case when (6.6) has the form:

$$\frac{\mathrm{d}x}{\mathrm{d}t} = h(x) + k(x)\Lambda(t), \tag{6.7}$$

where h and k are deterministic functions, sufficiently smooth to make permissible the mathematical steps we are going to need, and where $k(x)$ is a positive function. If $\Lambda(t)$ is a 'well-behaved' stochastic process, in the sense that its sample paths are smooth functions, (6.7) can be handled with the classical methods of the theory of ordinary differential equations and one can look for a solution $x(t)$ such that $x(0) = x_0$. Such a solution will be a stochastic process with sample paths all originating at x_0. However, in general a simple description of the solution $x(t)$ is not possible because $x(t)$ is non-Markov due to the assumed smoothness of the sample paths of $\Lambda(t)$. For $x(t)$ to be a Markov process we should instead deprive the sample paths of $\Lambda(t)$ of memory in the sense that, for instance, the random variables $\Lambda(t_1)$ and $\Lambda(t_2)$ should be uncorrelated for all $t_2 \neq t_1$, a situation clearly in contrast with the smoothness property of the sample paths. On the other hand, assuming such a lack of correlation creates serious mathematical difficulties concerning the interpretation of (6.7) because the sample paths of $x(t)$ may not admit of derivatives in the conventional sense. Actually, one suspects that the whole machinery of traditional calculus may be inadequate to handle equations such as (6.7). This is, indeed, the case. To overcome such difficulties new calculi have been devised, the most familiar ones being that of Ito and that of Stratonovich. While referring to any of the several specialized texts on this subject (for instance, those of Jazwinski, 1970; Soong, 1973; Arnold, 1974; or Wong and Hajek, 1985) for a precise formulation of the integration problem of stochastic differential equations and for an exposition of the necessary mathematical tools, we shall proceed heuristically to illustrate some instances frequently mentioned, especially in the biological literature. But first we need to introduce the notion of 'white noise'. To this purpose, let us return to the stochastic differential equation

$$\frac{dx}{dt} = h(x) + k(x)\Lambda(t) \tag{6.8}$$

earlier mentioned, but let us now assume that $\Lambda(t)$ is a stationary process with zero mean and with a rather narrow and peaked correlation function:

$$E[\Lambda(t)] = g_1 = 0, \tag{6.9a}$$

$$E[\Lambda(t_1)\Lambda(t_2)] = g_2(t_1,t_2) = g_2(t_2 - t_1), \tag{6.9b}$$

where $g_2(\tau)$ is appreciably non-zero only in the neighbourhood of $\tau = 0$ with a very sharp maximum at $\tau = 0$. More generally, for any group of instants $t_1, t_2, \ldots, t_n$ all lying close to each other we set:

$$E[\Lambda(t_1)\Lambda(t_2) \ldots \Lambda(t_n)] = g_n(t_1,t_2,\ldots,t_n), \tag{6.10}$$

and, again, assume that the nth-order correlation function g_n has a sharp maximum at $t_1 = t_2 = \ldots = t_n$, being otherwise effectively zero. Finally, we assume that when $t_1, t_2, \ldots, t_n$ are proximal to each other, and also when $t_{r+1}, t_{r+2}, \ldots, t_s$ are proximal but far from the group $t_1, t_2, \ldots, t_r$ and so on, then

$$E[\Lambda(t_1) \ldots \Lambda(t_r)\Lambda(t_{r+1}) \ldots \Lambda(t_s)\Lambda(t_{s+1}) \ldots \Lambda(t_p) \ldots]$$

$$= E[\Lambda(t_1)\ldots\Lambda(t_r)]E[\Lambda(t_{r+1})\ldots\Lambda(t_s)]E[\Lambda(t_{s+1})\ldots\Lambda(t_p)]\ldots$$

$$= g_r(t_1, \ldots, t_r) \, g_{s-r}(t_{r+1}, \ldots, t_s) \, g_{p-s}(t_{s+1}, \ldots, t_p)\ldots \tag{6.11}$$

where the functions g_n have already been qualitatively specified.

All these assumptions about the stochastic process $\Lambda(t)$ appearing in (6.8) may look rather artificial at this stage, but the motivation for them will soon emerge. With this in mind, let us perform a change of variable in (6.8) by setting:

$$y = \Phi(x), \quad x = \Phi^{-1}(y) \tag{6.12}$$

with

$$\Phi(x) = \int^x \frac{dz}{k(z)}. \tag{6.13}$$

Then (6.8) is changed into:

$$\frac{dy}{dt} = \frac{H(y)}{K(y)} + \Lambda(t),\tag{6.14}$$

upon setting

$$H(y) = h[\Phi^{-1}(y)],$$
$$K(y) = k[\Phi^{-1}(y)].\tag{6.15}$$

The advantage of this procedure is that we have constructed a stochastic process $y(t)$ defined by equation (6.14) in which $\Lambda(t)$ appears in a purely *additive way*. Note that (6.14) is of the same type as (6.5) for the velocity of a Brownian particle. Due to the above assumptions on $\Lambda(t)$, we now expect $y(t)$, and hence $x(t)$, to be Markov. Its transition p.d.f. $f_y(y,t \mid y_0)$ thus satisfies the differential form (3.10) of the Smolukowski equation that we now write as:

$$\frac{\partial f_y}{\partial t} = \sum_{n=1}^{\infty} \frac{(-1)^n}{n!} \frac{\partial^n}{\partial y^n} [B_n f_y].\tag{6.16}$$

Let us evaluate the infinitesimal moments B_n by using (6.14). First, we express the increment of y over a small time interval Δt by means of the approximation:

$$\Delta y \equiv y(t + \Delta t) - y(t) \simeq \frac{H(y)}{K(y)} \Delta t + \int_t^{t+\Delta t} \Lambda(\tau)d\tau,\tag{6.17}$$

where, here and in the following, the value of the process at time t is considered as fixed. Taking the expectation of both sides of (6.17), due to (6.9a), in the limit as $\Delta t \to 0$ we obtain

$$B_1(y) = \lim_{\Delta t \downarrow 0} \frac{1}{\Delta t} E[\Delta y] = \frac{H(y)}{K(y)}.\tag{6.18}$$

To calculate B_2 we now square both sides of (6.17):

$$(\Delta y)^2 \simeq O[(\Delta t)^2] + 2\Delta t \frac{H(y)}{K(y)} \int_t^{t+\Delta t} \Lambda(\tau)d\tau$$
$$+ \int_t^{t+\Delta t} \Lambda(\tau)d\tau \int_t^{t+\Delta t} \Lambda(\theta)d\theta.\tag{6.19}$$

Upon taking the expectations and after dividing by Δt, for small Δt we are left with:

$$\Delta t B_2 \simeq E[(\Delta y)^2] = \int_t^{t+\Delta t} d\tau \int_t^{t+\Delta t} d\eta g_2(\tau - \eta),\tag{6.20}$$

after making use of (6.9). Using the earlier specified qualitative behaviour of g_2, it then follows that

$$B_2 \simeq \frac{E[(\Delta y)^2]}{\Delta t} = \sigma^2, \tag{6.21}$$

with

$$\sigma^2 = \int_{-\infty}^{\infty} g_2(s)ds \tag{6.22}$$

and with the result becoming exact in the limit as $\Delta t \to 0$.

Proceeding along similar lines, it is not difficult to become convinced that due to the assumed properties (6.9) and (6.11) of $\Lambda(t)$ the following relationship holds:

$$\Delta t B_n(y) \simeq E[(\Delta y)^n] = o(\Delta t) \quad (n = 3, 4, \ldots). \tag{6.23}$$

Equation (6.16) thus becomes the Fokker–Planck equation

$$\frac{\partial f_y}{\partial t} = -\frac{\partial}{\partial y}[B_1(y)f_y] + \frac{\sigma^2}{2}\frac{\partial^2 f_y}{\partial y^2} \tag{6.24}$$

with $B_1(y)$ and σ^2 given by (6.18) and (6.21), respectively. The conclusion is that (6.14) can be thought of as defining a diffusion process $y(t)$ whose drift equals the deterministic part of the right-hand side of the equation while its infinitesimal variance depends exclusively on the characteristics $(g_2(\tau))$ of the random part of the equation. Furthermore, if we impose the condition that $P\{y(0) = y_0\} = 1$, with y_0 non-random, then the specification of such a diffusion process is unique.

Let us now examine the infinitesimal moments $A_n(x)$ of the Markov process $x(t)$ defined by (6.8). Denoting its transition p.d.f. by $f_x(x,t \mid x_0)$, we know that for small Δt we have:

$$\begin{aligned} A_n(x)\Delta t &\simeq \int (x' - x)^n f_x (x',\Delta t \mid x)dx' \\ &= \int [\Phi^{-1}(y') - x]^n f_x [\Phi^{-1}(y'),\Delta t \mid x]d[\Phi^{-1}(y')] \\ &= \int [\Phi^{-1} (y') - x]^n f_y [y',\Delta t \mid \Phi(x)]dy' \quad (n = 1, 2, \ldots), \end{aligned} \tag{6.25}$$

having made use of the one-to-one transformation (6.12) and of the relation

$$f_x(x',t \mid x) = \left[\frac{f_y(y',t \mid y)}{|dx'/dy'|} \right]_{y'=\Phi(x')} \tag{6.26}$$

between the transition p.d.f.'s of the processes $x(t)$ and $y(t)$. Let us now expand $\Phi^{-1}(y')$ as a Taylor series about the point $y = \Phi(x)$:

$$\Phi^{-1}(y') = \Phi^{-1}[\Phi(x)] + \alpha_1(x)[y' - \Phi(x)] + \frac{1}{2}\alpha_2(x)[y' - \Phi(x)]^2$$

$$+ \sum_{n=3}^{\infty} \frac{\alpha_n(x)}{n!} [y' - \Phi(x)]^n \qquad (6.27)$$

with

$$\alpha_n(x) = \frac{d^n\Phi^{-1}(y)}{dy^n}\bigg|_{y=\Phi(y)}. \qquad (6.28)$$

Since $\Phi^{-1}[\Phi(x)] = x$ and (6.15) holds, a straightforward application of the theorem on the derivative of the inverse function yields:

$$\begin{aligned}\alpha_1 &= k(x), \\ \alpha_2 &= k'(x)k(x),\end{aligned} \qquad (6.29)$$

where $k'(x)$ denotes $dk(x)/dx$. Making use of (6.29) and of (6.25) we obtain:

$$\Delta t\, A_1(x) \simeq k(x) \int [y' - \Phi(x)]\, f_y[y',\Delta t \mid \Phi(x)]dy'$$

$$+ \frac{1}{2} k'(x)k(x) \int [y' - \Phi(x)]^2\, f_y[y',\Delta t \mid \Phi(x)]dy'$$

$$+ \sum_{j=3}^{\infty} \frac{\alpha_j(x)}{j!} \int [y' - \Phi(x)]^j f_y[y',\Delta t \mid \Phi(x)]dy'. \qquad (6.30)$$

Therefore, in the limit as $\Delta t \to 0$, we find:

$$A_1(x) = k(x)B_1[\Phi(x)] + \tfrac{1}{2}k'(x)k(x)B_2[\Phi(x)]$$

$$+ \sum_{j=3}^{\infty} \frac{\alpha_j(x)}{j!} B_j[\Phi(x)], \qquad (6.31)$$

where the $B_n(y)$'s are given by (6.18), (6.21) and (6.23). Recalling (6.15) we thus find:

$$A_1(x) = h(x) + \frac{\sigma^2}{4} \frac{dk^2(x)}{dx}. \qquad (6.32)$$

Using the same procedure one can prove that

$$\begin{aligned}A_2(x) &= \sigma^2 k^2(x), \\ A_n(x) &= 0, \quad (n = 3, 4, \ldots).\end{aligned} \qquad (6.33)$$

By virtue of (6.32) this shows that the Markov process $x(t)$ defined by (6.8) is a diffusion process with drift and infinitesimal variance given by

$$A_1(x) = h(x) + \frac{\sigma^2}{4} \frac{dk^2(x)}{dx} \equiv h(x) + \frac{1}{4} \frac{dA_2}{dx}, \qquad (6.34a)$$

$$A_2(x) = \sigma^2 k^2(x). \qquad (6.34b)$$

Clearly, if k is a constant, $A_1(x)$ and $A_2(x)$ coincide with the corresponding functions determined earlier for the purely additive random noise case after rescaling the correlation function. We should, however, emphasize the determinant role played above by our assumptions on $\Lambda(t)$ required for (6.34) to hold. Note that any other stationary random function $\Lambda'(t)$ on the right-hand side of (6.8), with zero mean and with correlation functions $g'_n(t_1,t_2,\ldots,t_n) \neq g_n(t_1,t_2,\ldots,t_n)$, but with the same qualitative behaviour, would describe the same diffusion process $x(t)$ provided only that

$$\int_{-\infty}^{\infty} g'_2(\tau)\mathrm{d}\tau = \int_{-\infty}^{\infty} g_2(\tau)\mathrm{d}\tau. \qquad (6.35)$$

To obtain a one-to-one correspondence between $x(t)$ and $\Lambda(t)$, the latter should be better specified. This is usually done by considering the limiting case of $\Lambda(t)$, when

$$g_2(t_1,t_2) = g_2(t_2 - t_1) = \sigma^2\delta(t_2 - t_1), \qquad (6.36)$$

where $\delta(t)$ is the Dirac delta function and σ^2 is a constant, the only element of indeterminacy. Note that with the choice (6.36), relation (6.22) is satisfied. Let us further assume that the functions g_n appearing in (6.10) are such that for all integers $n \geq 0$ and for all t_1, t_2, ...

$$g_{2n+1}(t_1,t_2,\ldots,t_{2n+1}) = 0,$$

$$g_{2n}(t_1,t_2,\ldots,t_{2n}) = \sum g_2(t_i,t_j)g_2(t_k,t_h) \cdots, \qquad (6.37)$$

where the sum is taken over all the different ways in which one can divide the $2n$ instants t_1, t_2, ..., t_{2n} into n pairs.

As Wang and Uhlenbeck (1945) proved, if one assumes that $\Lambda(t)$ is a stationary process with correlation functions g_n satisfying (6.36) and (6.37) it follows that $\Lambda(t)$ is a *normal* process. However, this is a typical example in which the covariance matrix is singular due to (6.36) and (6.37). In particular, we have

$$\mathrm{Var}[\Lambda(t)] = g_2(0) = \infty,$$

which indicates that the sample paths of $\Lambda(t)$ are totally memoryless (and thus fluctuate infinitely rapidly) due to the assumed lack of correlation between the random variables $\Lambda(t)$ and $\Lambda(t + \Delta t)$, no matter how small Δt is or what t is. This peculiar stochastic process is called *white noise*.

Quite evidently, there is interest in stochastic differential equations such as (6.8) for the purpose of modelling biological and physical phenomena. The deterministic part of the equation

$$\frac{\mathrm{d}x}{\mathrm{d}t} = h(x) \qquad (6.38)$$

can be taken as describing the time course of the state of the system under study when all the relevant environmental and internal parameters are fixed. Adding the term $k(x)\Lambda(t)$ to the r.h.s. of (6.38) can then be viewed as equivalent to switching from the description of one single system to that of an ensemble of macroscopically identical systems, all starting at $x(0) = x_0$, such that the state of each varies in time as a sample path of the diffusion process specified by (6.34). The random term on the r.h.s. of (6.8) is usually interpreted as a perturbation due to the overall effect of the numerous microscopic, unknown, or only partially known, environmental or internal fluctuations of some of the parameters appearing in (6.38), for which a complete deterministic description is impossible or useless.

It should be emphasized that in any actual biological or physical situation the noise affecting the system's evolution would not be exactly 'white', whereas it is often reasonable to assume that it is stationary and that its correlation functions possess the qualitative features mentioned in the foregoing. It thus appears reasonable to conclude (Stratonovich, 1963, 1968) that for such a realistic noise, denoted by $\Lambda_R(t)$, the differential equation

$$\frac{dx_R}{dt} = h(x_R) + k(x_R)\,\Lambda_R(t) \tag{6.39}$$

leads us to a stochastic process $x_R(t)$ which is not exactly a diffusion process (because the infinitesimal moments A_3, A_4, ... are not exactly zero). However, while (6.8) is meaningful – because for such types of noise we may safely assume the differentiability of the sample paths of $x_R(t)$ – the diffusion process $x(t)$ specified by (6.34) can be looked upon as the limiting case of a sequence of processes $x_R(t)$ in which the actual 'coloured' noise becomes whiter and whiter. Therefore, writing (6.8) and interpreting $\Lambda(t)$ as white noise is a useful expedient for determining the limiting process $x(t)$. The goodness of the representation of the state of the system under study by $x(t)$, instead of $x_R(t)$, depends on how close the actual noise is to the white noise. More on this subject can be found in the quoted texts by Stratonovich, and in a fundamental paper by Wong and Zakai (1965).

According to (6.34) and to the above remarks, the Wiener process $W(t)$ can be thought of as the limit of the process $z(t)$ defined by the stochastic differential equation

$$\frac{dz}{dt} = \Lambda_R(t) \tag{6.40}$$

when $\Lambda_R(t) \to \Lambda(t)$. In this sense (and only in this sense) can $\Lambda(t)$ be formally interpreted as the derivative of the Wiener process. Therefore, we can write:

$$\frac{dx}{dt} = h(x) + k(x)\Lambda_R(t)$$
$$= h(x) + k(x)\frac{dz}{dt} \tag{6.41}$$

where $z(t)$ is the solution of (6.40). From (6.41) we also find

$$dx = h(x)dt + k(x)dz \neq h(y)dt + k(y)dW = dy, \tag{6.42}$$

where $y(t)$ *is not* equal to $x(t)$. The arbitrary identification of dy with dx in (6.42) and of $x(t)$ with the diffusion process with infinitesimal moments (6.34) is responsible for what is often incorrectly referred to as the Ito versus Stratonovich controversy (cf., for instance, Gray and Caughey, 1965; Mortensen, 1969; Arnold, 1974, Chap. 10).

It should be mentioned that an equation such as

$$dx = h(x)dt + k(x)dW, \tag{6.43}$$

which we have just derived heuristically, is called an Ito equation; this can be handled by means of a somewhat *ad hoc* calculus (Ito calculus) which differs in several fundamental ways from the one to which we are accustomed. Before elaborating on this, we mention that the solution, $x(t)$, of (6.43) is also a diffusion process. Its drift and infinitesimal variance are, however, given by

$$B_1(x) = h(x),$$
$$B_2(x) = \sigma^2 k^2(x). \tag{6.44}$$

Comparing (6.44) with (6.34) we thus see that $B_2(x) = A_2(x)$, while $A_1(x)$ differs from $B_1(x)$ by the term

$$\frac{\sigma^2}{4}\frac{dk^2(x)}{dx} \equiv \frac{1}{4}\frac{dB_2}{dx} = \frac{1}{4}\frac{dA_2}{dx}.$$

The only case where this difference vanishes is clearly when $k(x) =$ constant, i.e. when we are dealing with a purely additive noise.

Let us now return to equation (6.43) to provide a better sketch of its meaning and of the procedure to determine its solution. In particular, we shall see that, under certain conditions on the functions $h(x)$ and $k(x)$ appearing in (6.43), $x(t)$ is the diffusion process characterized by the drift and infinitesimal variance (6.44). To this purpose, we have to introduce two fundamental notions: the mean square (m.s.) Riemann integral of a stochastic process and the so-called 'stochastic' or 'Ito' integral.

6.1 m.s. Riemann integral

Let $x(t)$ be a stochastic process defined over $T = [t_0,+\infty)$ and let $[a,b]$ be an interval in T. Divide $[a,b]$ into n subintervals by a partition $a = t_0 < t_1 < \ldots < t_n = b$ and let

$$\delta_n = \lim_{0 \le i \le n-1} (t_{i+1} - t_i)$$

denote the maximum length of the subintervals. We now choose arbitrary points t'_i such that $t_i < t'_i < t_{i+1}$ for $i = 0, 1, \ldots, n - 1$ and consider the random variable y_n defined by

$$y_n = \sum_{i=0}^{n-1} x(t'_i)(t_{i+1} - t_i). \tag{6.45}$$

If the sequence of random variables $\{y_n\}$, $n = 1, 2, \ldots$ converges to a random variable y in the mean square sense[2] as $n \to \infty$ and $\delta_n \to 0$, then $x(t)$ is said to be m.s. Riemann integrable over $[a,b]$ and y is said to be the m.s. Riemann integral of $x(t)$, denoted by

$$y = \int_a^b x(t)dt. \tag{6.46}$$

A necessary and sufficient condition for a stochastic process $x(t)$ to be Riemann integrable is that its correlation function $g(t,s)$ $(= g(t - s)$ in this case) is Riemann integrable over $[a,b] \times [a,b]$.

If $x(t)$ is m.s. Riemann integrable over $[a,t]$ for any $t \in [a,b]$, then

$$y(t) = \int_a^t x(\tau)d\tau \tag{6.47}$$

has a finite variance for every $t \in [a,b]$:

$$E[y^2(t)] < +\infty. \tag{6.48}$$

Moreover, it is easily seen that $y(t)$ is continuous in the mean square sense.[3]

6.2 Stochastic integral (Ito calculus)

Ito calculus deals with the notion of integral of a process $k(t,\omega)$ with respect to the Wiener process $W(t,\omega)$, namely with the yet undefined expression

$$\int_a^b k(t,\omega)dW(t,\omega). \tag{6.49}$$

Since $W(t)$ is neither 'differentiable' nor 'of bounded variation', (6.50) cannot be defined in the usual sense. In other words, (6.49) cannot be defined as a limit of random variables of the type

$$y_n = \sum_{i=0}^{n-1} x(t'_i)\,\Delta W_i \quad t'_i \in [t_i, t_{i+1}], \tag{6.50}$$

with

$$\Delta W_i = W(t_{i+1}) - W(t_i), \quad \text{for } i = 0, 1, \ldots, n-1, \tag{6.51}$$

because (6.50) does not converge in the mean square sense. Actually, the convergence of y_n depends on the choice of the points t'_i, $i = 0, 1, \ldots,$ $n-1$. Let us consider the following example.

Define the random variables u_n and v_n:

$$u_n = \sum_{i=0}^{n-1} W(t_i)\Delta W_i, \tag{6.52a}$$

$$v_n = \sum_{i=0}^{n-1} W(t_{i+1})\Delta W_i. \tag{6.52b}$$

where ΔW_i is defined in (6.51). It is easy to see that (assuming for simplicity $\sigma^2 = 1$ and setting $\Delta t_i = t_{i+1} - t_i$, $i = 0, 1, \ldots, n-1$)

$$E[v_n - u_n] = \sum_{i=0}^{n-1} E[\Delta W_i^2]$$

$$= \sum_{i=0}^{n-1} \Delta t_i = b - a, \tag{6.53}$$

and

$$E[\{(v_n - u_n) - (b - a)\}^2]$$

$$= E[\{\sum_{i=0}^{n-1} (\Delta W_i^2 - \Delta t_i)\}^2]$$

$$= \sum_{i=0}^{n-1} \sum_{j=0}^{n-1} E[(\Delta W_i^2 - \Delta t_i)(\Delta W_j^2 - \Delta t_j)]$$

$$= \sum_{i=0}^{n-1} \{E[\Delta W_i^4] - \Delta t_i^2\}$$

$$= 2 \sum_{i=0}^{n-1} \Delta t_i^2 \leqslant 2\delta_n \sum_{i=1}^{n-1} \Delta t_i$$

$$= 2\delta_n(b - a), \tag{6.54}$$

where we have used for $i \neq j$

$$E[\Delta W_i^2 \, \Delta W_j^2] = \Delta t_i \Delta t_j$$

and for $i = j$

$$E[\Delta W_i^4] = 3\Delta t_i^2.$$

Accordingly,

$$\text{l.i.m.} (v_n - u_n) \equiv \lim_{n\to\infty} E[(v_n - u_n)^2] = b - a \neq 0, \qquad (6.55)$$

where l.i.m. is a shorthand notation for 'limit in mean square sense'. In other words, the two random variables (6.52a) and (6.52b) converge to different values in the mean square sense.

Ito (1944) defined the integral

$$\int_a^b k(t,\omega)dW(t,\omega)$$

as the m.s. limit of a sequence $\{y_n\}$ given by

$$y_n = \sum_{i=0}^{n-1} k(t_i,\omega)[W(t_{i+1},\omega) - W(t_i,\omega)]. \qquad (6.56)$$

The m.s. limit of (6.56) exists if[4]

(i) for any i ($i=0,1,\ldots,n-1$), $k(t_i,\omega)$ is independent of $W(t_{j+1}) - W(t_j)$ for $j = i, i + 1, \ldots, n$, and

(ii) $\int_a^b E[k^2(t,\omega)]dt < +\infty.$ \qquad (6.57)

It can be proved that $\int_a^t k(s,\omega)$, $dW(s,\omega)$, $t \in [a,b]$, is m.s. continuous with respect to t.

We can now approach the problem concerning the solution of Ito equation (6.43). To begin with, we set

$$x(t) = x_a + \int_a^t h(x)du + \int_a^t k(x)dW, \qquad (6.58)$$

where $h(x)$ and $k(x)$ are the functions defined in the foregoing and where the first integral in the r.h.s. of (6.58) is defined in the sense of m.s. Riemann integral and the second in the sense of Ito integral. We assume their existence.

Let us return to equation (6.43), that has been derived heuristically. Equation (6.58) can be viewed as an integral equation with respect to $x(t)$. We consider it as an integral form of (6.43), i.e. we assume that (6.58) is equivalent to (6.43). A process $x(t)$ that satisfies (6.58) is said to possess a stochastic differential given by (6.43).

We now come to the fundamental so-called *Ito lemma*. As we have mentioned, the Ito equation

$$dz(t,\omega) = h_0(t,\omega)dt + k_0(t,\omega)dW(t,\omega) \qquad (6.59)$$

is equivalent to

$$z(t,\omega) = z_a + \int_a^t h_0(u,\omega)du + \int_a^t k_0(u,\omega)dW(u,\omega), \qquad (6.60)$$

where $z_a = z(a,\omega)$ is the initial value of $z(t)$ independent of $h_0(t,\omega)$, $k_0(t,\omega)$ and $W(t,\omega)$, for $a < t$ and where h_0 and k_0 must satisfy some suitable conditions securing the existence of both integrals. Now let us consider a new process $x(t)$ generated by a (non-linear) transformation of $z(t)$:

$$x(t) = f(z(t),t). \qquad (6.61)$$

What is the process $x(t)$? Is there any Ito equation satisfied by $x(t)$?

Let f be, for instance, z^2, i.e. $f(z,t) = z^2$. Recall that $z(t)$ is the m.s. limit of

$$z_n = z_a + \sum_{i=0}^{n-1} h_0(t_i,\omega)\Delta t_i + \sum_{i=0}^{n-1} k_0(t_i,\omega)\Delta W_i, \qquad (6.62)$$

where we have set

$$a \equiv t_0 < t_1 < \ldots < t_n \equiv t,$$

and have set as before

$$\Delta t_i = t_{i+1} - t_i,$$

$$\Delta W_i = W(t_{i+1}) - W(t_i), \text{ for } i = 0, 1, \ldots, n - 1.$$

Using (6.62), $x(t)$ is given as the m.s. limit of x_n:

$$x_n = [z_a + \sum_{i=0}^{n-1} h_0(t_i,\omega)\Delta t_i + \sum_{i=0}^{n-1} k_0(t_i,\omega)\Delta W_i]^2$$

$$= z_a^2 + \left[\sum_{i=0}^{n-1} h_0(t_i,\omega)\Delta t_i\right]^2 + \left[\sum_{i=0}^{n-1} k_0(t_i,\omega)\,\Delta W_i\right]^2$$

$$+ 2z_a \sum_{i=0}^{n-1} h_0(t_i,\omega)\Delta t_i + 2z_a \sum_{i=0}^{n-1} k_0(t_i,\omega)\Delta W_i$$

$$+ 2 \sum_{i=0}^{n-1} h_0(t_i,\omega)\Delta t_i \sum_{j=0}^{n-1} k_0(t_j,\omega)\Delta W_j. \qquad (6.63)$$

Note that

$$\underset{n\to\infty}{\text{l.i.m.}} \left\{\sum_{i=0}^{n-1} h_0(t_i,\omega)\Delta t_i\right\}^2 = \left\{\int_a^t h_0(u,\omega)du\right\}^2$$

$$\underset{n\to\infty}{\text{l.i.m.}} \left\{\sum_{i=0}^{n-1} h_0(t_i,\omega)\Delta t_i \sum_{j=0}^{n-1} k_0(t_j,\omega)\Delta W_j\right\}$$

$$= \int_a^t h_0(u,\omega)du \int_a^t k_0(u,\omega)dW(u,\omega), \tag{6.64}$$

while

$$\left\{ \sum_{i=0}^{n-1} k_0(t_i,\omega)\Delta W_i \right\}^2$$

$$= 2 \sum_{j=0}^{n-1} \left[k_0(t_j,\omega) \sum_{i=0}^{j-1} k_0(t_i,\omega)\Delta W_i \right]\Delta W_j + \sum_{i=0}^{n-1} k_0^2(t_i,\omega)(\Delta W_i)^2.$$

Noting that

$$k_0(t_j,\omega) \sum_{i=0}^{j-1} k_0(t_i,\omega)\Delta W_i$$

is independent of ΔW_j, $j = 0, 1, \ldots, n-1$ and converges to

$$k_0(t_j,\omega) \int_a^{t_j} k_0(t,\omega)dW(t),$$

which, in turn, satisfies condition (6.57) for integrability in the Ito sense, we see that

$$\sum_{j=0}^{n-1} \left\{ k_0(t_j,\omega) \int_a^{t_j} k_0(t,\omega)dW(t) \right\}\Delta W_j$$

converges to

$$\int_a^t \left\{ k_0(s,\omega) \int_a^s k_0(u,\omega)dW(u) \right\}dW(s). \tag{6.65}$$

On the other hand, it can be proved that

$$E\left[\left\{ \sum_{i=0}^{n-1} k_0^2(t_i,\omega)(\Delta W_i^2 - \Delta t_i) \right\}^2 \right]$$

$$= 2 \sum_{i=0}^{n-1} E[k_0^4(t,\omega)]\Delta t_i^2 \leq 2\delta_n \sum_{i=0}^{n-1} E[k_0^4(t,\omega)]\Delta t_i$$

$$\rightarrow 2\left\{ \int_a^t E[k_0^4(u,\omega)]du \right\}\lim_{n\to\infty}\delta_n.$$

Hence, if $\int_a^t E[k_0^4(u,\omega)]du < \infty$, then $\sum_{i=0}^{n-1} k_0^2(t_i,\omega)\Delta W_i^2$ converges to $\int_a^t k_0^2(t,\omega)dt$ in the mean square sense. This, together with (6.64) and (6.65), implies that x_n converges to the process $x(t)$ defined by

$$x(t) = z_a^2 + \left[\int_a^t h_0(u,\omega)du \right]^2 + 2 \int_a^t k_0(s,\omega) \int_a^s k_0(u,\omega)dW(u)dW(s)$$

$$+ \int_a^t k_0^2(u,\omega)du + 2z_a \int_a^t h_0(u,\omega)du + 2z_a \int_a^t k_0(u,\omega)dW(u)$$

$$+ 2\int_a^t h_0(s,\omega)ds \int_a^t k_0(u,\omega)dW(u).$$

In other words,

$$dx(t) = 2\left[h_0(t,\omega) \int_a^t h_0(s,\omega)ds \right]dt + 2[k_0(t,\omega) \int_a^t k_0(s,\omega)dW(s)]dW(t)$$

$$+ 2z_a h_0(t,\omega)dt + 2z_a k_0(t,\omega)dW(t) + 2\left[h_0(t,\omega) \int_a^t k_0(s,\omega)dW(s) \right]dt$$

$$+ 2\left[\int_a^t h_0(s,\omega)ds \right]k_0(t,\omega)dW(t) + k_0(t,\omega)^2dt$$

$$= 2z(t)dz(t) + k_0^2(t,\omega)dt. \tag{6.66}$$

Relation (6.66) may not be consistent with one's intuition; due to the presence of the extra term $k_0^2(t,\omega)dt$. The origin of this extra term is $[dz(t)]^2$. In fact, the increment $dx(t)$ is

$$dx(t) = z(t + dt)^2 - z(t)^2$$

$$= [z(t) + dz(t)]^2 - z(t)^2$$

$$= 2z(t)dz(t) + [dz(t)]^2. \tag{6.67}$$

Hence, if one compares (6.67) with (6.66) and if one recalls that dW^2 is of order dt, one becomes convinced of the existence of the extra term $k_0^2(t,\omega)dt$. Indeed,

$$[dz]^2 = [h_0 dt]^2 + k_0^2 dW^2 + 2h_0 k_0 dtdW$$

$$= k_0^2 dt + o(dt). \tag{6.68}$$

In conclusion, in the calculation of the increment $dx(t)$ of a transformed process $x(t) = f(z(t),t)$, $[dz]^2$ cannot be neglected. This situation is expressed by the following.

Lemma 6.1 Ito's lemma (McKean, 1969). Consider a function $f = f(z_1,\ldots,z_n,t)$ defined on $\mathbb{R}^n \times [0,+\infty)$ with continuous partial derivatives

$$\frac{\partial f}{\partial t}, \frac{\partial f}{\partial z_i}, i = 1, 2, \ldots, n \quad \text{and} \quad \frac{\partial^2 f}{\partial z_i \partial z_j}, i, j = 1, 2, \ldots,$$

and consider n Ito equations: $dz_i(t) = h_i(z_i,\omega)dt + k_i(z_i,\omega)dW$, $i = 1, 2, \ldots, n$. Then $f(z_1(t),\ldots,z_i(t),t) = x(t)$ also provides an Ito equation:

$$dx(t) = f_0 dt + \sum_{i=1}^{n} f_i dz_i + \frac{1}{2} \sum_{i,j=1}^{n} f_{ij} dz_i dz_j, \tag{6.69}$$

where

$$f_0 = \frac{\partial f}{\partial t} [z_1(t), \ldots, z_n(t), t],$$

$$f_i = \frac{\partial f}{\partial z_i} [z_1(t), \ldots, z_n(t), t], \quad i = 1, 2, \ldots, n, \tag{6.70}$$

$$f_{ij} = \frac{\partial^2 f}{\partial z_i \partial z_j} [z_1(t), \ldots, z_n(t), t], \quad i, j = 1, 2, \ldots, n,$$

and

$$dz_i(t) dz_j(t) = k_i(t) k_j(t) dt. \tag{6.71}$$

For convenience, we shall call the solution of an Ito equation an 'Ito process'. According to Ito's lemma, we see that the totality of Ito processes is closed under any transformation f that satisfies the conditions stated in Ito's lemma.

We already know that an integral equation

$$x(t) = x_a + \int_a^t h(x) dt + \int_a^t k(x) dW \tag{6.58bis}$$

is equivalent to the Ito equation (6.43). Here we stress that the solution of (6.58) exists under Lipschitz and extra conditions on h and k and that it is unique depending on the initial value $x(a) = x_a$. A standard proof of this statement is based on the construction of the solution by means of successive approximation. For brevity, we omit the proof, which can be found elsewhere (see, for instance, Jazwinski, 1970). We should note also the following fact. In view of (6.58bis), one may see that $x(t)$ is continuous in t because of the sample path continuity of the Wiener process $W(t)$. Furthermore, $x(t)$ is a Markov process because $x(t + s)$ depends only on $x(s) = x_s$ and on $\{dW(u), s \leq u \leq t\}$. This implies that $x(t)$, i.e. the solution of the Ito equation, is a diffusion process. The drift and infinitesimal variance can be immediately calculated. In general, for a Wiener process with $\sigma^2 \neq 1$ from (6.43) there immediately follows:

$$\lim_{\Delta t \downarrow 0} \frac{1}{\Delta t} E[\Delta x(t) \mid x(t)=x] = h(x),$$

$$\lim_{\Delta t \downarrow 0} \frac{1}{\Delta t} E[\Delta x^2(t) \mid x(t)=x] = k^2(x),$$

in agreement with (6.44). The conclusion is that the Ito equation equivalent to equation (6.8) *is not* equation (6.43), but instead

$$dx(t) = \left[h(x) + \frac{\sigma^2}{2} k(x)k'(x) \right] dt + k(x)dW. \tag{6.72}$$

7 The first-passage-time problem

In the foregoing we have been concerned with the problem of describing the unfolding of a stochastic process $X(t)$ of the Markov type. In particular, we have taken into consideration the case of diffusion processes and have shown that in such case the transition p.d.f. of the process satisfies the diffusion equations (4.1) and (4.2). Actually, diffusion processes can also be defined as those Markov processes whose sample paths are continuous functions (cf., for instance, Arnold, 1974, Ch. 2 or Wong and Hajek, 1985, Ch. 5). Such a property – namely the continuity of the sample paths – plays an essential role for the validity of the forthcoming considerations. Hence, we shall henceforth confine our attention exclusively to diffusion processes.

So far, we have regarded the time variable as a parameter and have thus provided a description of the random variable $X(t)$ conditional on some initial value x_0 at an initial time t_0. However, one may assign a certain region of the state space and ask questions concerning the time necessary for the stochastic process to enter this region for the first time. Roughly speaking, this amounts to switching from the description of $X(t)$ to the description of $t(X)$, in which time is now regarded as a random variable whereas the space variable is considered as a parameter. More specifically, in the sequel we shall limit ourselves to considering a single state $\rho \neq x_0$ (accessible to $X(t)$) and define the following random variables:

$$T = \begin{cases} \inf_{t \geq t_0} \{t: X(t) > \rho \mid X(t_0) = x_0\}, & x_0 < \rho, \tag{7.1a} \\ \\ \inf_{t \geq t_0} \{t: X(t) < \rho \mid X(t_0) = x_0\}, & x_0 > \rho. \tag{7.1b} \end{cases}$$

The random variable T is called the first-passage time of $X(t)$ through the *threshold* or *boundary* ρ conditional upon $X(t_0) = x_0$. Hence, it also represents the time when first $X(t)$ enters the regions $x \geq \rho$ and $x \leq \rho$, respectively. The definitions (7.1) also hold when ρ is changed into a continuous function $S(t)$. This will be called a time-dependent threshold or boundary. In the sequel, we shall at times assume that $S(t)$ possesses a bounded derivative. Let us now set

$$g(\rho,t \mid x_0,t_0) = \frac{\partial}{\partial t} P\{T \leq t\}, \tag{7.2}$$

where T is defined by (7.1). The function g is the first-passage-time p.d.f. of $X(t)$ through ρ, conditional upon $X(t_0) = x_0$. It should, however, be remarked that T may be a dishonest random variable in the sense that the passage through ρ need not be a sure event. When this is the case, g is the first-passage-time p.d.f. conditional also upon the passage through ρ. Let us now define the following functions:

$$F(x,t \mid y,\tau) = P\{X(t) \leq x \mid X(\tau) = y\},$$ (7.3a)

$$A^{(\rho)}(x,t \mid y,\tau) = \begin{cases} P\{X(t) < x \text{ and } X(\theta) < \rho, \ \forall \theta < t \mid X(\tau) = y\}, x,y < \rho \\ P\{X(t) > x \text{ and } X(\theta) > \rho, \ \forall \theta < t \mid X(\tau) = y\}, \ x,y > \rho \end{cases}$$ (7.3b)

$$\alpha^{(\rho)}(x,t \mid y,\tau) = \frac{\partial}{\partial x} A^{(\rho)}(x,t \mid y,\tau).$$ (7.3c)

Clearly, (7.3a) is a transition distribution and

$$\frac{\partial F(x,t \mid y,\tau)}{\partial x} \equiv f(x,t \mid y,\tau).$$ (7.4)

Similarly, (7.3b) and (7.3c) define the transition distribution and the transition p.d.f. *in the presence of an absorbing boundary* at ρ, respectively. In the sequel we shall confine our attention to the case of a diffusion process $X(t)$ defined over the interval (r_1,r_2) with r_i $(i = 1,2)$ natural boundaries. We shall assume that $r_1 \leq x_0 < S(t_0) \leq r_2$, i.e. that the first passage through $\rho = S(t)$ occurs 'from below'. The opposite case, namely $x_0 > S(t_0)$, can be treated in a similar way. The functions (7.1)–(7.4) are related to one another by various identities. In particular, we have (Fortet, 1943):

$$f(x,t \mid x_0,t_0) = \int_{t_0}^{t} d\tau g[S(\tau), \tau \mid x_0,t_0] f[x,t \mid S(\tau),\tau]$$ (7.5)

holding for any $x_0 < S(t_0)$ and $x \geq S(t)$. Furthermore, the following relation holds:

$$\int_{r_1}^{S(t)} dx \alpha^{S(t)}(x,t \mid x_0,t_0) = 1 - \int_{t_0}^{t} g[S(\tau),\tau \mid x_0,t_0] d\tau.$$ (7.6)

Indeed, the left-hand-side term gives the probability that up to time t the boundary $S(t)$ has not yet been attained while the integral in the right-hand side equals the probability that $S(t)$ has been crossed before time t, the sum of these two probabilities being obviously unity. Finally, a relation between the free transition p.d.f. (7.4) and the probability current defined by (4.3) is provided by the continuity equation (4.4).

The first systematic approach to first-passage-time problems is due to Siegert (1951). Further extensions and results appear in a well-known article by Darling and Siegert (1953), where two-barrier problems were extensively studied for the case of constant boundaries.

Hereafter, we shall provide some examples leading to closed-form expressions of the first-passage-time p.d.f.'s for the Wiener and Ornstein–Uhlenbeck (OU) processes when the boundary is a constant. The same results will also be seen to follow at once by a more general procedure that will be sketched in Section 10 where use of integral equations, both for constant and for time-dependent boundaries, will also be considered. Section 8 will deal with a powerful tool to handle first-passage-time problems for constant boundaries and time homogeneous diffusion processes. i.e. with the Laplace transform method introduced by the aforenamed authors. In Section 9, the problem of determining the moments of the first-passage-time will be briefly discussed. Section 11 will be devoted to a rather thorough analysis of the behaviour of the first-passage-time p.d.f. and its moments for the OU process in the case of large boundaries and for large times.

Let us now return to the Wiener and Ornstein–Uhlenbeck processes defined in Section 5 and consider the problem of determining their first-passage-time p.d.f.'s through an assigned threshold value $S > X(t_0) = x_0$.

7.1 Wiener process

Consider first the case of a zero-drift Wiener process. Recalling (5.3), equation (7.5) reads:

$$\frac{1}{\sqrt{[2\pi(t - t_0)]}\sigma} \exp\left[-\frac{(x - x_0)^2}{2\sigma^2(t - t_0)}\right] = \int_{t_0}^{t} d\tau g(S,\tau \mid x_0,t_0)$$

$$\times \frac{1}{\sqrt{[2\pi(t - \tau)]}6} \exp\left[-\frac{(x - S)^2}{26^2(t - \tau)}\right], \quad (x > S). \tag{7.7}$$

Integrating both sides from S to $+\infty$, we thus obtain:

$$\int_{t_0}^{t} d\tau g(S,\tau \mid x_0,t_0) = \frac{2}{\sqrt{[2\pi(t - t_0)]}\sigma} \int_{S}^{+\infty} dx \exp\left[-\frac{(x - x_0)^2}{2\sigma^2(t - t_0)}\right] \tag{7.8}$$

or:

$$g(S,t \mid x_0,t_0) \equiv -2 \int_{-\infty}^{S} dx \frac{\partial}{\partial t} f(x,t \mid x_0,t_0), \tag{7.9}$$

where f is given by (5.3). Finally, making use of the Fokker–Planck equation (5.1), from (7.9) one easily obtains the closed-form expression:

$$g(S,t \mid x_0,t_0) = \frac{S - x_0}{t - t_0} f(S,t \mid x_0,t_0)$$

$$\equiv \frac{S-x_0}{\sqrt{[2\pi(t - t_0)^3]}\sigma} \exp\left[-\frac{(S-x_0)^2}{2\sigma^2(t - t_0)}\right], \quad (S > x_0). \tag{7.10}$$

By a similar argument, one can prove that for all $S \ne x_0$ one has:

$$g(S,t \mid x_0,t_0) = \frac{|S-x_0|}{\sqrt{[2\pi(t-t_0)^3]}\sigma} \exp\left[-\frac{(S-x_0)^2}{2\sigma^2(t-t_0)}\right]. \tag{7.11}$$

Note that a closed-form result similar to (7.9) holds for any diffusion process for which S is a symmetry point in the sense that:

$$f(x,t \mid S,\tau) = f(2S-x,t \mid S,\tau), \quad \forall \, x \in I. \tag{7.12}$$

Indeed, from (7.5) one obtains:

$$g(S,t \mid x_0,t_0) = -2 \int_{r_1}^{S} dx \, \frac{\partial}{\partial t} f(x,t \mid x_0,t_0). \tag{7.13}$$

Making use of (4.1), from (7.13) one obtains:

$$\begin{aligned} g(S,t \mid x_0,t_0) = 2\{&A_1(S)f(S,t \mid x_0,t_0) \\ &- \lim_{x \downarrow r_1} [A_1(x)f(x,t \mid x_0,t_0)]\} \\ &- A_2(S) \left.\frac{\partial f(x,t \mid x_0,t_0)}{\partial x}\right|_{x=S} \\ &+ \lim_{x \downarrow r_1} \frac{\partial}{\partial x} [A_2(x)f(x,t \mid x_0,t_0)]. \end{aligned} \tag{7.14}$$

If r_1 is natural boundary and if f and $\dfrac{\partial f}{\partial x}$ vanish sufficiently rapidly as x approaches r_1, (7.14) yields:

$$g(S,t \mid x_0,t_0) = 2 A_1(S)f(S,t \mid x_0,t_0) - A_2(S) \left.\frac{\partial f(x,t \mid x_0,t_0)}{\partial x}\right|_{x=S}. \tag{7.15}$$

We now turn to the case of the Wiener process with drift μ. Its transition p.d.f. is then given by (5.9) and satisfies equation (5.10). To determine the first-passage-time p.d.f. $g(S,t \mid x_0)$, we make use of (7.6). After differentiating both sides with respect to t and recalling (7.3c) we obtain:

$$g(S,t \mid x_0) = -\frac{\partial}{\partial t} A^{(S)}(S,t \mid x_0). \tag{7.16}$$

The transition distribution $A^{(S)}(S,t \mid x_0)$ can be obtained in the following way. First of all, we determine the transition function $\alpha^{(S)}(x,t \mid x_0)$ in the presence of an absorbing boundary at S by the so-called method of images. Namely, we express $\alpha^{(S)}(x,t \mid x_0)$ as the linear combination

$$\alpha^{(S)}(x,t \mid x_0) = f(x,t \mid x_0) + Af(x,t \mid 2S-x_0) \tag{7.17}$$

which is also a solution of (5.10) and satisfies the initial delta condition. Next, we impose the absorption condition (4.21) at S which, in the present case, reads:

$$\lim_{x \uparrow S} \alpha^{(S)}(x,t \mid x_0) = 0. \tag{7.18}$$

From (7.17) and (7.18) the constant A follows:

$$A = -\frac{f(S,t \mid x_0)}{f(S,t \mid 2S-x_0)} = -\exp\left[\frac{2\mu}{\sigma^2}(S - x_0)\right], \tag{7.19}$$

where use of (5.9) has been made. Hence:

$$\alpha^{(S)}(x,t \mid x_0) = \frac{1}{\sigma\sqrt{(2\pi t)}}\left\{\exp\left[-\frac{(x - x_0 - \mu t)^2}{2\sigma^2 t}\right]\right.$$
$$\left. - \exp\left[\frac{2\mu}{\sigma^2}(S - x_0) - \frac{(x - 2S + x_0 - \mu t)^2}{2\sigma^2 t}\right]\right\}. \tag{7.20}$$

By integrating both sides of (7.20) between $-\infty$ and S we then obtain:

$$A^{(S)}(S,t \mid x_0) = \frac{1}{2}\left[1 + \mathrm{Erf}\left(\frac{x-x_0 - \mu t}{\sigma\sqrt{(2t)}}\right)\right]$$
$$- \frac{1}{2}\exp\left[\frac{2\mu}{\sigma^2}(S - x_0)\right]\left[1 + \mathrm{Erf}\left(\frac{x - 2S + x_0 - \mu t}{\sigma\sqrt{(2t)}}\right)\right]. \tag{7.21}$$

From (7.16) and (7.21) we finally obtain:

$$g(S,t \mid x_0) = \frac{|S - x_0|}{t}f(S,t \mid x_0) \equiv \frac{|S - x_0|}{\sigma\sqrt{(2\pi t^3)}}\exp\left[-\frac{(S - x_0 - \mu t)^2}{2\sigma^2 t}\right], \tag{7.22}$$

which can be seen to hold for all $x_0 \ne S$.

Note that the crossing of S is a sure event if $x_0 < S$ and $\mu \ge 0$ or if $x_0 > S$ and $\mu \le 0$. Indeed, only in such cases does the function (7.22) integrate to unity.

7.2 Ornstein–Uhlenbeck process

The first-passage-time problem for the OU process cannot be solved by straightforward simple considerations similar to those exploited for the Wiener process. More will be said in Section 8. Here we limit ourselves to considering a very special case, namely when the threshold S is a symmetry point for the transition p.d.f. Recalling (5.15), we immediately see that $S = \mu/\delta$ is such a symmetry point for $f(x,t \mid x_0,t_0)$. Hence, relation (7.13) holds, with f specified by (5.15). Alternatively, use of (7.15) can be made. The result is:

$$g\left(\frac{\mu}{\delta},t \mid x_0\right) = \frac{2(\mu - \delta x_0)}{e^{\delta t} - e^{-\delta t}}f\left(\frac{\mu}{\delta},t \mid x_0\right),$$

where $f\left(\frac{\mu}{\delta},t \mid x_0\right)$ is obtained from (5.15).

8   The Laplace transform approach

Let $X(t)$ be a time-homogeneous diffusion process which possesses a transition p.d.f. $f(x,t \mid y)$ satisfying Kolmogorov's forward and backward equations (cf. Section 4):

$$\frac{\partial f(x,t \mid y)}{\partial t} = L_x^+[f(x,t \mid y)], \tag{4.16a}$$

$$\frac{\partial f(x,t \mid y)}{\partial t} = L_y^-[f(x,t \mid y)], \tag{4.16b}$$

where the differential operators L_x^+ and L_x^- are defined as follows:

$$L_x^+ = -\frac{\partial}{\partial x} b(x) + \frac{\partial^2}{\partial x^2} a(x), \tag{8.1a}$$

$$L_x^- = b(x)\frac{\partial}{\partial x} + a(x)\frac{\partial^2}{\partial x^2}, \tag{8.1b}$$

with $a(x) > 0$.

In what follows, we shall assume that the diffusion interval of the process $X(t)$ is $I = (r_1,r_2)$, $-\infty \leq r_1 < r_2 \leq +\infty$ and that both end-points r_i, $i = 1, 2$ are natural boundaries. Then, the initial condition (4.17)

$$\lim_{t \downarrow 0} f(x,t \mid x_0) = \delta(x - x_0) \tag{4.17}$$

determines the transition p.d.f. $f(x,t \mid x_0)$ uniquely. Moreover, since the boundaries r_1 and r_2 are natural,

$$f(r_1,t \mid y) = f(r_2,t \mid y) = 0, \quad \text{for any } y \in I, \tag{8.2a}$$

$$f(x,t \mid r_1) = f(x,t \mid r_2) = 0, \quad \text{for any } x \in I. \tag{8.2b}$$

(In the case of other boundary conditions, the discussion goes in a similar way.) In Section 7, we gave the integral equation (7.5) for the first-passage-time p.d.f. of a general diffusion process starting from x_0 through a time-varying boundary $S(t)$ by appealing to the (strong) Markov property of the process. Let us rewrite (7.5) assuming $x > S(t) > x_0$ or $x < S(t) < x_0$:

$$f(x,t \mid x_0,t_0) = \int_{t_0}^{t} d\tau g[S(\tau), \tau \mid x_0,t_0]f[x,t \mid S(\tau),\tau]. \tag{7.5}$$

In most cases, it is difficult to solve analytically this integral equation with respect to g and hence several numerical methods have been proposed, as we shall see in Section 10. However, if the considered process $X(t)$ is time-homogeneous (i.e. its transition p.d.f. satisfies (4.16) and (8.1)) and if the boundary is constant, i.e. $S(t) \equiv S$, then the transition p.d.f.'s and the first-passage-time p.d.f. appearing in (7.5) are replaced by $f(x,t \mid x_0)$,

$f(x,t-\tau \mid S)$ and $g(S,\tau \mid x_0)$, respectively. In this case, the integral equation (7.5) reads:

$$f(x,t \mid x_0) = \int_0^t d\tau g(S,\tau \mid x_0)f(x,t - \tau \mid S), \tag{8.3}$$

where we have assumed $t_0 = 0$.

Let $f_\lambda(x \mid y)$ and $g_\lambda(S \mid x_0)$ be the Laplace transforms of $f(x,t \mid y)$ and $g(S,t \mid x_0)$, respectively:

$$f_\lambda (x \mid y) = \int_0^\infty f(x,t \mid y)e^{-\lambda t}dt \tag{8.4}$$

and

$$g_\lambda(S \mid x_0) = \int_0^\infty g(S,t \mid x_0)e^{-\lambda t}dt \tag{8.5}$$

for $\text{Re}(\lambda) > 0$. Since the right-hand side of (8.3) is a convolution integral, the Laplace transform of (8.3) yields

$$f_\lambda(x \mid x_0) = g_\lambda(S \mid x_0) f_\lambda(x \mid S), \quad (x > S > x_0 \text{ or } x < S < x_0),$$

or

$$g_\lambda(S \mid x_0) = \frac{f_\lambda(x \mid x_0)}{f_\lambda(x \mid S)}, \quad (x > S > x_0 \text{ or } x < S < x_0). \tag{8.6}$$

The Laplace transform g_λ of the first-passage-time p.d.f. is thus expressed in terms of the Laplace transform f_λ of the process transition p.d.f. Hence our task is to obtain f_λ, the Laplace transform of the transition p.d.f. To this end, let us start with (4.16). The Laplace transforms of (4.16) yield:

$$[\lambda - L_x^+]f_\lambda(x \mid y) = \delta(x-y), \tag{8.7a}$$

$$[\lambda - L_y^-]f_\lambda(x \mid y) = \delta(x-y), \tag{8.7b}$$

where use of the relation

$$\int_0^\infty \frac{\partial f}{\partial t} e^{-\lambda t}dt = \lim_{\varepsilon \to 0} f(x,t \mid y)e^{-\lambda t}\bigg|_{t=\varepsilon}^{t=+\infty} + \lambda f_\lambda(x \mid y)$$

and of (4.17) has been made. The boundary conditions (8.2) reduce to

$$f_\lambda(r_1 \mid y) = f_\lambda(r_2 \mid y) = 0 \quad \text{for any } y \in I, \tag{8.8a}$$

$$f_\lambda(x \mid r_1) = f_\lambda (x \mid r_2) = 0 \quad \text{for any } x \in I. \tag{8.8b}$$

Note that the left-hand sides of (8.7a) and (8.7b) must contain terms which behave like delta functions since the right-hand sides are such. Taking this into account and integrating (8.7a) from $x = y - \varepsilon$ to $x = y + \varepsilon$ for small $\varepsilon(>0)$, we obtain

$$-\frac{d}{dx}\left[a(x)f_\lambda(x\mid y)\right]\Big|_{x=y-\varepsilon}^{x=y+\varepsilon} = 1$$

or

$$\frac{d}{dx}f_\lambda(x\mid y)\Big|_{x=y+\varepsilon} - \frac{d}{dx}f_\lambda(x\mid y)\Big|_{x=y-\varepsilon} = -\frac{1}{a(y)}, \tag{8.9a}$$

where we have assumed that $a(x)$ possesses a continuous first derivative. Similarly, integrating (8.7b) from $y = x - \varepsilon$ to $y = x + \varepsilon$, we obtain

$$\frac{d}{dy}f_\lambda(x\mid y)\Big|_{y=x-\varepsilon} - \frac{d}{dy}f_\lambda(x\mid y)\Big|_{y=x+\varepsilon} = -\frac{1}{a(x)}. \tag{8.9b}$$

Hence, instead of solving (8.7a) with boundary condition (8.8a) we solve the homogeneous equation

$$[\lambda - L_x^+]f_\lambda(x\mid y) = 0 \tag{8.10a}$$

with conditions (8.8a) and (8.9a). Likewise, we solve the equation

$$[\lambda - L_y^-]f_\lambda(x\mid y) = 0 \tag{8.10b}$$

with (8.8b) and (8.9b).

8.1   Solution of equation (8.7)

Solving equations (8.10) one obtains the so-called Green function. The reader familiar with this subject may go directly to equation (8.21).

It will be seen later that the solution of equation (8.10a) with conditions (8.8a) and (8.9a) coincides with that of equation (8.10b) with (8.8b) and (8.9b). Hence, it suffices to solve (8.10a) or (8.10b) with the corresponding conditions (8.8a) and (8.9a) or (8.8b) and (8.9b).

To begin with, let us consider the following equation:

$$L_x^+ w = \frac{d^2}{dx^2}\left[a(x)w\right] - \frac{d}{dx}\left[b(x)w\right] = 0. \tag{8.11}$$

Its solution is easily obtained as:

$$w(x) = \frac{c}{a(x)}\exp\left[\int^x \frac{b(z)}{a(z)}dz\right] \equiv Cw_0(x), \tag{8.12}$$

where C is an arbitrary integration constant. Next, let us consider the homogeneous equations:

$$[\lambda - L_x^+]u = 0, \tag{8.13a}$$

$$[\lambda - L_x^-]v = 0, \tag{8.13b}$$

and let us denote by $v_1(\lambda,x)$ and $v_2(\lambda,x)$ the fundamental solutions of (8.13b) which satisfy the boundary conditions:

$$v_1(\lambda,r_1) = 0, \quad v_2(\lambda,r_2) = 0. \tag{8.14}$$

Since v_1 and v_2 are fundamental solutions, the Wronskian

$$\Delta_x = v_1(\lambda,x)v_2'(\lambda,x) - v_1'(\lambda,x)v_2(\lambda,x) \tag{8.15}$$

does not vanish for any $x \in I$, where prime denotes differentiation with respect to x. Note that the Wronskian Δ_x defined in (8.15) satisfies the equation

$$a(x)\frac{d\Delta_x}{dx} + b(x)\Delta_x = 0. \tag{8.16}$$

Hence Δ_x takes the form:

$$\Delta_x = D \exp\left[-\int^x \frac{b(z)}{a(z)}\,dz\right], \tag{8.17}$$

where D is an integration constant to be determined in such a way that (8.17) coincides with (8.15) for a given pair of fundamental solutions v_i, $i = 1, 2$.

Let us show that we may choose the constants c_1 and c_2 as

$$\begin{aligned} c_2v_2(\lambda,x) &= c_1v_1(\lambda,x), \\ c_2v_2'(\lambda,x) - c_1v_1'(\lambda,x) &= -\frac{1}{a(x)}. \end{aligned} \tag{8.18}$$

Indeed, since $\Delta_x = v_1v_2' - v_1'v_2 \neq 0$ for any $x \in I = (r_1,r_2)$, the system of linear equations (8.18) with respect to c_1 and c_2 can be solved. The solution is

$$c_1 = -\frac{v_2(\lambda,x)}{\Delta_x}\frac{1}{a(x)} = -\frac{1}{D}w_0(x)v_2(\lambda,x),$$

$$c_2 = -\frac{v_1(\lambda,x)}{\Delta_x}\frac{1}{a(x)} = -\frac{1}{D}w_0(x)v_1(\lambda,x), \tag{8.19}$$

where the second equalities follow in view of (8.12) and (8.17).

Now for an arbitrary but fixed $x \in I$, let us set

$$f_\lambda(x \mid y) = \begin{cases} c_1v_1(\lambda,y), & y < x, \\ c_2v_2(\lambda,y), & y > x, \end{cases} \tag{8.20}$$

where c_1 and c_2 are given by (8.19). It can be checked that $f_\lambda(x \mid y)$ defined by (8.20) is the solution of (8.10b) satisfying the boundary conditions (8.8b). It can also be seen that $f_\lambda(x \mid y)$ defined by (8.20) satisfies condition (8.9b). In fact, for an arbitrary but fixed $x \in I = (r_1,r_2)$, $v_i(\lambda,y)$, $i = 1, 2$ are solution of (8.10b). Moreover,

$$f_\lambda(x \mid r_1) = c_1 v_1(\lambda, r_1) = 0,$$
$$f_\lambda(x \mid r_2) = c_2 v_2(\lambda, r_2) = 0,$$

and

$$\frac{\partial f_\lambda(x \mid y)}{\partial y}\bigg|_{y=x+\varepsilon} - \frac{\partial f_\lambda(x \mid y)}{\partial y}\bigg|_{y=x-\varepsilon}$$

$$= c_2 \frac{dv_2(\lambda, y)}{dy}\bigg|_{y=x+\varepsilon} - c_1 \frac{dv_1(\lambda, y)}{dy}\bigg|_{y=x-\varepsilon}$$

$$= c_2 v_2'(\lambda, x) - c_1 v_1'(\lambda, x) = -\frac{1}{a(x)}.$$

Next we shall prove that equation (8.13a) is satisfied by

$$u_i(\lambda, x) = -\frac{v_i(\lambda, x)}{a(x)\Delta_x} = -\frac{1}{D} w_0(x) v_i(\lambda, x), \quad i = 1, 2, \tag{8.21}$$

where Δ_x is the Wronskian defined by (8.15), $w_0(x)$ is defined in (8.12), and D is given in (8.17). By straightforward calculation, it can be seen that

$$J \equiv [\lambda - L_x^+](w_0 v_i) = \lambda w_0 v_i - [(a w_0 v_i)'' - (b w_0 v_i)']$$

$$= \lambda w_0 v_i - \{(a w_0)'' v_i + 2(a w_0)' v_i' + (a w_0) v_i'' - (b w_0)' v_i - (b w_0) v_i'\}.$$

In view of definition (8.12) of $w_0(x)$,

$$(a w_0)' = b w_0,$$
$$(a w_0)'' = (b w_0)'.$$

Hence

$$J = \lambda w_0 v_i - (a w_0) v_i'' - (b w_0) v_i'$$
$$= w_0[\lambda - L_x^-] v_i = 0, \quad i = 1, 2.$$

This implies that $f_\lambda(x \mid y)$ defined by (8.20) with (8.19) also satisfies equation (8.10a), if it is viewed as a function of x for a fixed $y \in I = (r_1, r_2)$. One may also check that the function $f_\lambda(x \mid y)$ thus defined satisfies the boundary conditions (8.8a) and condition (8.9a).

In conclusion, the solution of equation (8.7) with boundary conditions (8.8) is given by

$$f_\lambda(x \mid y) = \begin{cases} u_1(\lambda, x) v_2(\lambda, y), & x < y, \\ u_2(\lambda, x) v_1(\lambda, y), & x > y, \end{cases} \tag{8.22}$$

where $v_i(\lambda, x)$, $i = 1, 2$ are fundamental solutions of (8.13b) satisfying

$$v_1(\lambda, r_1) = v_2(\lambda, r_2) = 0$$

and where $u_i(\lambda,x) = -[1/a(x)\Delta_x]v_i(\lambda,x)$, $i = 1, 2$ with Δ_x defined in (8.15).

Note that $f_\lambda (x \mid y)$ defined in (8.22) automatically fulfils the condition

$$\int_{r_1}^{\gamma_2} f_\lambda (x \mid y)dx = \frac{1}{\lambda} \quad \text{for } y \in I, \tag{8.23}$$

which corresponds to the normalization condition:

$$\int_{r_1}^{\gamma_2} f(x,t \mid y)dx = 1 \quad \text{for } y \in I.$$

Accordingly, rewriting f_λ's in (8.6) in terms of the r.h.s. of (8.22), we obtain

$$g_\lambda(S \mid x_0) = \begin{cases} \dfrac{v_1(\lambda,x_0)}{v_1(\lambda,S)}, & S > x_0, \tag{8.24a} \\[3mm] \dfrac{v_2(\lambda,x_0)}{v_2(\lambda,S)}, & S < x_0. \tag{8.24b} \end{cases}$$

In the sequel we shall make use of the method sketched so far to obtain the Laplace transform of the first-passage-time p.d.f. for three well-known processes: the Wiener, Ornstein–Uhlenbeck and Rayleigh processes.

8.2 Wiener process $(a(x) = 1/2, b(x) = 0)$

Let us calculate the Laplace transform of the first-passage-time p.d.f. for the Wiener process starting from x_0 at $t = 0$ through a constant boundary S. In this case, $L_x^+ = L_x^- = (1/2)d^2/dx^2$ (i.e. the differential operator is self-adjoint) and the diffusion interval I is the whole line, i.e. $I = (-\infty,+\infty)$. Both boundaries, $r_1 = -\infty$ and $r_2 = +\infty$ are natural. The equation

$$\lambda v - \frac{1}{2}\frac{d^2v}{dx^2} = 0 \tag{8.25}$$

gives the fundamental solutions $v_1(\lambda,x) = e^{\sqrt{2\lambda}x}$ and $v_2(\lambda,x) = e^{-\sqrt{2\lambda}x}$, which satisfy the boundary conditions:

$$v_1 (\lambda,-\infty) = v_2(\lambda,+\infty) = 0.$$

The Wronskian Δ_x is given by

$$\Delta_x = .v_1v_2' - v_1'v_2 = -2\sqrt{2\lambda}.$$

Hence from (8.21)

$$u_i(\lambda,x) = \frac{1}{\sqrt{2\lambda}} v_i (\lambda,x), \quad i = 1, 2.$$

Accordingly

$$f_\lambda(x \mid y) = \begin{cases} \dfrac{1}{\sqrt{2\lambda}} \exp[\sqrt{2\lambda}(x - y)], & x < y, \\[2mm] \dfrac{1}{\sqrt{2\lambda}} \exp[-\sqrt{2\lambda}(x - y)], & x > y, \end{cases} \qquad (8.26)$$

and

$$g_\lambda(S \mid x_0) = \begin{cases} \exp[\sqrt{2\lambda}(x_0 - S)], & S > x_0, \\[2mm] \exp[-\sqrt{2\lambda}(x_0 - S)], & S < x_0. \end{cases} \qquad (8.27)$$

The inverse Laplace transform of the function $g_\lambda(S \mid x_0)$ given by (8.27) can be calculated to yield the well-known result:

$$g(S,t \mid x_0) = \frac{|S - x_0|}{\sqrt{(2\pi t^3)}} \exp\left[-\frac{(S - x_0)^2}{2t} \right] \qquad (8.27\text{bis})$$

8.3 Ornstein–Uhlenbeck process ($a(x) = \sigma^2/2$, $b(x) = \mu - \delta x$)

In this case, the diffusion interval is the whole line and $r_1 = -\infty$ and $r_2 = +\infty$ are again natural boundaries. Note that we now have:

$$[\lambda - L_x^-]v = \lambda v - (\mu - \delta x) \frac{dv}{dx} - \frac{\sigma^2}{2} \frac{d^2v}{dx^2} = 0. \qquad (8.28)$$

Set $x' = x - (\mu/\delta)$; then (8.28) is reduced to

$$\frac{\sigma^2}{2} \frac{\partial^2 v(x')}{\partial x'^2} - \sigma x' \frac{\partial v(x')}{\partial x'} - \lambda v(x') = 0.$$

In other words, an Ornstein–Uhlenbeck process with $a(x) = \sigma^2/2$ and $b(x) = \mu - \delta x$ is reduced to the one with $a(x) = \sigma^2/2$ and $b(x) = -\delta x$ by shifting the space variable by μ/δ. Hence, we set $\mu \equiv 0$ in (8.28) without loss of generality, and we consider the Ornstein–Uhlenbeck process with

$$[\lambda - L_x^-]v = \lambda v + \delta x \frac{dv}{dx} - \frac{\sigma^2}{2} \frac{d^2v}{dx^2} = 0. \qquad (8.29)$$

In order to solve equation (8.29), we perform the change of variable $z = (\sqrt{2\delta}/\sigma)x$. Then (8.29) is transformed into

$$\frac{d^2v}{dz^2} - z\frac{dv}{dz} - \frac{\lambda}{\delta}v = 0. \qquad (8.30)$$

Let us set further

$$v(z) = \exp(z^2/4)\, W(z).$$

From (8.29) we then obtain

$$\frac{d^2 W(z)}{dz^2} + \left(\frac{1}{2} - \frac{\lambda}{\delta} - \frac{z^2}{4}\right) W = 0. \tag{8.31}$$

The solutions of (8.31) are already known; they are the so-called parabolic cylinder functions or Weber functions. These are denoted by
$D_{-\lambda/\delta}(z)$ and $D_{-\lambda/\delta}(-z)$ (Erdelyi, 1953, vol. II, p. 116).

Taking account of the boundary conditions and restoring the original
variable x, we obtain

$$v_1(\lambda,x) = \exp\left[\frac{\delta x^2}{2\sigma^2}\right] D_{-\lambda/\delta}\left(-\frac{\sqrt{2\delta}}{\sigma}x\right),$$

$$v_2(\lambda,x) = \exp\left[\frac{\delta x^2}{2\sigma^2}\right] D_{-\lambda/\delta}\left(\frac{\sqrt{2\delta}}{\sigma}x\right). \tag{8.32}$$

The Wronskian Δ_x is

$$\Delta_x = v_1 v_2' - v_1' v_2 = -\frac{2\sqrt{\pi\delta}}{\sigma\Gamma(\lambda/\delta)} \exp\left[\frac{\delta x^2}{\sigma^2}\right]. \tag{8.33}$$

Using (8.21), we have

$$u_1(\lambda,x) = \frac{\Gamma(\lambda/\delta)}{\sigma\sqrt{\pi\delta}} \exp\left[\frac{\delta x^2}{2\sigma^2}\right] D_{-\lambda/\delta}\left(-\frac{\sqrt{2\delta}}{\sigma}x\right),$$

$$u_2(\lambda,x) = \frac{\Gamma(\lambda/\delta)}{\sigma\sqrt{\pi\delta}} \exp\left[-\frac{\delta x^2}{2\sigma^2}\right] D_{-\lambda/\delta}\left(\frac{\sqrt{2\delta}}{\sigma}x\right). \tag{8.34}$$

From (8.22) there follows

$$f_\lambda(x\,|\,y) = \begin{cases} \dfrac{\Gamma(\lambda/\delta)}{\sigma\sqrt{\pi\delta}} \exp\left[-\dfrac{\delta(x^2 - y^2)}{2\sigma^2}\right] D_{-\lambda/\delta}\left(-\dfrac{\sqrt{2\delta}}{\sigma}x\right) D_{-\lambda/\delta}\left(\dfrac{\sqrt{2\delta}}{\sigma}y\right), \\[4pt] \quad x < y, \\[8pt] \dfrac{\Gamma(\lambda/\delta)}{\sigma\sqrt{\pi\delta}} \exp\left[-\dfrac{\delta(x^2 - y^2)}{2\sigma^2}\right] D_{-\lambda/\delta}\left(\dfrac{\sqrt{2\delta}}{\sigma}x\right) D_{-\lambda/\delta}\left(-\dfrac{\sqrt{2\delta}}{\sigma}y\right), \\[4pt] \quad x > y, \end{cases} \tag{8.35}$$

and

$$g_\lambda(S\,|\,x_0) = \begin{cases} \exp\left[-\dfrac{\delta(S^2 - x_0^2)}{2\sigma^2}\right] \dfrac{D_{-\lambda/\delta}\left(-\dfrac{\sqrt{2\delta}}{\sigma}x_0\right)}{D_{-\lambda/\delta}\left(-\dfrac{\sqrt{2\delta}}{\sigma}S\right)}, & S > x_0, \quad (8.36a) \\[14pt] \exp\left[-\dfrac{\delta(S^2 - x_0^2)}{2\sigma^2}\right] \dfrac{D_{-\lambda/\delta}\left(\dfrac{\sqrt{2\delta}}{\sigma}x_0\right)}{D_{-\lambda/\delta}\left(\dfrac{\sqrt{2\delta}}{\sigma}S\right)}, & S < x_0. \quad (8.36b) \end{cases}$$

8.4 Rayleigh process

Consider the process $x(t)$ defined by

$$a(x) = \frac{\sigma^2}{2},$$

$$b(x) = \frac{K-1}{2}\frac{\sigma^2}{x} - \delta x, \quad \delta > 0,$$

(8.37)

over $I = (0,+\infty)$. The process is referred to as the Rayleigh process. We shall assume that K is an integer not less than 2 ($K \geqslant 2$) and that $x_i(t)$, $i = 1, 2, \ldots, K$ are mutually independent processes generated by the stochastic differential equations

$$dx_i(t) = -\delta x_i(t)dt + \sigma dW_i(t), \quad i = 1, 2, \ldots, K$$

$$(\delta > 0, \sigma > 0)$$

(8.38)

where $W_i(t)$, $i = 1, 2, \ldots, K$ are Wiener processes with independent and identical distribution functions. We shall then show that the process defined by (8.37) is identical to the process defined by

$$x(t) = (x_1(t)^2 + x_2(t)^2 + \ldots + x_K(t)^2)^{1/2}.$$

(8.39)

Indeed, let us calculate the infinitesimal moments for the process $x(t)$ defined by (8.39). The increment $\Delta x(t) \equiv x(t + \Delta t) - x(t)$ conditional upon $x(t) = x$ is given by

$$\Delta x(t) = \sum_{i=1}^{k} \frac{x_i}{x} \Delta x_i + \frac{1}{2x} \sum_{i=1}^{K} \Delta x_i^2 - \frac{1}{2x^3} \sum_{i,j=1}^{K} x_i x_j \Delta x_i \Delta x_j.$$

Taking into account that

$$\Delta x_i(t) = -\delta x_i \Delta t + \sigma \Delta W_i$$

and recalling that

$$\Delta x_i^2 \sim \sigma^2 \Delta t, \quad \Delta x_i \Delta x_j \sim 0, i \neq j,$$

we obtain

$$\Delta x(t) = -\frac{\delta \Delta t}{x} \sum_{i=1}^{K} x_i^2 + \frac{\sigma}{x} \sum_{i=1}^{K} x_i \Delta W_i + \frac{1}{2x} \sum_{i=1}^{K} \sigma^2 \Delta t$$

$$- \frac{1}{2x^3} \sum_{i=1}^{K} x_i^2 \sigma^2 \Delta t$$

$$= \left[\frac{K-1}{2}\frac{\sigma^2}{x} - \delta x\right]\Delta t + \frac{\sigma}{x} \sum_{i=1}^{K} x_i \Delta W_i.$$

This yields us

$$\lim_{\Delta t \downarrow 0} \frac{1}{\Delta t} E[\Delta x(t) \mid x(t) = x] = \frac{K-1}{2}\frac{\sigma^2}{x} - \delta x = b(x),$$

$$\lim_{\Delta t \downarrow 0} \frac{1}{\Delta t} E\{[\Delta x(t)]^2 \mid x(t) = x\} = \sigma^2 = 2a(x).$$

It is finally easy to check that

$$\lim_{\Delta t \downarrow 0} \frac{1}{\Delta t} E\{[\Delta x(t)]^n \mid x(t) = x\} = 0, \quad n = 3, 4, \ldots$$

Thus $x(t)$ defined by (8.39) with (8.38) is a diffusion process whose drift and infinitesimal variance are given by (8.37).

Furthermore, it can be seen that the boundary $r_1 = 0$ is an entrance boundary (see Section 4) where the process can start but never return, while $r_2 = +\infty$ is a natural boundary. In fact, the functions defined in (4.18) are now given by:

$$f(x) = \exp\left[-\int^x \frac{b(z)}{a(z)} \, dz\right] = \exp\left[-\int^x \frac{2}{\sigma^2}\left(\frac{K-1}{2} \frac{\sigma^2}{z} - \delta z\right) dz\right]$$

$$= x^{-(K-1)} \exp\left(\frac{\delta x^2}{\sigma^2}\right),$$

$$g(x) = \frac{2}{\sigma^2} x^{K-1} \exp\left(-\frac{\delta x^2}{\sigma^2}\right), \tag{8.40}$$

$$h(x) = f(x) \int^x g(z) dz,$$

$$k(x) = g(x) \int^x f(z) dz.$$

Let $I_1 \equiv (0, x')$ for any $x' \in I = (0, +\infty)$.

$$\int_{I_1} f(x) dx = \int_0^{x'} x^{-(K-1)} \exp\left(\frac{\delta}{\sigma^2} x^2\right) dx = \infty,$$

$$\int_{I_1} g(x) dx < \infty,$$

$$\int_{I_1} h(x) dx = \infty,$$

$$\int_{I_1} k(x) dx = \frac{2}{\sigma^2} \int_0^{x'} dx \, x^{K-1} \exp\left(-\frac{\delta}{\sigma^2} x^2\right) \int_0^x z^{-(K-1)} \exp\left(\frac{\delta}{\sigma^2} z^2\right) dz.$$

For small x,

$$\int_0^x z^{-(K-1)} \exp\left(\frac{\delta}{\sigma^2} z^2\right) dz \simeq \begin{cases} \dfrac{x^{-(K-2)}}{K-2}, & K \geqslant 3. \\[2mm] \ln x, & K = 2. \end{cases}$$

Hence for any integer $K \geqslant 2$,

$$\int_{I_1} k(x)dx < \infty.$$

Accordingly $r_1 = 0$ is an entrance boundary,[5] since $f(x) \notin L(I_1)$ and $k(x) \in L(I_1)$ (see Section 4). On the other hand, let $I_2 = (x',+\infty)$ for any $x' \in (0,+\infty)$. One may see that

$$f(x), g(x), k(x) \in L(I_2), \quad h(x) \notin L(I_2).$$

Hence $r_2 = +\infty$ is a natural boundary. Accordingly, we may impose the following boundary conditions for the transition p.d.f. $f(x,t\,|\,y)$ of the Rayleigh process:

$$f(0,t\,|\,y) = f(\infty,t\,|\,y) = 0,$$
$$f(x,t\,|\,\infty) = 0. \tag{8.41}$$

Note that $f(x,t\,|\,0)$ does not vanish because the boundary $r_1 = 0$ is entrance. However, the boundary $r_1 = 0$ is not attainable from any internal point of the diffusion interval, so that the transition p.d.f. $f(x,t\,|\,y)$, $y \in I$ is uniquely determined by the initial condition (4.17).

The function $w_0(x)$ is determined as solution of

$$L_x^+ w = \frac{\sigma^2}{2}\frac{d^2 w}{dx^2} - \frac{d}{dx}\left\{\left(\frac{K-1}{2}\frac{\sigma^2}{x} - \delta x\right)w\right\} = 0.$$

Thus

$$w_0(x) = x^{K-1}\exp\left(-\frac{\delta x^2}{\sigma^2}\right). \tag{8.42}$$

Equation (8.13b) is, in this case, given by

$$[\lambda - L_x^-]v = \lambda v - \left(\frac{K-1}{2}\frac{\sigma^2}{x} - \delta x\right)\frac{dv}{dx} - \frac{\sigma^2}{2}\frac{d^2 v}{dx^2}$$

or

$$\frac{d^2 v}{dx^2} + \left(\frac{K-1}{x} - \frac{2\delta}{\sigma^2}x\right)\frac{dv}{dx} - \frac{2\lambda}{\sigma^2}v = 0. \tag{8.43}$$

By the change of variable $z = \delta(x/\sigma)^2$, one can rewrite (8.43) as follows:

$$z\frac{d^2 v}{dz^2} + \left(\frac{K}{2} - z\right)\frac{dv}{dz} - \frac{\lambda}{2\delta}v = 0, \tag{8.44}$$

which is known to be the confluent hypergeometric equation (Erdelyi, 1953, vol. I, p. 252). One of the solutions of (8.44) is then given by

$$v_1(z) = \Phi\left(\frac{\lambda}{2\delta}, \frac{K}{2}; z\right), \tag{8.45}$$

where $\Phi(a,c;\,z)$ is the Kummer function defined as

$$\Phi(a,c; z) = \sum_{n=0}^{\infty} \frac{(a)_n}{(c)_n} \frac{z^n}{n!} \tag{8.46}$$

with

$$(\alpha)_0 = 1,$$
$$(\alpha)_n = \alpha(\alpha + 1) \ldots (\alpha + n - 1), \quad n \geqslant 1. \tag{8.47}$$

The other solution, which is linearly independent of $v_1(z)$, is given by

$$v_2(z) = \Psi\left(\frac{\lambda}{2\delta}, \frac{K}{2}; z\right), \tag{8.48}$$

where for non-integer c

$$\Psi(a,c; z) = \frac{\Gamma(1 - c)}{\Gamma(a - c + 1)} \Phi(a,c; z)$$
$$+ \frac{\Gamma(c - 1)}{\Gamma(a)} z^{1-c} \Phi(a-c+1, 2-c; z). \tag{8.49}$$

If c is an integer, i.e. $c = n + 1$, we have:

$$\Psi(a,n+1; z) = \frac{(-1)^{n-1}}{n!\Gamma(a - n)} \left\{ \Phi(a,n+1; z) \ln z \right.$$

$$+ \sum_{r=0}^{\infty} \frac{(a)_r}{(n + 1)_r} [\psi(a + r) - \psi(1 + r) - \psi(1 + n + r)]\frac{z^r}{r!} \right\}$$

$$+ \frac{(n - 1)!}{\Gamma(a)} \sum_{r=0}^{n-1} \frac{(a - n)_r}{(1 - n)_r} \frac{z^{r-n}}{r!}, \quad n = 0, 1, 2, \ldots \tag{8.50}$$

where $\psi(z) = $ d ln $\Gamma(z)/dz$ and where the last sum is to be omitted if $n = 0$. Note that

$$v_1(0) = \Phi\left(\frac{\lambda}{2\delta}, \frac{K}{2}; 0\right) = 1 > 0,$$

$$v_2(\infty) = \lim_{x \to \infty} \Psi\left(\frac{\lambda}{2\delta}, \frac{K}{2}; \frac{\delta x^2}{\sigma^2}\right) = 0,$$

due to the asymptotic behaviour of $\Phi(a,c; z)$ at $z = 0$ and of $\Psi(a,c; z)$ for large z. The Wronskian Δ_x can be seen to be:

$$\Delta_x = v_1(x)v_2(x)' - v_1(x)'v_2(x)$$

$$= \left[\Phi(a,c; z) \frac{d}{dz} \Psi(a,c; z) - \Psi(a,c; z) \frac{d}{dz} \Phi(a,c; z)\right]\frac{dz}{dx}$$

where we have set: $a = \lambda/(2\delta)$, $c = K/2$ and $z = \delta(x/\sigma)^2$. Now evaluation of the square brackets in the r.h.s. of the above equation yields:

$$\Delta_x = \frac{2\delta x}{\sigma^2}\left[-\frac{\Gamma(c)}{\Gamma(a)}\right]e^z\, z^{-c}$$

$$= 2\left(\frac{\delta}{\sigma^2}\right)^{1-K/2} x^{1-K}\left\{\exp\left[\frac{\delta x^2}{\sigma^2}\right]\right\}\left[-\frac{\Gamma(K/2)}{\Gamma(\lambda/2\delta)}\right] \tag{8.51}$$

where the original variable x appears in the r.h.s. Using (8.21), we obtain $u_i(\lambda,x)$, $i = 1, 2$.

In conclusion, we have

$$f_\lambda(x \mid y) =$$

$$
\begin{cases}
\dfrac{1}{\sqrt{\delta}\,\sigma}\dfrac{\Gamma(\lambda/2\delta)}{\Gamma(K/2)}\left(\dfrac{\delta x^2}{\sigma^2}\right)^{\frac{K-1}{2}}\exp\left[-\dfrac{\delta x^2}{\sigma^2}\right]\Phi\left(\dfrac{\lambda}{2\delta},\dfrac{K}{2};\dfrac{\delta x^2}{\sigma^2}\right)\Psi\left(\dfrac{\lambda}{2\delta},\dfrac{K}{2};\dfrac{\delta y^2}{\sigma^2}\right), & x < y, \\[3ex]
\dfrac{1}{\sqrt{\delta}\,\sigma}\dfrac{\Gamma(\lambda/2\delta)}{\Gamma(K/2)}\left(\dfrac{\delta x^2}{\sigma^2}\right)^{\frac{K-1}{2}}\exp\left[-\dfrac{\delta x^2}{\sigma^2}\right]\Psi\left(\dfrac{\lambda}{2\delta},\dfrac{K}{2};\dfrac{\delta x^2}{\sigma^2}\right)\Phi\left(\dfrac{\lambda}{2\delta},\dfrac{K}{2};\dfrac{\delta y^2}{\sigma^2}\right), & x > y,
\end{cases}
\tag{8.52}
$$

and

$$
g_\lambda(S \mid x_0) =
\begin{cases}
\dfrac{\Phi\left(\dfrac{\lambda}{2\delta},\dfrac{K}{2};\dfrac{\delta x_0^2}{\sigma^2}\right)}{\Phi\left(\dfrac{\lambda}{2\delta},\dfrac{K}{2};\dfrac{\delta S^2}{\sigma^2}\right)}, & S > X_0, \tag{8.53a} \\[4ex]
\dfrac{\Psi\left(\dfrac{\lambda}{2\delta},\dfrac{K}{2};\dfrac{\delta x_0^2}{\sigma^2}\right)}{\Psi\left(\dfrac{\lambda}{2\delta},\dfrac{K}{2};\dfrac{\delta S^2}{\sigma^2}\right)}, & S < X_0, \tag{8.53b}
\end{cases}
$$

9 The moments of the first-passage time

In this section, we shall consider the moments of the first-passage time T with density function $g(S,t \mid x_0)$. The kth moment of a p.d.f. $g(t)$ $(0 \leq t < \infty)$ is in general given by

$$m_k = \int_0^\infty t^k g(t)\mathrm{d}t. \tag{9.1}$$

Hence, $m \equiv m_1$ is the mean. The quantity

$$\mu_k = \int_0^\infty (t - m)^k g(t)\mathrm{d}t \tag{9.2}$$

is sometimes referred to as the kth central moment ($k = 1, 2, \ldots$). Clearly, μ_2 is the variance. The relationship between $\{\mu_k\}$ and $\{m_k\}$ is:

$$\mu_k = \sum_{j=0}^{k}\binom{k}{j}(-1)^j m_{k-j} m^j. \tag{9.3}$$

For a given p.d.f. $g(t)$, if every m_k defined by (9.1) exists, the sequence $\{m_k\}$ is called the moment sequence of $g(t)$. Conversely, for a given sequence $\{m_k\}$, the question arises whether one can determine a probability density function whose moment sequence coincides with $\{m_k\}$. This is known as the (Stieltjes) moment problem. Here we shall state without proof two theorems concerning the moment problem. Readers interested in the moment problem may refer, for instance, to Feller (1966) and Shohat and Tamarkin (1943).

Theorem 9.1 Suppose that the moments m_k ($k = 1, 2, \ldots$) of a random variable T (the first-passage time in our case) exist and that the series

$$\sum_{k=1}^{\infty} \frac{m_k}{k!} a^k$$

is absolutely convergent for some $a > 0$. Then the set of moments $\{m_k\}$ uniquely determines the distribution function of T.

A theorem which is directly connected with the Stieltjes moment problem is the following:

Theorem 9.2 A necessary condition for a given sequence $m_0 \equiv 1, m_1, m_2, \ldots$ to be a moment sequence of a p.d.f. defined on $[0, +\infty)$ is that

$$M_n \equiv |m_{i+j}|_{i,j=0}^{n} \geq 0, \tag{9.4a}$$

$$M_n' \equiv |m_{i+j+1}|_{i,j=0}^{n} \geq 0, \tag{9.4b}$$

Let $G(\lambda)$ be the Laplace transform of the p.d.f. $g(t)$

$$G(\lambda) = \int_0^{\infty} g(t)\, e^{-\lambda t} dt.$$

$G(\lambda)$ is also called the moment generating function. In fact,

$$m_k = (-1)^k \left. \frac{d^k G(\lambda)}{d\lambda} \right|_{\lambda=0}. \tag{9.5}$$

Hence, if $G(\lambda)$ is analytic around $\lambda = 0$, then the moments $\{m_k\}$ exist and are given by (9.5).

For instance, consider the Wiener process ($b(x) = 0$, $a(x) = 1/2$); as we know, the Laplace transform of the first-passage-time p.d.f. $g(S,t \mid x_0)$ of the process starting at x_0 through a constant boundary S is given by

$$g_\lambda(S \mid x_0) = \exp[-\sqrt{2\lambda} \mid S - x_0 \mid].$$

Since g_λ is not analytic around $\lambda = 0$, the moments $(m_k, k = 1, 2, \ldots)$ of $g(S,t \mid x_0)$ do not exist. One may check directly from (8.27bis) the non-existence of the moments.

The following facts are known about the moment generating function $G(\lambda)$:

(1) $G(\lambda)$ is a convex function of the real variable λ;
(2) Let $G_1(\lambda)$ and $G_2(\lambda)$ be the moment generating functions of the p.d.f.'s, $g_1(t)$ and $g_2(t)$ respectively. If for a positive number a,

$$G_1(\lambda) = G_2(\lambda), \quad |\lambda| < a$$

then

$$g_1(t) = g_2(t).$$

Apart from the general moment problem, one may often encounter in practice the requirement of determining the moments of a given random variable. Here let us consider practical methods to obtain the moments of first-passage-time p.d.f.'s.

9.1 Siegert formula

Let $f_{st}(x)$ be the steady state p.d.f. of a time-homogeneous diffusion process $X(t)$, $0 \leqslant t < +\infty$ defined on $I = (r_1,r_2)$ with r_i, $i = 1, 2$ being natural boundaries. The steady state p.d.f. is given by

$$f_{st}(x) = \frac{C}{a(x)} \exp\left[-\int_{r_1}^{x} \frac{b(z)}{a(z)}\, dz \right], \tag{9.6}$$

where C is the normalization constant. One can write the following equation for the transition p.d.f. $f(x,t \mid y)$:

$$f_{st}(y)\, \frac{\partial f(x,t \mid y)}{\partial t} = \frac{\partial}{\partial y}\left[a(y)f_{st}(y)\frac{\partial}{\partial y} f(x,t \mid y) \right]. \tag{9.7}$$

Integrating both sides in y from r_1 to z, one has

$$\frac{\partial f(x,t \mid z)}{\partial z} = \frac{1}{a(z)f_{st}(z)} \int_{r_1}^{z} f_{st}(y)\, \frac{\partial f(x,t \mid y)}{\partial t}\, dy.$$

Integrating now both sides in z from x_0 to S, one obtains:

$$f(x,t \mid S) - f(x,t \mid x_0) = \int_{x_0}^{S} \frac{dz}{a(z)f_{st}(z)} \int_{r_1}^{z} f_{st}(y)\, \frac{\partial f(x,t \mid y)}{\partial t}\, dy.$$

The Laplace transforms of both sides then yield:

$$f_\lambda(x \mid S) - f_\lambda(x \mid x_0) = \int_{x_0}^{S} \frac{dz}{a(z)f_{st}(z)} \int_{r_1}^{z} f_{st}(y)[\lambda f_\lambda(x \mid y) - \delta(x - y)]dy.$$

If $x > S > x_0$, $\delta(x - y) = 0$ for $S \geqslant y \geqslant x_0$. Hence, we obtain:

$$-\frac{1}{\lambda}\left[\frac{f_\lambda(x\mid x_0)}{f_\lambda(x\mid S)}-1\right] = \int_{x_0}^{S}\frac{dz}{a(z)f_{st}(z)}\int_{r_1}^{z}f_{st}(y)\frac{f_\lambda(x\mid y)}{f_\lambda(x\mid S)}\,dy.$$

Recalling (8.6), we have the relation

$$-\frac{1}{\lambda}[g_\lambda(S\mid x_0)-1] = \int_{x_0}^{S}\frac{dz}{a(z)f_{st}(z)}\int_{r_1}^{z}f_{st}(y)g_\lambda(S\mid y)dy. \qquad (9.8)$$

Suppose that $g_\lambda(S\mid x_0)$ is analytic around $\lambda = 0$; it can then be expanded as

$$g_\lambda(S\mid x_0) = \sum_{k=0}^{\infty}\frac{(-\lambda)^k}{k!}t_k(S\mid x_0) \qquad (9.9a)$$

$$= 1 - \lambda\sum_{k=0}^{\infty}\frac{(-\lambda)^k}{(k+1)!}t_{k+1}(S\mid x_0), \qquad (9.9b)$$

where $t_k(S\mid x_0)$ is the kth moment of $g(S,t\mid x_0)(k = 0, 1, \ldots)$ and where one should note that $t_0(S\mid x_0) = 1$. Substituting g_λ's in (9.8) with (9.9a) and (9.9b), one obtains

$$t_k(S\mid x_0) = k\int_{x_0}^{S}\frac{dz}{a(z)f_{st}(z)}\int_{r_1}^{Z}f_{st}(y)t_{k-1}(S\mid y)dy, \quad (k = 1, 2, \ldots)$$

$$t_0(S\mid x_0) = 1. \qquad (9.10)$$

This recursive relation is known as the Siegert formula (Siegert, 1951).

The moments of the first-passage time of the OU process through a constant boundary S can be obtained using this formula. The expression of $t_1(S\mid x_0)$ is given by Capocelli and Ricciardi (1971), while the expressions of $t_1(S\mid x_0)$, $t_2(S\mid x_0)$ and $t_3(S\mid x_0)$ are given by Sato (1978).

By differentiating (9.10) with respect to x_0, one easily obtains the differential equation

$$a(x_0)\frac{\partial^2 t_k(S\mid x_0)}{\partial x_0^2} + b(x_0)\frac{\partial t_k(S\mid x_0)}{\partial x_0} = -k\,t_{k-1}(S\mid x_0),$$

$$(k = 1, 2, \ldots). \qquad (9.11)$$

The kth moment $t_k(S\mid x_0)$ can be obtained recursively under the conditions

$$\lim_{x_0\uparrow S} t_k(S\mid x_0) = 0$$

and $\qquad\qquad\qquad\qquad\qquad\qquad\qquad\qquad\qquad\qquad\qquad (9.12)$

$$t_0(S\mid x_0) = 1.$$

9.2   An alternative formula for $t_k(S \mid x_0)$

We have already seen in Section 8 that the Laplace transform $g_\lambda(S \mid x_0)$ of the first-passage-time p.d.f. $g(S,t \mid x_0)$ is given by

$$g_\lambda(S \mid x_0) = \frac{f_\lambda(x \mid x_0)}{f_\lambda(x \mid S)} \quad \text{for } x > S > x_0 \text{ or } x < S < x_0.$$

In particular, if $x > S > x_0$, then

$$g_\lambda(S \mid x_0) = \frac{v_1(\lambda, x_0)}{v_1(\lambda, s)}, \quad S > x_0, \tag{8.24a-bis}$$

where $v_1(\lambda, x)$ is a solution of

$$[\lambda - L_x^-]v = 0$$

that satisfies the boundary condition

$$v_1(\lambda, r_1) = 0.$$

Note that $v_1(\lambda, x)$ as a function of a complex number λ is not necessarily analytic around $\lambda = 0$. Here we shall assume that $v_1(\lambda, x)$ can be expanded in the form

$$v_1(\lambda, x) = s(\lambda)\phi(\lambda, x), \tag{9.13}$$

where $\phi(\lambda, x)$ is an analytic function of λ around $\lambda = 0$ with $\phi(0, x) = 1$. The function $s(\lambda)$ may or may not be analytic around $\lambda = 0$. Then we have

$$g_\lambda(S \mid x_0) = \frac{\phi(\lambda, x_0)}{\phi(\lambda, S)}, \tag{9.14}$$

which in turn gives us

$$\frac{d^n}{d\lambda^n}[g_\lambda(S \mid x_0)\phi(\lambda, S)] = \frac{d^n}{d\lambda^n}\phi(\lambda, x_0).$$

As λ tends to 0, we have

$$\sum_{k=0}^{n}\binom{n}{k}(-1)^k t_k(S \mid x_0)\phi_{n-k}(S) = \phi_n(x_0), \tag{9.15}$$

where we have set

$$\phi_j(z) = \phi^{(j)}(0, z) \equiv \frac{d^j}{d\lambda^j}\phi(\lambda, z)\bigg|_{\lambda=0}.$$

In view of (9.15), one sees that $t_n(S \mid x_0)$ is expressed in terms of $t_k(S \mid x_0)$, $k = 0, 1, \ldots, n - 1$. Hence (9.15) can be solved directly. In fact, it can be written in the matrix form:

$$
\begin{pmatrix}
\phi_0(S) & 0 & & & & \\
2\phi_1(S) & \phi_0(S) & 0 & & \mathbf{0} & \\
3\phi_2(S) & 3\phi_1(S) & \phi_0(S) & 0 & & \\
\cdot & \cdot & & \cdot & & \\
\cdot & & \cdot & & \cdot & \\
\cdot & & & \cdot & & 0 \\
n\phi_{n-1}(S) & \binom{n}{n-2}\phi_{n-2}(S) & \ldots & \binom{n}{k}\phi_k(S) & \ldots & \phi_0(S)
\end{pmatrix}
\begin{pmatrix}
-t_1(S\,|\,x_0) \\
t_2(S\,|\,x_0) \\
\vdots \\
\vdots \\
\vdots \\
(-1)^n t_n(S\,|\,x_0)
\end{pmatrix}
$$

$$
= \begin{pmatrix}
\phi_1(x_0) - \phi_1(S) \\
\phi_2(x_0) - \phi_2(S) \\
\cdot \\
\cdot \\
\phi_n(x_0) - \phi_n(S)
\end{pmatrix}
$$

which yields

$$
t_n(S\,|\,x_0) = \begin{vmatrix}
\phi_1(S) & \phi_0(S) & 0 & & \mathbf{0} & \\
\phi_2(S) & 2\phi_1(S) & \phi_0(S) & 0 & & \\
\cdot & & \cdot & \cdot & & \\
\cdot & & & \cdot & \cdot & 0 \\
\cdot & & & & \cdot & \phi_0(S) \\
\phi_n(S) & n\phi_{n-1}(S) & \ldots & \binom{n}{k}\phi_k(S) & \ldots & n\phi_1(S)
\end{vmatrix}
$$

$$
- \begin{vmatrix}
\phi_1(x_0) & \phi_0(S) & 0 & & \mathbf{0} & \\
\phi_2(x_0) & 2\phi_1(S) & \phi_0(S) & 0 & & \\
\cdot & & \cdot & \cdot & & \\
\cdot & & & \cdot & \cdot & 0 \\
\cdot & & & & \cdot & \phi_0(S) \\
\phi_n(x_0) & n\phi_{n-1}(S) & \ldots & \binom{n}{k}\phi_k(S) & \ldots & n\phi_1(S)
\end{vmatrix}
$$

$$(n = 1, 2, \ldots) \qquad (9.16)$$

with $\phi_0(S) = 1$. For $n = 1, 2, 3$, we have from (9.16)

$$
\begin{aligned}
t_1(S\,|\,x_0) &= \phi_1(S) - \phi_1(x_0), \\
t_2(S\,|\,x_0) &= 2[\phi_1(S)]^2 - \phi_2(S) - 2\phi_1(S)\phi_1(x_0) + \phi_2(x_0), \\
t_3(S\,|\,x_0) &= 6[\phi_1(S)]^3 - 6\phi_1(S)\phi_2(S) + \phi_3(S) - \{6[\phi_1(S)]^2 \\
&\quad - 3\phi_2(S)\}\phi_1(x_0) + 3\phi_1(S)\phi_2(x_0) - \phi_3(x_0).
\end{aligned} \qquad (9.17)
$$

9.3 Case of OU process $[a(x) = \sigma^2/2, \ b(x) = -\delta x]$

As we have seen in Section 8, for $S > x_0$,

$$g_\lambda(S \mid x_0) = \frac{v_1(\lambda,x_0)}{v_1(\lambda,S)}, \quad S > x_0, \tag{8.24ter}$$

with

$$v_1(\lambda,x) = \exp\left[\frac{\delta x^2}{2\sigma^2}\right] D_{-\lambda/\delta}\left(-\frac{\sqrt{2\delta}}{\sigma}x\right), \tag{9.18}$$

and where $D_\lambda(z)$ is the parabolic cylinder function defined by (Erdelyi, 1953):

$$D_\lambda(z) = 2^{\frac{\lambda}{2}}\sqrt{\pi}\, e^{-\frac{z^2}{4}}$$

$$\times \left\{\frac{1}{\Gamma\left(\frac{1-\lambda}{2}\right)}\Phi\left(-\frac{\lambda}{2},\frac{1}{2};\frac{z^2}{2}\right) - \frac{\sqrt{2}z}{\Gamma\left(-\frac{\lambda}{2}\right)}\Phi\left(\frac{1-\lambda}{2},\frac{3}{2};\frac{z^2}{2}\right)\right\}. \tag{9.19}$$

In (9.19), $\Phi(\alpha,\gamma; z)$ is the Kummer function (see equation (8.46)).

Here let us set for brevity $\delta = 1$ and $\sigma^2 = 2$. The general case can be obtained from the case $\delta = 1$ and $\sigma^2 = 2$.

Thus, the function $v_1(\lambda,x)$ defined by (9.18) can be written as:

$$v_1(\lambda,x) = s(\lambda)\phi(\lambda,x),$$

where

$$s(\lambda) = \frac{\sqrt{\pi}2^{-\frac{\lambda}{2}}}{\Gamma\left(\frac{1+\lambda}{2}\right)}, \tag{9.20}$$

$$\phi(\lambda,x) = \Phi\left(\frac{\lambda}{2},\frac{1}{2};\frac{x^2}{2}\right) + \frac{\Gamma\left(\frac{1+\lambda}{2}\right)}{\Gamma\left(\frac{\lambda}{2}\right)}\sqrt{2}x\,\Phi\left(\frac{1+\lambda}{2},\frac{3}{2};\frac{x^2}{2}\right) \tag{9.21a}$$

$$= \sum_{n=0}^{\infty}\frac{(\sqrt{2}x)^n}{n!}\gamma_n(\lambda) \tag{9.21b}$$

with

$$\gamma_n(\lambda) = \frac{\Gamma\left(\frac{n+\lambda}{2}\right)}{\Gamma\left(\frac{\lambda}{2}\right)}, \quad (n = 0, 1, 2, \ldots). \tag{9.22}$$

Hence:

$$g_\lambda(S\,|\,x_0) = \frac{\phi(\lambda,x_0)}{\phi(\lambda,S)}, \quad S > x_0,$$

with ϕ defined in (9.13).

Note that $\phi(\lambda,z)$ is analytic around $\lambda = 0$ and satisfies the condition $\phi(0,z) = 1$. Therefore by evaluating

$$\phi_k(z) \equiv \frac{d^k}{d\lambda^k}\phi(\lambda,z)\Big|_{\lambda=0} = \sum_{n=0}^{\infty} \frac{(\sqrt{2}z)^n}{n!}\left\{ \frac{d^k}{d\lambda^k}\tau_n(\lambda)\Big|_{\lambda=0} \right\}, \tag{9.23}$$

one obtains $t_n(S\,|\,x_0)$ via (9.16). We note that:

$$\frac{d^k}{d\lambda^k}\tau_n(\lambda)\Big|_{\lambda=0} = \frac{k}{2^k}\Gamma\!\left(\frac{n}{2}\right)\rho_n^{(k)}, \quad (k = 1, 2, \ldots) \tag{9.24}$$

where

$$\rho_n^{(1)} = 1, \tag{9.25a}$$

and

$$\rho_n^{(k+2)} = \begin{vmatrix} \psi_0 & -1 & & 0 \\ \psi_1 & \psi_0 & -1 & \\ \psi_2 & 2\psi_1 & \psi_0 & -1 \\ \cdots & \cdots & & \cdots & \ddots & -1 \\ & & & & \ddots & \\ \psi_k & k\psi_{k-1} & \cdots & \binom{k}{j}\psi_j & \cdots & \psi_0 \end{vmatrix} \quad (k = 0, 1, 2, \ldots). \tag{9.25b}$$

In (9.25b), we have set

$$\psi_k = \psi^{(k)}\!\left(\frac{n}{2}\right) - \psi^{(k)}(1) \tag{9.26}$$

where

$$\psi(z) = \frac{1}{\Gamma(z)}\frac{d}{dz}\Gamma(z)$$

is the Di-gamma function. The first three moments $t_1(S\,|\,x_0)$, $t_2(S\,|\,x_0)$, and $t_3(S\,|\,x_0)$ are obtained from (9.17) by setting therein (Ricciardi and Sato, 1988):

$$\phi_1(z) = \frac{1}{2}\sum_{n=0}^{\infty}\frac{(\sqrt{2}z)^n}{n!}\Gamma\!\left(\frac{n}{2}\right),$$

$$\phi_2(z) = \frac{2}{2^2}\sum_{n=0}^{\infty}\frac{(\sqrt{2}z)^n}{n!}\Gamma\!\left(\frac{n}{2}\right)\left[\psi\!\left(\frac{n}{2}\right) - \psi(1)\right],$$

$$\phi_3(z) = \frac{3}{2^3} \sum_{n=0}^{\infty} \frac{(\sqrt{2}z)^n}{n!} \Gamma\left(\frac{n}{2}\right) \left\{ \left[\psi\left(\frac{n}{2}\right) - \psi(1) \right]^2 + \psi^{(1)}\left(\frac{n}{2}\right) - \psi^{(1)}(1) \right\}.$$

(9.28)

10   Algorithms for evaluation of first-passage-time p.d.f.s

In Section 8, we made use of equation (7.5) to write down the Laplace transform $g_\lambda(S \mid x_0)$ of a time-homogeneous diffusion process originating at x_0 through the constant boundary S. However, apart from some special cases, $g(S,t \mid x_0)$ cannot be obtained because of the difficulty of calculating the inverse Laplace transform of $g_\lambda(S \mid x_0)$. Furthermore, the methods of Section 8 cannot be extended to the cases of time-dependent boundaries. It is therefore desirable to design algorithms leading to a numerical evaluation of the function $g[S(t),t \mid x_0,t_0]$. The purpose of this section is to describe an algorithm that has proved to be particularly efficient and simple to use.

It should be explicitly pointed out that equation (7.5) is a first-kind Volterra integral equation in the unknown function $g[S(t),t \mid x_0,t_0]$ whose kernel exhibits a weak singularity at $\tau = t$. More specifically, let us rewrite (7.5) taking the limit $x \downarrow S(t)$. As proved by Fortet (1943), we then have:

$$f[S(t),t \mid x_0,t_0] = \int_{t_0}^{t} d\tau g[S(\tau),\tau \mid x_0,t_0] f[S(t),t \mid S(\tau),\tau]. \tag{10.1}$$

Since as τ approaches t the kernel $f[S(t),t \mid S(\tau),\tau]$ approaches a delta function, the singularity of such kernel at $\tau = t$ is evident. Moreover, one can prove that such a singularity is of the type $(t - \tau)^{-1/2}$, reflecting the property that the transition p.d.f. approaches that of Wiener process for small $t - \tau$ (see Fortet, 1943). The presence of this singularity makes the search for the solution algorithms of (10.1) not straightforward. An algorithm to evaluate the first-passage-time p.d.f. for the Wiener process and smooth varying boundaries is due to Durbin (1971). Other authors have successively proposed alternative numerical procedures (see, for instance, references in Buonocore *et al.*, 1987) with specific reference to the Wiener process. However, these methods can also be used for other types of diffusion processes whenever the latter can be transformed into the former by a suitable transformation (Ricciardi *et al.*, 1983).

In the sequel, for brevity we shall limit ourselves to describing an algorithm for the cases of Wiener and OU processes. However, the method we are going to describe can be extended to any diffusion process whose transition p.d.f. is known (Giorno *et al.*, 1989).

The idea on which the algorithm rests is to change (10.1) into an equation with a continuous kernel, so that it can be solved by the existing standard numerical methods. For brevity, we shall assume throughout $x_0 \equiv X(t_0) < S(t_0)$. We then have the following.

Lemma 10.1 Let $S(t)$ denote a function of class $C[t_0, +\infty)$ and let

$$\phi(x,t \mid y,\tau) \equiv \frac{d}{dt} F(x,t \mid y,\tau) \tag{10.2}$$

for all $y \in I$ and $\tau < t$. One then has:

$$g[S(t),t \mid x_0,t_0] = -2\phi[S(t),t \mid x_0,t_0]$$
$$+ 2 \int_{t_0}^{t} d\tau \, g[S(\tau),\tau \mid x_0,t_0]\phi[S(t),t \mid S(\tau),\tau]. \tag{10.3}$$

Proof Since by assumption $x_0 < S(t_0)$, by integration of both sides of (7.5) with respect to x between $S(t)$ and r_2 and by use of Fubini's theorem one obtains:

$$1 - F[S(t),t \mid x_0,t_0] = \int_{t_0}^{t} d\tau \, g[S(\tau),\tau \mid x_0,t_0]\{1 - F[S(t),t \mid S(\tau),\tau]\},$$
$$x_0 < S(t_0). \tag{10.4}$$

Taking the derivative of (10.4) with respect to t and making use of the relation (Fortet, 1943):

$$\lim_{\tau \uparrow t} F[S(t),t \mid S(\tau),\tau] = 1/2 \tag{10.5}$$

equations (10.3) follows.
We can now prove the following.

Theorem 10.1 Let $S(t)$, $k(t)$ and $r(t)$ be continuous functions in $[t_0,+\infty)$. Setting for all $y \in I$ and $\tau < t$

$$\psi[S(t),t \mid y,\tau]$$
$$= \phi[S(t),t \mid y,\tau] + k(t)f[S(t),t \mid y,\tau] + r(t)\{1 - F[S(t),t \mid y,\tau]\} \tag{10.6}$$

where ϕ is defined by (10.2), one has:

$$g[S(t),t \mid x_0,t_0] = -2\psi[S(t),t \mid x_0,t_0]$$
$$+ 2 \int_{t_0}^{t} d\tau \, g[S(\tau),\tau \mid x_0,t_0] \, \psi[S(t),t \mid S(\tau),\tau]. \tag{10.7}$$

Proof Substituting the function ϕ on the right-hand side of (10.3) with the function ψ defined by (10.6) we obtain:

$$-2\psi[S(t),t \mid x_0,t_0] + 2 \int_{t_0}^{t} d\tau\, g[S(\tau),\tau \mid x_0,t_0]\psi[S(t),t \mid S(\tau),\tau]$$

$$= -2\phi[S(t),t \mid x_0,t_0] + 2 \int_{t_0}^{t} d\tau\, g[S(\tau),\tau \mid x_0,t_0]\phi[S(t),t \mid S(\tau),\tau]$$

$$- 2k(t)\left\{ f[S(t),t \mid x_0,t_0] - \int_{t_0}^{t} d\tau\, g[S(\tau),\tau \mid x_0,t_0]f[S(t),t \mid S(\tau),\tau] \right\}$$

$$- 2r(t)\left\{ 1 - F[S(t),t \mid x_0,t_0] - \int_{t_0}^{t} d\tau\, g[S(\tau),\tau \mid x_0,t_0] \right.$$

$$\times \left. (1 - F[S(t),t \mid S(\tau),\tau]) \right\}.$$

Since the expressions in braces vanish due to (7.5) written for $x \equiv S(t)$ and to (10.4), recalling Lemma 10.1 the right-hand side reduces to $g[S(t),t \mid x_0,t_0]$.

Note that from Theorem 10.1 the integral equation discussed in Ricciardi *et al.* (1984) immediately follows by a special choice of the functions $k(t)$ and $r(t)$. Indeed, we have the following.

Corollary 10.1 If $S(t)$ is differentiable in $[t_0,+\infty)$, one has:

$$g[S(t),t \mid x_0,t_0] = 2j[S(t),t \mid x_0,t_0]$$

$$- 2 \int_{t_0}^{t} d\tau\, g[S(\tau),\tau \mid x_0,t_0]j[S(t),t \mid S(\tau),\tau] \qquad (10.8)$$

where the probability current $j(x,t \mid y,\tau)$ is defined as (Stratonovich, 1963):

$$j(x,t \mid y,\tau) = A_1(x)f(x,t \mid y,\tau) - \frac{1}{2}\frac{\partial}{\partial x}[A_2(x)\, f(x,t \mid y,\tau)]. \qquad (10.9)$$

Proof We write (10.6) with $r(t) \equiv 0$ and $k(t) \equiv -S'(t)$, with $S'(t) \equiv dS(t)/dt$. Recalling (10.2) one then has for all $u, v \in \mathbb{R}$:

$$\psi[S(t),t \mid u,v]$$

$$= \frac{\partial}{\partial t} \int_{r_1}^{S(t)} dx\, f(x,t \mid u,v) - S'(t)f[S(t),t \mid u,v]$$

$$= \int_{r_1}^{S(t)} dx\, \frac{\partial}{\partial t} f(x,t \mid u,v)$$

$$= \lim_{x \downarrow r_1} j(x,t \mid u,v) - j[S(t),t \mid u,v] = -j[S(t),t \mid u,v]$$

where use has been made of the continuity equation:

$$\frac{\partial f(x,t \mid y,\tau)}{\partial t} + \frac{\partial j(x,t \mid y,\tau)}{\partial x} = 0 \qquad (10.10)$$

(an alternative way of writing the Fokker–Planck equation due to definition (10.9)), and of the vanishing of the probability current at r_1. We now
set $-j[S(t),t \mid x_0,t_0]$ in place of $\psi[S(t),t \mid x_0,t_0]$ and $-j[S(t),t \mid S(\tau),\tau]$ in
place of $\psi[S(t),t \mid S(\tau),\tau]$ in equation (10.7). Hence, we finally obtain
equations (10.8).

We shall now separately consider the cases of Wiener and OU processes
to obtain some useful results.

10.1 The Wiener process

Let $\{W(t);\ t \geqslant t_0,\ t_0 \in \mathbb{R}\}$ be a Wiener process with drift, such that
$P\{W(t_0) = x_0\} = 1$, $E[W(t)] = x_0 + \mu(t - t_0)$ and $\mathrm{Cov}\{W(t), W(s)\} =$
$\sigma^2 \min(t,s)$ with $x_0 < S(t_0)$, $\mu,\ \sigma \in \mathbb{R}$. Then, for all $y \in \mathbb{R}$ and $\tau < t$ one
has (cf. (5.9)):

$$f(x,t \mid y,\tau) = [2\pi\sigma^2(t - \tau)]^{-1/2} \exp\left\{-\frac{[x - y - \mu(t - \tau)]^2}{2\sigma^2(t - \tau)}\right\} \quad (10.11)$$

so that:

$$F(x,t \mid y,\tau) = \frac{1}{2}\left\{1 + \mathrm{Erf}\left(\frac{[x - y - \mu(t - \tau)]}{[2\sigma^2(t - \tau)]^{1/2}}\right)\right\} \quad (10.12)$$

where $\mathrm{Erf}(z)$ denotes the error function:

$$\mathrm{Erf}(z) = \frac{2}{\sqrt{\pi}} \int_0^z dy\,\exp(-y^2). \quad (10.13)$$

Lemma 10.2 Let $S(t)$ be differentiable in $[t_0,+\infty)$. Then for the Wiener
process $W(t)$ and for all $y \in \mathbb{R}$ and $\tau < t$ one has:

$$\psi[S(t),t \mid y,\tau]$$

$$= f[S(t),t \mid y,\tau]\, h(t,\tau,y) + \frac{r(t)}{2}\left\{1 - \mathrm{Erf}\left(\frac{[S(t) - y - \mu(t - \tau)]}{[2\sigma^2(t - \tau)]^{1/2}}\right)\right\},$$

$$\quad (10.14)$$

where the function $h(t,\tau,y)$ is defined as follows:

$$h(t,\tau,y) = S'(t) - \frac{\mu}{2} - \frac{S(t) - y}{2(t - \tau)} + k(t). \quad (10.15)$$

Proof We first calculate the function ϕ given by (10.2). To this end we
set $x = S(t)$ in (10.12) and then differentiate both sides with respect to t to
obtain:

$$\phi[S(t),t \mid y,\tau] = \left(S'(t) - \frac{\mu}{2} - \frac{S(t) - y}{2(t - \tau)}\right)f[S(t),t \mid y,\tau]. \quad (10.16)$$

Equation (10.14) then follows from (10.6) and from (10.16).

Theorem 10.2 Let $S(t)$ be a $C^2[t_0,+\infty)$-class function and let $W(t)$ be the Wiener process. Then,

(i) $\lim\limits_{\tau\uparrow t} \psi[S(t),t \mid S(\tau),\tau] = 0$ iff $k(t) = \frac{1}{2} [\mu - S'(t)]$ and $r(t) \equiv 0$;

(ii) $\psi[S(t),t \mid S(\tau),\tau] = 0 \quad \forall t, \tau{:}t_0 \leqslant \tau < t$
   and $\lim\limits_{\tau\uparrow t} \psi[S(t),t \mid S(\tau),\tau] = 0$
   iff $S(t) = at + b$, $k(t) = \dfrac{\mu - a}{2}$ and $r(t) \equiv 0$, $a,b \in \mathbb{R}$.

Proof Assume first that the limit in (i) is zero. Since we have assumed that $S'(t)$ exists and is continuous for $t > t_0$, from (10.12) there follows:

$$\lim_{\tau\uparrow t} \frac{r(t)}{2} \left\{1 \pm \mathrm{Erf}\left(\frac{[S(t) - S(\tau) - \mu(t - \tau)]}{[2\sigma^2(t - \tau)]^{1/2}}\right)\right\} = \frac{r(t)}{2}. \qquad (10.17)$$

In order for $\lim\limits_{\tau\uparrow t} h[t,\tau,S(\tau)]f[S(t),t \mid S(\tau),\tau]$ to exist, one easily sees that, due to the divergence of $f[S(t),t \mid S(\tau),\tau]$ as τ approaches t, it must be:

$$\lim_{\tau\uparrow t} h[t,\tau,S(\tau)] = \lim_{\tau\uparrow t} \left[S'(t) - \frac{\mu}{2} - \frac{S(t) - S(\tau)}{2(t - \tau)} + k(t)\right] = 0,$$

which implies:

$$k(t) \equiv \frac{\mu - S'(t)}{2}. \qquad (10.18)$$

Using (10.18) and the assumption that $S(t)$ is a $C^2[t_0,+\infty)$-class function, by use of l'Hospital's rule one can then prove that

$$\lim_{\tau\uparrow t} h[t,\tau,S(\tau)]f[S(t),t \mid S(\tau),\tau] = 0. \qquad (10.19)$$

Hence, from (10.17) we see that it must also be $r(t) \equiv 0$, which concludes the proof of the necessity of (i). Vice versa, if (10.18) holds and if $r(t) \equiv 0$ it is immediately seen that the limit in (i) is zero, which proves the sufficiency of the condition. To prove (ii) we note that by assumption we have

$$\lim_{\tau\uparrow t} \psi [S(t),t \mid S(\tau),\tau] = 0. \qquad (10.20)$$

From (10.20) and from (10.14) and (10.15) it then follows that $r(t) \equiv 0$ and $k(t) = [\mu - S'(t)]/2$ so that one has:

$$\psi[S(t),t \mid S(\tau),\tau] = \frac{1}{2}\left[S'(t) - \frac{S(t) - S(\tau)}{(t - \tau)}\right]f[S(t),t \mid S(\tau),\tau]. \qquad (10.21)$$

However, the left-hand side of (10.21) vanishes by assumption for all $t_0 \leq \tau < t$ and for $\tau \uparrow t$. Hence, it must be that $S'(t) = [S(t) - S(\tau)]/(t - \tau)$, which implies that $S(t)$ is a linear function of t, i.e. $S(t) = at + b$. In turn, this implies $k(t) = (\mu - a)/2$, which proves the necessity of (ii). The sufficiency is immediately proved since from (10.14) and (10.15) it follows that $\psi[S(t),t \mid S(\tau),\tau] = 0$ for all $t_0 \leq \tau < t$ and for $\tau \uparrow t$ if one takes $S(t) = at + b$, $k(t) = (\mu - a)/2$ and $r(t) \equiv 0$.

Corollary 10.2 For the Wiener process $W(t)$ the first-passage-time p.d.f. through the linear boundary $S(t) = at + b$ is given by

$$g(at+b,t \mid x_0,t_0) = \frac{|at_0 + b - x_0|}{t - t_0} f(at+b,t \mid x_0,t_0),$$

$$(x_0 < at_0 + b). \tag{10.22}$$

Proof The proof follows from (10.7) and from (ii) of Theorem 10.2.

Corollary 10.3 Let $S(t)$ be a $C^2[t_0,+\infty)$-class function and let $W(t)$ be the Wiener process. If $k(t) = [\mu - S'(t)]/2$ and $r(t) \equiv 0$ then equation (10.7) possesses a unique continuous solution.

Proof Proof follows from the theory of integral equations (cf., for instance, Smithies, 1958) and from the remark that with such choice of $k(t)$ and $r(t)$ both functions $\psi[S(t),t \mid S(\tau),\tau]$ and $\psi[S(t),t \mid x_0,t_0]$ are continuous.

10.2 The OU process

Let $\{X(t); t \geq t_0, t_0 \in \mathbb{R}\}$ be the OU process characterized by the drift and infinitesimal variance $A_1(x) = \alpha x + \beta$ and $A_2(x) = \sigma^2$, α, β and $\sigma \neq 0$ being arbitrary real constants, and let $P\{X(t_0) = x_0\} = 1$. Then, for all $y \in \mathbb{R}$ and $\tau < t$ one has:

$$f(x,t \mid y,\tau) = \left\{ \frac{\exp[-2\alpha(t - \tau)]\alpha}{\pi\sigma^2[1 - e^{-2\alpha(t-\tau)}]} \right\}^{1/2}$$

$$\times \exp\left\{ -\frac{\alpha[(x + \beta/\alpha)\exp[-\alpha(t - \tau)] - (y + \beta/\alpha)]^2}{\sigma^2[1 - e^{-2\alpha(t-\tau)}]} \right\} \tag{10.23}$$

and

$$F(x,t \mid y,\tau) = \tfrac{1}{2}\{1 + \mathrm{Erf}[M(x,t,y,\tau)]\} \tag{10.24a}$$

with

$$M(x,t,y,\tau) = \left\{ \frac{\alpha}{\sigma^2[1 - e^{-2\alpha(t-\tau)}]} \right\}^{1/2} \{(x + \beta/\alpha)\exp[-\alpha(t - \tau)] - (y + \beta/\alpha)\}. \tag{10.24b}$$

Lemma 10.3   Let $S(t)$ be differentiable in $[t_0,+\infty)$. Then for the OU process $X(t)$ and for all $y \in \mathbb{R}$ and $\tau < t$ one has:

$$\psi[S(t),t \mid y,\tau] = f[S(t),t \mid y,\tau]H(t,\tau,y)$$
$$+ \frac{r(t)}{2}\{1 - \mathrm{Erf}[M(S(t),t,y,\tau)]\} \tag{10.25}$$

where the function $H(t,\tau,y)$ is defined as follows:

$$H(t,\tau,y) = S'(t) - \alpha[S(t) + \beta/\alpha] - \frac{\alpha\exp[-\alpha(t - \tau)]}{1 - \exp[-2\alpha(t - \tau)]}$$
$$\times \left\{[S(t) + \beta/\alpha]\exp[-\alpha(t - \tau)] - (y + \beta/\alpha)\right\} + k(t). \tag{10.26}$$

Proof   We calculate the function ϕ given by (10.2) by setting $x = S(t)$ in (10.24) and then take the derivative with respect to t:

$$\psi[S(t),t \mid y,\tau] = \left\{S'(t) - \alpha[S(t) + \beta/\alpha] - \frac{\alpha \exp[-\alpha(t - \tau)]}{1 - \exp[-2\alpha(t - \tau)]}\right.$$
$$\times \left.\{[S(t) + \beta/\alpha]\exp[-\alpha(t - \tau)] - (y + \beta/\alpha)\}\right\}f[S(t),t \mid y,\tau]. \tag{10.27}$$

Equation (10.25) then follows from (10.6) and from (10.27).

Theorem 10.3   Let $S(t)$ be a $C^2[t_0,+\infty)$-class function and let $X(t)$ be the OU process. Then,

(i) $\lim_{\tau \uparrow t} \psi[S(t),t \mid S(\tau),\tau] = 0$

 iff $k(t) = \frac{1}{2}[\alpha S(t) + \beta - S'(t)]$ and $r(t) \equiv 0$;

(ii) $\psi[S(t),t \mid S(\tau),\tau] = 0 \ \forall t, \tau: t_0 \leqslant \tau < t$
  and $\lim_{\tau \uparrow t} \psi[S(t),t \mid S(\tau),\tau] = 0$

 iff $S(t) = -\frac{\beta}{\alpha} + Ae^{\alpha t} + Be^{-\alpha t}$, $k(t) = B\alpha e^{-\alpha t}$,
  $A, B \in \mathbb{R}$ and $r(t) \equiv 0$.

Proof   Let us assume that the limit in (i) is zero. Then, due to the assumed continuity of $S'(t)$ for $t > t_0$, from (10.24) there follows:

$$\lim_{\tau \uparrow t}\frac{r(t)}{2}\{1 \pm \mathrm{Erf}[M(S(t),t,y,\tau)]\} = \frac{r(t)}{2}. \tag{10.28}$$

In order for $\lim_{\tau \uparrow t} H[t,\tau,S(t)]f[S(t),t \mid S(\tau),\tau]$ to exist, one then easily sees that, due to the divergence of $f[S(t),t \mid S(\tau),\tau]$ as τ approaches t, it must be:

$$\lim_{\tau \uparrow t} H[t,\tau,S(\tau)] = 0$$

which implies:

$$k(t) \equiv \frac{\beta + \alpha S(t) - S'(t)}{2}. \tag{10.29}$$

Using (10.29) and the assumption that $S(t)$ is a $C^2[t_0,+\infty)$-class function, by use of l'Hospital's rule one can then prove that:

$$\lim_{\tau \uparrow t} H[t,\tau,S(\tau)]f[S(t),t \mid S(\tau),\tau] = 0. \tag{10.30}$$

Hence, from (10.28) we conclude that also $r(t) \equiv 0$. The necessity of (i) is thus proved. Vice versa, if (10.29) holds and if $r(t) \equiv 0$ it is immediately seen that the limit in (i) is zero, the sufficiency of the condition being thus proved. To prove statement (ii) we make use of the assumption stating the vanishing of ψ as $\tau \uparrow t$. Recalling (10.25) and (10.26) it then follows that $r(t) \equiv 0$ and $k(t) = [\beta + \alpha S(t) - S'(t)]/2$ so that:

$$
\begin{aligned}
&\psi[S(t),t \mid S(\tau),\tau] \\
&= \left\{ \frac{S'(t) - \alpha S(t) - \beta}{2} - \frac{\alpha \exp[-\alpha(t - \tau)]}{1 - \exp[-2\alpha(t - \tau)]} [(S(t) + \beta/\alpha) \right. \\
&\quad \left. \times \exp[-\alpha(t - \tau)] - S(\tau) - \beta/\alpha] \right\} f[S(t),t \mid S(\tau),\tau].
\end{aligned} \tag{10.31}
$$

The assumed vanishing of the left-hand side of (10.31) for all $t_0 \leqslant \tau < t$ and for $\tau \uparrow t$ implies the vanishing of the expression in braces on the right-hand side, i.e.

$$S(t) = -\frac{\beta}{\alpha} + Ae^{\alpha t} + Be^{-\alpha t} \tag{10.32}$$

which, in turn, implies

$$k(t) = B\alpha e^{-\alpha t}. \tag{10.33}$$

The necessary part of (ii) is thus proved. The sufficiency is easily proved. Indeed, taking $S(t)$ and $k(t)$ as given by (10.32) and (10.33) and recalling (10.25) and (10.26) the stated vanishing of ψ follows.

Corollary 10.4 For the OU process $X(t)$ the first-passage-time p.d.f. through the hyperbolic boundary $S(t) = -\beta/\alpha + Ae^{\alpha t} + Be^{-\alpha t}$ is given by

$$
\begin{aligned}
&g(-\beta/\alpha + Ae^{\alpha t} + Be^{-\alpha t}, t \mid x_0, t_0) \\
&= 2\alpha \frac{|A \exp(\alpha t_0) + B \exp(-\alpha t_0) - x_0 - \beta/\alpha|}{\exp[\alpha(t - t_0)] - \exp[-\alpha(t - t_0)]} f[S(t),t \mid x_0,t_0] \quad (10.34)
\end{aligned}
$$

where f is given by (10.23) and $x_0 < -\beta/\alpha + Ae^{\alpha t_0} + Be^{-\alpha t_0}$.

Proof Proof follows from (10.7) and from (ii) of Theorem 10.3.

Corollary 10.5 Let $S(t)$ be a $C^2[t_0,+\infty)$-class function and let $X(t)$ be the OU process. If $k(t) = [\beta + \alpha S(t) - S'(t)]/2$ and $r(t) \equiv 0$ then equation (10.7) possesses a unique continuous solution.

Proof As in Corollary 10.3.

10.3 Daniels's boundary

As shown by Corollaries 10.2 and 10.4, suitable choices of $k(t)$ and $r(t)$ imply the vanishing of the kernel of equation (10.7), thus leading us to closed forms for $g[S(t),t \mid x_0,t_0]$. However, other closed-form expressions can be obtained by different choices of $k(t)$. An example is the following. Let $W(t)$ be the Wiener process with drift μ such that $P\{W(0) = 0\} = 1$ and let

$$S(t) = \frac{H}{2} + \mu t - \frac{\sigma^2 t}{H} \ln \frac{[c_1 + \sqrt{\Delta(t)}]}{2}, \tag{10.35}$$

with $\Delta(t) = c_1^2 + 4c_2 \exp(-H^2/\sigma^2 t)$, $H \neq 0$, $c_1 > 0$ and c_2 real numbers such that $c_1^2 + 4c_2 > 0$. Note that for $\mu = 0$ the function (10.35) is Daniels's boundary (Daniels, 1969).

By a procedure similar to that of Daniels, the transition p.d.f. with an absorbing boundary at $S(t)$ is found to be:

$$\begin{aligned} a^{[S(t)]}(x,t \mid 0,0) = (2\pi\sigma^2 t)^{-1/2} &\left\{ \exp\left[-\frac{(x - \mu t)^2}{2\sigma^2 t} \right] \right. \\ &- c_1 \exp\left[-\frac{(x - H - \mu t)^2}{2\sigma^2 t} \right] \\ &\left. - c_2 \exp\left[-\frac{(x - 2H - \mu t)^2}{2\sigma^2 t} \right] \right\}, \quad H[x - S(t)] \leq 0. \end{aligned} \tag{10.36}$$

From (7.6) we then obtain:

$$\begin{aligned} g[S(t),t \mid 0,0] = |H| [2\pi\sigma^2 t^3]^{-1/2} &\left\{ \exp\left[-\frac{(S(t) - \mu t)^2}{2\sigma^2 t} \right] \right. \\ &\left. - \frac{c_1}{2} \exp\left[-\frac{(S(t) - H - \mu t)^2}{2\sigma^2 t} \right] \right\}. \end{aligned} \tag{10.37}$$

Setting $r(t) = 0$ and $k(t) = \dfrac{\sigma^2}{2H} \ln\left[\dfrac{c_1 + \sqrt{\Delta(t)}}{2}\right] + \dfrac{H}{4t} - \dfrac{Hc_1^2}{2t[c_1 + \sqrt{\Delta(t)}]\sqrt{\Delta(t)}}$

in (10.7), we see that the first term on the right-hand side coincides with the right-hand side of (10.31), i.e.

$$g[S(t),t \mid 0,0] = 2|\psi[S(t),t \mid 0,0]|. \tag{10.38}$$

Hence, the above choice for $k(t)$ and $r(t)$ leads us to the closed-form expression (10.37) even though the kernel of equation (10.7) is non-zero. The fact is that the integral on the right-hand side of (10.7) is actually zero.

Let us now come to the solution of equation (10.7). Let $h > 0$ be the integration step and set $t = t_0 + kh$ ($k = 1, 2, \ldots$). Equation (10.7) then reads:

$$g[S(t_0+kh),t_0+kh \mid x_0,t_0] = -2\psi[S(t_0+kh),t_0+kh \mid x_0,t_0]$$

$$+ 2 \int_{t_0}^{t_0+kh} d\tau g[S(\tau),\tau \mid x_0,t_0]\psi[S(t_0+kh),t_0+kh \mid S(\tau),\tau],$$

$$(k = 1, 2, \ldots). \tag{10.39}$$

Hence, if

$$\lim_{\tau \uparrow t} \psi[S(t),t \mid S(\tau),\tau] = 0 \tag{10.40}$$

and approximating g_1 to g is given by

$$g_1[S(t_0+h),t_0+h \mid x_0,t_0] = -2\psi[S(t_0+h),t_0+h \mid x_0,t_0]$$

$$g_1[S(t_0+kh),t_0+kh \mid x_0,t_0] = -2\psi[S(t_0+kh),t_0+kh \mid x_0,t_0]$$

$$+ 2h \sum_{j=1}^{k-1} g_1[S(t_0+jh),t_0+jh \mid x_0,t_0]$$

$$\times \psi [S(t_0+kh),t_0+kh \mid S(t_0+jh),t_0+jh], \quad (k = 2, 3, \ldots), \tag{10.41}$$

where use of a composite trapezium rule has been made.

Theorem 10.4 Let (10.40) hold and set $T = t_0 + Nh$ with $N \in N_0$ and

$$\Delta_{kh} = g[S(t_0+kh),t_0+kh \mid x_0,t_0] - g_1[S(t_0+kh),t_0+kh \mid x_0,t_0],$$
$$(k = 1, 2, \ldots, N). \tag{10.42}$$

Then:

$$\lim_{h \downarrow 0} |\Delta_{kh}| = 0, \quad (k = 1, 2, \ldots, N; kh \text{ fixed}). \tag{10.43}$$

Proof From (10.39) and (10.41) we have:

$$\Delta_h = 2 \int_{t_0}^{t_0+h} d\tau g[S(\tau),\tau \mid x_0,t_0]\psi[S(t_0+h),t_0+h \mid S(\tau),\tau] \tag{10.44}$$

and:

$$\Delta_{kh} = 2 \int_{t_0}^{t_0+kh} d\tau g[S(\tau),\tau \mid x_0,t_0] \psi[S(t_0+kh),t_0+kh \mid S(\tau),\tau]$$

$$- 2h \sum_{j=1}^{k-1} g_1[S(t_0+jh),t_0+jh \mid x_0,t_0]$$

$$\times \psi[S(t_0+kh),t_0+kh \mid S(t_0+jh),t_0+jh], \quad (k = 2, 3, \ldots, N).$$
(10.45)

It is convenient to rewrite (10.45) as

$$\Delta_{kh} = 2h \sum_{j=1}^{k-1} \Delta_{jh} \psi[S(t_0+kh),t_0+kh \mid S(t_0+jh),t_0+jh] + \delta_{kh},$$
$$(k = 2, 3, \ldots, N),$$
(10.46)

where we have set:

$$\delta_{kh} = 2 \int_{t_0}^{t_0+kh} d\tau g[S(\tau),\tau \mid x_0,t_0] \psi[S(t_0+kh),t_0+kh \mid S(\tau),\tau]$$

$$- 2h \sum_{j=1}^{k-1} g[S(t_0+jh),t_0+jh \mid x_0,t_0]$$

$$\times \psi[S(t_0+kh),t_0+kh \mid S(t_0+jh),t_0+jh], \quad (k = 2, 3, \ldots, N).$$
(10.47)

From equations (10.44) and (10.46) the following inequalities immediately follow:

$$|\Delta_h| \leq \xi_N(h)$$
(10.48)

and:

$$|\Delta_{kh}| \leq hM \sum_{j=1}^{k-1} |\Delta_{jh}| + \xi_N(h), \quad (k = 2, 3, \ldots, N),$$
(10.49)

having set:

$$M = 2 \max_{t_0 \leq \tau \leq t \leq T} |\psi[S(t),t \mid S(\tau),\tau]|,$$

$$\delta_h = \Delta_h$$

and:

$$\xi_N(h) = \max_{1 \leq k \leq N} |\delta_{kh}|.$$
(10.50)

We now make use of some well-known inequalities (cf., for instance, Baker, 1978, pp. 925–6, Lemmas 6.2, 6.3) to write:

$$|\Delta_{kh}| \leq \xi_N(h)(1 + hM)^{k-1} \leq \xi_N(h)e^{khM}, \quad (k = 1, 2, \ldots, N).$$
(10.51)

We shall now prove that $\xi_N(h) \to 0$ as $h \to 0$. To this purpose we note that each δ_{kh} in (10.47) is the difference between the integral in the right-hand side and of an approximating Riemann sum with the partition

$$P = \{\eta_j = t_0 + jh/2, \quad (j = 0, 1, \ldots, 2k)\}, \tag{10.52a}$$

$$Q = \{\theta_0 = t_0; \theta_{2j-1} \equiv \theta_{2j} = t_0 + jh, \quad (j = 1, 2, \ldots, k - 1);$$
$$\theta_{2k-1} = t_0 + kh\}. \tag{10.52b}$$

Hence (cf. Baker, 1978, pp. 124–5) we have:

$$|\delta_{kh}| \leq 2kh\omega[(\psi g)_{kh}, h/2], \quad (k = 1, 2, \ldots, N), \tag{10.53}$$

where we have set:

$$(\psi g)_{kh} = \psi[S(t_0+kh), t_0+kh \mid S(\tau), \tau]g[S(\tau), \tau \mid x_0, t_0]$$

and where $\omega[(\psi g)_{kh}, h/2]$ is the modulus of continuity of $(\psi g)_{kh}$ in $[t_0, t_0+kh]$ for the parameter $\max_r \max\{\eta_{r+1}-\theta_r, \theta_r-\eta_r\} \equiv h/2$. From (10.53) with kh fixed we have:

$$\lim_{h \downarrow 0} |\delta_{kh}| = 0 \quad (k = 1, 2, \ldots, N)$$

showing together with (10.50) that $\lim_{h \downarrow 0} \xi_N(h) = 0$. The proof of the theorem then follows due to (10.51).

We point out that the Wiener and OU process condition (10.40) can be fulfilled as shown by Theorems 10.2 and 10.3. As for the speed of convergence of the present method, we limit ourselves to mentioning that the time $T_N(h)$ required to compute g_1 up to time $t_0 + Nh$ grows quadratically with N:

$$T_N(h) \sim (T_\psi + T_a + T_m)N^2/2,$$

where T_ψ is the time necessary to compute the function ψ and where T_a and T_m denote, respectively, the times required to perform an addition and a multiplication. This computation time is meaningfully shorter than that required to evaluate g by other existing numerical procedures (e.g. Anderssen *et al.*, 1973; Favella *et al.*, 1982; Ricciardi *et al.*, 1983). For instance, the computation time required by using a method such as in Favella *et al.* (1982) reduces by roughly 83% when our algorithm is implemented. However, the major advantage offered by our method rests on its extraordinary simplicity with respect to the other procedures. Indeed, it does not require use of large computing facilities but is suitable for implementation on personal computers. The underlying reason is that the kernel of equation (10.7) is now a continuous function due to assumption (10.40), whereas the kernel appearing in other numerical procedures exhibits a singularity. Some examples of implementation of the algorithm just described may be found in Buonocore *et al.* (1987). Its generalization to a wider class of diffusion processes is discussed elsewhere (Giorno *et al.*, 1989).

11   Asymptotic results

As we have already mentioned, it is difficult to obtain explicitly the first-passage-time p.d.f. $g_X(S,t \mid x_0)$ for a time-homogeneous diffusion process even through a constant boundary S except for a few cases. Various asymptotics may thus be studied to shed some light on the first-passage-time density of the process. The following cases may be of interest: (i) asymptotic moments for large boundary (more precisely, the asymptotic moments when S approaches one end of the diffusion interval); (ii) behaviour of g_X for large values of S; (iii) asymptotic behaviour of g_X for small times t; (iv) asymptotic behaviour of g_X for large times t. Here we confine ourselves to the study of the asymptotics of the first-passage time for the OU process through a constant boundary S. For simplicity we shall assume $S > x_0$, $\delta = 1$ and $\sigma^2 = 2$. For (i) and (ii), Nobile *et al.* (1985) showed that for a class of diffusion processes with steady state distribution the nth moment of the first-passage time approaches $n![t_1(S \mid x_0)]^n$ and that g_X thus tends to an exponential function with exponent given by $-t_1(S \mid x_0)$ as S becomes infinitely large. For the case (iii), one is led to believe that g_X behaves as g_W, where g_W is the first-passage-time density for the Wiener process through the same boundary S. Indeed, the diffusion process $X(t)$ starting at $t_0(=0)$ near the origin acts like the Wiener process. We shall analyse whether this is the case. For (iv), it will be shown that the first-passage-time p.d.f. for the OU process decays exponentially as t tends to infinity and the explicit form of the exponent will be given.

11.1   Asymptotic moments for large boundaries

We shall first provide the asymptotic expressions of the first-passage-time moments when the boundary S becomes very large. To this end, let us cite the following theorem (Nobile *et al.*, 1985):

Theorem 11.1   For a diffusion process with steady state distribution,

$$\lim_{S \to \infty} \frac{t_n(S \mid x_0)}{n![t_1(S \mid x_0)]^n} = 1. \tag{11.1}$$

We point out that this theorem can also be proved by noting that $\phi_k(S)/[\phi_1(S)]^k \to 0$ as $S \to \infty$ for $k = 2, 3, \ldots$ (see equation (9.16)). We also point out that due to the expression (9.17) one has:

$$\lim_{S \to \infty} \frac{t_1(S \mid x_0)}{\phi_1(S)} = 1. \tag{11.2}$$

Hence, (11.1) is equivalent to

$$t_n (S \mid x_0) \sim n![\phi_1(S)]^n \tag{11.3}$$

for large S, where $\phi_1(S)$ is defined by

$$\phi_1(S) = \left. \frac{d}{d\lambda} \phi(\lambda,z) \right|_{\lambda=0}. \tag{11.4}$$

In (11.4), the function $\phi(\lambda,z)$ in the case of the OU process is explicitly given by (9.21) as follows.

Making use of the asymptotic expansion of the Kummer function $\Phi(\alpha,\gamma; z)$ for large z (Erdelyi, 1953, vol. I, p. 278) in expression (9.21) of $\phi(\lambda,z)$ one has:

$$\Phi(\alpha,\gamma; z) = \frac{\Gamma(\gamma)}{\Gamma(\alpha)} e^z z^{\alpha-\gamma} [1 + O(z^{-1})]. \tag{11.5}$$

We then obtain

$$\phi(\lambda,z) = \frac{2e^{\lambda\log(z/\sqrt{2})}}{\Gamma(\lambda/2)} /g(z) [1 + O(z^{-1})], \tag{11.6}$$

where

$$g(z) = \frac{z}{\sqrt{2\pi}} \exp[-z^2/2]. \tag{11.7}$$

Hence,

$$\phi_1(z) = \phi^{(1)}(0,z) = g^{-1}(z)[1 + O(z^{-1})], \tag{11.8}$$

where we have used the relation: $\lim_{\lambda\downarrow 0} (\lambda/2)\psi(\lambda/2) = -1$. From (11.3) and (11.8), we obtain for large S:

$$t_n(S \mid x_0) \sim n!/[g(S)]^n, \quad (n = 1, 2, \ldots), \tag{11.9}$$

with $g(z)$ defined in (11.7). Hence, for a large boundary S, the mean first-passage time M, the variance V and the skewness Σ are given by:

$$\begin{aligned} M &\sim 1/g(S), \\ V &\sim 1/[g(S)]^2, \\ \Sigma &\sim 2, \end{aligned} \tag{11.10}$$

respectively. A table of M, V and Σ for $\theta = 1$ and $\mu = 2$ and for various values of S and x_0 was given in Cerbone *et al.* (1981). One may see that the values for large S given in the table coincide with those calculated via (11.10) with (11.7).

Note that a sequence $\{m_k\} = \{k![t_1(S \mid x_0)]^k\}$ can be a moment sequence and that it uniquely determines the density function (see Section 9 and Nobile *et al.*, 1985):

$$g(S,t \mid x_0) = \frac{1}{t_1(S \mid x_0)} \exp\left[-\frac{t}{t_1(S \mid x_0)}\right]. \tag{11.11}$$

Hence in the case of the OU process, as S tends to infinity the first-passage-time density approaches

$$g(t,S \mid x_0) \sim g(S) \, e^{-g(S)t}, \tag{11.12}$$

where $g(S)$ is defined in (11.7).

Next, let us return to the Laplace transform $g_\lambda(S \mid x_0)$ (see equation (8.36)) of the first-passage-time p.d.f. $g(t,S \mid x_0)$ of the OU process through a constant boundary S. Since we have assumed that $S > x_0$ and that $\delta = 1$ and $\sigma^2 = 2$, equation (8.36) becomes

$$g_\lambda(S \mid x_0) = \exp\left[\frac{S^2 - x_0^2}{4}\right] \cdot \frac{D_{-\lambda}(-x_0)}{D_{-\lambda}(-S)}, \quad S > x_0, \tag{11.13}$$

where $D_\lambda(z)$ is the parabolic cylinder function (cf. Sections 8 and 9).

If $0 = S > x_0$, the inverse Laplace transform of g_λ can exceptionally be calculated to give the well-known closed-form solution (Sato, 1978):

$$g(0,t \mid x_0) = \frac{2|x_0|}{\sqrt{2\pi}} \, (e^{2t} - 1)^{-3/2} e^{2t} \exp\left[-\frac{x_0^2}{2(e^{2t} - 1)}\right]. \tag{11.14}$$

Hence, in the sequel we shall assume $0 \neq S > x_0$ throughout.

Using the expression (9.9) of $D_\lambda(z)$, equation (8.36a) can also be rewritten as (cf. equation (9.14)):

$$g_\lambda(S \mid x_0) = \frac{\Omega(\lambda, x_0)}{\Omega(\lambda, S)}, \tag{11.15}$$

where

$$\Omega(\lambda, z) = \frac{1}{\Gamma\left(\dfrac{1 + \lambda}{2}\right)} \, \Phi\left(\frac{\lambda}{2}, \frac{1}{2}; \frac{z^2}{2}\right) + \frac{\sqrt{2}z}{\Gamma(\lambda/2)} \, \Phi\left(\frac{1 + \lambda}{2}, \frac{3}{2}; \frac{z^2}{2}\right) \tag{11.16a}$$

$$= \sum_{n=0}^{\infty} \frac{(\sqrt{2}z)^n}{n!} \, \frac{\Gamma\left(\dfrac{n + \lambda}{2}\right)}{\Gamma(\lambda/2)\Gamma\left(\dfrac{1 + \lambda}{2}\right)}, \tag{11.16b}$$

$\Phi(\alpha, \gamma; z)$ being the Kummer function (see equation (8.46)). We note that $\Omega(\lambda, z)$ is infinitely differentiable with respect to both variables λ and z.

Let us now suppose that the zeros $\lambda = \lambda_p$, $p = 0, 1, 2, \ldots$ of the function $\Omega(\lambda, z)$ with respect to λ for a given z are known. Then the Laplace transform g_λ can be inverted to give $g(S,t \mid x_0)$. Hence the investigation of the zeros of the function $\Omega(\lambda, z)$ with respect to λ is an essential task.

11.2 Zeros of $\Omega(\lambda,z)$

To begin with, we shall list properties of the function $\Omega(\lambda,z)$:

(1) $\Omega(\lambda,z)$ is positive for $\lambda > 0$. Hence, for a given z, a real positive zero λ_0 of $\Omega(\lambda,z)$ does not exist.

(2) For $p = 0, 1, \ldots$,

$$\Omega(-p,z) = \frac{(-1)^p}{2^{p/2}\sqrt{\pi}} H_p(z), \tag{11.17}$$

where $H_p(z)$ is the Hermite polynomial of order p:

$$H_p(z) = (-1)^p \exp\left(\frac{z^2}{2}\right) \frac{d^p}{dz^p} \exp\left(-\frac{z^2}{2}\right). \tag{11.18}$$

Hence, denoting the zeros of the Hermite polynomial of order p by $z_{p,k}$ ($k = 0, \pm 1, \ldots, \pm\frac{p-1}{2}$ if p is odd and $k = \pm 1, \pm 2, \ldots,$ $\pm\frac{p}{2}$ if p is even), we see that points $(-p,z_{p,k})$ are the zeros of $\Omega(\lambda,z)$.

(3) There exists a curve $\lambda = \lambda(z)$ in the lower half of the (z,λ)-plane such that $\Omega(\lambda,\lambda(z)) = 0$. The curve is open in the sense that both endpoints go to infinity (Ricciardi and Sato, 1988).

Figure 2 illustrates the curves $\lambda = \lambda_p(z)$, ($p = 0, 1, 2, \ldots$), that satisfy $\Phi(\lambda_p(z),z) = 0$. From property (2) and as shown in the figure, the curve $\lambda = \lambda_p(z)$ passes through the points determined from the zeros of the Hermite polynomials (hence, the curve $\lambda = \lambda_p(z)$ crosses the point $(-2p-1,0)$) and it approaches $\lambda = -p$ as z tends to infinity. The following property then emerges:

(4) Approximate solutions of $\Omega(\lambda,z) = 0$ near $z = 0$ are given by

$$\lambda = \lambda_p(z) = -2p - 1 + \frac{(2p+1)!!}{(2p)!!}\sqrt{\frac{2}{\pi}}z, \quad (p = 0, 1, 2, \ldots). \tag{11.19}$$

It can be also shown that

(5) approximate solutions of $\Omega(\lambda,z) = 0$ for large z are given by

$$\lambda = \lambda_p(z) = -p - \frac{z^p H_p(z)}{p!} g(z), \quad (p = 0, 1, 2, \ldots). \tag{11.20}$$

We have also the following

Conjecture For a given $z > 0$,

$$1 < \lambda_0(z) - \lambda_1(z) < \lambda_1(z) - \lambda_2(z) < \ldots$$
$$\ldots < \lambda_p(z) - \lambda_{p+1}(z) < \ldots < 2. \tag{11.21}$$

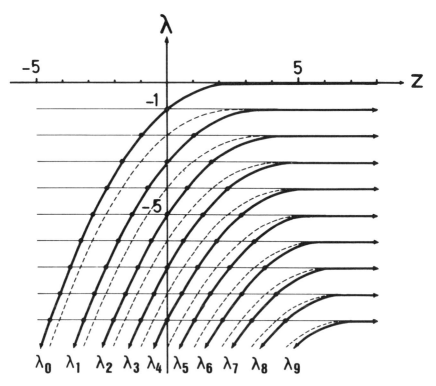

Fig. 5.2   Solution of $\Omega(\lambda,z) = 0$. Solid lines indicate the solutions of $\Omega(\lambda,z) = 0$, whereas dotted lines denote the extrema of $\Omega(\lambda,z)$. Dots show the zeros of Hermite polynomials.

11.3   First-passage-time p.d.f. as a sum of exponential functions

For a given z, let $\lambda = \lambda_p$, $p = 0, 1, 2, \ldots$ be the zeros of $\Phi(\lambda,z)$. Then we may write

$$g_\lambda(S \mid x_0) = \sum_{p=0}^{\infty} \frac{A_p(S \mid x_0)}{\lambda - \lambda_p(S)}, \tag{11.22}$$

where

$$A_p(S \mid x_0) = \frac{\Omega(\lambda_p(S),x_0)}{\Omega^{(1)}(\lambda_p(S),S)} \tag{11.23}$$

with

$$\Omega^{(1)}(\lambda_p(S),S) = \frac{\mathrm{d}}{\mathrm{d}\lambda}\Omega(\lambda,S)\bigg|_{\lambda=\lambda_p(S)} \tag{11.24}$$

In the right-hand side of (11.10), the numerator is calculated by using (11.3), while the denominator is given by

$\Omega^{(1)}(\lambda_p(S),S)$

$$= \frac{1}{2} \sum_{n=0}^{\infty} \frac{(\sqrt{2}S)^n}{n!} \frac{\Gamma\left(\dfrac{n + \lambda_p}{2}\right)}{\Gamma\left(\dfrac{\lambda_p}{2}\right)\Gamma\left(\dfrac{1 + \lambda_p}{2}\right)}$$

$$\times \left[\psi\left(\frac{n + \lambda_p}{2}\right) - \psi\left(\frac{\lambda_p}{2}\right) - \psi\left(\frac{1 + \lambda_p}{2}\right)\right], \tag{11.25}$$

with $\lambda_p = \lambda_p(S)$.

It follows that

$$g(S,t \mid x_0) = \sum_{p=0}^{\infty} A_p(S \mid x_0) \exp[\lambda_p(S)t]. \tag{11.26}$$

Note that

$$\Omega^{(1)}(\lambda_p(S),S) \begin{cases} > 0 & \text{for even } p, \\ < 0 & \text{for odd } p. \end{cases} \tag{11.27}$$

The signs of $\Omega(\lambda_p(S),x_0)$, $p = 0, 1, \ldots$ can be determined, for instance, with the aid of Figure 5.2. One may easily see that for $x_0 < S$, $A_0(S \mid x_0) > 0$. On the other hand, for a given value of S, $A_p(S \mid x_0)$, $p = 1, 2, \ldots$ can be positive or negative according to the value of x_0 ($<S$).

In the particular case $x_0 = 0$,

$$g(t,S \mid 0) = \sum_{p=0}^{\infty} A_p(S) \exp[\lambda_p(S)t], \tag{11.28}$$

where

$$A_p(S) = \left\{\frac{1}{2} \sum_{n=0}^{\infty} \frac{(\sqrt{2}S)^n}{n!} \frac{\Gamma\left(\dfrac{n + \lambda_p}{2}\right)}{\Gamma\left(\dfrac{\lambda_p}{2}\right)}\left[\psi\left(\frac{n + \lambda_p}{2}\right) - \psi\left(\frac{1 + \lambda_p}{2}\right)\right.\right.$$
$$\left.\left. - \psi\left(\frac{\lambda_p}{2}\right)\right]\right\}^{-1}, \tag{11.29}$$

with $\lambda_p = \lambda_p(S)$. The signs of $A_p(S)$ can be determined without difficulty.

11.4 Density for large t

Let us now discuss the asymptotic behaviour of the first-passage-time p.d.f. for large times. In view of (11.26), it is easy to see that for large t the function $g(t,S \mid x_0)$ can be approximated as

$$g(t,S \mid x_0) \sim A_0(S \mid x_0) \exp[\lambda_0(S)t], \tag{11.30}$$

where $\lambda = \lambda_0(S)$ is the curve satisfying $\Omega(\lambda_0(S),S) = 0$ and passing $(-1,0)$ in the (λ,z)-plane. Equation (11.30) shows that the first-passage-time density $g(S,t \mid x_0)$ approaches a single exponential function with negative exponent $\lambda_0(S)$ which is independent of the initial starting point x_0. This fact was also pointed out in Sato (1978).

11.5 Density for small times

For large λ, $g_\lambda(S \mid x_0)$ becomes

$$g_\lambda(S \mid x_0) = \exp[-\sqrt{\lambda}(S - x_0)], \quad S > x_0, \tag{11.31}$$

where we have used the asymptotic expansion of the parabolic cylinder function for large λ (see Erdelyi, 1953, vol. II, p. 123) in (10.36a). If $|z|$ is bounded and $|\arg(-\lambda)| \leq \frac{1}{2}\pi$, then for $|\lambda| \to +\infty$

$$D_\lambda(z) = \frac{1}{\sqrt{2}} \exp\left[\frac{\lambda}{2} \log(-\lambda) - \frac{\lambda}{2} - (\sqrt{-\lambda})z\right][1 + O|\lambda|^{-1/2}]. \tag{11.32}$$

Hence we may conclude that for small time t, $g(t,S \mid x_0)$ is approximated by

$$\frac{\dfrac{S - x_0}{2}}{\sqrt{2\pi}} t^{-3/2} \exp\left[-\frac{(S - x_0)^2}{4t}\right]. \tag{11.33}$$

This result implies, as expected, that the OU process starting at x_0 at $t_0 = 0$ behaves as the Wiener process (with variance $\mu = 2$) near the time origin.

We finally note that the same asymptotic form as (11.33) is obtained from (11.13) for the case $0 = S > x_0$ as far as small times t are concerned.

Notes

1 To simplify the notation, we shall denote by the same symbol the stochastic process and any of its realizations. For instance, $F(t)$ is either the force acting on a specific particle or the stochastic process $F(t,\omega)$ with ω varying over the ensemble. The interpretation will be clear from the context.

2 For a given sequence of random variables $\{x_n\}$, if there exists a random variable x such that

$$\lim_{n \to \infty} E[(x_n - x)^2] = 0 \tag{i}$$

$\{x_n\}$ is said to converge to x in the mean square sense. A necessary and sufficient condition for m.s. convergence is the Cauchy criterion:

$$\lim_{n,m\to\infty} E[(x_n - x_m)^2] = 0. \tag{ii}$$

In fact, since

$$(x_n - x_m)^2 \le 2(x_n - x)^2 + 2(x_m - x)^2,$$

(i) implies (ii). For brevity, we omit to show the converse.
3 A stochastic process $z(t)$ is said to be continuous in the mean square sense if

$$\lim_{h\to0} E[(z(t + h) - z(t))^2] = 0.$$

4 For a rigorous treatment of Ito calculus, one may see, for instance, Ito's original paper (1944), Jazwinski (1970) or Wong and Hajek (1985).
5 It can be proved that for the Rayleigh process with (8.37) the boundary $r_1 = 0$ is 'regular' if $0 < K < 2$ and is 'exit' if $K \le 0$.

References

Anderssen, K. S., De Hoog, F. R. and Weiss, R. (1973) On the numerical solution of Brownian motion processes, *Journal of Applied Probability*, **10**, 409–18.

Arnold, L. (1974) *Stochastic Differential Equations*, Wiley, New York.

Baker, C. T. H. (1978) *The Numerical Treatment of Integral Equations*, Oxford University Press, Oxford.

Buonocore, A., Nobile, A. G. and Ricciardi, L. M. (1987) A new integral equation of first-passage-time probability densities, *Journal of Applied Probability*, **19**, 784–800.

Capocelli, R. and Ricciardi, L. M. (1971) Diffusion approximation and first passage time problem for a model neuron, *Kybernetik*, **8**, 214–23.

Cerbone, G., Ricciardi, L. M. and Sacerdote, L. (1981) Mean variance and skewness of the first passage time for the Ornstein–Uhlenbeck process, *Cybernetics and Systems*, **12**, 395–429.

Daniels, H. E. (1969) The minimum of a stationary Markov process superimposed on a U-shaped trend, *Journal of Applied Probability*, **6**, 399–408.

Darling D. A. and Siegert, A. J. F. (1953) The first passage problem for a continuous Markov process, *The Annals of Mathematical Statistics*, **24**, 624–32.

Durbin, J. (1971) Boundary-crossing probabilities for the Brownian motion and Poisson processes and techniques for computing the power of the Kolmogorov–Smirnov test, *Journal of Applied Probability*, **8**, 431–53.

Erdelyi, A. (1953) *Higher Transcendental Functions*, vol. I, vol. II, McGraw-Hill, New York.

Favella, L., Reineri, M. T., Ricciardi, L. M. and Sacerdote, L. (1982) First passage time problems and some related computational methods, *Cybernetics and Systems*, **13**, 95–128.

Feller, W. (1952) Parabolic differential equations and semigroup transformations, *Annals of Mathematics*, **55**, 468–518.

Feller, W. (1954) Diffusion processes in one dimension, *Transactions of the American Mathematical Society*, **77**, 1–31.

Feller, W. (1966) *An Introduction to Probability Theory and its Applications, Vol. II*, Wiley, New York.

Fortet, R. (1943) Les fonctions aléatories du type de Markoff associées à certaines équations lineáires aux dérivées partielles du type parabolique, *Journal de mathématiques pures et appliquées*, **22**, 177–243.

Giorno, V., Nobile, A. G., Ricciardi, L. M. and Sato, S. (1989) On the evaluation of first-passage-time probability densities via nonsingular integral equations, *Advances in Applied Probability*, **21**, 20–36.

Gray, A. H. and Caughey, T. K. (1965) A controversy in problems involving random parametric excitation, *Journal of Mathematics and Physics*, **44**(3), 288–96.

Ito, K. (1944) Stochastic Integral, *Proceedings of the Imperial Academy, Tokyo*, **20**, 519–24.

Jazwinski, A. H. (1970) *Stochastic Processes and Filtering Theory*, Academic Press, New York.

Karlin, S. and Taylor, H. M. (1981) *A Second Course in Stochastic Processes*, Academic Press, New York.

McKean, H. P. (1969) *Stochastic Integrals*, Academic Press, New York.

Mortensen, R. E. (1969) Mathematical problems of modelling stochastic non-linear dynamic systems, *Journal of Statistical Physics*, **1**(2), 271–96.

Nobile, A. G., Ricciardi, L. M. and Sacerdote, L. (1985) Exponential trends of first-passage-time densities for a class of diffusion process with steady-state distribution, *Journal of Applied Probability*, **22**, 611–18.

Ricciardi, L. M. and Sato, S. (1988) First-passage-time density and moments of the Ornstein – Uhlenbeck process, *Journal of Applied Probability*, **25**, 43–57.

Ricciardi, L. M., Sacerdote, L. and Sato, S. (1983) Diffusion approximation and first passage time problem for a model neuron. II. Outline of a computation method, *Mathematical Biosciences*, **64**, 29–44.

Ricciardi, L. M., Sacerdote, L. and Sato, S. (1984) On an integral equation for first-passage-time probability densities, *Journal of Applied Probability*, **21**, 302–3.

Sato, S. (1978) On the moments of the firing interval of the diffusion approximated model neuron, *Mathematical Biosciences*, **39**, 53–70.

Shohat, J. A. and Tamarkin, J. D. (1943) *The Problem of Moments*, American Mathematical Society.

Siegert, A. J. F. (1951) On the first passage time probability function, *Physical Review*, **81**, 617–23.

Smithies, F. (1958) *Integral Equations*, Cambridge University Press, Cambridge.

Soong, T. T. (1973) *Random Differential Equations in Science and Engineering*, Academic Press, New York.

Stratonovich, R. L. (1963) *Topics in the Theory of Random Noise*, vol. I, Gordon & Breach, New York.

Stratonovich, R. L. (1968) *Conditional Markov Processes and their Applications to the Theory of Optimal Control*, Elsevier, New York.

Wang, M. C. and Uhlenbeck, G. E. (1945) On the theory of Brownian motion II, *Review of Modern Physics*, **17**, 323–42 (also in N. Wax (ed.) (1954) *Selected Papers on Noise and Stochastic Processes*, Dover, New York).

Wong, E. and Hajek, B. (1985) *Stochastic Processes in Engineering Systems*, Springer, New York.

Wong, E. and Zakai, M. (1965) On the convergence of ordinary integrals to stochastic integrals, *The Annals of Mathematical Statistics*, **36**, 1560–4.

Note added in proof

While this volume was in press, the following articles dealing with theoretical and computational problems on the evaluation of first-passage-time densities for one-dimensional diffusion processes have appeared:

Giorno, V., Nobile, A.G. and Ricciardi, L.M. (1989) A symmetry-based constructive approach to probability densities for one-dimensional diffusion processes. *Journal of Applied Probability*, **27**, 707–21.

Giorno, V., Nobile, A.G. and Ricciardi, L.M. (in press) On the asymptotic behaviour of first-passage-time densities for one-dimensional diffusion processes and varying boundaries. *Advances in Applied Probability*. Preprint No. 58, 1989.

Buonocore, A., Giorno, V., Nobile, A.G. and Ricciardi, L.M. (in press) On the two-boundary first-crossing-time problem for diffusion processes. *Journal of Applied Probability*. Preprint No. 67, 1989.

Buonocore, A. and Visentin, F. (1990) A simple algorithm for the evaluation of first-passage-time probability densities for one-dimensional diffusion processes. In *Proceedings of 10th European Congress on Cybernetics and Systems Research* (ed. R. Trappl), World Scientific Publishing Co., Singapore.

Giorno, V., Nobile, A.G. and Ricciardi, L.M. (1990) On the transition densities of diffusion processes with reflecting boundaries. In *Proceedings of 10th European Congress on Cybernetics and Systems Research* (ed. R. Trappl), World Scientific Publishing Co., Singapore.

6

Functionals of Brownian motion

Takeyuki Hida   *Department of Mathematics, Faculty of Sciences, Nagoya University, Chikusa-ku Nagoya 464, Japan*

1   Introduction

A very brief history of the mathematical theory of Brownian motion will be summarized in this section, where one can see how Brownian motion has become an important subject of pure mathematics and why it has so many significant applications in various fields of science such as quantum dynamics, biology, electrical engineering and so forth.

The story began in the year 1827, when Robert Brown discovered the highly irregular motion of pollen grains suspended in water. The cause of such a movement became known later; indeed the motion comes from the large number of collisions of the grains with molecules of the water.

The scientist who first established a mathematical theory of Brownian motion was Albert Einstein. He made some plausible assumptions to produce a mathematical formulation of this random phenomenon. He concluded that when the movement was projected onto a straight line, i.e. $\mathbb{R}^1$, the density function $u(x,t)$ of the grains at an instant t must satisfy the heat equation

$$\frac{\partial}{\partial t} u(x,t) = \frac{1}{2} D \frac{\partial^2}{\partial x^2} u(x,t), \quad x \in \mathbb{R}^1, t \geqslant 0, \tag{1}$$

where D is a constant which is proved to be

$$D = \frac{RT}{Nf} \tag{2}$$

with R a universal constant, T the absolute temperature, N the Avogadro number and f the coefficient of friction.

With the initial condition $U(x,0) = \delta(x - a)$, the solution of equation (1) is

$$u(x,t) = (2\pi Dt)^{-1/2} \exp\left[\frac{(x - a)^2}{2Dt}\right].$$

Namely, we are given a Gaussian distribution.

It is worth noting that Perrin (1913) used the formula (2) to obtain a good approximation of the Avogadro number from his experiments:

$$N \doteq 6 \times 10^{23}.$$

Let us now turn our eyes to a viewpoint from functional analysis. We should like to emphasize the importance of Lévy's work (1951) on the analysis of functionals on $L^2[0,1]$ launched in the 1910s, which actually have connections with present-day white-noise calculus. Before him, there were already influential works by Volterra and Pérès [1936], J. Hadamard and others; however, we can find very close connection to our approach in Lévy's works, in particular in Lévy (1951).

There, in the analysis on $L^2[0,1]$, it was natural to try to define the integration of functionals. Unfortunately, there is no Lebesgue-like measure on $L^2[0,1]$; instead, Lévy was able to introduce 'la valeur moyenne', which is an average, in a sense, of a functional. This idea, as we shall see later, leads us to introduce the measure of white noise and gives us suggestions for our analysis. What he did in this line is indeed a good motivation for our work.

Some years later, following Lévy's approach, Wiener (1923) introduced a probability measure, now called the 'Wiener measure', on the space of continuous functions. The Wiener measure is nothing but the probability distribution of a Brownian motion. A space of continuous functions with the Wiener measure is called Wiener space.

We are now in a position to give a mathematical definition of a Brownian motion, written as $\{B(t); t \in \mathbb{R}^2\}$, or more simply as $\{B(t)\}$. It is a system of random variables on a probability space, say $(\Omega, \mathbf{B}, P)$ such that:

(i) $\{B(t)\}$ is a Gaussian system, i.e. any finite linear combination of the $B(t)$'s is Gaussian in distribution;
(ii) the difference $B(t + h) - B(t)$ has mean 0 and variance $|h|$;
(iii) $B(0) = 0$.

The analysis on a Wiener space is, intuitively speaking, the analysis of functionals of a Brownian motion. Brownian motion is, of course, the most basic stochastic process, therefore we understand that the analysis on a Wiener space is important not only in functional analysis, but also in probability theory. It should be noted here that profound properties of a Brownian motion were investigated by Lévy, and his book published in

1948 (second and enlarged edition 1965) is the most important literature.

Returning to the Wiener space, we know that much progress was made by Cameron and Martin (1944). At present, there are many mathematicians working on infinite-dimensional calculus on the Wiener space; indeed, that calculus is one of the most active fields in modern mathematics.

Meanwhile, Lévy's functional analysis on $L^2[0,1]$ has become a very interesting field both in analysis and in probability theory. Now one may ask if there is a connection between Lévy's functional analysis and Brownian motion. These may appear unrelated, but they are in fact two aspects of the same thing. This fact will be seen in the following sections where functionals of Brownian motion, call them Brownian functionals, are analysed.

There are several reasons why Lévy's functional analysis is now revisited. Among others, (i) taking 'la valeur moyenne' can be rephrased, at least in spirit, as having integration with respect to the measure of white noise (the time derivative of Brownian motion) which is introduced on a space of generalized functions; (ii) new tools from analysis have now been provided – one is the $\mathcal{T}$- or $\mathcal{S}$-*transform* of Brownian functions, and the other is the *infinite-dimensional rotation* group. In connection with the rotation group we may say that our calculus has an aspect that is the harmonic analysis arising from the infinite-dimensional rotation group. A development of Lévy's functional analysis along these lines is exactly what we are going to discuss in the present chapter. One can also see that the analysis has many applications with wide range of spectrum, and in reality, we are very much stimulated by questions arisen from those applications.

2   White noise and Brownian functionals

We are going to discuss the analysis of functionals of Brownian motion. They are expressed in the form

$$f(B(t); t \in \mathbb{R}^1).$$

As is easily seen from the definition, Brownian motion has independent increments; that is, increments $\Delta_j B$ over non-overlapping intervals Δ_j are mutually independent. We therefore prefer the formal expression:

$$\varphi(\dot{B}(t); t \in \mathbb{R}^1), \quad \dot{B}(t) = \frac{\mathrm{d}}{\mathrm{d}t}B(t), \tag{3}$$

since $\{\dot{B}(t)\}$ is viewed as a continuous analogue of a sequence of i.i.d. (independent identically distributed) random variables. Unfortunately, $\{\dot{B}(t)\}$ is no ordinary stochastic process, but it is a generalized process.

We shall, however, often use an expression like (3) in what follows because of the great advantage of using i.i.d. variables.

Before we come to the analysis, we have to establish the notion of a functional with formal expression (3). For this purpose we first introduce the probability distribution of $\{\dot{B}(t)\}$. Since a sample function of $\dot{B}(t)$ is a generalized function, a space E of test functions will be provided in advance to have a smeared variable $\dot{B}(\xi) \equiv \langle \dot{B}, \xi \rangle$, $\xi \in E$. The $\dot{B}(\xi)$ may be understood as $- \int \xi'(t) B(t) dt$. With this remark the characteristic functional $C(\xi)$ is easily obtained:

$$C(\xi) \equiv E[e^{i\dot{B}(\xi)}] = \exp\left[-\tfrac{1}{2}\|\xi\|^2\right], \quad \xi \in E, \; \| \; \|:L^2(\mathbb{R}^1)\text{-norm.}$$

If the basic space E is taken to be a nuclear space such that

$$E \subset L^2(\mathbb{R}^1) \subset E^*, \; E^* = \text{the dual space of } E, \quad (\text{a Gel'fand triple})$$

then the Bochner–Minlos theorem guarantees the existence and the uniqueness of the probability measure μ on E^* such that

$$C(\xi) = \int_{E^*} e^{i\langle x,\xi \rangle} d\mu(x), \quad \xi \in E, \tag{4}$$

where $\langle \; , \; \rangle$ is the canonical bilinear form connecting E and E^*. This measure μ is nothing but the probability distribution of $\{\dot{B}(t)\}$, so that almost all x in E^* is viewed as a sample function of $\dot{B}(t)$, which is of course a generalized function (see, e.g. Hida, 1980a).

The Hilbert space $L^2(E^*,\mu) \equiv (L^2)$ is therefore a realization of a collection of functionals of the form (3) with finite variance. A member of (L^2) can now be called a *Brownian functional*.

Note that for any fixed ξ, $\langle x,\xi \rangle$ is a functional in (L^2), and at the same time it is a random variable on (E^*,μ) which is Gaussian $N(0,\|\xi\|^2)$ in distribution. We then come to polynomials in $\langle x,\xi \rangle$'s. Once the variables x, having been smeared by test functions in the form $\langle x,\xi \rangle$, are given, polynomials in $\langle x,\xi \rangle$'s are thought of as most basic functionals.

Let us collect, in particular, all the Hermite polynomials in the $\langle x,\xi \rangle$, $\xi \in E$, of the same degree, say degree n. The closed linear subspace spanned by them will be denoted by $\mathcal{H}_n$. It is proved that $\mathcal{H}_n$, $n \geqslant 0$, are mutually orthogonal since the basic measure μ is the Gaussian and Hermite polynomials of different degree are orthogonal with respect to the Gaussian measure. The algebra generated by exponential functions of the form $\exp[\alpha\langle x, \xi \rangle]$ $\alpha \in \mathbb{C}$ is dense in (L^2) and so is the set of polynomials in $\langle x,\xi \rangle$'s. More specifically, the collection of all Hermite polynomials in $\langle x,\xi \rangle$'s is dense in (L^2). Hence we can see that the direct sum of $\mathcal{H}_n$'s is in agreement with the entire space (L^2). Thus we have obtained a Fock space

$$(L^2) = \sum_{n=0}^{\infty} \oplus \mathscr{H}_n. \tag{5}$$

The subspace $\mathscr{H}_n$ is often called the *homogeneous chaos* of degree n, and a member of $\mathscr{H}_n$ is often referred to as a *multiple Wiener integral* of degree n (see Itô, 1951; Hida, 1980a).

Having established the Hilbert space of Brownian functionals, we now introduce two basic tools from analysis.

2.1 Integral representation or $\mathscr{T}$-transform

Brownian functions have been rigorously defined, but they do not have, in general, visualized expressions. A nice representation would, therefore, be requested. It is in fact given by the following $\mathscr{T}$-transform:

$$(\mathscr{T}\varphi)\,(\xi) = \int_{E^*} e^{i\langle x,\xi\rangle}\varphi(x)d\mu(x), \quad \varphi \in (L^2). \tag{6}$$

Set

$$\mathbb{F} = \{(\mathscr{T}\varphi)\,(\xi): \varphi \in (L^2)\}.$$

Obviously, $\mathbb{F}$ is a vector space. It is possible to topologize $\mathbb{F}$ so as to be isomorphic to a reproducing kernel Hilbert space with kernel $C(\xi - \eta)$, $(\xi,\eta) \in E \times E$.

Theorem 1   The $\mathscr{T}$-transform gives an isomorphism

$$\mathbb{F} \cong (L^2). \tag{7}$$

To prove this theorem, we observe the $\mathscr{T}$-transforms of

$$\varphi(x) = \sum_j a_j \exp\,[i\langle x,\eta_j\rangle] \quad \text{and} \quad \psi(x) = \exp\,[-i\langle x,\eta\rangle].$$

They are given by

$$(\mathscr{T}\varphi)(\xi) = \sum_j a_j C(\xi + \eta_j) \quad \text{and} \quad (\mathscr{T}\psi)(\xi) = C\,(\xi - \eta).$$

respectively. Since $\mathbb{F}$ is the reproducing kernel Hilbert space with kernel $C(\xi - \eta)$, $(\xi,\eta) \in E \times E$, then

$$\left(\sum_j a_j C(\cdot + \eta_j),\ C(\cdot - \eta)\right)_{\mathbb{F}} = \sum_j a_j C(\eta + \eta_j)$$

has to be true. We also have

$$(\varphi,\psi)_{(L^2)} = \sum_j a_j C(\eta + \eta_j).$$

Noting that the algebra generated by exponential functions of $\langle x, \xi \rangle$'s is dense in (L^2) we come to the isomorphism (7).

If the $\mathcal{T}$-transform is restricted to the subspace $\mathcal{H}_n$, then the following theorem is established. It gives us a good representation of Brownian functionals, as was expected; and it plays the most important role in our analysis.

Theorem 2 For $\varphi(x) \in \mathcal{H}_n$ we have

(i) $(\mathcal{T}\varphi)(\xi) = i^n C(\xi) U(\xi)$

  with

$$U(\xi) = \int \ldots \int_{\mathbb{R}^n} F(u_1, \ldots, u_n) \xi(u_1) \ldots \xi(u_n) du^n, \tag{8}$$

  F: symmetric L^2-function (notation: $F \in \widehat{L^2(\mathbb{R}^n)}$);

(ii) $\|\varphi\|_{(L^2)} = \sqrt{n!} \|F\|_{L^2(\mathbb{R}^n)}$;

(iii) the correspondence $\varphi \leftrightarrow F$ is bijective.

This theorem may be written in short, and even in a formal way, in the form

$$\mathcal{H}_n \cong \sqrt{n!}\ \widehat{L^2(\mathbb{R}^n)} \quad \text{under } \mathcal{T}, \tag{9}$$

and hence

$$(L^2) \cong \sum_n \oplus \sqrt{n!}\ \widehat{L^2(\mathbb{R}^n)}. \tag{9'}$$

Proof We start with an exponential function given by the generating function of the Hermite polynomials:

$$\varphi(x) = \exp\left[2t\frac{\langle x, \eta \rangle}{\sqrt{2}} - t^2\right] = \sum_{0}^{\infty} \frac{t^k}{k!} H_k\left(\frac{\langle x, \eta \rangle}{\sqrt{2}}\right),$$

where $\|\eta\| = 1$. The $\mathcal{T}$-transform of $\varphi(x)$ is

$$(\mathcal{T}\varphi)(\xi) = e^{-t^2} \int \exp\left[-\sqrt{2}t\langle x, \eta \rangle + i\langle x, \xi \rangle\right] d\mu(x)$$

$$= \exp\left[-\tfrac{1}{2}\|\xi\|^2 + i\sqrt{2} + (\eta, \xi)\right]$$

$$= C(\xi) \sum_{k=0}^{\infty} \frac{(i\sqrt{2t})^k}{k!} (\eta, \xi)^k,$$

where $(\ ,\ )$ is the inner product in $L^2(\mathbb{R}^1)$. Compare the terms of t^k in the expansions of φ and $\mathcal{T}\varphi$ to prove

$$\left(\mathcal{T}H_k\left(\frac{\langle x, \eta \rangle}{\sqrt{2}}\right)\right)(\xi) = C(\xi)(i\sqrt{2})^k (\eta, \xi)^k.$$

This relation can be generalized to that for a functional of the form

$$\varphi(x) = \prod_j H_{k_j}\left(\frac{\langle x,\eta_j\rangle}{\sqrt{2}}\right),$$ finite product, where $\{\eta_j\}$ is a complete ortho-

normal system in $L^2(\mathbb{R}^1)$ such that $\{\eta_j\} \subset E$. Such a polynomial is called a Fourier–Hermite polynomial based on $\{\eta_n\}$. Now write

$$\xi = \sum_j t_j\, \eta_j + \xi',$$

where ξ' is orthogonal to the η_j's involved in the above expression of $\varphi(x)$. Then, we have

$$(\mathscr{T}\varphi)(\xi) = \int \exp\left[i\sum_j t_j\,\langle x,\eta_j\rangle + i\langle x,\xi'\rangle\right]\prod_j H_{k_j}\left(\frac{\langle : \eta_j\rangle}{\sqrt{2}}\right)d\mu(x)$$

$$= \int \exp[i\langle x,\xi'\rangle]\, d\mu(x) \prod_j \int \exp[it_j\langle x,\eta_j\rangle]$$

$$\times\, H_{k_j}\left(\frac{\langle x,\eta_j\rangle}{\sqrt{2}}\right)d\mu(x)$$

(since $\langle x,\eta_j\rangle$'s and $\langle x,\xi'\rangle$ are mutually independent)

$$= C(\xi') \prod_j e^{-\frac{1}{2}t_j^2}(\sqrt{2}\mathrm{i})^{k_j}(\eta_j,t_j\eta_j)^{k_j}.$$

Noting that $t_j = (\eta_j,\xi)$ and that $\|\xi\|^2 = \sum_j t_j^2 + \|\xi'\|^2$, we have

$$(\mathscr{T}\varphi)(\xi) = (\sqrt{2}\mathrm{i})^n C(\xi)\int\cdots\int_{\mathbb{R}^n}\left[\,\eta_1(t_1)\ldots\eta_1(t_{k_1})\eta_2(t_{k_1+1})\ldots\right]$$

$$\times\, \xi(t_1)\xi(t_2)\ldots\xi(t_n)dt_1dt_2\ldots dt_n,$$

where $n = \sum_j k_j$. The function in the bracket [ ] together with the constant $(\sqrt{2})^n$ is denoted by $\widetilde{F}(t_1,\ldots,t_n)$ and is symmetrized:

$$F(t_1,\ldots,t_n) = \frac{1}{n!}\sum_\pi \widetilde{F}(t_{\pi(1)},t_{\pi(2)},\ldots,t_{\pi(n)}),$$

where $\sum_\pi$ denotes the sum extending over all permutations π of $\{1,2,\ldots,n\}$. It is easy to see that

$$\|\widetilde{F}\|_{L^2(\mathbb{R}^n)} = 2^{n/2},$$

$$\|\widetilde{F}\|_{L^2(\mathbb{R}^n)} = \left(\prod_j k_j!\right)^{1/2}(n!)^{-1}\, 2^{n/2}.$$

While

$$\|\varphi\|_{(L^2)} = \left(\prod_j k_j!\right)^{1/2} 2^{n/2}.$$

Thus, we have the expression (8) and (ii) in the theorem for a Fourier–Hermite polynomial. Since such polynomials of degree n span the whole space $\mathcal{H}_n$, we can easily prove (8) and (ii) for a general φ in $\mathcal{H}_n$.

The assertion (iii) is almost obvious from the discussion above. Thus, we have completely proved the theorem.

In view of the formula (8), the representation $\mathcal{H}_n$-functionals in terms of $\widehat{L^2(\mathbb{R}^n)}$-functions, as indicated by (9), is called the *integral representation* of φ, and $U(\xi)$ is called the *U-functional* associated with φ. For a general φ, we express it in the form $\varphi = \Sigma\varphi_n$, $\varphi_n \in \mathcal{H}_n$, and associate $U_n(\xi)$ with each φ_n. Then the sum $\sum_n U_n(\xi)$ is the *U-functional* associated with φ.

Remark 1 The $\mathcal{T}$-transform is not quite an infinite-dimensional analogue of the ordinary Fourier transform on $L^2(\mathbb{R}^n)$. For one thing, $\mathcal{T}$ carries (L^2)-functional not into (L^2) but to the reproducing kernel Hilbert space. Needless to say, some roles of the ordinary Fourier transform are played by $\mathcal{T}$.

Remark 2 This remark is significant. Since the exponential function $e^{i\langle x,\xi\rangle}$ has enough analytic properties, it may be viewed as a test function. In fact, the algebra generated by the exponential functions is dense in (L^2). Therefore, the $\mathcal{T}$-transform, viewed as the inner product of such an exponential function as $e^{-i\langle x,\xi\rangle}$ and a Brownian functional $\varphi(x)$, gives the idea of having a generalized functional in place of the (L^2)-functional $\varphi(x)$. Actually, we shall do this from Section 5 onwards.

Remark 3 An engineer once told me that a random function such as $\varphi(x)$ is, in general, not manageable by a computer, while the associated U-functional, which is a sure (i.e. non-random) functional of a C^∞-function ξ can be dealt with by a computer. This is one of the significant advantages of the use of the $\mathcal{T}$-transform.

2.2 Infinite-dimensional rotation group

Before we give the definition, let us make a naive observation. Let $\{\xi_n\}$ be a complete orthonormal system in $L^2(\mathbb{R}^1)$ such that $\xi_n \in E$ for every n. Then we are given a system of independent indentically distributed, indeed

$N(0,1)$, random variables $\langle x,\xi_n \rangle$, so that the strong law of large numbers tells us that

$$\frac{1}{N} \sum_{n=1}^{N} \langle x,\xi_n \rangle^2 \to 1 \quad \text{a.e.} \quad x \in E^*,$$

or

$$\sum_{n=1}^{N} \langle x,\xi_n \rangle^2 \sim N \quad \text{for large } N. \tag{10}$$

Also the mapping

$$x \to \langle x,\xi_n \rangle, \quad n \geq 1,$$

gives, so to speak, a coordinate representation of x. Thus, roughly speaking, (10) means that, if we let $N \to \infty$, almost all x is sitting on, as it were, an infinite-dimensional sphere $S^\infty(\sqrt{\infty})$ with centre at the origin and with radius $\sqrt{\infty}$.

On the other hand, the fact that each coordinate $\langle x,\xi_n \rangle$, viewed as a random variable on the probability space (E^*,μ), has the same probability distribution $N(0,1)$ suggests to us that the measure μ looks like a uniform probability measure on the sphere $S^\infty(\sqrt{\infty})$. In a sense, this really is the case.

Following Yoshizawa (1969), we now introduce an infinite-dimensional rotation group.

Definition A linear transformation g acting on E is called a *rotation* of E if it satisfies

(i) g is an isomorphism of E,
(ii) $\|g\xi\| = \|\xi\|$ for every $\xi \in E$.

The product of the two rotations g_1 and g_2 can be defined as

$$(g_1 \cdot g_2)\xi = g_1(g_2\xi), \quad \xi \in E. \tag{11}$$

With this product the collection $O(E)$ of all the rotation of E forms a group.

Definition The group $O(E)$ is called the *rotation group* of E. If E is not specified, it is simply called an *infinite-dimensional rotation group* and is denoted by O_∞.

For any $g \in O(E)$ its adjoint g^* is defined in a usual manner. Using the fact that $\langle x,g\xi \rangle$, for any fixed $x \in E^*$, is a continuous linear functional of ξ, we can find x^*, which we shall denote by g^*x, such that

$$\langle x,g\xi \rangle = \langle x^*,\xi \rangle \equiv \langle g^*x,\xi \rangle.$$

It is easy to see that the collection

$O^*(E^*) \equiv \{g^*; g \in O(E)\}$

forms a group and that

$$O^*(E^*) \cong O(E) \tag{12}$$

under the correspondence

$g^* \leftrightarrow g^{-1} \in O(E).$

Since g^* is a transformation on E^*, we can define the product g^* and μ:

$d(g^*\mu)(x) = d\mu(g^*x).$

Theorem 3   For any $g^* \in O^*(E^*)$ we have

$$g^*\mu = \mu. \tag{13}$$

Proof   The characteristic functional of $g^*\mu$ is

$$\int e^{i\langle x,\xi\rangle} d(g^*\mu)(x) = \int e^{i\langle x,\xi\rangle} d\mu(g^*x)$$

$$= \int e^{i\langle g^{*-1}x,\xi\rangle} d\mu(x) = \int e^{i\langle x,g^{-1}\xi\rangle} d\mu(x)$$

$$= e^{\frac{1}{2}\|g^{-1}\xi\|^2} = C(\xi).$$

This proves the assertion (13).

In view of Theorem 3, the group $O^*(E^*)$ has a more direct connection with probability theory than $O(E)$, while the latter is easier to deal with because it is a transformation group on E, which is more easily visualized than E^*. We shall therefore discuss mainly the group $O(E)$ in what follows.

3   Applications of the integral representation

The integral representation established in the last section has many applications not only to stochastic processes having realizations in (L^2) but also to functional analysis and other related fields. We shall now show some typical applications.

3.1   Stochastic differential equations

Consider a bilinear case

$$dX(t) = -\lambda X(t)dt + (bX(t) + c)dB(t), \quad \lambda > 0, \tag{14}$$

with an assumption that

$$EX(t) \equiv 0. \tag{15}$$

We may assume that $\{X(t)\}$ is a curve in the Hilbert space (L^2). Associated with $X(t)$ is a U-functional depending on t. We denote it by $U_t(\xi)$. Then, the equation (14) can be paraphrased in the form

$$\frac{d}{dt} U_t(\xi) = -\lambda U_t(\xi) + \xi(t)(b U_t(\xi) + c), \quad t \in \mathbb{R}^1. \tag{16}$$

The solution is

$$U_t(\xi) = c \, \exp\left[-\lambda t + b \int_{-\infty}^{t} \xi(u) du\right] \int_{-\infty}^{t} \xi(u) \, \exp\left[\lambda u - b \int_{-\infty}^{u} \xi(v) dv\right] du.$$

The solution $X(t)$ to (14), in fact a stationary process, is therefore given by

$$X(t) = \sum_{n=1}^{\infty} \frac{cb^{n-1}}{n!} e^{-\lambda t} \int_{-\infty}^{t} \cdots \int_{-\infty}^{t} \exp[\lambda \min_{1 \leq j \leq n} u_j] dB(u_1) \, \cdots \, dB(u_n). \tag{17}$$

Remark   In the expression (17) we have used the traditional notation $dB(u_1) \cdots dB(u_n)$ to denote a multiple Wiener integral. In Section 6 a more general description as well as a general notion of stochastic integral will be introduced.

3.2   The Kac formula

We first extend a linear functional of x, which is of the form $\langle x, \xi \rangle$, $\xi \in E$, to the case where ξ is taken to be an $L^2(\mathbb{R}^1)$-function. Let f be an $L^2(\mathbb{R}^1)$-function. Then it is approximated by a sequence $\{\xi_n\}$ of members of E, i.e.

$$\xi_n \to f \quad \text{in} \quad L^2(\mathbb{R}^1).$$

Then $\{\langle x, \xi_n \rangle\}$ forms a Cauchy sequence in (L^2):

$$\int_{E^*} |\langle x, \xi_n \rangle - \langle x, \xi_m \rangle|^2 d\mu(x) = \|\xi_n - \xi_m\|^2 \to 0, \quad n, m \to \infty.$$

Hence, there is a member in (L^2) (in fact in $\mathcal{H}_1$) which is a limit of the $\langle x, \xi_n \rangle$ in $\mathcal{H}_1$. The limit is independent of the choice of $\{\xi_n\}$, so that it may be denoted by $\langle x, f \rangle$, although $\langle x, f \rangle$ is no longer continuous in x.

With a particular choice of $L^2(\mathbb{R}^1)$-function f to be $\chi_{[0,t]}$ the indicator function of the interval $[0,t]$, we have a version of a Brownian motion $B(t)$:

$$B(t) = B(t,x) = \langle x, \chi_{[0,t]} \rangle, \quad t \geq 0. \tag{18}$$

Lemma For a bounded continuous function f we set

$$u(a) = \int d\mu(x) \int_0^\infty e^{-\alpha t} f(a + B(t)) dt, \quad \alpha > 0, \ a \in \mathbb{R}, \tag{19}$$

with the Brownian motion given by (18). Then we have

$$\left(-\frac{1}{2}\frac{d^2}{da^2} + \alpha\right) u(a) = f(a). \tag{20}$$

Proof $u(a) = \int_0^\infty e^{-\alpha t} \int_{-\infty}^\infty f(y) \frac{1}{\sqrt{2\pi t}} \exp\left[-\frac{(y-a)^2}{2t}\right] dy dt.$

Use the fact that the Laplace transform of a Gaussian kernel with variance t is

$$\frac{1}{\sqrt{2\alpha}} \exp[-\sqrt{2\alpha}|y|],$$

to obtain

$$u(a) = \int_{-\infty}^a + \int_a^\infty \left\{\frac{1}{\sqrt{2\alpha}} \exp[-\sqrt{2\alpha}\,|a-y|] f(y)\right\} dy.$$

Take the second derivative of $u(a)$ to see

$$u''(a) = 2\alpha u(a) - 2f(a).$$

Theorem 4 Let f be as in the lemma, and let V be bounded and non-negative. Set

$$v(a) = \int d\mu(x) \int_0^\infty e^{-\alpha t} f(B_a(t)) \exp\left[-\int_0^t V(B_a(s)) ds\right] dt, \tag{21}$$

where $B_a(t) = B(t) + a, \ a \in \mathbb{R}^1$. Then we have

$$\left[\alpha - \frac{1}{2}\frac{d^2}{da^2} + V(a)\right] v(a) = f(a). \tag{22}$$

Proof First show that

$$v(a) - u(a)$$

$$= -\int d\mu(x) \int_\infty^0 e^{-\alpha t} f(B_a(t)) \int_0^t V(B_a(t)) \exp\left[-\int_s^t V(B_a(u)) du\right] ds dt,$$

where $u(a)$ is a function given by (19). Then we can prove the equality

$$v(a) - u(a) = -\int_0^\infty e^{-\alpha t} dt \int V(B_a(t)) v(B_a(t)) d\mu(x)$$

and conclude, by using the lemma, that

$$\left[\alpha - \frac{1}{2}\frac{d^2}{da^2}\right]v(a) - f(a) = -V(a)v(a).$$

3.3 Stochastic area

Let $B(t) = \{B_1(t), B_2(t); \; t \geq 0\}$ be a two-dimensional Brownian motion. Lévy (1940) wished to define the area $S(T)$ of the region enclosed by the Brownian curve in the interval $[0,T]$ and the chord connecting the origin with the point $B(T)$. He actually gave the following integral:

$$S(T) = \frac{1}{2}\int_0^T \{B_1(t)dB_2(t) - B_2(t)dB_1(t)\}. \tag{23}$$

If the Brownian curve were smooth, the integral would express the area in the usual sense. Unfortunately, the Brownian curve is not smooth, so it does not define an area. The attempt to define the area eventually gave the idea of the stochastic integral (Lévy, 1941, 1952; see also Lévy (1948) Section 7).

In our set-up, $S(T)$ can be viewed as a member in $\mathcal{H}_2 \subset (L^2)$. This can be seen in the following manner. Set

$$B_1(t) = B_1(t,x) = \langle x, \chi_{[0,t]} \rangle,$$
$$B_2(t) = B_2(t,x) = \langle x, \chi_{[-t,0]} \rangle, \quad t \geq 0.$$

The stochastic integral

$$\int_0^T B_1(t)\,dB_2(t)$$

is understood as the limit (in the mean square sense) of the sum

$$\sum_i B_1(t_i^n)\Delta_i^n B_2, \qquad \Delta_i^n B_2 = B_2(t_{i+1}^n) - B_2(t_i^n),$$
$$t_0^n = 0 < t_1^n < t_2^n < \cdots < t_n^n = T, \tag{23_n}$$

as $n \to \infty$ (tacitly we assume that the above partition of $[0,T]$ becomes finer and finer and $\max_i |t_{i+1} - t_i| \to 0$). The existence of the limit is almost obvious.

Similarly we can define

$$\int_0^T B_2(t)\,dB_1(t)$$

and we have $S(T)$.

The sum (23_n) is certainly a member of $\mathcal{H}_2$, so that the limit (23) is still in $\mathcal{H}_2$.

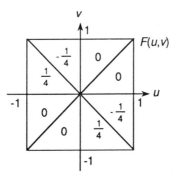

Fig. 6.1   Kernel function associated with $S(1)$

For simplicity we set $T = 1$. Then, observing that each term in (23_n) has the kernel function $\frac{1}{2}(\chi_{[0,t_i]}(u)\chi_{\Delta_i^n}(v) + \chi_{\Delta_i^n}(u)\chi_{[0,t_i]}(v))$ (note that we must have a symmetrized kernel), we can easily see that the kernel function $F(u,v)$ associated with $S(1)$ is given as illustrated in Figure 1. The kernel $F(u,v)$, which is real and symmetric, serves as a symmetric integral operator of Hilbert–Schmidt type acting on $L^2(\mathbb{R}^1)$. Simple computations show that the operator F has eigenvalues

$$\lambda_n = 2(2n - 1)\pi, \quad n = 0, \pm1, \pm2, \ldots$$

and that their multiplicity is always double. Using this fact, we can compute the characteristic function of the random variable $S(1)$. It is given by

$$E(e^{itS(1)}) = \int e^{itS(1,x)} d\mu(x) = 1/\cosh\frac{t}{2}.$$

(See the following Section 3.3' for actual computations. A general theory is discussed there.)

Note   Because of the importance of the concept of a stochastic area, it appears in many fields of mathematics (see e.g. Arato *et al.*, 1961; Gaveau, 1977; also note Diego de Falco's result (1987) that is applied to quantum mechanical orbitual angular momentum).

3.3'   Quadratic functionals

The investigation of Lévy's stochastic area suggests that we discuss more general functionals in $\mathscr{H}_2$ with real-valued kernel $F(u,v)$ in $L^2(\mathbb{R}^2)$.

Let $\varphi(x)$ be a real-valued $\mathscr{H}_2$-functional. Then the kernel $F(u,v)$ is also real-valued. As in the case of $S(1)$ we can appeal to the Hilbert–Schmidt theory to obtain

$$F(u,v) = \sum_n \frac{1}{\lambda_n} \eta_n(u)\eta_n(v) \tag{24}$$

where $\{\lambda_n, \eta_n; \ n \geqslant 1\}$ is the eigensystem of the integral operator F, namely

$$\lambda_n \int F(u,v)\eta_n(v)dv = \eta_n(u),$$

$$\int \eta_n(u)\eta_m(u)du = \delta_{n,m}.$$

The U-functional has to be expressed in the form

$$U(\xi) = \int \int E(u,v)\xi(u)\xi(v)dudv$$

$$= \sum_n \frac{1}{\lambda_n} (\eta_n,\xi)^2.$$

We note that the monomial $(\eta_n,\xi)^2$ is the U-functional of the Fourier-Hermite polynomial of the form $\langle x,\eta_n\rangle^2 - 1$. We therefore have

$$\varphi(x) = \sum_n \frac{1}{\lambda_n} (\langle x,\eta_n\rangle^2 - 1). \tag{25}$$

Here is an important remark. Since $\{\eta_n\}$ is an orthonormal system in $L^2(\mathbb{R}^1)$, the collection $\{\langle x,\eta_n\rangle; \ n \geqslant 1\}$ is a system of *independent* identically distributed random variables, and so is $\{\langle x,\eta_n\rangle^2 - 1; \ n \geqslant 1\}$. The formula (25) shows that $\varphi(x)$ has an expansion into a series of independent random variables, whose distributions are well known (the centred χ^2-distribution up to a constant). The characteristic function of $\varphi(x)$, viewed as a random variable on (E^*,μ), is obtained by

$$E(e^{it\varphi}) = \int \exp\left[it\sum_n \frac{1}{\lambda_n}(\langle x,\eta_n\rangle^2 - 1)\right]d\mu(x)$$

$$= \prod_n \int \exp\left[\frac{it}{\lambda_n}(\langle x,\eta_n\rangle^2 - 1)\right]d\mu(x)$$

(since $(\langle x,\eta_n\rangle^2 - 1)$, $n \geqslant 1$, are independent)

$$= \prod_n \left\{\left(1 - \frac{2it}{\lambda_n}\right)^{-1/2}\exp\left[-\frac{it}{\lambda_n}\right]\right\}.$$

The product in the last formula is in agreement with the reciprocal of the square root of the modified Fredholm determinant $\delta(2it; F)$ expressed in terms of eigenvalues. Thus we have proved

$$E(e^{it\varphi}) = \delta(2it; F)^{-1/2}. \tag{26}$$

3.4 Exponential of a quadratic functional

Let φ be as in Section 3.3'. Set

$$f(x) = \exp[i\varphi(x)].$$

With the notation of Section 3.3', we have

$$f(x) = \exp\left[i\sum_1^\infty \lambda_n^{-1}(\langle x,\eta_n\rangle^2 - 1)\right].$$

To compute the $\mathscr{T}$-transform $(\mathscr{T}f)(\xi)$, we expand ξ in the form

$$\xi = \sum_n a_n\eta_n + \xi'$$

where $a_n = (\xi,\eta_n)$ and ξ' is orthogonal to the η_n's. We now note again that $\{\langle x,\xi'\rangle, \langle x,\eta_n\rangle;\ n \geq 1\}$ is a system of independent Gaussian random variables. We therefore have

$$(\mathscr{T}f)(\xi) = \int_{E^*} \exp[i\langle x,\xi'\rangle]d\mu(x)$$

$$\times \int_{E^*} \exp\left[i\sum_n a_n\langle x,\eta_n\rangle + i\sum_n \lambda_n^{-1}(\langle x,\eta_n\rangle^2 - 1)\right]d\mu(x)$$

$$= \int \exp[i\langle x,\xi'\rangle]d\mu(x)\prod_n\int\exp[ia_n\langle x,\eta_n\rangle + i\lambda_n^{-1}(\langle x,\eta_n\rangle^2 - 1)]d\mu(x)$$

$$= C(\xi')\prod_n\left\{(2\pi)^{-1/2}\int\exp[ia_nt + (i\lambda_n^{-1} - 2^{-1})t^2]dt\cdot\exp[-i\lambda_n^{-1}]\right\}$$

$$= C(\xi')\prod_n\left\{(1-2i\lambda_n^{-1})^{-1/2}\exp(-i\lambda_n^{-1})\exp\left[-\frac{a_n^2}{2(1 - 2i\lambda_n^{-1})}\right]\right\}$$

$$= C(\xi')\delta(2i;\ F)^{-1/2}\exp\left[\sum_n\frac{-i\lambda_n^{-1}a_n^2}{1 - 2i\lambda_n^{-1}}\right]\exp\left[-\frac{1}{2}\sum_n a_n^2\right]$$

$$= C(\xi)\delta(2i;\ F)^{-1/2}\exp\left[\sum_n\frac{-i\lambda_n^{-1}a_n^2}{1 - 2i\lambda_n^{-1}}\right]$$

where we have used the equality $\|\xi\|^2 = \sum_n a_n^2 + \|\xi'\|^2$.

Hence we have

$$(\mathscr{T}f)(\xi) = C(\xi)\delta(2i;\ F)\exp\left[i\sum_n\frac{(\eta_n,\xi)^2}{-\lambda_n + 2i}\right]$$

$$= C(\xi)\delta(2i;\ F)\exp\left[\int\int\tilde{F}(u,v)\xi(u)\xi(v)dudv\right]. \tag{27}$$

The second equality is simply a rephrasing of the first equality just proved. That is, we have introduced a new kernel function $\widetilde{F}(u,v)$ which is an $L^2(R^2)$-function and is characterized as an integral operator in such a way that

(a) $F\widetilde{F} = \widetilde{F}F$;
(b) $F, \widetilde{F}$ have the same range;
(c) $\widetilde{F}(-1 + 2iF) = iF$.

Remark Let $\varphi(x)$ be the same functional as in Section 3.3'. We can also think of a real exponential function of $\varphi(x)$:

$$g(x) = \exp[\varphi(x)].$$

In this case, we need to think of a condition for $g(x)$ to be an (L^2)-functional. A necessary and sufficient condition for this is that the kernel $F(u; v)$ of the integral representation of φ has no eigenvalue λ_n with $0 \leq \lambda_n \leq 4$.

4 Infinite-dimensional rotation group $O(E)$

The rotation group $O(E)$, introduced in Section 2 as a tool of our analysis on (L^2), is really a large group. With any reasonable topology, like the compact-open topology (it seems to be fitting, because $O(E)$ is a transformation group acting on the topological space E), we can see that the group $O(E)$ is neither compact nor locally compact. We shall therefore consider only several subgroups of $O(E)$ and discuss their interesting roles in probability theory or even in some other fields like Lie group theory, functional analysis, or quantum field theory.

4.1 Finite-dimensional rotations

Let F be a finite-dimensional, say n-dimensional, subspace of E. Let g be a transformation on E such that

$g|_F$ (the restriction of g to F) is a rotation of F, and

$g|_{F^\perp}$ is the identity I,

where $F^\perp$ is the orthogonal complement of F in E. Then g is a member of $O(E)$. Now set

$$G(F) = \{g; g|_F \in SO(n), g|_{F^\perp} = I\}.$$

Then, obviously $G(F)$ is a subgroup of $O(E)$ and we have

$$G(F) \cong SO(n). \tag{28}$$

Further, if we take an increasing sequence F_n of finite, say n-dimensional subspaces of E, we can easily think of an inductive limit of the $G_n = G(F_n)$, $n \geq 1$:

$$G_\infty = \bigvee_n G_n, \qquad G_\infty \subset O(E).$$

Of course, such a limit depends on the choice of a sequence $\{F_n\}$. We often choose the F_n in such a way that for a given complete orthonormal system $\{\xi_n\}$ in $L^2(\mathbb{R}^1)$ with $\xi_n \in E$ for every n, we take E_n to be an n-dimensional subspace of E spanned by ξ_j, $1 \leq j \leq n$.

Any g belonging to G_∞ is called a *finite-dimensional rotation* of E and the group G_∞ itself is called the group of finite-dimensional rotations. We are now going to discuss the roles of the finite-dimensional rotations.

Let $\{\xi_n\}$ be a complete orthonormal system in $L^2(\mathbb{R}^1)$ such that $\xi_n \in E$ for every n. Take a two-dimensional rotation $\tilde{g}_\theta$, $\theta \in [-\pi, \pi]$, say a rotation of (ξ_j, ξ_k)-plane. It gives a member g_θ of O_∞ and it determines a two-dimensional rotation g_θ^* as its adjoint, acting on E^*. We are then given a one-parameter group U_θ, $\theta \in [-\pi, \pi]$, of unitary operators on (L^2), which is defined by

$$(U_\theta \varphi)(x) = \varphi(g_\theta^* x), \tag{29}$$

and satisfies

$$\begin{aligned} U_{\theta+2\pi} &= U_\theta, \\ U_\theta U_{\theta'} &= U_{\theta''}, \quad \theta + \theta' \equiv \theta'' \bmod 2\pi, \\ U_0 &= I \text{ (identity)}. \end{aligned} \tag{30}$$

In exactly the same manner as in the analysis on $\mathbb{R}^2$, we have the infinitesimal generator of $\{U_\theta\}$ expressed in the form

$$\langle x, \xi_j \rangle \frac{\partial}{\partial \xi_k} - \langle x, \xi_k \rangle \frac{\partial}{\partial \xi_j}, \tag{31}$$

where $\partial/\partial\xi_k$ means the partial differential operator in the variable $\langle x, \xi_k \rangle$.

With this observation we are naturally led to the infinite-dimensional Laplace–Beltrami operator, which is a quadratic form of the operators of the form (31) with $i, j = 1, 2, \ldots$, and is a negative operator on (L^2), commutes with all finite-dimensional rotations, and annihilates constants. Such an operator, denote it by Δ, is to be (up to a positive constant factor)

$$\Delta = \sum_j \left(\frac{\partial^2}{\partial \xi_j^2} - \langle x, \xi_j \rangle \frac{\partial}{\partial \xi_j} \right). \tag{32}$$

Proposition For φ in $\mathcal{H}_n$, we have

$$\Delta \varphi = -n\varphi. \tag{33}$$

The proof comes from the formula for Hermite polynomials,

$$H_n''(x) - 2xH_n'(x) = -2nH_n(x),$$

and from the fact that $\mathcal{H}_n$ is spanned by all the Hermite polynomials in $\langle x, \xi_n \rangle$'s of degree n.

In fact, if φ is a Fourier–Hermite polynomial based on the $\{\xi_n\}$ expressed in the form

$$\varphi(x) = \prod_j H_{k_j}\left(\frac{\langle x, \xi_j \rangle}{\sqrt{2}}\right), \quad \Sigma k_j = n,$$

then

$$\Delta\varphi = \sum_j \left(\frac{\partial^2}{\partial \xi_j^2} - \langle x, \xi_j \rangle \frac{\partial}{\partial \xi_j}\right) \prod_j H_{k_j}\left(\frac{\langle x, \xi_j \rangle}{\sqrt{2}}\right)$$

(the sum extends only over a finite number of j's appearing in the product)

$$= \sum_j (-k_j) H_{k_j}\left(\frac{\langle x, \xi_j \rangle}{\sqrt{2}}\right) \prod_{i \ne j} H_{k_i}\left(\frac{\langle x, \xi_j \rangle}{\sqrt{2}}\right)$$

$$= -n \prod_j H_{k_j}\left(\frac{\langle x, \xi_j \rangle}{\sqrt{2}}\right).$$

In view of the property (33), the operator $-\Delta$, which is familiar in quantum dynamics, is often called the *number operator*. Sometimes, Δ is called the (infinite-dimensional) *Ornstein–Uhlenbeck operator*, because it is the infinitesimal generator of the semigroup associated with the infinite-dimensional Ornstein–Uhlenbeck process. We also call Δ the infinite-dimensional *Laplace–Beltrami operator*, since it is viewed as an infinite-dimensional analogue of the spherical Laplacian operator.

So far, we have observed the operator Δ that is characterized by G_∞. There are several areas of study to which the group G_∞ contributes directly; for instance, to the ergodic property of the measure μ, irreducible unitary representations of G_∞ on the spaces $\mathcal{H}_n$, and others. In spite of the importance of G_∞ in white-noise analysis, G_∞ can occupy only (a small) part of the entire rotation group $O(E)$.

Remark The group G_∞ is not essentially changed when the basic nuclear space E is replaced by others, even where the time-parameter space $\mathbb{R}^1$ is changed to $\mathbb{R}^d$, i.e. the case where $E \subset L^2(\mathbb{R}^d)$.

4.2 The Lévy group

As in Section 4.1, we take a complete orthonormal system $\{\xi_n\}$ and fix it. Let π be a permutation of positive integers. Define a transformation g_π on E by

$$g_\pi \xi = \sum_n a_n \xi_{\pi(n)} \quad \text{for} \quad \xi = \sum_n a_n \xi_n.$$

Consider a collection

$$\mathscr{G} = \{g \in O(E); \quad g = g_\pi, \quad \forall \, \varepsilon > 0, \, \exists \, N(\varepsilon) \text{ such that} \\ \forall \, n > N(\varepsilon), \quad \mathscr{N}(i \leq n; \, \pi(i) > n) < \varepsilon n\},$$

where $\mathscr{N}(\dots)$ means the number of the element in the bracket. Obviously $\mathscr{G}$ forms a discrete group (see Lévy, 1951) and is called the *Lévy group*.

Let G be a continuous group, which is a subgroup of $O(E)$, generated by G_∞ and $\mathscr{G}$:

$$G = G_\infty \vee \mathscr{G}.$$

Then, G_∞ is an invariant subgroup of G. The factor group G/G_∞ has a very close connection with the Lévy Laplacian Δ_L acting on the space of generalized Brownian functionals. In a sense, Δ_L can be characterized by G/G_∞.

Remark Recently, Obata (1988) has proved the following interesting properties concerning the characterization of the Lévy group. Namely, the Lévy group $\mathscr{G}$ consists of all permutations of natural numbers such that each member preserves both the upper and the lower densities of any subsets of natural numbers. Furthermore, it coincides with the isotropy group for a certain functional on l^2. The maximal permutation group which commutes with the Lévy Laplacian Δ_L can be described in terms of a certain linear functional and it contains the Lévy group $\mathscr{G}$.

4.3 Whiskers

The definition of a whisker will be given later. Let us start with the *shift*, which will be seen to be the most important whisker. Let S_t, $t \in \mathbb{R}^1$, be an operator defined by

$$(S_t \xi)(u) = \xi(u - t). \tag{34}$$

With the usual choice of a nuclear space E, it is easily seen that S_t belongs to $O(E)$ and

$$S_t S_s = S_{t+s}, \tag{35}$$
$$S_t \to I, \text{ as } t \to 0,$$

hold. That is, $\{S_t; \, t \in \mathbb{R}^1\}$ is a continuous one-parameter subgroup of $O(E)$.

The adjoint of S_t will be denoted by T_t; $S_t^* = T_t$. Then $\{T_t; \, t \in \mathbb{R}^1\}$ again forms a one-parameter group, and by Theorem 3, the equality

$$T_t \mu = \mu$$

holds. Thus we have obtained a *flow* (one-parameter group of measure-preserving transformations) $\{T_t\}$ on (E^*, μ).

Definition The flow $\{T_t;\ t \in \mathbb{R}^1\}$ given above is called the *flow of Brownian motion*.

Theorem 5 The flow of Brownian motion is ergodic.
More precisely:

Theorem 6 The flow $\{T_t;\ t \in \mathbb{R}^1\}$ has σ-Lebesgue spectrum on the subspace $(L^2) \ominus \mathcal{H}_0 = \sum_{n=1}^{\infty} \oplus \mathcal{H}_n$.

What Theorem 6 means is the following. Define U_t by

$$(U_t\varphi)(x) = \varphi(T_t\, x). \tag{36}$$

Then $\{U_t;\ t \in \mathbb{R}^1\}$ is a continuous one-parameter unitary group acting on (L^2). Hence, Stone's theorem says that U_t admits a spectral representation of the form

$$U_t = \int e^{it\lambda} dE(\lambda), \tag{37}$$

where $\{E(\lambda);\ \lambda \in \mathbb{R}^1\}$ is a resolution of the identity I on (L^2), that is,

(i)   each $E(\lambda)$ is a projection operator,
(ii) $E(\lambda)E(\lambda') = E(\lambda \wedge \lambda')$, where $\wedge$ means the minimum,
(iii) $E(\lambda + 0) = E(\lambda)$,
(iv) $E(+\infty) = I,\ E(-\infty) = 0$.

We are now ready to speak of the spectral type $\{d\rho_n\}$ of a unitary group $\{U_t\}$ on a separable Hilbert space $\mathcal{H}$ with a spectral representation of the form (37). The Hellinger–Hahn theorem asserts that $\mathcal{H}$ is decomposed into at most a countable number of cyclic subspaces $\mathcal{H}_n$ (which means that there is an element f_n of $\mathcal{H}_n$ such that $\{U_t f_n;\ t \in \mathbb{R}^1\}$ spans the subspace $\mathcal{H}_n$):

$$\mathcal{H} = \sum_n \oplus \mathcal{H}_n$$

and U_t on $\mathcal{H}_n$ is isomorphic to the multiplication by $e^{i\lambda t}$ on $L^2(\mathbb{R}^1, d\rho_n)$, with $\rho_n(\lambda) = \|E(\lambda)f_n\|^2$; namely, there exists an isometry V from $\mathcal{H}_n$ onto $L^2(\mathbb{R}^1, d\rho_n)$ such that

$$(VU_t V^{-1}g)(\lambda) = e^{it\lambda}g(\lambda),\quad g \in L^2(\mathbb{R}^1, d\rho_n). \tag{38}$$

In addition, $\mathcal{H}_n$'s are chosen in such a way that the sequence $\{d\rho_n\}$ is non-increasing

$$d\rho_1 \gg d\rho_2 \ldots \gg d\rho_n \gg \ldots,$$

where $\gg$ means the right-side measure is absolutely continuous with respect to the left-side measure. With this restriction, the type of the sequence $\{d\rho_n\}$ gives a unitary equivalence. Let the support of the measure $d\rho_n$ be denoted by Λ_n. Obviously, Λ_n is decreasing; $m(\lambda) \equiv \max\{n; \lambda \in \Lambda_n\}$ is referred to as the *multiplicity* of λ.

Theorem 6 says that the space $\sum\limits_{1}^{\infty} \oplus \mathcal{H}_n$ is decomposed into countably many cyclic subspaces of the $\{U_t\}$ defined by (36) and that all the $d\rho_n$ are equivalent to the Lebesgue measure.

Proof of Theorem 6 First we note that the operator U_t on (L^2) commutes with the projection down to the subspace $\mathcal{H}_n$. Another remark is that the action of U_t on $\varphi(x)$ implies a transformation of the associated U-functional:

$$U(\xi) \rightarrow U(S_t\xi). \tag{39}$$

(i) We first restrict U_t to $\mathcal{H}_1$. Let φ be in $\mathcal{H}_1$ and let F be the kernel associated with φ. Then $U_t\varphi$ has the U-functional of the form

$$\int F(u)\xi(u - t)du$$

by (39). That is, $F(u)$ changes to $F(u + t)$.

With these relations in mind we now take φ in $\mathcal{H}_1$ such that the Fourier transform $\hat{F}(\lambda)$ of the kernel F never vanishes. Then the family $\{e^{it\lambda}\hat{F}(\lambda); t \in \mathbb{R}^1\}$ spans the entire space $L^2(\mathbb{R}^1)$; so does $\{F(u + t); t \in \mathbb{R}^1\}$. Hence $\mathcal{H}_1$ itself is a cyclic subspace, and $d\rho_1$ can be taken to be Lebesgue measure.

(ii) On $\mathcal{H}_2$ the action of U_t corresponds to a one-dimensional shift of the kernels:

$$F(u_1,u_2) \rightarrow F(u_1+t,u_2+t), \tag{40}$$

which also comes from (39). By change of variables

$$(u_1,u_2) \rightarrow (v_1,v_2), \quad v_1 = \frac{u_1 + u_2}{2}, \quad v_2 = \frac{u_1 - u_2}{2},$$

we have

$$F(u_1,u_2) = \widetilde{F}(v_1,v_2) \rightarrow \widetilde{F}(v_1+t,v_2).$$

The symmetric property of $F(u_1,u_2)$ in u_1 and u_2 turns into that of $\widetilde{F}(v_1,v_2)$ in v_2; i.e. $\widetilde{F}(v_1,-v_2) = \widetilde{F}(v_1,v_2)$. With this choice of variables we can see that the space $\widehat{L^2(\mathbb{R}^2)}$ has direct sum decomposition into cyclic subspaces of the form $\{F(u_1,u_2) = \widetilde{F}(v_1,v_2) = f(v_1)\xi_n(v_2); f \in L^2(\mathbb{R}^1)\}$,

$n = 1, 2, \ldots,$ where $\{\xi_n\}$ is an orthonormal system and each ξ_n generates a subspace of $L^2(\mathbb{R}^2)$ involving symmetric functions. The subspaces thus obtained are mutually orthogonal. Also, we can see that the transformation (40) (or (40′)) is reduced to the shift of $f(v_1)$ so that we are given the same situation as in (i). We therefore conclude that all the $d\rho_n$ are equivalent to the Lebesgue measure on $\mathbb{R}^1$ and the multiplicity is countably infinite. Such a case is simply called σ-*Lebesgue*.

(iii) For $\mathscr{H}_n$, $n \geqslant 3$, the trick used in (ii) can be applied with slight modification, and as a result, we can prove that the spectral type is σ-Lebesgue in this case also. Thus the theorem is proved.

Application, the Wiener expansion   As an application of Theorem 6, we can discuss the so-called Wiener expansion. Suppose we are given a black box which permits white-noise input. Then, observing the output, we wish to identify the given black box. The *basic ideas* are: (i) white noise carries enough information to analyse the black box: (ii) the black box in question can be expressed as a Brownian functional, indeed nonlinear functional of white noise; and (iii) the time development is taken into account when the input–output relation is observed; this means that the shift would be used in the analysis on each cyclic subspace where the well-known linear filtering theory can be applied.

Suppose that φ in (L^2) is a mathematical description of the unknown black box. Then φ is assumed to be non-anticipating and is expressible as

$$\varphi = \sum_{k=0}^{\infty} \varphi_k, \quad \varphi_k \in K_k, \quad \varphi_0 = E(\varphi) = \text{const.}, \tag{41}$$

according to the cyclic subspace expansion: $(L^2) \ominus \{1\} = \sum_{k=1}^{\infty} \oplus K_k$.

The $\{T_t\}$ has simple Lebesgue spectrum on each cyclic subspace K_k. Note that the output is expressed as $U_t\varphi$. The ergodic theorem tells us that

$$\varphi_0 = E(\varphi) = \lim_{T-S\to\infty} \frac{1}{T-S} \int_S^T U_t\varphi dt. \tag{42}$$

Now use the facts that

$$K_k \cong L^2(\mathbb{R}^1, \rho_k'(\lambda)d\lambda), \quad \rho_k'(\lambda) \neq 0, \text{ a.e.} \tag{43}$$

If, in particular, $\varphi \leftrightarrow f$ under the isomorphisms (43), then

$$U_t\varphi(x) \leftrightarrow e^{it\lambda}f(\lambda). \tag{44}$$

Here we remark that the black box never forecasts, i.e. is non-anticipating, which means that $\varphi(x)$ is a functional of $\langle x, \xi \rangle$'s with support of $\xi \subset (-\infty, 0]$. Let us take φ_k, $k \neq 0$, in (41), and compute the covariance function $\gamma(h)$:

$$\gamma(h) = \int U_{t+h}\varphi_k \cdot U_t\varphi_k \mathrm{d}\mu = \int U_h\varphi_k \cdot \varphi_k \mathrm{d}\mu$$

which is, again by the ergodic theorem, equal to

$$\lim_{T-S\to\infty} \frac{1}{T-S}\int_S^T (U_{t+h}\varphi_k \cdot U_t\varphi_k)\mathrm{d}h. \tag{45}$$

The correspondence (44) implies that

$$\gamma(h) = \int e^{ih\lambda}|f(\lambda)|^2\rho_k'(\lambda)\mathrm{d}\lambda.$$

Therefore, once the limit (45) is known for every h, the exact form of $|f(\lambda)|^2\rho_k'(\lambda)$ is known. Since $\rho_k'(\lambda)$ is a known function that never vanishes on $\mathbb{R}^1$, we know the function $|f(\lambda)|^2$. Also there is a well-known technique (in the theory of stationary stochastic processes) that tells us how to factorize $|f(\lambda)|^2$ (cf. the so-called Karhunen theory, or see Hida, 1980a), we know the function $f(\lambda)$. Namely we know φ_k. This shows how the recipe works.

We have known significant roles of the shift, which actually comes from the shift transformation of the time variable. The most important remark made now is that the shift describes the propagation of the time so that it plays a dominant role when we discuss actual phenomena that change as time goes by.

The next step is to look for a new one-parameter subgroup of $O(E)$ which also comes from a transformation group of the time variable and which must have a good probabilistic meaning. A well-known example of such a group is the *dilation* $\{\tau_t\}$, sometimes called the tension. It is given by

$$(\tau_t\xi)(u) = \xi(e^tu)e^{t/2}, \quad t \in \mathbb{R}^1. \tag{46}$$

Obviously $\{\tau_t\}$ is a one-parameter subgroup of $O(E)$. In addition it has a nice relationship with the shift $\{S_t\}$. In fact, $\{S_t\}$ is transversal to $\{\tau_t\}$:

$$S_t\tau_t = \tau_s S_{t\exp[s]}. \tag{47}$$

A probabilistic role may be illustrated in such a way that a Gaussian process $\{U_t\}$ given by

$$U_t \equiv U(t,x) = \langle \tau_t^*x, \chi_{[0,1]} \rangle, \quad t \in \mathbb{R}^1 \tag{48}$$

is an Ornstein–Uhlenbeck Brownian motion with covariance function $\gamma(h) = \exp[-\frac{1}{2}|h|]$.

We are now in a position to discover, systematically, other one-parameter subgroups of $O(E)$ which are also defined by change of time variable. For this purpose we have to specify the basic nuclear space E.

Let $\overline{\mathbb{R}^1}$ be a one-point compactification of $\mathbb{R}^1$ isomorphic to the circle S^1. Set

$$D_0 = \left\{ \xi \in C^\infty; \xi\left(\frac{1}{u}\right)\frac{1}{|u|} \in C^\infty \right\}.$$

It is a nuclear space isomorphic to $C^\infty(S^1)$ and to $C^\infty(\overline{\mathbb{R}^1})$.

Definition   A one-parameter subgroup $\{g_t, t \in \mathbb{R}^1\}$ of $O(D_0)$ is called a *whisker* if

(i) each g_t is expressed in the form

$$(g_t\xi)(u) = \xi(\psi_t(u))\sqrt{|\psi'_t(u)|},$$

where $\psi_t(u)$ is a diffeomorphism of $\overline{\mathbb{R}^1}$ for every t;

(ii) $g_t g_s = g_{t+s}$;

(iii) g_t is continuous in t.

As is easily seen, the shift and the dilation are examples of a whisker.

The requirement (ii) above is equivalent to $\psi_t(\psi_s(u)) = \psi_{t+s}(u)$, which is a translation equation. We therefore see that $\psi_t(u)$ is in general expressed in the form

$$\psi_t(u) = f\{f^{-1}(u) + t\}, \tag{49}$$

where f is a diffeomorphism of $\overline{\mathbb{R}^1}$. Thus the infinitesimal generator $\alpha = \left.\dfrac{d}{dt} g_t\right|_{t=0}$ can be expressed in the form

$$\alpha = a(u)\frac{d}{du} + \frac{1}{2} a'(u) \tag{50}$$

where $a(u) = f'[f^{-1}(u)]$.

With this expression of a generator α of $\{g_t\}$ one can discuss commutation relations among whiskers in terms of generators. Explicit forms of generators of the shift and the dilation are given below

$$s \equiv \left.\frac{d}{dt} S_t\right|_{t=0} = -\frac{d}{du}, \tag{51}$$

$$\tau \equiv \left.\frac{d}{dt} \tau_t\right|_{t=0} = u\frac{d}{du} + \frac{1}{2}, \tag{52}$$

respectively. The relations of these with another whisker with the generator α are expressed by

$$[\alpha, s] = a'(u)\frac{d}{du} + \frac{1}{2}a''(u),$$

$$[\alpha, \tau] = (a(u) - ua'(u))\frac{d}{du} - \frac{1}{2}ua''(u).$$

Observing these commutation relations, and noting the expressions (51) and (52), it is suggested that we introduce a third generator expressed in the form

$$\kappa = u^2 \frac{d}{du} + u. \tag{53}$$

This is the generator of the one-parameter group $\{k_t; t \in \mathbb{R}^1\}$ given by

$$\kappa_t : \xi(u) \rightarrow \xi\left(\frac{u}{-tu+1}\right)\frac{1}{|-tu+1|}, \quad t \in \mathbb{R}^1. \tag{54}$$

A member of the whisker $\{\kappa_t\}$ is called a *special conformal transformation*.

Let us recall our choice of the basic nuclear space E to be D_0. With this choice it can be proved that $\{\kappa_t; t \in \mathbb{R}^1\}$ is a one-parameter subgroup of $O(D_0)$ although the transformation

$$u \rightarrow \frac{u}{-tu+1}$$

has singularity at $u = -1/t$.

Having established three whiskers and their generators, we now come to the commutation relations in question. They are given by

$$\left.\begin{array}{l} [\tau, s] = -s, \\ [\tau, \kappa] = \kappa, \\ [s, \kappa] = -2\tau. \end{array}\right\} \tag{55}$$

We can therefore see that the three one-parameter subgroups $\{S_t\}$, $\{\tau_t\}$ and $\{\kappa_t\}$ generate a three-dimensional subgroup, denote it by G_p, of $Q(D_0)$, and that G_p is isomorphic to the Lie group $PGL\ (2,\mathbb{R})$.

Now one may ask what is the probabilistic role of the group G_p. Before answering this question, let us briefly mention the projective invariance of Brownian motion. Suppose we are given a 'Brownian bridge'. To fix the idea, we consider the unit time interval $[0,1]$. The Brownian bridge on the time interval $[0,1]$ is a modification of a Brownian motion such that starting from the origin as the ordinary Brownian motion it returns to the origin at instant 1. Such a process is realized, for instance, by

$$X(t) = B(t) - tB(1), \quad 0 \le t \le 1.$$

Let us normalize it:

$$Y(t) = \frac{X(t)}{\sigma(t)}, \quad \sigma(t) = V[E(X(t)^2)], \quad t \in (0,1).$$

Lévy (1948) claimed that, if $p(t)$ is a projective transformation carrying the interval $(0,1)$ onto itself, then the two processes

$$\{Y(t); 0<t<1\} \quad \text{and} \quad \{Y(P^{-1}(t)); 0<t<1\}$$

are the same Gaussian process. The proof is easy since the covariance
function of $Y(t)$ is expressed in the form

$$E(Y(t)Y(s)) = \left\{\frac{1-t}{1-s}\Big/\frac{s}{t}\right\}^{1/2}, \quad 0 < s < t < 1,$$

namely, it is the square root of the anharmonic ratio of the four numbers
$(0,s,t,1)$, so that $Y(p^{-1}(t))$ should have the same covariance function.

   We now note that the projective transformation p induces a member g_p
of G_p:

$$g_p\colon \xi(u) \to \xi(p(u))\sqrt{|p'(u)|}.$$

Take an $L^2(\mathbb{R}^1)$-function $f(\cdot\,; t)$:

$$f(u; t) = \sqrt{\frac{1-t}{t}}\, \chi_{[0,t]}(u)\, \frac{1}{1-u}.$$

Then we see that $\{\langle x, f(\cdot\,; t)\rangle;\ t \in (0,1)\}$ and $\{\langle x, f(\cdot\,; p^{-1}(t))\rangle;\ t \in (0,1)\}$ are realizations in $\mathscr{H}_1$ of the Gaussian processes $\{Y(t);\ t \in (0,1)\}$ and $\{Y(p^{-1}(t));\ t \in (0,1)\}$, respectively, since $f(u,t)$ satisfies the relation

$$g_p f(u; t) = f(u; p^{-1}(t)).$$

Therefore the above two processes should be the same process because
we have

$$\langle x, f(\cdot\,; p^{-1}(H)\rangle = \langle x, g_p f(\cdot\,; t)\rangle$$
$$= \langle g_p^* x, f(\cdot\,; t)\rangle.$$

Now we have given an interpretation to the projective invariance of
Brownian motion in terms of the infinite-dimensional rotation group (see
Hida *et al.*, 1968; Hida, 1980a).

5   Generalized Brownian functionals

5.1   Extension of $\mathscr{H}_n$

Let us remind ourselves that we have preferred to take white noise $\{\dot{B}(t)\}$
to be the system of variables of Brownian functionals. Once the variables are given, the most basic class of functions has to be the set of
polynomials in those variables, i.e. in $\dot{B}(t)$'s in the present case. Unfortunately, those polynomials cannot be ordinary (L^2)-functionals.

   Take, for instance, $\dot{B}(t)^2$. The approximation to it may be taken to be
$(\Delta B/\Delta)^2$, where $B(t)$ is realized as $\langle x, \chi_{[0,t]}\rangle$. The U-functional associated
with $(\Delta B/\Delta)^2$ is $1/\Delta^2 \int\int \chi_\Delta(u,v)\xi(u)\xi(v)dudv + 1/\Delta$. While the Hermite
polynomial $\varphi_\Delta = (\Delta B/\Delta)^2 - 1/\Delta$ gives us

$$U_\Delta(\xi) = \frac{1}{\Delta^2} \int \int \chi_{\Delta^2}(u,v) \xi(u) \xi(v) \, du \, dv.$$

Let $\Delta \to \{t\}$; then

$$U_\Delta(\xi) \to \xi(t)^2.$$

With this simple observation, we can think of a generalized Brownian functional which is viewed as a 'limit' of φ_Δ as $\Delta \to \{t\}$, since $\xi(t)^2$ can be associated as its *U*-functional.

A generalization of this trick is to take a Hermite polynomial in $\dot{B}(t)$ instead of a power of $\dot{B}(t)$. For example, $\dot{B}(t)^n$ should be modified to be

$$n! H_n(\dot{B}(t); 1/dt) \tag{56}$$

with which $\xi(t)^n$ is associated as *U*-functional. Such a modification is called *additive renormalization*.

Remark Hermite polynomial with parameter σ^2 is defined by

$$H_n(x; \sigma^2) = \frac{(-\sigma^2)^n}{n!} \exp(x^2/2\sigma^2) \frac{d^n}{dx^n} \exp(-x^2/2\sigma^2).$$

Note that the kernel function of $U(\xi) = \xi(t)^n$ is $\delta(u_1 - t)\delta(u_2 - t)$ $\ldots \delta(u_n - t)$ (*n*-times tensor product of δ-function). With this important example one can proceed to introduce a class $\mathcal{H}_n^{(-n)}$, which is an extension of $\mathcal{H}_n$, involving Hermite polynomials in $\dot{B}(t)$'s of degree n.

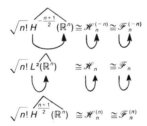

Fig. 6.2 Definition of space of generalized Brownian functionals

Figure 6.2 tells us how to define the space $\mathcal{H}_n^{(-n)}$. Note that $\widehat{H^p}(\mathbb{R}^n)$ $= H^p(\mathbb{R}^n) \cap \widehat{L}^2(\mathbb{R}^n)$, where $H^p(\mathbb{R}^n)$ is the Sobolev space of order p and $\widehat{H^{-p}}(\mathbb{R}^n)$ is the dual space of $\widehat{H^p}(\mathbb{R}^n)$. The symbol $\mathcal{F}_n$ stands for the collection of *U*-functionals associated with the members in $\mathcal{H}_n$, and $\mathcal{F}_n$ is topologized so as to be isomorphic to $\mathcal{H}_n$. Other symbols are to be understood in an obvious way.

A member in $\mathcal{H}_n^{(-n)}$ is called a *generalized Brownian functional of degree n*.

5.2 Finite-dimensional analogue

On extending the space (L^2) we have freedom to form a direct sum of the $\mathcal{H}_n^{(-n)}$'s. One may think of a trick in the finite-dimensional case, in particular the case of S^1. An $L^2(S^1)$-function has Fourier series expansion, where coefficients are square-summable. While those of a generalized function may be slowly increasing. This motivates the following.
Set

$$(L^2)_{\{C_n\}}^+ = \left\{ \psi = \sum_n \psi_n;\ \psi_n \in \mathcal{H}_n^{(n)},\ \sum_n C_n^{-2}\|\psi_n\|_n^2 < \infty \right\},$$

$$\|\ \ \|_n : \mathcal{H}_n^{(n)}\text{-norm},$$

where C_n (>0) is decreasing monotonically. The space $(L^2)_{\{C_n\}}^+$ is a Hilbert space with the norm $\|\psi\| = (\sum C_n^{-2}\|\psi_n\|_n^2)^{1/2}$ and it is taken to be a space of test functionals. Define $(L^2)_{\{C_n\}}^-$ by

$$(L^2)_{\{C_n\}}^- = \text{the dual space of } (L^2)_{\{C_n\}}^+.$$

The bilinear form connecting $(L^2)_{\{C_n\}}^+$ and $(L^2)_{\{C_n\}}^-$ will be denoted by an angle bracket $\langle\ ,\ \rangle$.

Definition A member of $(L^2)_{\{C_n\}}^-$ is called a *generalized Brownian functional*.

Notation To denote the space $(L^2)_{\{C_n\}}^-$ we often use the notation

$$\sum_{n=0}^{\infty} \oplus\ C_n \mathcal{H}_n^{(-n)}. \tag{57}$$

If $\{C_n\}$ is not necessarily specified, we omit $\{C_n\}$ and simply write $(L_2)^-$.

Example 1 A delta function of Brownian motion. Set

$$\varphi(x) = \delta_0(B(t) - y),\quad y \in \mathbb{R}^1, \tag{58}$$

where $B(t)$ is realized by $\langle x, \chi_{[0,t]}\rangle$. Use the fact that the Fourier transform of the delta function is a constant function $(2\pi)^{-1/2}$ to obtain

$$\varphi(x) = \frac{1}{2\pi}\int \exp[-i\lambda(B(t) - y)]d\lambda.$$

Then, the $\mathcal{T}$-transform is applied. It is easy to see that

$$(\mathcal{T}\varphi)(\xi) = C(\xi)g(t;\ y)\exp\left[\frac{iy}{t}\int_0^t \xi(u)du + \frac{1}{2t}\left(\int_0^t \xi(u)du\right)^2\right], \tag{59}$$

where $g(t;\ y) = \frac{1}{\sqrt{2\pi t}}\exp\left[-\frac{1}{2t}y^2\right]$. The kernel of the $\mathcal{H}_n$-component is given by

$$g(t;\ y) \cdot \frac{H_n(y/\sqrt{2t})}{n!(2t)^{n/2}} \chi_{[0,t]^n}.$$

It can therefore be proved that $\varphi(x)$ given by (58) is a member of $(L^2)^-_{\{1/n\}}$ but not in (L^2).

Example 2   Exponential function of $\alpha \dot{B}(t)$, $\alpha \in \mathbb{R}^1$. It should be modified in such a way that

$$:e^{\alpha \dot{B}(t)}: = e^{\alpha \dot{B}(t) - \alpha^2/2dt}. \tag{60}$$

In fact, the associated U-functional is $\exp[\alpha \xi(t)]$. The expression above is obtained by taking *multiplicative renormalization* by the amount $\exp[-\alpha^2/2dt]$, which is an agreement with the additive renormalization if we observe the Taylor series expansion:

$$:e^{\alpha \dot{B}(t)}: = \sum_n \frac{\alpha^n}{n!} : \dot{B}(t)^n : .$$

Example 3   The following generalized functional is viewed as an infinite-dimensional analogue of the Gauss kernel of $\mathbb{R}^n$.

$$\varphi = :\exp\left[c \int_0^t \dot{B}(u)^2 du\right]: \quad \text{Re } c' < \frac{1}{2}.$$

The necessary renormalization is the multiplicative one. The associated U-functional is of the form

$$U(\xi) = \exp\left[c' \int_0^t \xi(u)^2 du\right], \quad c' = \frac{c}{1 - 2c}.$$

The proof of this result immediately comes from the computations of Section 3.4 and the remark that follows.

6   Causal calculus

The causal calculus means the calculus of Brownian functionals where the time development is always taken into account explicitly and is expressed in terms of the $\dot{B}(t)$.

Once again let us remember that $\{\dot{B}(t)\}$ has been taken to be the system of variables of (generalized) Brownian functionals. It is therefore quite reasonable to think of a partial differential operator such as $\partial/\partial \dot{B}(t)$. In order to make concrete such an operator we shall use U-functionals and their functional derivatives. Variation of φ in $\dot{B}(t)$ can be rephrased by the variation of U in $\xi(t)$. This suggests to us to use the Fréchet derivative of U as a counterpart of the derivative of φ, where formal expressions of the derivatives of φ turn into concrete formulae in functional analysis.

Definition   Let $U(\xi)$ be the U-functional associated with φ. Then, φ is $\dot{B}(t)$-differentiable if and only if U is Fréchet differentiable and the derivative $\partial U(\xi)/\partial \xi(t)$ is a U-functional of some $(L^2)^-$-functional, call it φ_t'. In this case we denote

$$\varphi_t' \equiv \frac{\partial}{\partial \dot{B}(t)}\varphi \equiv \partial_t\varphi.$$

Example 1   For $\varphi = \int f(u):\dot{B}(u)^2: du$, f being bounded continuous, we have $U(\xi) = \int f(u)\xi(u)^2 du$. Then

$$\frac{\delta U(\xi)}{\delta \xi(t)} = 2f(t)\xi(t), \tag{61}$$

which is to be a U-functional associated with $2f(t)\dot{B}(t)$. Hence

$$\partial_t\varphi = 2f(t)\dot{B}(t). \tag{62}$$

Following Kubo and Takenaka (1980–2), introduce the adjoint operator ∂_t^* of the ∂_t by using $\langle\,,\,\rangle$ connecting $(L^2)^+$ and $(L^2)^-$:

$$\langle \partial_t\varphi, \psi \rangle = \langle \varphi, \partial_t^*\psi \rangle.$$

Theorem 7   (i) The operator ∂_t is an annihilation operator:

$$\partial_t: \mathcal{H}_n^{(n)} \to \mathcal{H}_{n-1}^{(n-1)}$$

and ∂_t^* is a creation operator:

$$\partial_t^*: \mathcal{H}_n^{(-n)} \to \mathcal{H}_{n+1}^{(-n-1)}.$$

∂_t is weakly continuous on $\mathcal{H}_n^{(n)}$, while ∂_t^* is strongly continuous on $\mathcal{H}_n^{(-n)}$.

(ii) The canonical commutation relations hold:

$$[\partial_t, \partial_s^*] = \delta_s(t)I,$$
$$[\partial_t, \partial_s] = [\partial_t^*, \partial_s^*] = 0.$$

(iii) Multiplication by $\dot{B}(t)$ is expressible as

$$\dot{B}(t) \cdot = \partial_t^* + \partial_t.$$

Remark   A conventional notation $\delta_t(t) = 1/dt$ is often used in the actual calculation. To prove the theorem, the following lemma is useful.

Lemma   For $\mathcal{T}$ in $\mathcal{H}_n^{(-n)}$ with kernel $F(u_1, \ldots, u_n) \in \widehat{\mathcal{H}^{-(n+1)/2}}\,(\mathbb{R}^n)$ we have kernels

$$n(\delta_{t^*}F)(u_1,u_2,\ldots,u_{n-1}) \quad \text{for } \partial_t\varphi, \tag{63}$$
$$\delta_t \hat{\otimes} F(u_1,u_2,\ldots,u_{n+1}) \quad \text{for } \partial_t^*\varphi,$$

provided, for $\partial_t\varphi$, the convolution $\delta_{t^*}F$ of $\delta_t(u_n)$ and $F(u_1,\ldots,u_n)$ is well-defined.

The proof of the lemma comes from direct computations of the Fréchet derivative.

Theorem 8 Let φ and f be an $(L^2)^-_{\{C_n\}}$-functional and an $L^2(\mathbb{R}^1)$-function, respectively. Assume that $C_{n+1}^2 \leqslant C_n^2/(n+1)$. Then the integral

$$\Phi = \int f(u)\partial_u^*\varphi du \tag{64}$$

is well-defined, and the Φ belongs to $(L^2)^-_{\{C_n\}}$.

If, in particular, φ is in $\mathcal{H}_n^{(-n)}$ with kernel $F(u_1,\ldots,u_n)$ then Φ given by (64) is a member of $\mathcal{H}_{n+1}^{(-n-1)}$ with kernel $f \hat{\otimes} F$.

An important remark follows.

Remark The integral (64) may be written as

$$\int \partial_u^*(f(u)\varphi)du$$

and, even further, $f(u)\varphi$ may be replaced by φ_u. If φ_u is an ordinary Brownian functional and if it is non-anticipating, i.e. φ_u is a functional of $\dot{B}(s)$, $s \leqslant u$, then the integral $\int \partial_u^*\varphi_u du$ is in agreement with the Itô-type stochastic integral. The advantage of the stochastic integral of the form (64) is that the integrand is not necessarily non-anticipating.

With this remark we can now say that the causal calculus, using the differential operators ∂_t's and the stochastic integrals, can be carried out like ordinary differential and integral calculus on $\mathbb{R}^n$.

Example 2 Let f be a polynomial of the form $f(x) = \sum_1^N a_k x^k$. A problem in biology gave us the equation

$$\frac{d}{dt}X(t) = -\lambda X(t) + f(\dot{B}(t))(bX(t) + c), \quad \lambda > 0,$$

which has only formal significance since multiplication by $f(\dot{B})$ is involved. We may understand it as

$$\frac{d}{dt}X(t) = -\lambda X(t) + f(\partial_t^*)(bX(t) + c). \tag{65}$$

This equation can be dealt with within the space $(L^2)^-$. In fact, (65) is rephrased in terms of U-functional as in Section 3.1; namely, we have

$$\frac{d}{dt} U_t(\xi) = -\lambda U_t(\xi) + f(\xi(t)) (bU_t(\xi) + c).$$ (66)

The solution is

$$U_t(\xi) = c \, \exp\left[-\lambda t + b \int^t f(\xi(u)) du\right] \int^t f(\xi(u)) \, \exp\left[\lambda u - b \int^u f(\xi(v)) dv\right] du,$$

and for $X(t)$ itself we obtain

$$X(t) = \sum_1^\infty \frac{cb^{n-1}}{n!} e^{-\lambda t} \int^t \cdots \int^t \exp\left[\lambda \min_{1 \le j \le n} u_j\right] M_f(du_1) \dots M_f(du_n),$$ (67)

where $M_f(du) = \sum_1^N a_k : \dot{B}(u)^k : du$. The integral in (67) can be defined as the traditional stochastic integral with respect to $dB(u)$. We may use the operators ∂_u^*'s in such a way that

$$M_f(du) = \sum_1^N a_k (\partial_u^*)^{k_1} du$$

to carry out the integration in (67).

An equation involving the $\frac{d}{dt}$, ∂_t, ∂_t^*, like equation (65), is called a *stochastic functional differential equation.*

Example 3 The delta function $\varphi_t = \delta_0(B(t) - y)$ established in Example 1 in Section 5 has the U-functional of the form

$$U_t(\xi) = g(t; y) \exp\left[\frac{y}{t} \int_0^t \xi(u) du - \frac{1}{2t} \left(\int_0^t \xi(u) du\right)^2\right].$$

(Note the difference from $(\mathcal{T}\varphi_t)(\xi)$.) It satisfies

$$\frac{\delta U_t(\xi)}{\delta \xi(s)} = \begin{cases} \frac{1}{t}\left(y - \int_0^t \xi(u) du\right) U_t(\xi), & s < t. \\ 0 & , & s > t. \end{cases}$$

This means that φ_t satisfies the following stochastic functional differential equation:

$$\partial_s \varphi_t = \begin{cases} \frac{1}{t}\left(y - \int_0^t \partial_u^* \, du\right)\varphi_t, & s < t. \\ 0 & , & s > t. \end{cases}$$ (68)

with an additional requirement:

$$\langle \varphi_t, 1 \rangle = g(t; y). \tag{69}$$

Conversely, we can prove that (68) and (69) should characterize the delta function φ_t.

Remark We now observe that φ_t defines the local time of Brownian motion. Intuitively, this fact is quite reasonable. We are, in fact, able to give a correct interpretation. Kubo (1983) has proved that, even in the case where a function $F(x)$ has the second derivative $F''(x)$ only as a generalized function, we can still establish a formula

$$F(B(t)) - F(B(s)) = \int_s^t F'(B(u))dB(u) + \frac{1}{2}\int_s^t F''(B(u))du, \quad t > s,$$

which is viewed as a generalization of the Itô formula, by regarding $F''(B(u))$ as a generalized Brownian functional. Now take $F(u)$ to be $|u - y|$. Then we have

$$|B(t) - y| - |B(s) - y| - \int_s^t \text{sign } (B(u) - y)dB(u)$$

$$= \frac{1}{2}\int_s^t 2\delta_0(B(u) - y)du \left(= \int_s^t \varphi_u du \right).$$

The left-hand side is the known formula for the local time of a Brownian motion.

Example 4 Again consider a Gauss kernel

$$\varphi = : \exp\left[-\frac{1}{2}\int_T \dot{B}(u)^2 du \right]:, \quad T: \text{ finite interval.}$$

Then

$$U(\xi) = \exp\left[-\frac{1}{4}\int_T \xi(u)^2 du \right],$$

and hence

$$\frac{\delta U(\xi)}{\nu\xi(t)} = -\frac{1}{2}\xi(t)U(\xi), \quad t \in T, \tag{70}$$

which means

$$2\partial_t \varphi = -\partial_t^* \varphi, \quad t \in T,$$

or equivalently

$$\partial_t \varphi = -\dot{B}(t)\varphi, \quad t \in T, \tag{71}$$

(remembering that $\dot{B}(t) \cdot = \partial_t^* + \partial_t$).

With an additional condition

$$\langle \varphi, 1 \rangle = 1 \tag{72}$$

the stochastic functional differential equation (71) determines the Gauss kernel.

We then proceed to second-order differential operators, in particular Lévy's Laplacian Δ_L operator (Lévy, 1951).

The following expression of Lévy's Laplacian Δ_L is due to H.-H. Kuo (private communication):

$$\Delta_L \varphi = \int \partial_t^2 \varphi (dt)^2, \quad \varphi \in (L^2)^-. \tag{73}$$

Originally, the Δ_L was given by Lévy (1951) for functionals on the Hilbert space $L^2[0,1]$. Let $L^2[0,1]$ be replaced by E to fit our analysis. Denote the Fréchet derivative $\delta U(\xi)/\delta\xi(t)$ by $U'_\xi(t)$. If its variation is expressible as

$$\delta U'_\xi(t) = U''_{\xi^2}(t)\delta\xi(t) + \int U''_{\xi\eta}(t,s)\delta\xi(s)ds$$

then Lévy's definition of the Laplacian Δ_L has to be

$$\Delta_L U = \int U''_{\xi^2}(t)dt. \tag{74}$$

If the use of generalized functions is permitted for the expression of $\delta U'_\xi(t)$ in the integral form such as

$$\delta U'_\xi(t) = \int [U''_{\xi^2}(s)\delta_0(s - t) + U''_{\xi\eta}(t,s)]\delta\xi(s)ds, \tag{75}$$

then the second-order Fréchet derivative may formally be expressed as the inner product of [ ] in (75) and $\delta(s - t)$, where s is the variable and t is fixed. We may write $\langle \delta(\cdot - t), \delta(\cdot - t)\rangle = 1/dt$, so that we have the second-order Fréchet derivative

$$-\frac{\delta U'_\xi(t)}{\delta\xi(t)} = U''_{\xi^2}(t)\frac{1}{dt} + U''_{\xi\eta}(t,t)$$

which corresponds to $\partial_t^2 \varphi$. Thus the formula (73) is acceptable to us, as was suggested by (74).

Example 5 For $\varphi = \int f(u) : \dot{B}(u)^2 : du$ in Example 1, we have

$$\partial_t \varphi = 2f(t)\dot{B}(t),$$

$$\partial_t^2 \varphi = 2f(t)\frac{1}{dt}.$$

Hence

$$\Delta_L \varphi = 2 \int f(t) dt \quad (\text{trace!}),$$

where f is tacitly assumed to be integrable.

Example 6 Let φ be a Gauss kernel:

$$\varphi = \; : \exp\left[c \int_0^T \dot{B}(u)^2 du \right] :$$

Then,

$$\Delta_L \varphi = 2c' T \varphi, \quad c' = \frac{c}{1 - 2c}.$$

In order to speak of the domain $\mathscr{D}(\Delta_L)$ of Lévy's Laplacian, we introduce a class of normal functionals following Lévy's idea.

A generalized Brownian functional φ in $\mathscr{H}_n^{(-n)}$ is called a *normal functional* of degree n if the associated U-functional is of the form

$$U(\xi) = \int \cdots \int F(u_1, \ldots, u_p) \xi(u_1)^{n_1} \ldots \xi(u_p)^{n_p} du_1 \ldots du_p, \; \Sigma n_j = n,$$

(76)

where F is an ordinary integrable function. Set

$$\aleph_n = \{\varphi: \text{normal and of degree } n\},$$

and set

$$\aleph = \sum_n \aleph_n \subset (L^2)^-.$$

The domain of Δ_L is now taken to be

$$\mathscr{D}(\Delta_L) = \{\varphi = \Sigma\varphi_n; \; \varphi_n \in \aleph_n, \; \Sigma\Delta_L\varphi_n \text{ converges in } (L^2)^-\} \subset \aleph.$$

Remark 1 For further discussion on the Lévy Laplacian Hida and Saito (1988).

Remark 2 Heuristically, Δ_L on $L^2[0,1]$ was given in such a way that for a suitable choice of a complete orthonormal system $\{\xi_n\}$, Δ_L is given by the following operator $\widetilde{\Delta}_L$:

$$\widetilde{\Delta}_L = \lim_{N\to\infty} \frac{1}{N} \sum_{n=1}^N \frac{\partial^2}{\partial\xi_n^2}.$$

Let us restrict our attention to the unit time interval $[0,1]$ and deal with normal functionals of the form

$$U(\xi) = \int_0^1 \cdots \int_0^1 F(u_1, \ldots, u_p) \xi(u_1)^{n_1} \ldots \xi(u_p)^{n_p} du_1 \ldots du_p.$$

And let $\{\xi_n\}$ be a complete orthonormal system in $L^2[0,1]$ which is equally dense in the sense of Lévy (1951, Part III); that is,

$$\lim_{N\to\infty} \frac{1}{N} \sum_{n=1}^{N} \xi_n(u)^2 \to 1 \quad \text{in} \quad L^1[0,1].$$

Then, the operator $\widetilde{\Delta}_L$ is in agreement with the expression (73). Indeed if $\xi = \Sigma a_j \xi_j$ then $U(\xi)$ can be thought of as a function of $(a_1, a_2, \dots)$: $U(\xi) \equiv U(a_1, a_2, \dots)$. Hence

$$\frac{\partial}{\partial \xi_j} U(\xi) \equiv \frac{\partial}{\partial a_j} U(a_1, a_2, \dots)$$

($\equiv$ means 'may be identified with'). Therefore, if $\widetilde{\Delta}_L$ is applied to the above functional $U(\xi)$ with F continuous, then we have

$$\widetilde{\Delta}_L U(\xi) \equiv \lim_n \frac{1}{n} \sum_{j=1}^{n} \frac{\partial^2}{\partial a_j^2} U(a_1, a_2, \dots)$$

$$= \sum_k n_k(n_k - 1) \int_0^1 \dots \int_0^1 F(u_1, \dots, u_k, \dots, u_p) \xi(u_1)^{n_1} \dots$$

$$\times \lim_{N\to\infty} \sum_{n=1}^{N} \xi_n(u_k)^2 \left(\Sigma a_j \xi_j(u_k) \right)^{n_k - 2} \dots \xi(u_p)^{n_p} du_1 \dots du_k \dots du_p$$

$$= \sum_k n_k(n_k - 1) \int_0^1 \dots \int_0^1 F(u_1, \dots, u_k, \dots, u_p) \xi(u_1)^{n_1} \dots$$

$$\times \xi(u_k)^{n_k - 2} \dots \xi(u_p)^{n_p} du_1, \dots du_k \dots du_p.$$

This result demonstrates our assertion. Incidentally, we note that the operator $\widetilde{\Delta}_L$ commutes with the operators V_g acting on the U-functional defined by

$$V_g U(\xi) \equiv U(g\xi), \quad g \in G,$$

where G is the group generated by the Lévy group and finite-dimensional rorations (see Section 4.2).

Remark 3 By using the operators ∂_t and ∂_t^* we can rephrase the number operator Δ given by (32):

$$\Delta = \int \partial_t^* \partial_t \, dt. \tag{32'}$$

With this expression, Δ becomes an operator acting on (L^2). Its domain $\mathscr{D}(\Delta)$ is now defined to be wide enough. We may take it so as to include all the normal functionals. If φ is a normal functional and is in $\mathscr{H}_n^{(-n)}$, then we still have equation (33):

$$\Delta \varphi = -n\varphi.$$

7 Multi-dimensional parameter case

Many topics can be discussed in parallel to those of the case of one-dimensional parameter. A crucial difference will, however, be seen when we come to the whiskers of the rotation group.

Take the basic nuclear space E to be

$$D_0(\mathbb{R}^d) = \{\xi \in C^\infty(\mathbb{R}^d); \ \xi\left(\frac{u}{|u|^2}\right)|u|^{-d} \in C^\infty(\mathbb{R}^d)\}.$$

Then we are given

(i) the measure μ of white noise on E^* with the characteristic functional

$$C(\xi) = \exp\left[-\tfrac{1}{2}\|\xi\|^2\right], \ \| \ \| \text{ the } L^2(\mathbb{R}^d)\text{-norm},$$

(ii) the rotation group $O(E)$.

In what follows we shall mention only significant differences from the results in the earlier sections on the one-dimensional parameter case.

7.1 Generalized functionals

To define the space $\mathscr{H}_n^{(-n)}$ we use again the Sobolev space $\overparen{H^{-(dn+1)/2}(\mathbb{R}^{dn})}$ where $\wedge$ means symmetric in n d-dimensional variables. The space $(L^2)^-_{\{C_n\}}$ is defined in exactly the same manner as in the case $d = 1$.

7.2 Rotation group

Finite-dimensional subgroups are also similar to the case of $d = 1$, so there are no more interesting facts. But whiskers are different, and indeed subgroups of $O(E)$ involving them have more complicated and naturally more interesting structure.

A whisker is, as in Section. 4.3, a one-parameter subgroup $\{g_t\}$ of $O(E)$ expressible as

$$(g_t\xi)(u) = \xi(\psi_t(u))\left|\frac{\partial}{\partial u}\psi_t(u)\right|^{1/2}, \quad u \in \mathbb{R}^d, \tag{77}$$

where

$$\frac{\partial}{\partial u}\psi_t = \left(\frac{\partial \psi_t^i}{\partial u_j}\right)^n_{i,j=1}, \quad \psi_t = (\psi_t^1, \dots, \psi_t^d).$$

The group property requires

$$\psi_t(\psi_s(u)) = \psi_{t+s}(u),$$

which implies

$$\psi_t(u) = f^{-1}(f(u) + tc), \quad c \in \mathbb{R}^d,$$

with a diffeomorphism f of $\overline{\mathbb{R}^d}$. The infinitesimal generator α of the g_t is expressed in the form

$$\alpha = (a, \nabla) + \tfrac{1}{2}(\nabla, a) \tag{78}$$

where $a = a(u)$ is a vector-valued function $c'(\partial f^{-1}/\partial u)$ evaluated at a vector $f(u)$.

Starting from the shifts $\{S_t^j; t \in \mathbb{R}^1\}, j = 1, 2, \ldots, d,$

$$(S_t^j \xi)(u_1, \ldots, u_d) = \xi(u_1, \ldots, u_j - t, \ldots, u_d) \tag{79}$$

we shall be in search of other whiskers which have good relations with each other. Thus the following whiskers are obtained (see Hida *et al.*, 1985):

(i) isotropic dilation τ_t:

$$(\tau_t \xi)(u) = \xi(e^t u)e^{td/2}, \quad t \in \mathbb{R}^1; \tag{80}$$

(ii) rotations on $\mathbb{R}^d$, whose generators are

$$\gamma_{i,j} = u_j \frac{\partial}{\partial u_k} - u_k \frac{\partial}{\partial u_j}, \quad j \neq k; \tag{81}$$

(iii) special conformal transformations $\{\kappa_t^j; t \in \mathbb{R}^1\}, j = 1, 2, \ldots d.$

$$(\kappa_t^j \xi)(u) = \left(\frac{u_1}{\beta(t,u)}, \ldots, \frac{u_j - t|u|^2}{\beta(t,u)}, \ldots, \frac{u_d}{\beta(t,u)} \right) |\beta(t,u)|^{-d/2}, \tag{82}$$

where $\beta(t,u) = 1 - 2tu + t^2|u|^2.$

Remark 1 Non-isotropic dilations are not fitting. For one thing, they generate, with other whiskers mentioned above, an infinite-dimensional subgroup of $O(E)$.

Remark 2 Let w be the reflection operator given by

$$(w\xi)(u) = \xi\left(\frac{u}{|u|^2} \right)|u|^{-d}.$$

Then we have

$$\kappa_t^j = w S_t^j w.$$

The infinitesimal generators of the S_t^j, τ_t, κ_t^j are

$$s_j = -\frac{\partial}{\partial u_j},$$

$$\tau = (u, \nabla) + \frac{d}{2},$$

$$\kappa_j = 2u_j(u,\nabla) - |u|^2\frac{\partial}{\partial u_j} + d\cdot u_j,$$

respectively. The satisfy the following commutation relations:

$$[\jmath_i,\jmath_j] = 0, \; [\kappa_i,\kappa_j] = 0, \; [\tau,\gamma_{i,j}] = 0;$$
$$[\jmath_i,\kappa_i] = -2\tau, \; [\jmath_i,\kappa_j] = 2\gamma_{i,j} \; (i \neq j);$$
$$[\jmath_i,\tau] = \jmath_i, \; [\kappa_i,\tau] = -\kappa_i;$$
$$\begin{cases} [\gamma_{i,j},\gamma_{j,l}] = \gamma_{i,l}, \\ [\gamma_{i,j},\gamma_{k,l}] = 0, & (i,j,k,l \text{ different}). \end{cases}$$
$$\begin{cases} [\gamma_{i,j},\kappa_j] = \kappa_i, \\ [\gamma_{i,j},\kappa_k] = 0 & (i,j,k \text{ different}). \end{cases}$$
$$\begin{cases} [\gamma_{i,j},\jmath_j] = \jmath_i, \\ [\gamma_{i,j},\jmath_k] = 0, & (i,j,k \text{ different}). \end{cases}$$

As suggested by these commutation relations, we can prove that the shifts, the isotropic dilation, the rotations on $\mathbb{R}^d$ and the special conformal transformations form a $\frac{1}{2}(d+2)(d+1)$-dimensional subgroup, denote it by $C(d)$, of $O(E)$ and that it is isomorphic to the group $SO(d+1,1)$. This subgroup $C(d)$ is called the d-dimensional *conformal group*.

It can also be proved that the conformal group is maximal among the finite-dimensional subgroups of $O(E)$ consisting of whiskers and involving the d shifts and the isotropic dilation.

Remark The projective invariance of Brownian motion established in Section 4 can be generalized in this case by using the group $C(d)$. Now we may call this property the *conformal invariance* of white noise. For related topics in physics see Todorov *et al.* (1978).

8 Concluding remarks

To close this chapter, three remarks follow in order.

8.1 F. Oosawa's examples

F. Oosawa's examples (private communication) describing the movement of primitive animals suggest questions that can be considered in a simplified version of our set-up.

8.1.1 *Two independent fluctuations*
Suppose that two independent fluctuations, denote them by $\{\dot{B}_1(t)\}$ and $\{\dot{B}_2(t)\}$, are involved in the stochastic differential equation describing the movement in question. Let, for instance, the equation

$$\frac{dX(t)}{dt} = (-\lambda + \alpha \dot{B}_1(t))X(t) + ce^{\beta \dot{B}_2(t)}, \quad \lambda > 0, \tag{83}$$

be given. Denote by ∂_t' and $\partial_t'^*$ the operators that come from $\{\dot{B}_1(t)\}$ and let ∂_t and ∂_t^* come from $\{\dot{B}_2(t)\}$. Then, we should like to understand (83) as

$$\frac{dX(t)}{dt} = (-\lambda + \alpha \partial_t'^*)X(t) + ce^{\beta \partial_t^*}1. \tag{84}$$

The solution to (84) is now easy to obtain; it is expressible as

$$X(t) = c\int_{-\infty}^{t} \exp\left[-(\lambda + \alpha^2/2)(t-u)\right]\exp\left[\alpha(B_1(t) - B_1(u))\right]:e^{\beta \dot{B}_2(u)}:du, \tag{85}$$

where $:e^{\beta \dot{B}(u)}:du$ can be understood as a generalized random measure.

In a similar manner we can discuss a somewhat difficult case where $\partial_t'^*$ in (84) is replaced by $(\partial_t'^*)^2$ so that the friction coefficient of $X(t)$ appears positive in the expression.

8.1.2 *Asymmetry*

Suppose that there are involved exponential-type fluctuations

$$e^{\pm \alpha E(t)}, \quad \alpha > 0,$$

where $E(t)$ is an Ornstein–Uhlenbeck process, denote it by $E(t)$ $= \int_{-\infty}^{t} e^{-\lambda(t-u)} \dot{B}(u)du$. If such fluctuations act exponentially, we may replace them with the operators

$$D(\pm\alpha) \equiv \exp\left[\pm \alpha \int_{-\infty}^{t} e^{-\lambda(t-u)}\partial_u^* du\right].$$

With this understanding, consider the differential equation

$$\frac{d}{dt}X(t) = -k_+D(-\alpha)X(t) + k_-D(+\alpha)(1 - X(t)), \quad k_\pm > 0. \tag{86}$$

Now we may assume that $X(t)$ is a member of the space $(L^2)^-$. Hence, associated with $X(t)$ is a U-functional denoted by $U_t(\xi)$. Set

$$L_t(\xi) = \exp\left[\alpha \int_{-\infty}^{t} e^{-\lambda(t-u)}\xi(u)du\right].$$

Using these notations, the equation (86) turns into

$$\frac{d}{dt}U_t(\xi) = -k_+L_t(-\xi)U_t(\xi) + k_-L_t(\xi)(1 - U_t(\xi)). \tag{87}$$

The solution to this equation is

$$U_t(\xi) = k_- \exp\left[-\int_{-\infty}^t k_+ L_u(-\xi) + k_- L_u(\xi) du\right]$$

$$\times \left[c + \int_{-\infty}^t L_u(\xi) e^{\int_{-\infty}^u (k_+ L_v(-\xi) + k_- L_v(\xi)) dv} du\right]. \tag{88}$$

It is hard to obtain an explicit solution, $X(t)$, expressed by a stochastic integral; however, it is possible to show some properties of $X(t)$ through the formula (88). For example, asymmetry in time of the movement of primitive animals may be illustrated by using the solution (88).

8.2 Ricciardi's example

L. M. Ricciardi (private communication) has proposed a stochastic differential equation of the form

$$\frac{d}{dt} X(t) + aX(t) = (bX(t) + c)Y(t), \quad t \geq 0, \ (a > 0), \tag{89}$$

where $Y(t)$ is a centred Gaussian process, which is not white, i.e. a coloured noise with $Y(0) = 0$.

To solve the equation, we first make the coloured noise white. That is, let the Gaussian process $Y(t)$ be expressed in the form

$$Y(t) = \int_0^t F(t,u)\dot{B}(u)du \tag{90}$$

with the crucial restriction that

$$\mathcal{B}_t(Y) = \mathcal{B}_t(\dot{B}) \quad \text{for every } t, \tag{91}$$

where $\mathcal{B}_t(Y)$ is the smallest σ-field with respect to which the $Y(s)$, $s \leq t$, are measurable, and $\mathcal{B}_t(\dot{B})$ is similarly defined. Such a representation does exist if $Y(t)$ has unit multiplicity and satisfies some trivial assumptions.

Remark A representation of the form (90) with the property (91) is called a canonical representation of $Y(t)$. A canonical representation of a Gaussian process, if it exists, is essentially unique.

Assuming the existence of the canonical representation of $Y(t)$, we can see that $X(t)$, the solution to (89), is viewed as a curve in (L^2). To make the situation simple, let us assume further that $b = 0$ and $X(0) = \alpha$ (const.). The U-functional $U_t(\xi)$ associated with $X(t)$ has to satisfy

$$\begin{cases} \dfrac{d}{dt} U_t(\xi) + aU_t(\xi) = c\displaystyle\int_0^t F(t,u)\xi(u)du, \\ U_0(\xi) = \alpha. \end{cases} \tag{92}$$

This equation can easily be solved, and we have

$$U_t(\xi) = e^{-at}\left[\alpha + c\int_0^t e^{au}\int_0^u F(u,v)\xi(v)dvdu\right].$$

This means that

$$X(t) = e^{-at}\left[\alpha + c\int_0^t e^{au}\int_0^u F(u,v)\dot{B}(v)dvdu\right]. \tag{93}$$

It is noted that $\mathscr{B}_t(x) = \mathscr{B}_t(\dot{B})$ holds for every t, so that the above formula is fitting for applications such as prediction and filtering. Also, the case $b \neq 0$ can be dealt with in a similar manner.

8.3   An application to quantum field theory

In Theorem 7 we obtained the canonical commutation relations in the case where the degree of freedom is combinuously infinite. Also, the expression of the Gauss kernel discussed in Section 6 suggests to us to apply to the well-known $P(\phi)$-theory (see Simon, 1974).

We have hopes that many applications to quantum field theory will be found in our theory of causal calculus.

Acknowledgements

I am grateful to Prof. Luigi M. Ricciardi, the Chairman of the Dottorato di Ricerca in Mathematica Applicata ed Informatica of the Naples University, for inviting me to give this series of lectures within the CNR-JSPS Cooperative Programme. The financial support of the Italian Ministry of Education (MPI) is also gratefully acknowledged.

References

Arato, M., Kolmogorov, A. N. and Sinai, Ya. G. (1962) Evaluation of the parameters of a complex stationary Gauss–Markov process, *Soviet Math. (Doklady)*, **3**, 1368–71.

Cameron, R. and Martin, W. T. (1944) Transformations of Wiener integrals under translations, *Ann. Math.*, **2**, 45, 386–96.

de Falco, Diego (1987) Lévy's stochastic area in stochastic mechanics. BiBoS Notes Nr. 245/87, University of Bielefeld.

Gaveau, B. (1977) Principle de moindre action, propagation de la chaleur et estimées sous elliptiques sur certain groupes nilpotents, *Acta Mathematica*, **139**, 95–153.

Hida, T. (1980a) *Brownian Motion* (English edn), Springer, Berlin.

Hida, T. (1980b) Causal analysis in terms of white noise. In *Quantum Fields – Algebra, Processes*, L. Streit (ed.), Springer, Berlin, pp. 1–19.

Hida, T. (1983) Causal calculus and an application to prediction theory. In *Prediction Theory and Harmonic Analysis. The Pesi Masani Volume*, V. Mandrekar and H. Salehi (eds), North-Holland, Amsterdam, pp. 123–30.

Hida, T. and Saito, K. (1988) White noise analysis and the Lévy Laplacian. In *Stochastic Processes in Physics and Engineering*, S. Albeverio *et al.* (eds), Reidel, Dordrecht, pp. 177–84.

Hida, T., Lee, K.-S. and Lee, S.-S. (1985) Conformal invariance of white noise, *Nagoya Mathematics Journal*, **98**, 87–98.

Hida, T., Kubo, I., Nomoto, H. and Yoshizawa, H. (1968) On projective invariance of Brownian motion, *Pub. Res. Inst. Math. Sci. Kyoto Univ.*, **A4**, 595–609.

Itô, K. (1951) Multiple Wiener integral, *Journal of the Mathematical Society of Japan*, **3**, 157–69.

Kubo, I. (1983) Itô formula for generalized Brownian functionals, *Springer Lecture Notes in Control and Information Science*, **49**, 156–66.

Kubo, I. and Takenaka, S. (1980–2) Calculus on Gaussian white noise, *Proceedings of the Japan Academy*, **56A**, 376–80, 411–16, **57A**, 433–7, **58A**, 186–9.

Kuo, H.-H. (1983) Brownian functionals and applications, *Acta Applicandae Mathematicae*, **1**, 175–88.

Lévy, P. (1940) Le mouvement brownien plan, *Amer. J. Math.*, **62**, 487–550.

Lévy, P. (1941) Intégrales stochastiques, *Soc. Math. de France, Sud-Est*, **25**, 67–74.

Lévy, P. (1948) *Processus stochastiques et mouvement brownien* (2nd edn, 1965), Gauthier-Villars, Paris.

Lévy, P. (1951) *Problèmes concrets d'analyse fonctionnelle*, Gauthier-Villars, Paris.

Lévy, P. (1952) Intégrales de Stieltjes généralisées, *Ann. Soc. polonaise de Math.*, **25**, 17–26.

Obata, N. (1988) Density of natural numbers and the Lévy group, *J. Number Theory*, **30**, 288–97.

Perrin, J. (1913) *Les atomes*, Félix Alcan, Paris.

Simon, B. (1974) *The P(φ)$_2$ Euclidean (Quantum) Field Theory*, Princeton University Press, Princeton, NJ.

Streit, L. and Hida, T. (1983) Generalized Brownian functionals and the Feynman integral, *Stochastic Processes and their Applications*, **16**, 55–69.

Todorov, I. T., Mitcher, M. C. and Petkova, V. B. (1978) *Conformal Invariance in Quantum Field Theory*, Scuola Normale Superiore, Pisa.

Volterra, V. and Pérès, J. (1936) *Théorie générale des fonctionnelles*, Gauthier-Villars, Paris.

Wiener, N. (1923) Differential space, *Journal of Mathematics and Physics*, **2**, 131–74.

Wiener, N. (1938) The homogeneous chaos, *American Journal of Mathematics*, **60**, 897–936.

Yoshizawa, H. (1969) Rotation group of Hilbert space and its application to Brownian motion, *Proceedings of the International Conference on Functional Analysis and Related Topics, Tokyo*, pp. 414–23.

7

Random semicontinuous functions

Gabriella Salinetti   *Dipartimento di Statistica, Probabilità e Statistiche Applicate, Università di Roma 'La Sapienza', 00185 Roma, Italy*
and
Roger J.-B. Wetts   *Department of Mathematics, University of California at Davis, Davis, Calif. 95616, USA*

This chapter introduces a new approach to the description and analysis of stochastic phenomena. It parts company from the classical approach when the realizations are infinite-dimensional in nature. We shall be mostly concerned with questions of convergence and the description of the probability distributions associated with such phenomena.

We begin with a brief review of the classical theory for stochastic processes, bringing to the fore some of the shortcomings of such an approach. In the second part of the paper we deal with the epigraphical approach that relies on the modelling of the 'paths' of the stochastic phenomena by semicontinuous functions. We conclude with a discussion and a comparison of the two theories, and the application to the convergence of stochastic processes.

1   Stochastic processes: the classical view

A *stochastic process*, with values in the extended reals, is a collection $\{X_t, t \in T\}$, of extended real-valued random variables indexed by T and defined on a probability space $(\Omega, \mathscr{A}, \mu)$. Here, and in the next few sections, we take T to be a subset of $\mathbb{R}$. It is a *discrete process*, if T is a discrete subset of $\mathbb{R}$, in which case, without loss of generality we can always identify T with $\mathbb{Z}$ (the integers) or $\mathbb{N}$ (the natural numbers).

The probability measure associated to $\{X_t, t \in T\}$ is usually defined in terms of its finite-dimensional distributions. For any finite subset $\{t_1, \ldots, t_q\} \subset T$, the q-dimensional random vector

$$(X_{t_1}, X_{t_2}, \ldots, X_{t_q})$$

defined on $(\Omega, \mathscr{A}, \mu)$ with values in $\bar{\mathbb{R}}^q = [-\infty, \infty]^q$ has the probability measure defined by the correspondence

$$P_{t_1, \ldots, t_q}(B): = \mu\{\omega \in \Omega \mid (X_{t_1}(\omega), \ldots, X_{t_q}(\omega)) \in B\}$$

where $B \in \bar{\mathscr{B}}^q$ is a Borel subset of $\bar{\mathbb{R}}^q$. The family of probability measures

$$\{P_I, I \in \mathscr{I}(T)\}$$

where $\mathscr{I}(T)$ is the collection of all finite subsets of T, is the family of *finite-dimensional distributions* of the stochastic process $\{X_t, t \in T\}$.

This approach is attractive for a number of reasons, in particular because of its immediate simplicity, at least as far as the definition is concerned. But in many cases, the price must be paid at a later stage, and sometimes there are technical, and even conceptual, difficulties that can be directly traced back to this 'finite-dimensional' approach to stochastic processes.

In a functional setting, the classical approach leads to the following framework. To every $\omega \in \Omega$, there corresponds a function (*sample path, realization*):

$$t \mapsto X_t(\omega): T \to \bar{\mathbb{R}}.$$

The stochastic process $\{X_t, t \in T\}$ can be viewed as map from Ω into $\bar{\mathbb{R}}^T$; we now identify $\bar{\mathbb{R}}^T$ with the space of all extended real-valued functions defined on T. The family of finite-dimensional distributions assigns a probability to all subsets of the type

$$B_I: = \{x \in \bar{\mathbb{R}}^T \mid (x(t_1), \ldots, x(t_q)) \in B\}$$

where $B \in \bar{\mathscr{B}}^q$, $I = \{t_1, \ldots, t_q\} \in \mathscr{I}(T)$. The sets B_I are *cylinders* (with finite-dimensional base) and they form a field on $\bar{\mathbb{R}}^T$. The finite-dimensional distributions assign a measure to each set of this field through the identity:

$$P(B_I) = P_I(B).$$

It can be shown, as done by Daniell and Kolmogorov, that this measure P can be uniquely extended to the σ-field, denoted by $\bar{\mathscr{R}}^T$, generated on $\bar{\mathbb{R}}^T$ by the family of cylinders. We can thus pin down a unique probability measure associated to the stochastic process $\{X_t, t \in T\}$. From this viewpoint, two stochastic processes are then *equivalent* if they have the same finite-dimensional distributions, that is, they identify the same probability measure on $\bar{\mathbb{R}}^T$.

2 Some questions, some examples

One of the shortcomings of this approach is that no attention is paid to (possible) topological properties of the realizations of the process. In many applications, we may be interested in developing a calculus for processes that have very specific properties, whose paths may very well belong to a subset of $\mathbb{R}^T$ of measure zero. The two following examples illustrate many of the difficulties.

Example 2.1 Suppose $V:\Omega \to (0,\infty)$ is a random variable with continuous distribution function. For all $t \in \mathbb{R}$, prob $[V = t] = 0$. Let $T = \mathbb{R}_+$ and $\{Y_t, t\in T\}$, $\{Y'_t, t\in T\}$ be two stochastic processes such that

for all $\omega \in \Omega$: $Y_t(\omega) = Y'_t(\omega) = 0$,
except that: $Y_t(\omega) = -1$ if $V(\omega) = t$.

These two processes are equivalent, although the realizations of $\{Y'_t\}$ are continuous with probability 1, and those of $\{Y_t\}$ are continuous with probability 0.

One may be templed to view the phenomena illustrated by Example 2.1 as just another example of the fact that random variables that have the same distribution are not necessarily almost surely equal. But in this case there is something more that enters into play. Let $C(T)$ denote the *set of continuous functions* defined on T and values in $\mathbb{R}$. Thus, we could reformulate our earlier observation, in the following terms:

$$\mu[Y'_. \in C(T)] = 1, \quad \text{and} \quad \mu[Y_. \in C(T)] = 0,$$

but, as we shall now see, neither $C(T)$ nor its complement – the space of functions with discontinuities – belong to $\mathscr{R}^T$. The preceding expressions make sense only because

$$\{\omega \in \Omega \mid Y'_.(\omega) \in C(T)\} = \Omega \in \mathscr{A} \quad \text{and}$$
$$\{\omega \in \Omega \mid Y_.(\omega) \notin C(T)\} = \Omega \in \mathscr{A}.$$

But in terms of the probability distributions P and P' on $\mathscr{R}^T$ induced by $\{Y_t\}$ and $\{Y'_t\}$ respectively, the expressions $P'(C(T)) = 1$, and $P(C(T)) = 0$ do not make sense because neither P' nor P are defined for the set $C(T)$. To see this, simply observe that since $P = P'$, the above would imply

$$1 = P(\bar{\mathbb{R}}^T) = P(C(T) \cup (\bar{\mathbb{R}}^T \backslash C(T))$$
$$= P'(C(T)) + P(\bar{\mathbb{R}}^T\backslash C(T)) = 1 + 1 = 2!$$

Observe also that the paths of both processes are bounded. But again in terms of P, or equivalently P', we cannot characterize boundedness since

$\{x \in \mathbb{R}^T \mid 0 \leqslant x(t) \leqslant 1, \text{ for all } t \in T\} \notin \mathcal{R}^T.$

Example 2.2 The Poisson Process. Let $\{X_n, n = 1, \ldots\}$ be a stochastic process $(T = \mathbb{N})$ where

X_1 is the waiting time for the first event,

and for $n = 2, \ldots$

X_n is the waiting time between $(n - 1)$th and nth event.

Then, the time of occurrence of the nth event is

$S_n\!: = X_1 + \ldots + X_n.$

Under the assumption that the event

$$0 =: S_0 < S_1 < \ldots < S_n < \ldots, \; \operatorname{Sup}_n S_n = \infty \tag{2.1}$$

has probability 1, on this subset of Ω, we define the random variables

$$N_t\!: = \max[n\colon S_n \leqslant t] \tag{2.2}$$

that records the (random) number of events that occur in the interval $[0,t]$; if ω is not in the set specified by (2.1), we set $N_t(\omega)\!: = 0$. It is well known, see Billingsley (1979) for example, that if the $\{X_n, n=1, \ldots\}$ are independent with the same exponential distribution, then $\{N_t, t \geqslant 0\}$ is the *Poisson* stochastic process.

For every ω, the realization

$t \mapsto N_t(\omega)\colon \Omega \to \mathbb{R}_+$

is a non-decreasing, integer-valued function.

Let $\mathbb{Q} \subset \mathbb{R}$ be the rationals, and let $\varphi\colon [0,\infty) \to \mathbb{Q}$ be such that $\varphi(t)\!: = t$ if $t \in \mathbb{Q}$, and $\varphi(t)\!: = 0$ otherwise. Now, define

$M_t(\omega)\!: = N_t(\omega) + \varphi(t + X_1(\omega)).$

For all $t \in [0,\infty)$

$\mu\{\omega \mid \varphi(t + X_1(\omega)) \neq 0\} = \mu[X_1 \in \mathbb{Q} - t] = 0,$

since $\mathbb{Q} - t$ is a countable subset of $\mathbb{R}_+$ and X_1 is absolutely continuous (with respect to the Lebesgue measure). Thus

$\mu\{\omega \mid M_t(\omega) = N_t(\omega)\} = 1$

and the stochastic process $\{M_t, t \in \mathbb{R}_+\}$ has the same family of finite-dimensional distributions as $\{N_t, t \in \mathbb{R}_+\}$. However, for all ω, the realizations $t \mapsto M_t(\omega)$ are everywhere discontinuous, neither monotone nor integer-valued!

We are basically in the same situation as in Example 2.1. The realizations of $\{N_t\}$ all lie in

$$\{x \in \mathbb{R}^{[0,\infty)} \mid x \colon [0,\infty) \to \mathbb{N}, \ x(s) \leqslant x(t) \quad \text{whenever } s \leqslant t\}$$

which does not belong to $\mathscr{R}^T$.

All of this comes from the fact that a subset B of $\mathbb{R}^T$ cannot lie in $\mathscr{R}^T$ unless there exists a countable subset S of T with the property: if $x \in B$ and $x(t) = y(t)$ for all t in S then $y \in B$ (Billingsley, 1979, Theorem 36.3).

This means that any set of the type

$$\{x \in \mathbb{R}^T \mid x(t) \in F \quad \text{for all } t \in T' \subset T\}$$

where $F \subset \mathbb{R}$ is closed, are not necessarily in $\mathscr{R}^T$, since they usually cannot be obtained as *countable* intersections of sets in $\mathscr{R}^T$. This is especially important when it comes to the study of functionals of stochastic processes. For a stochastic process $\{X_t, t \in T\}$, let

$$J(\omega) = \inf_{t \in T} X_t(\omega),$$

then for all $\alpha \in \mathbb{R}$,

$$\{\omega \mid J(\omega) \geqslant \alpha\} = \{\omega \mid X_{\cdot}(\omega) \in S_\alpha\}$$

where

$$S_\alpha = \{x \in \bar{\mathbb{R}}^T \mid \quad \text{for all } t \in T, \ x(t) \geqslant \alpha\},$$

but $S_\alpha \notin \bar{\mathscr{R}}^T$, and thus J is not even measurably related to the stochastic process $\{X_t\}$. This point is brought home by considering the two equivalent processes of Example 2.1. Here, both

$$J_1 := \inf_{t \in T} Y_t, \quad \text{and } J_1' \colon \inf_{t \in T} Y_t'$$

turn out to be measurable functions from Ω into $[0,1]$ but in no way 'equivalent', since

$$J_1 \equiv -1, \quad \text{and } J_1' \equiv 0.$$

These are some of the simplest examples we know that clearly suggest that the class $\mathscr{R}^T$ is often too small to obtain an appropriate probabilistic description of stochastic processes. The applications should, of course, dictate the framework to use in any particular situation. In the next sections, we show that there is a rather general approach that allows us to avoid some of the objections that one may have to this 'simple' definition of stochastic processes.

3 Some topological considerations

From a topological viewpoint, the shortcomings of the 'finite-dimensional distributions' description of stochastic processes come from the fact that

$\mathbb{R}^T$ does not take into account the underlying topology of T. The σ-field $\mathcal{R}^T$ is not in general a Borel field, although the first step in the construction of $\mathcal{R}^T$ is topological in nature. We can think of $\mathcal{R}^T$ as generated by the class of measurable rectangles

$$\{x \in \mathbb{R}^T \mid (x(t_1), \ldots, x(t_k)) \in G_1 \times \ldots \times G_k\}$$

as $(t_1, \ldots, t_k)$ ranges over $\mathcal{I}(T)$ and the G_1 ranges over $\mathcal{G}(\mathbb{R})$, the open subsets of $\mathbb{R}$.

This class of measurable rectangles is the base for the product topology on $\mathbb{R}^T$ but in general $\mathcal{R}^T$ is not the Borel field with respect to the product topology. Unless T is a countable space, the product topology never has a countable base (Matheron, 1975, Theorem 6). If B_π denotes the Borel field generated by the open sets of the product topology, we have that

$$\mathcal{R}^T \subset \mathcal{B}_\pi$$

with equality if T is countable. For example, if $T \subset \mathbb{R}$ is an open interval, let $\mathcal{A}$ be the subset of $\mathbb{R}^T$ that consists of the constant functions with values in $[0,1]$. Then $\mathcal{A}$ belongs to $\mathcal{B}_\pi$ but not to $\mathcal{R}^T$.

The 'classical' approach essentially ignores the topology with which T is endowed, in favour of the discrete topology. And since, with respect to the discrete topology, all functions in $\mathbb{R}^T$ are continuous, there is no way to distinguish between those realizations that we identify as continuous (with respect to the usual topology on $\mathbb{R}$) and any other realizations, that are also 'continuous' but now with respect to the discrete topology.

One general approach, that allows us to include (at least to our knowledge) all interesting stochastic processes, and which skirts around all of the inherent difficulties of the 'classical' approach, is to think of stochastic processes as random lower (or upper) semicontinuous functions. The realizations of such processes are then lower (or upper) semicontinuous functions, a rather large class of functions that should include nearly all possible applications. And for this class, there is a natural choice of topology, and an approach that avoids most of the pitfalls of the 'finite-dimensional distributions' approach.

For any function $x: T \to \bar{\mathbb{R}}$, the *epigraph* of x is the subset of the product space $T \times \mathbb{R}$ defined by

$$\text{epi } x = \{(t, \alpha) \mid \alpha \geq x(t)\}.$$

To any stochastic process $\{X_t, t \in T\}$ we can associate its *epigraphical representation*, i.e. the set-valued map defined as follows:

$$\omega \mapsto \text{epi } X_.(\omega) = \{(t, \alpha) \mid \alpha \geq X_t(\omega)\}.$$

For any finite set $I = \{(t_1, \alpha_1), \ldots, (t_q, \alpha_q)\}$ in $T \times \mathbb{R}$, we have

$$\{x \in \mathbb{R}^T \mid (x(t_1) > \alpha_1, \ldots, x(t_q)) > \alpha_q\}$$
$$= \{x \in \mathbb{R}^T \mid \text{epi } x \cap I = \varnothing\}. \tag{3.1}$$

Since $\mathcal{R}^T$ is the minimal σ-field generated by sets of the type

$$\mathcal{R}^T = \sigma - \{\{x \in \mathbb{R}^T \mid x(t_1) \leqslant \alpha_1, \ldots, x(t_q) \leqslant \alpha_q\},$$
$$[(t_1,\alpha_1), \ldots,(t_q,\alpha_q)] \in \mathcal{I}(T \times \mathbb{R})\}$$

with $\mathcal{I}(T \times \mathbb{R})$ the finite subsets of $T \times \mathbb{R}$. From (3.1) it also follows that

$$\mathcal{R}^T = \sigma - \{\{x \in \mathbb{R}^T \mid \text{epi } x \cap I \neq \varnothing\}, I \in \mathcal{I}(T \times \mathbb{R})\}.$$

The sets of $\mathcal{I}(T \times \mathbb{R})$ form a base for the discrete topology of $T \times \mathbb{R}$, and they are also compact with respect to this topology.

In the epigraphical view, the 'classical' approach defines a stochastic process $\{X_t, t \in T\}$ with domain $(\Omega,\mathcal{A},\mu)$ as a measurable map from $(\Omega,\mathcal{A})$ into $(\mathbb{R}^T,\mathcal{R}^T)$ where measurability means that

$$\{\omega \in \Omega \mid \text{epi } X_.(\omega) \cap K \neq \varnothing\} \in \mathcal{A} \tag{3.2}$$

for all subsets K of $T \times \mathbb{R}$, that are compact with respect to the discrete topology. This highlights the source of the limitations of the classical approach; it is not able to identify the topological properties of the realizations beyond those that can be identified by the discrete topology. The preceding relation also suggests the remedy to use, in order to bring the topology of T into the probabilistic description of the process. Instead of working with the discrete topology on $T \times \mathbb{R}$, we could equip $T \times \mathbb{R}$ with a topology that would be more appropriate for the application at hand.

Let us return to Example 2.1 with $T = \mathbb{R}_+$. If P and P' denote the probability measures induced by Y and Y' respectively, then

$$\mu\{\omega \mid \text{epi } Y_.(\omega) \cap K = \varnothing\} = P\{x \in \mathbb{R}^T \mid \text{epi } x \cap K = \varnothing\}$$
$$= P'\{x \in \mathbb{R}^T \mid \text{epi } x \cap K = \varnothing\}$$
$$= \mu\{\omega \mid \text{epi } Y'_.(\omega) \cap K = \varnothing\}$$

for all subsets K of $T \times \mathbb{R}$ that are compact for the discrete topology. The situation is completely different if compact refers to the 'natural' topology, i.e. the usual topology on $\mathbb{R}^2$ relative to $T \times \mathbb{R}$. It is easy to verify that for any $\beta \in (-1,0)$ and $[\alpha_1,\alpha_2] \subset T$, we have that

$$\mu\{\omega \mid \text{epi } Y'_.(\omega) \cap ([\alpha_1,\alpha_2] \times [-1,\beta]) = \varnothing\} = 1$$

and

$$\mu\{\omega \mid \text{epi } Y_.(\omega) \cap ([\alpha_1,\alpha_2] \times [-1,\beta]) = \varnothing\}$$
$$= \mu\{\omega \mid V(\omega) \notin [\alpha_1,\alpha_2]\} < 1.$$

This time, the 'induced' probability measures will be different, but of course they cannot be defined on $\mathcal{R}^T$, that in the classical approach is the 'universal' functional space for dealing with stochastic processes.

4 Separability, measurability and stochastic equivalence

The epigraphical approach focuses its attention on the sets of the type:

$$\{\omega \in \Omega \mid \mathrm{epi}\ X_{\cdot}(\omega) \cap K \neq \varnothing\},$$

to define measurability, as well as to serve as building blocks in the definition of the probability measure associated with the process $\{X_t, t \in T\}$. Let $\mathcal{K}_\tau$ denote the class of compact subsets of $T \times \mathbb{R}$ where τ is the product topology generated by τ_1 on T and the usual topology on $\mathbb{R}$. *Measurability* of the process $\{X_t, t \in T\}$ will now mean: for all K in $\mathcal{K}_\tau$,

$$\{\omega \in \Omega \mid \mathrm{epi}\ X_{\cdot}(\omega) \cap K \neq \varnothing\} \in \mathcal{A}. \tag{4.1}$$

This condition is closely related to the classical notion that the process is measurable, which means that

$$(\omega, t) \mapsto X_t(\omega) \text{ is } (\mathcal{A} \otimes \mathcal{B}\ (T))\text{-measurable} \tag{4.2}$$

where $\mathcal{B}(T)$ is the Borel field on T generated by the τ_1-open sets. In Section 6, we shall show that for stochastic processes with lower semicontinuous realizations, these two conditions are equivalent. We bring this fact to the fore at this time, because to require that a process be measurable is a standard condition used to overcome some of the difficulties created by the classical definition. By definition any stochastic process is $\mathscr{R}^T$-measurable, but not necessarily in terms of (4.2) or (4.1). This follows from the fact all sets that are compact with respect to the discrete topology are also τ-compact.

Closely related to the notion of measurability of a stochastic process is that of the *separability* of a stochastic process, as introduced by Doob. Among the major shortcomings of the class $\mathscr{R}^T$ is the fact that subsets of the type

$$\{x \in \overline{\mathbb{R}}^T \mid x(t) \in F, t \in T' \subset T\} \tag{4.3}$$

where F is a closed subset of $\mathbb{R}$, do not necessarily belong to $\overline{\mathscr{R}}^T$. One circumvents the potential difficulties by requiring that the stochastic process $\{X_t, t \in T\}$ be *separable*, i.e. there exists an everywhere dense countable subset D of T and a μ-null set $N \subset \Omega$ such that for every open set $G \subset T$ and closed subset F of $\mathbb{R}$, the sets

$$\{\omega \in \Omega \mid X_t(\omega) \in F \text{ for all } t \in G \cap D\}$$

and

$$\{\omega \in \Omega \mid X_t(\omega) \in F \text{ for all } t \in G\}$$

differ from each other at most on a subset of N (Gikhman and Skorohod, 1969).

In terms of the realizations of the stochastic process $\{X_t, t \in T\}$, separability means that for all $\omega \in \Omega \backslash N$, the function $t \mapsto X_t(\omega)$ is D-separable (Billingsley, 1979), i.e. for every t in T there exists a sequence $\{t_n, n = 1, \ldots\}$ such that

$$t_n \in D, \; t = \lim_n t_n, \quad \text{and} \quad X_t(\omega) = \lim_n X_{t_n}(\omega);$$

in other words, for every $\omega \in \Omega \backslash N$, the realization is completely determined by its values on D. A stochastic process separable with respect to D is $\mathscr{R}^D$-measurable, and one may reasonably assume that the fact that D is countable removes the 'discrepancies' connected with 'uncountabilities'. Of course not all stochastic processes are separable. Process $\{Y_t\}$ of Example 2.1 is not separable, although the equivalent stochastic process $\{Y_t'\}$ is separable. In fact, given any finite-valued process there always exists an equivalent process defined on the same probability space that is separable [Billingsley, 1979, Theorem 38.1].

At first, it may appear that it is possible to restrict the study of stochastic processes to those that are separable, but there is some hidden difficulty. Separability is defined in terms of a reference set D. For the convergence of stochastic processes, it would be necessary to prove first that there exists a set D with respect to which all elements of the sequence (or net), as well as the limit process, are separable. Moreover, the existence of an equivalent separable process does not mean that the functionals defined on these processes will in any way be comparable; think about the processes $\{Y_t\}$ and $\{Y_t'\}$ of Example 2.1 and the sup functional, see Section 2. Separability only guarantees that sets of the type (4.1) are measurable and that their probability can be determined by the family of finite-dimensional distributions. If $\{X_t, t \in T\}$ is not separable, nothing can be said *a priori* about sets of the type (4.1), and no additional information is gained from the fact that there is an equivalent separable stochastic process. Thus a functional of the stochastic process involving sets of type (4.1) cannot be analysed in terms of the same functional defined on an equivalent stochastic process.

Roughly speaking, separability is an attempt at recovering the topological structure of T, *a posteriori*. The approach developed in the next sections takes the topological structure of T directly into account.

5   The epigraphical approach

The earlier sections have pointed out the shortcomings of the 'classical' approach by reformulating it in terms of the epigraphical representation of the process. We have seen that the inherent weaknesses of this approach can be overcome by requiring that the stochastic process satisfy the stronger measurability condition

$$\{\omega \in \Omega \mid \text{epi } X_{\cdot}(\omega) \cap K \neq \varnothing\} \in \mathscr{A} \quad \text{for all } K \in \mathscr{K}_\tau \tag{5.1}$$

which take into account the topological structure of T.

All that follows is devoted to the study of stochastic processes that satisfy condition (5.1) and have lower semicontinuous (l.sc.) realizations, i.e.

$$t \mapsto X_t(\omega) \text{ is l.sc. on } T, \quad \text{for all } \omega \in \Omega. \tag{5.2}$$

Such stochastic processes, with possibly the values $+\infty$ and $-\infty$, are called *random l.sc. functions*. In another setting, such functions are known as *normal integrands*, and much of the theory developed by Rockafellar (1971, 1976) for normal integrands can be transposed to the present context. Many of the questions raised in the earlier sections seem to find their natural formalization in terms of the properties of random l.sc functions and the associated epigraphical behaviour. This leads us also to consider the associated *random closed set*

$$\omega \mapsto \text{epi } X_{\cdot}(\omega): \Omega \rightrightarrows \mathbb{R}. \tag{5.3}$$

For each ω, the set epi $X_{\cdot}(\omega)$ is a closed subset of $T \times \mathbb{R}$ since the functions $t \mapsto X_t(\omega)$ are l.sc., and the measurability of this set-valued function follows from condition (5.1).

All of this suggests defining a topology for the space of (extended real-valued) l.sc. functions in terms of the epigraphs, the *epi-topology*. We shall see that the corresponding Borel field provides us with the desired interplay between topological properties and measurability. We follow the development that was initiated in Salinetti and Wets (1986) and review here some of the main features of that theory.

At first it may appear that the requirement that the process has l.sc. paths is a rather serious limitation, at least if we use this framework for the study of general stochastic processes. This is not the case. Of course, stochastic processes with continuous realizations fit into this class, but also any càd-làg process (continuous from the right, limits from the left) admits a trivial modification that makes it a stochastic process with l.sc. paths. Although we restrict ourselves to the l.sc. case, it is clear that all the results have their counterpart in the upper semicontinuous (u.sc.) case, replacing everywhere epigraph by *hypograph*.

Crucial to the ensuring development is the fact that for stochastic processes that are l.sc. random functions, we can introduce a notion of convergence which is not only the appropriate one if we are interested in the extremal properties of the process, as well as for many related functionals, but also provides in many situations a more satisfactory approach to the convergence of stochastic processes as the standard functional approach.

6 The epigraphical random set

Henceforth, we work in the following setting

$(\Omega, \mathscr{A}, \mu)$ a *complete* probability space,
(T, τ_1) a locally compact separable metric space,
$(\omega, t) \mapsto X_t(\omega): \Omega \times T \to \bar{\mathbb{R}}$ a *random l.sc. function*.

By this we mean that

(i) for every ω, the realization $t \mapsto X_t(\omega)$ is l.sc. with values in the extended reals;
(ii) the map $(\omega, t) \mapsto X_t(\omega)$ is $(\mathscr{R} \otimes \mathscr{B}_1)$-measurable, where $\mathscr{B}_1$ is the Borel field on T.

The associated epigraphical random set, is the map

$$\omega \mapsto \operatorname{epi} X_.(\omega): \Omega \rightrightarrows \mathbb{R}$$

that takes values in the closed subsets of $T \times \mathbb{R}$, including the empty set.

The product space $T \times \mathbb{R}$ is given the product topology of τ_1 with the natural topology on $\mathbb{R}$, we denote it by τ. Thus $(T \times \mathbb{R}, \tau)$ is a locally compact separable metric space. Let

$\mathscr{F} = \mathscr{F}(T \times \mathbb{R})$ denote the closed subsets of $T \times \mathbb{R}$,
$\mathscr{G} = \mathscr{G}(T \times \mathbb{R})$ denote the open subsets of $T \times \mathbb{R}$,
$\mathscr{K} = \mathscr{K}(T \times \mathbb{R})$ denote the compact subsets of $T \times \mathbb{R}$.

For any subset C of $T \times \mathbb{R}$, let

$$\mathscr{F}^C := \{F \in \mathscr{F} \mid F \cap C = \varnothing\}, \quad \mathscr{F}_C := \{F \in \mathscr{F} \mid F \cap C \neq \varnothing\}.$$

The topology $\mathscr{T}$ generated by the subbase of open sets

$$\{\mathscr{F}^K, K \in \mathscr{K}\}, \quad \text{and} \quad \{\mathscr{F}_G, G \in \mathscr{G}\} \tag{6.1}$$

makes the topological (hyper)space $(\mathscr{F}, \mathscr{T})$ regular and compact, see e.g. Dolecki *et al.* (1983, Proposition 3.2). If T has a countable base, so does $(\mathscr{F}, \mathscr{T})$, see e.g. Matheron (1975, Theorem 1.2.1) and Dolecki *et al.* (1983) in which case a base for $\mathscr{T}$ is given by the open sets of the type

$$\{\mathscr{F}^{\operatorname{cl}B_1 \cup \ldots \cup \operatorname{cl}B_s} \cap \mathscr{F}_{B_{s+1}} \cap \ldots \cap \mathscr{F}_{B_q}, q \text{ finite}\} \tag{6.2}$$

where cl C denotes the *closure* of C, and the

$$\{B_i, i = 1, \ldots, q\}$$

come from a countable base of open sets for $T \times \mathbb{R}$. The *Borel field*, generated by the $\mathscr{T}$-open subsets of $\mathscr{F}$, will be denoted by $\mathscr{B}(\mathscr{F})$, It is easy to see that it can be generated from the subbase of open sets (6.1), and in the countable-base case by the restricted class (6.2), cf. Matheron (1975) and Salinetti and Wets (1981).

We can also view the epigraphical random set as a random variable defined on Ω and values in $\mathscr{E}$, the subset of $\mathscr{F}$, *consisting of the sets that are epigraphs*. It is easy to verify that $\mathscr{E}$ is a closed subset of $\mathscr{F}$, and thus with the $\mathscr{T}$-relative topology, it inherits all the properties of $\mathscr{F}$. The map

$$\omega \mapsto \text{epi } X_{.}(\omega)\colon \Omega \to \mathscr{E}$$

is *measurable* (is a *random set*), if for all $K \in \mathscr{K}$,

$$(\text{epi } X_{.})^{-1}(K) = \{\omega \in \Omega \mid \text{epi } X_{.}(\omega) \cap K \neq \varnothing\} \in \mathscr{A}. \tag{6.3}$$

This is equivalent (Rockafellar, 1976; Salinetti and Wets, 1981) to any one of the following conditions:

$(\text{epi } X_{.})^{-1}(F) \in \mathscr{A}$ for all $F \in \mathscr{F}$,
$(\text{epi } X_{.})^{-1}(B) \in \mathscr{A}$ for all closed balls B of $T \times \mathbb{R}$,
$\omega \mapsto \text{epi } X_{.}(\omega)$ admits a Castaing representation (see below),
graph $(\text{epi } X_{.}) \in \mathscr{A} \otimes \mathscr{B}_1$,
$\omega \mapsto \text{epi } X_{.}(\omega)\colon \Omega \to \mathscr{F}$ is $\mathscr{B}(\mathscr{F})$-measurable.

Each one of these characterizations catches a special aspect of the measurability of the epi $X_{.}$. To have measurable graph corresponds to having $\{X_t, t \in T\}$ a measurable stochastic process. The fact that the random (closed) sets admit a Castaing representation generalizes the notion of separability of a stochastic process. And the last one induces on $(\mathscr{F}, \mathscr{B}(\mathscr{F}))$, more precisely on $(\mathscr{E}, \mathscr{B}(\mathscr{E}))$, a distribution. From the definitions, it is immediate to verify (Rockafellar, 1971, Proposition 1) that

Theorem 6.1 The stochastic process $\{X_t, t \in T\}$ with l.sc. realizations is measurable if and only if $(\omega, t) \mapsto X_t(\omega)$ is a random l.sc. function, or still, if and only if $\omega \mapsto \text{epi } X_{.}(\omega)$ is a random closed set.
  A countable collection of measurable functions $\{(x_k, \alpha_k)\colon \Omega \to T \times \mathbb{R}, k = 1, \ldots\}$ is a *Castaing representation* (Rockafellar, 1976) of epi $X_{.} \in \mathscr{A}$ if

$$\{\omega \mid \text{epi } X_{.}(\omega) \neq \varnothing\} := \text{dom epi } X_{.} \in \mathscr{D},$$

and for all $\omega \in \text{epi } X_{.}$,

$$\text{cl}(\cup_k \{x_k(\omega), \alpha_k(\omega)\}) = \text{epi } X_{.}(\omega).$$

We now show that the fact that the random closed set epi $X_{.}$ admits a Castaing representation is an extension of the notion of separability for the stochastic process $\{X_t, t \in T\}$. The key fact is the following.

Theorem 6.2 Any real-valued separable stochastic process $\{X_t, t \in T\}$ with l.sc. realizations is a measurable process.

Proof (due to G. Pflug).   In view of Theorem 6.1, and the equivalent definitions of measurability (for random sets), it suffices to exhibit a countable collection of measurable functions

$$(x_k, \alpha_k) : \Omega \to T \times \mathbb{R}, \quad k = 1, \ldots$$

such that for all $\omega \in \Omega$,

$$\text{epi } X_\cdot(\omega) = \text{cl}\{\cup_k(x_k(\omega), \alpha_k(\omega))\}.$$

Suppose $D = \{d_i, i \in I\} \subset T$ is the countable set with respect to which $\{X_t, t \in T\}$ is separable, and let $A = \{a_j, j \in J\}$ be a countable dense subset of $\mathbb{R}$. Let $\{(x_1, \alpha_{ij}) : \Omega \to T \times \mathbb{R}, i \in I, j \in J\}$ be a countable collection of random functions defined by

$$x_i(\omega) = d_i,$$
$$\alpha_{ij}(\omega) = a_j \text{ if } X_{d_i}(\omega) \le a_j,$$
$$= \inf \{n \in \mathbb{N} \mid X_{d_i}(\omega) \le n\} \text{ otherwise.}$$

The α_{ij} are measurable, and moreover, from the lower semicontinuity of the realizations,

$$\text{epi } X_\cdot \subset \text{cl}(\cup_{ij}(x_i, \alpha_{ij})).$$

To complete the proof, we need only to check the reverse inclusion for any $\omega \in \Omega \backslash N$, where N is a μ-null subset of Ω such that every realization of $X_\cdot(\omega)$ is D-separable. Let $(t, \alpha) \in \text{epi } X_\cdot(\omega)$. Separability implies that there exists $\{d_i, i \in I'\}$ converging to t such that $X_t(\omega) = \lim_i X_{d_i}(\omega)$. Then

$$\alpha = \lim_{i,j} \alpha_{ij}(\omega),$$

when we choose the α_{ij} such that

$$\min[\alpha, X_{d_i}(\omega)] \le \alpha_{ij}(\omega) \le \min[\alpha, X_{d_i}(\omega)] + 1/j.$$

The converse of this theorem does not hold. A counter-example would be the process $\{Y_t, t \in T\}$ as defined in Example 2.1 with $T = \mathbb{R}_+$.

Remark 6.3   In Section 4, we indicated that separability was introduced to recover the measurability of the sets

$$\{\omega \in \Omega \mid X_t(\omega) \in F, \quad \text{for all } t \in G \subset T\}$$

where $F \subset \mathbb{R}$ is closed and G is τ_1-open, we should note that there are of course no measurability problems if $(\omega, t) \mapsto X_t(\omega)$ is a random l.sc. function. And thus in that context, separability is mostly an irrelevant concept.

7 Distributions and distribution functions

In Section 6, we have seen that to each random l.sc. function we can associate an epigraphical random closed set. As we shall show now, to each random closed set there corresponds a distribution function, which in turn will allow us to define the 'distribution function' of a random l.sc. function. Let us denote by Γ a random closed set, defined on Ω and with values in the closed subsets of $T \times \mathbb{R}$. Let P denote the distribution of Γ, i.e. the probability measure induced on $\mathcal{B}(\mathcal{F})$ by the relation

$$P(B) = \mu\{\omega \mid \Gamma(\omega) \in B\} \tag{7.1}$$

for all $B \in \mathcal{B}(\mathcal{F})$.

Since the topological space $(F, \mathcal{B}(\mathcal{F}))$ is metrizable – see Section 6 – every probability measure defined on $\mathcal{B}(\mathcal{F})$ is regular (Attouch, 1984, Theorem 1.1), and thus is completely determined by its values on the open (or closed) subsets of $\mathcal{F}$. If we assume that $\mathcal{F}$ has a countable base – and for this it suffices that $\mathcal{T}$ has a countable base – every open set in $\mathcal{F}$ is the countable union of elements in the base, obtained by taking finite intersection of the elements in the subbase. Thus, it will certainly be sufficient to know the values of P on the subbase (6.1) to completely determine P. This observation will bring us to the notion of a distribution function for the random closed set Γ (Salinetti and Wets, 1986).

First observe that the restriction of P to the class $\{\mathcal{F}_K, K \in \mathcal{K}\}$ defines a function D on $\mathcal{K}$ through the relation:

$$D(K) = P(\mathcal{F}_K) = \mu\{\omega \mid \Gamma \cap K \neq \varnothing\} \tag{7.2}$$

for all $K \in \mathcal{K}$. This function has the following properties:

$$D(\varnothing) = 0; \tag{7.3}$$

for any decreasing sequence $\{K_\nu, \nu = 1, \ldots\}$ in $\mathcal{K}$, the sequence

$$\{D(K_\nu), \nu = 1, \ldots\} \text{ decreases to } D(\lim K_\nu); \tag{7.4}$$

for any sequence of sets $\{K_\nu, \nu = 0, \ldots\}$, the functions $\{\Delta_n, n = 0, 1, \ldots\}$ defined recursively by

$$\Delta_0(K_0) = 1 - D(K_0),$$
$$\Delta_1(K_0; K_1) = \Delta_0(K_0) - \Delta_0(K_0 \cup K_1), \text{ and for } n = 2, \ldots \tag{7.5}$$

$$\Delta_\nu(K_0; K_1, \ldots, K_\nu) = \Delta_{\nu-1}(K_0; K_1, \ldots, K_{\nu-1}) - \Delta_{\nu-1}(K_0 \cup K_\nu; K_1; \ldots, K_{\nu-1}),$$

take on their values in $[0, 1]$.

The properties of D on $\mathcal{K}$ are essentially the same as those of the distribution function of a 1- or n-dimensional random variable. Property (7.4) is the same as right-continuity, whereas (7.3) corresponds to the continuity at $-\infty$ for a distribution function on the real line. Property (7.5) can be viewed as an extension of the notion of monotonicity. In view of this, and the fact (Salinetti and Wets, 1986, Choquet's Theorem 1.3) that any function $D: \mathcal{K} \to [0,1]$ that satisfies the conditions (7.3), (7.4), (7.5) uniquely determines a probability measure on $\mathcal{B}(\mathcal{F})$, we call D the *distribution function* of Γ.

The fact that we can restrict the domain of definition of D to the subclass $\mathcal{K}^{ub}$ of $\mathcal{K}$ is very useful in a number of applications, where

$$\mathcal{K}^{ub} = \{\text{finite union of closed balls with positive radii}\};$$

note that $\varnothing \in \mathcal{K}^{ub}$ as the union of an empty collection. This comes from the fact that the properties of $(\mathcal{F},\mathcal{T})$ enable us to generate $\mathcal{B}(\mathcal{F})$ from the family

$$\{\mathcal{F}_K, K \in \mathcal{K}^{ub}\};$$

in fact, for all $K \in \mathcal{K}$, we have

$$K = \cap \{K' \mid K' \supset K, K' \in \mathcal{K}^{ub}\}$$

and

$$\mathcal{F}_K = \bigcap_{\substack{K' \supset K \\ K' \in \mathcal{K}^{ub}}} \mathcal{F}_{K'};$$

and consequently

$$D(K) = P(\mathcal{F}_K) = \inf_{\substack{K' \supset K \\ K' \in \mathcal{K}^{ub}}} P(\mathcal{F}_{K'}) = \inf_{\substack{K' \supset K \\ K' \in \mathcal{K}^{ub}}} D(K').$$

The (probability) *distribution function* of a random lower semi-continuous function $(\omega,t) \mapsto X_t(\omega)$ is the distribution function of its epigraphical random set. Since the random set takes its values in the (hyper) space of epigraphs we could reformulate it in the following terms: let C be a τ_1-compact subset of T, and $\alpha \in \mathbb{R}$, then

$$D(C,\alpha) := \mu\{\omega \mid \inf_{t \in C} X_t(\omega) \le \alpha\}$$

defined on (the compact subsets of T) $\times \mathbb{R}$ can be used instead of the usual definition of D on the compact subsets of $T \times \mathbb{R}$.

8   ... and finite-dimensional distributions!

Let us consider $\{X_t, t \in T\}$ a measurable stochastic process with l.sc. realizations, then epi $X_\cdot : \Omega \rightrightarrows T \times \mathbb{R}$ is a closed random set with distribution function $D: \mathcal{K} \to [0,1]$. Any finite set $I = \{(t_1, \alpha_1), \ldots, (t_h, \alpha_h)\} \subset T \times \mathbb{R}$ is τ-compact, and thus we have

$$D(I) = \mu\{\omega \in \Omega \mid \text{epi } X_\cdot(\omega) \cap I \ne \phi\}.$$

In particular, if we fix t, then for all $\alpha \in \mathbb{R}$

$$D(\{(t,\alpha)\}) = \mu\{\omega \in \Omega \mid X_t(\omega) \leqslant \alpha\} = P_t((-\infty, \alpha])$$

where P_t refers to the 1-dimensional probability measure of the random variable X_t. Similarly, if we fix $t_1, \ldots, t_q$, then

$$P_{t_1,\ldots,t_q}((-\infty, \alpha_1] \times \ldots \times (-\infty, \alpha_q])$$

$$= \mu\{\omega \mid X_{t_1}(\omega) \leqslant \alpha_1, \ldots, X_{tq}(\omega) \leqslant \alpha_q\}$$

$$= \Sigma_{i=1}^q D(\{(t_i,\alpha_i)\}) - \Sigma_{\substack{i,j \\ i=j}} D(\{(t_i,\alpha_i), (t_j,\alpha_j)\})$$

$$+ \ldots + (-1)^{h+1} D(\{(t_1,\alpha_1), \ldots, (t_q,\alpha_q)\})$$

The following theorem is now immediate.

Theorem 8.1 If $\{X_t, t \in T\}$ is a measurable stochastic process with l.sc. realizations, the finite-dimensional distributions are completely determined by D, or equivalently by the restriction of D to the finite subsets of $T \times \mathbb{R}$.

Of course, the converse of this theorem does not necessarily hold. Take for example the process $\{Y_t, t \in T\}$ of Example 2.1 with $T = \mathbb{R}_+$ and let $K = [t_1, t_2] \times [-\frac{1}{2}, -\frac{3}{4}]$, where $0 < t_1 < t_2$. Then $D(K) = \mu\{\omega \mid V(\omega) \in [t_1, t_2]\} > 0$, but $D(I) = 0$ for any finite subset I of K. The family of finite-dimensional distributions, that assigns a value to D for every finite subset of K, does not allow us to make any reference about the value to assign to $D(K)$.

Remark 8.2 Note that the standard consistency conditions for the family of finite-dimensional distributions could actually be derived from the 'monotonicity' property (7.5) of the distribution function D. Thus, we can think of this family of finite-dimensional distributions itself as a distribution function, but defined on the finite subsets of $T \times \mathbb{R}$. This suggests another approach to Kolmogorov's consistency theorem via Choquet's theorem.

The fact that a compact set $K \subset T \times \mathbb{R}$ cannot be obtained as a countable union of finite sets is a topological fact that leads to a probabilistic discrepancy in the example involving the process $\{Y_t, t \in T\}$.

Definition 8.3 The distribution function of a random l.sc. function is said to be *inner separable*, if to any $K \in \mathcal{K}$ and $\varepsilon > 0$, there corresponds a finite set $I_\varepsilon \subset K$ such that $D(K) < D(I_\varepsilon) + \varepsilon$.

The basic difference between separability of a stochastic process and the inner separability of its distribution is that separability is aimed at the reconstruction of sets through 'finite sets', whereas inner separability is aimed at the reconstruction of the probabilistic content of the sets in terms of the probability associated to finite sets.

Proposition 8.4 (Salinetti and Wets, 1986, Proposition 4.6). Suppose $\{X_t, t \in T\}$ is a measurable stochastic process with l.sc. realizations. If it is separable, then its distribution function is inner separable. Moreover, if its distribution function is inner separable, its values on $\mathcal{K}$ are completely determined by its values on the finite subsets of $T \times \mathbb{R}$.

This last assertion is an immediate consequence of the definition of inner separability.

9   Weak convergence and convergence in distribution

We show that for random l.sc. functions, weak convergence of the probability measures corresponds to the convergence of the distribution functions at the 'continuity' sets.

By ν, we index the members of a sequence of stochastic processes, the induced probability measures on $\mathcal{B}(\mathcal{E})$, or the corresponding distribution functions on $\mathcal{K} = \mathcal{K}(T \times \mathbb{R})$; by $\mathcal{B}(\mathcal{E})$ we mean the Borel field $\mathcal{B}(\mathcal{F})$ restricted to $\mathcal{E}$. With $\nu = \infty$, or simply without index, we refer to the limit element of the sequence. We have seen that for every $K \in \mathcal{K}$:

$$D^\nu(K) = P^\nu(\mathcal{E}_K) = \mu\{\omega \in \Omega \mid \text{epi } X^\nu(\omega) \cap K \neq \phi\}.$$

Since $\mathcal{E}_K$ is a closed subset of $\mathcal{F}$–$\mathcal{E}$ is a closed subset of $\mathcal{F}$–, we can easily obtain from the Portemanteau theorem (Attouch, 1984) that

Proposition 9.1 If P^ν converges weakly to P, then for all $K \in \mathcal{K}$

$$\lim_{\nu \to \infty} \sup D^\nu(K) \leq D(K). \tag{9.1}$$

Unless $P(\text{bdy } \mathcal{E}_K) = 0$, the probability measure attached to the *boundary* of $\mathcal{E}_K$, we cannot guarantee that

$$\lim_{\nu \to \infty} \inf D^\nu(K) \geq D(K), \tag{9.2}$$

i.e. unless K is a 'continuity' point of D in a sense to be defined below. Note that 'continuity sets' of D must correspond to P-continuity sets and that the class of sets for which this continuity is defined must at least be a convergence determining class (Attouch, 1984).

Definition 9.2 An increasing sequence $\{K^n, n=1, \ldots\}$ of compact sets is said to *regularly converge* to K if

$$K = \text{cl } \cup_{n=1}^{\infty} K^n \quad \text{and} \quad \text{int } K \subset \cup_{n=1}^{\infty} K^n; \tag{9.3}$$

where int S denotes the interior of the set S.

Definition 9.3 A distribution function $D: \mathcal{K} \to [0,1]$ is *distribution-*

continuous at K, if for every regularly increasing sequence $\{K^n, n=1, \ldots\}$ to K,

$$D(K) = \lim_{n \to \infty} D(K^n). \tag{9.4}$$

The *distribution-continuity set* $\mathscr{C}_D$ of D, is the subset of $\mathscr{K}$ on which D is distribution-continuous.

Proposition 9.4 (Salinetti and Wets, 1986, Lemma 1.11).   For any $K \in \mathscr{K}$,

   (i) *if* (P(bdy $\mathscr{E}_K$) $= 0$, then $K \in \mathscr{C}_D$;
   (if) $K \in \mathscr{C}_D$ *and* $K = \mathrm{cl}(\mathrm{int}\, \mathscr{K})$, *then* P(bdy $\mathscr{E}_K$) $= 0$.

Assuming that (T, τ_1) has a countable base, let $\mathscr{K}_{\mathbb{Q}}^{\mathrm{ub}} \subset \mathscr{K}^{\mathrm{ub}}$ be such that $\mathscr{K}_{\mathbb{Q}}^{\mathrm{ub}}$ is the finite union of balls that determine a countable basis for $(T \times \mathbb{R}, \tau)$. We have

$$\mathscr{K}^{\mathrm{ub}} \cap \mathscr{C}_D = \mathscr{K}^{\mathrm{ub}} \cap \{K \mid P(\text{bdy } \mathscr{E}_K) = 0\},$$

and if T has a countable base

$$\mathscr{K}_{\mathbb{Q}}^{\mathrm{ub}} \cap \mathscr{C}_D = \mathscr{K}_{\mathbb{Q}}^{\mathrm{ub}} \cap \{K \mid P(\text{bdy } \mathscr{E}_K) = 0\}.$$

This allows us to rephrase weak-convergence of probability measures in terms of the pointwise convergence of the distribution functions.

Theorem 9.5 (Salinetti and Wets, 1986, Theorem 1.15).   For the family of random l.sc. functions $\{X_., X_.^\nu, \nu = 1, \ldots\}$, equivalently of measurable stochastic processes with l.sc. realizations, we have that the P^ν converge weakly to P if and only if for all $K \in \mathscr{K}^{\mathrm{ub}} \cap \mathscr{C}_D$, (and if (T, τ_1) has a countable base, for all $K \in \mathscr{K}_{\mathbb{Q}}^{\mathrm{ub}} \cap \mathscr{E}_D$):

$$D(K) = \lim_{\nu \to \infty} D^\nu(K).$$

We refer to this type of convergence, as *convergence in distribution* of the stochastic processes $\{X_t^\nu, t \in T\}$ to $\{X_t, t \in T\}$, and denote it by $X_.^\nu \xrightarrow{\text{i.d}} X_.$.

10   Convergence in distribution and convergence of the finite-dimensional distributions

In the classical approach to the study of stochastic processes, convergence of stochastic processes is defined in terms of the convergence of the finite-dimensional distributions, that we denote by

$$X_.^\nu \xrightarrow{\text{f.d.}} X_..$$

In view of the comments in Section 8, we cannot expect that $X_{\cdot}^{\nu} \xrightarrow{\text{f.d}} X_{\cdot}$ implies that $X_{\cdot}^{\nu} \xrightarrow{\text{i.d}} X_{\cdot}$, but the converse could reasonably be conjectured, see Theorem 8.1. However, in general this implication also fails. The reason is that for finite sets $K \subset \mathcal{K}$, the notions of distribution-continuity and continuity of the corresponding finite-dimensional distribution do not coincide.

Remark 10.1   This can all be traced back to the relationship between the epitopology and the pointwise-topology. Equivalence is obtained in the presence of equi-semicontinuity (Salinetti and Wets, 1986, Section 3), see also Doleck; *et al.* (1983) for details.

The passage from convergence in distribution to convergence of the finite-dimensional distributions and vice versa, is based on the possibility of 'approximating' the values of the distribution function for compact sets K by finite sets, *independent of ν*, and conversely.

Definition 10.2   The family of distribution functions $\{D; D^{\nu}=1, \ldots\}$ on $\mathcal{K}$ is *equi-outer regular* at the finite set $I \subset T \times \mathbb{R}$, if to every $\varepsilon > 0$ there corresponds a compact set $K_{\varepsilon} \in \mathcal{K}^{\text{ub}} \cap \mathcal{C}_{\text{D}}$ with $K_{\varepsilon} \supset I$ such that for $\nu = 1, \ldots$

$$D^{\nu}(K_{\varepsilon}) < D^{\nu}(I) + \varepsilon, \text{ and } D(K_{\varepsilon}) < D(I) + \varepsilon.$$

Now, let $\mathcal{C}_{\text{f.d.}}$ denote the finite subsets of $T \times \mathbb{R}$, i.e.

$$\mathcal{C}_{\text{f.d.}} \subset \{I = \{(t_1, \alpha_1), \ldots, (t_q, \alpha_q)\}, q \text{ finite}\},$$

such that the distribution function of the vector $(X_{t_1}, \ldots, X_{t_q})$ is continuous at $(\alpha_1, \ldots, \alpha_q)$.

Definition 10.3   The family of distribution functions $\{D; D^{\nu}, \nu=1, \ldots\}$ on $\mathcal{K}$ is *equi-inner separable* at $K \in \mathcal{K}$, if to every $\varepsilon > 0$, there corresponds a finite set I_{ε} such that

$$D(K) < D(I_{\varepsilon}) + \varepsilon, \quad \text{and } D^{\nu}(K) < D^{\nu}(I_{\varepsilon}) + \varepsilon$$

for $\nu = 1, \ldots$; see Definition 8.3.

Theorem 10.4 (Salinetti and Wets, 1986, Corollary 4.6).   Suppose $\{X; X^{\nu}, \nu=1, \ldots\}$ is a collection of random l.sc. functions. Then $X_{\cdot}^{\nu} \xrightarrow{\text{i.d.}} X$ implies $X_{\cdot}^{\nu} \xrightarrow{\text{f.d.}} X_{\cdot}$ if and only if $\{D, D^{\nu}, \nu=1, \ldots\}$ is equi-outer regular on $\mathcal{C}_{\text{f.d.}}$. And $X_{\cdot}^{\nu} \xrightarrow{\text{f.d.}} X_{\cdot}$ implies $X_{\cdot}^{\nu} \xrightarrow{\text{i.d.}} X_{\cdot}$ if and only if $\{D; D^{\nu}, \nu=1, \ldots\}$ is equi-inner separable.

11 Bounded random l.sc. functions

Applications usually require us to restrict our attention to a subclass of processes that possess further properties beside lower (or upper) semi-continuity. From the point of view of the epigraphs, this means that the realizations now belong to $\mathscr{E}'$ a subset of $\mathscr{E}$. Let $\mathscr{T}'$ be the relative $\mathscr{T}$-topology on $\mathscr{E}'$. Then the topological space $(\mathscr{E}',\mathscr{T}')$ inherits a number of the properties of $(\mathscr{F},\mathscr{T})$ (Kelley, 1955). In particular, if $(\mathscr{F},\mathscr{T})$ is metric with countable base, then $(\mathscr{E}',\mathscr{T}')$ is metric with countable base. Thus, in principle all the earlier results still apply to $(\mathscr{E}',\mathscr{T}')$, and the theory of weak-convergence on separable metric spaces can be used to obtain convergence criteria. In particular, recall the following.

Theorem 11.1 Prohorov. The sequence $\{P^\nu, \nu=1,\ldots\}$ of probability measures on $\mathscr{B}(\mathscr{E}')$ is tight if and only if every subsequence contains a further subsequence that weakly converges to a probability measure.

This means that the sequence $\{P^\nu, \nu=1,\ldots\}$ is relatively compact. A subset $\mathscr{S}$ of $\mathscr{E}'$ is $\mathscr{T}'$-compact if and only if it is a $\mathscr{T}$-closed subset of $\mathscr{E}$, see Section 6.

We now deal with bounded processes. We use this class to illustrate the potential application of the 'epigraphical' approach to specific classes of stochastic processes. To begin with, let us observe the following.

Lemma 11.2 For all $\alpha \in \mathbb{R}_+$

$$\mathscr{E}_\alpha = \{\text{epi } x \mid \sup_{t \in T} |x(t)| (t) \leqslant \alpha\} \subset \mathscr{E}$$

is $\mathscr{T}$-compact. And hence, any collection of probability measures $\mathscr{P}$ on $\mathscr{B}(\mathscr{E}')$ such that for every $\varepsilon > 0$, there exists $\alpha \geqslant 0$ such that for all $P' \in \mathscr{P}$

$$P'(\mathscr{E}_\alpha) > 1 - \varepsilon,$$

is tight.

Proof The first assertion follows from (Dolecki *et al.*, 1983, Section 4) and the second one from the definition of tightness (Parthasaraty, 1967).

Let

$$\mathscr{E}^\#: = \{\text{epi } x \mid \sup_{t \in T} |x(t)| \leqslant \alpha^\#\}$$

be the space of epigraphs associated to l.sc. functions that are bounded below and above by $\alpha^\#$. From Lemma 11.2, and Theorem 11.1, it follows directly that

Proposition 11.3 Any collection $\mathscr{P}$ of probability measures on $\mathscr{B}(\mathscr{E}^{\#})$ is tight, and hence every subsequence has a convergent subsequence.

12   An application to goodness-of-fit statistics

Let us consider the basic case of independent observations $(\xi_1, \xi_2, \ldots, \xi_\nu)$ from the uniform distribution on $[0,1]$. Let us define the empirical process

$$U_t^\nu(\omega) = \begin{cases} F^\nu(\omega, t) - t, & \text{if } 0 < t < 1, \\ 0 & \text{otherwise.} \end{cases}$$

where for every ω, $F^\nu(\omega, \cdot)$ is the empiral distribution (taken left-continuous) determined by the sample $(\xi_1, \ldots, \xi_\nu)$. The realizations $U_{\cdot}^\nu(\omega)$ are l.sc. on $[0,1]$ (with respect to the natural topology on $\mathbb{R}$); this comes from the fact that F^ν is a left-continuous piecewise constant distribution function on $\mathbb{R}$. It is also easy to verify that the function

$$(\omega, t) \mapsto U_t^\nu(\omega) : [0,1]^\nu \times [0,1] \to [-1,1]$$

is measurable. Redefining the underlying sample space to be $[0,1]^\infty$, and making the obvious identifications, we have that for all $\nu = 1, \ldots$

$$(\omega, t) \mapsto U_t^\nu(\omega) = [0,1]^\infty \times [0,1] \to [-1,1]$$

is a random l.sc. function. We are here in the case when for all $\nu = 1, \ldots$

$$\text{epi } U_{\cdot}^\nu \subset \{\text{epi } x \mid -1 \leqslant x(t) \leqslant 1, \ t \in [0,1]\} =: \mathscr{E}'.$$

Moreover, for all ν, the corresponding distribution functions $\{D^\nu, \nu=1, \ldots\}$ are inner-separable at K, for all K in $\mathscr{K}^{ub}$. This follows from the inner-separability of the distribution function associated to the stochastic process $\{\mathscr{F}^\nu(\cdot, t), \ t \in [0,1]\}$. Since, we may as well take for balls the products of intervals, we see that epi $F^\nu(\omega) \cap ([t_1, t_2] \times [\alpha_1, \alpha_2])$ only if $\mathscr{F}^\nu(\omega, t_2) \leqslant \alpha_1$, since F^ν is monotone non-decreasing. Thus for any finite collection of balls, the value of the associated distribution function is determined by its values on some finite set.

By Proposition 8.4, and the fact that the values of D^ν on $\mathscr{K}^{ub}$ determine uniquely its values on $\mathscr{K}$, we know that the finite-dimensional distributions completely determine D^ν. Moreover, from Proposition 11.3, since the $\{U_t^\nu, t \in T\}$ are (equi-)bounded, the associated probability measures are tight. This means that there always exists a subsequence

$$\{D^{\nu_k}, k=1, \ldots\} \text{ converging to } D,$$

(i.e. $U_{\cdot}^\nu \overset{\text{i.d.}}{\longrightarrow} U_{\cdot}$).

Observe that independence has not played any role up to now. If the $\{\xi_k, k=1, \ldots\}$ are i.i.d., by the law of large numbers, for every $I = (t_1, \ldots, t_q)$, the finite-dimensional distributions converge in distribution to the q-dimensional distribution of the random vector identically zero. And thus the limit process $\{U_t, t \in T\}$ must be a stochastic process whose realizations are such that

$$U_t(\omega) = 0 \quad \text{for all } t \in [0,1],$$

and for all $\omega \in \Omega \backslash N$ where N is a set of measure 0.

Actually a somewhat stronger result does hold. From, the strong law of large numbers, for every $t \in T$

$$U_t^\nu = F^\nu(\cdot, t) - t \to 0 \quad \text{a.s.,}$$

i.e. there exists a set N_t of measure 0, such that

$$U_t^\nu(\omega) = F^\nu(\omega, t) - t \to 0 \quad \text{for all } \omega \in \Omega \backslash N_t. \tag{12.1}$$

We shall show that almost surely

$$\text{epi } U. = \lim_{\nu \to \infty} \text{epi } U_{\cdot}^\nu$$

Let $S = \{t_1, t_2, \ldots\}$ be a countable dense subset of $T = [0,1]$. Then by (12.1), we have that

$$U_{t_k}^\nu(\omega) = F^\nu(\omega, t_k) - t_k \to 0 \quad \text{for all } \omega \in \Omega \backslash N$$

where N is the null set

$$N: = U_{k=1}^\infty N_{t_k}.$$

Now, it is an exercise in epi-convergence to show that for every $\omega \in \Omega \backslash N$

$$\limsup_{\nu \to \infty} \text{epi } U.(\omega) \subset \text{epi } U. \subset \liminf_{\nu \to \infty} \text{epi } U_{\cdot}^\nu(\omega),$$

where $\limsup_{\nu \to \infty}$ and $\liminf_{\nu \to \infty}$ are the superior and inferior limits of sets (Dolecki *et al.*, 1983; Salinetti and Wets, 1986). In fact it suffices to show that for all $\omega \in \Omega \backslash N$, $t \in [0,1]$

$$\text{for all } t_k \to t, \ (k) \subset (\nu): \liminf_{k \to \infty} U_{t_k}^k(\omega) \geqslant 0, \tag{12.2}$$

and

$$\text{there exists } t_\nu \to t: \limsup_{\nu \to \infty} U_{t_\nu}^\nu(\omega) \leqslant 0. \tag{12.3}$$

Condition (12.3) is immediate. For, let $t \in T$, $\varepsilon > 0$ and take $t_\nu \in S$ with $t_\nu \in [t, t+\varepsilon)$. We have

$$F^\nu(\omega, t) - t \leqslant F^\nu(\omega, t_\nu) - t_\nu + \varepsilon.$$

Hence

$$\limsup_{\nu \to \infty} (U_t^\nu(\omega) = F^\nu(\omega, t) - t) \leqslant \varepsilon,$$

and since $\varepsilon > 0$ is arbitrary, (12.3) follows.

Now let $t_k \to t$ and (ν_k) be a subsequence of (ν). For any $\varepsilon > 0$, fix

$t_\varepsilon \in D$ such that $t_\varepsilon \in (t-\varepsilon, t]$. Since $t_k \to t$, there is k_ε such that for all $k \geqslant k_\varepsilon$,

$$t_\varepsilon < t_k < t_\varepsilon + \varepsilon.$$

Thus for all $v \in (v_k)$ with $v \geqslant v_{k_\varepsilon}$, for all $\omega \in \Omega \backslash N$, we have

$$F^v(\omega, t_k) - t_k \geqslant F^v(\omega, t_\varepsilon) - t_\varepsilon - \varepsilon,$$

since F^v is monotone increasing with respect to t. This implies that for all $\omega \in \Omega \backslash N$,

$$\liminf_{k \to \infty} U_{t_k}^{v_k}(\omega) \geqslant -\varepsilon.$$

Since $\varepsilon > 0$ is arbitrary, it yields (12.2).

Almost sure epi-convergence implies convergence in distribution (Salinetti and Wets, 1986, Section 3) and thus

$$U_\cdot^v \xrightarrow{\text{i.d.}} U_\cdot.$$

The Glivenko–Cantelli theorem is a corollary of epi-convergence in distribution, as we see next.

Theorem 12.1 (Glivenko and Cantelli). $\sup_{t \in [0,1]} |U_t^v(\omega)| \to 0$, a.s.

Proof   Suppose, to the contrary, that for some $\omega \in \Omega \backslash N$, and $\varepsilon > 0$, there is a subsequence (v_k) of (v) such that $\sup_t |U_t^{v_k}(\omega)| > \varepsilon$. This means that there exists for each k, t_k such that $|U_{t_k}^{v_k}(\omega)| > \varepsilon$. Passing to a subsequence if necessary, let t be the limit of $\{t_k, k=1, \ldots\}$, then

$$\text{either} \quad U_{t_k}^{v_k}(\omega) > \varepsilon, \quad \text{or} \quad U_{t_k}^{v_k}(\omega) < -\varepsilon.$$

If the second inequality occurred infinitely often, then for some subsequence we would have that

$$\liminf_{k' \to \infty} U_{t_{k'}}^{k'}(\omega) < -\varepsilon,$$

which does contradict the epi-convergence of the $U_\cdot^v$ to $U_\cdot$. If $U_{t_k}^{v_k}(\omega) > \varepsilon$ infinitely often, then

$$\varepsilon \leqslant \limsup_{k \to \infty} U_{t_k}^{v_k}(\omega).$$

If $t' = 1$ then $t_k \leqslant 1$ and $t_k > 1 - \varepsilon/2$ for k sufficiently large. The preceding inequality then implies that

$$\varepsilon \leqslant \limsup_{k \to \infty} U_{t_k}^{v_k}(\omega) \leqslant \limsup_{k \to \infty} U_1^{v_k}(\omega) + \frac{\varepsilon}{2} = \frac{\varepsilon}{2},$$

recall that $U_1^v(\omega) = 0$, see the definition. If $t' \in [0,1]$, there exists $\varepsilon' > 0$, $2\varepsilon' < \varepsilon$ such that for k sufficiently large

$t' - \varepsilon' < t_k < t' + \varepsilon'.$

Then, from the proof given for (12.3), it follows that

$$\varepsilon \leq \limsup_{k \to \infty} U_{t_k}^{v_k}(\omega)$$

$$\leq \limsup_{k \to \infty} [U_{t' + \varepsilon'}(\omega) + 2\varepsilon'] < \varepsilon.$$

This is again a contradiction, and the proof is complete.

References

Ash, R. (1972) *Real Analysis and Probability*, Academic Press, New York.

Attouch, H. (1984) *Variational Convergence for Functions and Operators*, Pitman, Boston.

Billingsley, P. (1979) *Probability and Measure*, Wiley, New York.

Dolecki, S., Salinetti, G. and Wets, R. (1983) Convergence of functions: equisemicontinuity, *Transactions of the American Mathematical Society*, **276**, 409–29.

Gikhman, I. I. and Skorohod, A. V. (1969) *Introduction to the Theory of Random Processes*, W. B. Saunders, Philadephia.

Kelley, J. L. (1955) *General Topology*, Van Nostrand, New York.

Matheron, G. (1975) *Random Sets and Integral Geometry*, Wiley, New York.

Parthasaraty, K. R. (1967) *Probability Measures on Metric Spaces*, Academic Press, New York.

Rockafellar, R. T. (1971) Convex integral functionals and duality, in *Contributions to Nonlinear Analysis*, E. Zarantonello (ed.), Academic Press, New York, pp. 215–36.

Rockafellar, R. T. (1976) Integrals functionals, normal integrands and measurable selections, in *Nonlinear Operators and Calculus of Variations*, L. Waelbroeck (ed), Lecture Notes in Mathematics 543, Springer, Berlin, pp. 157–207.

Salinetti, G. and Wets, R. (1981) On the convergence of closed-valued measurable multifunctions, *Transactions of the American Mathematical Society*, **266**, 275–89.

Salinetti, G. and Wets, R. (1986) On the convergence in distribution of measurable multifunctions (random sets), normal integrands, stochastic processes and stochastic infima, *Mathematics of Operations Research*, **11**, 385–419.

Name index

Aczél, J. 110, 111, 115, 119, 123, 124, 165
Aho, A. V. 7, 61
Anderssen, K. S. 275, 283
Arato, M. 299, 328
Arimoto, S. 111, 113, 165
Arnold, L. 225, 231, 239, 283
Ash, R. 353
Attouch, H. 343, 346, 353

Babu, C. C. 165
Backer, E. 168
Baker, C. T. H. 274, 283
Belis, M. 122, 165
Ben-Bassat, M. 111, 124, 135, 143, 165
Benois, M. 69, 104
Berg, P. W. 202, 203
Berstel, J. 62, 67, 74, 104
Bertsch, M. E. 185, 203
Billingsley, P. 333, 334, 338, 353
Blatt, D. W. E. 191, 203
Blumer, A. 111, 165
Boekee, D. E. 135, 148, 165, 168
Bouchon, B. 122, 165
Boxma, Y. 168
Brian, W. J. 182, 186, 203
Brzozowski, J. A. 101, 102, 104
Büchi, J. R. 103, 104
Buneman, P. 18, 61
Buonocore, A. 264, 275, 283, 285
Burbea, J. 151, 165

Cameron, R. 288, 328
Campbell, L. L. 110, 166
Capocelli, R. M. 108, 109, 124, 148, 151, 155, 164, 166, 259, 283
Caughey, T. K. 231, 284
Cerbone, G. 277, 283
Charvát, F. 113, 167
Chaundy, T. W. 117, 118, 166
Chen, C. H. 134, 135, 166
Chu, J. T. 136, 166
Chueh, J. E. 136, 166
Clark, D. P. 177, 182, 184, 203
Cohen, R. S. 104
Comins, H. N. 191, 203
Cook, S. A. 49, 54, 61
Cull, P. 1, 6, 47, 61

Daniels, H. E. 272, 283
Darling, D. A. 240, 283
Daróczy, Z. 110, 111, 123, 124, 165
de Falco, D. 299, 328
De Hoog, F. R. 283
De Luca, A. 118, 155, 156, 157, 160, 161, 164, 166
DeCurtins, J. 47, 61
Dejean, F. 99, 104
Devijver, P. A. 147, 148, 150, 166
Dolecki, S. 340, 351, 353
Durbin, J. 264, 283

Ebanks, B. R. 155, 156, 157, 159, 166

Ecklund, E. F. Jr. 6, 61
Eilenberg, S. 62, 69, 87, 104
El-Sayed, A. B. 124, 166
Elgot, C. C. 73, 103, 104
Emptoz, H. 155, 156, 157, 166
Endler, J. A. 204
Erdelyi, A. 251, 254, 262, 277, 282, 283

Favella, L. 275, 283
Feller, W. 215, 216, 257, 284
Ferreri, C. 123, 166
Fife, P. C. 171, 203
Fleming, W. H. 191, 194, 203
Fliess, M. 69, 105
Fortet, R. 240, 264, 284

Gallager, R. G. 111, 151, 166
Garey, M. R. 53, 54, 61
Gargano, L. 166
Gaveau, B. 299, 328
Gikhman, I. I. 337, 353
Giorno, V. 264, 275, 284, 285
Gray, A. H. 231, 284
Greene, D. H. 61
Guiaşu, S. 122, 165, 167
Gurney, W. S. C. 173, 203
Gurtin, D. 203
Gurtin, M. E. 179, 203
Györfi, L. 147, 167

Hajek, B. 225, 239, 283, 285
Hardy, G. H. 116, 167
Hartley, R. V. L. 107, 167
Hashiguchi, K. 62, 90, 95, 105
Havrda, J. 113, 167
Hellman, M. E. 136, 167
Henneman, W. H. 99, 100, 105
Hida, T. 286, 289, 290, 309, 312, 321,
    324, 328, 329
Hilhorst, D. 203
Hopcroft, J. E. 7, 61
Horowitz, E. 61

Ito, K. 225, 234, 283, 284, 290, 329
Ito, Y. 176, 203

Jazwinski, A. H. 225, 238, 283, 284
Jelinek, F. 111, 167
Johnson, D. S. 53, 54, 61

Kailath, T. 135, 167
Kanal, L. N. 134, 135, 167

Kapur, J. N. 112, 167
Karlin, S. 215, 284
Karp, R. M. 49, 55, 61
Kawanabe, H. 183, 186, 203
Kawasaki, K. 191, 200, 203, 205
Kelley, J. L. 353
Kerridge, D. F. 123, 167
Kieffer, J. C. 111, 167
Kleene, S. C. 62, 67, 85, 105
Knast, R. 102, 104
Knopfmacher, J. 155, 156, 157, 167
Knuth, D. E. 61
Kolmogorov, A. N. 331, 328
Kosaka, M. 172, 203
Kovalevski, V. A. 135, 167
Kubo, H. 172, 204
Kubo, I. 319, 329
Kuno, T. 204
Kuo, H.-H. 320, 329

Ladner, R. 103, 105
Lallement, G. 62, 105
Lee, K.-S. 329
Lee, S.-S. 329
Levin, S. A. 171, 190, 204
Levins, R. 198, 204
Levy, L. 18, 61
Lévy, P. 287, 298, 305, 320, 322, 329
Littlewood, J. E. 167
Longo, G. 122, 167
Loo, S. G. 155, 156, 157, 167
Lothaire, M. 105

MacArthur, R. H. 198, 204
MacCamy, R. C. 179, 203
McEliece, R. J. 109, 167
McGregor, J. L. 202, 203
McKean, H. P. 237, 284
McKnight, J. D. Jr. 67, 105
McLeod, J. B. 117, 118, 166
McMurtrie, R. E. 204
McNaughton, R. 103, 105
Marshall, A. W. 161, 167
Martin, W. T. 288, 328
Mascle, J. P. 105
Mathai, A. M. 110, 167
Matheron, G. 335, 340, 353
May, R. H. 191, 204
Mezei, G. 69, 73, 104
Mimura, M. 171, 204
Mitcher, M. C. 329
Mittal, D. P. 114, 168

Morisita, M. 171, 172, 173, 176, 177, 178, 183, 200, 204
Mortensen, R. E. 231, 284
Murray, J. D. 171, 204

Nagylaki, T. 191, 204
Namba, T. 191, 204
Nemetz, T. 147, 167
Neyfeh, A. H. 192, 204
Nisbet, R. M. 173, 191, 203
Nobile, A. G. 276, 277, 283, 284, 285
Nomoto, H. 329
Nyquist, H. 107, 167

Obata, N. 305, 329
Okubo, A. 171, 174, 179, 185, 190, 204
Olkin, I. 161, 167
Oosawa, F. 325

Pacala, S. 191, 204
Pan, V. 61
Papert, S. 103, 105
Parker, D. S. Jr. 111, 167
Parthasaraty, K. R. 353
Pattle, R. E. 179, 204
Peletier, L. A. 203
Pérès, J. 287, 329
Perrin, J. 287, 329
Perrot, J. F. 105
Petkova, V. B. 329
Pflugg, G. 342
Picard, C. F. 110, 122, 168
Pin, J.-E. 62, 74, 75, 87, 99, 100, 102, 104, 105
Polya, G. 167

Rao, C. R. 151, 165, 168
Rathie, P. N. 110, 112, 167, 168
Raviv, J. 111, 124, 136, 143, 165, 167
Reineri, M. T. 283
Rènyi, A. 108, 110, 111, 116, 168
Ricciardi, L. M. 165, 200, 206, 259, 263, 264, 266, 275, 279, 283, 284, 285, 327, 328
Rierra, T. 156, 168
Rockafellar, R. T. 339, 341, 353
Rogers, H. 1, 53, 61
Roughgarden, J. 191, 192, 204

Sacerdote, L. 283, 284
Sahni, S. 61
Saito, K. 321, 329
Sakarovitchi, J. 71, 74, 75, 105, 106

Salinetti, G. 330, 339, 340, 343, 344, 346, 347, 351, 352, 353
Sant'anna, A. P. 109, 124, 136, 151, 168
Sato, S. 206, 259, 263, 279, 282, 284
Schneider, K. 111, 167
Schur, I. 162, 168
Schützenberger, M. P. 69, 99, 104, 106
Sedgewick, R. 61
Shannon, C. E. 107, 109, 122, 168
Sharma, B. D. 114, 118, 123, 157, 159, 168
Shigesada, N. 170, 175, 179, 191, 192, 204, 205
Shohat, J. A. 257, 284
Sibson, R. 151, 168
Siegert, A. J. F. 240, 259, 283, 284
Simon, B. 328, 329
Simon, I. 97, 101, 106
Sinai, Ya.G. 328
Skorohod, A. V. 337, 353
Smithies, F. 269, 284
Soong, T. T. 225, 284
Stassen, V. 24, 61
Stratonovich, R. L. 225, 230, 266, 284
Straubing, H. 100, 101, 102, 104, 105, 106
Streit, L. 329

Takenaka, S. 329
Tamarkin, J. D. 257, 284
Taneja, I. J. 107, 109, 110, 111, 118, 123, 124, 136, 143, 147, 157, 166, 168
Taylor, H. M. 215, 284
Teramoto, E. 174, 191, 200, 203, 205
Termini, S. 118, 155, 156, 157, 160, 164, 166
Thérien, D. 100, 105, 106
Thomas, W. 102, 106
Todorov, I. T. 325, 329
Toussaint, G. T. 147, 168
Traub, J. F. 61
Trillas, E. 156, 168
Trouborst, P. N. 147, 168

Uhlenbeck, G. E. 229, 285
Ullman, J. D. 7, 61
Utida, S. 205

Vaccaro, U. 166
Vajda, I. 148, 159, 168
van der Lubbe, J. C. A. 117, 136, 148, 165, 168

van Der Pyl, T. 114, 124, 169
Varma, R. S. 112, 169
Visentin, F. 285
Volterra, V. 287, 329

Walsh, T. R. 15, 61
Wang, M. C. 229, 285
Watanabe, S. 177, 178, 182, 184, 205
Weiss, R. 283
Wets, R. J.-B. 330, 339, 340, 343, 344,
  346, 347, 351, 352, 353
Wiener, N. 107, 169, 287, 329

Winograd, S. 36, 61
Wirth, N. 47, 61
Wong, E. 225, 230, 239, 283, 285
Wozniakowski, H. 61

Yamaguti, M. 171, 204
Yoshizawa, H. 294, 329
Yosida, T. 205

Zadeh, L. 155, 169
Zakai, M. 230, 285

Subject index

absorbing boundary 216, 240, 272
accessible boundary 216
additivity 110, 126
  generalized 118, 126, 157
  pseudo 126
  strong 127
algorithm 1, 48, 82, 264
  approximation 57
  backtrack 42, 57
  best 4
  correct 2
  deterministic 50
  divide-and-conquer 6, 21–31, 41
  exhaustive 52, 56
  Gaussian elimination 25
  Huffman 111
  iterative 3, 10, 20, 29, 47
  matrix multiplication 25
  minimal space 13
  non-deterministic 50, 59
  polynomial multiplication 25, 30
  polynomial time 50
  probabilistic 57
  reasonable 49
  recursive 3–10, 19, 29
  sorting 39
  Strassen's 24
  unreasonable 49
alphabet 63
ant-lion 171
automaton 76
  finite 78
  minimal 84
  recognizable 86
  trim 84

backward equation 212
Bayes rule 134
Bayesian distance 113
Bayesian probability of error 111
Bochner–Minlos theorem 289
Boolean algebra 65, 88, 101
Borel field 335–40
bound 147, 155
  best-case 35
  entropy-type 151
  Fano-type 108, 146
boundary classification 216
Brownian
  bridge 311
  curve 298
  functional 288, 308, 317
  generalized functional 313
  motion 223, 286, 311, 319

canonical representation 327
Cantor diagonal proof 54
Castaing representation 341
causal calculus 315
Chapman-Kolmogorov equation 209
Choquet's theorem 344
coding rate 110

coding theorem 110
coefficient
  Bhattacharyya 111
  diffusion 179
  dispersion 173
coloured noise 327
complexity
  space 7
  time 7
concatenation 70
confluent hypergeometric function 254
conformal group 325
conformal invariance 325
congruence 82
conservation equation 213
continuity equation 175, 185, 240, 266
Cook's theorem 54
correlation function 222, 232
cost
  logarithmic 8
  uniform 8
covariance function 308
covariance matrix 220, 229

Daniel's boundary 272
diffusion equation 212, 220
  time-homogeneous 215
diffusion interval 213–19, 244
diffusion process 212–39, 253
  temporally homogeneous 214
diffusivity 178, 184
dispersal process 191
dispersion measure 155–62
distance
  Bayesian 113
  Bhattacharyya 113
  generalized 146
  measure of 108, 135
divergence measure 109, 135, 151
drift 212–38, 253
Dyck's reduction 68

Eilenberg's theory 82
entrance boundary 216, 253
entropy
  α-log 121, 136, 159
  binary 158
  cubic 135
  dispersion 163
  γ- 113
  generalized 108, 117, 135
  hypo- 123, 138

logarithmic 157
  measure 159
  of degree β 113, 118, 135
  of degree (α, β) 121, 136, 159
  of fuzzy set 118, 155
  of order 1 and degree β 114
  of order α 108, 114, 135, 141
  of order α and degree β 114, 135,
    145
  quadratic 113, 135, 159
  Renyi 112
  Shannon 108–36
  sine 121, 136
  trigomometric 123, 136
  -type bound 151
environment density 172
environmental potential 173, 185, 196
epi-convergence 351
  almost-sure 351
epi-topology 339
epigraph 335–49
epigraphical random set 340
epigraphical representation 335, 338
equilibrium state 175
ergodic 306
error
  Bayesian probability of 111
  bound 108, 135, 146
  function 221, 243, 267
  probability of 134, 147, 151
exhaustive search 41
exit boundary 216, 283

Fano-type bound, *see* bound
FFT 27
first-passage time 239
  moments of 256–63
  p.d.f. 239–81
flow of Brownian motion 306
Fock space 289
Fokker-Planck equation 213–41, 267
fuzzy set theory 108, 122

Gaussian
  distribution 287
  elimination algorithm 25
  kernel 297, 319
  process 207, 220, 229, 327
Gini's index 113
Glivenko-Cantelli theorem 351
growth rate 194

halting problem 54
Hamiltonian path 42, 45, 52, 55, 58
Hellinger-Hahn theorem 306
homogeneous chaos 290
Huffman algorithm, see algorithm
hyperbolic boundary 271
hypograph 339

inaccessible boundary 216
independence inequality 128
independent increment 219
induced probability measure 336
induction 66, 80
inductive proof, 3, 19, 31
inequality
    among entropies 129
    generalized Fano-type 132
    independence 128
    Shannon 136
infinitesimal generator 303, 324
infinitesimal moment 211–30, 252
infinitesimal variance 211–38, 253, 269
information measure 112, 135
Ito calculus 225, 231, 283
Ito equation 231–7
Ito formula 319
Ito lemma 234, 237
Ito-type stochastic integral 317

Kac formula 296
Karhunen theory 309
Kleene's theorem 67, 85
knight' tour problem 45
Kolmogorov backward equation 244
Kolmogorov consistency theorem 345
Kolmogorov equation 213, 217
Kolmogorov forward equation 244
Kummer function 254, 262, 277

language 71
    rational 86
    recognizable 82–102
    star-free 89, 102
    variety of 88
Lévy group 304, 322
Lévy-Laplacian 305, 320
linear filtering theory 308
local time 319
logarithmic cost criterion 8
logistic growth 193
Lotka-Volterra equation 189

Markov process 207, 238
Markov property 208
mean square sense (m.s.) 232
    continuity 232
    convergence 232, 283
    differentiability 232
    limit 234
    Riemann integral 231
method of images 242
Mezei's theorem 70
moment generating function 257
monoid 63
    aperiodic 101
    finite 78
    free 83
    of transition 85
    quotient 82
    syntactic 82–102
Morisita's equation 182
Morisita's experiment 176
morphism 78
    monoid 94
    natural 82
    of semigroup 63
    surjective 71, 104
multiple Wiener integral, see Wiener
multiple-scale method 191, 197
multi-species system 196
mutual information 111

natural boundary 216–21, 240, 250
natural morphism 82
natural projection 71
niche-partitioning theory 198
noiseless coding theory 122
non-anticipating 317
normal functional 321
normal process, see Gaussian process
NP-complete problem 54, 59
n-queens problem 47
nuclear space 309
    basic 304, 323
number operator 304

Oosawa's example 325
operation
    Boolean 69, 89
    rational 90
    star 103
optimization problem 52, 57
Ornstein-Uhlenbeck (OU)

Brownian motion 308
    operator 304
    process 221, 241–82, 304, 326

$p(\phi)$-theory 328
parabolic cylinder function 251, 262, 278
pattern recognition 108, 124, 136
perturbation procedure 201
phase-plane diagram 185
Poisson process 333
population density 172, 178, 185
population pressure 173, 181
probability measure 330, 337, 349
probability current 213, 240, 266
probability density function (p.d.f.) 207
    of first-passage-time 239–56, 265, 282
    steady state 214, 258
probability flow 216
probability space 330
    complete 340

random
    function 207, 224
    l.sc. function 339–50
    set 340
    variable 330
    vector 330
Rayleigh process 249, 252–6, 283
realization 331–9
recursivity 110, 123
    generalized 127
reflecting boundary 221
reflection condition 221
reflection operator 324
regression equation 178
regular boundary 216, 283
Rényi entropy 112
Ricciardi's example 327
rotation group 294, 323
    infinite-dimensional 288, 312
running time 4, 7, 19–31, 41, 48
    average-case 31, 38
    best-case 31, 38
    worst-case 31, 38

S-structure 103
sample path 216, 224, 239, 331
satisfiability problem 43
Schur concavity 130

Schutzenberger's theorem 89, 99
search problem 110
segregation 182, 200
    mutual 182
    process 182
    selective 182
    spatial 185
selective segregation 182
self information 109
semigroup 63
    free 63, 87
    morphism of 63
    quotient 63, 87
semilinear 69
semiring 64, 74
separability 337, 345
    measure of 134
separable
    equi-inner 346
    inner 345
Shannon entropy 108–36
Shannon inequalities 136
    generalized 131
Shannon information measure 108
shift 305
Siegert formula 259
Simon's theorem 101
singular process 215
Smolukovski equation 209, 226
spatial segregation 185
spectral representation 306
standard Wiener process 220
star operation 103
star height 98
star-free language 89, 102
star-height problem 99
state 76
stationarity 218
stationary distribution 175, 185
stationary process 225
statistical pattern recognition 108, 124, 136
stochastic
    area 298
    differential equation 225, 252, 295, 325
    integral 298
    process 207, 330, 337, 342
Stone's theorem 306
Strassen's algorithm 24
Stratonovich calculus 225

Straubing's hierarchy 102
Straubing's theorem 100
subgroup 68
subsemigroup 63
symmetry 114, 126, 157
syntactic monoid 82–102
system
  ecological 190
  multi-species 196
  two-species 193

tension 308
test function 289
tie-breaking rule 46
time complexity 7
time-dependent boundary 239, 269
time-homogeneous diffusion equation 215
time-homogeneous diffusion process 241, 276
total absorption 218
total reflection 218
Towers of Hanol problem 6–10, 29
transition p.d.f. 208–72
travelling salesman problem 52
Turing machine 51
two-barrier problem 240

two-species system 193

U-functional 293, 307, 326
uncertainty 109
uniform cost criterion 8
unitary operator 303
unreasonable algorithm, *see* algorithm

weak subadditivity 128
Weber function 251
weighted entropy 138
whiskers 305, 323
white noise 225
  coloured 327
  measure of 287
white-noise analysis 304
white-noise calculus 287
Wiener
  expansion 308
  measure 287
  multiple integral 290
  process 220, 230–82
  process with drift 220, 242, 267, 272
  space 287
word 63
worst case running time 31, 38

yes/no problem 49